LEGAL ASPECTS OF
CORRECTIONS
MANAGEMENT
THIRD EDITION

Clair A. Cripe, AB, JD

General Counsel (Retired)
Federal Bureau of Prisons
Former Adjunct Professor
George Washington University, National College of Law

Michael G. Pearlman, MS, JD

Legal Administrative/Correctional Program Officer (Retired)
Federal Bureau of Prisons
Adjunct Professor
George Mason University

Daryl Kosiak, JD

Regional Counsel (Retired)
North Central Region, Federal Bureau of Prisons
Instructor, Department of Political Science and Sociology
Northern State University
Aberdeen, South Dakota

JONES & BARTLETT
LEARNING

World Headquarters
Jones & Bartlett Learning
5 Wall Street
Burlington, MA 01803
978-443-5000
info@jblearning.com
www.jblearning.com

Jones & Bartlett Learning books and products are available through most bookstores and online booksellers. To contact Jones & Bartlett Learning directly, call 800-832-0034, fax 978-443-8000, or visit our website, www.jblearning.com.

Production Credits

Publisher: Cathleen Sether
Acquisitions Editor: Sean Connelly
Editorial Assistant: Caitlin Murphy
Director of Production: Amy Rose
Production Assistant: Alyssa Lawrence
Marketing Manager: Lindsay White
Manufacturing and Inventory Control
 Supervisor: Amy Bacus

Composition: Laserwords Private Limited, Chennai, India
Cover Design: Scott Moden
Rights and Permissions Manager: Katherine Crighton
Rights and Photo Research Supervisor: Anna Genoese
Cover Image: © David R. Frazier Photolibrary, Inc./
 Alamy Images
Printing and Binding: Malloy, Inc.
Cover Printing: Malloy, Inc.

Some images in this book feature models. These models do not necessarily endorse, represent, or participate in the activities represented in the images.

Library of Congress Cataloging-in-Publication Data
Cripe, Clair A.
 Legal aspects of corrections management / Clair Cripe, Michael Pearlman, and Daryl Kosiak.—[3rd ed.]
   p. cm.
 Includes index.
 ISBN-13: 978-1-4496-3940-2 (pbk.)
 ISBN-10: 1-4496-3940-2 (pbk.)
1. Correctional law—United States. 2. Prisoners—Civil rights—United States. 3. Corrections—United States. I. Pearlman, Michael G. II. Kosiak, Daryl. III. Title.
 KF9728.C76 2012
 344.7303'5—dc23

2011036485

6048

Printed in the United States of America
22 21 20 19 18 10 9 8 7 6 5

Contents

Preface

With this, the third edition of *Legal Aspects of Corrections Management*, we present an updated discussion of the law which most forcefully impacts the operations of corrections. It is a voluminous body of law—court cases, statutes, regulations, and standards. And it is of course a body of law that is constantly changing, and expanding.

By far the most important legal influences and constraints on corrections are those coming from the courts. The book first presents an introduction to the workings of the courts, with an emphasis on Supreme Court decisions, as these decisions define corrections law throughout the country. First, there is a description of how the legal system works in the United States, the nature of the criminal justice system, and how legal conflicts and issues get into courts. In those organizational respects, there has been little change over recent years. How the courts have ruled upon those legal complaints that are brought to them is the main focus of the book.

The law of the U.S. Constitution is the major thrust of judicial actions in this area. Those constitutional rulings form the central part of the book. The Supreme Court has by now given us guidelines on most areas, where the practices of corrections are impacted by provisions of the Constitution. This third edition presents those governing Supreme Court decisions. Plus, it updates the case law with recent court rulings, including applications of the Supreme Court's guidance by courts at lower levels.

To some extent in reaction to those court rulings, the legislative branch (particularly the U.S. Congress) has given us statutes which regulate and circumscribe correctional practices, as well as the very basic aspect of going to court. This edition presents that group of recent enactments. Attention is also given to changes in professional standards which have come to influence correctional policies. There are expanded examples of state corrections policy, updates in such areas as interstate compacts and collateral consequences of convictions, and discussions of employee law and standards of conduct.

We welcome to the authorship team a third member, Daryl Kosiak. Like the other two of us (Mike Pearlman and myself), Daryl is an attorney with first-hand knowledge of corrections law, and has experience teaching the law of corrections in the classroom, both to college students and to corrections workers. That experience, we believe, reflects what has always been the goal of our writing—to serve as a teaching and learning tool for those studying this area of criminal justice, and to be a ready reference for the corrections practitioner.

Clair A. Cripe

Acknowledgments

We would like to thank the following reviewers for their input in the revision of this text:

Paul R. Bowdre, Western Nebraska Community College

Terry D. Edwards, University of Louisville

Michael D. Frazier, University of Texas at Dallas

Paige H. Gordier, Lake Superior State University

Catherine A. Jenks, University of West Georgia

Linda Keena, University of Mississippi

Junius H. Koonce, Edgecombe Community College

Anastasia Lawrence, University of Texas at Brownsville

Larry A. MacDonald, Oakland Community College

Richard Tewksbury, University of Louisville

Adrienne C. Watts, Wayne County Community College District, Detroit, Michigan

I Sources of Corrections Law

In Part I (Chapters 1 through 4), we look at the background of corrections and of the law. In Chapter 1, we provide a brief introduction, review the organization of the text, and look at a broad and general history of the law and how our legal system in the United States works. In Chapter 2, we focus on the criminal justice system. We also take our first look at the field of corrections—how it fits into the bigger criminal justice picture and the different components that make up the field of corrections. In Chapter 3, we focus on the specific legal provisions that are most often encountered in corrections litigation. Chapter 3 examines the types of legal actions that are most often used by prisoners or other offenders to complain about their conditions and treatment. When one of those legal actions is filed, the corrections worker may find himself going to court. Chapter 4 discusses, in a more practical manner, the legal steps that should be anticipated and that will likely be experienced in a corrections lawsuit.

Virtually any kind of corrections activity performed in any of the various corrections agencies and facilities may be the subject of a lawsuit. In this first part of the text, we try to set the stage for a better understanding of what "corrections law" means, where it comes from, and how it affects the individual corrections worker. These introductory chapters describe the sources of this area of the law. The sources are found in American law itself and in its intersection with the practical workings of corrections agencies, in their huge variety and complexity.

1

An Introduction to the Law and to the Legal Aspects of Corrections Management

The judicial Power of the United States, shall be vested in one supreme Court, and in such inferior Courts as the Congress may from time to time ordain and establish.

U.S. Constitution, Article III, Section 1

Chapter Outline

- Organization of the Text
- The Law
- Historic Origins
- Branches of Government
- The Court System
  - Federal Courts
  - State Courts
- Criminal and Civil Law

Our purpose is to tell you about the greatness of our legal system and how important its influence has been on corrections in the United States. There, that's done. Now, the rest of this volume will be dedicated to qualifying that overreaching statement and explaining what the law means to the corrections practitioner. The truth of the matter is that, in the past 50 years, the law has had more of an impact on corrections than any other factor or force. More than new programs. More than research. More than studies and developments in criminology, rehabilitation methods, or any theories of punishment and sentencing. The law has also had more of an impact on corrections than management theory and even new technologies.

Court rulings have directly impacted the operations of corrections facilities. They have also changed the way managers have had to think about their decision making, on matters great and small. In setting their priorities in running institutions and community programs, corrections administrators must take legal considerations into account. This means that, from academic study to the day-to-day work of the corrections officer, legal rulings have been absorbed into the corrections field.

It has not been easy for corrections professionals to accommodate the legal "intrusions." It is still not easy. Corrections professionals know their business. They know what the problems are and what needs to be done. The last thing they ever needed was a bunch of uninformed, or ill-informed, outsiders (that is how corrections workers saw them—the lawyers and the judges) to make their work more complicated and unpredictable.

As the legal "revolution" in corrections occurred, particularly in the 1960s and 1970s, corrections managers resented the intrusion of the law into their work. That resentment was deep-seated and bitter. With time, most of them grasped (although they never liked the fact) that they needed advice that would help them get along with the courts with the least possible confrontation and the least amount of outside intrusion. Inmate litigation became endemic and, for most people working in adult corrections, litigation was accepted as an inevitable part of corrections operations and management.

Those old-liners, the hard-nosed administrators and workers of the 1960s and 1970s, are now mostly retired from the profession. They have been replaced by managers who, from the time they came to work, had to face the realities of litigation and court involvement. Given their druthers, most of them would prefer the simpler task of running prisons and jails without legal intrusions, but they know that this is not possible in the world of corrections in the United States. (We are careful to specify "in the United States," because no other country, to our knowledge, experiences anything close to the level of involvement of the courts in corrections that occurs in this country.)

This brings us to the purpose of writing this text. It is designed to serve as a teaching reference for those who are going to work in corrections or those who want to know more about this part of the criminal justice field. At the same time, it should serve as a reference tool for today's corrections workers who need and want to know what they must do to run corrections facilities with minimal legal entanglements.

We personally know some of those hard-nosed wardens and commissioners who were working in the 1960s when the first cases came down. They were required to revise practices that had been assumed to be solidly justified and impervious to outside review. It was not easy being a corrections lawyer, preaching a new sermon of caution and concern based upon a scripture of constitutionality. Corrections lawyers were roundly disliked, even though they worked for the government and were proposing what was deemed to be best for the protection of corrections principles and corrections workers.

In the intervening decades, thousands of lawsuits and hundreds of court decisions have defined legal constraints on corrections policies and practices. For example, in the year 2010, 25,058 prisoner civil rights and prison condition lawsuits were filed in the 94 United States District Courts.[1] Most important, the U.S. Supreme Court, over time, has produced (at the rate of about one or two decisions per year) the central constitutional guidelines.

There is an expression that "prisons reflect society"; this refers to the view that what one sees in the "free world" exists in some form or other within the correctional environment. Accordingly, there is no aspect of correctional life and work, to our knowledge, that has not been the subject of litigation. Many areas, over time, have been ruled to be outside the realm of judicial review. This text focuses on those areas that are inside that realm: those areas where lawyers and judges will insist on compliance with constitutional or other legal standards.

■ Organization of the Text

This text presents the accumulated legal developments (constraints) in a format that is created with the corrections practitioner in mind. It begins with general discussions of what the law is and in what areas it interfaces with corrections. Most of the text is a detailed presentation of what the law has said about specific areas of corrections operations and practices.

First, we look at the background of corrections and of the law. Next, we look at constitutional law. This is a discussion of those areas of corrections work in which different provisions of the U.S. Constitution have been examined to see whether they define or limit what may be done by corrections officials. In many areas, there are now Supreme Court decisions, which provide the authoritative word and interpret the U.S. Constitution on corrections issues. In many respects, this is one of the most exciting aspects of corrections. The following provisions of the U.S. Constitution will be covered:

- Inmate access to the courts
- The First Amendment: inmate correspondence, inmate association rights, visiting, and religion
- The Fourth Amendment: search and seizure and privacy
- The due process provisions of the Fifth and Fourteenth Amendments, as they apply to such areas as inmate discipline, classification, transfers, personal injuries, and property loss
- The Fourteenth Amendment as it applies to equal protection for female offenders and others
- The Eighth Amendment as it applies to the death penalty and other sentencing issues, conditions of confinement, cruel and unusual punishment, and health care

Our look at constitutional law also includes a discussion of probation and parole, community corrections, and fines. Finally, we will look at law that governs corrections by means other than the Constitution and at corrections issues that are somewhat outside the central core of managing prisons.

For each subject covered, there are other resources to assist the reader in obtaining an understanding of the material, along with a general summary and "Thinking About It" questions, which are relevant to the covered material. To help you find important statements of the law as you look through this text, holdings of cases and statements of important legal principles are given in boldface font. On every Supreme Court opinion, you can expect to find a boldface presentation of the important statements of the Court in that case. If there are such important statements of the law in other cases (or in statutes), these will be presented in boldface font, as well.

Near the end of this text, there is a glossary of key terms that defines words and terms that are often found in corrections, criminal justice, or the law. The glossary is followed by an alphabetical listing of cases. The Table of Cases also provides the page number(s) where the case can be found within the text.

We note that throughout the text, the words *he* and *she* and the words *his* and *her* are used interchangeably. The use of these terms reflects the significant number of women working in the corrections field. During the year 2005, women accounted for 33% of the employees in correctional facilities under state or federal authority.[2]

Our hope is that this text will serve as a handy reference to the corrections professional and as a valuable teaching resource for the criminal justice professor and student. It must be understood that this text is a digest—it distills into a comparatively small volume what has become an overwhelmingly large body of law. Our goal has been to make this text an understandable collection of essential and representative court decisions, combined with some background on the various aspects of corrections on which those decisions touch.

■ The Law

What is the law? There is no need to get bogged down with various definitions. Legal scholars do not agree on definitions, and they, in fact, propose different ones. Let us say the law is the set of principles and rules laid down to determine the rights and duties of a state's citizens (*state* is used here in the sense of any level of autonomous government) and to resolve disputes between those citizens. The law has binding legal force.

Central to nearly all legal systems, and certainly to ours in the United States, is the judiciary. **Courts** are the voice of legal authority. The courts interpret and administer the laws, and they determine the specific rights and duties of citizens. (Note that the courts are central to the legal system of government, not to all of government. As we will see, there are three branches of government, and they are theoretically of equal importance.)

■ Historic Origins

American law derives mainly from English law, which in turn derived historically from Roman law, with some influences from the Normans, the Scandinavians, and church (**canon**) law. After the American Revolution, in the late 1700s, there was reaction against many things English, including legal decisions and procedures. In general, however, law in the United States adopted English concepts and legal language. Louisiana brought along its French law tradition, much of which continues there. Several southwestern and western states include a Spanish influence, particularly in property matters.

English law relied very heavily on the decrees, orders (sometimes called **writs**), and **decisions** of its judges. Together, these judicial pronouncements constitute the **common law**.[3] As part of the revolutionary break from English rule in 1776, the former colonies, now states, adopted written **constitutions** as the prime statement and source of the law. The same was done for the federal government in the "supreme law" of the land, the U.S. Constitution. The reliance on written constitutions was the most significant break from English legal tradition. Today, it is still the most significant difference between English and American law, which are in most other respects closely related.

■ Branches of Government

The constitutions of the United States and of each of the individual states establish three branches of government:

1. The legislature, which enacts laws
2. The executive branch, which enforces and carries out the laws
3. The judiciary, which interprets and applies the laws

These very basic descriptions of the functions of the three branches do not take into account some governmental activities that do not fall clearly into one category or another. For our study, however, these broad definitions allow us to see the basis for the activities of government and the conflicts that almost inevitably come out of them.

The functions of the three branches of government also give rise to two important principles of our American government. One is the separation of powers, which holds that each branch should perform its own function and should not intrude into the functions of the other two independent branches. A second major principle is one of **checks and balances**, which establishes, by constitutional requirements, procedures whereby each branch has some constraints on each of the other two. An example is the process of appropriating money: only the legislature (Congress) can impose taxes and raise money for the government to spend. Thus, the executive branch cannot carry out any activity it wishes, unless the money for it is appropriated. But the president must approve, in turn, any appropriation of money, and can veto an appropriation.

Another underpinning of the American government is the establishment of a national (**federal**) government, along with the recognition of the political independence of each state. This system leads to certain hierarchical principles: federal law prevails in conflicts with state or local law.[4] The U.S. Constitution is the highest source of law, over statutes, treaties, and regulations. Thus, the U.S. Constitution is the highest law in the country.[5]

> **This Constitution, and the Laws of the United States which shall be made in Pursuance thereof; and all Treaties made, or which shall be made, under the Authority of the United States, shall be the supreme Law of the Land; and the Judges in every State shall be bound thereby, any Thing in the Constitution or Laws of any State to the Contrary notwithstanding.**
>
> U.S. Constitution, Article VI, Clause 2

In the same manner, the constitution of a state is, for that state, the supreme source of law. The legislature of each state enacts laws within the framework of its constitution (as does the federal legislature, the Congress).

In the early decades of the United States, laws were principally derived from common law (judicial) decision making. Legislatures were not very active. This changed during the late 1800s (from the Civil War on), and the national Congress and the state legislatures became more and more active in the 20th century. The courts did not back off from their historic role, though, so the American legal system is truly a mixture of the elements of common law development (with its emphasis on judicial decisions), along with **statutes** and **regulations**.

■ The Court System

Federal Courts

Under the U.S. Constitution, judicial authority is given to "one supreme Court, and in such inferior Courts as the Congress may from time to time…establish" (Article III, Section 1). Thus, the U.S. Supreme Court is the only court established by the Constitution. The Constitution specifies neither the number of members who will sit on the Supreme Court (it has varied from 6 to 10), nor the qualifications of Court members or the Court's precise **jurisdiction** (what kinds of **cases** it will review).

The lower federal courts are established by statute. Typically, the federal courts are courts of "general jurisdiction." This means that, unlike courts in many other countries and in some states, the same courts handle civil matters (involving private rights), criminal cases (involving offenses against all), equity-type cases (involving the spirit of fairness[6]), and most commercial matters (involving business and commerce).[7]

The first level of federal courts includes the U.S. District Courts. These are the federal courts in which **trials** are held and federal cases are initially filed and disposed of. Every state has at least one federal district. Larger states may have several district courts. Thus, there are, in some states, Northern, Southern, Eastern, Western, Middle, or Central Districts. California, Texas, and New York each have four districts, which is the greatest number of districts in any one state.

There are usually several judges appointed to sit in each district. Cases are heard before a single judge.[8] Assisting the U.S. district judges on many matters, but not with the same wide authority, are U.S. magistrate judges. (These may be thought of as assistant judges or junior judges, although they will not appreciate us saying so!)

The district court's role is to receive **evidence** about the "facts of the case" (establishing who did what). Higher-level courts will not retry a case, but instead serve as a forum for review and **appeal**. This review process is one reason why cases with factual similarities can have different results.

Appeals from the decisions of the federal district courts are taken to U.S. Courts of Appeals. Each **court of appeals** has jurisdiction over several states. Appeals from all the district courts in those states are taken to the designated court of appeals. The geographic area that a court of appeals covers is called a "circuit." The circuits are numbered, and there are now 11 numbered federal circuits.[9] For example, all federal appeals from Maine, New Hampshire, Massachusetts, and Rhode Island (plus Puerto Rico) are taken to the U.S. Court of Appeals for the First Circuit. Appeals from the U.S. District Courts in Vermont, New York, and Connecticut go to the Second Circuit Court of Appeals. In common usage, these courts are sometimes called "circuit courts." You will hear, as a common abbreviation, something like, "That case was decided in the Eighth Circuit," which means the U.S. Court of Appeals for the Eighth Circuit decided the case. **Figure 1-1** is a map showing the breakdown of the United States into federal judicial circuits.

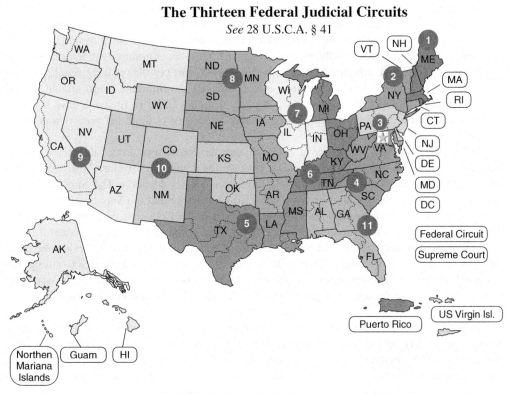

The Thirteen Federal Judicial Circuits
See 28 U.S.C.A. § 41

Figure 1-1 The Thirteen Federal Judicial Circuits.
Source: United States Courts. *Court Locator.* Available from http://www.uscourts.gov/court_locator.aspx.
[19 February 2011]

In most cases, when appeals are taken, the lawyers for each side file **briefs**, arguing their cases in writing, and later they argue their cases orally before the court of appeals. There are usually three judges who sit and decide each case at the appellate level. Sometimes, in special matters and because of the importance of the case, it will be heard by all members of that particular court. This is called a hearing **en banc**. Cases are decided by a majority of the judges who sit on the case. One judge is designated to write the **opinion** of the court. If not all the judges agree, the disagreeing judge or judges will often write a dissenting opinion. (This practice of writing majority and dissenting opinions goes on in the Supreme Court, as well. With nine justices voting, there are many more dissenting opinions in the Supreme Court.)

It is the **majority opinion** that prevails for the individual case the judges are deciding. That opinion also becomes the prevailing law, or **precedent**, on any legal matter that is decided by that case. It is the governing law for that circuit, and it will be followed by all courts in that circuit when that particular legal question arises in the future. It is not binding in other circuits but may be looked to for guidance by other courts. Through this procedure, you can see that there may be disagreeing opinions or legal conclusions in different circuits. This does happen, and such disagreements are often grounds for taking cases to the Supreme Court. Only the Supreme Court can resolve differences between the lower federal courts of appeals.

The U.S. Supreme Court is the highest and final federal appellate court. There is a direct appeal to the Supreme Court on only a few kinds of cases (for example, if a federal law, or a state law of statewide application, is found by a lower court to be unconstitutional, that decision can be appealed directly to the Supreme Court).[10] Most cases come to the Supreme Court by means of **certiorari**, which means that the Supreme Court certifies that the legal question raised by the case is of considerable importance and that the Supreme Court should decide that question. As noted, one frequent basis for the Supreme Court to review a case is that it presents a question that has caused a conflict or difference of opinion between two or more courts of appeals.

When a party loses its case in a court of appeals and it wants the Supreme Court to consider and reverse that decision, it files a petition for a writ of certiorari, which is a legal paper asking the Supreme Court to review the lower court's decision. The Supreme Court votes (in chambers—not in public) on whether the case is one that the Supreme Court should consider. If four or more justices vote to review the case, the Court issues an order certifying the case to be heard in the Supreme Court. This is called granting a writ of certiorari. If, as in most cases that are petitioned to the Supreme Court, the justices do not vote to review the case, the writ of certiorari is denied. Each year, several thousand cases (about 5,900 during the 12-month period ending September 30, 2010) are taken by petition to the Supreme Court. The Court votes to accept the appeal or grant certiorari in relatively few cases (165 during the above 12-month period).[11]

Cases in the Supreme Court, like the appellate courts, are considered by a process that involves each party submitting written briefs and then arguing the case orally before the Court. All cases in the Supreme Court are considered by all nine justices of the Court. (Sometimes a justice disqualifies himself or herself because of some prior involvement, or there may be a vacancy on the Court that remains unfilled. Thus, some cases are decided by eight or fewer justices.)

The Supreme Court still sits in a "term of court," as virtually all courts once did. The term of the Supreme Court runs from October through June. Lower federal courts no longer have such terms. Federal judges at all levels (the Supreme Court and district and appeals courts) are appointed by the president, with the advice and consent of the Senate (meaning their appointments must be approved in the Senate by affirmative vote). They serve for life and can be removed only by impeachment. This contrasts with the states, where many judges are elected to their offices.

State Courts

Each state has a similar hierarchy of courts, which is structured much like the federal system. There are, in every state, levels of trial courts and appellate courts. That is as far as a general statement can go, because there is a huge difference among states regarding how their court systems are organized and named. You will have to investigate the state of interest to you regarding what the courts at different levels are called.

For example, **trial courts** may be called circuit courts (typically for counties), district courts, superior courts, or municipal courts (in larger cities). There may be courts authorized to handle certain specialized kinds of cases at the first level, such as juvenile courts, probate courts, domestic relations courts, and traffic courts. In some jurisdictions, all of these special matters and all kinds of cases—civil and criminal—are handled in the trial courts, which we then call **courts of general jurisdiction**. It is becoming more and more common, especially in counties and cities of larger populations, to reduce the burdens on the trial courts by having matters of smaller import taken to small-claims courts (for civil matters with limited jurisdiction, such as those involving matters of up to $5,000) or police courts or magistrates or justices of the peace (for criminal matters, with jurisdiction to impose small sentences such as fines or short jail terms of 10 days or less). Persons often appear in these small-claims courts or traffic courts without counsel, which tends to save money and speed up the process.

Most states have two levels of appellate courts. The middle level is called a court of appeals, an appellate division, or some similar name. A few states (Delaware, Maine, Montana, Nevada, New Hampshire, Rhode Island, South Dakota, Vermont, West Virginia, and Wyoming) do not have an intermediate appellate court and have only one level of appeal. The final level of appeal in the state is usually the **supreme court** of that state, with a few exceptions (exceptions include the Court of Appeals in New York, where the supreme court is a first-level court; the Supreme Judicial Court in Massachusetts; the Court of Appeals in Maryland; the Supreme Judicial Court Sitting as Law Court in Maine; and the Supreme Court of Appeals in West Virginia). These appellate-level courts handle appeals in all kinds of cases, both civil and criminal. Only Texas and Oklahoma have supreme appellate courts that are divided—one for civil and one for criminal cases.[12]

As noted previously, state judges at all levels are elected in many states. In some states, judges are appointed by the governor or by legislative election.[13] The means of selecting state judges, particularly by election, has been the subject of criticism and debate. In many states, the judges do not run as nominees of political parties, making them (theoretically) separated from the partisan political process. Also, especially upon re-election, judges may run unopposed, reducing the political effects on their offices.

▪ Criminal and Civil Law

Matters of the law are divided, for study and for practical concerns, into divisions or topics. A division is often made between criminal and civil matters of the law. What difference does it make? It is not purely an academic question. We have noted that, in some jurisdictions, certain courts only consider one kind of case or the other, civil or criminal. Some lawyers specialize in **criminal law,** and others practice only **civil law**. There are different rules of procedure in federal and in many state courts that govern criminal trials and proceedings, as opposed to civil ones.

Examples of different rules include those for **burden of proof**. For criminal cases, the standard is proof beyond a reasonable doubt; the evidence must be entirely convincing in establishing the defendant's guilt. In civil cases, the usual standard is proof by a preponderance of the evidence; the evidence must show a greater likelihood that the person did, as opposed to did not do, the act as charged. This is also referred to as the "greater weight" of the evidence. The reason for this dual standard and for the higher standard of proof in criminal trials is that, in a criminal case, the defendant is facing the loss of freedom (**liberty**).[14]

Crimes are those acts that are described by a state (that is, a government) in its laws or regulations as prohibited activities, for the protection of its citizens. Every citizen has a duty to conform to those standards of conduct. A violation of that duty, or commission of such a prohibited act, is a crime, and the violator (the criminal or the **offender**) is subject to punishment. It is important to note that the description of criminal acts and the punishment authorized for them are matters of legislation and not judicial (common) law. A crime is a violation of a duty owed to the state and all its citizens. Court actions are thus brought by state officials, called prosecutors (often district or state attorneys), on behalf of all citizens in that state. There are, of course, wide ranges of criminal activities, from the practically trivial (parking and small traffic matters) to violations of the most horrendous nature (homicides, espionage, and other violent behaviors).

Crimes are often divided into the more serious, called **felonies**, and the less serious, called **misdemeanors**, for procedural reasons (such as the type of punishment upon **conviction** or the kinds of court procedures that apply). The most common dividing line between felonies and misdemeanors is the maximum **penalty** authorized for the particular offense. As a general rule, if a crime carries a penalty of more than one year in prison, it is a felony; if it carries a penalty of one year or less, it is a misdemeanor. There are, in some criminal systems, offenses of even lesser importance than misdemeanors, such as **petty offenses** (which may be punishable only by fines or by jail terms of 30 days or less, as examples).

Civil law is the entire body of law that is not criminal—that is, it deals with duties owed by one person to another and not to the state. (This area of noncriminal law is also sometimes called "private law.") The two most common kinds of civil law are contracts and torts. Contracts law is the set of rules established to deal with promises made by one person to another. (In all of these discussions, it should be remembered that, for most purposes, a "person" may be a corporation, business, or an agency, as well as an individual human being.) At one time, contracts law was governed primarily by court decisions and precedents—that is, by common law. Over time, legislatures have enacted more and more rules with respect to contracts, so that the law today is a large mix of common law and legislation.

Torts law covers other types of duty owed by one person to another (that is, other than duties owed by contracts) and is the means by which an **injury** or harm caused can be remedied through a legal action. We will discuss torts in more detail later. It is noted here that in civil law, both for contracts and for torts, the remedy that is most often sought by the injured person is damages—that is, money; though in some cases, specific performance (of a contract) or injunctive relief (to force action or to restrain it) may be the remedies sought. All of these are now considered to be civil actions (and almost all of the litigation in the corrections field is civil, not criminal.)

Some actions may be a violation both of criminal law and civil duties owed to others. For example, **assault** may lead to a civil suit, whereby an individual attempts to recover money damages for the harm inflicted by a wrongful action. The same activity, investigated by the police, may be the basis for a prosecutor bringing a criminal prosecution for assault.

Civil actions are usually initiated when an **attorney** files a legal paper—a **complaint**—on behalf of his client, asking for damages because of a wrong inflicted or a duty violated by another person. The person bringing the action is the **plaintiff**; the person sued is the **defendant**. By contrast, criminal cases are brought by a **grand jury** (handing up an indictment) or by a prosecutor (filing a bill of information or some other title in lesser cases). The case is brought by the state (or the people of the state) against a defendant, who is charged with wrongdoing. (Of course, there may be multiple defendants involved in criminal activity. In a civil case, there may also be more than one plaintiff and more than one defendant.) Class actions are civil cases in which, for purposes of economy, a plaintiff or a group of plaintiffs who have the same legal complaints against a defendant (or defendants) may be joined together by a court into a single class; one plaintiff or several are allowed to proceed with the lawsuit on behalf of all the others, who are notified of the proceedings. A decision or judgment in a class action is entered on behalf of all the plaintiffs and is binding on all the parties.

While criminal law and civil law are the two major components of the law, the law may be categorized in other ways. Any one or all of the following may be evident in criminal or civil litigation.

Case law is the common law that was discussed earlier. It refers to decisions of courts published in law books (called reporters). A significant portion of this text includes a discussion of case law.

Statutory law is the body of law created by the acts of the various legislatures, including Congress. Examples of such laws, discussed later in this text, are the Prison Litigation Reform Act and the Interstate Agreement on Detainers.

Administrative law is a body of law created by administrative agencies (for example, departments of justice and state regulatory agencies). These laws, discussed with statutory law, are seen in the form of rules, regulations, orders, and decisions. Administrative law is often developed to more effectively carry out statutory law.

Procedural law refers to the methods by which a legal right or duty is enforced (for example, entering a plea, presenting evidence, or establishing jurisdiction).

Substantive law is the whole area of the law that creates and defines legal rights and obligations (for example, tort law and criminal law).

SUMMARY

- Law in the United States is principally derived from English law, which in turn was largely based on judicial rulings, collectively called the common law. A major difference between the United States and England is that the supreme law of the land in the United States is the Constitution. Each of the states also has a written constitution, which is the highest law of that state.

- In the federal, state, and local governments, there are three branches: legislative, executive, and judicial. Each of these branches has separate powers, which are spelled out in the respective constitutions.

- Laws of the federal government are the highest laws of the country. The U.S. Supreme Court is the highest court of the country.

- In the federal government, the levels of courts are trial courts, called U.S. District Courts; appellate courts, called U.S. Courts of Appeals (designated primarily by numbered circuits); and the U.S. Supreme Court.

- Cases in the Supreme Court are usually considered when at least four justices of the Court agree to review a case by granting a writ of certiorari (certifying the case's importance to be heard in the Supreme Court). Only a small percentage of cases that are petitioned (appealed) to the Supreme Court are actually reviewed by the Court. In a few cases, there is a right of direct appeal to the Supreme Court; the kind of direct appeal we will see occasionally in this text is that in which a federal law, or a state law of statewide application, is found by a district court to be unconstitutional.

- Each state has similar levels of courts: trial courts at the county, city, or town level; appeals courts (in most states); and a supreme court, which is the final judicial authority for cases brought under state laws.

- Legal matters are divided into criminal law and civil law. Criminal law is used for the prosecution of offenders who violate statutes that define conduct or activity that is prohibited because it is offensive to the state's citizens. Upon conviction of any such crimes, sanctions (sentences) are imposed, as authorized by the state's criminal statutes. Civil law comprises the rest of the law—that is, all the law that is not criminal. There are many kinds of civil law, but the most common are contracts law (the duties owed by one person to another because of promises made) and torts law (the remedies the law provides for injuries done by one person to another, other than by contract violation). The law may be further categorized into such areas as case, statutory, administrative, procedural, and substantive law. Any of these may appear within the context of criminal and civil litigation.

KEY TERMS

administrative law: The body of law created by administrative agencies (such as regulatory agencies). These laws are seen in the form of rules, regulations, orders, and interpretive decisions.

appeal: A request by either party that a case be removed from a lower court to a higher court in order for a trial proceeding to be reviewed by the higher court. It also refers to the review by an appeals court of a lower court's proceedings or outcome.

assault: The unlawful intentional infliction, or attempted or threatened infliction, of injury upon another. (Also defined as an unlawful physical attack by one person upon another.)

attorney: A person trained in the law, admitted to practice before the bar of a given jurisdiction, and authorized to advise, represent, and act for other persons in legal proceedings. (Used interchangeably with lawyer or counsel.)

brief: A written document prepared by counsel that presents facts, discussion of contested issues, legal references, and arguments pertaining to the case before a trial court or an appellate court.

burden of proof: The necessity of proving a fact or facts in dispute in a case. The obligation a party has to introduce sufficient evidence to convince the trier of fact that an essential fact or conclusion is true.

canon law (church law): The body of law established by religious organizations, and administered by religious officials, for the determination of rights and liabilities under matters subject to religious jurisdiction.

case (legal proceedings): The court proceeding, whether civil or criminal, in all its aspects. Also used to refer to a report of a court decision in legal publications, such as court reporters.

case law: The cumulated law, as given in the decisions of courts. The aggregate of reported cases on a particular subject, from a particular source, or in toto.

certiorari: A writ issued by a superior court to an inferior court of record that orders the certification of the records and proceedings in the case, so that the record (the case) may be reviewed for any error and corrected, as needed. A form of appellate review. (Now used principally to apply to reviews by the U.S. Supreme Court of actions by lower courts. To obtain a Supreme Court review, an applicant files a petition for a writ of certiorari.)

chancery (court of chancery): A court to hear cases in equity (in England and some places in the United States).

checks and balances: Procedures established by constitutional requirements, whereby each of the three branches of government has some constraints on the other two.

civil law: The body of law that determines private rights and liabilities, as distinguished from criminal law.

common law: Those principles and rules, applicable to government and individuals, that do not rest for their original authority on statutes but on statements (rulings) found in decisions of courts. In a broader sense, it is sometimes used to refer to the Anglo-American system of justice and legal concepts.

complaint (civil procedure): The initial pleading filed in court, by which a legal action is commenced. This is the pleading that sets out a claim for relief, including the factual and legal grounds for such relief.

constitution: A statement of the fundamental laws or principles that are agreed on to govern a nation, a state, an organization, or a society.

conviction: A judgment of a court, based either on the verdict of a jury, judicial officer, or on the guilty plea of the defendant, that the defendant is guilty of the offense for which he has been tried.

court: An agency or individual officer of the judicial branch of government, authorized or established by statute or constitution, which has the authority to decide controversies in law and disputed matters of fact brought before it.

court of appeals: A court that does not try cases, but rather hears appeals.

court of general jurisdiction: A court that has the legal authority to try all civil cases and criminal offenses, including all felonies.

crime (criminal offense): An act committed or omitted in violation of a law forbidding or commanding it, for which an adult can be punished, upon conviction, by incarceration or other penalties, or for which a juvenile can be brought under the jurisdiction of a juvenile court and adjudicated as a delinquent or transferred to adult court.

criminal law: The entire body of law—statutes, court opinions, rules—that defines offenses against the state, sets rules for their prosecution, and authorizes sanctions for committing offenses.

decision: A determination or conclusion reached by a court. Usually used to refer to the written report of a court that states its conclusion or determination of the case. The decision reached by a court is reflected in its opinion. (See that definition.)

defendant: A person against whom a criminal proceeding is undertaken or a person against whom a civil legal action is brought.

en banc (courts): A proceeding in which all members of a particular court will participate in hearing and deciding a case.

equity (courts): An alternative, established in English law, to the ordinary forms of civil law and justice. The emphasis in equity is to provide fair and just results in cases in which the common law or ordinary laws do not appear adequate. Equity concentrates on the persons who are present in court without trying to establish rights to govern other cases. (In the United States, in most jurisdictions, equity and law have been combined in courts of general jurisdiction.)

evidence: Any type of proof that is presented at trial, consisting of witnesses' testimony, records, documents, and other physical objects. Used to prove (or disprove) a fact relevant to the case being tried.

federal: Pertaining to the national government of the United States of America. The government of a community of independent states, joined in a union having central and predominant authority.

felony: A criminal offense punishable by death or by incarceration in a confinement facility for a period of which the lower limit is prescribed by statute in a given jurisdiction, typically more than one year.

grand jury: A body of persons who have been selected and sworn to investigate criminal activity and the conduct of public officials and who hear evidence and legal advice from a prosecutor against an accused person to determine whether there is sufficient evidence to bring that person to trial. The decision of a grand jury that there is sufficient evidence for trial results in an indictment or "true bill," which is "handed up" by the grand jury.

injury: Any wrong or damage done to another's person, rights, reputation, or property.

jurisdiction: The precise geographic territory, subject matter, or person(s) over which lawful authority may be exercised, as defined by constitutional provisions or by statute.

liberty: Freedom from restraints. As provided in the Fifth and Fourteenth Amendments, no person shall be deprived of "life, liberty, or property, without due process of law."

majority opinion: The opinion of an appellate court in which the majority of its participating members join. It therefore is the controlling opinion for the case.

misdemeanor: An offense usually punishable by incarceration in a local confinement facility (jail) for a period of which the upper limit is prescribed by statute in a given jurisdiction; the period is less than that of a felony and is typically limited to a year or less.

offender: An adult who has been charged with (strictly, that person is an alleged offender) or convicted of a criminal offense.

opinion (court): The statement by a judge or a court of the decision reached in a case. It is usually given in writing and typically sets out the issue(s) presented in the case, the facts of the case, the law that applies, and the reasoning used to reach a conclusion or judgment.

penalty: The punishment that is affixed by law or by judicial decision to the commission of a particular offense. It may be death, imprisonment (which may be a prison sentence or a jail sentence), an alternative facility sanction, a fine, restitution, or a loss of civil privileges. (Also called a sanction or punishment.)

petty offense: A minor criminal offense that is triable by a magistrate or subjudicial officer, without a jury. (The definition of the offenses so triable will be made by statute. In some places, it may include misdemeanors.)

plaintiff: The party who initiates a civil action. The person who files a complaint in court. (Technically, also the prosecutor, the state, or the United States in a criminal action, but it is seldom used in that context.)

precedent: A court decision that provides authoritative guidance or principle for a later case that has a similar question of law. A determination of a point of law made by a court, which is to be followed by a court of the same rank or of lower rank in a subsequent case that presents the same legal problem.

procedural law: Methods of proceeding, typically in a court, by which a legal right or duty is enforced. Distinguished from substantive law, which defines the rights, responsibilities, and duties of persons.

regulation: An order by competent authority, most often an agency of the executive branch, setting rules for actions that are under the agency's control.

statute: An act of a legislature declaring, commanding, or prohibiting something.

statutory law: The body of law created by the acts of the legislatures.

substantive law: The whole area of law that creates and defines legal rights and obligations. Distinguished from procedural law, which is the methods of proceeding by which a legal right or duty is enforced.

supreme court: An appellate court at the highest level in most states and in the federal court system. The court of last resort in the particular jurisdiction. The U.S. Supreme Court is the highest court in the federal court system and the highest court in the nation.

trial: The examination of issues of fact and law in a case or controversy, beginning when the jury has been selected in a jury trial, the first witness is sworn, or the first evidence is introduced in a court trial, and concluding when a verdict is reached or the case is dismissed.

trial court: A judicial officer who is authorized to conduct trials. (Usually used to distinguish from appeals courts.)

writ: An order requiring a specified act to be performed.

ENDNOTES

1. Administrative Office of the U.S. Courts. *2010 Annual Report of the Director: Judicial Business of the United States Courts.* Table C-2A. Washington, DC: U.S. Government Printing Office, 2011.
2. Stephan, J. *Census of State and Federal Correctional Facilities, 2005.* Appendix table 12. Washington, DC: Bureau of Justice Statistics, U.S. Department of Justice, October 2008.
3. There was, in English law, equity law alongside common law. **Equity** dealt with matters of "doing the right thing" (keeping the "King's conscience"), particularly in hardship cases. Separate courts, called **chancery courts**, handled equity matters. In equity cases, courts ordered specific performance or injunction rather than money damages, and they developed maxims rather than decisions. Equity was used when common law did not provide an adequate remedy. Equity law was also taken from English law and incorporated into American law. However, in most jurisdictions in the United States, equity and common law have been merged, so that both kinds of cases are heard in the same courts. The equity concept persists in some different legal language, in some differences in philosophical approaches to cases, and in procedural differences, such as the fact that there is a right to a jury trial only in common law cases and not in equity matters, which are decided by the judge alone. (This explains why there is no jury in injunction cases.)
4. Conflicts between federal and state or local law can serve as another example of the checks and balances concept. For example, in 2001, the federal government challenged the state of Oregon's Death with Dignity Act, which authorized physician-assisted suicide. The federal government took the position that assisting in a suicide is not a "legitimate medical purpose" and authorized federal drug agents to identify and punish doctors who assisted in helping terminally-ill patients to die. In April 2002, a U.S. district court rejected the government's directive; in September 2002, the government asked the Court of Appeals for the Ninth Circuit to strike down the Oregon law. In May 2004, the Ninth Circuit upheld the state law, stating that the "[U.S.] Attorney General's unilateral attempt to regulate general medical practices historically entrusted to state lawmakers...far exceeds the scope of his authority." The U.S. Supreme Court granted the government's petition for certiorari. In January 2006, the Supreme Court affirmed the Court of Appeals decision and upheld the state law, stating, "the statute [Controlled Substances Act] manifests no intent to regulate the practice of medicine generally. The silence is understandable given the structure and limitations of federalism, which allow the States " 'great latitude under their police powers to legislate as to the protection of the lives, limbs, health, comfort, and quiet of all persons.' " *Gonzales v. Oregon*, 546 U.S. 243 (2006).
5. According to the constitutions of the states, or by legislation, local governmental jurisdictions of many levels are created, including counties, townships, and cities. In most cases, each of these levels of government also has a type of legislature (a board of supervisors or a county or city council), an executive (a sheriff, a mayor, or a town manager), and a judicial system (circuit courts, city courts, or magistrates). Thus, the three-branch concept of government prevails at all levels in our country.
6. See endnote 3.

7. There are some specialized courts in the federal system, such as customs courts, tax courts, and military courts-martial. These trial-level courts have counterpart appellate courts. These specialized courts are not of concern to us in this study, because they do not deal with corrections matters, with the exception of the military courts—including the Court of Military Appeals—which do deal with sentencing and corrections litigation.

8. There are some rare exceptions. One that we see in the corrections field is the requirement (by statute) that when a state law is under review as to its constitutionality, a panel of three district judges is convened to rule on that question.

9. In addition, and as an exception to the numbering rule for circuits, there are two courts of appeals that sit in the District of Columbia. The U.S. Court of Appeals for the District of Columbia Circuit hears appeals from the U.S. District Court for the District of Columbia. The Federal Circuit Court hears appeals from specified federal boards and administrative courts.

10. There are an even smaller number of cases that may, by direction of the Constitution (Article III, Section 2), be brought directly and from the beginning into the Supreme Court. These are cases that involve ambassadors and those in which a state is a party. There have been a few such cases, which involved such matters as disputes between states about their boundaries or the allocation of water from rivers. Because the Supreme Court is not a trial court and has no procedure to take testimony or receive evidence, it has usually appointed a special master to conduct such a trial on its behalf.

11. Administrative Office of the U.S. Courts. *2010 Annual Report of the Director: Judicial Business of the United States Courts.* Table B-2. Washington, DC: U.S. Government Printing Office, 2011.

12. National Center for State Courts. *State Court Web sites.* Accessed January 15, 2011, http://www.ncsc.org/information-and-resources/browse-by-state/statecourtwebsites.aspx. Under the states listed, there is a court structure chart.

13. American Judicature Society. *Methods of Judicial Selection.* Accessed January 15, 2011, http://www.judicialselection.us.

14. Different burden of proof standards can lead to different results, even with the same basic facts. Perhaps the best known example is the O. J. Simpson case, where the former football great was found not guilty of murder in the criminal trial but had a monetary judgment entered against him in the civil trial, which was based on the same set of facts.

2 Corrections and the Criminal Justice System

It is the mission of the Federal Bureau of Prisons to protect society by confining offenders in the controlled environments of prisons and community-based facilities that are safe, humane, cost-efficient, and appropriately secure, and that provide work and other self-improvement opportunities to assist offenders in becoming law-abiding citizens.

Mission Statement of the Federal Bureau of Prisons

Chapter Outline

- The Police
- Arrest and Release
- Prosecution
- The Courts
- Sentencing
- Corrections
  - Probation
  - Fines
  - Restitution
  - Electronic Monitoring
  - Community Service and Creative Sentencing

In this chapter, we take a quick and broad look at the criminal justice system in the United States and how corrections, as a discipline, fits into that system. Because there are many areas where the different components of criminal justice interrelate, it would be desirable to coordinate planning and working between those components. In practice, unfortunately, and in most jurisdictions there is very little coordination between the different components. That lack of coordinated planning also is evident in most legislatures, where programs and appropriations are historically pursued in one area, with little attention paid to how legislative action may affect other criminal justice areas.

One example of such lack of attention to coordinated planning is a fairly common one: the enactment of new criminal statutes that increase the penalties for crimes without consideration of the impact that action will have on police, prosecutors' offices, the courts, and corrections. For example, the implementation of determinate sentencing and the abolishment of parole have clearly achieved a "get tough on crime" stance.

To illustrate, we can look at the state of Florida. Between 1993 and 2007, the state's inmate population grew from 53,000 to over 97,000. A number of state correctional policies and practices contributed to this growth. In 1995, Florida's legislature abolished **good time** credits and discretionary release by the parole board. The legislation required every inmate to serve 85% of his sentence. A "zero tolerance" policy also was put in place, requiring probation officers to report every offender who violated any condition of supervision and increasing prison time for these "technical violations." From this legislative action, the number of violators in Florida's prisons increased by an estimated 12,000.[1] A by-product of this increase is the need for additional expenditures. This impacts the state's budgetary resources, as those newly expended funds can detract from the funds that are available for other programs.

At the same time, practices such as determinate sentencing and the abolishment of parole have produced the unintended consequence of lessening the motivations for inmates to abide by institution regulations and work toward their release. This places an increased burden on prison administrators to maintain institution security and good order. Some state governments and state legislatures have tried to provide a more comprehensive process by creating criminal justice planning agencies for an entire state or by better organizing committee work and legislative drafting in the legislature. On the federal level, legislation has been introduced in the United States Congress proposing the establishment of the National Criminal Justice Commission. The legislation gives the commission the responsibility for doing a comprehensive review of all areas of the criminal justice system, including criminal justice costs, practices, and policies of federal, state, local, and tribal governments.[2]

Criminal law deals with violations of duties that citizens owe to the society at large. By enactments of the legislature, certain conduct is described as prohibited and violative of societal standards. Such conduct is, by those legislative actions, declared to be criminal. These legislative enactments, taken together, constitute the "criminal law" for a specific jurisdiction. When conduct is declared to be criminal, the statute that defines the crime also sets the punishments (or range of punishments) that accompany that particular crime.

The legislature, whether state or federal (or even local, in cases where counties, towns, or cities have been given limited authority to legislate on criminal matters), also defines the procedure by which crimes are investigated, prosecuted, and punished. In law schools, courses are often given in these two areas: criminal law, which examines the substantive law of criminal activities, definitions of different crimes, and classification of crimes; and criminal procedure, which is the study of the agencies and actions of criminal law enforcement, prosecution, court proceedings, and criminal sanctions. These procedures, as well as the agencies and individuals that pursue them, make up the criminal justice system.

Figure 2-1 shows the principal elements in the criminal justice system in the United States. There may be variations of this system in individual states, but the major components are the same: police, prosecution, courts, and corrections.

What is the sequence of events in the criminal justice system?

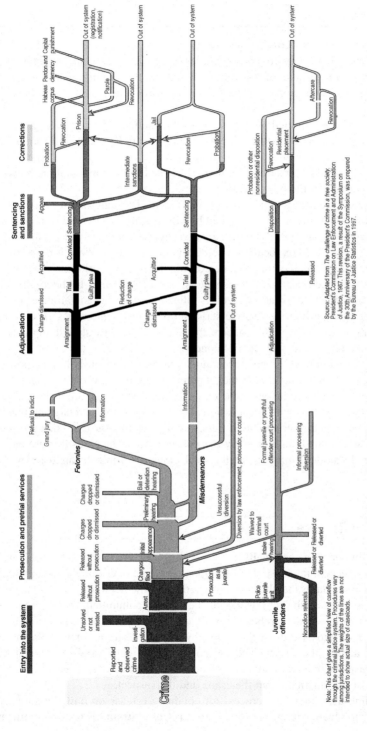

Figure 2-1 The criminal justice system. The above diagram illustrates the sequence of events in the criminal justice system. To link to a description of one of the areas shown, go to http://bjs.ojp.usdoj.gov/content/largechart.cfm and click on the section of interest.

Source: Bureau of Justice Statistics, United States Department of Justice. Available from http://bjs.ojp.usdoj.gov/content/largechart.cfm

■ The Police

The role of the police in our criminal justice system is to prevent, detect, and investigate crime and apprehend offenders. This role is sometimes called law enforcement. The police carry out this role within the constraints of constitutional and statutory requirements and with the overriding principle that their work is done for the protection and welfare of the citizenry as a whole.

Crimes may be committed within sight of the police. Most crimes, however, are not observed by the police. Some of these are reported to the police, and some are never reported. The police are given authority to prevent crimes, enforce the criminal law, investigate criminal activities, turn investigative material over to prosecutors for initiating criminal prosecutions, and work with prosecutors in the prosecution of cases.

Police have great discretion in investigative matters. Through training and experience, they learn that certain crimes may best be handled by informal discussion. Some reported crimes are investigated vigorously and swiftly; others are investigated summarily or not at all. These investigative decisions are based on local enforcement policy, which, in turn, is derived from a range of sources, including available police resources and the relative seriousness of different crimes as viewed by the police department, prosecutors, and local courts. In theory, the views of the police department, prosecutors, and the courts reflect the opinions and attitudes of the citizenry in that jurisdiction regarding the relative seriousness of different crimes. The criminal justice system, after all, is founded on the concept that the criminal law should appropriately punish those who violate prescribed standards of conduct.

Because of the volume of crime in most jurisdictions and seriously limited police resources, the discretionary action of police is, in fact, a potent element of law enforcement. Decisions not to investigate or decisions to handle some cases of misconduct that are technically criminal by informal resolution, such as with a discussion and warning, result in a large number of criminal matters that proceed no further into the system. Adding together the cases that are never reported and those that are handled "in-house" by the police (that is, the cases that are not referred for prosecution), only a small minority of the total cases of criminal conduct is pursued in the courts.[3]

■ Arrest and Release

Of significant importance, especially to the accused, is the decision to hold the suspect in custody. Taking a person into custody based upon suspicion of criminal conduct is called **arrest**. There are precise standards that the police use to decide whether a person may be arrested. These involve such elements as the seriousness of the offense committed, the record of the suspect, actions of the suspect when apprehended, and, certainly, what action has been taken in comparable cases. If taken into custody by the police (by physical restraint, such as placing in handcuffs and placing in a cell), the suspect will be advised of his or her right to remain silent and to contact and consult with an attorney. The suspect will also be booked. This is the entry into the police records of information about the crime and the suspect.

At this point, there may be a process for obtaining **release on bail**. An attorney will often move promptly to obtain bail or have the suspect **released upon his own recognizance** (that is, without any bail or any **bond** having to be posted). Depending on the crime and local procedures, this may be obtained in some cases without court review. Otherwise, the application for release will be made at the initial court appearance or as soon thereafter as possible.

■ Prosecution

Another component with great discretionary authority is the prosecution.[4] The police bring to the prosecutor's office their records of investigation, which include the complaint made (by the victim or others); statements of witnesses; other evidence gathered; in some cases, a statement by the accused (confession); the prior record of the accused; and, usually, recommendations for prosecution. The **prosecutor** weighs this information and makes a decision about proceeding. Weak cases may be dropped here or sent back for further investigation. More complex cases may remain under continuing investigation by the police. However, such a case may be referred to the prosecutor for preliminary review regarding the strength of the case or to meet time requirements to bring the accused into court for an initial appearance while he is under arrest.

If the prosecutor decides that there is sufficient evidence to proceed, she will initiate the formal steps of prosecution. What these steps are depends on the nature of the crime and what category of seriousness it falls into. This in turn may vary from one jurisdiction to another. (As with all of these criminal justice procedures, this discussion is based on the most common practice. The reader should always be alert to the fact that circumstances may be different in a particular local jurisdiction.)

If the offense is a minor one—that is, a petty offense—the prosecutor files a complaint, an **information**, or a criminal charge, and the defendant is taken promptly before a lower court (a magistrate, a commissioner, or a justice of the peace). Note that once **charges** are filed, the person accused of the criminal act has become a defendant—a party in a criminal proceeding. The title of the case will typically read, "*The People of the State*" or "*The State of (name of the state) versus (name of the accused), defendant.*" For minor crimes, the proceedings are usually quick; the defendant is advised of his rights and asked for his plea. Even if the defendant denies the charges, the case will usually proceed quickly. If a trial is requested, an early trial date will be set, but sufficient time for attorneys to prepare and to obtain the presence of necessary witnesses must be allowed. If the defendant is found guilty (by plea or by trial), penalties are proportionally smaller (usually limited to fines or short jail terms) for minor offenses.

If the offense is a greater one, then the crime is considered to be either a misdemeanor or a felony. As noted previously, in most jurisdictions, misdemeanors are offenses that carry penalties of up to one year in prison. Felonies are offenses that carry penalties of more than one year in prison. For misdemeanors, prosecutors can almost always file the charges by signing an information or similar prosecutive document. For felonies, an **indictment** is one method of charging the accused, and this requires taking the evidence before a grand jury, which decides whether there is sufficient evidence to take the accused to trial, and, if there is, the grand jury hands up an indictment. (Some states have no grand juries. Other jurisdictions seldom use them.) It is common for a defendant who is charged with a felony to be asked to waive indictment and to agree to proceed by information. Thus, only a small number of prosecutions nationwide originate with grand jury action.

Soon after arrest, defendants are brought before the lower (preliminary) judicial authority, where they are told their rights, the assignment of **counsel** is discussed (if they have not retained an attorney), and the sufficiency of the charges is preliminarily reviewed (by a judicial official, ensuring, for the first time, review of the evidence by someone outside the prosecution and police offices). Whether by indictment, information, or other official prosecutor's charges, the case is formally and publicly filed in the court system at this time. After an information or indictment is filed, the defendant is taken before the criminal court for arraignment.

At **arraignment**, the accused person is brought before the court and is asked to enter a plea of "guilty" or "not guilty." Arraignment is conducted in open court and consists of reading the indictment or information to the defendant or otherwise providing him with the substance of the charges against him. At arraignment, the court makes certain that indigent defendants (persons without funds) are provided counsel. Here also the defendant elects whether to have a **trial by jury** or **trial by judge** alone.

After reviewing the evidence presented at this preliminary stage, the court may order some charges to be dismissed for insufficient evidence or some charges to be reduced to lesser offenses. From these earliest stages, the defense counsel will negotiate with the prosecutor to get charges dropped or reduced, either on the basis of the strength of the case or in return for entering a guilty plea. The defense counsel will file motions with the court, challenging the legality of the prosecution papers, sometimes challenging arrest or other police actions, or challenging the propriety of detention.

■ The Courts

After the initial papers are filed with the clerk of the court, the judge assigned to the criminal matter has jurisdiction over the disposition of the case.

> **In all criminal prosecutions, the accused shall enjoy the right to a speedy and public trial, by an impartial jury of the State and district wherein the crime shall have been committed, which district shall have been previously ascertained by law, and to be informed of the nature and cause of the accusation; to be confronted with the witnesses against him; to have compulsory process for obtaining witnesses in his favor, and to have the Assistance of Counsel for his defence.**
>
> U.S. Constitution, Amendment 6

> **No person shall be ... deprived of life, liberty, or property, without due process of law.**
>
> U.S. Constitution, Amendment 5

> **No State shall make or enforce any law which shall abridge the privileges or immunities of citizens of the United States; nor shall any State deprive any person of life, liberty, or property, without due process of law; nor deny to any person within its jurisdiction the equal protection of the laws.**
>
> U.S. Constitution, Amendment 14

Every criminal court must ensure that constitutional standards for **criminal proceedings** and **due process** are met. If the defendant pleads guilty, the court makes sure that the action of the defendant in pleading guilty is understood by him and is voluntarily made. If he pleads not guilty, the case proceeds to trial. If the defendant elects not to have a jury, the court will hear the trial and make the decision as to the defendant's guilt. If there is a jury, the judge supervises all proceedings, makes rulings on evidence and procedural matters, and instructs the jury about the law that applies to their deliberations. A defendant found not guilty is, of course, released (unless there are other charges pending on which to hold him). A defendant found guilty is then ready for sentencing.

The corrections component involvement in the criminal justice process can begin as early as the arrest stage if the suspect is detained in jail, and for some, pretrial release may include aspects of correctional supervision. But for many criminal defendants, the corrections stage of criminal justice becomes involved at sentencing. Sentencing is the legal process that anticipates the correctional function. In many cases, corrections authorities may be involved in the sentencing itself. But sentencing is a judicial function; only courts impose **sentences,** as authorized by the criminal statutes.[5] It is true that, in some jurisdictions, sentencing reforms in recent years have diminished the wide authority of sentencing judges by prescribing mandatory or determinate sentences. In most cases, these procedures reduce the range of sentences that may be imposed by the judges. There is usually a formula, in states that have adopted determinate sentencing, under which elements of criminal conduct are described and assigned values, which are then used (in charts or by other means) to arrive at a narrow range of sentences. Judges may be allowed to go above or below these sentence guides, for reasons that are found in the record and that are based on circumstances that are particularly mitigating or aggravating, in comparison to the average case. Where such sentencing guidelines have not been adopted,[6] judges are typically given (by the legislature, through the criminal statute) a wider range of penalties that may be imposed. While many judges object to the restrictions placed on their wide discretion as a result of sentencing guidelines or **mandatory sentences**, others welcome the attempts to ensure more consistent results in sentencing from case to case across all courts in the jurisdiction.

■ Sentencing

To assist in their sentencing decisions, it has become common in many jurisdictions for the courts to request sentencing reports regarding individual defendants. The Supreme Court has made it clear that individualizing sentences to fit particular defendants is an approved practice. *Williams v. New York*, 337 U.S. 241 (1949). In that case, the Court also emphasized that the sentencing procedure is more relaxed than the strict procedural and evidentiary requirements of due process at the criminal trial itself:

> [A] sentencing judge…exercise[s] a wide discretion in the sources and types of evidence used to assist him in determining the kind and extent of punishment to be imposed within limits fixed by law…Highly relevant—if not essential—to his selection of an appropriate sentence is

> the possession of the fullest information possible concerning the defendant's life and charac-
> teristics... [M]odern concepts individualizing punishment have made it all the more necessary
> that a sentencing judge not be denied an opportunity to obtain pertinent information by a
> requirement of rigid adherence to restrictive rules of evidence properly applicable to the trial.

The Court repeatedly emphasized the importance of individualizing sentences in modern
sentencing philosophy. The reason for this was also stated by the Court:

> Retribution is no longer the dominant objective of the criminal law. Reformation and
> rehabilitation of offenders have become important goals of criminal jurisprudence.

Note that this was said in a case where the Supreme Court upheld the imposition of the
death penalty. But *Williams* is still good law, and it is often cited to sustain rulings about the
relaxed nature of sentencing portions of criminal trials and importance of getting as much information as possible about the defendant in order to fit the sentence to the individual. To assist
the courts in this process, the Supreme Court recognized the value of the sentencing report:

> Under the practice of individualizing punishments, investigational techniques have been
> given an important role. [The reports of probation workers] have been given a high value
> by conscientious judges who want to sentence persons on the best available information
> rather than on guesswork and inadequate information.

Presentencing reports are often sought, particularly in felony cases. In earlier days, these
reports usually came from the prosecutor and perhaps from the defense. To obtain a fairer, more
balanced, and more consistent report, such reports are today usually sought from a judicial office,
the probation office, or even from the corrections department. Sometimes these reports are commenced before the defendant is found guilty. More often, the judge orders a report to be prepared
following the defendant's entering of a guilty plea or after conviction. This report usually reviews
the criminal conduct of the defendant but focuses more on social, educational, psychological,
medical, and family background and needs. These, together with the criminal record that is
always available from the police and prosecution, are used to enable the court to impose a more
informed sentence:

> The aim of the [federal] presentence investigation is to provide a timely, accurate, objective, and
> comprehensive report to the court. The report should have enough information to assist the court
> in making a fair sentencing decision and to assist corrections and community corrections officials
> in managing offenders under their supervision.[7]

As an example, one of your authors, who was working as a casemanager in a prison facility,
received a telephone call from a person asking to talk with a specific inmate. The caller said he
wanted to personally inform the inmate that the inmate's mother had died. From checking the
presentence report, the caseworker learned that the inmate's mother had actually passed on several
years earlier. The report is also used by staff to confirm family relationships (such as the inmate's
spouse, siblings, and children) for making decisions on inmate visits and correspondence.

Appendix 1 provides a model **presentence report**, which shows the kind of language that would be used in providing a good report to the sentencing judge. This model report is very detailed and involves complicated criminal activity. It shows the range of information a judge needs in order to make an informed sentencing decision.

This inevitably brings us to the question: What is the purpose of sentencing? Although some criminal statutes have attempted to address this ultimate penological question, most legislation is silent, or ambiguous, about the purpose of punishment. The historic and traditional answer to the question is that we sentence criminal offenders for **retribution**, **incapacitation**, **deterrence** (general and individual), and **rehabilitation**. When a judge sees rehabilitation as the primary purpose to be achieved in sentencing, the presentence report, with its detailed information about the defendant, is of the greatest use. For incapacitation, retribution, or general deterrence, the details of the defendant's psychological or educational background may be viewed as irrelevant, except for possible mitigation or aggravation in exceptional cases.

In any event, the final answers regarding the purposes of sentencing have not yet been made. Criminal justice authorities, and especially legislatures, have not reached an agreement about which of the grand purposes (individually or in combination) are most justified in sentencing. The debate continues, and what is certain is that judges and the public, as well as professors and legislators, hold widely varying views about the proper purposes of punishment. What we can report also is that emphasis on one sentencing goal or another seems to shift from decade to decade. Rehabilitation as a primary goal was widely taught in schools beginning in the 1930s and after. It was finally adopted by many judges and legislatures in the 1950s and 1960s. By the 1980s, serious questions were raised regarding its validity as a correctional purpose. The questions were raised by academicians, correctional practitioners, and judges. As a result—and as a result too of public reaction to constantly increasing criminal activity—there was a swing of the pendulum in the 1980s and 1990s toward retribution and incapacitation as the justifiable (and more clearly achievable) goals of sentencing. In the first part of the 21st century, there is a belief that imprisonment is warranted for persons committing the most serious criminal acts (e.g., violent crimes) but that alternatives should be considered for persons posing a minimal risk to the community. The American Correctional Association (ACA) is the leading professional association in the correctional area. In August 2010, the ACA approved a new public correctional policy that, with respect to criminal sentencing, said:

> The length of a term of incarceration resulting from a criminal conviction should be only as long as necessary to accomplish the objectives of punishment... This will optimize the cost to the taxpayers... minimize any deleterious effects of imprisonment, and maximize the chances for the successful reintegration of offenders into the community after release and also ensure that the public's interest in the long-term incarceration of habitual, violent and predatory sexual offenders is preserved.[8]

Corrections

Corrections is the collection of agencies that perform those functions that carry out the sentencing orders of criminal courts. It is the last component in the continuum of criminal justice activities of the criminal justice system. Included in corrections are (1) the probation authority, (2) **jails** (at least to the extent that they carry out short sentences, usually called jail terms), (3) the agencies that perform community corrections functions, (4) prisons, and (5) paroling authorities. Under our definition, those who collect **fines** and **restitution** money (often clerks of court) and those who assist in supervising offenders in the community (which may include police) are also part of corrections. But the five authorities listed are the principal, traditional components of corrections.

Sentences in the United States range from fines, restitution, community service, probation supervision, suspended sentences, and terms of imprisonment, to execution in capital cases. Corrections agencies carry out all of these sentences. Fines and restitution are typically paid by the defendant to the clerk's office or another judicial office, so involvement of a corrections agency in such cases is minimal as long as payments are made.

Probation is a type of sentence that allows the defendant to remain in the community, and it usually allows him to stay at his home and keep his job. The defendant who is placed on probation is required to report regularly to a probation officer, who counsels the probationer and helps in crises. There are always conditions imposed by the court that govern the activities of the defendant. Violations of these may result in a negative report to the court. If these are serious enough, the probationer may be called into court to determine whether the probation should be revoked. Courts rely heavily on the insights and judgment of the probation officers on these matters. In most cases, if probation is revoked, the defendant can be sent to prison at that time. Nonpayment of fines or restitution may also result in the defendant being called before the court to face possible jail terms as sanctions.

It should be noted that, for all of these components of corrections for **adults**, there are similar components in the **juvenile** justice system. From probation to **incarceration,** specialized juvenile agencies handle delinquency cases in the criminal justice system.

In recent years, there has been much said and written about "alternatives to imprisonment." In truth, there have always been alternatives to imprisonment (probation being the main one), but because of the attention, legislatures and courts have looked to additional ways to sentence. Why? There are many reasons. Because of crackdowns on sentencing (longer sentences for many offenses, especially involving violence), prisons have become more crowded. Prisons are expensive to build and run. For lesser offenders, at least, it seems to make sense to use anything that might work instead of prison. But what will work? This is not the place to air the claims and counter-claims that have been made or examine the limited studies and evidence that sometimes accompany them. Here are descriptions of some of the alternatives that have been tried.

Probation

Probation is a commonly used sanction and is often used for first- or second-time offenders and those involved in lesser crimes. The essence of probation is that the defendant is allowed to remain in the community, while also remaining under some degree of supervision by a **probation officer**. Usually, a judge imposes a term of imprisonment upon a defendant and suspends the execution of it so long as the defendant satisfactorily completes a designated period of time under supervision. Less common are suspensions of sentences involving fines or other penalties or the suspension of the imposition of a sentence, allowing the judge (upon revocation of probation) to impose any sentence that could have been imposed at initial sentencing.

There are usually general conditions imposed upon the **probationer** that are used in all similar cases. (For example: do not commit any offense, do not use drugs, and maintain steady employment.) In addition, very specific conditions geared to the individual defendant may be used. (For example: do not go to the Main Street Tavern, where there are bad influences; get training in welding to improve your employment opportunities; and pay restitution of $150 per month to the victims from whom you embezzled money.) Appendix 2 lists mandatory, standard, special, and other conditions that may be imposed as a condition of a person's supervised release in one group of courts (federal).

Although many people (in the media, in the public, and even in the judiciary) do not consider probation a sanction, but rather as a "slap on the wrist" that allows criminals to get off free, probation is properly viewed as an alternative sanction, carrying varying degrees of restraint on liberty. In many jurisdictions, more than half of the persons who are sentenced receive probation. In fact, more persons are on probation supervision in the United States than are in prison. At the end of 2009, over 7.2 million adults were under some kind of adult correctional supervision in the United States. Of these, over 4.2 million were on probation, 819,000 were on parole, 760,000 were in jails, and over 1.5 million were in state and federal prisons.[9]

Probation officers have a difficult job. One of the major problems they face is the large numbers of persons whom they are expected to supervise. Sometimes, the numbers run to 200 offenders or more per officer. For example, the average standard probation **caseload** in Georgia in fiscal year 2008 was 250, and in Rhode Island, probation and parole officers assigned to general caseloads have caseloads of approximately 190 offenders.[10] This usually means that officers look after the most demanding problem probationers, and many probationers are left unsupervised. At best, many probationers report in every month or so by telephone, which serves as their supervision.

There are many degrees of supervision within the realm of probation. At one extreme is *unsupervised probation*, which is virtually an oxymoron, given the definition we have provided that says that supervision is the essence of probation. Still, with overloads of probationers, we have noted that many officers do minimal supervision on many cases. It is an official recognition of this fact that prompts some courts to approve of probation for some defendants without any supervisory contact at all. In effect, unless the probationer is picked up for a new offense, probation is dormant. At the other extreme is intensive probation, in which a court requires much more frequent contacts between probation officer and probationer. This level of contact necessarily requires smaller caseloads for the probation officer, and if there are resources for this in the jurisdiction, *intensive probation* is a more meaningful alternative for some defendants who would otherwise go to prison.[11] The fact of the matter is that there are many well-trained officers in this country who, with additional resources, could make probation a strong and viable sentencing alternative. It is the most reliable and potentially the most valuable type of community corrections.

(Warning: it is important to distinguish between probation and parole. Probation is a sanction, imposed by a judge at sentencing. **Parole** is release from a term of imprisonment by a paroling authority. They are similar in that both probationers and parolees are released into the community and placed under the supervision of government officers; in some jurisdictions, the same officers supervise both probationers and parolees. But the status of probationers and the status of parolees are very different, both in their initial placement and in their revocation. Both placement and revocation of probationers are done by the sentencing court. The placement into parole and revocation of parole—returning the parolee to prison—are done by the paroling authority, which is usually an independent administrative board or a commission appointed by the executive, typically by the governor of the state.)

Fines

For many offenses, fines may be used in lieu of or in addition to jail or prison terms. For crimes at the bottom end of the severity scale (traffic offenses), fines have become the accepted method of punishment. In some other countries, fines are used more often than in the United States. The advantages of fines are that they are punitive; fairly easy to administer; and fairly easy to fit into a sentencing schedule, with ranges of severity. The disadvantages are that fines are seen as being unavailable for many defendants who are indigent, and they are viewed by some as being not punitive enough for high-income defendants (such as drug dealers or wealthy white-collar defendants). Using fines for the latter types of defendants is often seen as an example of rich people being able to buy their way out of criminal difficulties.

Restitution

Restitution is an attempt in the criminal system to make the injured "whole," to even the balance that has been unjustly tipped by the criminal act. (This is much the same kind of balancing that is the basis of administering justice, with monetary awards as damages, in the civil field.) Victims may feel that restitution is a satisfying type of sentence, because they personally receive something for their injuries.

Every state gives courts statutory authority to order restitution. In over one-third of the states, courts are required to order restitution unless there are compelling or extraordinary circumstances. An example is Florida, which provides that "[i]n addition to any punishment, the court shall order the defendant to make restitution to the victim for: 1) Damage or loss caused directly or indirectly by the defendant's offense; and 2) Damage or loss related to the defendant's criminal episode, unless it finds clear and compelling reasons not to order such restitution."[12]

Restitution sanctions are some of the oldest kinds of sentences used.[13] The concept is one of leveling benefit and loss; the defendant must pay back his ill-gotten gains, either directly to the victim or to some place (such as a victims' fund) where it can be used for the good of those harmed by criminal activity. The U.S. Department of Justice report on ordering restitution[14] identifies an issue that impacts restitution. This is the presence of conflicting directives on restitution within a state; for example, states may give the victim the right to restitution but may fail to require that courts order restitution. Some other identified restitution problems include the victim's failure to request restitution, the difficulty in calculating loss, and the defendant's inability to pay.

As with fines, there are frequent problems in making sure restitution is paid. This is partly because payments are being made over time. In addition, many offenders who were ordered to pay are confined and unable to make significant payments until they are released or placed in a work program; other factors can include limited assets, difficulty in securing and maintaining employment, and the lack of skills to get higher paying jobs. Efforts are being made by the states to enforce restitution orders, including improved monitoring of restitution payments; the attachment of state payments to the defendant; the revocation of probation or parole for willful failure to pay; and using state entities or private collection agencies to collect restitution (any collection fee can be added to the amount of the debt).[15]

Electronic Monitoring

With technological advances, new methods of community sanctions are inevitable. Electronic monitoring is one that has now been tried in many jurisdictions. The theory is that, with huge supervision loads and difficulty in keeping track of probationers, electronic monitoring does what a probation officer cannot do—keep constant track of the whereabouts of the offender. This, in theory, helps to enforce the conditions of probation that relate to where the probationer can be, whether at home or at work, or at limited other places (such as school, church, or social places). There is usually a bracelet or anklet that transmits to a telephone connection, signaling that the person is at home or has left the approved area. Although there are some equipment and administrative costs associated with running such programs, they are, of course, far less expensive than the cost of imprisonment. Some argue that, for persons at the lower end of the imprisonment spectrum, electronic monitoring provides public protection and a degree of sanction that justify its use as an alternative to prison.[16]

Community Service and Creative Sentencing

To avoid prison as a sanction and to give more clout to the noncustodial sentence, some courts regularly use an order for **community service** or for some type of work or activity that is intended to "teach a lesson." Sometimes, these sanctions are used often enough (such as requiring offenders who have committed less serious offenses to work in the parks for a certain number of days) that they have become established alternative sanctions. We also read about them in the press, in instances in which a judge is reported to have used a "creative" order to fit the criminality of a particular offender. A slumlord is ordered to live for two weeks in one of his filthy apartments and to clean it up, or an attorney is ordered to give talks to high school classes on the benefits of the American legal system. These examples illustrate an inherent problem in such sentencing: it is eccentric and departs from a system that aims for consistency as a goal to promote fair sentencing. It also tends to be used for the affluent offender. Creativity probably needs to be encouraged, but creative ideas should be incorporated into sentencing standards to avoid any further disparity in our sentencing structure.

SUMMARY

- The criminal justice system in the United States is divided into four components: police, prosecution, courts, and corrections.

- Police prevent, detect, and investigate crimes and apprehend offenders. Different levels of crimes are handled by the police with different levels of intensity. There is considerable discretion given to the police in carrying out their functions.

- When a suspect is taken into custody, this is called an arrest. An arrested person will be taken before a judicial authority to obtain release on bail or on recognizance.

- Police take their records of investigation to prosecutors. Prosecutors evaluate the investigative material and, if they determine there is sufficient evidence to proceed, they will take steps to file charges (by indictment from a grand jury, information, or criminal complaint). Felonies, which typically carry penalties of more than one year in prison, may be initiated by indictments. Lesser offenses (misdemeanors or petty offenses) are initiated by information or criminal complaints.

- Once charges are filed, the criminal court is responsible for seeing to it that a speedy and fair trial is conducted. The procedural rules for guaranteeing fair trials (due process) are complex. If the defendant is convicted, which may be by jury trial or by the court alone, he may be sentenced according to the criminal statutes in the jurisdiction.

- Many courts use sentencing reports, from the probation office or another source, to assist in sentencing, especially in higher-penalty cases. The Supreme Court has encouraged the individualization of sentences.

- Corrections agencies carry out the sentences of the criminal courts. The field of corrections includes probation authorities, jails, community corrections agencies, prisons, and parole authorities. (There are also juvenile corrections counterparts to all of these criminal corrections agencies for adults.)

- Fines and restitution orders are other types of sentences, but they are usually enforced by officials within the judicial system (such as clerks of court) and so are not included within traditional "corrections agency" definitions. Electronic monitoring, community service, and other "creative sentencing" alternatives have been employed in recent years. These are typically supervised and enforced by one of the traditional corrections agencies.

THINKING ABOUT IT

How would you decide the following true case? In May 2002, a father of 13 children unintentionally left his 21-month-old daughter in a car seat in the family's van. She was in the car seat for seven hours before being discovered. The child died of hyperthermia. The father, a civil engineer who was very active in the church, was convicted. He could have received a prison sentence of 15 years. The jury, however, recommended a 12-month sentence, believing the father had no intent to hurt the child but also feeling he had to be punished for the death. You are the judge—what would you do? What is the purpose of sentencing in this case?

KEY TERMS

adult: A person who is within the original jurisdiction of a criminal court rather than a juvenile court because his age at the time of an alleged criminal act was above a statutorily specified limit.

arraignment: The appearance of a person (soon after arrest or after charges have been lodged) before a court in order that the court may inform him of the accusation(s) against him and that he may enter his plea to the charges.

arrest: Taking a person into custody by authority of the law for the purpose of charging him with a criminal offense or initiating juvenile proceedings, terminating with the recording of a specific offense.

bond (appearance bond): A written promise by a financially responsible person to pay the bail sum if the offender does not follow the terms of release. See also release on bail.

caseload (corrections): The total number of clients registered with a corrections agency, or with an individual officer within an agency, during a specified time period. (Usually refers to persons under probation or parole supervision or those assigned to caseworkers inside a corrections facility.)

charge: A formal allegation that a specific person has committed a specific offense.

community service: A sentence (or alternative to sentencing) in which the offender performs work benefiting a charity, government operation, or another organization; the work is approved by the sentencing court as being in the public's (or community's) interest.

corrections: A generic term that includes all government agencies, facilities, programs, procedures, personnel, and techniques concerned with the investigation, intake, custody, confinement, supervision, or treatment of alleged or adjudicated adult offenders, juvenile delinquents, or status offenders.

counsel: A person trained in the law, admitted to practice before the bar of a given jurisdiction, and authorized to advise, represent, and act for other persons in legal proceedings. (Used interchangeably with lawyer or attorney.)

criminal proceedings: Proceedings in a court of law, undertaken to determine the guilt or innocence of an adult accused of a crime.

deterrence: The act, or theory, of stopping action by frightening the potential actor. In penology (sentencing philosophy), deterrence refers to the discouragement of crime because of fear of its consequences (the sanctions that may be imposed). There are two aspects of deterrence: specific (or individual) deterrence—discouragement of the individual offender; and general deterrence—discouragement of a large number of persons who might consider the criminal conduct but who might be convinced not to engage in that conduct because of its adverse consequences, as shown by the punishment of others.

due process (due process of law): Exercise of the powers and authority of government in those ways that are prescribed by settled principles of law. There is a wide range of principles and procedures that may be prescribed (that is, process that may be due) according to the nature of the proceedings. The minimum process (principles and procedures) requires adequate advance notice of the proceeding, an opportunity to be heard and to assert one's rights, and consideration before a person or tribunal that is authorized by law to hear and determine the matter, according to established rules of good order.

fine: A penalty imposed on a convicted person by a court that requires payment of a specified sum of money.

good time: An award, authorized by statute, that reduces the length of time an inmate must spend in prison. It is given for satisfactory conduct in prison. There may also be authorization for *extra good time*, an additional award for particularly meritorious or outstanding actions or behavior. Good time does not usually reduce the total length of the sentence. Initially conceived as an incentive for good behavior, it has become virtually an automatic award in most places, lost only when the inmate misbehaves (withholding good time for current awards, forfeiture of good time for accumulated awards). In a few jurisdictions, the good time allowance may reduce the maximum term of the sentence or even the parole eligibility date (the earliest date the inmate can be considered for parole release).

incapacitation: The inability to act. In penology (sentencing philosophy), the justification for a term of imprisonment on the grounds that it renders the offender unable to commit offenses during the time of his imprisonment.

incarceration: Imprisonment. Confinement in a jail or prison.

indictment: A formal, written accusation made by a grand jury and filed in a court, alleging that a specified person has committed a specific offense.

information: A formal, written accusation made by a prosecutor and filed in a court, alleging that a specified person has committed a specific offense.

jail: A confinement facility, usually administered by a local law enforcement agency, such as a sheriff's department (that is intended for adults but may sometimes contain juveniles) which persons are being detained pending adjudication or are committed, after adjudication, for a short period of time (usually a year or less).

juvenile: A person subject to juvenile court proceedings or certain other special status or treatment because his age is below the statutorily specified limit of adulthood.

parole: The status of an offender who has been conditionally released from a confinement facility prior to the expiration of his sentence and placed under the supervision of a parole agency. The various aspects of parole—such as which inmates are eligible for parole and when, who is the paroling authority, the setting of parole standards (conditions), and the authority to revoke parole and to terminate parole—are defined by statute.

presentence report: The document resulting from an investigation undertaken by a probation agency or other designated authority, at the request of a criminal court, into the past behavior, family circumstances, and personality of an adult who has been convicted of a crime, in order to assist the court in determining the most appropriate sentence. (For a juvenile, the same kind of report is called a predisposition report.)

probation: The conditional freedom granted by a judicial officer to an alleged offender or an adjudicated adult or juvenile, as long as the person meets certain conditions of behavior, for a given period of time. The conditions and period of time are set by the judicial officer. The offender is released into the community, under the supervision of a probation officer.

probation officer: An employee of a probation agency whose primary duties include one or more of the probation agency functions.

probationer: A person required by a court or probation agency to meet certain conditions of behavior as required by a sentence or disposition of probation.

prosecutor: An attorney employed by a government agency or subunit, whose official duty is to initiate and pursue criminal proceedings on behalf of the government against persons accused of committing criminal offenses.

rehabilitation: Restoring an offender to a law-abiding lifestyle. In penology (sentencing philosophy), rehabilitation refers to the theory that a purpose of sentencing is to help the offender live a crime-free life in the community. To that end, a corrections agency is expected to have rehabilitation programs, which improve the offender's prospects of being a productive and law-abiding citizen.

release on bail: The release, by a judicial officer, of an accused person who has been taken into custody, upon his promise to pay a certain sum of money if he fails to appear in court as required, the promise of which may or may not be secured by the deposit of an actual sum of money or property.

release on own recognizance: The release, by a judicial officer, of an accused person who has been taken into custody, upon his promise to appear in court as required for criminal proceedings.

restitution: Compensation or reparation by one person for loss or injury caused to another. In criminal law, a court sanction requiring restoration by the offender to a person of that of which he has been wrongfully deprived, or payment by the offender of some monetary amount to the wronged person (victim) to compensate for injury or loss caused by criminal conduct.

retribution: In sentencing philosophy, the theory that every crime deserves a concomitant punishment.

sentence (criminal law): The penalty (sanction) imposed by a court on a convicted person. This includes a court decision to suspend (defer) the imposition or the execution of a penalty and place the defendant on probation.

sentence, mandatory: A statutory requirement that a certain penalty, a certain minimum penalty, or a penalty with severe restrictions (such as no parole eligibility) shall be imposed and executed upon certain convicted offenders.

trial by judge (court trial): A trial in which there is no jury and a judicial officer determines the issues of fact as well as the law in the case.

trial by jury (jury trial): A trial in which a jury determines the issues of fact in a case and renders a verdict.

ENDNOTES

1. Pew Center on the States, *One in 100: Behind Bars in America 2008* (Washington, DC: The Pew Charitable Trusts, February 2008) 9–10. This report noted that while crime in Florida did drop during this time, crime also dropped as much or more in other states that had not increased, or had even shrunk, their prison systems.

2. 112th Congress (2011-2012). *S. 306, National Criminal Justice Commission Act.* Accessed June 11, 2011, http://www.govtrack.us/congress/bill.xpd?bill=s112-306. This legislation was first introduced in 2009. In January 2010, it was approved by the Senate Judiciary Committee. In July 2010, the bill passed the U.S. House of Representatives but did not pass in the Senate. It was reintroduced in the 112th Congress on February 8, 2011.

3. Further, even if arrested and charged, many persons are not convicted and sentenced. The California Department of Corrections report, *Dispositions of Adult Felony Arrests, 1997*, shows that of the 326,768 felony arrests that year, only about 66% of those who had complaints filed against them were found guilty and sentenced. About 13% of those who were arrested for felonies were imprisoned. Allen, H. and Simonsen, C. *Corrections in America—An Introduction*, 9th ed (Upper Saddle River, NJ: Prentice Hall, 2001), 106.

4. The title for this agency varies. In federal courts, each district has a U.S. Attorney, who has prosecutorial authority. In the states, prosecutions are pursued at the county or city (or town) level. These prosecutors are called state's attorneys, district attorneys, prosecuting attorneys, city attorneys, or other titles, depending on the location.

5. A few jurisdictions have used a sentencing procedure in which courts merely commit the defendant to another agency, and the length of sentence is determined by that agency. An example was the sentencing of young offenders to the California Youth Authority. Once found guilty, a youth was sent to the correction agency, which determined how long was needed for the rehabilitation of the offender. These indeterminate sentences have usually been tied to rehabilitation models, in which case corrections experts, rather than the courts, are thought to be better qualified to decide how long the offender should remain in custody.

6. In 2008, the National Center for State Courts issued a research report on "Assessing Consistency and Fairness in Sentencing." The report indicates at least 20 states and the District of Columbia have sentencing guidelines. These guidelines are described as "a relatively new reform effort to encourage judges to take specific legally relevant elements into account in a fair and consistent way when deciding whether a convicted offender should be imprisoned, and if so, for what length of time." Guidelines may be either advisory (voluntary) or mandatory (more presumptive—stricter requirements for departure from the guidelines, tighter sentencing ranges, more vigorous appellate review). National Center for State Courts. *Assessing Consistency and Fairness in Sentencing* (Williamsburg, VA: National Center for State Courts, 2008), 1.

7. Administrative Office of the U.S. Courts. *The Presentence Investigation Report.* Publication 107, Office of Probation and Pretrial Services. Revised March 2006., accessed June 11, 2011, http://www.fd.org/pdf_lib/publication%20107.pdf>.

8. American Correctional Association. "Public Correctional Policy on Criminal Sentencing and Early Release from Confinement." *Corrections Today* 72(5) (2010): 86–87.

9. Glaze, L. *Correctional Populations in the United States, 2009.* Table 1. Washington, DC: Bureau of Justice Statistics, U.S. Department of Justice, 2010.

10. Georgia Department of Corrections. *Field Operations.* Accessed January 15, 2011, http://www.dcor.state.ga.us/Divisions/Corrections/ProbationSupervision/FieldOperations.html. Also Rhode Island Department of Corrections. *Probation and Parole: Overview of Units.* Accessed January 15, 2011, http://www.doc.ri.gov/probation/overview.php.

11. Some studies indicate that intensive probation results in more violations—which could be explained by the fact that probationers placed on intensive probation are more at risk (more likely to commit violations), or that greater supervision uncovers more technical violations.

12. Office of Justice Programs. *Ordering Restitution to the Crime Victim.* Washington, DC: Office for Victims of Crime, U.S. Department of Justice, 2002.

13. The *Code of Hammurabi*, dating from about 1750 B.C., included the following: "Anyone trespassing upon the land of another and cutting wood therefrom, shall pay to the owner thereof one-half 'mine' of gold." Baum, H. M., ed. *Records of the Past*, Vol. 2. (Philadelphia: Patterson & White, 1903), 74.

14. See endnote 12.

15. Office of Justice Programs. *Restitution: Making It Work.* Washington, DC: Office for Victims of Crime, U.S. Department of Justice, 2002. Also: Colorado Judicial Department. *Restitution—Background and Highlights May 2005.* Accessed January 15, 2011, http://www.courts.state.co.us/userfiles/File/Self_Help/Victim_Restitution/may05restitution.pdf.

16. A publication from the International Association of Chiefs of Police (IACP) notes electronic monitoring may also be used for individuals posing a higher risk. The publication states that law enforcement agencies are beginning to get funding from state legislatures to begin Global Positioning Satellite (GPS) sex offender tracking programs. IACP. *Tracking Sex Offenders with Electronic Monitoring Technology.* Alexandria, VA: International Association of Chiefs of Police, 2008.

3 Habeas, Torts, and Section 1983

The essence of habeas corpus is an attack by a person in custody upon the legality of that custody. The traditional function of the writ is to secure release from illegal custody.

In 1670, the Chief Justice of England was able to say, in ordering the immediate discharge of a juror who had been jailed by a trial judge for bringing in a verdict of not guilty, that "the writ of habeas corpus is now the most usual remedy by which a man is restored again to his liberty, if he have been against law deprived of it."

U.S. Supreme Court, *Preiser v. Rodriguez*

Chapter Outline

- Habeas Corpus
- Torts
- Section 1983

Although corrections is part of the criminal justice system, most of the litigation that affects corrections officials is in the civil area. Remember that within the legal system the law is divided into two main types: criminal and civil. In some jurisdictions, there are different courts that handle criminal and civil matters. Usually, there are different rules that govern criminal cases as opposed to civil cases. There are also different standards of evidence in the two kinds of trials. As you may remember, in a criminal case, the defendant is facing the loss of freedom (his liberty), thus, a higher standard of proof is required. There are, especially in larger jurisdictions, different lawyers who specialize in handling the different kinds of cases. The civil law is for adjudication of controversies between individual, private parties. The criminal law is for the administration of criminal laws, the end goal of which is the punishment of wrongs done to the public.

Corrections staff are sometimes involved in criminal cases. As we have seen, probation officers make sentencing reports to judges at the sentencing stage of criminal trials. If probationers, or other defendants who are in some kind of community program, do not meet the conditions of their probation or community placement, the probation officers or others who supervise the offenders will go into court to report on their status. That court is usually the criminal court that originally tried and sentenced the defendant. Jail and corrections officers will also go into court as witnesses in criminal cases, typically in cases in which offenses (such as escape or assault) have been committed in the jail or prison facility.

Except for the comparatively small number of appearances in criminal cases, such as those we have just mentioned, corrections staff will be seen mostly in civil court cases, not criminal. Most of this text is a review of the kinds of cases that make up corrections litigation. This area of the law is sometimes called "prisoners' rights." The dockets in many jurisdictions in this country, especially in those jurisdictions where a large prison facility is located, are clogged with many lawsuits filed by prisoners or others serving sentences. In this chapter, we will look at the major kinds of cases that make up correctional law litigation.

From 1980 to 1996, the number of prisoner petitions filed by federal and state inmates in U.S. district courts rose from 23,287 in 1980 to a high of 68,235 in 1996. In 1996, the Prison Litigation Reform Act (PLRA) was enacted. The PLRA has had an impact in reducing the amount of prisoner litigation, as intended. For example, during 2000, 58,257 prisoner petitions were filed in U.S. district courts. In 2010, this number was further reduced to 51,901.[1] These decreases occurred even though there was an increase in both state and federal prison populations. At year-end 1996, there were approximately 1.18 million prisoners under the jurisdiction of federal or state adult prison authorities. This grew to 1.39 million in the year 2000 and 1.61 million in the year 2009.[2] In the years between 1996 and 2009, the prison population increased approximately 36%. During this same period, petitions filed in U.S. district courts by federal and state prisoners dropped by about 30%. Today, there are some who believe the PLRA has been "too effective," preventing judicial consideration of meritorious issues.[3]

■ Habeas Corpus

Habeas corpus is one of the oldest kinds of court actions, going far back into English law. It is recognized, and guaranteed, in the U.S. Constitution:

> **The Privilege of the Writ of Habeas Corpus shall not be suspended, unless when in Cases of Rebellion or Invasion the public Safety may require it.**
>
> U.S. Constitution, Article I, Section 9

Availability of the writ is also assured in state constitutions, where it is sometimes called "the great writ of liberty."

A habeas corpus action is started when a prisoner (or detainee) files a **petition**, asking for relief. The matter complained about must be the legality of imprisonment (or detention). The relief sought is release from illegal confinement. The petition should be filed against the person or authority who is the official custodian. The person filing the paper (for our purposes, a prisoner) is called a **petitioner**; the custodian (in prisoner rights cases, the **warden** or **superintendent**) is called the **respondent** in the case. (This is in contrast to other civil cases, where the action is usually started by filing a paper called a complaint; the parties in such a case are the plaintiff and the defendant. In Appendix 3, there is a copy of a 1997 complaint filed in the

United States District Court for the District of Columbia. The complaint states the facts as alleged by the claimant, the violative claims that are being made, and the relief that the plaintiff wishes the court to grant.)

In a habeas action, the court will then order the respondent to show cause why a writ of habeas corpus should not issue (why the prisoner should not be released). Habeas corpus is regarded as an urgent legal action; the **response** by the custodian is usually required within a very short time (often 10 days or less), and all actions by the court are usually taken in a prompt manner. Habeas corpus actions are treated as emergency matters and, as such, go to the top of court dockets, ahead of other types of civil cases. After an attorney for the custodian (the respondent) responds, the court may dismiss the petition, hold a hearing to obtain more information, or grant the request and issue a writ. (Note that only courts can issue writs! In prisons and jails, we often hear of inmates who file writs; they are called writ-writers. This is poor nomenclature, and bad use of language, because only judges—and not inmates—have legal authority to write writs.)

Now, we must review some technical and very legalistic information. **Habeas corpus** is Latin for "have the body." It is an order directed to the person with custody, commanding him to "have," or produce, the body of the person who is in custody before the court. In fact, there are several types of habeas corpus, and all of them have Latin names. The common one is the writ of *habeas corpus ad subjiciendum*. When we use the term *habeas corpus* by itself, this is the type we mean. It is used, as we have just seen, to review the legality of the **confinement** of the detainee or prisoner. Two other types are encountered occasionally in corrections: *habeas corpus ad prosequendum* is a writ issued by a court, ordering the custodian to bring the prisoner before the court for purposes of prosecution; *habeas corpus ad testificandum* is an order to bring a prisoner before the court to give evidence in a court case. Some courts still use these kinds of writs to bring prisoners to court, although, as the decades go by, fewer and fewer courts are using these ancient (and foreign language) styles of orders.

A habeas corpus action will ordinarily be filed in the court where the prisoner is being held—that is, the court with jurisdiction over the custodian (the warden, for example) and the prisoner.[4] Relief in habeas corpus is release from custody. It traditionally meant total release from confinement. In more recent years, it has also been used to achieve release from limited confinement or a particular type of confinement. (For example, a prisoner may use habeas corpus to claim that his placement in **segregation** in an institution was illegal. If he is successful, the court may order his release but only into the regular prison population.)

Habeas corpus is not the proper action to test the guilt or innocence of the person in custody. (That is properly accomplished in the court where he is prosecuted or in appeals from judgments of that court.) Damages are not awarded in habeas corpus actions. Habeas corpus is, however, one of the tools almost always used by attorneys for persons under death sentence to challenge the propriety of that status.

There are federal statutes that spell out the authority of federal courts to issue writs of habeas corpus. These statutory provisions are contained in Title 28 of the U.S. Code.[5] There are provisions for federal prisoners to seek habeas corpus relief, which are found under Title 28, U.S. Code, Section 2241. There are also provisions that authorize federal courts to consider applications from state prisoners for release under Title 28, U.S. Code, Section 2254. As a general rule, federal courts are not quick to jump into habeas matters involving state prisoners; they usually defer to the states to take care of such problems in their own courts, as the federal law contemplates.

In an effort to limit a prisoner's ability to file petitions in federal court, Congress, in 1996, passed the Antiterrorism and Effective Death Penalty Act (AEDPA). AEDPA made several amendments to the habeas corpus requirements. For example, an amended Section 2254 provides that federal habeas corpus relief is only available to a state prisoner if the petitioner has exhausted the remedies that are available for such relief in the state where he is confined or detained; if there is no available state exhaustion process; or if there are circumstances that exist to make the process ineffective to protect the rights of the applicant. This section further allows federal courts, upon finding that the application for a writ of habeas corpus has no merit, to dismiss the application even if there has been no **exhaustion** at the state level. Another example of the amendments occurs in Section 2255 and establishes a one-year period of limitation for a federal prisoner to file a motion attacking the legality of his sentence. The section specifies when the limitation period begins to run.

As suggested above, one objective of AEDPA was to promote the finality of criminal convictions and sentences. Contrary to its intent, AEDPA may have resulted, at least initially, in a higher number of petitions filed in U.S. district courts, especially with respect to petitions filed by state inmates using Section 2254. In April 1997, the year following passage of AEDPA, the number of habeas corpus petitions filings by state prisoners had increased from 1.1 per 1,000 inmates per month to 3.4 per month—an increase of 2,600 petitions. The lowest number of habeas corpus filings by state prisoners since 1996 (fiscal years) was in 2010, when 17,042 petitions were filed by state prisoners in U.S. district courts. This is 20% above the 1996 level but a drop of 17% from 1997. One reason for the significant increase in 1997 was for prisoners to get within AEDPA's requirement that petitions be filed within the one-year period of limitation specified in the statute.[6] See **Figure 3-1.**

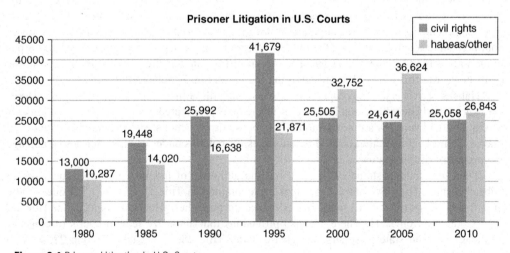

Figure 3-1 Prisoner Litigation in U.S. Courts.

■ Torts

A **tort** is a private wrong or injury for which a court will provide a remedy in the form of damages. It is also an ancient remedy in English law (and the word itself derives from Latin or Roman origins). A tort always involves a violation of some duty owed to the person injured—other than by agreement of the parties (that is, by contract). These are the two main areas of the civil law: torts and contracts.

There are three elements in any tort action: (1) a legal duty owed by the defendant to the plaintiff, (2) a breach of that duty, and (3) injury (damage) as a proximate result of the breach of duty. The duties that are owed have been established by law and go back to principles of the common law. Some are defined (in more recent times) in legislation, but even those are based on, and are interpreted by, court rulings.

Torts may be either intentional or negligent. In intentional torts, the wrong is done by someone who intends to do what the law has declared to be wrong. In negligent torts, the wrong is done by someone who fails to exercise the degree of care that is required by the law in performing acts that are otherwise permissible.

The most common type of tort that we encounter in our everyday lives today is probably the accident that is caused by the negligent operation of an automobile. The injury caused may involve property damage, personal injury, or both. Every driver has a duty to operate a vehicle safely and in accordance with rules of the road, and every driver must learn and adhere to those rules. Failure to use proper or "reasonable" care in the operation of a vehicle is a breach of duty, and, if it causes injury to another person, it is a tort. The injured party may file suit for the injury suffered and, in doing so, becomes a plaintiff against the defendant who has injured him.

There are two types of **damages** that may be recovered in a civil tort suit: compensatory damages and punitive damages (although some states do not allow punitive damages in tort actions). Compensatory damages are awarded to cover the actual monetary loss suffered by the plaintiff. In cases of property damage, these would include the costs of restoring or repairing the property. In cases of personal injury, compensatory damages would include medical bills, lost wages, pain and suffering, and an estimate of future losses in these same categories. Punitive damages are designed to punish the defendant for severely bad conduct. Here, more than simple **negligence** is required; a defendant may have shown gross negligence (acting recklessly) or willful negligence (acting intentionally to cause harm) in order to justify an award of punitive damages. There are also nominal damages, which are damages of small amounts that are awarded when a tort has technically been committed, but the judge or jury deciding on the amount of damages believes that a minimal award is the most just result. Again, the relief given in a tort action is an award of money. There is no injunctive relief in tort suits, and attorney fees are not usually given in common law tort suits.

The most frequently encountered common law torts are assault, **battery**, **false imprisonment**, **libel**, and **defamation.** Negligent loss of someone else's property is also a tort, as is medical malpractice. These last two are the kinds most often encountered in corrections facilities, although assault and battery are also the basis of some prisoner suits.

In English law, the **sovereign** (the king or queen) could not be sued in its (his or her) own courts, unless the sovereign gave permission to be sued. After all, the courts were a part of the sovereignty and, as such, could not be used to attack the sovereign. Over the centuries, the courts became more and more independent, but the principle of sovereign immunity continued. It was carried over into the United States, where the legal principle states that the sovereign (the government) cannot be sued without its permission. Most governments have abandoned strict sovereign immunity. Today, the federal government permits tort actions to be brought (with strict statutory restrictions), and most state governments permit some kinds of tort actions against the state. These are usually called tort claim acts. In most cases, they require administrative claims first to be made against the government. If those are not successful, the injured party may be able to go into court to pursue the tort action.

For some time, even though there was a Federal Tort Claims Act, there was some question as to whether federal prisoners could sue the U.S. government for tort injuries. Lower courts had ruled both ways—that they could and that they could not. The Supreme Court finally ruled that federal inmates could use the Tort Claims Act in *United States v. Muniz*, 374 U.S. 150 (1963). Two cases were decided under *Muniz*: one dealing with injuries suffered by an inmate who was assaulted during a prison disturbance (Muniz), and a second case dealing with an inmate who went blind (Winston) as a result of alleged medical malpractice by government doctors. Those two kinds of cases happen to be the most common kinds of tort claims arising out of federal prison operations, except for claims for damaged or lost property.[7]

■ Section 1983

What we have just examined in the preceding section are common law torts. There is another major group of legal actions available to prisoners, sometimes called constitutional torts. These are torts in the sense that they represent injuries or harm suffered by a person because of wrongful actions by another. They are not common law torts, however, because they are not included in the body of torts that have been developed by court rulings (common law) over the centuries. Instead, they are injuries caused by a violation of rights guaranteed by the Constitution. They are recognized and authorized as court suits by a federal statute, which is contained in the Civil Rights Act of 1871. This law is codified in Title 42, U.S. Code, Section 1983:

> **Every person who, under color of any statute, ordinance, regulation, custom, or usage, of any State or Territory or the District of Columbia, subjects, or causes to be subjected, any citizen of the United States or other person within the jurisdiction thereof to the deprivation of any rights, privileges, or immunities secured by the Constitution and laws, shall be liable to the party injured in an action at law, suit in equity, or other proper proceeding for redress.**

Most states also have provisions in state law that allow suits to be brought for injuries sustained as a result of violations of state constitutional guarantees.

Although it was enacted in 1871, the federal Civil Rights Act was not used much until the civil rights litigation explosion of the 1950s and the prisoner rights litigation explosion of the 1960s. Since then, it has been the most frequently used type of lawsuit in corrections litigation.

Lawsuits under Section 1983 allege that state officials have deprived the prisoners of their constitutional rights. Examples include the right to due process in disciplinary hearings (Fifth and Fourteenth Amendments) in *Wolff v. McDonnell*, 418 U.S. 539 (1974); access to law libraries in *Bounds v. Smith*, 430 U.S. 817 (1977); and access to health care (Eighth Amendment) in *Estelle v. Gamble*, 429 U.S. 97 (1976). Thousands of these suits are filed in federal courts each year. Why has this law been so popular? There are several reasons. As we have seen, habeas corpus and torts have limited scope and are limited in the kinds of relief they make available. Section 1983 allows broad relief, in law, equity, or any "other proper proceeding." This has resulted in suits in which both damages and injunctive relief are commonly sought, and often given, in Section 1983 actions.

There are two main kinds of injunctive relief: (1) *restrictive injunctions*, in which defendants are enjoined (that is, they are legally ordered to stop) from doing things they have been wrongfully doing; and (2) *mandatory injunctions*, in which defendants are required to do things they should have been doing. If plaintiffs can show that government authorities have not been following constitutional requirements, it may be most valuable to obtain **injunctions**, either to stop them from doing something (ordering prison officials to stop putting people into a segregation unit that is inadequately heated, for example) or to require them to start doing something (ordering prison officials to adequately heat the segregation unit in winter, for example).

State prisoners also brought suits in federal court using the Civil Rights Act, because the federal courts (at least in the 1960s and 1970s) were seen, in most jurisdictions, as being more liberal, and more likely to rule in favor of prisoners than state courts. Also, the law as it applies to prisons became more established, over time, in federal courts, and prisoners in one jurisdiction could use rulings in other parts of the country as leverage to get favorable rulings in their own situations. As already noted, a state prisoner is barred from bringing a habeas corpus action in a federal court unless the prisoner has already used the state remedies that are available to litigate the same matter. This was confirmed in *Wilwording v. Swenson*, 404 U.S. 249 (1972), and *Preiser v. Rodriguez*, 411 U.S. 475 (1973).

The Supreme Court, in *Heck v. Humphrey*, 512 U.S. 477 (1994), held that a state inmate's claim for damages is not cognizable (capable of being tried or examined) under Section 1983 if a judgment for the plaintiff would imply that the conviction or sentence was invalid, unless the inmate could show that such conviction or sentence had already been invalidated. The question in *Edwards v. Balisok*, 520 U.S. 641 (1997), was whether an inmate's challenge to the procedures used to deprive him of **good time** credits was cognizable under Section 1983. Balisok, a Washington State prison inmate, was charged with and found to have committed four prison rule infractions, for which he was punished by segregated confinement and a loss of 30 days good time credit. He filed a Section 1983 action requesting, in part, a declaration that the disciplinary hearing procedures used by state officials violated due process, and requesting compensatory and punitive damages because they used those procedures. He did not request that his good time be restored, as *Preiser* held that the exclusive remedy in federal court for an inmate seeking this substantive relief is a writ of habeas corpus.

Balisok's main allegation was that he was not allowed to present a defense through specifically identified witnesses who had exculpatory evidence. He further alleged that the action of excluding witnesses was a consequence of the deceit and bias of the hearing officer. The Supreme Court noted the following:

> **The due process requirements for a prison disciplinary hearing are in many respects less demanding than those for criminal prosecution, but they are not so lax as to let stand the decision of a biased hearing officer who dishonestly suppresses evidence of innocence.**

The Supreme Court held that Balisok's claim for declaratory relief and monetary damages, based on allegations of deceit and bias by the decision maker, could invalidate the punishment that was imposed, and it was therefore not cognizable under Section 1983. In such instance, habeas corpus would be the appropriate judicial remedy.

In a **per curiam** opinion in *Muhammad v. Close*, 540 U.S. 749 (2004), the Supreme Court held that *Heck* did not apply to prison disciplinary issues where the inmate's complaint poses no challenge to his conviction or to the duration of his sentence. In *Muhammad*, the inmate's amended complaint sought compensatory and punitive damages for his pre-disciplinary hearing detention. It did not challenge the disciplinary finding of insolence or the action taken because the inmate was found to be insolent.

In *Wilkinson v. Dotson*, 544 U.S. 74 (2005), two state prison inmates challenged their parole status (eligibility for parole in the first case, suitability for parole in the second). The inmates separately brought suit under 42 U.S.C. § 1983, claiming Ohio's parole procedures violated the Federal Constitution. The district courts held that relief had to be sought through habeas corpus. On appeal, the Sixth Circuit consolidated the two cases and reversed the lower courts, holding that the actions could occur under Section 1983. In affirming the Sixth Circuit, the Supreme Court held:

> *Heck* **specifies that a prisoner cannot use § 1983 to obtain damages where success** *would necessarily* **imply the unlawfulness of a (not previously invalidated) conviction or sentence. And** *Balisok*... **demonstrates that habeas remedies do not displace § 1983 actions where success in the civil rights suit** *would not necessarily* **[emphasis added] vitiate the legality of (not previously invalidated) state confinement.**

The connection between the constitutionality of the inmate's parole proceedings and release from confinement was seen by the Court as too tenuous to require a suit in habeas corpus. Litigation success for either inmate did not mean release, but rather at most a new eligibility review or new parole hearing. Since such action does not clearly demonstrate the invalidity of confinement or its duration, the inmates could proceed under 42 U.S.C. § 1983.[8]

Let's look more closely at the provisions of the Civil Rights Act. Under 42 U.S.C. § 1983, a suit can be brought by any person who claims his constitutional rights have been abridged. This person (the plaintiff) can sue an offending person, who can be any government official or corrections staff member. Such actions may not be brought against the state itself or corrections agencies (although municipal corporations have been held to be "persons" and may be sued[9]). The persons sued must be operating under color of state law. Section 1983 defendants are thus always state employees or officials (or, as we will see later, persons functioning just as if they were state employees, such as doctors under contract who provide medical services to state prisoners.)

Can a state divest itself of jurisdiction over Section 1983 suits seeking monetary damages from corrections officers? Believing that damage suits filed by inmates against state correction officers were largely "frivolous and vexatious," New York enacted Correction Law § 24. The law effectively stripped its courts of jurisdiction over such damage claims, requiring these claims to be brought in the court of claims, with the claim being made against the state. The impact of this change meant the inmate would be suing a different defendant (the state), there would be different relief (no right to attorney fees or to seek punitive damages or injunctive relief), and that there would be different procedural protections (not entitled to a jury trial). The law's focus was narrow in scope, as it did not prevent the trial courts that generally exercise jurisdiction over Section 1983 suits from continuing to do so against other state officials. In *Haywood v. Drown*, 556 U.S. __ (2009), the question was whether that "exceptional treatment of a limited category of § 1983 claims is consistent with the Supremacy Clause of the United States Constitution."

In *Haywood*, a state prison inmate began Section 1983 actions against several New York state correctional employees, alleging violation of his civil rights relating to inmate disciplinary proceedings and an altercation. The trial court dismissed the action, saying that under Correction Law § 24, the court did not have jurisdiction. Both the intermediate appellate court and the state court of appeals (the state's highest appellate court) affirmed. The court of appeals rejected the inmate's claim that Correction Law § 24's jurisdictional restriction was contrary to the Supremacy Clause. The court held that the law treated state and federal actions against correction officers in the same manner (neither can be brought), and is best characterized as a "neutral state rule."

The Supreme Court reversed.

[A]lthough States retain substantial leeway to establish the contours of their judicial systems, they lack authority to nullify a federal right or cause of action they believe is inconsistent with their local policies. "The suggestion that [an] act of Congress is not in harmony with the policy of the State, and therefore that the courts of the State are free to decline jurisdiction, is quite inadmissible, because it presupposes what in legal contemplation does not exist."

It is principally on this basis that Correction Law § 24 violates the Supremacy Clause. In passing Correction Law § 24, New York made the judgment that correction officers should not be burdened with suits for damages arising out of conduct performed in the scope of their employment. Because it regards these suits as too numerous or too frivolous (or both), the State's longstanding policy has been to shield this narrow class of defendants from liability when sued for damages...The State's policy, whatever its merits, is contrary to Congress' judgment that *all* persons who violate federal rights while acting under color of state law shall be held liable for damages.

In its opinion, the Court also addressed the New York court of appeals' holding that Correction Law § 24 was constitutional because it treated both federal and state claims the same.

Although the absence of discrimination is necessary to our finding a state law neutral, it is not sufficient. A jurisdictional rule cannot be used as a device to undermine federal law, no matter how evenhanded it may appear.

The Court also commented on the fact that the state held inappropriate for its trial courts only certain types of lawsuits—those seeking damages relief against correction officers.

> **We therefore hold that, having made the decision to create courts of general jurisdiction that regularly sit to entertain analogous suits, New York is not at liberty to shut the courthouse door to federal claims that it considers at odds with its local policy.**

> **Our holding addresses only the unique scheme adopted by the State of New York—a law designed to shield a particular class of defendants (correction officers) from a particular type of liability (damages) brought by a particular class of plaintiffs (prisoners)...Correction Law § 24 is effectively an immunity statute cloaked in jurisdictional garb.**

Section 1983, which only covers state officials, cannot be used to sue federal employees. However, the Supreme Court, in an act of judicial legislation, held that this was unfair and further held that persons can sue federal officials for violations of constitutional rights. *Bivens v. Six Unknown Federal Narcotics Agents*, 403 U.S. 388 (1971). The complaint in that case alleged that on November 26, 1965, agents of the Federal Bureau of Narcotics, acting under claim of federal authority, entered the petitioner's apartment without warrant, searched the apartment, and arrested the petitioner on narcotics charges—all without probable cause. In 1967, the petitioner sued, alleging the arrest was made unlawfully, unreasonably, and contrary to law. He sought monetary damages from each of the agents.

The district and appeals courts ruled for the government, holding that the complaint failed to state a federal cause of action. In reversing, the Supreme Court held that an individual could sue a federal agent for an arrest and home search that were alleged to be illegal. The Court further held that the actions of the federal agents in violation of the Fourth Amendment's prohibition against unreasonable search and seizure were a "federally protected interest" and not one better handled under state tort law, as the federal government had argued. This case authorizes persons to sue for constitutional civil rights violations against federal officials in the same way that Congress had authorized such suits against state officials in Section 1983.[10]

For some time, there was a question about whether the "Bivens doctrine," which allowed civil rights suits against federal agents, applied only to violations of the Fourth Amendment, because the *Bivens* case itself dealt with allegations of illegal search and seizure. Later, the Supreme Court made it clear that such suits (claiming constitutional violations) could be brought for violations of the **due process clause** (Fifth Amendment), as in *Davis v. Passman*, 442 U.S. 228 (1979). They also could be brought against prison officials for claims of cruel and unusual punishment (Eighth Amendment), *Carlson v. Green*, 446 U.S. 14 (1980). Thus, federal prisoners bring **Bivens actions,** not Section 1983 actions. (Throughout this text, you will often see these lawsuits referred to simply as "Section 1983" or "Bivens" suits. This is just shorthand for the entire statutory or case cite, because those two kinds of actions are so common in corrections law, and the majority of decisions discussed in this book were decided under one or the other of those two authorities.) In practice, the two kinds of legal actions are otherwise identical, and all the provisions and court rulings under one kind of suit (Section 1983 or Bivens) may be used in the other.

In practice and in fact, using Section 1983 actions, although limited to suits against individual officials, has been very effective. This is because rulings that defendants have violated constitutional rights and relief in money damages or injunction, or both, carry considerable impact, and they often bring about the correction of what have been unconstitutional actions or conditions. Thus, the impact of a successful Section 1983 lawsuit often is much broader than just the victory for the individual plaintiff.

One significant aspect of a Section 1983 or Bivens suit is that a judgment in favor of the prisoner plaintiff may mean that the individual official defendant must pay a monetary award from her own financial resources. While the employee may receive representation by the government, be held not liable for monetary damages by the court, or, if held liable, receive indemnification from the government, these are not automatic occurrences.

SUMMARY

- There are three types of legal actions that cover nearly all of the lawsuits brought by inmates to complain about the conditions under which they are being held, sue for money damages because of injuries they have suffered, or complain about other matters related to their status as offenders. The three commonly used actions are habeas corpus (petitions by prisoners seeking release from custody because of some illegality in their confinement); torts (tort claims or lawsuits by prisoners seeking money damages for injuries or losses sustained because of wrongful actions by a corrections employee); and Section 1983 (complaints by prisoners alleging violations of constitutional rights and asking for money damages or injunctive relief, pursuant to 42 U.S.C. § 1983).

- Habeas corpus is an ancient remedy, which was taken from English law, and is guaranteed in the U.S. Constitution. Section 1983 (and Bivens lawsuits for federal prisoners) is the most commonly used legal action to challenge prison and jail conditions. Tort Claims Acts are used for common law tort actions in those jurisdictions in which the government has waived its sovereign immunity, allowing suits to be brought against the government. The most frequently encountered tort claims in prisons involve money damages for negligent loss of or damage to an inmate's property, injuries suffered because of assaults caused by the negligence of corrections officers or staff, and medical malpractice claims.

THINKING ABOUT IT

When stepping out of the shower, inmate Smith slips on a bar of soap. He falls, injuring his back. The injury occurs in the presence of Officer Jones. Inmate Smith blames Officer Jones for his injury. If inmate Smith decides to file a lawsuit, he has the best chance of success under which of the three types of inmate lawsuits?

KEY TERMS

battery: The unlawful use of force against the person of another. Technically, offensive touching or bodily injury to another person.

Bivens action: An action in federal court, alleging a civil rights violation by federal officials. Named for a Supreme Court opinion (*Bivens v. Six Unknown Federal Narcotics Agents*) that allows a lawsuit for such federal agents' violations equivalent to the lawsuits authorized by 42 U.S.C. § 1983 for violations of civil rights by persons operating under color of state law.

confinement: The status of being in secured custody, where the person is not free to come and go, unless escorted.

damages: Monetary awards in civil cases, given by court order (judgment) to a person who has been harmed by another.

defamation: A tort involving the unprivileged publication of false statements, which result in injury to another. The injury suffered may be contempt, ridicule, hatred, or damage to reputation.

due process clause: The constitutional statement that protects persons from certain governmental actions unless prescribed rules and procedures are followed. There are two such clauses in the U.S. Constitution; these appear in the Fifth Amendment (for federal government actions) and in the Fourteenth Amendment (for state actions). Almost all state constitutions also have such clauses.

exhaustion: A requirement that relief must be pursued in another procedure or place before it can be pursued in a particular court. Used especially for *exhaustion of administrative remedies* (requiring that such remedies be used, where they are available, before a lawsuit is filed) and *exhaustion of state remedies* (requiring that state remedies be pursued before federal actions are undertaken).

false imprisonment: A tort involving the unlawful restraint by one person of the physical liberty of another. (May also be a crime.)

good time: An award, authorized by statute, that reduces the length of time an inmate must spend in prison. It is given for satisfactory conduct in prison. There may also be authorization for *extra good time*, an additional award for particularly meritorious or outstanding actions or behavior. Good time does not usually reduce the total length of the sentence. Initially conceived as an incentive for good behavior, it has become virtually an automatic award in most places, lost only when the inmate misbehaves (withholding good time for current awards, forfeiture of good time for accumulated awards). In a few jurisdictions, the good time allowance may reduce the maximum term of the sentence or even the parole eligibility date (the earliest date the inmate can be considered for parole release).

habeas corpus: A writ (a court process or order) of ancient origin, used to obtain immediate relief by release from illegal confinement or custody. (Technically, this is the writ of *habeas corpus ad subjiciendum*. Other writs of habeas corpus are used to obtain a person in custody before a court, for prosecution [*habeas corpus ad prosequendum*] or for testifying [*habeas corpus ad testificandum*].)

injunction (court order): A writ (order) to restrain a person from doing that which he should not do or requiring him to do that which he should do. (The latter is sometimes called a mandatory injunction or mandamus.) This relief is entered to avoid irreparable injury (under the "rules of conscience" of an equity court) to any individual's person, property, or other rights.

libel: Defamation (see that definition) by means of print, writing, pictures, or signs. A publication that is injurious to the reputation of another.

negligence: The failure to use such care as a reasonably prudent person would use under the same or similar circumstances. In the law, it is the doing of something that a prudent person would not have done or the failure to do something that a prudent person would have done. It is the failure to live up to that standard of conduct that the law expects in order to protect other persons against unreasonable risk of harm.

per curiam: Literally, "by the court." Used to denote an opinion of the whole court, rather than one written (as is usual) by a particular judge. Often used for a brief announcement of the disposition of a case, without a full opinion.

petition (legal proceeding): A document filed in a court having civil or general jurisdiction, asking that special relief within the jurisdiction of that court be granted. Used in habeas corpus proceedings as the document filed by a person who is in custody, asking for release from custody. Used in the Supreme Court as the document filed by a person requesting that the court issue a writ of certiorari, indicating that the case will be reviewed by that court.

petitioner: The party who files a petition.

respondent: The party who files a response.

response: The pleading filed by the respondent in an equity action. An answer to a petition (such as a petition for a writ of habeas corpus) or other proceeding in equity or to a petition (for writ of certiorari) in the Supreme Court.

segregation (corrections): The separation of inmates in correctional facilities from the regular population. It is usually done for disciplinary reasons, but it may be done for a variety of other reasons, such as awaiting transfer, for protection, or pending investigation. Also used to denote the place (the separate unit) in a facility where inmates are housed separately and under tighter control. This place is known in different facilities as disciplinary detention, administrative detention, punitive detention, segregation, isolation, and (colloquially) the hole.

sovereign: The person (ruler) or body (government) in which supreme authority is vested. Sovereign immunity is the immunity (see that definition) of the sovereign from liability.

superintendent: In corrections, the person in charge of a correctional facility. In most places, it is used as the title for the manager of a lower security correctional facility. (Similar to warden—see that definition.)

tort: A wrong. An injury to the person or property of another, outside of any contractual agreement. A breach of duty that the law (by statute or by common law) has said is owed to another person. (Some acts may be either crimes or torts or both—crimes are offenses against the public, whereas torts are injuries to private persons, which may be pursued in civil courts.)

warden: Historically, a guardian; a keeper of wards. Today, used principally as the title of the person in charge (the chief executive officer) of a correctional facility. (In many jurisdictions, used for the title of such a person in a maximum or medium security facility, whereas superintendent is used for lower security facilities.)

ENDNOTES

1. Maguire, Kathleen, ed. *Sourcebook of Criminal Justice Statistics*, Table 5.65.2010. Accessed November 3, 2011, http://www.albany.edu/sourcebook/pdf/t5652010.pdf. In both 2000 and 2010, approximately 80% of the filings were done by state prisoners and 20% by federal prisoners. Note that these numbers are for filings in U.S. district courts, and do not reflect actions in state courts.
2. Beck, A. and Mumola, C. *Prisoners in 1998* (Washington, DC: Bureau of Justice Statistics, U.S. Department of Justice, 1999), 1. Also see Glaze, L. *Correctional Populations in the United States, 2009* (Washington, DC: Bureau of Justice Statistics, U.S. Department of Justice, 2010), Appendix Table 1.
3. In *Woodford v. Ngo*, 548 U.S. 81 (2006), the Supreme Court held that the PLRA requires the proper exhaustion of administrative remedies for inmate grievances before inmates bring Section 1983 actions into federal courts. A criticism of *Woodford* is that the ruling holds that the PLRA prevents the filing of even meritorious claims if an inmate fails to meet the prison's procedural grievance filing requirements.
4. This holding dates back to *Braden v. 30th Judicial Circuit Court of Kentucky*, 410 U.S. 484 (1973). Braden was indicted in Kentucky in 1967 on two criminal counts. He escaped from the custody of Kentucky and remained at large until he was later arrested in Alabama. He was convicted in Alabama and confined within that state. Though he was located in Alabama, he filed a habeas corpus action in Kentucky, which was granted by the district court in that state. The court of appeals reversed, holding that the law requires the prisoner be within the territorial limits of the district court. Stating that the writ is directed to and served on the "jailer," not the prisoner, the Supreme Court reversed, holding that "the language of § 2241(a) requires nothing more than that the court issuing the writ has jurisdiction over the custodian."
5. Federal laws are compiled, for ease of use, in a collection of books called the *U.S. Code*. (The *U.S. Code Annotated* is just another version of this collection, which includes commentary and court decisions printed with each section to show what has been done with each particular section.) The entire body of statutes is divided into titles. Each title deals with a different subject matter. Title 28, which we refer to here, deals with the judiciary and court matters. Within each title, there are chapters and sections. These divisions are also made for ease of use and to make individual subjects easier to find. When referencing federal statutes, we will provide the title number followed by the section number. (For example, 28 U.S.C. § 2241 stands for Title 28, U.S. Code, Section 2241).
6. Information regarding AEDPA is taken primarily from 28 U.S.C. §§ 2241–2255 (2006). Also see Scalia, J. *Prisoner Petitions Filed in U.S. District Courts, 2000, with Trends*

1980–2000 (Washington, DC: Bureau of Justice Statistics, U.S. Department of Justice, 2002), 5. Also see the *Sourcebook of Criminal Justice Statistics* Table 5.65.2010, cited in endnote 1 above.

7. Prison systems routinely take temporary custody of the personal property of prisoners, including at those times when prisoners are transferred between facilities. During these transfers, some personal property of the prisoner may be lost or damaged while in the possession of prison officials. To compensate prisoners for such losses, if caused by a negligent act or the omission of a prison employee, various administrative procedures have been developed. An example of this type of administrative procedure is Title 31, U.S.C. Section 3723, which permits a prisoner to submit a claim to the Bureau of Prisons for personal property that was lost or damaged as a result of the negligence of a federal employee. Claims may not exceed $1,000 and must be presented within one year of the loss. The U.S. Supreme Court, in *Ali v. BOP*, 552 U.S. 214 (2008), ruled that federal prisoners could not use the Federal Torts Claims Act (FTCA) to seek damages from the United States for the loss or damage to personal property while in the possession of BOP employees as Congress had expressly precluded consideration of these types of claims under the FTCA.

8. In *Skinner v. Switzer,* 562 U.S. __ (2011), the Supreme Court considered whether "a convicted state prisoner seeking DNA testing of crime scene evidence" could make such a claim under a Section 1983 civil rights action, or whether it must be done in a petition for a writ of habeas corpus. In allowing for a Section 1983 action, the Court, referring to its decisions in *Heck* and in *Wilkinson*, said "[s]uccess in his suit for DNA testing would not 'necessarily imply' the invalidity of his conviction. While test results might prove exculpatory, that outcome is hardly inevitable;…results might prove inconclusive or they might further incriminate Skinner."

9. *Monell v. Department of Social Services*, 436 U.S. 658 (1978).

10. In *Pollard v. GEO Group Inc.*, 607 F.3d 583 (9th Cir. 2010), the U.S. Court of Appeals for the Ninth Circuit held that *Bivens* "allows a federal prisoner to recover for violations of his constitutional rights by employees of private corporations operating federal prisons." The court held that the employees of GEO, a private prison corporation, do act under color of federal law for purposes of *Bivens* liability. This holding conflicts with the Fourth Circuit opinion in *Holly v. Scott*, 434 F.3d 287, 294 (4th Cir. 2006). *Holly* held that employees of private corporations operating federal prisons do not fall within the scope of *Bivens*, and that such employees are not federal actors. These two circuit decisions are an example of a "split in the circuits," meaning two or more court of appeals make contrary holdings, each holding applying within its own circuit. The Supreme Court decided this issue with a decision in *Minneci v. Pollard*, 565 U.S. __ (2012). The Court held that Pollard could not assert a *Bivens* claim, that his "Eighth Amendment claim focuses upon a kind of conduct that typically falls within the scope of traditional state tort law. And in case of a privately employed defendant, state tort law provides an 'alternative, existing process' capable of protecting the constitutional interests at stake." The Court said "the prisoner must seek a remedy under state tort law."

4 | Going to Court

Prison officials must be free to take appropriate action to ensure the safety of inmates and corrections personnel and to prevent escape or unauthorized entry. They should be accorded wide-ranging deference in the adoption and execution of policies and practices that in their judgment are needed to preserve internal order and discipline and to maintain institutional security.

U.S. Supreme Court, *Bell v. Wolfish*

Chapter Outline

- You Are Summoned
- Getting Representation
- Step by Step
- Not Going to Trial
- Trial
- Appeal

This chapter involves the serious matter of having to appear in a court proceeding, either as a **witness** or as a party in a case. The reader should consider it as a guidebook for getting prepared for such a court appearance, whether it is about to happen or even if it may never occur. If you are working in the corrections field, it is a fact of your work life that you may have to go to court. This may occasionally be necessary in criminal cases, for which you may be called as a witness. An example is where you are a responding officer when an inmate seriously assaults another person (staff, inmate, or visitor) and that assault is being criminally prosecuted. It is more likely, however, that you will be called as a witness for a civil case. An example is where an inmate sues prison officials, claiming their actions under prison policy are denying her adequate medical care. We see another example in Appendix 3, where the inmate's complaint concerned his being denied access to electric or electronic musical instruments.

Much more serious is when you are yourself sued. This is likely to be in a Section 1983 (constitutional tort) case, unless you are a warden or otherwise legally a custodian, in which case it may be either a habeas corpus action or a Section 1983 action, depending on the nature of the complaint and the kind of relief that is requested. Appendix 4 provides an example of an inmate filing a complaint under the Civil Rights Act, 42 U.S.C. § 1983. (Note: this inmate's complaint worked its way through the judicial system, up to and including the United States Supreme Court.)

It is, of course, unsettling to be sued. For persons in virtually all other walks of life, it is unusual to be sued. For those working in corrections, an environment where an inmate's actions and choices need to be more controlled to better ensure institution security, discipline, and good order, and the protection of persons, including the public, it has almost become commonplace. Being sued is nothing to be taken lightly, and in this chapter we will try to put the corrections lawsuit in perspective.

■ You Are Summoned

You will first know you are being sued when you receive a **summons** or **waiver of summons** (this may go by a different name in some jurisdictions). The summons may be served by an official of the court. (In a federal Section 1983 case, a U.S. Marshal is responsible for serving the summons; in a local state court, it may be someone from the sheriff's office.) A summons may also be served by certified mail.

Attached to the summons is the complaint (or petition or whatever legal document has been filed in court to start the lawsuit). The complaint (see Appendix 4) states who is bringing the action (the plaintiff) and who is being sued (the defendant or, more likely, defendants). It also contains the allegations made by the plaintiff. From now on, for ease of discussion, we will consider the lawsuit to be made by a prison inmate against a correctional officer. (Note: An inmate also could decide to sue more than one person; for example, the inmate could sue several workers at the prison, from the warden down through correctional supervisors and some line corrections staff.) The prisoner, in a Section 1983 action, will state that certain actions have been taken that amount to violations of his constitutional rights. There may be references to specific statutes (showing the jurisdiction of the court to consider this kind of case) and court rulings (showing there is a constitutional right that has been recognized), but these are not strictly necessary, especially in an inmate suit. The most important component of a complaint is the statement of facts—the allegations by the plaintiff of the things that have violated his rights.[1] (Courts are more lenient in reviewing the language of papers filed by inmates, because inmates are allowed to do their own research and legal drafting. They are also allowed to file their actions **pro se**—that is, on their own behalf, without the assistance of attorneys.) Finally, the complaint will state what kind of **relief** (injunction, declaratory relief, and/or money damages) the plaintiff is seeking.

The summons (issued by the court) will also indicate that the defendant has a specified amount of time (often 30 days) in which to answer the complaint.[2] This notice of "time to answer" is most important, because it sets a legal deadline for the defendant to be sure that an answer is filed in the court.

■ Getting Representation

What next? Getting representation is the most basic, and important, step for the defendant. What is *not* done: The defendant must not seek out or talk to the plaintiff. Even if it is someone who is seen at work at the prison or jail every day, the defendant should avoid all confrontations with the plaintiff. The defendant should never discuss the lawsuit with the prisoner–plaintiff. It is possible that the prisoner will try to engage in conversation about the court case, but this should be avoided. If it is too difficult to avoid the prisoner who has sued, the defendant may want to ask for a transfer to another post or shift to avoid the problem. It is also not advisable for the defendant to contact the court, or any official at the courthouse, about the case. Of course, the defendant should not attempt to answer the complaint himself.

If you are sued and there are a number of defendants, you will undoubtedly know and work with some or all of them. It is all right to talk to them. Ask them if they have been served with a summons (or whether there was a waiver of summons), and discuss how you are going to get representation. Even if the suit looks frivolous or ridiculous, or if you know nothing about the facts of the complaint, the only way to get rid of it is to have a lawyer file the necessary papers to get it dismissed. Failure to do this could result in a court judgment against you. Doing nothing is the worst thing that the defendant can do. It is hoped that you have been advised, during training or elsewhere at your work, about how to get a lawyer to represent you. In some agencies, there are lawyers on the staff, and perhaps even assigned to the facility where you work, who do this legal work. In many agencies, representation is provided by the attorney general's office (for state corrections workers). In counties, it is commonly provided by the county attorney or solicitor. Some jurisdictions even provide a way to get representation by private attorneys, who are paid by the government. Due to the importance of this aspect, new correctional employees should always ask during staff training sessions about procedures if they are sued in a work-related matter.

You should also notify your supervisor about the lawsuit. Your agency may have a formal procedure (such as a form or written report) to do this, or oral reporting may be enough. It is important for a number of reasons that supervisors and prison managers know that you have been sued. It may be necessary for you to take time from work in order to consult with your lawyer or go to court. A lawsuit may affect your working relationship with plaintiff–inmates. Also, if you don't know or aren't sure how to get a lawyer, the supervisor should help you with the steps necessary to get representation.

Be sure to keep all papers, including the envelope (noting the date and time received) in which the papers were mailed or carried and any notes you may make. When you go to see your lawyer, take all the papers you have that relate to the case. Because of the strict time deadlines, you should obtain representation as soon as possible after you are served. From then on, it is the responsibility of the lawyer to meet deadlines, take necessary legal steps to protect your interests, notify you of any developments in the case, and get necessary information from you to prepare the case. If at any time you are not aware of what is happening, you should not hesitate to ask your lawyer. It is her responsibility to represent you, and part of that responsibility is answering your questions and keeping you advised of important court dates and rulings. If your case does go to trial, your lawyer will represent you in the courtroom and, if need be, on appeal. But the most important thing is for the lawyer to get actively involved right at the beginning, because most prisoner suits are dismissed at an early stage, and only a small number actually go to trial.

All of this discussion, of course, assumes that you are entitled to representation. Every state has rules about the standards for representing employees. In the vast majority of cases, corrections staff are represented at no expense by government lawyers. In a very few cases, there may be a determination that a defendant is not entitled to representation by the state. This will usually be because the corrections employee acted in a blatantly offensive manner (as shown by investigation and not merely by an inmate's allegations) or acted totally outside the scope of any policies governing his duties. The defendant must be notified of any such determination. Still, he must obtain representation. In such a situation, he must find a private attorney to represent him.

In order to determine whether an employee is entitled to representation, there is an important standard used called the **scope of employment** (also known by other names, such as "scope of duties" or "line of duty"). This concept is used to set the boundaries and determine whether the employee was acting properly and in such a manner that the government will take responsibility for his actions. It is also used to decide other very important questions, such as indemnification in the case of adverse judgment in a lawsuit and the responsibility of the government (in case of tort claims) for the actions of its agents. **Figure 4-1** shows how such determinations may be made. The circles show different factors that define the responsibilities

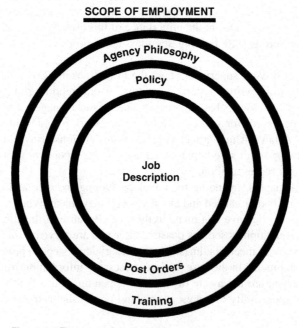

Figure 4-1 The scope of employment.

of each employee. The outer circle defines the boundary of an employee's duties. If the employee goes beyond that boundary, he will be considered to be "outside the scope" of his employment. He will then be on his own to obtain counsel and to face any other legal ramifications of his actions. The determining factors (and the elements in the concentric circles that define an employee's duties) may vary from one agency to another. But they are important for each corrections employee to know, at every level, in order to determine what is expected of him on the job and what extent his employer (the government) will defend and support his actions.

Some prison workers carry liability insurance to cover their actions while at work. If a worker is insured, he must notify the insurance company, which will likely provide an attorney or give instructions about how the worker is to get representation. As long as the worker's actions are covered by the terms of the policy, the insurance carrier will pay for lawyers' fees and for any judgment that may result in a case. You can see, of course, that insurance coverage may present some complications. For example, there may be other defendants in the case who do not have insurance or there may be requests for injunctive relief, which the insurance company has no responsibility or authority to address. A less apparent concern is the possibility that an insurer may feel it is appropriate to settle the suit by making a nominal payment to the inmate, rather than undergo the time and expense of prolonged litigation. Such a practice can be detrimental to prison administration, as it could serve as an incentive for inmates to file more lawsuits, regardless of merit, or it may undermine sound policy or practice.

■ Step by Step

As we have indicated, your attorney will review those papers that have been filed in court and will decide the best steps to take to protect your interests. Your answer to the complaint is called just that—an **answer**. A defendant may file a motion to dismiss the complaint and/or for summary judgment prior to filing an answer. That paper must be filed by the deadline indicated by the court, unless an extension is obtained. The attorney will undoubtedly want to get a report from you about the incident or actions complained about. This may be done by asking for a written report, having an interview with you, or both. From these, and any other papers and reports that may have been prepared about the matter, the lawyer will prepare and file an answer with the court. It is also likely that the attorney will file **motions** with the court to dismiss the case because of defects in it. This may be pursued for a wide variety of reasons: because you were not properly served (notified) of the complaint, because the court has no jurisdiction to consider such a case, or (very frequently) because what the inmate alleges does not entitle him to any judicial relief, even if the facts are true. These motions to dismiss are quite technical, but they are very important to protect you. The lawyer should send you a copy of any such papers she files for you. If you do not get these copies, you should feel free to ask for them.

If the case is not dismissed by the court at this early stage, you will enter a phase of the proceedings called **discovery.** There are four principal kinds of discovery.

1. **Interrogatories**: These are written questions that an attorney for one side submits to the other side. (Interrogatories may also be submitted to possible witnesses who have information about the case.) If you receive interrogatories, you may sit down with your attorney and, taking your time, prepare answers to be filed. Your attorney, looking at what may be best for your defense, may decide that it would be advantageous to ask the inmate, or witnesses, what the facts are. For this reason, she may then send interrogatories to the plaintiff or to witnesses.

2. **Depositions**: These are questions asked in person and under oath and their responses, with a court reporter taking down all that is said. It is similar to examining a witness in a courtroom, except there is no judge present, so the questions tend to be more freewheeling. The deposition is usually taken in a lawyer's office, not in the courthouse. In a civil case, it is common for a plaintiff to take the deposition of a defendant, and vice versa. (In prisoner suits, however, discovery is not nearly as common as it is in other civil actions.) Depositions of key witnesses in civil cases who are not parties are also usually taken. By taking a deposition or asking interrogatories, an attorney tries to nail down what testimony the other side has to offer. This process gives a good indication of the strengths and weaknesses of the witnesses and of the overall case.

3. **Motions to produce documents**: These entail just what the title says: one party obtains from the other any documents that may be relevant to the case. (What may not be obtained are attorney papers; these are the lawyer's work product, such as the notes taken at your interview, and are not available to the other side.)

4. **Requests for admissions:** These also are just what the title says: one party asks the other whether it is true that certain facts exist. These requests will refer to specific facts that are relevant to the case. They may be used to confirm that certain vital facts are clearly true and are not contested by either side. They also may be used to see whether certain things can be eliminated from controversy (and possibly from the trial) by getting the other side to agree on what the facts are.

All types of discovery have time deadlines. These deadlines must be met; otherwise, assistance will be sought from the court to compel the discovery, or even a default of the entire case may be ordered.

With good discovery, an attorney may obtain virtually the entire factual and evidentiary case that the other side may use. This is done purposely, to encourage parties to find out what kind of case the other side has (strengths and weaknesses) and further, to encourage settlement of cases. If an attorney has accomplished thorough discovery and a case does go to trial, there should be few surprises.

■ Not Going to Trial

We noted previously that an attorney will file motions to dismiss a case, based on the original papers that are filed. If these are not successful, and the case proceeds toward trial, other motions will likely be filed. The most common is the motion for **summary judgment**. To support this motion, the attorney will often file affidavits from her client or from witnesses. **Affidavits** are sworn written statements containing information relevant to the case. The attorney will argue that her party is entitled to win the case based on the law governing the case because the facts shown in affidavits (plus depositions or other discovery) are not in dispute and do not require trial. The opposing side will respond, asserting why summary judgment is not appropriate (and probably asking for summary judgment for his client instead).

The court will rule on the motion for summary judgment, either denying it (usually, denial is on the grounds that there are still disputed facts to be resolved) or granting it. If it is granted to the defendant, the case is dismissed. If it is granted to the plaintiff, the court must decide what relief (such as money damages, injunction, or other relief) is appropriate.

As a result of the preparation of the case and as the trial gets closer, parties (and especially attorneys for the parties) feel pressure to settle cases without going to trial. Many judges will call attorneys in and urge them to try to settle the case. If an attorney has found that her case is weak, her client is not strong on the controlling facts, or the judge is obviously leaning toward the other side, she may talk to her client about getting something out of the case by settling, usually with a compromise instead of a significant ruling and judgment for the other side. This kind of compromise settlement is probably not as common in prisoner cases, for a number of reasons: inmates may see the issue purely as either a win or loss, with nothing in between (less than a total win) being acceptable; injunctive relief may require a significant change in agency policy or practice, which management may not be willing to consider; money damages are usually recoverable only from the individual worker's pocket, so that even a comparatively small settlement is seen as unacceptable; or agreement to even a small award may require admission by prison staff of violation of constitutional rights as to certain activities, which may be considered totally unacceptable because of the precedent it sets, both for this defendant and especially for other inmate–plaintiffs. It is only in rare instances where settlement in prison cases is in the best interests of the defendant(s), such as where the case is factually weak or the law is unclear.

■ Trial

If the case is not dismissed or settled, it will proceed to trial, which is very different from what you may have seen on television or in the movies. A hearing date is set by the judge, at which time the attorneys for both sides will appear in the courtroom, usually with their clients present (although this is not required in a civil case). At the time set, the attorney should ensure that her case is ready, the documentary evidence is available, and the witnesses are prepared to testify. A trial may proceed with or without a jury. A **jury** is a group of citizens who decide what the facts are—they are solely fact finders. Some cases are tried without a jury—that is, by the judge alone. There is never a jury in habeas corpus cases. In torts and Section 1983 cases, the parties are usually entitled to a jury. If both sides waive jury trial (and there may be good tactical reasons for doing this, such as a history of juries not being favorable in your locality), the judge will hear the case. Then the judge becomes the trier of fact and also decides (as she does in all cases) what law applies to the facts of the particular case.

If you are a defendant in the case, you will likely be called as a witness. Or you may be called to testify because you have information relevant to the outcome of someone else's case. If you are "summoned," or called to testify, you again must notify your superiors, who will have to arrange to allow you to go to court. And, most important, you should contact the attorney who is calling you to testify and discuss with her your role as a witness. As a matter of good trial preparation, the attorney should be in touch with you and set up an appointment to talk about your testimony, but, because of the press of business, this may not happen. If this is the case, you should, by all means, get in touch with her.

There are a number of rules and reminders that apply to your conduct as a witness in a court case.[3] It is hoped that your attorney will go over these with you. Sometimes, because of the press of time—and corrections trial lawyers tend to be very busy indeed—the attorney will not have time to go over things in detail. You should always ask for time to go over your testimony and time to ask questions about the case that may be of special concern to you. Here are some very basic rules:

- Review any records and reports that are available to you that relate to the facts of the case. Specifically, review any records, reports, written statements, and depositions that you may have given. Do not memorize your testimony, as such testimony will sound rehearsed and may cause the jury to lose confidence in your testimony.

- Dress and act professionally. Consult with your attorney about the propriety or expectation of wearing your uniform at trial if you wear one at work, especially in criminal trials in which you are a witness. Limit facial gestures to presenting a pleasant but serious focus. There should be no smirks, grimaces, or similar expressions. It is very important that you demonstrate that you take the proceedings seriously.

- Try to remain as calm as possible. Take the amount of time you need to think about your answers. Speak clearly and loud enough so that you can be heard by all jurors. Speak directly to the judge or jury as much as possible. Do not allow an opposing attorney to get you angry.

- Answer only the question, exactly as it is given to you. Do not volunteer additional information. You do not have the right to object to a question—your attorney will do that if it is objectionable. If you do not understand a question, you do have the right to ask your attorney or the judge for clarification. Answer as briefly as you can.

- If you do not know the answer, say so. There is nothing wrong with this. Do not try to come up with information you are not sure about, just because a question has been asked. Tell the truth, no matter what. If a wrong or misleading answer has been given, clarify your answer as soon as you realize the error.

- In response to a question, it is permissible to say you have discussed your testimony before trial with your attorney and other appropriate parties.

- Be courteous. If the judge or an attorney interrupts, stop talking and wait for someone to tell you to go on. A judge may sometimes ask you questions or give you some advice or instructions. Listen to these closely, and then go on.

- When your testimony is over, you should leave the courtroom, unless you are a party to the case. If you are the defendant in the case, you should go back to the defense table and sit with your attorney.

- If you are a party in the case, we have noted already that you are permitted to be in the courtroom during the trial. If you want to leave, consult with your attorney about this. If you are called as a witness, and you want to sit in the courtroom after (or before) you have testified, ask the attorney who called you if this is permitted. Sometimes, witnesses are excluded from sitting in the courtroom, except when they are testifying. (The attorney should let you know before you go on the witness stand whether there is a local rule that excludes you from sitting in on the trial after you have finished testifying.)

At the end of all testimony, the attorneys will argue the case, summarizing the points that are most important and favorable to their clients. If there is a jury, the judge will give **instructions** to the jury. These are the rules that they must use to decide the facts of the case. After deliberating, the jury returns a **verdict**. This decides liability in the case—whether the defendant is liable or whether the plaintiff has failed to prove the defendant to be liable. If the defendant wins, the case is dismissed. Judgment is entered for the defendant(s). If the plaintiff wins, the court proceeds to the next stage, which is deciding on the appropriate relief to be given. If the relief requested is money damages, the jury will be used and instructed about how to decide on appropriate damages. If there is no jury, the judge decides this as well. After the verdict and the damages are decided, the court enters a **judgment** in the case. This is the official court order, which states the outcome and is filed in the court records.

▓ Appeal

The attorney for the losing party will usually file motions in an attempt to set aside the verdict and judgment that have been entered. If these are not successful (and they usually are not), a notice of appeal is filed. There is a strict time limit for this to be done.

In a civil case, either side may appeal if it is dissatisfied with the outcome. (In a criminal case, as a general rule, only the defendant can appeal a loss.) If you are a defendant, the government will again provide representation for you if the plaintiff appeals or to take an appeal if you have lost. Often, certain lawyers specialize in handling appeals, and others try the cases in the lower courts. Again, be sure to make inquiries about whether your interests are being protected. Do not hesitate to contact the attorney who has been assigned to handle the appeal of your case.

There are many names for the courts that handle appeals. In federal courts and in many states, they are called courts of appeals. The case in appellate court will be handled by filing papers (briefs and motions). The court will set a date for the case to be argued. A court of appeals usually consists of three or more judges. A lawyer for each side will argue the case. Most of these arguments are based solely on the legal merits of what has gone on in the trial court. Courts of appeals do not ordinarily review the facts of the case in regard to whether the verdict is correct. Only the issue of whether certain facts should *not* have been considered and the issue of whether there is enough evidence in the record to support the verdict will be reviewed.

Although arguments in appellate courts are open to the public, you will not likely appear there. A court of appeals takes no testimony; it only hears legal arguments, and these tend to be technical (and pretty boring!). However, if you want to hear your case when it is argued, you have a right to attend. You should ask your attorney about the time and place.

Judgments that are approved (affirmed) in the appellate courts are returned as final. If the appellate court finds significant mistakes have been made, it will return the case to the trial judge, along with instructions about how to proceed. Sometimes, the case will have to be tried over. This is called a **reversal** and a **remand** (sending the case back to the trial court for corrections to be made, which may mean trying the case over from the beginning).

There is technically opportunity for appeal to the supreme court of a state, if it is a state trial, or of the United States, if it is a federal trial. As discussed earlier, the U.S. Supreme Court will agree to look at a case only if there is a substantial legal question that should be addressed. This happens very rarely. There is, in practice, a right of appeal up to the first level of appeal, the appellate court. The decision of that court is, in most cases, the final decision on the case. "I'm going to take this case all the way to the Supreme Court" is more attorney bravado and posturing than a legal certainty.

SUMMARY

- This chapter is presented as a guide to be used by the corrections worker in the event that he is sued.

- A corrections lawsuit (most commonly under Section 1983) is commenced when an inmate files a complaint. Each named defendant is served with a summons and the complaint. In the federal courts and some state courts, service of the summons may be waived by the defendant.

- The person being sued (the defendant) should take the summons or waiver, and any relevant records he has in his possession, to the attorney who is responsible for representing staff members in the case. That attorney will provide information about local court procedures, answer questions about the case, and take necessary steps to file the appropriate papers (an answer and motions) in court.

- If the case is not dismissed by the court, the next stage of the case is discovery. Discovery is not as frequently used in prisoner suits as in other civil lawsuits. The purpose of discovery is to find out all the information one can about the other side's case. Types of discovery are interrogatories, depositions, motions to produce documents, and requests for admissions.

- An attorney will continue to try to avoid trial by the use of pretrial motions. One of the most commonly used at this stage is the motion for summary judgment. This motion argues that there are no facts in dispute that would necessitate a trial and therefore the attorney's client should win the case on the basis of the undisputed facts and the law that governs the case.

- If the case goes to trial, it may be before the trial judge alone or with a jury. The jury decides only the facts of the case; the verdict (either in favor of the plaintiff or the defendant); and, if the verdict is for the plaintiff, the amount of damages to be awarded.

- A person called as a witness should go over his prospective testimony with the attorney who is calling him as a witness and should adhere to the rules for being a good witness (some important rules are set out in the chapter).

- A party who loses a case may take an appeal if the attorney who represents that party thinks there is any good argument to be made that a mistake was made in any part of the trial. No testimony or evidence is taken in an appeals court. That court decides the appeal based on written records (including a transcript of the trial) sent up by the trial court. Attorneys for each side submit written briefs, making their arguments about the case, and usually are allowed to argue the case before the judges (most commonly, there are three judges) of the appellate court.

THINKING ABOUT IT

Officer Smith is a five-year employee of the Department of Corrections. He has earned very good work evaluations and is in line for a promotion. He often works in the cell block and walks down the tiers past each inmate's cell. On May 12, as he walks by inmate Johnson's cell, Johnson throws a piece of feces at Officer Smith, hitting him in the face. Smith yells for Johnson's cell to be opened. When it is, Smith enters the cell and hits Johnson in the face. Smith then leaves the cell, yelling for the door to be closed. Inmate Johnson sues Officer Smith, alleging assault. The officer denies the assault, saying that his actions were appropriate to gain control of Johnson. Officer Smith requests representation. Will the government agree to represent the officer? Why or why not?

KEY TERMS

affidavit: A written statement of facts, confirmed by oath or affirmation of the person making it (the affiant).

answer (civil procedure): The pleading filed by the defendant, responding to the plaintiff's allegations in the complaint. It is a written statement that sets out the defendant's factual and legal grounds for his defense.

deposition: The testimony of a witness taken under oath, not in open court, in response to oral questions, pursuant to a rule or order that authorizes such questioning. The testimony is transcribed and is usually intended for use at a later trial.

discovery (court procedure): A procedural tool or remedy used to compel an adverse party or a witness to answer allegations and interrogatories, disclose facts within his knowledge, or produce documents or records, all of which are designed to help the requesting party to better prepare and present his case.

instructions: Rules and directions the trial judge gives to a jury to use in their deliberations on the facts of the case.

interrogatories (court procedure): A method of discovery. Written questions about facts of a case that an attorney submits in advance of trial to persons who are believed to have knowledge about those facts.

judgment: The statement of the decision of a court, amounting to final disposition of the case at that level. It is sometimes made orally in a courtroom, but it is finalized by entry into the records of the court. In a criminal case, it is an official, recorded statement that the defendant is convicted or acquitted of the offense charged.

jury, trial jury, petit jury: A body of persons, the number of which is defined by constitution, statute, or court rules, that is selected according to law, sworn to determine certain matters of fact in a criminal action, and sworn to render a verdict of guilty or not guilty (in a criminal case). (In civil cases, a jury, as defined by statute or by court rules, decides certain matters of fact and renders a verdict for either the plaintiff or the defendant, including, in most cases, the amount of damages that are awarded to the prevailing party.)

motion: An oral or written request made by a party to any action, before, during, or after a trial, that a court issue a ruling or an order on any matter of procedure or substance related to the case.

motion to produce documents (court procedure): A method of discovery. A motion to obtain from the opposing side any documents that may be relevant to the case.

pro se: Acting as one's own attorney in legal or administrative proceedings.

relief (court procedure): A broad term used to describe the assistance, redress, or benefit that a complainant wishes to receive from a court. Examples are orders of injunction, declaratory relief, and money damages.

remand: To send back. To return the person or matter to the place from which it came.

requests for admissions (court procedure): A method of discovery. Written statements of facts about a case; these statements are formally sent to the opposing party, who is asked to admit or deny that certain facts are true. Those which are admitted usually will be accepted by the court as having been established and as not requiring proof at trial.

reverse: To overturn by contrary judgment or decision. To set aside, repeal, or revoke.

scope of employment: The boundaries that define the actions that an employee (or agent) is expected to perform and the manner in which those actions are to be performed.

summary judgment: The court's disposition of a case summarily—that is, without the need for a trial. Based on the facts shown in the pleadings and by affidavits, a court's determination that judgment can be entered before trial because the facts necessary to decide the case are already clearly presented and are not controverted, so that trial (which is intended to resolve disputed facts) is unnecessary.

summons: A written order issued by a judicial officer requiring a person accused of a criminal offense to appear in a designated court at a specified time to answer a charge. Also, an order in a civil case to respond or answer in court.

verdict: In criminal proceedings, the decision made by a jury (in a jury trial) or by a judicial officer (in a court trial) that a defendant is either guilty or not guilty of the offense for which he has been tried. In civil proceedings, the decision made by a jury or judicial officer in favor of the claim of the plaintiff or the counterclaim or defense of the defendant.

waiver of summons: A process authorized in federal courts and some state courts allowing a plaintiff to request the defendant to waive service of the summons, eliminating some costs of the litigation. A defendant who waives service of summons is still required to respond or answer to the complaint.

witness: A person who directly perceives an event or thing or who has expert knowledge relevant to a case. Also, such a person who is called to testify in a hearing or trial.

ENDNOTES

1. The importance of the factual statement in a civil rights complaint is shown in *Ashcroft v. Iqbal,* 556 U.S. __ (2009). In that case, the Supreme Court held that "...[Iqbal's] complaint fails to plead sufficient facts to state a claim for purposeful and unlawful discrimination against petitioners [Attorney General Ashcroft and FBI Director Mueller]."
2. Defendants in federal court who waive service of summons get 60 days to respond after the request for waiver is sent to them.
3. Your agency or your attorney may have instructions that will assist you in preparing for testifying. There are some good publications that provide advice, as well. A good one is published by the professional association for corrections workers, the American Correctional Association: Collins, W. *Correctional Law for the Correctional Officer.* 5th ed. (Alexandria, VA: American Correctional Association, 2010), 173–175.

Constitutional Law of Corrections

We now begin to look at "The Law of Corrections." Until the 1960s, the courts generally had a "hands-off" philosophy toward intervening in correctional matters. Perhaps this position is best shown by the statement in the 1871 Virginia case, *Ruffin v. Commonwealth*, 62 Va. 21 Gratt. 790 (1871): "[A]s a consequence of his crime [he] not only forfeited his liberty, but all his personal rights except those which the law in its humanity accords to him. He is for the time being the slave of the State."

In 1967, The President's Commission on Law Enforcement and Administration of Justice, in its *Task Force Report: Corrections*, stated the following:[1]

> **A variety of rights and privileges are traditionally lost upon conviction of a crime. While before conviction the Government must justify every assertion of authority, after conviction such assertions stand on a different footing…And virtually all of an offender's activities may be subject to regulation by correctional officials, particularly in institutions. He has no absolute right to see friends or relatives or to do any of a multitude of things that the rest of society takes for granted.**

> **Yet it is inconsistent with our whole system of government to grant such uncontrolled power to any officials, particularly over the lives of persons. The fact that a person has been convicted of a crime should not mean that he has forfeited all rights to demand that he be fairly treated by officials.**

This 1967 report correctly noted that there were "increasing signs that the courts are ready to abandon their traditional hands-off attitude." In 1961, the Supreme Court, in *Monroe v. Pape*, 365 U.S. 167 (1961), said that in passing the Civil Rights Act of 1871, Congress intended to provide a remedy to parties deprived of their constitutional rights, privileges, and immunities by an official's abuse of his position. As applied, this Act allowed inmates to sue public officials for monetary damages and injunctive relief, if their clearly established constitutional rights were violated.

Some prison cases during this era clearly showed such violations. Cases arose from "vicious and brutal staff behavior, literal torture of inmates, overcrowded, dark, vermin-infested facilities, and other deprivations of fundamental freedoms."[2] While these conditions certainly did not exist at all correctional institutions, the fact they existed at any of them validated some inmate claims and contributed to court intervention. In *Wolff v. McDonnell*, 418 U.S. 539 (1974), the Supreme Court stated the following:

> **Lawful imprisonment necessarily makes unavailable many rights and privileges of the ordinary citizen … But though his rights may be diminished by the needs … of the institutional environment, a prisoner is not wholly stripped of constitutional protections when he is imprisoned for crime. There is no iron curtain drawn between the Constitution and the prisons of this country.**

In Part II (Chapters 5 through 17), we look at constitutional law. This includes a discussion of those areas of corrections work in which different provisions of the Constitution have been examined to see whether they define or limit what may be done by corrections officials. In many areas, there are now Supreme Court decisions, which provide the authoritative word by interpreting the U.S. Constitution on corrections issues. There are also additional court decisions presented from lower courts (mostly federal but also some state), which give history of litigation in the area under discussion, interpret or extend the Supreme Court ruling, or, in some cases, present constitutional interpretation on points on which the Supreme Court has not yet ruled.

Some have called the court rulings on these corrections matters "the law of prisoners' rights." Although prisoners' rights are discussed in Chapter 5 as a generic category, we do not use that phrase here for the discussion of the law for two reasons. First, the field of corrections encompasses more than prisons and prisoners. Even if the area of "prisons and prisoners" is interpreted to include jails and pretrial detainees (and much of the law on prisons does apply to jails, as discussed in Chapter 20), there are also issues of probation and parole, juveniles and young offenders, and community corrections that do not neatly (or properly) fit under the phrase "prisons and prisoners." Second, using the term "prisoners' rights" implies the emphasis on concern for the law as it could be used or interpreted for the benefits or rights of prisoners. The law in this area is more complex. As many people have pointed out, the law of corrections in virtually all areas of concern becomes a balancing of interests: the interests of prisoners on one hand and the interests of corrections managers on the other. Of course, it is natural for prisoners (and their advocates) to seek the greatest benefits and privileges they can obtain in the prison setting. But there are valid concerns that must be weighed on the other side. And it is that balancing of interests that many judges missed in the early days (the 1960s and 1970s) of the "correctional law revolution." It took many years of litigation to obtain recognition in the law that individual freedoms in prisons had to be limited, for the good of the prison as a whole—that is, to obtain orderly running, security, and safety in corrections facilities. We try to present faithfully the development of those counterbalancing interests: the interests of prisoners and of their keepers. The interests are not always hostile; in many cases, they coincide or come close to matching. It is fairer though to title this discussion the Law of Corrections, rather than to say it is the Law of Prisoners' Rights.

Supreme Court decisions are presented in this part in some detail. Often, the facts of a case are helpful in our study of how the law in a particular area developed. The reasoning of the

Court may also be useful. (Note: if you see the word "Court" used with a capital "C," we are referring to the U.S. Supreme Court. Lower courts are referred to with a small "c," except when an official name is used, as in "the U.S. Court of Appeals for the Eighth Circuit.") The most important thing of all is the court's holding—what it concludes is the governing legal principle for that area of the law. As already noted, to help you find important statements of the law as you look through the book, holdings of cases and statements of important legal principles are given in **boldface font**. On every Supreme Court opinion, you can expect to find boldface presentation of the important statements of the Court in that case. The few exceptions are instances in which the Supreme Court decision does not contain a ruling or language that is vital to understanding the "law of corrections." If there are such important statements of the law in other cases (or in some chapters, in statutes), they will be presented boldly.

For every case discussed, there will be a citation of the case given; this allows the reader to find the whole case in a court reporter or other resource, if reading the whole case (or more of it than is presented here) is desired. Contrary to practice in legal writing, we do not give page numbers for the quotations from cases and ordinarily do not indicate the vote on court decisions or the discussions contained in dissenting or concurring opinions. Those practices may be helpful in legal writing and discussions that give a fuller picture of the case. We skip them, however, because they are contrary to the purposes of this text; they would tend to clutter the discussion, and perhaps even cloud the issues, for non-attorney readers who just want to know "the law." In every case, it is the holding of the majority that is presented in boldface font. You can rely on this material to be "the law" of that case.

The sheer volume of "the law" in this area is huge. No book can present all of "the law of corrections." Such a collection would not be a book, but a long shelf of books, because the number of reported opinions on corrections matters now stretches into the many hundreds. Any author or teacher must select the cases that will give the reader the best understanding of the current state of the law. We have tried to select cases that touch on the wide variety of issues that may be of interest to corrections workers and to students in this field. We have also selected cases in which the law has spoken in some authoritative way (that is, more than just a lonely judicial voice in some isolated court). Besides the leading and controlling Supreme Court opinions, we also have included a smattering of opinions from lower courts to give the reader an idea of the issues that have been considered historically and those that are being considered currently in the courts.

As with all such legal discussions, the reader and the corrections worker must remember that only the Supreme Court (or federal law) speaks for the whole country. The holdings of the Supreme Court on corrections matters govern those areas of corrections work, constitutionally and legally. If the Supreme Court has not given a conclusive ruling on a particular question of concern, then an inquiry must be made as to whether a local court (such as a federal circuit court, district court, or state court) has made a ruling on that question. If there is no Supreme Court ruling and no ruling by a court that controls in your jurisdiction, the matter is still open to litigation, and the law is not settled. If a court in another location (such as a court of appeals in another part of the country or a supreme court in another state) has spoken on the issue, that ruling may be informative about how the law may be interpreted, but it is not binding or settled law for your local jurisdiction.

Let us onward, to The Law!

ENDNOTES

1.   President's Commission on Law Enforcement and Administration of Justice. *Task Force Report: Corrections* (Washington, DC: U.S. Government Printing Office, 1967), 82–83.
2.   Harris, M. and Spiller Jr., D. *After Decision: Implementation of Judicial Decrees in Correctional Settings.* (Washington, DC: National Institute of Law Enforcement and Criminal Justice, Law Enforcement Assistance Administration, U.S. Department of Justice, 1977), 22.

5 | A General View of Prisoners' Rights Under the Constitution

The problems of prisons in America are complex and intractable, and, more to the point, they are not readily susceptible of resolution by decree.

U.S. Supreme Court, *Procunier v. Martinez*

Chapter Outline

- The Nature of Prisons
- Section 1983 and the Constitution
- Defenses: How Does the Corrections Worker Protect Himself?
- Inmate Grievances
- The Prison Litigation Reform Act
- Prisoners' Rights

This chapter sets the stage for the detailed study of the constitutional law as it applies to corrections management and operations. We will first look at prison itself, the structure and the people (inmates and staff) within its walls. We then will look at the means that prisoners use to pursue their rights in courts. Most of this pursuit, over the past three decades, has been through the guarantees of rights contained in the U.S. Constitution. We look at the statutory channel (42 U.S.C. § 1983) that is used to assert those constitutional rights and to complain about violations of those rights in federal courts. We then shift focus to look at prisoners' rights litigation from the viewpoint of corrections workers and the various ways corrections staff can protect themselves from being found responsible for violating the constitutional rights of inmates.

■ The Nature of Prisons

Here are three statements from prison systems of different size:

[The Florida Department of Corrections' mission is to] protect the public safety, to ensure the safety of Department personnel, and to provide proper care and supervision of all offenders under our jurisdiction while assisting, as appropriate, their re-entry into society. (Florida had 103,915 sentenced prisoners under its jurisdiction as of December 31, 2009.)

The [Virginia] Department of Corrections enhances public safety by providing effective programs, re-entry services, and supervision of sentenced offenders in a humane, cost-efficient manner, consistent with sound correctional principles and constitutional standards. (Virginia had 38,059 sentenced prisoners under its jurisdiction as of December 31, 2009.)

The mission of the North Dakota State Penitentiary is to protect the public by maintaining proper custody of the offenders sentenced by the courts; to provide a safe and healthy environment for staff and inmates; and to offer the best work, education, and treatment programs possible, encouraging inmates to make the needed changes to be law abiding and successful in society. (The state of North Dakota had 1,486 sentenced prisoners under its jurisdiction as of December 31, 2009.)[1]

These statements are representative of mission statements for most correctional agencies, whether there are 1,000 or 100,000 inmates. Protecting the public, providing a safe and humane environment, and providing inmates the opportunities for self-improvement are common elements of these statements.

As of December 31, 2009, there were 1,613,740 inmates under the jurisdiction of state and federal correctional authorities.[2] Twenty-six states reported increases in population. However, in 2009, only two states reported population increases of at least 5%.[3] In 2002, there were 17 states that reported increases of at least 5%.[4] In 2009, 24 states reported population decreases, with 6 states reporting decreases of at least 4%. Men are about 14 times more likely than women to be in prison. At year-end 2008, over 52% of sentenced inmates under state jurisdiction were serving time for violent crimes. Perhaps more reflective of the times is that violent offenders made up 60% of the growth in state prison population from 2000 through 2008.[5] The growth in the violent offender inmate population may result in more confrontations and behavioral incidents, giving prison officials increased management and litigation concerns.

Inmates are generally housed in one of three types of prisons:

Maximum (Close, High) security is characterized by a perimeter of double fences or a wall and outside patrols or towers (see **Figure 5-1**). Inside, there is cell housing, highly controlled movement, direct supervision, and regular searches of inmates and housing areas. These prisons have a high staff-to-inmate ratio. Super maximum security prisons fall within the maximum security category and have highly restrictive conditions. They ordinarily house those persons who have shown that they are unable to adjust to a maximum security setting. Examples include extremely assaultive inmates, gang members, and inmates who have killed other inmates or staff.

Medium security is usually characterized by a perimeter of single or double fences and external patrols. Inmate housing may be in cells or secure dormitories. Work and self-improvement programs are available. Internal inmate movement is often unescorted but frequently supervised. Regular searches of inmates and housing areas are conducted.

Minimum security is characterized by a perimeter of a single fence or no fence, and there are no towers and less frequent patrols. Inmates are assigned to room or dormitory housing and are allowed a greater degree of unrestricted movement. These facilities generally have a relatively

Figure 5-1 A guard's tower at Fort Ord Prison.
Source: © Kimber Rey Solana/ShutterStock, Inc.

low staff-to-inmate ratio. Inmates in these facilities may participate in outside work and/or program assignments. These facilities often are called prison camps.

In addition to these **classifications**, there may also be administrative institutions. These facilities have a specific purpose and may house inmates of different security levels. Examples include prison medical centers and detention facilities (see **Figure 5-2**). Detention facilities house inmates in various stages of the criminal justice process, including many pretrial inmates.

In determining an inmate's institution placement, the objective of the staff is to assign an inmate to the least restrictive environment that still provides appropriate control. Over the years, efforts have been made to standardize this process—for example, by assigning point totals to various factors (such as age, prior record, and nature of offense) and then designating an

Figure 5-2 A corrections building in Chicago, Illinois.
Source: © Benkrut/Dreamstime.com

institutional placement based on the inmate's total points. Within this context, however, the professional judgment of the staff continues to be a significant component of the designation process.

A prison, in essence, is a community unto itself, with very specific outer boundaries, such as a fence or wall. The interior components of a prison also resemble a community: there is an organizational control structure (prison administration), along with those living under its guidelines (inmates). There are various work assignments and, usually, educational opportunities. There are those who abide by prison rules and those who don't—and for those who don't, there is an enforcement mechanism (an institution disciplinary system). There is a store (prison commissary), where inmates may purchase selected items, often from their institution earnings. There may be television, movies, and other recreational opportunities. There are visiting and telephone privileges; of course, these are more limited than in the outside world. No matter the "amenities" offered, the one item that is not available is arguably the most important: the freedom to come and go at will.

In discussing confinement, it is important to remember that prison is not a housing of choice. To run effectively, institutions require a high degree of uniformity in rules and control, in such things as lights on and lights out, meal times, work schedules, and free-time activity. "Treat people firmly but fairly" is a common expression within a prison environment. To do otherwise is seen as creating a potentially disruptive situation within the prison. For example, allowing each inmate to decide what and how much property he can keep would create a situation of "haves" and "have-nots" and encourage the development of an underground marketplace, as well as produce potential safety, sanitation, and fire hazards. This would create dissension among the inmates and make it more difficult to maintain institutional security, discipline, and good order.

Over 35 years ago, Gresham Sykes wrote about the "pains of imprisonment."[6] While his focus was on a maximum security prison, the "pains" identify aspects of prison life that may exist in all prisons:

Deprivation of liberty: The inmate's conviction and subsequent confinement may be seen by the inmate as a deliberate rejection by the community. Within the prison, his movement is further restricted.

Deprivation of goods and services: While the inmate's basic needs are met, this is done within the highly structured confinement of the institution. Gone is his opportunity to choose to buy a hamburger at a fast food restaurant. His is a material impoverishment.[7]

Deprivation of heterosexual relationships: The lack of these opportunities can be frustrating and can affect the inmate's image of himself.

Deprivation of autonomy: The nature of an institution, as noted, requires a high degree of uniformity and consistency to operate smoothly. To accomplish this, the inmate is subject to a variety of institution rules that are intended to control his behavior. Dependence, as opposed to independence, is the expected condition.

Deprivation of security: The prison houses the inmate with other convicted criminals, many of whom may have violent histories. This can affect an inmate's feeling of well-being. Physical assaults, or threats of them, may be prevalent.

Each of these deprivations may affect an inmate's self-concept and lead the inmate to develop coping mechanisms. Litigation is one such mechanism. For some inmates, litigation can serve as a means to keep one's mind active or to "get back at the system." Here are four reasons why lawsuits may be filed by prisoners:

Fact: There is a justified reason for suit. An example is litigation by an inmate who has a serious medical condition and is deprived of his right to medical care.

Frustration: The inmate feels she has no other option available. An example is litigation by an inmate who feels she has a valid issue but is unable to get a response from someone in authority.

Fancy: The inmate thinks litigation might be a "fun" thing to do and feels there is nothing to lose. An example is litigation by an inmate who wants an additional slice of bacon served with his breakfast meal.

Fiction: The inmate asserts an untruth. An example is litigation by an inmate who does not like a staff member and files suit, making false allegations, as a type of harassment.

As noted earlier, regardless of the reason for the litigation, staff must treat all litigation seriously. Failure to do this can result in a suit without merit suddenly receiving credibility.

The most vital component of prison management is prison staff. The great majority of corrections workers are conscientious and want to do the best job possible. Their job differs from most others in that their "client" (the inmate) is not entering into this relationship by choice. Every inmate (or almost every inmate[8]) is opposed to his confinement and often is looking for ways to gain an extra benefit or test the system. An inmate often has a propensity to act out or challenge authority. In a position of authority, correctional staff must be trained how to handle a variety of situations, exercise supervision, and use good interpersonal communication skills. When a staff member lets her guard down, difficulty can arise, and it usually will.

■ Section 1983 and the Constitution

Title 42 of the U.S. Code, Section 1983, establishes a cause of action for persons to bring suit against government officials, based on alleged violations of constitutional rights. Over the past 35 years, this type of action remains a common type of lawsuit brought by prisoners nationwide. (Remember that Section 1983 is unavailable to federal prisoners, because Section 1983 refers to constitutional violations by state officials, but federal inmates have an equivalent remedy in Bivens actions.)

For a number of reasons, Section 1983 suits have become the most prevalent type of legal action against government officials, and they have been used to establish most of the constitutional rights of prisoners that have been defined by the courts—especially by the U.S. Supreme Court—in the past 35–40 years. This is not to say that common law torts and habeas corpus are not important. They provide avenues for court review of prisoner complaints in many hundreds of cases every year, but they provide a much more limited scope of review. Section 1983 actions have provided, in a variety of constitutional claims, the means to achieve a wider scope of judicial review of prison activities and programs. Section 1983 also provides broader relief, especially in the way of injunctive relief and monetary relief. It can be used for class action lawsuits, which challenge prison policies on a broad scale. It can also be brought before federal courts, where, historically, prisoners have found friendlier forums than in many state courts. (Remember too that most states have similar provisions in state law, whereby state prisoners can challenge prison conditions under provisions of the state constitution. As federal courts became more conservative in the 1980s and 1990s, and as decisions of the U.S. Supreme Court in that period prescribed more pro-government standards for federal courts to use in handling claims of constitutional violations, and with the Prison Litigation Reform Act, prisoners turned more frequently, at least in some states, to their local courts for relief under the provisions of state law, including the state's constitution.)

The most important source of prisoners' rights is still the U.S. Constitution, and the U.S. Supreme Court, as the final arbiter and definer of constitutional provisions, is still the most important source of definitions of prisoners' rights.

For a selection of clauses in the U.S. Constitution that have been used most frequently in prisoner litigation, see **Box 5-1**. You will note that most of these are from the first 10 amendments of the Constitution, commonly known as the **Bill of Rights**. There are also some other provisions that are used in prisoner litigation (remember that the right to petition for the writ of habeas corpus is guaranteed in Article I of the Constitution). The provisions in the Bill of Rights, however, are the ones used most often.

■ Defenses: How Does the Corrections Worker Protect Himself?

In Section 1983 actions, if the prisoner shows that there has been a violation of his constitutional rights, one form of relief (and this type is almost always sought by the prisoner–plaintiff) is monetary damages. These damages are assessed against the individual defendant who has been found responsible for the constitutional violation. These may involve punitive, as well as compensatory, damages. The amounts awarded (by a jury or judge) may be very small but may also be, in some cases, very large. If the worker is not covered by insurance or a state policy of indemnification, the personal judgment against him will have to be paid out of his own pocket. This may threaten any savings he has, his future earnings, his ability to obtain a loan, and even his home or other property held in his name.

For this and other reasons, the corrections worker and corrections agencies must be very concerned about prisoner lawsuits. There is no immunity against being sued. What can the worker do to protect his assets?

The first rule for the corrections worker is to follow policies, and the instructions of supervisors. Because there are many good reference sources of sound policy today, and because most corrections agencies have legal counsel to advise them and to review policy issuances to be sure that they are constitutionally defensible, a corrections worker must assume that the policies of her agency are good, in accordance with current judicial rulings and statutory provisions. A principal duty of any attorney who is assigned to provide legal advice and assistance to a correctional agency or facility is to make certain that policies are constitutionally and statutorily sound. Also, when a court ruling (any U.S. Supreme Court ruling and lower court ruling that is applicable to the agency's location) is made, it must be immediately reviewed so that any changes to agency policy can be drafted, if changes are required in order to bring agency practices into line with the new ruling.

Box 5-1 Articles of Amendment to the Constitution of the United States

Amendment 1

Congress shall make no law respecting an establishment of religion, or prohibiting the free exercise thereof; or abridging the freedom of speech, or of the press; or the right of the people peaceably to assemble, and to petition the Government for a redress of grievances.

Amendment 4

The right of the people to be secure in their persons, houses, papers, and effects, against unreasonable searches and seizures, shall not be violated, and no Warrants shall issue, but upon probable cause, supported by Oath or affirmation, and particularly describing the place to be searched, and the persons or things to be seized.

Amendment 5

No person shall be held to answer for a capital, or otherwise infamous crime, unless on a presentment or indictment of a Grand Jury, except in cases arising in the land or naval forces, or in the Militia, when in actual service in time of War or public danger; nor shall any person be subject for the same offence to be twice put in jeopardy of life or limb; nor shall be compelled in any criminal case to be a witness against himself, nor be deprived of life, liberty, or property, without due process of law; nor shall private property be taken for public use, without just compensation.

Amendment 6

In all criminal prosecutions, the accused shall enjoy the right to a speedy and public trial, by an impartial jury of the State and district wherein the crime shall have been committed, which district shall have been previously ascertained by law, and to be informed of the nature and cause of the accusation; to be confronted with the witnesses against him; to have compulsory process for obtaining witnesses in his favor, and to have the Assistance of Counsel for his defence.

Amendment 8

Excessive bail shall not be required, nor excessive fines imposed, nor cruel and unusual punishments inflicted.

Amendment 14, Section 1

All persons born or naturalized in the United States and subject to the jurisdiction thereof are citizens of the United States and of the State wherein they reside. No State shall make or enforce any law which shall abridge the privileges or immunities of citizens of the United States; nor shall any State deprive any person of life, liberty, or property, without due process of law; nor deny to any person within its jurisdiction the equal protection of the laws.

As a practical matter, the staff member should, of course, follow policy to be in step with the professional expectations of the agency's management. As a legal matter, the staff member should follow policy to ensure compliance with legal standards and especially to avoid liability in the event of inmate lawsuits. Further, being able to show that an action taken was strictly according to agency policy is ordinarily a good defense if the staff member is ever sued. This holds true even if the policy is later determined to be inaccurate or wrong. By following policy, the staff member is operating within the scope of employment and according to what prison management says is proper.

A second rule is to obtain, or provide, good training. As the field of corrections has become more complex and more affected by court rulings and other legal factors, it has become more important for corrections managers to provide good training to ensure that staff members will act consistently and in accord with agency policy and constitutional requirements. It is important for supervisors at all levels to be aware of those practices that are constitutionally mandated and to inform staff members, particularly those who are new, about the accepted and expected way to perform their duties.

This is not to say that all staff must receive legal training or instruction by lawyers (although, in recent years, this has become more and more prevalent in corrections training). However, at a minimum, staff must learn, and supervisors must therefore know, the areas of performance in which there are the greatest exposures to constitutional liability. Corrections workers at every level must be aware of the importance of acting at all times in a professional manner; these days, this means learning, and passing on to subordinates, the legal requirements of the job. (Studying this text, or taking a course or seminar using this text as a reference, may be a good step in obtaining legally oriented professional training.)

A third rule is to become familiar with the law in your jurisdiction that directly affects your job. Whatever the specialty—security, casework, education, personnel matters, parole, health care—the corrections worker should know the law that is applicable to that special kind of work. In any agency, the worker should study the statutes that govern the agency as a whole and those statutes that specifically govern the worker's special area. Further, the worker should learn about the court rulings that interpret prisoners' rights and staff responsibilities in any area where the official regularly works. To do this, the worker follows the second and first rules: get good training from someone who knows legal rulings and constraints, and be sure to follow policies, which are written to incorporate legal requirements.

A fourth rule to ensure a good defense when sued is to find a good mentor. The new worker especially should, of course, follow instructions from supervisors at all times and will, with time, learn the accepted ways of performing according to agency standards. It often happens that there is a particular supervisor around, an "old hand," who is particularly good at conveying agency policies and practices and who may also know sufficient legal information to advise the new worker of the best way to do things. A related piece of advice is that, no matter how much education you may have had and how much you think you may know from other experiences, when you first go to work in a prison, watch and listen. There is nothing you may have learned from the classroom or your other work experiences that will prepare you thoroughly for work inside a prison. Be patient, learn from the good and respected workers around you, and you will, in time, have the understanding and credibility to be a respected corrections professional yourself, serving as a role model and mentor to others.[9]

A fifth rule is to keep good records. It is hoped that the training for all staff members, whether in classrooms or on the job, will emphasize the need for, and the way to write and to maintain, good records. Whether it is filling out the forms that are routinely required to cover certain staff actions or writing a special report to record what happened in an unusual circumstance, there is nothing more important to the lawyer in defending an action than having good, clear, reliable records of what happened, whatever the nature of the lawsuit. If you are called on later to testify in a trial or to help investigators get all the facts about an occurrence, good records are invaluable to refresh your memory and to establish a more reliable, factual basis for what transpired some weeks or months earlier.

Having good knowledge of the law, being well trained in the job, keeping good records, and knowing agency policies and adhering to them are the basic lines of defense for the corrections worker. They serve to ensure that staff activity is lawful to start with and then, if there is an inmate suit, they provide the best legal defense to protect the worker against losing the case.

■ Inmate Grievances

Another method of protection for the worker is the inmate **grievance** system. It serves to protect in a practical way, as well as legally.

> The purpose of the [Florida Department of Corrections] grievance procedure is to provide an inmate with a channel for the administrative settlement of a grievance. In addition to providing the inmate with the opportunity of having a grievance heard and considered, this procedure will assist the department by providing additional means for internal resolution of problems and improving lines of communication. This procedure will also provide a written record in the event of subsequent judicial or administrative review.

> The purpose of this standard operating procedure (SOP) is to increase the safety and security of Idaho Department of Correction (IDOC) correctional facilities by providing offenders a process to voice complaints about policies, division directives, SOPs, field memorandums, conditions of confinement, employee actions, actions of other offenders, medical, and other incidents occurring within the jurisdiction of the Department. An effective grievance process gives offenders the ability to voice concerns, helps IDOC staff increase adherence to policy and procedure, and aids in the discovery of unworkable, impractical, or inconsistent practices.[10]

The concept underlying an inmate grievance system is that inmates will have complaints about their treatment and that there is some benefit in providing a means for them to channel those complaints in a uniform manner. It is good for inmates to receive answers to their complaints, even though the answers may not be what they wanted to hear. The mere fact of providing a response provides the inmate with a sense of being recognized and may reduce feelings of frustration. It also may prevent the development of a new feeling—anger—that may arise when no response to a complaint is received.

Corrections agencies have come to accept a grievance system for inmates as a sound correctional tool.[11] In the past, particularly in the 1970s, there was experimentation with a variety of systems to provide a mechanism for the inmate to raise complaints and achieve an informal resolution of those complaints. In this sense, "informal" means resolution without violence, direct confrontation, and the inmate going to court to file a formal legal complaint.

Such mechanisms included attempts at mediation or arbitration, with rules and procedures that brought them just short of court actions. A few states tried using an ombudsman, a system that, by definition, used an outside party to review and investigate complaints. Such a person has authority only to recommend changes in policy or action. Some corrections facilities turned to hearing panels—a committee of staff members who heard complaints from the inmates and had authority to recommend, or in some cases to order, corrective action. There were a few instances in which inmates were included on such hearing panels and were even allowed to vote on the outcome. Some states also tried using inmate advisory groups, which are committees composed entirely of inmates that review complaints and recommend action. These groups were also used for other matters, such as reviewing new policy and reviewing disciplinary actions taken. These attempts to incorporate direct inmate involvement in institution activities and problems, although based on enthusiastic ideas about democratic training for the inmates and participatory management, were neither notably successful nor widely adopted.

The system that has been adopted nearly universally (that is, in all of the states, the federal government, and many of the city and county systems), at least in large corrections systems, is the written grievance system. Typically, there are published rules in such a system that provide for: (1) the opportunity for any inmate to file a written grievance; (2) time limits for filing the grievance and for responding to it; (3) a description of the kinds of actions that may be the subject of grievances or those that may not (in many states, disciplinary sanctions are not grievable, for example); (4) emergency handling of certain complaints, such as medical or personal injury complaints or impending loss of property; (5) safeguards against reprisals that might be taken against inmates for using the system; and (6) at least one level of appeal from initial disposition of the complaint—usually, an appeal to the headquarters-level of the system. **Figure 5-3** contains flow charts diagramming two of the inmate grievance processes used by the Arizona Department of Corrections.

As a practical matter, using such written inmate grievances provides a number of benefits. It alerts staff to problem areas in the institution. It spotlights those matters that are of greatest inmate concern. It may point out an individual officer or an isolated activity where corrective action may be needed. It serves, when run properly, to diffuse inmate resentment and hostility. It often lessens the number of lawsuits that are filed. When lawsuits are filed, it provides a quick record to attorneys and the courts of what has been done already to address the complaint. It may provide a statistical basis, either grossly or precisely, to assess programs, policies, or activities that need more careful review and possible revision. It gives the corrections agency the chance to address its problems of management and operation and to correct them internally, without having the courts step in and order corrective action of the courts' preference.[12]

There are weaknesses to the system. It does not provide all kinds of relief—usually the only relief is corrective action for the aggrieved inmate. Money damages are not necessarily available. Injunctive relief is rare, taken only in those cases mentioned in the preceding paragraph in which management recognizes an ongoing problem that needs correction. Often, it fails to cover some of the greatest complaints of inmates, such as serious disciplinary action or medical

ATTACHMENT A
DEPARTMENT ORDER 802

Inmate Grievance - Standard Grievance Process

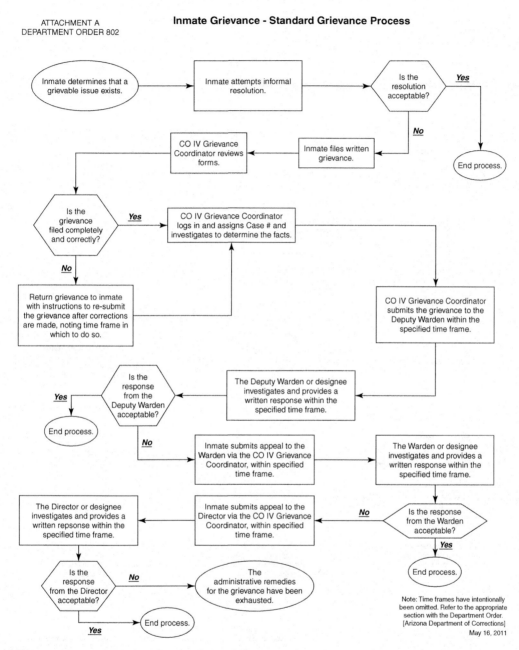

Figure 5-3 Inmate Grievance—Standard Grievance Process.
Source: Provided Courtesy of Arizona Department of Corrections.

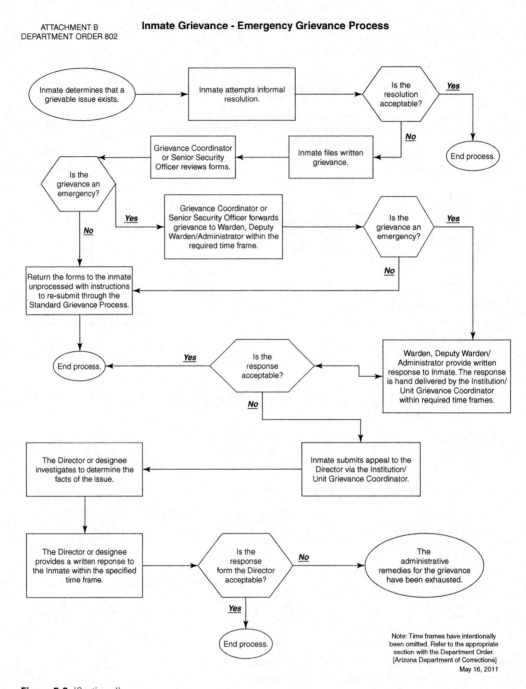

ATTACHMENT B
DEPARTMENT ORDER 802

Inmate Grievance - Emergency Grievance Process

Note: Time frames have intentionally
been omitted. Refer to the appropriate
section with the Department Order.
[Arizona Department of Corrections]
May 16, 2011

Figure 5-3 (Continued)

malpractice. Inmates may try to undermine the system—by filing great numbers of complaints, for example—to try to clog up the system or exhaust the patience of the staff, or by filing frivolous complaints. Inmates may file complaints that they know are without merit, have no basis in fact, are repetitious of claims that have already been addressed, or are otherwise written in bad faith.[13] Time limits to respond to inmates' grievances may drag on and be discouraging. Inmates may perceive that corrective relief is never given. As with any program, its success depends on the positive intent of the staff who administer it and the support of management. However, on balance, for a wide range of prison complaints, the written grievance system is recognized as a very useful tool.

Besides the practical benefits, the courts too have generally recognized that an administrative grievance system is a desirable mechanism. Many courts have encouraged corrections agencies to adopt such systems. The primary reason, no doubt, has been a desire to cut down on the large number of prisoner lawsuits that are filed. It is especially believed that the trivial matters that can be the subject of lawsuits, which can quickly clog up the courts' time, should be disposed of internally at the prison, and not at the courthouse. A side benefit is that, if and when a case does come to court, there will be a written record already made, which can be attached to the agency's response and may allow for quick resolution of the case on the pleadings.

For these reasons, many courts have required use of the grievance system before the inmate pursues a lawsuit. This is called an exhaustion requirement, which means that, if the agency has a grievance system (and if the subject matter of the lawsuit is covered by the grievance system), the inmate will be required to "exhaust" his administrative grievance remedy before he comes into court. As to Section 1983 actions, however, the Supreme Court has held, in *Edwards v. Balisok*, 520 U.S. 641 (1997), "that § 1983 contains no judicially imposed exhaustion requirement... [A]bsent some other bar to the suit, a claim either is cognizable under § 1983 and should immediately go forward, or is not cognizable and should be dismissed." In the next section, we discuss provisions of the Prison Litigation Reform Act, which establish "some other bar," that is, some constraints on using Section 1983 for prisoner lawsuits.

▩ The Prison Litigation Reform Act

In 1996, the Prison Litigation Reform Act of 1995 (PLRA) was signed into law.[14] That federal statute (in Title 42, U.S. Code, Section 1997e) made several significant changes to prisoner litigation in federal courts. With regard to suits relating to prison conditions, the Act provided the following:

> No action shall be brought with respect to prison conditions under ... (42 U.S.C. § 1983), or any other Federal law, by a prisoner confined in any jail, prison, or other correctional facility until such administrative remedies as are available are exhausted.

The PLRA also placed other limitations on prisoner suits:

- frivolous, malicious, and ill-founded suits could be dismissed without requiring exhaustion of administrative remedies;

Box 5-2

United States Court of Appeals
FOR THE DISTRICT OF COLUMBIA CIRCUIT
PRISON LITIGATION REFORM ACT NOTICE

Pursuant to the Prison Litigation Reform Act, new requirements have been placed on prisoners proceeding pro se when filing appeals in Federal courts. The most significant restrictions relate to filing *in forma pauperis* and filing successive claims.

PROCEEDING *IN FORMA PAUPERIS*

28 U.S.C. § 1915 requires a prisoner to pay the appropriate filing fee ($450 for a petition for review from an agency decision or an original action or $455 for an appeal from the district court) when filing an appeal *in forma pauperis*. The court must assess and collect from your prison account a partial filing fee of 20% of the greater of:

(1) the average monthly deposits to your prison account; or

(2) the average monthly balance in your prison account for the six-month period preceding the filing of the notice of appeal.

Thereafter, you are required to make monthly payments of 20% of the preceding month's income. The agency having custody of your account is required to forward payments from your account to the Clerk of the court each time the amount in your account exceeds $10.00, until the filing fee is paid.

If you are attempting to proceed *in forma pauperis* on appeal from a district court order in a civil case, you must seek leave to do so from the district court in the first instance. (Note that the district court's authorization to proceed in that court *in forma pauperis* is effective only for proceedings in the district court and does not carry over to proceedings in this court.) If the district court denies leave to proceed *in forma pauperis* on appeal, you may seek leave to do so from this court. If the district court grants leave to proceed *in forma pauperis* on appeal, you must submit to this court a certified copy of the trust fund account statement for the six-month period preceding the filing of the notice of appeal and the consent to collection of fees form. In an original action or agency case, you must also submit a completed motion for leave to proceed on appeal *in forma pauperis* form.

Under 28 U.S.C. § 1915, you may be required to pay the appropriate filing fee in full, even if the complaint is dismissed prior to the collection of the entire filing fee.

SUCCESSIVE CLAIMS

Pursuant to the Prison Litigation Reform Act, unless a prisoner claims to be in "imminent-danger of serious physical injury," he or she may not file a civil action or pursue a civil appeal *in forma pauperis* if the prisoner has, on three or more occasions while incarcerated or detained in any facility, brought an action or appeal in a court of the United States that was dismissed on the grounds that it is frivolous, malicious, or failed to state a claim upon which relief may be granted." 28 U.S.C. § 1915(g).

- attorney fees were limited;
- no federal civil action could be filed by an inmate for mental or emotional injury while in custody without a prior showing of physical injury;
- an inmate seeking to proceed *in forma pauperis* (without funds, and therefore excused from paying filing fees or other court fees) would have to submit records showing the lack of funds in his prison account in order to avoid payment of fees (see **Box 5-2** for the information sheet on proceeding *in forma pauperis* provided by one appeals court);
- court orders for relief from prison conditions were strictly limited to correct only the violation of rights shown by the particular plaintiff–inmate;
- consent decrees were limited in the scope of relief that could be ordered; and
- the use and authority of special masters in prison cases were limited.

These amendments to federal statutes, and particularly to Section 1983 actions, are being tested in the courts. (See Appendix 5 for one district court's "Instructions for filing a Complaint by a Prisoner Under the Civil Rights Act, 42 U.S.C. § 1983.") Meanwhile, the PLRA has achieved the main intent of the act, which is reducing the volume of prisoner rights suits brought in federal courts.

Let's now look at the Court's handling of the PLRA's exhaustion requirement. Several Supreme Court decisions are relevant to this discussion. In *Booth v. Churner*, 532 U.S. 731 (2001), the Court said that an inmate must complete a prison administrative process capable of addressing the inmate's complaint and providing a form of relief, even if that process does not provide for requested monetary relief. The Court said that the congressional focus was on the exhaustion of "processes," not the forms of relief.[15] The next year, in *Porter v. Nussle*, 534 U.S. 516 (2002), the Court held that the PLRA's exhaustion requirement applies to *all* prisoner suits about prison life.

> **Beyond doubt, Congress enacted § 1997e(a) to reduce the quantity and improve the quality of prisoner suits; to this purpose, Congress afforded corrections officials time and opportunity to address complaints internally before allowing the initiation of a federal case. In some instances, corrective action taken in response to an inmate's grievance might improve prison administration and satisfy the inmate, thereby obviating the need for litigation…In other instances, the internal review might "filter out some frivolous claims."…And for cases ultimately brought to court, adjudication could be facilitated by an administrative record that clarifies the contours of the controversy.**

In *Woodford v. Ngo*, 548 U.S. 81 (2006), the Supreme Court examined whether the PLRA's exhaustion requirement requires *proper* exhaustion of administrative remedies. In *Woodford*, the inmate filed his grievance outside the prison policy's required time period, resulting in prison officials rejecting the inmate's grievance. The PLRA's statutory language provides that an inmate may not sue under 42 U.S.C. § 1983 "until such administrative remedies as are available are exhausted." The inmate, taking the statutory language as written, argued that it does not matter why administrative remedies are no longer available, only that they are no longer available. The issue before the

Court was whether an inmate satisfies the PLRA exhaustion requirement by filing an untimely or otherwise procedurally defective administrative grievance. The Court held it did not.

> **Proper exhaustion demands compliance with an agency's deadlines and other critical procedural rules because no adjudicative system can function effectively without imposing some orderly structure on the course of its proceedings … The benefits of exhaustion can be realized only if the prison grievance system is given a fair opportunity to consider the grievance … A prisoner who does not want to participate in the prison grievance system will have little incentive to comply with the system's procedural rules unless noncompliance carries a sanction … For example, a prisoner wishing to bypass available administrative remedies could simply file a late grievance without providing any reason for failing to file on time. If the prison then rejects the grievance as untimely, the prisoner could proceed directly to federal court … We are confident that the PLRA did not create such a toothless scheme.[16]**

In *Jones v. Bock*, 549 U.S. 199 (2007), the Court considered whether inmates were required to specially plead or show exhaustion in their complaints, or whether exhaustion was an affirmative defense that the defendant must plead and show. Prior to *Jones,* there was a split in the circuits on this issue. The Court noted that the PLRA, while dealing extensively with the issue of exhaustion, did not address the issue of whether exhaustion had to be pleaded by the inmate or claimed by the defendant as an affirmative defense. In the absence of the PLRA addressing this aspect, the Court held that the usual practice was to be followed and that this meant prison officials needed to raise the issue as an affirmative defense.

> **The PLRA dealt extensively with the subject of exhaustion … but is silent on the issue whether exhaustion must be pleaded by the plaintiff or is an affirmative defense. This is strong evidence that the usual practice should be followed, and the usual practice under the Federal Rules is to regard exhaustion as an affirmative defense.**

The Court held that since the PLRA does not require plaintiffs to plead exhaustion, such a result must be achieved by amendment to the Federal Rules (or by amendment of the act), and not by judicial interpretation.[17]

Jones also held that the Sixth Circuit erred in ruling that an inmate's exhaustion was inadequate under the PLRA when a person later sued by the inmate is not named in the first grievance step. The Supreme Court said the PLRA did not impose such a requirement; rather, the PLRA required the inmate to comply with the agency's prison grievance process. Since the prison procedures did not mention naming particular officials, the Sixth Circuit's rule requiring this as part of the exhaustion process was not warranted. Finally, the Court held that the Sixth Circuit erred in holding that an inmate's entire claim had to be dismissed if any one claim was not properly exhausted, again pointing out that this action was not required by the PLRA. The Court observed that the effect of a total exhaustion rule might be having inmates file various claims in separate lawsuits to avoid this potential problem. Such action was seen as contrary to a main purpose of the PLRA: reducing the number of inmate suits. If a complaint contains both good and bad claims, the court moves forward with the good and leaves the bad behind.

■ Prisoners' Rights

If, despite the efforts that have been described (which in many cases may be helpful in avoiding a lawsuit), the corrections worker finds herself involved in a court action, the steps outlined in a review of court appearances come into play. Again (it cannot be overemphasized), the first step and the most important way to defend a case is to obtain representation, establish good communication with counsel, and cooperate with counsel in all stages of the legal case until its conclusion.

In order to work effectively and legally, avoid lawsuits wherever possible, and have a good working relationship with counsel, the staff must be knowledgeable of the law. For torts, habeas corpus, and state or local relief, this requires knowledge of local laws and policies. For the most common legal action, as well as the most threatening (because of the risk of personal judgments and broad injunctive relief), corrections staff, in defense against Section 1983 actions in federal courts, must be aware of constitutional requirements. The balance of Part II of this book (Chapters 6 through 17) discusses the constitutional requirements that have been placed on corrections workers. On the other side of the coin, these are the prisoners' constitutional rights, as defined at this time.

This text focuses on the constitutional principles established by the Supreme Court, which are contained in a group of cases that, taken together, form the body of "corrections law," or prisoners' rights. There are many decisions—hundreds in the lower federal courts and hundreds more in state courts—that further define prisoners' rights. Because the Supreme Court, in interpreting the Constitution as it applies to different areas of inmate activities, is setting the standards that are applicable nationwide in every jurisdiction and that are the yardstick for measuring constitutional liability under 42 U.S.C. § 1983, we will usually present the Supreme Court decisions as "the law" in any subject area. Lower court decisions will be covered occasionally, because they take prisoners' rights questions into new or expanded areas not yet addressed by the Supreme Court. The reader, and especially any corrections worker, is warned (again) that, besides the Supreme Court decisions, the rulings in local jurisdictions, whether from state courts (for state agencies) or from federal appellate or district courts (for state or federal workers), are also binding as to legal requirements, in practice and in court litigation in that jurisdiction.

SUMMARY

- A prison is a special community with very specific outer boundaries. The interior components of a prison also resemble a community. To run effectively, prisons require a high degree of uniformity. The prison environment, by its very nature, may contribute to the filing of litigation.

- Prisoners' rights are principally those rights that are guaranteed under the U.S. Constitution and that apply to the situations in which inmates find themselves. Those rights are primarily pursued in the courts through a federal civil rights statute, 42 U.S.C. § 1983 (and the equivalent, Bivens suits, for federal inmates).

- In Section 1983 suits, inmates usually seek monetary damages. Courts may also give injunctive relief in such suits. Money damages are awarded against the individual officials who have been shown to be responsible for violating constitutional rights. Corrections staff, therefore, must be concerned, individually, about the impact of civil rights lawsuits that may be brought against them.

- The first, and leading, rule for corrections workers is to follow agency policy. Policy should always be written to include any current requirements guaranteed by the Constitution, as interpreted by the courts. It is the responsibility of agency administrators and lawyers to make sure that policy does reflect, at a minimum, those constitutional guarantees.

- Other rules for corrections workers are to get good training in all aspects of the job; to become familiar with the law (statutory and court rulings) that directly affects the job; to identify and follow a good mentor; and to keep good records of work performed and of any unusual incidents.

- Inmate grievance systems have been adopted by virtually all corrections agencies. These provide benefits to corrections staff and management and to inmates in many cases. Courts have encouraged the use of administrative grievance systems. As interpreted by the Supreme Court, the exhaustion requirement of the Prison Litigation Reform Act of 1995 applies to all prisoner suits about prison life (*Porter v. Nussle*). The Court also has held that the PLRA requires the proper exhaustion of administrative remedies for inmate grievances before inmates bring Section 1983 actions into federal courts (*Woodford v. Ngo*).

- When lawsuits are filed against corrections workers, they must work closely with counsel in defense of the lawsuits.

THINKING ABOUT IT

Inmate Lyon was denied permission by state prison officials to participate in Jewish services held at the prison. The prison chaplain told the inmate that the exclusion was based on the recommendation of a Jewish consultant (a rabbi). Lyon then wrote a memo, attempting to informally resolve the issue. The prison's deputy warden responded, stating that, while Lyon could attend Jewish services, he would not be allowed to participate. The deputy warden said that "Jewish experts" had suggested that prison inmates should not be converted to Judaism. In place of conversion, Lyon could engage in a course of Jewish study.

Lyon filed a Section 1983 suit against state prison officials, claiming the denial of participation in Jewish services and holidays violated his constitutional rights. Prison officials argued for dismissal, citing the inmate's failure to exhaust his administrative remedies as required by the PLRA. Lyon admitted he did not follow the prison grievance procedure, saying that this was because he had been told by the prison chaplain and the deputy warden that the exclusion decision rested in the hands of "Jewish experts," not with state prison officials. In effect, Lyon argued that administrative remedies were not available within the meaning of the relevant statutory language, because the prison chaplain and deputy warden prevented his exhaustion of those remedies. How do you think the appeals court ruled? This case was reported as *Lyon v. Vande Krol*, 305 F.3d 806 (8th Cir. 2002).

KEY TERMS

Bill of Rights: A common term for the first 10 amendments to the U.S. Constitution.

classification (corrections): The systematic arrangement, usually prescribed by written policy, of persons or things into similar groups, based on specified criteria. There are two principal subjects of classification in corrections: (1) correctional facilities, or portions of facilities, usually grouped by security level (such as minimum, medium, maximum, high, or low) or special purpose (such as pretrial status, protective custody, or medical or mental health facilities); (2) inmates, whereby offenders are grouped according to their backgrounds, special needs, legal status, and custody requirements (reflecting any requirements for special security precautions).

grievance (corrections): A complaint filed by an inmate in an informal procedure, which is reviewed in a mechanism established by a corrections agency. Relief may be given for conditions or actions that are found in the review process to have been wrongful.

in forma pauperis: Literally, in the nature of a pauper. Indigent; lacking funds to pay certain fees or costs in court.

ENDNOTES

1. Florida Department of Corrections Mission Statement. Accessed June 13, 2011, http://www.dc.state.fl.us/about.html. Also Virginia Department of Corrections Mission Statement. Accessed June 13, 2011, http://www.vadoc.state.va.us. Also North Dakota Department of Corrections Mission Statement for its State Penitentiary. Accessed June 13, 2011, http://www.nd.gov/docr/about/missions.html. The population numbers are from West, H., Sabol, W., and Greenman, S. *Prisoners in 2009* (Washington, DC: Bureau of Justice Statistics, U.S. Department of Justice, 2010), Appendix Table 4.

2. The prison population reported is the number of prisoners under the *jurisdiction* or legal authority of state and federal correctional officials. This number includes persons held in prison or jail facilities outside of the state or federal prison system (in local jails, or inmates in transit—for example, going to court). It is worth noting that there is also a prison population count of prisoners under the *custody* of state and federal correctional officials. In 2009, this number was 1,524,513. It represents the number of inmates physically housed in state and federal correctional facilities regardless of which entity has the legal authority, as well as state and federal inmates in privately operated facilities. The number also may include juveniles held in adult facilities in the six states that have combined jail–prison systems. See Glaze, L. *Correctional Populations in the United*

States, 2009 (Washington, DC: Bureau of Justice Statistics, U.S. Department of Justice, December 2010), 1.

3. See endnote 1 above, *Prisoners in 2009.* Appendix Table 1.

4. Harrison, P. and Beck, A. *Prisoners in 2002* (Washington, DC: Bureau of Justice Statistics, U.S. Department of Justice, 2003), 3.

5. See endnote 1 above, *Prisoners in 2009.* Table 7, and Appendix Tables 1 and 9.

6. Sykes, G. M. *The Society of Captives* (Princeton, NJ: Princeton University Press, 1974), 63–83.

7. To illustrate the deprivation of goods and services, one of your authors once served as chairman of an inmate classification committee. These meetings ran for several hours and members took turns bringing in doughnuts for the committee. On a day when your author was bringing doughnuts into the meeting, he was approached by an inmate who was serving a life sentence. The inmate asked for a doughnut and was advised they were for committee members. Your author must have given the inmate the erroneous impression he could have a doughnut if any were left when committee members took their lunch break. Several hours later, the committee did break, and there was the inmate, waiting. When told no doughnuts were left, the inmate's face "dropped," and he said words to the effect of, "Do you know how long it has been since I had a doughnut?"

8. Occasionally, there are inmates who are not opposed to being confined. The reasons vary: there may be a desire to complete a beneficial prison vocational training program; some inmates feel they are better cared for or have more secure living conditions within the prison than they do on the outside.

9. This is especially true when you are young and just beginning in the field. Depending on your particular job, you may be making an equivalent or even a higher salary than the "old hand." For long-term success and effective performance, it is critical to respect this person's experience and knowledge. You also will find that once you have attained this hands-on experience and training, the integration of book knowledge will occur more naturally.

10. Florida Department of Corrections. *Inmate Grievance Procedure.* Rule Chapter 33-103. Accessed January 6, 2011, http://www.dc.state.fl.us/secretary/legal/ch33/. Also the Idaho Department of Corrections. *Grievance and Informal Resolution Procedure for Offenders.* Accessed June 13, 2011, http://www.idoc.idaho.gov/sites/default/files/webfm/documents/about_us/policies_and_forms/policypublic/3160201001.pdf. Prison grievance policies offer a credible, timely, and effective means of staff–inmate communication with the intent of resolving issues at the lowest possible level.

11. In a survey of adult correctional agencies, 44 agencies reported activities in their grievance systems. Those 44 agencies reported, for the year 2000, a total of 826,533 grievances filed. Of these, 407,656 were formally resolved at the initial step in the grievance process, and 274,831 were appealed beyond the initial step. Camp, G. and Camp, C. *The 2001 Corrections Yearbook—Adult Corrections,* (Middletown, CT: Criminal Justice Institute, 2002), 40–41.

12. One agency (the Federal Bureau of Prisons) reported that 28,756 administrative remedy (grievance) requests were answered by its institutions in fiscal year 2009, with 6.2% of these granted. 17,175 of those were appealed to the next level (region) and answered, with 3.7% granted. 7,429 of those were appealed to the highest level (central office) and answered, with 1.3% granted. As shown, and as might be expected, there were fewer filings at each

level. This is indicative of an inmate being successful at a prior level(s) and also suggests that many inmates understood and accepted the response even when not favorable. The drop in the percentage of grants at each level is reflective of the prior reviews and the grants resulting from these. Federal Bureau of Prisons. *State Of The Bureau 2009 – The Bureau's Core Values* (Washington, DC: Federal Bureau of Prisons, U.S. Department of Justice, 2010), 12–13. As a general comment, many correctional agencies have informal resolution prior to their formal administrative remedy process. It is probable that many inmates receive a favorable resolution or a satisfactory explanation at this level and do not proceed further.

13. States use various means to maintain the effectiveness of their grievance system. Examples include the training of staff, limiting the number of filings an inmate may make over a given time period, and setting up procedures to address an inmate's abuse of the system. An inmate who abuses the grievance system (for example, an inmate who files emergency grievances that are not emergencies or who files a malicious grievance—intentionally falsifying information with the intent to do harm) may be subject to restrictions on filing grievances. Restrictions may include limiting the number of grievances that the inmate may file over a set period of time and taking disciplinary action against an inmate for a demonstrated pattern of abuse.

14. In 1980, prior to passage of the PLRA, Congress, in part to recognize the usefulness of prison grievance procedures, enacted amendments to the Civil Rights statute (Section 1983) in the Civil Rights of Institutionalized Persons Act (CRIPA). This statute (in § 1997e(a) and (b)) provided, in part, that a court could suspend a Section 1983 action if the inmate had not used an available grievance system. There were two strong limitations to the suspension of a case: the action was suspended for a maximum of 90 days, and the grievance system must have been certified by the U.S. Attorney General or by a federal district court. This certification was to be based on a determination that the system was in compliance with the minimum standards of the act. Essential standards were an advisory role for inmates and staff in formulating, implementing, and operating the system; time limits for staff replies; and safeguards against reprisals. The 1996 passage of the PLRA amended CRIPA. The previous limitation provisions, allowing for up to a 90-day suspension of a Section 1983 action to allow for grievance exhaustion, and requiring compliance with the minimum standards for certification, were removed. In the September 27, 1995 Congressional Record (S14413), Senator Dole, in introducing the legislation, said one purpose of the legislation is, "to address the alarming explosion in the number of frivolous lawsuits filed by State and Federal prisoners." Title 42, United States Code, Section 1997e reads, "[n]o action shall be brought with respect to prison conditions under section 1983...or any other Federal law... until such administrative remedies as are available are exhausted." The new language of the PLRA makes exhaustion mandatory, not discretionary as it was in CRIPA.

15. *Booth* provides a good example of the evolution of the law. In *McCarthy v. Madigan*, 503 U.S. 140 (1992), the Supreme Court held that exhaustion of the Bureau of Prisons inmate grievance procedure was not required, since the procedure did not give the requested monetary relief. The Court then said, "Congress, of course, is free to design or require an appropriate administrative procedure for a prisoner to exhaust his claim for money damages." The PLRA, in 42 U.S.C. § 1997e(a), does just that. In 2001, the Court in *Booth* said the PLRA's statutory history confirms Congress meant to require exhaustion of

administrative procedures regardless of the "fit" between a prisoner's requested relief and the administrative remedies possible.

16. A criticism of *Woodford* is that the ruling holds that the PLRA prevents the filing of even meritorious claims if an inmate fails to meet the prison's procedural requirements for filing a grievance. At the time of this book's preparation, efforts were being made to modify various PLRA provisions, including the exhaustion requirement. One example is the Prison Abuse Remedies Act of 2009. This bill was introduced in the House of Representatives on December 16, 2009. As to the exhaustion requirement, the proposed legislation provides for courts to allow up to a 90-day stay for nonfrivolous claims relating to prison conditions. This stay allows prison officials to consider such claims through the administrative process. In April 2010, the legislation was referred to the Subcommittee on Crime, Terrorism, and Homeland Security but did not go beyond that point and never became law during the 111th (2009–2010) Congress.

17. This could be another example of the evolution of the law (see endnote 15 above). In *Jones,* the Court is stating that requiring a plaintiff to plead exhaustion is a result to be obtained by an amendment of the Federal Rules, not by judicial action.

6 Access to Courts

It is fundamental that access of prisoners to the courts for the purpose of presenting their complaints may not be denied or obstructed.

U.S. Supreme Court, *Johnson v. Avery*

Chapter Outline

- Opening the Gates
- *Ex parte Hull*
- *Johnson v. Avery*
- *Shaw v. Murphy*
- *Bounds v. Smith*
- *Lewis v. Casey*
- *Murray v. Giarratano*
- *Wolff* and *Martinez*
- Frivolous Complaints and Frequent Filers

We will begin our look at the constitutional provisions that protect the rights of prisoners by discussing in this chapter how inmates get into court to get their complaints heard. Are there protections or guarantees that apply to the filing of prisoner complaints in the courts? If so, where are they found, and how far do they go? How much do prison authorities have to do, or what are they restrained from doing, according to the constitutional rights of prisoners to have access to the courts?

We ask you to look in that list of Amendments to the Constitution provided in Box 5-1 and look for the provision that you think gives to prisoners the right to get into court, even when they are confined in prison. (We ask you to do that, with the assurance that what we have given you there are the provisions in the Constitution that are used to ensure rights to prisoners and to measure the extent of those rights.)

There is nothing that addresses such a right, is there? Indeed, the courts (including the Supreme Court) have not always been careful to specify where such a right is found in the

Constitution. But, as we will see in this chapter, the courts—and most important, the Supreme Court—have found that prisoners do have a right of access to the courts.

There is a right in Article I, Section 9 of the Constitution to seek a writ of habeas corpus. This is a specific guarantee of constitutional protection. But what of other complaints and wrongs done to prisoners? Habeas corpus provides only special relief—release from illegal confinement. And prisoners have many complaints; indeed, the great majority of their complaints are not the basis for habeas corpus relief, that is, these complaints would not entitle them to be released from custody.

■ Opening the Gates

It is frequently said that, until the 1960s, the courts had a "hands-off" attitude toward prisons and prisoner complaints. By "hands-off" we mean that, except for a few cases of habeas corpus, courts did not look behind the walls of prisons to examine the way prisoners were treated. Running the prisons was considered to be the business of wardens and those charged with keeping control of those in custody and not the business of the judiciary.

Federal courts in the 1960s opened the gates to prisoners—they started taking their hands off and looking more closely at matters behind prison walls.

■ *Ex Parte Hull*

This is not to say that hands were kept completely off before 1960. In a landmark case that is still an important guide for corrections officials, the Supreme Court said the following in *Ex parte Hull*, 312 U.S. 546 (1941):

> **[T]he state and its officers may not abridge or impair petitioner's right to apply to a federal court for a writ of habeas corpus.**

Michigan had a regulation that required prisoners to submit all legal documents to an institution office for review before they could be mailed to court. If "properly drawn," the papers would be forwarded to court. If not, they would be returned to the inmate. Hull, a Michigan inmate, tried to send a petition for a writ of habeas corpus to the Supreme Court. It was refused for mailing, as was a later letter to the Court. (How, you may ask, did Hull get into court? He somehow managed to get another paper to his father, who filed it with the clerk of the Court.) The Supreme Court, while not giving Hull relief on his habeas corpus petition, struck down the Michigan regulation. This is a leading ruling for the principle that prison officials may not screen, censor, or interfere with an inmate's mailings and submissions to courts.[1]

The Supreme Court, however, while giving us a leading principle on prisoners' rights, did not identify where in the Constitution it found the protection for prisoners that it summarily (and unanimously) defined. One may surmise that the protection was inherent in the habeas corpus provision (Article I, Section 9), which we have already discussed. If that is the source of the protection, it leaves the question: Do the constitutional protections for accessing federal courts apply only to habeas corpus petitions and not to other types of actions, such as suits for constitutional violations under Section 1983? We will look at that question again, as later opinions are given by the Supreme Court on prisoner access to courts.

■ *Johnson v. Avery*

The leading case on prisoner access to the courts, and one that can be noted as a leading part of the abandonment of the "hands-off" doctrine in the 1960s, is *Johnson v. Avery*, 393 U.S. 483 (1969). Johnson, a Tennessee inmate, was disciplined for violating a prison regulation that stated, "No inmate will advise, assist or otherwise contract to aid another, whether with or without a fee, to prepare Writs or other legal matters."[2] The trial court (the U.S. District Court in Middle Tennessee) found that the regulation was invalid on the grounds that it was an interference with inmates' access to federal habeas corpus relief. On appeal, the Sixth Circuit Court of Appeals reversed, finding that the State of Tennessee was pursuing a legitimate purpose in preserving prison discipline and in limiting the practice of law to licensed attorneys. The Supreme Court accepted the appeal (the petition for writ of certiorari) to decide whether the state limitation on prisoner legal activities was valid. In the prison vernacular, the practice of one inmate helping another with legal work is called "jailhouse lawyering," so the Supreme Court had to decide whether it was legally permissible for Tennessee to prohibit "jailhouse lawyering."

At the outset, the Court identified its opinion as being based on concern for protecting the writ of habeas corpus. Thus, this case, like *Ex parte Hull*, is based constitutionally on the provision guaranteeing the writ of habeas corpus.

> **[I]t is fundamental that access of prisoners to the courts for the purpose of presenting their complaints may not be denied or obstructed.**

There were other earlier cases, the Court noted, that had relied on this principle. For example, according to *Smith v. Bennett*, 365 U.S. 708 (1961), a state may not make the writ available only to prisoners who can pay a filing fee. Also, a state must furnish a transcript of court proceedings to a prisoner who cannot afford to pay for that transcript when the prisoner says it is needed in order to pursue subsequent legal action. *Long v. District Court*, 385 U.S. 192 (1966).

In a statement of legal principle that was given as an aside (we call this a **dictum**), the Supreme Court said that Tennessee could not have a regulation that would forbid illiterate or poorly educated prisoners to file habeas corpus petitions. In this case, because Tennessee did not have any other source of assistance (other than the jailhouse lawyer) for such prisoners, in effect it was doing just that by prohibiting prisoners from assisting one another with legal filings. The Court noted (we would call this taking judicial notice of facts, which are not proved in the record) that prisons have "a high percentage of persons who are totally or functionally illiterate." A crucial fact seemed to be that Tennessee did not provide any alternative kind of legal assistance for such illiterate persons to file petitions for relief. (The Court noted that some states did provide assistance to prisoners to help in drafting habeas corpus petitions. In some states, the public defender system provided attorneys who would assist with preparing petitions. One state (several more now) used senior law students to assist prisoners. A few states have even paid attorneys to be of assistance to inmates at the prison.)

The Court further stated that there can be abuses when inmates provide legal assistance to other inmates. To help control this problem, the state could place restrictions and restraints on the "jailhouse lawyering" activities—for example, by having limitations on the time and place for such activities and prohibiting the giving of any consideration (money or other favors) for the assistance provided by another inmate. Nonetheless, the Court said:

> [U]nless and until the State provides some reasonable alternative to assist inmates in the pre-
> paration of petitions for post-conviction relief, it may not validly enforce a regulation such
> as that here in issue, barring inmates from furnishing such assistance to other prisoners.

■ Shaw v. Murphy

In *Shaw v. Murphy*, 532 U.S. 223 (2001), the Supreme Court looked further at the issue of "jailhouse lawyering" and reasonable alternatives. Murhpy, a Montana State Prison inmate working as an inmate law clerk, wanted to help a maximum security inmate who was charged with assaulting a correctional officer. Although prison rules did not allow this help (because of separate housing locations), the inmate law clerk wrote a letter to the charged inmate, saying, "I do want to help you with your case... Don't plead guilty because we can get at least 100 witnesses to testify that [the officer] is an over zealous guard who has a personal agenda to punish...inmates." Prison staff reviewed the correspondence and charged the inmate law clerk with violating prison rules, including interference with due process hearings. A hearing was held and Murphy was found to have committed the prohibited act. A sanction was imposed. (This was internal disciplinary punishment.) Murphy sued, seeking injunctive and declaratory relief under 42 U.S.C. § 1983. He claimed, in part, a violation of his First Amendment rights, including the right to provide legal assistance to other inmates.

The U.S. District Court in Montana dismissed the claim. The Ninth Circuit Court of Appeals reversed, saying there was a First Amendment right of association, because the law clerk was giving legal advice relevant to the second inmate's defense. The Supreme Court reversed, holding that inmates do not have a special First Amendment right to provide legal assistance to other inmates. Such contacts between inmates are subject to the standard stated in *Turner v. Safley*, 482 U.S. 78 (1987). *Turner*, discussed in some detail in a review of the First Amendment as it applies to inmate mail, allows restrictions on an inmate's constitutional rights if those restrictions are reasonably related to legitimate penological objectives. The inmate failed to show that the prison restrictions were not related to such objectives.[3]

■ Bounds v. Smith

Another leading case on prisoner access to courts is *Bounds v. Smith*, 430 U.S. 817 (1977). The Supreme Court in *Bounds* took the principles of *Johnson v. Avery* and expanded them into broader guarantees of constitutional protections.

At the outset, the *Bounds* Court stated the question it was addressing: "whether States must protect the right of prisoners to access to the courts by providing them with law libraries or alternative sources of legal knowledge." The Court, however, did not answer that question thoroughly, but it did give us more guidance about the right of accessing the courts.

In *Johnson v. Avery* and in *Ex parte Hull*, the Supreme Court had said that the state could not impede or restrict an inmate's right of access to courts. In *Bounds*, the Court held that the state must take some steps to assist inmates if they did not have alternative means of getting legal assistance.

This lawsuit came out of North Carolina, which had a large number of prison facilities spread over the state. (At the time of the suit, there were 13,000 inmates in 77 prison units; 65 of those units had fewer than 200 inmates each.) The district court had found that the state did not have any type of assistance to help inmates prepare their petitions to the courts. That court required the state to come up with a plan to fulfill its duty to ensure access to the courts. The district court noted that the state could choose to implement a program that provided lawyers, law students, or public defenders to provide assistance or provided law libraries for inmates to do the work themselves.

North Carolina responded with a plan to provide seven libraries in facilities around the state. Inmates who needed to work on their legal matters would be transported to one of these central libraries to work one full day (or longer, if necessary) on their legal research and writing. The state drew up a list of books that would be provided in each library, along with standard legal forms, writing paper, typewriters, and access to copying machines. Almost by default, that plan has become the constitutional standard for prison law libraries, because it was the one presented in the case considered by the Supreme Court.[4]

Inmates objected to this plan, saying it did not go far enough. They sought more books, a library at every institution, and legal counsel for assistance in addition to the libraries. The district court approved the state plan and held that the state did not have to provide legal assistance in addition to the libraries. On appeal, the Fourth Circuit Court of Appeals affirmed. The appeals court approved the ruling of the district court and the state's plan for law libraries, with one amendment: it required the state to ensure that female inmates would have access rights to library facilities similar to the men's.

The Supreme Court affirmed the lower court's ruling and, in effect, the constitutionality of the North Carolina law library plan. In its arguments before the Supreme Court, the state contended that its only obligation (under *Johnson v. Avery*) was not to interfere with inmate "writ writers" and not to restrict communications to the courts (under *Ex parte Hull*). The Court rejected those contentions and said more was required:

> **[O]ur decisions have consistently required States to shoulder affirmative obligations to assure all prisoners meaningful access to the courts ... We hold, therefore, that the fundamental constitutional right of access to the courts requires prison authorities to assist inmates in the preparation and filing of meaningful legal papers by providing prisoners with adequate law libraries or adequate assistance from persons trained in the law.**

You can see that law libraries are not constitutionally required—provided that the state has an alternative means of "adequate" legal assistance. What would such an alternative be? The Court noted that briefs in the case suggested these alternatives: training inmates as paralegal assistants to work under lawyers' supervision; using paralegals and law students; having a program of volunteer attorney assistance; hiring lawyers on a part-time or full-time staff basis; or using legal assistance organizations, public defenders, or legal service offices. As an aside, the Court observed that using attorneys or legal services programs would be preferable to having inmate writ writers, because the inmates who do legal work for other inmates could generate internal disciplinary problems. The Court said that it would not endorse any particular plan, however. In fact, it encouraged local experimentation, with the overriding requirement that any plan would have to provide adequate, meaningful assistance to meet constitutional standards.

Let us return to our question: Does the constitutional standard of court access apply only to habeas corpus actions (as would seem to be the limits of the holdings in *Hull* and *Johnson*)? The Court in *Bounds* expanded the principle of prisoner access to courts, but it fell short because it did not define exactly what kind of legal activities were covered. Some language in *Bounds* seems very broad indeed. The Court stated, for example, "[P]risoners have a constitutional right of access to the courts," and "States [have] obligations to assure all prisoners meaningful access to the courts." But the citations to earlier cases supporting those statements deal with habeas corpus petitions, or with attacks on convictions. Nor did this Court identify the constitutional provision that supports the principle on which it was insisting. The closest we get is this statement of the question to be decided: Do the state's programs give to inmates the opportunity "to present claimed violations of fundamental constitutional rights to the courts"? The Court's discussion seems to infer, if not conclude, that the legal assistance requirements apply to habeas corpus petitions and to civil rights (constitutional) complaints.

We have to conclude that *Bounds* held that access to the courts is guaranteed for habeas corpus and for Section 1983 actions. Whether it applies to "lesser" activities, such as common law torts and personal legal matters (such as researching domestic relations cases, for example) was not decided. Our conclusion is supported by this statement in the opinion: "[T]his Court has 'constantly emphasized' [that] habeas corpus and civil rights actions are of 'fundamental importance…in our constitutional scheme' because they directly protect our most valued rights."

While a close and careful reading of *Bounds* would seem to limit the Court's **holding** to habeas corpus and Section 1983 actions, in practice, there is no distinction made in most prisons about what kinds of legal matters the inmates are working on. Because it is improper for officials to scrutinize an inmate's legal work (other than perhaps to do the most cursory examination of legal papers to be sure that they are, in fact, of a legal nature) or to interfere in any way with legal papers being sent to courts, inmates are allowed to work on any kind of legal matter. Also, because only a very few jurisdictions have an alternative legal assistance program, such as the Supreme Court encouraged be explored in *Bounds*, almost every prison in the country has a law library (see **Figure 6-1**).

There may be a wide variety in the size (and thoroughness) of the lawbook collections in prison libraries. Small institutions (and most jails) usually have comparatively small collections—much smaller than the one specified in *Bounds*. But the average law library in prisons is probably pretty close to the one proposed by North Carolina in *Bounds*. (Some are much larger, and, in some states, there may even be several in a single institution.) What a bonanza for the lawbook publishers! Lawbooks are expensive; statute and case reporter collections contain many books, and those books must be constantly updated. (Another problem and expense is the mutilation or loss of books—in colleges, public libraries, and prisons, books are frequently damaged or stolen. A major difference is that those in prisons must be restored or a constitutional question is raised!) The Supreme Court recognized that there is a serious economic impact for the state in providing

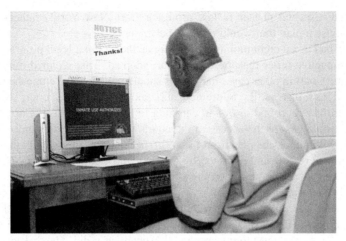

Figure 6-1 An inmate using a computer in the library at the maximum
security prison Tecumseh State Correctional Institution in Nebraska.
Source: © Mikael Karlsson/Alamy Image

a prison law library. Most states and localities, however, have chosen to install law libraries rather than pursue any of the alternative legal assistance programs suggested by the Court.

Recent technological changes have occurred which may alter the way prisoners access legal materials. In some prisons, paper book law libraries have been replaced with **electronic law libraries**. An electronic law library provides access to the same types of material as in a traditional paper library, with the difference being the format. Electronic law libraries may increase the availability of legal resources because of reduced cost and elimination or reduction in theft or destruction of resources. Electronic libraries take up less physical space, but they do involve inmate access to computer terminals and also instruction to inmates in the computer skills and research techniques needed to locate relevant material.

Lewis v. Casey

In 1996, the Supreme Court, in *Lewis v. Casey*, 518 U.S. 343 (1996), modified its holdings and decision in *Bounds*. A lower federal court had held that the Arizona Department of Corrections was not meeting *Bounds* standards and that its law libraries and other legal assistance provided to inmates were inadequate. That court ordered Arizona to provide more training to library staff, update its legal materials, provide better photocopying services, provide better library access for lockdown prisoners, keep its libraries open during expanded times specified by the court, and prepare a videotape on legal research for inmates. Also, bilingual inmates had to be located and trained as legal assistants to help non-English speaking inmates. The Ninth Circuit Court of Appeals affirmed that judgment.

The Supreme Court, in a part (Section III) of the opinion in *Lewis* in which eight of the nine justices joined, found that the district court order was far too broad and intrusive. The lower court had failed "to accord adequate deference to the judgment of the prison authorities," and had instead used a special master (a law professor from New York!) rather than the prison authorities to devise a plan that would provide better services.

The **master** had taken eight months to investigate the Arizona legal program and then drew up a 25-page injunctive order that the lower court adopted. This violated numerous warnings from the Supreme Court in other cases that courts should not become "enmeshed in the minutiae of prison operations." Instead, the Supreme Court said that the lower court should have acted as the North Carolina court had in *Bounds*, turning to the Department of Corrections to devise a program that would ensure the access to the courts that the court demanded. The plan from North Carolina, with minor changes from the court, became the approved plan for implementation and for ultimate review and approval by the Supreme Court in *Bounds*. Here, "[t]he State was entitled to far more than an opportunity for rebuttal, and on that ground alone this order would have to be set aside."

However, there was much more that the Supreme Court found objectionable in the lower court's actions. First, the Court said, there had not been a sufficient showing by inmates of actual injury to justify the district court to intervene as drastically as it did. The district court had found "a systemic *Bounds* violation," meaning that the whole Arizona prison system was failing to meet *Bounds* standards for legal assistance. Instead, the Supreme Court pointed out, there were only two inmates who, from the record, were shown to have been injured (by not getting their legal matters drafted or filed). The lower court was especially concerned with illiterate and non-English speaking inmates because of their inability to get into court with their complaints. The Supreme Court indicated that the remedy devised by the lower court should have been limited to the injuries that were shown to have been sustained by the two injured inmates. Those two instances "were a patently inadequate basis for a conclusion of systemwide violations and imposition of systemwide relief."

> *Bounds* **did not create an abstract, free-standing right to a law library or legal assistance ... [T]he inmate therefore must ... demonstrate that the alleged shortcomings in the library or legal assistance program hindered his efforts to pursue a legal claim.**

Yet another, and perhaps even more important, holding of *Lewis* was that the *Bounds* opinion had been taken too far:

> **[S]everal statements in** *Bounds* **went beyond the right of access recognized in the earlier cases on which it relied ... These statements appear to suggest that the State must enable the prisoner to discover grievances, and to litigate effectively once in court ... [W]e now disclaim [those suggestions]. To demand the conferral of such sophisticated legal capabilities upon a mostly uneducated and indeed largely illiterate prison population is effectively to demand permanent provision of counsel, which we do not believe the Constitution requires.**

The Court went on to specify what kinds of cases are covered by the prisoners' rights to have access to courts. Besides habeas corpus, earlier cases indicated that inmates could pursue direct appeals from their convictions. *Wolff* (discussed later in this chapter) extended prisoner access rights "only slightly" to vindicate "basic constitutional rights," namely, civil rights actions under 42 U.S.C. § 1983. That is as far as the Supreme Court would go; inmates do not have to be aided to bring, and to effectively pursue, all kinds of legal actions, the Court said in *Lewis*.

In other words, *Bounds* does not guarantee inmates the wherewithal to transform them-selves into litigating engines capable of filing everything from shareholder derivative actions to slip-and-fall claims. The tools it requires to be provided are those that the inmates need in order to attack their sentences, directly or collaterally, and in order to challenge the conditions of their confinement. Impairment of any other litigating capacity is simply one of the incidental (and perfectly constitutional) consequences of conviction and incar-ceration.

Thus, with *Lewis v. Casey*, the guidelines of *Bounds* are severely limited, although the Court in *Lewis* did not say that it was overruling *Bounds*. Also, with a hearty slap at the freewheeling actions of the district judge in this case, the Supreme Court once more emphasized the message of deference to prison authorities that the courts should be, but often are not, showing in their handling of prison matters.

Today, states use various approaches to provide inmates with legal assistance. For example, the Washington state department of corrections' policy says "[o]ffenders will have access to a Law Library and/or the resources of a Law Library, assistance from persons trained in the law, or access to legal services contractors." With respect to inmate assistance in legal matters, the policy, in part, provides:

One offender may confer with another offender in researching and preparing legal pleadings. No offender may represent, attend, hear, or participate in another offender's legal matter before a legal tribunal unless called upon as a witness...An offender cannot, under any circumstances, receive any form of favor or payment for the time, efforts, equipment, or materials used in assist-ing another offender...Offenders may assist each other in preparing legal documents in the Law Library...unless there is a legitimate penological interest precluding such contact.

This policy provides an example of accommodating an inmate's right to legal assistance, while also addressing the concerns prison officials have to protect security and good order in the institution.[5]

■ *Murray v. Giarratano*

In *Murray v. Giarratano*, 492 U.S. 1 (1989), inmates who were on death row in Virginia claimed that they had a constitutional right to counsel in order to pursue collateral attacks on their con-victions and sentences. The Supreme Court acknowledged that, in earlier cases, such as *Gideon v. Wainwright*, 372 U.S. 335 (1963), it had ruled that, under the Sixth and Fourteenth Amendments, defendants had the right to counsel at trials on criminal felony charges. This meant that the government would have to provide counsel for defendants who were indigent. The Court also had ruled, in *Douglas v. California*, 372 U.S. 353 (1963), that there was a similar right to counsel, whom the government would have to appoint for indigents, for an initial appeal from conviction and sentence. But, in *Pennsylvania v. Finley*, 481 U.S. 551 (1987), the Supreme Court had held that the state did not have to provide counsel for indigent prisoners who were seeking post-conviction relief (by collateral attacks on their convictions and sentences).

One question that remained—and the one that was considered in *Murray*—was whether inmates under death sentence were entitled to counsel in order to pursue collateral attacks after their initial appeals. Lower courts had ruled that they were constitutionally entitled to such legal assistance, and four justices in *Murray* agreed with that conclusion. This was primarily based on the decision of the Supreme Court in *Bounds,* which required assistance to be provided to inmates to give them meaningful access to the courts. But the majority of the Court in *Murray* held that their ruling in *Pennsylvania v. Finley* had been correct and that it also applied to persons on death row, as well as those serving ordinary sentences of imprisonment.

> **In *Finley* we ruled that neither the Due Process Clause of the Fourteenth Amendment nor the equal protection guarantee of "meaningful access" required the State to appoint counsel for indigent prisoners seeking state postconviction relief...[W]e now hold that *Finley* applies to those inmates under sentence of death as well as to other inmates, and that holding necessarily imposes limits on *Bounds*.**

■ *Wolff* and *Martinez*

The Supreme Court has dealt with inmates' legal activities in two other cases. By coincidence, these two cases are primarily known for their rulings in other areas of constitutional law. But the Court disposed of court-access issues in both of them, with clear holdings regarding prisoners' rights. Those two cases, *Wolff* and *Martinez,* are also similar in that they both deal with issues of attorney–client (when the client is an inmate) contacts. Attorney–client communication is another aspect of prisoners' access to the courts.

A fundamental principle of our legal system is the right of a person to have confidential communications with his attorney. This principle clearly does not end just because the client is in prison. Whether the attorney is representing the inmate on an appeal of the criminal conviction that placed his client into prison, on constitutional claims about the conditions of the inmate's confinement, or on any of the whole range of civil matters in which inmates may be involved, professional legal contacts—in person, by phone, or by mail—are necessary.

Attorneys are considered to be "officers of the court," bound by codes of ethics governing their work. As officers of the court, they are entitled to a degree of special deference to their status, and they, in turn, must take their professional responsibilities seriously. In some circumstances, attorneys have violated the trust that is given to them in their capacity as members of the bar. (For more detail, see the case of *U.S. v. Novak*, 531 F.3d 99 (1st Cir. 2008), which serves as an explicit example of the violation of trust by an attorney. The focus of *Novak*, however, is the Fourth Amendment search and seizure provision.)

Prisons and jails have administrative and security concerns, which lead to some restrictions on prisoners having contacts with their lawyers. The prisoners and the lawyers may not be very understanding about these restrictions and the reasons for having them. What has to be arrived at is a balance between the government's needs to ensure proper oversight of all inmate activities, including legal ones, for the security and orderly running of the institution and the needs of attorneys and inmates to have adequate and specially protected opportunities for communication, in visits, phone calls, and correspondence. *Wolff* and *Martinez* address some of the specific ways in which that balance is to be achieved in a corrections setting.

Wolff v. McDonnell, 418 U.S. 539 (1974), is known as the leading case on inmate discipline. The bulk of the opinion deals with prison disciplinary requirements. In a separate section (Section VII) of the decision, the Court addressed a Nebraska regulation that governed the inspection of attorney mail addressed to inmates. The state originally provided that all incoming mail would be opened and inspected. During the course of the litigation, Nebraska modified its position to say that mail from attorneys to inmates could be opened (but not read) to inspect for contraband, so long as it was done in the presence of the inmates. The Eighth Circuit Court of Appeals had ruled that attorney mail could only be inspected by feeling it or fluoroscoping it; it could be opened only in "appropriate circumstances," presumably when officials had good grounds to suspect, from other circumstances, that there was contraband enclosed. Also, there was a question in the case about how far the prison officials had to inquire to identify mail as coming from attorneys. The holding of the Court regarding such attorney mail follows:

> **We think it entirely appropriate that the State require any such communications to be specially marked as originating from an attorney, with his name and address being given, if they are to receive special treatment.**

With respect to the issue of the "special treatment" given to attorney mail—that is, opening the mail only in the presence of the inmate—as opposed to general correspondence, which can be opened (and read) by prison staff for inspection and security purposes, the Court said:

> **As to the ability to open the mail in the presence of inmates, this could in no way constitute censorship, since the mail would not be read ... The possibility that contraband will be enclosed in letters, even those from apparent attorneys, surely warrants prison officials' opening the letters ... [W]e think [state officials], by acceding to a rule whereby the inmate is present when mail from attorneys is inspected, have done all, and perhaps even more, than the Constitution requires.**

Oh my—what does the Court mean when it says that perhaps this is more than the Constitution requires? Why does the Court have to tempt us into such speculation about just what the Constitution does require? That phrase has never been fully explained by the Supreme Court or tested much in the lower courts. Today, most prison authorities take the *Wolff* decision holdings as their guidance. If anything, they may be more liberal in dealing with mail between attorneys and inmates. For example, they may not require the special attorney markings on the envelope that *Wolff* says can be required, and some may not even open mail marked as coming from an attorney (especially in lower security institutions).

Another legal issue raised by some prisoners is whether a prison policy of opening and inspecting legal mail out of the presence of the inmate violates the inmate's First Amendment free speech rights rather than access to the courts. One lower federal court has ruled that this practice and policy did violate the Constitution. In the wake of the 9-11 terrorist attacks, there were instances of public officials receiving letters contaminated with the anthrax virus. To prevent the introduction of biological toxins, prison officials determined that incoming special mail would be opened and inspected outside of the presence of the inmate, protecting the institution, staff, and inmates. The court of appeals in *Jones v. Brown*, 461 F.3d 353 (3rd Cir. 2006), held that opening and inspecting incoming legal mail out of the presence of the inmate stripped the communication of its confidentiality and burdened the prisoner's constitutional rights. The court supported its position with language in *Wolff v. McDonnell* that stated the only way to ensure a prisoner's legal mail is not read by correctional officials is to conduct the inspection in the presence of the inmate. The court of appeals then used the weighing factors identified in *Turner v. Safley* to conclude that prison officials had failed to demonstrate "a valid, rationale connection" between the new policy and a legitimate governmental interest. The court ruled that prison officials failed to demonstrate that the risks posed immediately after the 9-11 attacks still required this on-going abridgment of the prisoner's rights.

Can officials read the incoming mail from attorneys? Lower courts have split on this issue, but most cases (and most prisons) follow the Supreme Court guidance, saying that the opening of the mail is only for the purpose of ensuring that no contraband is enclosed and not for reading the content of any communications. If improper enclosures or content are discovered, the mail could be refused for delivery to the inmate. *Wright v. McMann*, 460 F.2d 126 (2nd Cir. 1972). The attorney mail, after all, is protected only for the conveyance of legal discussions. If it is used for other purposes, it has no more protection than ordinary mail. If it is used for improper purposes (enclosing any contraband, such as money or drugs, or for discussing criminal proposals, such as escape plans or future criminal activity), it should be forwarded to law enforcement officials for possible prosecution. Improper use of the mail by an attorney, or by anyone in his office, would be grounds for placing restrictions on the legal mail of that attorney and possibly of that inmate.

In Section VIII of *Wolff v. McDonnell*, the Court also addressed the issue of legal assistance provided to Nebraska inmates. To meet *Johnson v. Avery* requirements, the warden at the Nebraska Penal Complex appointed an inmate who had some knowledge of legal matters to assist inmates. The warden limited legal assistance to the work of this one advisor. The Court did not decide whether this one advisor was sufficient but agreed with the Eighth Circuit that the case should be remanded (sent back) to the district court to ascertain whether the help given was sufficient or whether other inmates also would have to be permitted to give legal help. The Court did address the question of whether legal assistance to inmates is limited to the preparation of habeas corpus petitions (as *Hull* and *Johnson* seemed to limit them). The Court noted that "the demarcation line between civil rights actions and habeas petitions is not always clear." The Court said:

> **The right of access to the courts, upon which *Avery* was premised, is founded in the Due Process Clause and assures that no person will be denied the opportunity to present to the judiciary allegations concerning violations of fundamental constitutional rights.**

Thus, we have a ruling that these access-to-courts opinions apply to the preparation and submission of habeas corpus and civil rights (Section 1983) actions, the standard that was picked up on by the Court again in *Bounds*.

In *Procunier v. Martinez*, 416 U.S. 396 (1974), the main part of the decision dealt with inmate mail restrictions. That case is known for being the lead, opening case in the Supreme Court on the issue of regulating prisoner correspondence. This case also contains a ruling on the issue of attorney visits. The question presented in the case was whether it was proper for the state (California) to restrict attorney visiting privileges to members of the bar and licensed private investigators. (California has a system of licensing legal investigators who provide investigative assistance to lawyers. Have you seen any of them in action in movies or TV shows? They were recognized as being of such help to attorneys that they were also granted the special visiting privileges given for legal visits.) The lower court had ruled that this state regulation was "an unjustifiable restriction on the right of access to the courts." It struck down the regulation, and the Supreme Court agreed:

> **The constitutional guarantee of due process of law has as a corollary the requirement that prisoners be afforded access to the courts in order to challenge unlawful convictions and to seek redress for violations of their constitutional rights.**

Inmates and lawyers wanted the regulation stricken, because they wanted to be able to use law students or paralegals to visit the prisons and to interview inmate clients. Although the Court conceded that the prisoner-access-to-courts doctrine did not require officials to adopt every proposal that prisoners might want to facilitate their legal activities, there was no showing, in this case, that a less restrictive regulation, allowing student and paralegal activities, would not be possible. The Court agreed that any such requested practices must be weighed against the legitimate interests of penal administration. Here, there was nothing to show that allowing the "attorney helpers" would unduly burden the prison task of screening and monitoring visitors.

As a result, prisons today must allow paralegals and law students, as well as any other professional assistants (such as the investigators in California), to have legal visits in the same manner as attorneys. As a practical matter, the attorney must identify the individual who is to have the visit, because that person is visiting in the place of the attorney, and the attorney is responsible for supervising the work (and the professional behavior) of the assistant.

There is one special caveat: prisoners who are charged with crime have additional protection under the Sixth Amendment. (Please look at the language of that amendment; you will see that it is prefaced by the phrase, "In all criminal prosecutions.") Assistance of counsel is mentioned specifically as a guarantee for pretrial criminal defendants. Courts are very protective of these pretrial rights of detainees. Reading the mail, or even opening the mail, of pretrial defendants is very risky. The best advice is to check with local authorities, because any pretrial defendant is held under the authority of the local criminal court. In most jurisdictions, the criminal court judges will be especially protective of attorney–client communications. Attorney visits to clients awaiting trial also receive a higher degree of protection (more frequent visiting times may be required, for example). Attorney contacts, by visits, mail, or phone calls, must be carefully protected, according to the expectations and rulings of the local courts, so as not to jeopardize the prosecution of criminal cases.

■ Frivolous Complaints and Frequent Filers

This chapter clearly shows that inmates have a right of access to the courts, but what about those inmates who abuse this process? Responding to inmate litigation can be very time-consuming and, where individual staff members are sued, can impact staff members professionally (disrupting the performance of their duties at work) and possibly even personally (such as complicating the approval of a loan). Prison litigation is also very burdensome to the courts. Although legal recourse is appropriate for substantive claims, what about those lawsuits where "no evidentiary hearing is required in a prisoner's case...when the factual allegations are incredible"?[6]

The Prison Litigation Reform Act (PLRA), in Title 28, U.S. Code, Section 1915A, requires a court to review, preferably before docketing or as soon as practicable thereafter, an inmate's complaint in a civil action in which the inmate is seeking redress from a government entity or officer or employee of a government entity. Section 1915A(b) *requires* the court to dismiss an inmate's complaint or any portion of it, if it is frivolous, malicious, fails to state a claim upon which relief can be provided, or seeks monetary relief from a defendant who has immunity.

Another provision of the PLRA (in Title 28, U.S. Code, Section 1915) requires an inmate who wishes to bring a civil action or file an appeal *in forma pauperis* (claiming lack of funds to pay certain costs) to pay the full amount of the filing fee. The PLRA allows for this to be paid on a time payment plan.[7] Although the statute allows for filing without payment if the inmate has no assets and no means by which to pay the initial partial filing fee in Section 1915(b)(4), payment is required when such funds exist. Institution staff are required to withdraw the funds and send them to the court to pay the inmate's filing fee obligation.

An additional modification is found in Section 1915(g). This section of the PLRA significantly limits an inmate who wants to proceed *in forma pauperis* from filing a new civil action or appealing a judgment in a civil action if on three or more prior occasions ("three strikes") while confined she had brought an action in a court of the United States that was dismissed on the grounds that it was frivolous, malicious, or failed to state a claim on which relief might be granted.[8] The only exception to the Section 1915(g) provision is where the inmate is under "imminent danger of serious physical injury." In *Malik v. McGinnis*, 293 F.3d 559 (2nd Cir. 2002), the Second Circuit held that the statutory intent was to make an exception for cases in which the danger existed at the time the complaint was filed; its focus was to prevent impending harm, not to revisit a harm that had already occurred and was past.

SUMMARY

- Inmates have a right of access to the courts, which prison officials may not obstruct. This was based, in the earlier Supreme Court decisions, on the constitutional guarantee of the writ of habeas corpus *(Ex parte Hull; Johnson v. Avery)*.

- Access to the courts is also guaranteed for suits claiming civil rights violations, under 42 U.S.C. § 1983 *(Bounds v. Smith; Wolff v. McDonnell)*. Prisoner access rights also have for a long time been guaranteed for direct appeals from convictions *(Lewis v. Casey)*.

- A state may not forbid inmates to assist other inmates in legal matters ("jailhouse lawyering"), unless there is an alternative method of assistance provided, particularly for illiterate inmates, who must also have a means to get their petitions to court *(Johnson v. Avery)*.

- Inmates do not have a special First Amendment right to provide legal assistance to other inmates. Such contacts between inmates are subject to the standard stated in *Turner v. Safley* and *Shaw v. Murphy*.

- Inmates must be provided a law library to assist them in preparing their legal papers, unless there is an alternative legal assistance program provided (*Bounds v. Smith*).

- The broad legal assistance holdings of *Bounds* were severely limited in the later decision of *Lewis v. Casey*. The Supreme Court criticized the federal trial court in *Lewis* for not deferring to the judgment of the prison authorities regarding what kind of law library and legal assistance program could be provided. Further, the relief provided (a sweeping, detailed legal assistance plan) was considered to be far too broad, based on the limited legal complaints that had been proved. It was held that the lower court should have provided limited relief to correct the violations shown, rather than mandate a system-wide plan of corrective action. Finally, constitutional requirements for legal assistance to inmates are limited to direct appeals from convictions, habeas corpus actions, and lawsuits under Section 1983, and, as to those, the government need only ensure that there is assistance for the initial preparation and filing of papers, not for later litigating steps.

- When *Bounds v. Smith* was decided, access to an adequate law library meant access to an area with many paper volumes of statutes and case decisions. Some states have moved to providing access to these materials in an electronic format, and a very modern prison law library may consist of few books but several computer terminals which provide access to the materials which were formerly available in paper books.

- Counsel need not be provided to inmates in collateral attacks on their sentences, even in death penalty cases (*Murray v. Giarratano*).

- Attorney mail requires more protection than ordinary mail, but (as long as it is identified as attorney mail on the envelope) it may be opened and inspected (not read) in the presence of the inmate. This serves the security concerns of the prison and protects the confidentiality of the contents of the mail (*Wolff v. McDonnell*).

- Legal visits also require special protections. Not only attorneys, but also paralegals, legal investigators, and law students who are under the attorneys' supervision are entitled to legal visits with the attorneys' inmate clients (*Procunier v. Martinez*).

- Recent legislative actions and court interpretations have resulted in procedures (requiring inmates to pay filing fees; mandating court dismissal of frivolous claims; and "three strikes" provisions) to curtail inmate abuses of court filings.

THINKING ABOUT IT

In April 1992, correctional officers found homemade weapons (including two toothbrushes with razor blades attached to them) in an inmate's cell. This was the third time the inmate had been found to possess such weapons. After a disciplinary hearing, the inmate was placed in disciplinary segregation. Upon release, he was moved to the prison's highest security level, an Intensive Management Unit (IMU). The inmate filed a Section 1983 action against 18 prison officials, complaining, in part, that he had no direct access to the prison law library (he did have use of a law library correspondence system that provided legal materials within 24 hours), that photocopy and notary services were too slow and expensive, and that he was denied contact visits with his attorney. Was the inmate successful in his suit? See *Keenan v. Hall*, 83 F.3d 1083 (9th Cir. 1996).

KEY TERMS

dictum (plural, dicta): A statement in a court opinion that is not essential to support the decision. A legal principle or conclusion (in an opinion) that is not necessary to the decision of the case.

electronic law library: A method of providing legal materials, such as statutes and court opinions, in an electronic format, rather than in paper volumes.

holding: The legal principle decided by a court's opinion or ruling.

master (court procedure): A person appointed by a court to assist in specified duties in a particular case. The duties to be performed are spelled out in an order and often include the gathering of facts and the taking of testimony. A master will then prepare a report of his actions for the court.

ENDNOTES

1. In *Houston v. Lack*, 487 U.S. 266 (1988), the Supreme Court held that an inmate's appeal was considered "filed" on the date it was dropped into the prison mailbox. The inmate is unable to travel to the courthouse to file the appeal; in fact, the inmate can do little else but hand her complaint to prison officials for mailing. The inmate does not have any discretion in this process.

2. Note that prison authorities, in writing this regulation, perpetuated the common mistake made in prison circles, among inmates and staff, of calling the papers prepared by inmates "writs." As discussed earlier, only courts write, or sign, writs. Inmates prepare petitions, asking the courts to issue writs. That is the proper nomenclature for habeas corpus proceedings.

3. The Court remanded (sent back) to the lower court the issue of whether the inmate had overcome the presumption that prison officials had acted reasonably. In its ruling, the Supreme Court pointed out that prison officials had offered the charged inmate the assistance of another law clerk.

4. Regarding law books, the North Carolina plan proposed that the library would contain North Carolina statutes and reporters (the books that contain state court rulings, particularly at the appellate levels); court rules; the federal code, in certain frequently used titles (*U.S. Code Annotated,* Titles 18, 28, and 42); the *Supreme Court Reporter* (from 1960 to present) and federal court reporters (for those same years); *Black's Law Dictionary;* and several legal reference books in the areas of habeas corpus, criminal law, and prisoners' rights. This pretty

closely conforms, the Court noted, to minimum collections for law libraries in prisons, as drawn up and recommended by the American Correctional Association, the American Bar Association, and the American Association of Law Libraries.

5. State of Washington Department of Corrections. *Legal Access for Offenders.* Accessed February 13, 2011, http://www.doc.wa.gov/policies/default.aspx?show=500>.

6. The Seventh Circuit noted that facts alleged by inmates may be unbelievable, because they are nutty or delusional! This is the language used in *Gladney, Jr. v. Pendleton Correctional Facility and Indiana Department of Corrections*, 302 F.3d 773 (7th Cir. 2002). The complaint alleges "that on numerous occasions over a span of three years unnamed guards at three different prisons unlocked the door to the plaintiff's [inmate] cell while he was asleep, allowing inmates to come in and drug and sexually assault him. He slept through all these outrages and only discovered what had happened when one day he noticed a needle mark under his lip. When he visited the prison infirmary to have the mark attended to, the medical personnel claimed not to see the mark because they were trying to make him think that he was delusional."

7. Please refer to Chapter 5, Box 5-2, for the information sheet provided by one appeals court on the PLRA's requirements for an inmate filing *in forma pauperis.*

8. This restriction does not apply to an inmate who can pay the filing fee. In that instance, the court will screen the civil complaint as provided in Section 1915A.

7 First Amendment: Inmate Mail

When a prison regulation or practice offends a fundamental constitutional guarantee, federal courts will discharge their duty to protect constitutional rights.

U.S. Supreme Court, *Procunier v. Martinez*

We have been sensitive to the delicate balance that prison administrators must strike between the order and security of the internal prison environment and the legitimate demands of those on the "outside" who seek to enter that environment, in person or through the written word.

U.S. Supreme Court, *Thornburgh v. Abbott*

Chapter Outline

- Prison Mail: The Background
- *Procunier v. Martinez*
- *Procunier v. Navarette*
- *Turner v. Safley*
- Correspondence in Foreign Languages
- *Thornburgh v. Abbott*
- *Beard v. Banks*
- *Bell v. Wolfish*
- National Security Issues
- Inmate Postage
- Nude Photos

The First Amendment to the U.S. Constitution contains this phrase:

Congress shall make no law ... abridging the freedom of speech.

Freedom of speech is one of the most cherished, and frequently discussed, freedoms set out in our Constitution. But, you will notice, the phrase only applies to "Congress." Is it therefore only applicable to the federal government? No, not really. The First Amendment does refer to the federal Congress, and, for many years, it was not clear whether there was any such protection in the states (apart from state constitutions, most of which have similar provisions to the U.S. Bill of Rights). But, in a series of opinions (e.g., *Rankin v. McPherson*, 483 U.S. 378 (1987)), the U.S. Supreme Court has held that this provision of the First Amendment applies to the states as well, through the operation of the due process clause of the Fourteenth Amendment. Therefore, decisions of the Supreme Court that interpret the First Amendment apply to the federal government and all state governments.

It is sometimes even said that freedom of speech is of the highest concern, and deserving of the highest degree of protection, in our country. It has been said that the First Amendment is a "preferred" amendment, containing the most important kinds of constitutionally protected liberties. There is no set of priorities stated in the Constitution, of course, and on the face of it, all provisions are of the same degree of importance. What is meant by these statements is that the protections of the First Amendment are fundamental to our most cherished freedoms and therefore deserve the highest degree of concern in the courts when those freedoms are threatened. Although the First Amendment freedoms are of extremely high importance, they are not absolute. All of them have restrictions and limitations. The Supreme Court and lower courts have addressed what, if any, First Amendment rights are retained by prisoners and the extent to which these rights may be restricted or limited by prison officials.

■ Prison Mail: The Background

In the 1960s, the federal courts started abandoning their long-standing, hands-off attitude toward prisons. By the end of that decade, there was a torrent of prisoner litigation, challenging all kinds of prison conditions and practices. It is not surprising that many of those challenges dealt with the First Amendment.

A prime subject of inmate litigation was correspondence. Many lawsuits focused on personal, social correspondence—that is, mail sent between inmates and persons such as family and friends outside the prisons. There was a flurry of court decisions dealing with such mail.

While inmates asserted their rights to the protections of the First Amendment, prison officials insisted that prison was a completely different world from that on the outside, requiring considerable restrictions on inmate mail. Some of the matters prison officials were particularly concerned about included letters that discussed direct affronts to security (such as plans for escape); enclosures (such as maps or money) that could be used in illegal ventures; contents of correspondence that discussed or planned other illegal activities (such as robberies to be committed on release, the retrieval of stolen money secreted somewhere before confinement, or threats against government officials); contents of letters that expressed viewpoints that, in the prison setting, could be inflammatory (such as an encouragement to riot, or racial or religious statements that would be likely to incite some readers to extreme actions); and pornographic content (whether in the letters themselves or, more likely, in enclosures of publications, photos, or drawings). Some authorities did not like, for obvious reasons, communications that were critical of staff (and particularly of the warden or other high officials), and they took steps to restrict them.

The practice of restricting the content of mail is sometimes called "censorship." Censorship has become an emotion-packed word, partly because of our strongly held feelings about the importance of freedom of speech, so it is commonly used by those who are opposed to any restraints on speech. (Speech, you will notice, is not limited to its usual meaning of verbal, spoken communication; it also covers any kind of communication of thoughts and ideas, such as publications, written words, and even artistic representations and physical actions that communicate ideas.) In careful usage, the word *censorship* refers to the act of officials who have the authority to remove objectionable content from printed or artistic content. It has also been used to refer to the act of military authorities who review and "censor" mail, removing those portions that are thought to be threatening or damaging in any way. The Supreme Court, and other courts, are usually (but not always) careful to avoid using the word *censorship*, because it carries within it the negative connotation of interfering with a basic freedom.

What does "censorship" mean in a prison setting? Some people picture prison officials opening mail and poring over every word to make sure there is nothing objectionable. In practice, this is pretty far from the truth. So much mail is received and sent by inmates of the typical prison or jail that the thorough review of all mail is impractical.[1] What is practical? What is done most often is to (1) search the contents of incoming mail for contraband and (2) identify those inmates (or groups of inmates) who are of most concern as security threats and look closely at their mail. Examples of such inmates of high concern are gang members, inmates who have escape histories, and inmates involved in large-scale drug or other criminal activities.

Incoming mail presents the greatest concern, because prison officials must carefully control what is introduced into the facility. What is sent out of the prison is of less concern, because once it leaves the premises it no longer poses a direct threat to internal security. It is true that in some institutions, particularly smaller ones, and especially ones of higher security, the contents of mail—both incoming and outgoing—are scanned closely. But if there is not enough staff time to inspect every piece of mail carefully, authorities can save staff time by concentrating on those inmates who must be watched most closely and hope to intercept those things that pose the greatest risks. In the final analysis, the main purpose of monitoring inmate mail is deterrence—knowing that their mail will be opened and that it may be read (assuming that it *will* be read), inmates and their outside correspondents will be deterred from sending improper content in their mail (or so it is hoped by prison officials).[2]

This is not to say that officials have no interest in what is sent out of the prison or in the mail of the run-of-the-mill prisoner. If only communications to and from selected, high-risk inmates are subjected to close review, those inmates can ask (or coerce) other inmates to send out or receive information that they do not want intercepted. In addition, in the interest of running an orderly prison, it is good for staff to know if inmates are having particularly upsetting problems. In many places, officers on the night shifts, when sitting at their desks, are given mail to review to gain more knowledge about inmates under their supervision, as well as to look for more serious things such as security breaches or plans for criminal activity.

In the past few years, some correctional agencies have made electronic mail services available to inmates, without the inmate having internet access. Using e-mail eliminates the risk of contraband items being smuggled into the facility within mail sent to inmates. As with other inmate correspondence, the e-mail's contents are reviewed pursuant to agency policy. The use of e-mail provides inmates with another means of communicating, along with regular mail, telephone, and visiting.[3]

■ *Procunier v. Martinez*

In California, state prison officials adopted regulations that instructed inmates not to write letters that unduly complained or magnified their grievances. The regulations declared as contraband any writings "expressing inflammatory political, racial, religious or other views or beliefs." They said inmates "may not send or receive letters that pertain to criminal activity; are lewd, obscene, or defamatory; contain foreign matter, or are otherwise inappropriate."

Procunier v. Martinez, 416 U.S. 396 (1974), was a **class action**—meaning that it was a combined lawsuit brought on behalf of all persons who were in a similar situation: in this case, all of the inmates in prisons of the California Department of Corrections. A class action is designed to save court time and to keep costs down by having a single presentation of the issues and a consolidated review of the legal status of the plaintiffs and their common complaints.

This case was unusual in that it was first considered by a three-judge federal court in the Northern District of California. You will recall that there is a nearly universal principle in our judicial system that the first, or trial, level of cases is presided over by a single judge. Congress has enacted an exception, providing for three judges to sit in review of a case in federal court when the lawsuit challenges the constitutionality of a statewide law (or a regulation that has the effect of a statewide law). There is another unusual provision for such cases: if the state law is held unconstitutional (as it was in *Martinez* by the three-judge panel), the state may take a direct appeal to the Supreme Court, avoiding the ordinary route of taking an appeal to a circuit court of appeals and then petitioning the Supreme Court for a writ of certiorari.

In *Procunier v. Martinez*, the Supreme Court, for the first time, addressed the issue of the rights of inmates to be free of restrictions on their mail under the First Amendment. The Court noted that, historically, there was a hands-off attitude in federal courts toward prison matters. The Court here put that concept officially to rest, saying that federal courts must "take cognizance of valid constitutional claims whether arising in a federal or state institution."

> **When a prison regulation or practice offends a fundamental constitutional guarantee, federal courts will discharge their duty to protect constitutional rights.**

The Court then noted that many lower courts had been addressing freedom of speech restrictions in prison regulations. A wide range of standards had been adopted in various courts to deal with these complaints. Some courts took a hands-off posture, deferring to prison needs for censorship of mail. Another standard was that the restrictions on correspondence would have to be supported by a "rational and constitutionally acceptable concept of a prison system." (That standard certainly did not give much guidance to either side about what kind of restrictions would be allowed or tossed out.) In another court, a similar position was adopted, in which a restriction would be upheld if it was "reasonably and necessarily [related] to the advancement of some justifiable purpose." Stricter courts required that, to support a restriction of correspondence, there must be a "compelling state interest" or, at the strictest extreme, a "clear and present danger" to support First Amendment regulation by the government, even in a prison setting.

It was exactly because of these kinds of wide disagreements and varying standards in the lower courts that Supreme Court review was established in the first place. But here, as in many other areas of constitutional standards, the Supreme Court did not necessarily adopt one lower court's analysis and run with it. First, the Court in *Procunier v. Martinez* noted that prisoner mail had been identified as an aspect of "prisoners' rights." However, in the case of prison mail, the Court noted that restrictions on the mail were of concern to other people besides the prisoners. So it refrained from going so far as to decide whether a person's right to free speech survives imprisonment. Both parties to correspondence have an interest in having their mail delivered and read, the Court said. The person outside the prison has an interest in receiving or sending mail, and "it is plain that [the outside person's] interest is grounded in the First Amendment's guarantee of freedom of speech." As to restrictions on First Amendment liberties, there may be some restrictions if they are imposed "in furtherance of legitimate governmental activities."

The Court then issued its guidelines for such prison cases:

> **One of the primary functions of government is the preservation of societal order through enforcement of the criminal law, and the maintenance of penal institutions is an essential part of that task. The identifiable governmental interests at stake in this task are the preservation of internal order and discipline, the maintenance of institutional security against escape or unauthorized entry, and the rehabilitation of the prisoners.... [T]he legitimate governmental interest in the order and security of penal institutions justifies the imposition of certain restraints on inmate correspondence.**

The Court gave some examples of "order and security" concerns that would justify censorship, including letters concerning escape plans or other proposed criminal activity, and letters in code. The guidance of the Court was given in this language:

> **[C]ensorship of prisoner mail is justified if the following criteria are met. First, the regulation or practice in question must further an important or substantial governmental interest unrelated to the suppression of expression... [Prison officials] must show that a regulation authorizing mail censorship furthers one or more of the substantial governmental interests of security, order, and rehabilitation. Second, the limitation of First Amendment freedoms must be no greater than is necessary or essential to the protection of the particular governmental interest involved.**

Applying these standards, the Court affirmed the action of the district court, rejecting the California regulations. Those prison rules were found to be too broad and too vague. They had been used to suppress unwanted criticism and did not establish clear restrictions based on prison concerns about security and order.

The Supreme Court also agreed with the district court in requiring state officials to take procedural safeguards when mail was rejected. This procedure requires that an inmate be notified when a letter is rejected, the author of any letter is given some opportunity to protest the rejection, and such protests are reviewed by someone other than the person who originally disapproved the correspondence. As a result, such procedures for protest and review must be built into any prison's correspondence policies and practices.

■ *Procunier v. Navarette*

In a case decided just a few years later, the Supreme Court, in *Procunier v. Navarette*, 434 U.S. 555 (1978), showed the importance of following court rulings. Mr. Procunier (the Director of the California Department of Corrections) and other state officials were sued under 42 U.S.C. Section 1983. The inmate, Navarette, sued them, claiming interference with his outgoing mail. He claimed that the officials failed to mail several correspondence items he had written in 1971 and 1972.

The officials claimed **immunity** from this lawsuit. This is what we call qualified immunity. (It is in contrast to absolute immunity, which protects legislators, judges, prosecutors, and jury members from being sued at all for actions taken in connection with their official duties.) It is the leading defense available to officials in the executive branch, such as prison officials, in Section 1983 actions. By the time of this case, the qualified immunity doctrine had been settled in several cases. For example, in the case of *Scheuer v. Rhodes*, 416 U.S. 232 (1974), the Court ruled as follows:

> **[A] qualified immunity is available to officers of the executive branch [if their action is based on] the existence of reasonable grounds for the belief formed at the time and in light of all the circumstances, coupled with good-faith belief.**

This principle was explained further in *Wood v. Strickland*, 420 U.S. 308 (1975).
However, in *Navarette,* the Court summarized:

> **[T]he immunity defense would be unavailing to petitioners [prison officials] if the constitutional right allegedly infringed by them was clearly established at the time of their challenged conduct, if they knew or should have known of that right and if they knew or should have known that their conduct violated the constitutional norm.**

Applying this standard, the Supreme Court agreed with the prison officers that in 1971 and 1972, when the conduct complained of in this lawsuit took place, there was no established First Amendment right of prisoners, and thus there was no basis for rejecting the qualified immunity defense. Reviewing the cases of the Supreme Court and of federal courts in California, there was no judicial ruling that gave a clearly established constitutional right protecting Navarette's correspondence. Therefore, the petitioners were entitled to the immunity defense as a matter of law, because they had no obligation to know at the time that their conduct was in violation of a constitutional right.

Another ground that the courts could have used to reject the qualified immunity defense would have been that the officials acted with "malicious intention," intending to deprive the prisoner of a constitutional right or intending to cause him injury. The Court concluded that there was no issue of malicious intent, because even the prisoner's claims alleged only negligent and inadvertent interference with his mail.

It should be noted that if the actions complained of had occurred in 1977 or 1978 (or today), there would be a very different outcome. Qualified immunity would not be immediately available. Courts would have to look at the officials' conduct and hold it up against established constitutional standards on correspondence, which by then had been set in *Procunier v. Martinez* (in 1974) and in succeeding cases.

▓ *Turner v. Safley*

Another major Supreme Court decision on inmate mail is *Turner v. Safley*, 482 U.S. 78 (1987). There were two Missouri regulations under review in *Turner.* The first regulation governed correspondence between inmates. The authorities allowed correspondence with immediate family members in other institutions and correspondence between inmates (in different institutions) about legal matters. Other correspondence between inmates was generally disapproved.

The Court applied the principles of *Procunier v. Martinez,* observing that courts must take cognizance of the valid constitutional claims of inmates. Noting that prisoners have the right to petition for redress of their grievances and to have access to the courts (another type of correspondence that is specially protected) under *Johnson v. Avery*, 393 U.S. 483 (1969), the Court emphasized that prisoners are not barred by their prison walls from seeking the protections of the Constitution. On the other side, however, the Court acknowledged (as it did in *Martinez*) that courts are not good places to deal with problems of prison administration.

> **[T]he problems of prisons in America are complex and intractable, and, more to the point, they are not readily susceptible of resolution by decree.**

> **Running a prison is an inordinately difficult undertaking that requires expertise, planning, and the commitment of resources, all of which are peculiarly within the province of the legislative and executive branches of government. Prison administration is, moreover, a task that has been committed to the responsibility of those branches, and separation of powers concerns counsel a policy of judicial restraint.**

> **[W]hen a prison regulation impinges on inmates' constitutional rights, the regulation is valid if it is reasonably related to legitimate penological interests. In our view, such a standard is necessary if "prison administrators ... and not the courts, [are] to make the difficult judgments concerning institutional operations."**

[The Court in *Turner* quoting *Jones v. North Carolina Prisoners' Union*, 433 U.S. at 128.]

In *Turner*, the Court identified the following factors as important in determining the reasonableness of the prison regulation, which impacts constitutional rights:

[T]here must be a "valid, rational connection" between the prison regulation and the legitimate governmental interest put forth to justify it.

[A court must examine] whether there are alternative means of exercising the right that remain open to prison inmates.

[Courts must also look at] the impact accommodation of the asserted constitutional right will have on guards and other inmates, and on the allocation of prison resources generally.

[T]he absence of ready alternatives is evidence of the reasonableness of a prison regulation.

Applying these concepts to the Missouri regulation barring inmate-to-inmate correspondence, the Court said the justification for the regulation by prison officials was based on concern that mail between prisons could be used to communicate escape plans and to arrange assaults, retribution, and other violence. There was also a growing concern in Missouri (and in many prison departments) about prison gangs. One way to help control this problem, according to the state, was to transfer gang members into different prisons and then to restrict their correspondence. Other inmates were in protective custody, under threat of violence from some inmates; allowing free communication between inmates in different facilities could place additional risk on the safety of these protected inmates. After applying the four determining factors noted above, the Court concluded that the Missouri regulation did not deprive inmates of all means of expression; rather, it stopped communications only with a limited group of persons—those of particular concern to prison officials. To allow the requested correspondence could result in less liberty and safety to others, both inmates and staff. Lastly, the Court noted there was no obvious, easy alternative to the adopted policy. Therefore, the Court held that "the prohibition on correspondence is reasonably related to valid corrections goals." The Missouri regulation was declared to be constitutionally valid.

The second part of the *Turner* opinion deals with another Missouri regulation, which banned inmate marriages. Prison officials claimed that marriages could lead to "love triangles" and did not carry any constitutional protection in the first place. The Supreme Court disagreed. The right to marry had been recognized as a fundamental right, under *Zablocki v. Redhail*, 434 U.S. 374 (1976). This right carries over into a prison setting, the Supreme Court said.

Authorities argued that restrictions on marrying in prison were necessary because of legitimate security and rehabilitation concerns. Although the right to marry could be subject to necessary restrictions inherent in incarceration, the Supreme Court ruled that there are still benefits that could accrue as the result of inmate marriages.

[W]e conclude that these [several beneficial elements of marriage] are sufficient to form a constitutionally protected marital relationship in the prison context.

The Court held that the Missouri regulation, presenting almost a complete ban on inmate marriages, was an exaggerated response to the security concerns of officials. The prison regulations were found to be not reasonably related to legitimate prison interests. Missouri could regulate the time and place and other incidents of the marriage relationship. (The Court suggested that it approved of the Federal Bureau of Prisons rule, which generally permitted marriages but allowed a warden to deny marriage if it was found to constitute a threat to security or order of the prison or to public safety. What are the differences between these two approaches? Can you think of examples when the federal restriction would be properly applied?) The Missouri ban on prison marriages was found to be invalid.

The Sixth Circuit Court of Appeals, in *Toms v. Taft*, 338 F.3d 519 (6th Cir. 2003), extended the *Turner* holding on inmate marriages by requiring Ohio state authorities to assist an inmate who wanted to marry someone outside the prison. Ohio law required both parties seeking a marriage license to personally appear in the probate court to make an application. The local judge had indicated that he would be willing to appoint either an employee of the institution or an employee of the probate court to serve as a deputy clerk for the purpose of issuing the marriage license. The prison warden, however, declined the inmate's request to allow someone at the prison to act as a deputy clerk, stating, "I do not see myself or the institution being involved in this process," other than allowing for a brief marriage ceremony if a marriage license was obtained. The federal court disagreed with Ohio officials, stating the following:

> **[A] refusal to aid a prisoner in exercising his right to marry, where such refusal completely frustrates the right, can amount to a "prison regulation" under *Turner*. Therefore, such refusals must be reasonably related to legitimate penological interests ... [T]he distinction between actively prohibiting an inmate's exercise of his right to marry and failing to assist is untenable in a case in which the inmate's right will be completely frustrated without officials' involvement ... The inmate's right to marry may be curtailed only where the officials' refusal to assist the inmate is reasonably related to legitimate penological interests.**

■ Correspondence in Foreign Languages

Another special concern of prison administrators is the use of a language other than English in inmate correspondence. This issue (which has not been decided in the Supreme Court) was addressed in the case of *Thongvanh v. Thalacker*, 17 F.3d 256 (8th Cir. 1994). Thongvanh, a native of Laos, was an inmate at the Iowa Men's Reformatory. He was able to speak some English, but some family members (particularly his parents and grandparents) could not. Iowa officials had a rule that all correspondence, incoming and outgoing, had to be written in English. This, of course, was so that it could be monitored.

Thongvanh brought a Section 1983 action, alleging violation of his First Amendment (free speech) rights, due process, and equal protection. At trial, a jury found that there were violations of his rights and awarded him $4,000. The court of appeals affirmed that judgment.

Although the court of appeals conceded that Iowa officials had legitimate security concerns regarding the inspection of mail, that court found that officials had not shown why correspondence in Lao could not be translated and then checked. Thongvanh had been allowed to correspond with his parents and grandparents in Lao but only with them. There was a refugee service center that provided translations to the Iowa Reformatory for those letters. It was also noteworthy that Spanish speaking inmates were excepted from the English-only mail policy. As in many prisons, there was a staff member who was able to translate Spanish correspondence. Also, the evidence showed that there was an exception made for a German speaking inmate who was allowed to correspond in German.

After considering this evidence and applying the standards of *Turner v. Safley*, the appeals court found (1) the inmate's right under the First Amendment to free expression was clearly abridged, (2) limiting correspondence in Lao to Thongvanh's parents and grandparents was arbitrary and not reasonably related to a legitimate government interest, and (3) this inmate was not treated the same as other inmates similarly situated (those who spoke Spanish and German).

The court's opinion in this case did not clearly specify what constitutional standards were applied to arrive at this verdict against Iowa prison officials. From what was stated, it is fair to assume that there were two constitutional standards violated: First Amendment freedom of speech (under *Turner* standards because there was an alternative available in Iowa to allow the speech to occur) and equal protection under the Fourteenth Amendment (because Thongvanh was, without good justification, treated so differently from other inmates who were allowed to correspond in languages other than English).

With respect to both of those conclusions, a key factor, no doubt, was that Iowa officials could obtain translations of the inmate's correspondence into and out of Lao. What this opinion did not address was what obligation, if any, the prison officials had to locate a translation service for mail written in Lao. What if the refugee service translators had not been available? How far would officials have to go to find translators for Lao or any other language? And if the service was not free (as the refugee service was), how much would the government be obligated to pay to achieve foreign-language translation for this or any other inmate?

Ortiz v. Fort Dodge Correctional Facility, 368 F.3d 1024 (8th Cir. 2004), concerned an inmate who was allowed to correspond in Spanish with a sister in Mexico City, as this was the only way they could communicate. He was not allowed to correspond in Spanish with other family members who lived in the United States, nor could he receive letters written in Spanish from these persons. This ban lasted three months, at which time the prison changed its policy to allow inmates to correspond in their preferred language. Ortiz filed suit asking for compensatory and punitive damages for the three months during which he could not write or receive letters in Spanish. The district court, applying the *Turner* factors, found in favor of the prison and Ortiz's unit manager, holding that the former policy was reasonably related to a penological interest. The appeals court affirmed. The *Ortiz* courts distinguished *Thongvanh,* saying that Ortiz did not identify a cost-free way for the prison to accommodate him. Ortiz did not present at trial what it would cost to hire an interpreter, whether the prison had Spanish speaking employees, whether other prisons could have provided interpretation services, or whether a social service agency was willing to translate the letters on the inmate's behalf. The lack of such information failed to meet *Turner's* third and fourth factors, which require an evaluation of the alternatives to the existing regulation and their impact on the prison, inmates, and non-inmates. No ready alternative at a minimal cost was presented. The distinction between the cases? In *Thongvanh*, information was presented to show that a translation service had offered, at no cost, to translate the letters into English.

In another appellate-level case, *Kikumura v. Turner*, 28 F.3d 592 (7th Cir. 1994), the court reviewed a Federal Bureau of Prisons policy at the U.S. Penitentiary in Marion, Illinois, which acted to exclude publications in Japanese. (During the course of the litigation, the policy shifted somewhat, and officials at the penitentiary were able to find an employee in another prison who could screen the materials published in Japanese and return them.) The trial court had found that there was no clearly established constitutional right for an inmate to receive a publication in a foreign language and granted qualified immunity to Warden Turner. The appeals court upheld that ruling. (Whether Iowa officials would have been protected by qualified immunity in the *Thongvanh* case—because there was no clearly established right to receive foreign-language mail when their action was taken—was not addressed in that court opinion.) Because of procedural complexities and errors, the appeals court sent the case back for further consideration on the issue as to whether the original, total ban on the receipt of Japanese materials violated Kikumura's constitutional rights, which would have entitled him to injunctive or declaratory relief.

▪ *Thornburgh v. Abbott*

Another type of inmate mail is the receipt of publications—magazines, newspapers, books, and clippings from those materials. In general, a prisoner may receive such publications in two ways: (1) by subscription or (2) as separate mailings from family or friends.

The Federal Bureau of Prisons had regulations that allowed inmates to receive publications from outside the prison but authorized local prison authorities to reject incoming publications that were found to be "detrimental to the security, good order, or discipline of the institution or if [they] might facilitate criminal activity." Wardens were cautioned not to reject publications solely on the grounds of religious, philosophical, political, social, or sexual content, or if the content was unpopular or repugnant.

The term *publication* was defined as including books, magazines, newspapers, and other materials such as brochures, flyers, and catalogs. The regulation gave some examples of publications that could be found to pose a threat to security—for example, those depicting how to make or use weapons, ammunition, or bombs; those depicting how to make alcoholic beverages or how to manufacture drugs; those encouraging activities that could lead to group violence or disruption; those providing instruction in the commission of criminal activity; and (the most controversial example and the one most contested in the case) those containing sexually explicit material that posed a threat to the security, good order, or discipline of the institution or facilitated criminal activity. (Under the last standard, if you were a warden, what material would you exclude?) An instruction of the Bureau of Prisons gave additional guidance for this pornography standard: wardens could reject material that depicted homosexuality, sado-masochism, or bestiality but only if it was found to pose a threat to the security of the local institution (the overriding standard for any material). Sexually explicit material involving children could always be excluded, because the mailing of it is per se (in and of itself) a violation of federal laws.

In a class action, *Thornburgh v. Abbott*, 490 U.S. 401 (1989), addressed challenges to these regulations by inmates and by some publishers. The Supreme Court quickly identified that the inmates (and the publishers) had First Amendment interests in receiving (and sending) the contested publications. First, the Court addressed the question of what standard of review should be applied to these kinds of First Amendment rights. The Court said the standard to be applied was the one in *Turner v. Safley*, not the one in *Procunier v. Martinez*, because the latter case was limited in its analysis and application. The Court observed that outgoing mail (which may be the focus of the *Martinez* opinion) is not as great a security concern as incoming mail.

The mail regulations in the *Thornburgh* case were based on a concern for prison security, which is a purpose "central to all other corrections goals," the Court said. It was a legitimate governmental objective, and the regulation restricting inmate First Amendment rights was neutral in its application—that is, it was applied without regard to the content of the expression. Further, the Court liked the fact that determinations for rejections of publications were made on individualized bases: the Bureau of Prisons required each individual magazine or book or newspaper to be examined. Inmates were not kept from subscribing to certain titles; only individual issues of a subscription could be excluded, based on a finding that those issues contained material that posed a risk to the institution's security. Using the *Turner* language, the Bureau of Prisons' regulation was found not to be exaggerated, and it was permissible, because there was no obvious alternative that could achieve the same result (of keeping such publications out of prison).

Applying the *Turner* standard, the Court concluded that the government regulations were "reasonably related to legitimate penological interests." The regulations were upheld as constitutionally valid.[4]

■ *Beard v. Banks*

In this case, which is an extension of the ruling in *Thornburgh v. Abbott*, the Supreme Court considered whether it was a violation of the First Amendment for Pennsylvania authorities to withhold newspapers, magazines, and personal photographs from inmates who were in a Long Term Segregation Unit. This was done, prison officials said, to motivate the inmates to adopt better behavior.

The district court found that the prison rule was acceptable and was supported by the evidence officials presented. The court of appeals reversed, holding that the prison's regulation could not be "supported as a matter of law by the record in this case."

The Supreme Court, in *Beard v. Banks*, 548 U.S. 521 (2006), reversed the appellate court and agreed with the district court's conclusion. It held that the state's justification to motivate improved behavior by inmates was a legitimate governmental purpose under *Turner v. Safley* requirements:

The articulated connections between newspapers and magazines, the deprivation of virtually the last privilege left to an inmate, and a significant incentive to improve behavior, are logical ones.

The Court further said that the material presented by prison officials was sufficient to show that the policy was reasonable and inquiring into the other three factors discussed in *Turner* would not be particularly useful.

Applying language it had used in *Overton v. Bazzetta*, 539 U.S. 126 (2003), which related to visitation rights, the Court concluded:

[W]ithholding such privileges "is a proper and even necessary management technique to induce compliance with the rules of inmate behavior, especially for high-security prisoners who have few other privileges to lose."

The Court added that the court of appeals had placed too high an evidentiary burden on Beard, the secretary of the department of corrections, failing to provide sufficient deference to the judgment of prison officials on these matters of prison management.

In the absence of evidence contrary to or conflicting with the rationale of prison authorities, the Court concluded that the policy was constitutional within the standards set by *Turner.*

■ *Bell v. Wolfish*

In another case that is also something of an adjunct to the *Thornburgh v. Abbott* decision, the Supreme Court dealt with the constitutionality of a regulation limiting the receipt of books and magazines. *Bell v. Wolfish*, 441 U.S. 520 (1979), is primarily known and cited as a case dealing with conditions in jails, particularly with double-celling (crowding) in jails. *Bell* also dealt with a challenge to a Federal Bureau of Prisons regulation that required inmates (most of whom were pretrial detainees but some of whom were prisoners serving sentences) to receive such publications only from the publisher (thus, the "publisher-only" rule). The Bureau of Prisons justified this restriction on the grounds of security concerns; it was claimed that books and magazines were too hard to examine thoroughly for contraband, and the greatest risk for the introduction of contraband in such materials was when they were sent by family and friends. By limiting the sender to publishers, it was thought that the threat of contraband would be minimized. During the course of the litigation, the Bureau of Prisons amended its rule to allow paperback books and magazines to be sent in by family and friends. Hardback books were still limited to a "publisher-only" restriction.

The Supreme Court found the regulation to be a reasonable response to "an obvious security problem." The Court noted that there were other ways for inmates to obtain reading materials (mainly, from a prison library). The rule had nothing to do with the content of the materials and therefore was content-neutral (always a First Amendment concern of the courts). The same concern over security, in support of the regulation, applied to both pretrial detainees and to convicted inmates. The prison regulation was upheld.

■ National Security Issues

A special interest arises from the confinement of certain types of inmates, such as spies and terrorists. In the mid-1990s, the Federal Bureau of Prisons implemented rules governing inmates associated with national security issues and acts of violence and terrorism (Title 28, Code of Federal Regulations, Sections 501.2 and 501.3). These sections authorize the implementation of special administrative measures (which govern such areas as the inmate's correspondence, interviews with representatives of the news media, use of telephone, and visiting) to prevent disclosure of classified information (for national security cases) and to protect persons against the risk of death or serious bodily injury (for acts of violence and terrorism).

For example, in the case of an inmate convicted of espionage, the inmate may have knowledge about practices and procedures used by government agencies. The "shelf life" of this information may extend many years beyond the inmate's conviction. If the information became known, the safety of United States operatives could be in danger. To address this concern, the mail, telephone conversations, and visiting activities of such an inmate may be subject to increased limitations or scrutiny under this regulation.

The section of the rule (28 CFR 501.3) on prevention of acts of violence and terrorism authorizes, under stringent procedures, "the monitoring or review of communications between [a particular inmate] and attorneys or attorneys' agents who are traditionally covered by the attorney–client privilege, for the purpose of deterring future acts that could result in death or serious bodily injury to persons, or substantial damage to property that would entail the risk of death or serious bodily injury to persons."

In *United States v. Stewart*, 590 F.3d 93 (2nd Cir. 2009), en banc re-hearing denied, 597 F.3d 514 (2nd Cir. 2010), the court of appeals upheld the validity of the section 501.3 special administrative measures as applied to communications between defendant Stewart (an attorney) and her client, Omar Abdel Rahman, a prisoner convicted of terrorist acts. The court of appeals described Rahman's status as follows:

> Rahman is serving a life sentence in a maximum security prison for terrorism-related crimes of seditious conspiracy, solicitation of murder, solicitation of an attack on American military installations, conspiracy to murder, and a conspiracy to bomb. He is subject to "Special Administrative Measures" (SAMs) restricting his ability to communicate with persons outside of the prison in which he is incarcerated so as to prevent him from continuing to lead terrorist organizations.

Attorney Stewart signed documents saying she understood the restrictions imposed by the SAMs and agreed to abide by its terms (for example, not to use her meetings, correspondence, or phone calls with Rahman to pass messages between third parties and Rahman). After agreeing to the limitations imposed by the special administrative measures, Stewart facilitated communication of information to third parties in violation of those measures, resulting in the prosecution of herself and others. She was sentenced to 10 years in federal prison for her conduct.

Inmate Postage

Does the First Amendment entitle an inmate to free writing material and postage? The Supreme Court has not addressed this question, but lower federal courts have. In *Van Poyck v. Singletary*, 106 F.3d 1558 (11th Cir. 1997), the Department of Corrections policy in Florida provided indigent inmates with free postage and writing materials to mail one first-class letter per month, for such mailing to occur on a specific day, and for an inmate to receive a maximum of 15 stamps from a person outside the prison. Another rule limited the number of stamps an inmate could possess at any one time to 20. The inmates alleged a violation of their First Amendment, freedom of speech rights.

The Eleventh Circuit held that the First Amendment does not require prison officials to give indigent inmates unlimited free postage and materials for nonlegal mail. The Court also supported the limitation on the number of stamps received and possessed by inmates, holding that the rule was related to the legitimate security interest of eliminating the exchange of contraband among inmates.

In *Davidson v. Mann*, 129 F.3d 700 (2nd Cir. 1997), an inmate challenged a New York state prison rule that limited the number of stamps an inmate could purchase to 50 every two weeks— or to 50 per month for an inmate in special housing (ordinarily disciplinary) status. This was claimed to be a First Amendment violation of the inmate's right to send outgoing nonlegal mail. The appeals court, using the *Turner* standard, ruled in favor of the state, saying the regulation was rationally related to legitimate penological objectives. The limits on the number of stamps were seen as legitimately furthering the goal of avoiding thefts and disputes. It was also commented that inmates in New York had the choice of prioritizing their mailings or showing extenuating circumstances to warrant an exception being made.

Nude Photos

Inmate Giano challenged the Clinton, New York Correctional Facility policy that prohibited the possession of nude or seminude photos of inmates' spouses or girlfriends. He brought a Section 1983 action, claiming that the policy infringed on his First Amendment rights. *Giano v. Senkowski*, 54 F.3d 1050 (2nd Cir. 1995). Officials at Clinton allowed inmates to receive other erotic literature (such as *Playboy* magazine), but they justified the exclusion of wives' or girlfriends' photos on the grounds that possession of such photos could cause violent confrontations between inmates if they were passed around the institution or if they were possessed by the wrong inmates. Officials said that the possibility of those confrontations posed a threat to the safety, security, and good order of the institution.

Giano's girlfriend sent four photos to him; two of them were seminude. Under the prison's policy, an employee who went through the incoming mail took out the two seminude photos and sent the rest of the mail to Giano. The confiscated photos were added to Giano's personal property, which was to be stored and then given to him upon his release. The Second Circuit said that this action and this policy by Clinton officials did not violate the First Amendment.

"Prison officials must be given latitude to anticipate the probable consequences of certain speech, and must be allowed to take reasonable steps to forestall violence," the court said.

Other courts, it was noted, had recognized this same problem. The Ninth Circuit, in *Pepperling v. Crist*, 678 F.2d 787 (9th Cir. 1982), accepted the proposition that nude photos of wives or girlfriends are "highly emotionally charged and often lead to violent altercations among prisoners." Another court, in *Trapnell v. Riggsby*, 622 F.2d 290 (7th Cir. 1980), upheld the ban on nude photos of wives and girlfriends on the grounds that many offenders had assaultive behavior records and "the highly emotionally charged nature of the photographs" increased the likelihood of violence. The court in *Giano* concluded that the policy at Clinton was based on a valid, rational concern about maintaining prison order and security. The court, in something approaching a humorous aside, noted the proposition that "one man's pornography may be another's keepsake." But the court was also helped to reach its conclusion by the fact that the inmate had other links to his girlfriend, including ordinary correspondence and other permissible photos.

SUMMARY

- Freedom of speech, guaranteed in the First Amendment, is a freedom that is highly protected in the courts, but it is not an absolute freedom.

- Prison officials have concerns about the content of mail—both sent and received by inmates. Contraband enclosures and illegal content in communications are the main concerns.

- The Supreme Court recognized the mail sent by outside correspondents to inmates to be "speech," protected by the First Amendment. But the Court also ruled that prison officials could restrict such correspondence if it was necessary in order to further a "legitimate government interest." The government interests that could justify restrictions on correspondence are the preservation of internal order and discipline, maintenance of institutional security, and rehabilitation of prisoners (*Procunier v. Martinez*).

- In a civil rights action (under Section 1983), a prison official is protected against liability (is given qualified immunity) if the actions he took interfering with inmate correspondence were taken before the law governing such correspondence had been clearly established (*Procunier v. Navarette*).

- Conceding the very difficult problems that are inherent in running prisons, the Supreme Court held that prison officials had good security reasons to prohibit inmates from writing to inmates in other institutions in most cases (*Turner v. Safley*). In the same case, however, the Court said prison authorities had not shown justification to ban inmate marriages. The Court provided a four-part test for examining First Amendment challenges.

- Regarding correspondence in foreign languages, the Supreme Court has not yet ruled on the obligation of prisons to allow such correspondence. A lower court indicated that, in a case in which a translation service was available and correspondence had been allowed for other languages, prohibiting some mail in Lao was not permissible (*Thongvanh v. Thalacker*). Another lower court indicated that an official was protected by qualified immunity in a case involving receipt of Japanese publications, because the law in this area had not been clearly established (*Kikumura v. Turner*).

- The Supreme Court upheld a regulation that allowed local prison officials to reject incoming publications (magazines, newspapers, etc.) if they were found to be detrimental to the security or good order of the institution or if they might facilitate criminal activity (*Thornburgh v. Abbott*).

- A prison regulation banning newspapers, magazines, and personal photos to incorrigible, recalcitrant inmates housed in a highly restrictive housing unit was upheld as a proper and even necessary management approach to induce compliance with the rules of inmate behavior, especially for high-security prisoners who have few other privileges to lose (*Beard v. Banks*).

- Special administrative measures (covering such areas as inmate correspondence, news media interviews, telephone use, and visiting) have been implemented to prevent disclosure of classified information (for national security cases) and protect persons against the risk of death or serious bodily injury (for acts of violence and terrorism). An appeals court has upheld such measures in a case involving acts of violence and terrorism (*United States v. Stewart*).

- Courts of appeals have decided that prison officials may limit (for nonlegal mail) the number of stamps provided to an indigent inmate and may also limit the number of stamps that an inmate may purchase or have in her possession (*Van Poyck v. Singletary; Davidson v. Mann*).

- Federal courts upheld a New York policy that prohibited nude or seminude photos of spouses or girlfriends to be sent in to inmates (*Giano v. Senkowski*).

THINKING ABOUT IT

A prison inmate writes his brother, saying there is a "beetled eye'd bit__ back here who enjoys reading people's mail." The letter continues, saying the staff member was hoping to read a letter "someone wrote to their wife talking dirty sh__, so she could go in the bathroom and masturbate." (Note: the last two letters of *bit__* and *sh__* were blackened out.) The letter was reviewed by prison staff under agency policy, and the inmate was punished under the institution's disciplinary policy. The inmate sued, claiming a violation of First Amendment rights. How do you think the court should rule? See *Loggins v. Delo*, 999 F.2d 364 (8th Cir. 1993).

KEY TERMS

class action: An action brought by one (or a few) plaintiff(s) on behalf of a large group of persons, all of whom have similar interests in pursuing the action.

immunity: Exemption by law. Freedom from a duty, or from liability, because actions are protected by law. Immunity from criminal prosecution may be either transactional immunity or use immunity. Transactional immunity provides immunity from prosecution for an offense to which a witness's compelled testimony relates. Use immunity bars a person's compelled testimony and its fruits from being used in any manner in connection with the criminal prosecution of the person.

ENDNOTES

1. In *United States of America v. Stotts*, 925 F.2d 83 (4th Cir. 1991), the U.S. Court of Appeals for the Fourth Circuit noted that the federal prison system was processing more than 156,000 pieces of mail a week. In 1990, the federal prison system reported its inmate population as totaling about 59,000. In 2002, the federal prison system housed over 137,000 inmates in 102 institutions. (Federal Bureau of Prisons. *State Of The Bureau 2002—Accomplishments and Goals.* Washington, DC: Federal Bureau of Prisons, U.S. Department of Justice, 31, 56.) An Office of Inspector General report (Report Number I-2003-002) stated, on page vi, that "[i]nstitution mailrooms process up to 3,000 pieces of mail daily, with double that amount or more on a Monday (because there is no mail delivery on weekends) and during holiday periods."

2. Reminiscent of an old movie scene, one of your authors recalls a letter that an inmate tried to mail. The inmate asked the person receiving the letter to send the inmate a food item (believed to be a cake) and place a gun within that food item.

3. Another recent approach to inmate mail is the policy of some jails to require that postcards be used for the mailings.

4. While the *Thornburgh* case judicially decided the issue of receiving sexually oriented publications under First Amendment protection, the U.S. Congress has legislatively taken action to limit such publications. In Section 615 of the Commerce, Justice, State Appropriations Act of 2000 (Public Law 106-113), Congress said: "None of the funds made available in this Act to the Federal Bureau of Prisons may be used to distribute or make available any commercially published information or material to a prisoner when it is made known to the Federal official having authority to obligate or expend such funds that such information or material is sexually explicit or features nudity." In effect, this language prevents federal prison staff from delivering these publications to inmates, even if the inmate has a subscription. The Bureau of Prisons January 2003 policy on Incoming Publications requires such a publication to be returned to the publisher or sender, with notification of

the administrative appeal process. (For more information in this area, please go to http://www.bop.gov. Once on that website, click on "Policy/Forms" and select the 5000 series. The policy on incoming publications is located at 5266.10.) How did inmates and publishers react to these restrictions? In an earlier version (1996) of the restrictions, three inmates with subscriptions, along with the affected publishers, sued in a free-speech challenge. The U.S. District Court for the District of Columbia enjoined enforcement, finding it facially invalid under the First Amendment. The DC Circuit Court of Appeals, applying *Turner*, reversed in *Amatel v. Reno*, 156 F.3d 192 (DC Cir. 1998). In June 1999, the U.S. Supreme Court, without comment, declined to review the court of appeals' decision.

8 | First Amendment: Inmate Association Rights and Visiting

The fact of confinement and the needs of the penal institution impose limitations on constitutional rights, including those derived from the First Amendment, which are implicit in incarceration. Perhaps the most obvious of the First Amendment rights that are necessarily curtailed by confinement are those associational rights that the First Amendment protects outside of prison walls.

U.S. Supreme Court, *Jones v. North Carolina Prisoners' Labor Union*

Chapter Outline

- Freedom of Association
- *Jones v. North Carolina Prisoners' Labor Union*
- Inmates and the News Media: *Pell v. Procunier; Saxbe v. Washington Post*
- *Houchins v. KQED, Inc.; Garrett v. Estelle; Hammer v. Ashcroft; Smith v. Coughlin*
- Inmate Visits
- *Block v. Rutherford*
- *Kentucky Department of Corrections v. Thompson*
- *Overton v. Bazzetta*
- Conjugal Visits
- Artificial Insemination

In this chapter, we will look at another right that is protected by the First Amendment of the Constitution. Although it is not as well-known as the freedoms of speech, press, and religion, which are all also contained in the First Amendment, there is an association right that is found in that amendment. Most inmates obviously have an interest in keeping in contact with family and friends. One way to do that is through correspondence. In this chapter, we will look at the contacts that inmates maintain or establish through organizations, associations, and especially through visiting.

◼ Freedom of Association

Again, we ask you to look in the First Amendment for the right to freedom of association. Other than the right to peaceably assemble, it does not appear there, does it? But the Supreme Court has found such a right in the First Amendment (which is applicable to the states by the Fourteenth Amendment).

In *Roberts v. United States Jaycees*, 468 U.S. 609 (1984), the Supreme Court said that there are two kinds of freedom of association protected by the Constitution. The first protects the rights of individuals "to enter into and maintain certain intimate human relationships." This particularly refers to family relationships and the need to protect them and the inherent need for seclusion from others in such relationships (that is, a right to privacy). Where does the Constitution give such protection? The Supreme Court said, "because the Bill of Rights is designed to secure individual liberty, it must afford the formation and preservation of certain kinds of highly personal relationships a substantial measure of sanctuary from unjustified interference by the State." Well, okay, if you say so—but this is another example of the Supreme Court conducting a somewhat free-ranging interpretation of the Constitution, rather than a strict construction of the First Amendment's language. (Not that any of us find fault with the protection of intimate family relationships. That is one thing that liberals, conservatives, and middle roaders would seem to agree on.)

But there is not much need for this kind of associational protection in prisons, because prisoners obviously forfeit their rights to close, intimate family relationships as an aspect of their incarceration. (An exception might be those few states that allow "conjugal visitation"—the permission to receive visits from spouses in a more or less private place in the prison, such as a small apartment or a trailer. See the discussion of that kind of association later in this chapter.)

For the second kind of association protected by the Constitution, the Supreme Court has recognized that citizens have a right to engage in "expressive association." This is the right to gather together (in "peaceable assembly") to take part in those activities that are specifically protected by the First Amendment: the right to speak, the right to worship, and the right to petition the government for redress of grievances.

This brings us to the central questions of this chapter: To what extent do prisoners retain any associational right under the Constitution, and to what degree can prison authorities restrict or ban those associational activities?

◼ *Jones v. North Carolina Prisoners' Labor Union*

In the late 1960s and early 1970s, there was a movement to organize U.S. prisoners into prisoners' unions. This movement was based, in name and philosophy, on the U.S. labor union movement. The state of North Carolina experienced the organization of inmates in many of its institutions into a "Prisoners' Labor Union." The union's stated purposes were "to seek through collective bargaining ... to improve ... working condition, ... to work towards the alteration or elimination of practices and policies of the Department of Correction which it did not approve of, and to serve as a vehicle for the presentation and resolution of inmate grievances." The state originally tolerated inmates forming and joining this union, but as its size grew to some 2,000 members in

40 different prisons, the North Carolina Department of Correction issued a regulation prohibiting the solicitation of members, banning union meetings in the prisons, and forbidding bulk mailings about the union from outside sources.

The union filed suit, challenging the regulation and seeking an injunction against its enforcement, pursuant to 42 U.S.C. § 1983. Because it was a challenge to the constitutionality of the statewide regulation, a three-judge district court was convened to hear the lawsuit. That court found the regulation unconstitutional in many respects and enjoined its enforcement. The state took a direct appeal of that judgment to the Supreme Court, which issued its opinion in *Jones v. North Carolina Prisoners' Labor Union*, 433 U.S. 119 (1977).

The Supreme Court in *Jones* noted that the district court had based its review of the state regulation on three constitutional provisions: freedom of speech and freedom of association under the First Amendment, and equal protection of the laws under the Fourteenth Amendment. The entire decision of the Supreme Court is permeated with its criticism of the district court's approach; the Court held that the lower court did not give "appropriate deference to the decision of prison administrators." Although the Court noted that constitutional rights can be claimed by prisoners, it emphasized that the needs of prisons "impose limitations on constitutional rights," even those found in the First Amendment. The Supreme Court said that courts must recognize the "wide-ranging deference to be accorded the decisions of prison administrators." The district court had given particular emphasis to the fact that North Carolina had permitted inmates to be members of the union, so it would perforce have to allow solicitation of membership. As to bulk mailings of union literature and meetings of inmate union members, the district court especially relied on the equal protection clause. The court held that because prison officials allowed other groups, such as the Jaycees, Alcoholics Anonymous, and the Boy Scouts, to have meetings and receive literature, they could not "pick and choose" and try to limit union activities simply because they disliked the message of this group or its purposes.

The Supreme Court, however, found North Carolina's approach to be reasonable. The state had permitted membership in the union, because it assumed that each prisoner could choose to believe whatever he wanted to believe. Officials had concluded that concerted group activity by the union, or the solicitation of membership, would pose problems and frictions in the operation of the state's prisons. The Supreme Court said that "[t]he ban on inmate solicitation and group meetings, therefore, was rationally related to the reasonable, indeed to the central, objectives of prison administration."

As to speech rights, the Court held that those rights were "barely implicated in this case." The only mail question was that of bulk mailings, and the advantage of those would be cost savings. Those savings did not fundamentally affect free speech values, because there were other channels of outside informational flow by the union. Nor did the ban on the solicitation of membership improperly impair free speech rights. Solicitation is more than just the simple expression of ideas; it would be, in this case, an invitation to engage in a prohibited activity. (A North Carolina statute separately made illegal any collective bargaining for inmates with respect to pay, work hours, or other conditions of their incarceration. Given this law on the books, the position of the corrections department permitting membership in the union, besides complicating the case, was a questionable one from the outset.) It was not only reasonable but necessary for the prison officials to control union activities, and that was permissible under the First Amendment free speech clause.

The Supreme Court said that association rights might have been more implicated in this case than speech rights. However, association rights are "necessarily curtailed by the realities of confinement." Further, the Court held:

> They [association rights] may be curtailed whenever the institution's officials, in the exercise of their informed discretion, reasonably conclude that such associations, whether through group meetings or otherwise, possess the likelihood of disruption to prison order or stability, or otherwise interfere with the legitimate penological objectives of the prison environment.

The Court recognized that preserving order in the prison was a paramount concern. The district court had rejected prison officials' concerns, because that court said those concerns were speculative rather than concrete. The Supreme Court rejected this approach taken by the district court:

> Prison life, and relations between the inmates themselves and between the inmates and prison officials or staff, contain the ever-present potential for violent confrontation and conflagration. Responsible prison officials must be permitted to take reasonable steps to forestall such a threat, and they must be permitted to act before the time when they can compile a dossier on the eve of a riot.

The Supreme Court also rejected the equal protection analysis of the district court. Conceding that other organizations had been allowed to operate more freely than the union, the Court found this justified. Officials had demonstrated a rational basis (note this language—this case is known for its reliance on rationality and reasonableness as the standards for judging the propriety of prison officials' actions) for different approaches, distinguishing different kinds of prison organizations. Alcoholics Anonymous and Jaycees were allowed to operate in many prisons because they were seen as serving rehabilitative purposes, and they had worked "in harmony with the goals and desires of the prison administrators." The union, of course, differed greatly and critically from those other organizations in these respects, because its stated intent was to pursue an adversarial relationship with authorities. The Supreme Court pointed out that a prison is not a public forum and does not require the protections that have been given to such forums in other cases. When it comes to different groups within prisons, the Court required discretion to be honored:

> [T]he courts should allow the prison administrators the full latitude of discretion, unless it can be firmly stated that the two groups [those permitted and those disallowed] are so similar that discretion has been abused. That is surely not the case here. There is nothing in the Constitution which requires prison officials to treat all inmate groups alike.

■ Inmates and the News Media: *Pell v. Procunier; Saxbe v. Washington Post*

In a case involving visitation (the language of which was cited and relied on in the *Jones* case), inmates in California sought to have a California regulation declared unconstitutional. The regulation prohibited face-to-face interviews between individual inmates and any representatives of the news media. The media joined in the case, arguing that the freedom of the press, which is guaranteed in the First Amendment, had also been violated by the state action. A three-judge district court found that the state policy unconstitutionally infringed the inmates' rights under the First and Fourteenth Amendments. Because the press could enter institutions to observe conditions and to interview inmates in a random manner, and because the inmates were given interview rights under its ruling, the district court did not award any additional protections to the media. A direct appeal was taken to the Supreme Court.

In *Pell v. Procunier*, 417 U.S. 817 (1974), and in another case that decided the same question on the same day, *Saxbe v. Washington Post*, the Supreme Court decided the issue of entitlement to media interviews by looking at the two sets of interests presented by the two types of parties involved in this litigation.

First, as to the inmates who wanted to have individual interviews, the state regulation clearly restricted one kind of communication they would like to have under the First Amendment. The Court concluded that this restriction was permissible. It was noted that inmates had other means of communication available—they could send and receive mail, and this was permitted with members of the news media, as well as with family and friends. They also were allowed to have visits—not with the news media but with family, friends, attorneys, and clergy. A major concern in these cases always had been that there could be terrible treatment of an inmate or horrible conditions inside a prison, which could be sealed off from outside knowledge by the prison walls and prison restrictions. These alternative methods of communication by mail and visits, whereby inmates could communicate their complaints and grievances, ensured that the authorities did not erect an absolute barrier to knowledge about prison conditions.

> **[T]he institutional objectives furthered by that regulation [banning face-to-face media interviews] and the measure of judicial deference owed to corrections officials in their attempt to serve those interests are relevant in gauging the validity of the regulation. Accordingly, in light of the alternative channels of communication that are open to prison inmates, we cannot say on the record in this case that this restriction on one manner in which prisoners can communicate with persons outside of prison is unconstitutional.**

Second, the media representatives argued that the limitation on press interviews violated their rights under the freedom of press guarantee of the First Amendment (extended to the states by the Fourteenth Amendment). Again, the Supreme Court was impressed that California authorities were not trying to conceal conditions inside prisons, because the press and members of the public were allowed to visit and take tours of prison facilities. During tours, journalists could stop and speak to any inmates they encountered and could discuss with them any subject. The sole limitation was the ban on interviews with specifically requested individual inmates. This restriction was adopted in 1971 in response to a violent episode that authorities felt was at least partly attributable to face-to-face interviews. When they were permitted, it was found that the press concentrated on a few inmates, who as a result became "public figures" and gained notoriety and influence among their fellow inmates.

In the companion case, *Saxbe v. Washington Post*, 417 U.S. 843 (1974), the Federal Bureau of Prisons justified a similar ban on individual interviews on a similar theory, called the "big wheel" theory. Prison experience had taught them that a few inmates, already or potentially notorious, were spotlighted by the press attention and through "their repeated contacts with the press tend to become the source of substantial disciplinary problems that can engulf a large portion of the population at a prison." It is noteworthy that the holding stated in *Pell* and followed in *Saxbe* was a strictly legal one and a shocker to many in the media:

> **[T]he First Amendment does not guarantee the press a constitutional right of special access to information not available to the public generally ... Newsmen have no constitutional right of access to the scenes of crime or disaster when the general public is excluded. Similarly, newsmen have no constitutional right of access to prisons or their inmates beyond that afforded the general public.**

Applying this constitutional standard to the Federal Bureau of Prisons regulation, the Court held that, because members of the news media were given access to information available to the general public (and the public did not have a right to individual interviews with selected inmates), there was no violation of the First Amendment.

The Supreme Court holdings in *Pell* and *Saxbe* are especially significant for the support they give to prison security and good order against strong First Amendment claims. One underlying principle in the orderly running of prisons is that inmates should be treated the same, so far as possible. (In this sense, prison is or should be a great equalizer.) To do otherwise can easily lead to unrest or animosity, as inmates perceive that preferred treatment is given to another inmate or group of inmates. This is the principle behind the "big wheel" theory.

According to this theory, if an inmate is given special attention in the media or has her writings published in newspapers or magazines, that special attention brings special notoriety within the prison. This can lead to hostility toward someone who has gained special status or who is seen as having brought negative attention to the facility or a tightening of conditions as the result of publicity. Pressures may be placed on her to tell the stories or complaints of other inmates in order to avoid negative reactions if she does not. Staff members at the prison may also treat the inmate differently; there is especially a concern that they will be reluctant to deal with the "big wheel" inmate as strictly in accord with policy as they do with others. This fear of notoriety or exposure of staff in the media has been called a "chilling effect," as the result of such an inmate who gets special media attention.[1]

■ *Houchins v. KQED, Inc.; Garrett v. Estelle; Hammer v. Ashcroft; Smith v. Coughlin*

In *Houchins v. KQED, Inc.*, 438 U.S. 1 (1978), the Supreme Court reviewed an attack by a television station on a refusal by a sheriff to allow journalists to visit and photograph a portion of the county jail where a prisoner had committed suicide and conditions were allegedly very bad. The Court reaffirmed the principle of *Pell* and *Saxbe*, saying that the First Amendment does not require the sheriff to give the media access to government information, and the media did not have any right of special access to the county jail that was any greater than that given to the public generally.

Another offshoot of *Pell v. Procunier,* involving a question of narrow application but of some interest, was *Garrett v. Estelle*, 556 F.2d 1274 (5th Cir. 1977). The question there was whether the media had the right to film and televise executions. Garrett, a news reporter, asked prison officials for permission to film the first execution to take place in Texas under its new **capital punishment** statute. The request was denied, pursuant to a Texas statute that prohibited press access to death row inmates and at executions. (Texas did revise its position during the litigation to allow press pool representatives at the execution, but filming was still disallowed.) The Court of Appeals for the Fifth Circuit (the Supreme Court has not decided this question) ruled that the First Amendment does not require the news media to have access to matters that are not accessible to the public generally, citing *Pell.* The state contended that televising an execution would amount to reinstating public executions, which had been stopped in Texas in 1920. (The Supreme Court, much earlier, in *Holden v. Minnesota*, 137 U.S. 483 (1890), had upheld the right of a state to restrict attendance at executions, rather than make them public.) The court upheld the right of Texas to continue a policy that barred the access of the media to film executions.[2]

A related issue arose when prison officials modified a policy to no longer allow face-to-face media interviews with death row inmates. In *Hammer v. Ashcroft*, 570 F.3d 798 (7th Cir. 2009) (en banc), cert denied 559 U.S. __ (2010), a prisoner on death row in a federal institution sued various prison officials, alleging this prohibition violated his rights under the First Amendment and the equal protection component of the due process clause of the Fifth Amendment.

When the federal government opened its death row, interviews were allowed (for the first nine months). Shortly after the broadcast of a television interview with a death row prisoner, the policy was reevaluated, and a decision was made to prohibit all death row offenders from this type of media communication.[3]

The Seventh Circuit Court of Appeals, in an en banc decision, rejected the inmate's claim that allowing prison officials discretion to permit face-to-face interviews in situations other than death row, while having a blanket prohibition for death row, violated the equal protection clause. The court, noting that the "Special Confinement Unit" was one of the most secure areas of the federal prison system, held that the Constitution is not offended by applying greater restrictions to maximum security prisoners than those requiring less security.

The court also considered arguments made by correctional administrators, and accepted as legitimate by the Supreme Court in *Pell v. Procunier* and *Saxbe v. Washington Post*, that media interviews with prisoners can turn those interviewed into celebrities within the prison. Relying on the principle established in *Saxbe v. Washington Post,* that prisoners who are interviewed may "tend to become the source of substantial disciplinary problems that can engulf a large portion of the population at a prison," the court held that the regulation satisfied the "reasonably related to legitimate security interests" standard set forth in *Turner v. Safley,* 482 U.S. 78 (1987).

The prisoner's last contention, that the restriction was motivated by a desire to silence prisoners who might criticize prison officials or prison conditions, was also rejected. This appellate court found that the challenged rule was objectively reasonable and thus was permissible under *Turner* standards. The court also noted that prisoners on death row retained other means of communicating with the outside world about prison conditions, including correspondence with the media and the filing of lawsuits.

Limits placed by the state on other kinds of associational rights have also been upheld. For example, in *Smith v. Coughlin*, 748 F.2d 783 (1984), the Second Circuit Court of Appeals upheld

New York's restriction on visits to death row inmates, which limited visiting to family members only and did not allow visits with friends and acquaintances.

■ Inmate Visits

We have already touched on the rights of inmates to special visits, for example, those with the news media. Another example is with attorneys and their representatives. In addition to special visits, all prisons and jails have some provision for visiting. In more secure institutions, visiting may be very limited regarding both the list of approved visitors and also the frequency of visits.

A facility (prison or jail) will typically advise new arrivals during the orientation process about the visiting and correspondence rules. As with mail, a prisoner will be asked to list those family members and close friends with whom he would like to visit. (This same process may also apply to telephone calls in facilities where telephone contact is permitted but limited to a certain list of persons, limited in frequency, and limited in length of calls.) If an inmate has an additional particular person, such as a member of the clergy, with whom he would like to visit, he may place that person's name on the list also. The list is reviewed to see if there are any names that present special problems. (Some of the most disruptive scenes in the visiting room have taken place when an inmate received visits from a wife and a girlfriend at the same time!) Investigations may be made into the backgrounds of some visitors, especially in high security facilities or with highly notorious inmates. These may include checks for criminal records or even general background checks (with the police or probation officers) in the inmate's or requested visitor's community.

Visits in prisons and jails are of two kinds: contact and noncontact. In a contact visit, the inmate and his visitor are seated, perhaps at a table or in facing chairs, in a visiting area where physical contact is possible. During such visits, the visitors, at least, are allowed to get up and get a drink of water, go to the restroom, or possibly get a snack out of a vending machine. These visits are supervised by a visiting room officer, who is typically seated to observe activities anywhere in the room, and perhaps also by camera monitors. Noncontact visits (these are the ones usually depicted on film) are those where the inmate and the visitor are unable to have physical contact, usually because they are seated facing each other with a glass partition separating them. Conversation is allowed by a grill opening in the glass or a telephone used on each side. Noncontact visits are common in detention facilities (see **Figure 8-1**). On the other hand, contact visiting is the norm in most prisons. In some prisons and jails, visiting is further "normalized" by allowing children to play in the visiting room or an adjoining play area. Other prisons and jails do not allow small children to visit. Some places, especially in warmer climates, allow visiting outdoors; this is usually limited to low security institutions.

The main concern regarding visiting on the part of prison staff is the passing of contraband in the visiting area. Noncontact visiting tends to minimize the opportunity for a visitor to leave contraband at the institution. Why, then, do prisons allow contact visiting? Prison life is harsh and leads to many tensions, including the stress of enforced separation from family and friends. The visit with a loved one is a way to relieve those tensions and to encourage a more tranquil adjustment by most inmates, according to most prison officials. However, visiting is not always tranquil—for example, in the case when a wife walks in and sees the inmate visiting with a

Figure 8-1 A man visiting a woman in prison.
This is an example of a noncontact visit.
Source: © Comstock/Thinkstock

girlfriend. Not all visitors are pacifying—for example, a heated argument with a spouse, brother, or criminal acquaintance can occur easily in a prison visiting room. But, on balance, most prison managers would rather allow visiting, even frequent or crowded visiting, than not.

Nevertheless, contraband does get passed, by any means the ingenuity of the inmate and his visitor can devise. It may be passed from mouth to mouth during a kiss when first meeting for the visit (most places allow a hug and a kiss at the start and the end of a visit). It may be passed from hand to hand during a visit. Contraband also may be hidden somewhere in the visiting area (such as in a wastebasket, on the underside of a chair, in a vending machine, or in a restroom) to be retrieved by the inmate (or his inmate friend) later on.

Besides surveillance of the visiting area—by staff on the scene and perhaps by camera monitors—other security steps must be taken. The visitor is warned of the consequences of introducing contraband and may be required to check any belongings (such as a duffel bag, fanny pack, or purse) at the front entrance. The visitor will often be required to pass through a metal detector on the way to the visiting area. The inmate is searched before the visit and strip-searched after the visit. His clothing is also thoroughly searched before he is allowed back inside the facility. Areas where visitors have access (such as the restroom, under chairs, and in waste containers) are carefully searched after the visiting period. Small children have even been used to carry contraband (such as drugs, money, and ammunition) into the prison in their diapers or candy containers.

■ *Block v. Rutherford*

The leading case on inmate visiting, *Block v. Rutherford*, 468 U.S. 576 (1984), arose out of the Los Angeles County Jail. The sheriff had a policy that allowed only noncontact visits by pretrial detainees with their spouses, relatives, and friends. A group of detainees brought a class action under 42 U.S.C. Section 1983, challenging that policy. The district court found that denying inmates the right to embrace their wives or children (which they are not allowed to do in non-contact visiting) from time to time during the weeks or months they were awaiting trial was an impermissible burden. That court (and the court of appeals in affirming) found that the loss of some contacts during visitation was punitive and an exaggerated response to security concerns of jail officials. The Supreme Court reversed the lower courts' actions.

Because the case involved pretrial detainees and not prison inmates, the courts used the standard set out in *Bell v. Wolfish*, 441 U.S. 520 (1979). From *Bell*, the standard set by the Supreme Court is whether the challenged practice or condition amounts to punishment of the inmate: "A court must decide whether the disability is imposed for the purpose of punishment or whether it is but an incident of some other legitimate governmental purpose." (In practical and legal effect, the same outcome can be expected in prison cases, because both jails and prisons use the same process to detect unconstitutionality. They must determine whether there is a legitimate government interest, usually related to security, that can justify the restriction on otherwise permissible and even constitutionally protected activity.) The Supreme Court in *Block* said:

> **The question before us, therefore, is narrow: whether the prohibition of contact visits is reasonably related to legitimate governmental objectives.**

The Court easily detected "a valid, rational connection between a ban on contact visits and internal security of a detention facility." Even the lower courts acknowledged that contact visits open an institution to the introduction of drugs, weapons, and other contraband. Visitors could conceal contraband items and transfer them during the close contact that is permitted in contact visiting. The fact that it was unconvicted, pretrial detainees rather than convicted prisoners who were involved did not sway the Supreme Court (although this was a factor that influenced the decisions of lower courts on this and many other pretrial issues). As in *Bell*, the Court concluded that there was no reason to conclude "that pretrial detainees pose any lesser security risk than convicted inmates." Although the Court conceded that visits from family and friends are impor-tant to inmates, it drew the following conclusion:

> **[T]he Constitution does not require that detainees be allowed contact visits when respon-sible, experienced administrators have determined, in their sound discretion, that such visits will jeopardize the security of the facility.**

What the Supreme Court did not decide was whether inmates have the right under the Con-stitution to have visits in the first place. Stated another way, could visits be banned altogether?

▨ *Kentucky Department of Corrections v. Thompson*

In *Kentucky Department of Corrections v. Thompson*, 490 U.S. 454 (1989), Kentucky officials had adopted a policy that excluded certain prison visitors. This policy covered such persons as those under the influence of alcohol or drugs, those with a record of disruptive conduct, those who were directly related to the inmate's criminal conduct, and those whose presence would constitute a clear and present danger to an institution's security. The Kentucky State Reformatory at LaGrange adopted even more restrictive grounds for excluding visitors, including former "residents" (inmates) at the facility and former employees. Inmates at the Reformatory and inmates at the State Penitentiary at Eddyville brought a class action under Section 1983, challenging the enforcement of these visiting regulations.

Some visitors were barred from visiting for violations of some part of the visiting rules. These suspension "orders" were entered without any kind of hearing. The constitutional challenge centered on whether it was a violation of due process of law to terminate or suspend visiting privileges without a hearing. The lower courts in *Thompson* had said that there was a protected constitutional interest for prisoners to receive visits. This constitutional right required the prison officials to adopt some procedures whereby a prisoner would receive notice of and the reasons for any action to exclude a visitor, as well as an opportunity to respond. These procedures were called "minimum due process procedures." The Supreme Court reversed the lower courts' rulings.

We will not enter here into a detailed discussion of the due process analysis made by the Supreme Court. In summary, the Court said that, in order to claim due process protection, there had to be a liberty interest provided in either of two places: in the due process clause itself (in the Constitution) or in the laws of the state. In this case, the suspension of visiting privileges was not guaranteed by the due process clause. It was not inherent in the Constitution itself. In several cases, the Court had rejected the idea that any changes in conditions of confinement that adversely affected inmates were sufficient to invoke due process, merely because of that adverse impact.

Whether state law had created enforceable liberty interests is a more difficult question to address, and it is made even more difficult by a 1995 Supreme Court decision in the inmate discipline case of *Sandin v. Conner*, 515 U.S. 472 (1995). The answer, according to the Court here in *Thompson*, turned on whether the state had adopted "substantive predicates" to guide or limit its discretion in decision making. Another analysis turned on whether the state's regulations had "explicitly mandatory language," which required a certain outcome. That is, if the regulation said that when certain conditions or predicates were present a particular outcome had to follow, then the state had created a liberty interest. In the case of such mandatory conditions or predicates, the state would have created the expectation on the part of citizens (including prisoners) that certain facts, conditions, or actions would lead to a certain result. The *Sandin* case has overruled that analysis, which found due process created "outside the Constitution" by the state's statutory or regulation language. *Sandin* was an inmate discipline case, but the decision has raised serious doubt regarding the use of the *Thompson* analysis and standard in any prison cases.

Applying those somewhat complex standards, the Court in *Thompson* concluded that the Kentucky regulations did not have the "requisite mandatory language." They did not require a particular result to follow when certain conditions were met. The policy issuance started with the phrase, "Administrative staff reserves the right to allow or disallow visits." Visitors might be excluded if they fell into one of the listed categories, but they did not have to be excluded. Therefore, the regulations were saved from creating a liberty interest, which would have been protected by the due process clause. The Supreme Court ruled that Kentucky was not required to hold a hearing in order to terminate visiting privileges.

The Supreme Court thus came oh-so-close to addressing whether there is a constitutional right to visiting, but it did not decide that question. Justice Anthony Kennedy, in a concurring opinion (agreeing with the majority decision we just discussed), raised a concern that the Kentucky case involved only a denial of visiting to certain visitors and not a ban on all prison visitations. He expressly cautioned that a ban on all visiting would have raised a different question, not yet decided, about whether a total ban is unconstitutional. The most we have is an inference in the majority opinion that, if there were sound security reasons, a ban would probably be constitutional. However, that ultimate, broadest issue has not been decided by the Supreme Court. (But see *Overton v. Bazzetta* in the next section.) In addition, as pointed out earlier, for the stability and safe running of the institution, virtually all prison administrators concede the value of allowing inmate visitation. Therefore, the conditions for having a challenge in court on a total ban are not too likely to occur. What has happened in practice is that all visiting is suspended during an institutional emergency, such as the aftermath of a riot or massive disruption. That is a temporary situation and if challenged would likely be supported by the courts as a necessary reaction to the emergency, in furtherance of legitimate but temporary security concerns of the administration.

■ *Overton v. Bazzetta*

In the early 1990s, the population of Michigan prisons increased, leading to an increase in prison visitation, which strained the resources available for prison supervision and control. Prison officials found it more difficult to maintain order during visiting and prevent smuggling or drug trafficking. Substance abuse also increased. In response to these concerns about prison security, in 1995, the Michigan Department of Corrections revised its visitation policies. Under its new regulations, visitors had to be named on an approved visitor list.[4] The list contained a number of restrictions: Minors under 18 years of age could not be placed on the visiting list unless they were the children, stepchildren, grandchildren, or siblings of the inmate. If an inmate's parental rights had been terminated, the child could not visit. A child who was approved to visit had to be accompanied by an adult who was an immediate family member of either the child or the inmate or was the child's legal guardian. A former inmate could not visit unless he was a member of the inmate's immediate family and had the warden's prior approval. Inmates who committed multiple substance abuse violations were not allowed to receive any visitors, other than attorneys and members of the clergy. An inmate with the no-visitor restriction could request reinstatement of his visiting privileges after two years. The decision on the reinstatement rested with the warden.

Inmates, their friends, and their family members filed a Section 1983 action, alleging that the visiting restrictions violated the First, Eighth, and Fourteenth Amendments. The case, *Overton v. Bazzetta*, 539 U.S. 126 (2003), was certified as a class action. The focus of the litigation was on noncontact visits.

Both the district court and the appeals court ruled that the restrictions on noncontact visits were invalid. The Supreme Court disagreed. In considering whether the regulations infringed on a constitutional right of association, the Court concluded:

> **The very object of imprisonment is confinement. Many of the liberties and privileges enjoyed by other citizens must be surrendered by the prisoner. An inmate does not retain rights inconsistent with proper incarceration ... And, as our cases have established, freedom of association is among the rights least compatible with incarceration.**

> **We need not attempt to explore or define the asserted right of association at any length or determine the extent to which it survives incarceration because the challenged regulations bear a rational relation to legitimate penological interests.**

Holding the challenged regulations to be rationally related to a legitimate penological objective (the *Turner v. Safley* standard), the Court held it was not necessary to consider the extent to which the right of association survives incarceration. The Court noted that it accords substantial deference to the professional judgment of prison administrators, as these are the persons who define the goals of a corrections system and determine the most appropriate means to accomplish those goals.

> **The burden, moreover, is not on the State to prove the validity of prison regulations but on the prisoner to disprove it.**

> ***Turner* does not impose a least-restrictive-alternative test, but asks instead whether the prisoner has pointed to some obvious regulatory alternative that fully accommodates the asserted right while not imposing more than a *de minimis* cost to the valid penological goal.**

In the last part of its opinion, the Court held that the visiting restriction for inmates with two substance-abuse violations was not cruel and unusual punishment in violation of the Eighth Amendment. The withdrawal of visitation privileges for these inmates for a limited period was viewed as a regular means of effecting prison discipline. The Court further concluded that the regulation did not present any of the other concerns raised by the Eighth Amendment: it did not create inhumane prison conditions; deprive inmates of basic necessities or fail to protect their health or safety; involve the infliction of pain or injury; or amount to deliberate indifference to the basic needs of the inmates.

■ Conjugal Visits

Early in this chapter, there was a reference to **conjugal visits**. A few states[5] allow such visits, during which an inmate and his or her spouse (or, in some places, unmarried partner) are allowed some degree of privacy, during which they can engage in acts of sexual intimacy. The Supreme Court has not ruled on any request to permit such visiting as a matter of constitutional entitlement.

A case that may be somewhat suspect because of its age, but which is still one of the few reported cases ruling on the right to conjugal visitation, is *Payne v. District of Columbia*,

253 F.2d 867 (DC Cir. 1958). In *Payne,* a court in the District of Columbia rejected a claim by an inmate's wife that she was legally entitled to conjugal visits with her inmate husband.

In *Lyons v. Gilligan,* 382 F.Supp. 198 (N.D. OH, 1974), inmates of the Marion, Ohio Correctional Institution and their wives brought a Section 1983 action to require conjugal visiting, claiming that they were denied constitutional rights of privacy (the intimate familial, associational rights referred to early in this chapter) and that they were thereby being cruelly and unusually punished. As to punishment, the court concluded that the absence of conjugal visitation was not excessive punishment, but only a customary concomitant of incarceration. When and if additional states should adopt family visiting, there might be an "evolving standard of decency," which would require courts to address whether the denial of conjugal visits is a constitutional violation. But with the current standards of visiting, there was no constitutional right found by this court.

Perhaps a more intriguing argument is that raised by the claim in the *Lyons* case that authorities were denying inmates and their wives access to bedroom activities, which constituted an unwarranted invasion of their privacy. The federal court rejected that argument, saying that the cases that had recognized a privacy right in the First Amendment were distinguishable:

> **[T]he right of privacy on which plaintiffs rely is bottomed on the need to ensure private citizens that the police will not intrude upon their most intimate affairs. It does not follow, however, that because the state cannot pass criminal laws the enforcement of which will require such intrusion, the state is obligated by the Constitution to create private places for the conduct of marital relations . . . [I]mprisonment of persons convicted of crimes is not tantamount to an intrusion into the prisoner's home.**

The court concluded that there was no constitutional violation when authorities failed to provide for conjugal visits, thereby preventing acts of sexual intimacy between prisoners and their wives during their visits.

A conjugal visitation program in New York State gained court approval in *Matter of Mary of Oakknoll v. Coughlin,* 475 N.Y.S.2d 644 (NY App. Div. 1984). Some inmates complained that the program was limited to those inmates (and their spouses) who could show a valid marriage certificate to verify their married status. The court upheld the program and its restrictions. That court noted that there was no constitutional right to conjugal visitation. Prison officials had the authority, the court said, to authorize visiting programs. Conjugal visiting was, in effect, just one type of visiting. The standards for visiting of any type were for the officials to determine, based on their corrections experience and judgment. Another federal court later confirmed that the commissioner of corrections in New York had discretion to determine what the prison visitation program should be and which inmates would be able to participate in the conjugal visitation program. *Cromwell v. Coughlin,* 773 F.Supp. 606 (S.D. NY 1991).

An example of a current conjugal visitation program is that operated by the Mississippi Department of Corrections (MDOC).

> Conjugal visits are offered to inmates under the care of MDOC. However, there are strict guidelines and procedures. Conjugal visits are only allowed to eligible legally married inmates (married is defined as the union of a man and a woman). The spouse of the inmate must provide proof of

marriage. Common law marriages are not considered legal marriages as defined by MDOC, and therefore do not qualify for conjugal visit privileges.

Inmates that qualify for conjugal visits are those that are "A" or "B" custody (minimum custody levels) and maintain an acceptable level of good behavior. In addition, eligible inmates cannot have a rule violation report (a report that is written after a rule is broken such as fighting, swearing, etc.) in the last 6 months.

Inmates that are identified to be at risk of transmitting HIV or any other sexually transmitted disease (syphilis, gonorrhea, etc.) to a non-infected person are not eligible for conjugal visits. Inmates are given one hour for a conjugal visit and provided with the following items: soap, condoms, tissue, sheets, pillowcase, face towel and a bath towel. The inmate and spouse are searched before and after each visit for security reasons.[6]

■ Artificial Insemination

There is a fundamental right to procreation, as determined by the Supreme Court in *Skinner v. Oklahoma*, 316 U.S. 535 (1942). Interestingly, one of the six states (California) that allows conjugal visits refused an inmate's request to artificially inseminate his wife.

In *Gerber v. Hickman*, 291 F.3d 617 (9th Cir. 2002), Gerber, a 41-year-old man serving a sentence of 100 years to life plus 11 years, asked to receive a plastic collection container along with a prepaid return mailer from a laboratory; he wanted to be allowed to ejaculate into the container and to have the filled container returned to a laboratory in the prepaid mailer by overnight mail or have it picked up by his counsel. The inmate said he would pay all costs for this procedure.

The inmate sued when his request was denied.[7] The district court in California dismissed the suit for failure to state a claim, ruling that an inmate does not have a constitutional right to procreate and that such a right is "fundamentally inconsistent with incarceration." The Court of Appeals for the Ninth Circuit affirmed:

> **[T]he Supreme Court in *Turner* recognized that an inmate's right to marry while in prison did not include the inmate's right to consummate the marriage while in prison or to enjoy the other tangible aspects of marital intimacy … [T]he Court clearly stated that the right to marry "is subject to substantial restrictions as a result of incarceration," and that inmate marriages are formed "in the *expectation* that they *ultimately* will be fully consummated." … The Court plainly envisioned that while the intangible and emotional aspects of marriage survive incarceration, the physical aspects do not.**

The Ninth Circuit's decision, however, was not unanimous. A dissenter said there was nothing in the record to show that the right to have a child was fundamentally inconsistent with incarceration; he would have remanded the case for further proceedings to determine whether legitimate penological objectives justified the restriction. A second dissenter suggested that, by allowing conjugal visiting, the state did not intend to deprive an inmate of the right to procreate. This dissenter believed that this decision suggested that the state's denial was nothing more than "the ad hoc decision of prison authorities."

An earlier Missouri case, *Goodwin v. Turner*, 908 F.2d 1395 (8th Cir. 1990), offered at least a partial response to the "ad hoc" reference in the *Gerber* dissent. In *Goodwin*, a male inmate sought habeas corpus relief after denial by the Federal Bureau of Prisons of his request that he be allowed to artificially inseminate his wife. In denying the request, the Court of Appeals for the Eighth Circuit, applying *Turner v. Safley*, said the prison regulation met the reasonable relationship standard:

> **[I]f the Bureau [of Prisons] were forced to allow male prisoners to procreate, whatever the means, it would have to confer a corresponding benefit on its female prisoners. The significant expansion of medical services to the female population and the additional financial burden of added infant care would have a significant impact on the allocation of prison resources generally and would further undercut the Bureau's limited resources for necessary and important prison programs and security.**

SUMMARY

- The Supreme Court has recognized that the associational rights that persons would have in the "free world" may be limited by prison officials' concerns about prison order and stability (*Jones v. North Carolina Prisoners' Labor Union*). The fact that other organizations, such as the Boy Scouts and Alcoholics Anonymous, were allowed to organize and meet in prisons did not mean that a labor union was constitutionally entitled to organize and meet under equal protection analysis. The Court held that the prison authorities had reasonable grounds for distinguishing between the groups and were not required to treat all groups alike.

- Prison regulations that banned interviews by the news media of individual inmates were upheld by the Supreme Court. Under the freedom of press guarantee of the First Amendment, members of the news media have no more right of access to prisons than the general public (*Pell v. Procunier; Saxbe v. Washington Post*). Extending the ruling about limited access by the media to prisons and jails, a federal appeals court upheld a Texas rule that excluded news media from filming executions (*Garrett v. Estelle*). Prison officials may create a blanket exclusion of face-to-face media interviews for death row inmates, while permitting such interviews with offenders in other prisons (*Hammer v. Ashcroft*).

- Visiting in prisons and jails is a valued activity. There are two kinds of visits: contact and noncontact. In noncontact visits, a physical barrier (usually glass) remains between the inmate and his visitor; in contact visits, there is no such barrier, and inmates and their visitors are seated in ordinary chairs and are permitted to have some degree of physical contact.

- The Supreme Court upheld a policy at the Los Angeles County Jail that only allowed non-contact visiting by detainees with their family and friends who visited. The Court said that there is no constitutional requirement for contact visits and that jail administrators had good security reasons to limit visits (*Block v. Rutherford*).

- In another visiting case, the Supreme Court ruled that prison officials were not required to provide a hearing before terminating the visiting privileges of persons who were deemed to pose a threat to institutional security or the orderly running of the visiting room (*Kentucky Department of Corrections v. Thompson*). The holding of that case is probably still valid, although the reasoning the Court used is cast in doubt by a 1995 Supreme Court decision in *Sandin v. Conner.*

- The Supreme Court ruled that where a regulation bears a reasonable relation to legitimate penological interests, a visiting policy that limits visits by an inmate's children and places other restrictions on visits was constitutionally permissible (*Overton v. Bazzetta*).

- Conjugal visits are allowed in a few states. There is little in the way of constitutional law on conjugal visitation. The Supreme Court has not had any case ruling on this issue; however, one federal court ruled that there is no constitutional right to conjugal visits *(Lyons v. Gilligan)*. In New York, courts ruled that visiting policies were up to the prison officials and that it was permissible for New York to limit conjugal visits to spouses (*Matter of Mary of Oakknoll v. Coughlin; Cromwell v. Coughlin*).

- There are few legal cases on the right of prisoners to pursue artificial insemination. Appeals courts have so far applied the *Turner* standard and have held that requests for artificial insemination may be denied by prison authorities, based on their legitimate penological concerns (*Gerber v. Hickman; Goodwin v. Turner*).

THINKING ABOUT IT

Inmate John Doe is in a same-sex relationship with a person in the community. In the correctional facility where Doe is incarcerated, family members, including spouses, may kiss and hug during visits. Doe's correctional facility also has a rule that persons of the same sex may not engage in such physical contact unless they are relatives or immediate family. Correctional officials adopted the rule to promote institution security on the grounds that inmates identified as homosexuals could be targeted for physical, sexual, or verbal abuse. Doe and the community person bring suit in federal court challenging the rule as violative of their rights under the First Amendment and the Equal Protection clause. Under *Turner v. Safley*, how do you think the court will rule? *Whitmire v. Arizona*, 298 F.3d 1134 (9th Cir. 2002).

KEY TERMS

capital punishment: The sanction of the death penalty. Now used only with great procedural protections, in cases where it is authorized by criminal statute.

conjugal visits: Visits with a spouse. In corrections, the term has come to refer to programs that allow an inmate and spouse to be together in separate facilities, away from the common visiting room, where they have more privacy and the opportunity for sexual intimacy.

ENDNOTES

1. In *Jordan v. Pugh*, 504 F.Supp. 2d 1109, (D. CO 2007), an inmate housed in the Administrative Maximum Unit, Florence, Colorado challenged the Federal Bureau of Prisons (BOP) rule prohibiting an inmate from being published under a byline, alleging that the rule was an unconstitutional violation of the First Amendment. The prohibition was based on the "big wheel" theory. In its opinion, the district court said: "[a]t trial, the BOP presented no evidence of any instance where an inmate who published under a byline in the news media became a 'big wheel,' or more importantly, became a security risk."

   The court held that the "existence of a 'big wheel' security risk arising from an inmate's bylined publication in the news media is undocumented and speculative." Using both the two-part *Martinez* test (whether the restriction further an important or substantial governmental interest unrelated to the suppression of expression and is no broader than necessary to protect the particular governmental interest) and the four-part *Turner v. Safley* test (rational connection between the regulation and a legitimate, neutral penological objective; whether alternative means exist; impact of the accommodation; and whether there were alternatives that could be applied at a de minimis cost), the court found the regulation violated the First Amendment rights of prisoners. (Note: The Bureau of Prisons current rule (Title 28, Code of Federal Regulations, Section 540.20) has removed language prohibiting an inmate from publishing under a byline.)

2. In *Entertainment Network, Inc. v. Lappin*, 134 F.Supp.2d 1002 (S.D. IN 2001), an internet content provider sued, seeking to do a live internet broadcast of the execution of Timothy McVeigh (the Oklahoma City bomber, see endnote 3 below). This court reaffirmed the position that the press has no constitutional right of access to prisons or prison inmates beyond that given to the general public.

3. The inmate had bombed the Murrah Federal Building in Oklahoma City, killing 168 people. He was seen by authorities as using the television appearance to "justify and extol terrorism."

4. Members of the clergy and attorneys on official business could visit without being listed.

5. The *2002 Corrections Yearbook* reported that six states allowed conjugal visits. These were California, Connecticut, Mississippi, New Mexico, New York, and Washington. Camp, C. G., ed. *The 2002 Corrections Yearbook—Adult Corrections* (Middletown, CT: Criminal Justice Institute, 2003), 149. In some states, this type of visiting program may be known as family visiting or family reunion.

6. Mississippi Department of Corrections. *Conjugal Visits*. Accessed February 6, 2011 from http://www.mdoc.state.ms.us/conjugal_visits.htm.

7. Title 15, California Code, Section 3174(e)(2) denied family visits for inmates "sentenced to life without the possibility of parole [or] sentenced to life, without a parole date established by the Board of Prison Terms."

9 First Amendment: Religion

Inmates clearly retain protections afforded by the First Amendment, including its directive that no law shall prohibit the free exercise of religion.

U.S. Supreme Court, *O'Lone v. Shabazz*

Chapter Outline

- Establishment of Religion
- Faith-Based Initiatives
- *Cruz v. Beto*
- Freedom to Exercise Religion in Prisons
- *O'Lone v. Shabazz*
- Religious Freedom Restoration Act (RFRA)
- Religious Land Use and Institutionalized Persons Act of 2000 (RLUIPA)
- Other Free Exercise Issues in Prisons
  - Diet
  - Grooming
- Unusual Religious Groups

Another of the highly protected rights of the First Amendment, and the first one mentioned there, is religion:

Congress shall make no law respecting an establishment of religion, or prohibiting the free exercise thereof.

The language of this phrase applies to "Congress," and, therefore, to the federal government. The Supreme Court uses the Fourteenth Amendment to apply the religion phrases to the states. This is not one phrase but two: the establishment clause and the free exercise clause. The government cannot (1) establish religion or (2) prohibit the exercising of one's religion. Although there are two freedoms protected, the press—and sometimes even teachers and the courts—are not careful to distinguish which of the "freedom of religion" phrases is being used. The kind of protection is different under each one.

As an exercise in your understanding of "establishment" as opposed to "free exercise," consider the following, which are some of the most publicized issues decided under the First Amendment. Which of these were decided under the establishment clause, and which were decided under the free exercise clause?

1. persons handing out religious material in an airport terminal
2. conscientious objection—not having to serve in the military because of religious reasons
3. putting a nativity scene on the courthouse lawn
4. polygamy—being allowed to have several wives
5. paying for chaplains in the military with government funds
6. persons driving around a quiet residential neighborhood with religious messages blaring from a speaker on their truck
7. prayer, or Bible readings, in public schools[1]

■ Establishment of Religion

The establishment of religion clause is rarely discussed in law and practice. In corrections law, there are very few cases under the establishment clause.

One of the most interesting religion cases was *Theriault v. Carlson*, 339 F.Supp. 375 (N.D. GA 1973) and 495 F.2d 390 (5th Cir. 1974); also *Theriault v. Silber*, 391 F.Supp. 578 (W.D. TX 1975); and many other reported cases involving inmate–plaintiff Theriault. In *Theriault v. Carlson*, Theriault and another inmate, while confined in the Atlanta Penitentiary, challenged federal authorities to allow them to practice their religion. These inmates had created a religion called Church of the New Song (CONS—its membership was restricted to those in prison!). They wrote scriptural texts and demanded group meetings and other activities. Although most of these claims in court were based on the "free exercise" clause, one claim was tied to the establishment clause: Theriault asked to be paid as a chaplain of his group, like other prison chaplains. If this didn't happen, he claimed that prison authorities should terminate religious programs funded by the government (chapels, Bibles, and Korans paid for with government money and the paid employment of chaplains on the staff).

The federal court (the main discussion on establishment is in the original district court decision in northern Georgia) held that it was permissible to have chaplaincy programs in prisons. The court likened them to those in the military, which had already been upheld by the courts. (We will look at the other claims of Theriault in the "free exercise" section later in this chapter.)

There is language in a leading Supreme Court decision that provides good guidance regarding what government should or should not do under the First Amendment. In *Abington School District v. Schempp*, 374 U.S. 203 (1963), the Supreme Court held:

> **The state must be steadfastly neutral in all matters of faith, and neither favor nor inhibit religion … [H]ostility, not neutrality, would characterize the refusal to provide chaplains and places of worship for prisoners and soldiers cut off by the state from all civilian opportunities for public communion.**

Because *Abington* was a school-prayer case and did not involve prisons, this language endorsing chaplains and chapels for the military and prisons is dictum and not the case holding. It is a strong indication, however, and a strong discouragement to litigating this issue, that the Court does not consider the use of public monies for chaplaincy programs in prison to be a violation of the establishment clause. The first sentence of the previous quotation is a generic constitutional admonition for governments to use in assessing their position in questions concerning the "establishment of religion."

The establishment clause does not specifically identify prohibited conduct, but *Abington*, and other Supreme Court decisions, such as *Everson v. Board of Education*, 330 U.S. 1 (1947), provide guidance. In *Everson*, the Court noted:

> **The 'establishment of religion' clause of the First Amendment means at least this: Neither a state nor the Federal Government can set up a church. Neither can pass laws which aid one religion, aid all religions, or prefer one religion over another. Neither can force nor influence a person to go to or to remain away from church against his will or force him to profess a belief or disbelief in any religion ... Neither a state nor the Federal Government can, openly or secretly, participate in the affairs of any religious organizations or groups and vice versa.**

Bowen v. Kendrick, 487 U.S. 589 (1988), addresses another establishment question. *Bowen* concerned a challenge to the Adolescent Family Life Act, which allowed federal grants to public or nonprofit private organizations or agencies for services and research in the area of premarital adolescent sexual relations and pregnancy. Noting the complexity of the problem, the act named a number of entities, including religious organizations, whose involvement was seen as important. The district court had held that the act violated the establishment clause because it provided for the involvement of religious organizations in the federally funded programs. The case was appealed directly to the Supreme Court. The Court held that the act, on its face, did not violate the establishment clause. The Court held that if both secular and religious objectives influence the government's practice, there is no violation of the establishment clause, provided the government's expressed purposes are sincere. These holdings have a direct relevance to the current focus on faith-based initiatives, which have been government-sponsored programs that take place in corrections.

■ Faith-Based Initiatives

Within two weeks of taking office in 2001, President George W. Bush issued Executive Orders 13198 and 13199. Respectively, these orders (1) covered agency responsibilities with respect to faith-based and community initiatives and (2) established the White House Office of Faith-Based and Community Initiatives (White House OFBCI). The White House OFBCI was to "establish policies, priorities, and objectives for the Federal Government's comprehensive effort to enlist, equip, enable, empower, and expand the work of faith-based and other community organizations to the extent permitted by law." Selected federal agencies (specifically, the Attorney General and the Secretaries of Education, Labor, Health and Human Services, and Housing and Urban Development) were directed to establish a Center for Faith-Based and Community Initiatives, whose purpose would be to "coordinate department efforts to eliminate regulatory, contracting, and other programmatic obstacles to the participation of faith-based and other community organizations in the provision of social services." Additional executive orders on this subject have been issued since January 2001, including President Obama's February 2009 amendment to Executive Order 13199.[2]

As you recall, we previously said that only a few prison cases are brought under the establishment clause. However, with the recent introduction of faith-based initiatives in a number of states, as well as in the federal government, new challenges to the establishment clause have arisen. Those in support of faith-based programs in prison suggest that such programs can help an inmate learn self-restraint and become a better citizen upon release. These program goals certainly appear worthwhile and are secular in nature. The issue in prison litigation may focus on exactly how this is achieved and whether the programs violate the First Amendment's establishment clause.

One example of a challenge to faith-based initiatives occurred in the Iowa state correctional system. The Iowa Department of Corrections (DOC), starting in 1999, contracted with a religious-based organization to provide programming with the purpose of providing "a positive influence in prison" and to assist prisoners, upon release, in becoming "contributing members of society." *Americans United for Separation of Church and State v. Prison Fellowship Ministries, Inc.*, 509 F.3d 406 (8th Cir. 2007). The program included both study and work based on Christian values, but a participant did not have to be Christian to participate. Participants in the program were housed in a separate unit. Participation in the program was voluntary and there were no incentives, such as early release. Until July 2007, DOC funding made up 30–40% of the religious program's operating cost. The contracts required government funds cover only "the non-religious aspects" or "the non-sectarian portion."

In analyzing whether the program violated the establishment clause of the First Amendment, the court of appeals addressed two issues: Did the state act with the purpose of inhibiting or advancing religion? Did the aid have the effect of advancing or inhibiting religion? Relying upon an earlier Supreme Court opinion, *Agostini v. Felton*, 521 U.S. 203 (1997), both the district court and the court of appeals concluded that the state's intention was secular—to offer inmates comprehensive programs and reduce recidivism—with no purpose of either advancing or inhibiting religion. As to the second issue, the district court found, and the court of appeals agreed, that the program, as implemented in Iowa, advanced and endorsed religion in violation of the establishment clause. The court specifically noted that the program was "dominated by Bible study, Christian classes, religious revivals, and church services." The court concluded that for an inmate to enter the program and use the government funding, the inmate had to agree to "productively participate in a program that is Christian-based." The court found that the program violated the establishment clause of the First Amendment.[3]

■ Cruz v. Beto

For many years, the only guidance from the Supreme Court on prison religion issues was in *Cruz v. Beto*, 405 U.S. 319 (1972). This was a per curiam decision of the Court, meaning that it was a summary opinion without full-blown analysis and discussion, as would be found in the regular opinions of the Court. (This per curiam decision was somewhat unusual in that two justices only concurred in the case and one justice dissented. Such divisions are uncommon in per curiam decisions.) This was a Section 1983 action by Cruz, a Texas inmate, who claimed to be a Buddhist. He was not allowed to use the prison chapel, or to correspond with a Buddhist religious advisor, and could not share his religious materials with other inmates. For his attempts to hand out literature, he was punished by being placed in solitary confinement. He also objected to other religious programs that provided Jewish and Christian Bibles and religious classes and services. The district court dismissed Cruz's complaints without a hearing, and the Fifth Circuit Court of Appeals affirmed.

The Supreme Court, although conceding that prison officials must be given wide latitude in the running of prisons (it was this deference to prison administrators' discretion that led the lower courts to dismiss the complaints), said that prison complaints based on constitutional challenges must be more closely examined. In this case, the complaints had been summarily dismissed, and the Court said that that was too hasty.

> **If Cruz was a Buddhist and if he was denied a reasonable opportunity of pursuing his faith comparable to the opportunity afforded fellow prisoners who adhere to conventional religious precepts, then there was palpable discrimination by the State against the Buddhist religion.**

This sounds like an "equal protection" analysis, reasoning that if Texas allows activities by one religious group, it must (constitutionally) be prepared to offer similar activities to other religions. Again, it is not a fully-developed opinion—but it is a statement of law from the Supreme Court, and it is therefore binding as a constitutional standard. In addition, the Court clearly said that the First Amendment (the religion clause) was applicable to persons in prison.

■ Freedom to Exercise Religion in Prisons

"It is a matter of some interest to correctional administrators and to lawyers that the 'correctional law revolution' can be traced to religious cases—specifically, to cases brought by Black Muslim prisoners in the early 1960s."[4] The courts had a "hands-off" attitude toward prisons for many decades. In more recent times, courts have reversed this attitude, and, indeed, there are literally thousands of prisoners' rights lawsuits filed, and many hundreds decided every year, even in the face of the discouragement intended by the Prison Reform Litigation Act. It is our assertion that this opening-up of the courts to review prison programs and activities can be traced to the "Black Muslim" litigation in federal courts in the early 1960s. This religious group, led at the time by Elijah Muhammad (a former federal inmate himself), gained followers among black inmates, as well as many black citizens in the community, particularly in the large cities—Chicago, New York, Los Angeles, Washington, DC, and others. Although there were a few prisoners' rights cases before 1961, they were sporadic and led to no body of case law that protected the rights of prisoners in any significant area.

The Black Muslims made demands for prison authorities to recognize their group and allow religious activities. Some states denied that the Nation of Islam (the Black Muslims) was a religion and litigated this issue. (The early cases from New York State, for example, showed that approach to the litigation, contesting whether the Nation of Islam was, in fact, a religion.) If it was not a religion, it would not be entitled to First Amendment protection at all. Courts have been notably reluctant to tackle this issue of what is, in fact, a religion, though one court did address the issue and concluded that the Black Muslim faith was indeed a religion.[5]

Once that entry issue was decided, there was a flurry of complaints and demands from Black Muslim inmates, particularly in California, New York, and the District of Columbia. These dealt with the rights to hold services; pursue religious instruction; have visits from religious leaders; have correspondence with religious persons in the community; obtain religious writings; wear religious medals and other apparel (shawls, robes, kufis, sandals); and obtain funding for chaplains or other religious assistance and materials. As a result of this litigation, and of concessions by prison administrators because of the pressures of the litigation, Black Muslims were permitted to engage in a range of activities in prisons, at least in those jurisdictions with large urban populations where the lawsuits were brought.

■ *O'Lone v. Shabazz*

For many years, the only Supreme Court ruling on prison religious activities was its 1972 decision in *Cruz v. Beto.* There was some guidance from lower federal courts in cases dealing with free exercise claims by various religious groups in the community, and the lower courts were embroiled in many prison cases that raised religious issues. In *O'Lone v. Shabazz*, 482 U.S. 342 (1987), the Supreme Court finally gave a clear ruling on prisoners' free exercise rights in prison.

Shabazz and other Muslim inmates at a state prison in New Jersey filed suit, claiming that prison regulations interfered with their ability to attend Jumu'ah prayers in the institution. Because of security concerns and demands on staff time, prison officials prohibited inmates who were working on outside work details from coming back inside the prison during the day, except for emergencies. This prevented Muslims on the outside work details from attending Jumu'ah service, which the parties agreed was a religious dictate (the most important service of the week) of their sincerely held religious beliefs. The district court had held that the challenged prison rules were permissible, because they advanced the goals of security, order, and rehabilitation. The court of appeals reversed, saying that the free exercise rights of the prisoners had been violated without the state showing whether some method of accommodation could be achieved, taking into account the prison's concerns about crowding, understaffing, and the possibilities of disruption.

The Supreme Court rejected this ruling of the court of appeals, which would have required prison officials to prove there was "no reasonable method" that would have accommodated these inmates' rights to observe "a central religious practice." The Supreme Court emphasized that the courts should respect and defer to the judgment of the prison officials. Regarding the restrictions imposed in this case, the Court found that prison officials acted reasonably and with good cause. Looking at the reasons for the adoption of the prison policy, the Court found that there were no obvious, easy alternatives to the policy that New Jersey officials had adopted.

In *O'Lone*, the Supreme Court set out the standards that govern analysis of prisoners' constitutional claims:

> **To ensure that courts afford appropriate deference to prison officials, we have determined that prison regulations alleged to infringe constitutional rights are judged under a "reasonableness" test less restrictive than that ordinarily applied to alleged infringements of fundamental constitutional rights** [Citing ***Jones v. North Carolina Prisoners' Labor Union***]. **We recently restated the proper standard: "[W]hen a prison regulation impinges on inmates' constitutional rights, the regulation is valid if it is reasonably related to legitimate penological interests."** [Citing ***Turner v. Safley*, 482 U.S. 78 (1987)**]

New Jersey had a legitimate interest in maintaining security and order at the prison, the Supreme Court said, which led officials to adopt the policy that restricted inmates' rights to exercise their religion freely by attending Jumu'ah prayers. This reasonable restriction, in furtherance of a legitimate penological objective, the Court ruled, outweighed the First Amendment claim of inmates to practice their religion.

■ Religious Freedom Restoration Act (RFRA)

Having obtained a ruling from the Supreme Court that explained the standards for weighing the free exercise claims of prisoners, one would have thought that the matter was then just to apply those standards to the individual claims that would be raised under the First Amendment. We would ask, "Who, in our governmental system, has the authority to overturn the rulings of the Supreme Court?" Considering anything you have heard and read about our judicial system, you would probably answer, "No one has authority to overrule the Supreme Court." Especially on any question of interpretation of the U.S. Constitution, the Supreme Court is the final authority, and there is no further appeal.

This principle, however, was challenged by the U.S. Congress. In 1993, Congress enacted the Religious Freedom Restoration Act (RFRA is codified at Title 42, U.S. Code, Section 2000bb). This law was proposed and enacted specifically to overturn the standard for weighing governmental authority as opposed to individuals' religious freedoms, as set out in *O'Lone* and other rulings of the Supreme Court on religious matters. According to its statement of purpose in enacting RFRA, Congress cited its unhappiness with the 1990 ruling in the case of *Employment Division v. Smith*, 494 U.S. 872 (1990). There, the Supreme Court had pulled back from its earlier rulings that government would have to show a compelling interest in order to justify restrictions on the free exercise of religion. While not citing the Supreme Court decision in *O'Lone*, Congress had been made aware of the prison ruling and asked to exempt correctional facilities from RFRA. That request, in the form of an amendment, was rejected in a vote on the floor of Congress.

RFRA provides the following:

> Government may substantially burden a person's exercise of religion only if it demonstrates that application of the burden to the person—(1) is in furtherance of a compelling governmental interest; and (2) is the least restrictive means of furthering that compelling governmental interest.

"Government" as used in the law was defined (in Section 2000bb-2) as any agency or official of the United States, any state, or any subdivision of a state. Thus, by very specific language, Congress directed courts to use its interpretation of the First Amendment free exercise clause and not that of the Supreme Court.

This federal law raised a very serious question about the separation of powers of the government and whether Congress can enact a different interpretation of the Constitution than that given by the Supreme Court. Also, our government is one of specifically delegated powers, and there is nothing in the Constitution (specifically, in Article II of the Constitution, which sets out the powers of the federal Congress) that gives to the legislature the authority to interpret the Constitution or review the constitutional rulings of the Supreme Court.

City of Boerne v. Flores, 521 U.S. 507 (1997), dealt with a decision by local zoning officials in Texas to deny religious leaders a building permit to enlarge a church. The denial was based on an ordinance governing historic preservation in an area encompassing the church. The church's archbishop sued in U.S. district court, challenging the denial of the permit under RFRA. The trial court held that Congress, by enacting RFRA, had exceeded its constitutional powers. The Fifth Circuit Court of Appeals reversed, saying the act was constitutional, and the case went to the Supreme Court. That Court held that RFRA "exceeds Congress' power."

> **Congress does not enforce a constitutional right by changing what the right is. It has been given the power [in Section 5 of the Fourteenth Amendment] "to enforce," not the power to determine what constitutes a constitutional violation.**
>
> **The power to interpret the Constitution in a case or controversy remains in the Judiciary.**
>
> **It is for Congress in the first instance to "determin[e] whether and what legislation is needed to secure the guarantees of the Fourteenth Amendment," and its conclusions are entitled to much deference... Congress' discretion is not unlimited, however, and the courts retain the power... to determine if Congress has exceeded its authority under the Constitution. Broad as the power of Congress is under the Enforcement Clause of the Fourteenth Amendment, RFRA contradicts vital principles necessary to maintain separation of powers and the federal balance.**

The federal government has taken the position that the Court's decision in *Boerne* was limited to state and not federal action. Accordingly, for federal agencies and activities, the test contained in RFRA (whether compelling government interests are involved and whether they are upheld by the least restrictive means) remains the standard for free exercise claims raised under the First Amendment. For states, the former test for prison matters was reinstated: whether the government restriction is reasonably related to legitimate penological interests (as stated in *O'Lone* and *Turner*).[6]

◼ Religious Land Use and Institutionalized Persons Act of 2000 (RLUIPA)

Did *Boerne* then put this issue to rest? Apparently not. In September 2000, the Religious Land Use and Institutionalized Persons Act of 2000 was enacted (RLUIPA is codified in Title 42, U.S. Code, Section 2000cc), and it is applicable to state programs which use federal funding. The act focuses on two areas: (1) the protection of land use, when it is used for religious exercise and (2) the protection of religious exercise by institutionalized persons. Both contain the RFRA language the Supreme Court, in *Boerne*, had held unconstitutional as specifically applied to the states. RLUIPA prohibits states from imposing a substantial burden on the religious exercise of a person unless the government shows that imposing the burden furthers a compelling government interest and is the least restrictive means of furthering that compelling interest.

RLUIPA is a congressional effort to achieve its RFRA purposes by narrowing the focus to show a greater federal interest, one that Congress apparently believes is within its enforcement powers under Section 5 of the Fourteenth Amendment. As applied to institutionalized persons, the statute applies where the substantial burden on religious activity occurs in a program or activity that receives federal financial assistance or where the substantial burden would affect (or removal of that substantial burden would affect) commerce with foreign nations, among the states, or with Indian tribes.

As applied to institutionalized persons, would the Supreme Court find RLUIPA constitutional? In *Cutter v. Wilkinson*, 544 U.S. 709 (2005), current and former Ohio prison inmates, identifying themselves as followers of "nonmainstream" religions, claimed Ohio prison officials failed to allow their religious exercise, and that such denial was a violation of RLUIPA, section 3. This section prohibits state governments from imposing a substantial burden on an institutionalized person's religious exercise unless the government demonstrates that the burden placed on the person furthers "a compelling governmental interest" and does so by "the least restrictive means." In response, Ohio prison officials countered the inmates' claims under RLUIPA, arguing that the act violated the establishment clause of the First Amendment.

The district court rejected Ohio's argument, saying that on the "thin record before it, the court declined to find…that enforcement of RLUIPA, inevitably, would compromise prison security. The court of appeals reversed, holding that section 3 "impermissibly advance[es] religion by giving greater protection to religious rights than to other constitutionally protected rights."

The Supreme Court reversed, saying:

RLUIPA thus protects institutionalized persons who are unable freely to attend to their religious needs and are therefore dependent on the government's permission and accommodation for exercise of their religion.

The Court first established the premise that exercise of religion involves not only beliefs, but also the performance of physical acts, including assembling with others for worship and participating in religiously motivated activity. In recognizing the need of correctional administrators to balance correctional goals against religiously motivated activities, the Court said:

We do not read RLUIPA to elevate accommodation of religious observances over an institution's need to maintain order and safety.

The court further commented that lawmakers supporting RLUIPA were mindful of this need and that the lawmakers anticipated "that courts would apply the Act's standard with 'due deference to the experience and expertise of prison and jail administrators in establishing necessary regulations and procedures to maintain good order, security and discipline, consistent with consideration of costs and limited resources.'"[7] RLUIPA's requirements did not compel prison officials to accommodate a prisoner's religious observances at the expense of these interests.

In concluding that RLUIPA did not violate the establishment clause of the First Amendment, the Court noted that for more than 10 years the Federal Bureau of Prisons had operated under the compelling governmental interest standard (established by RFRA, discussed earlier in this chapter) "without compromising prison security, public safety, or the constitutional rights of other prisoners."

A final comment on *Cutter*. In *Cutter,* Ohio officials made a **facial challenge** to the constitutionality of a RLUIPA provision. This type of challenge claims that the statute itself is unconstitutional. Ohio did not claim unconstitutionality under the facts of any specific inmate cases. The district court, noting the underdeveloped record, said a finding "that it is *factually impossible* to provide the kind of accommodations that RLUIPA will require without significantly compromising prison security or the levels of service provided to other inmates cannot be made at this juncture." The Supreme Court agreed.

Another issue that RLUIPA generated was whether a prison inmate could seek money damages for violations of the statute directly from the state. Under the concept of sovereign immunity, most sovereign governments (the federal and state governments) waived their sovereign immunity for certain types of suits (e.g., torts). In *Sossamon v. Texas,* 563 U.S. __ (2011), a state prisoner sued several defendants, including the state of Texas, alleging that a state policy which prohibited inmates from participating in group religious activities in the prison chapel and some inmates on disciplinary restrictions from participating in group religious activities violated the prisoner's free exercise of religion rights under RLUIPA. The prisoner sought injunctive relief and money damages both from individual state officials and the state itself. The state argued that it had not waived its sovereign immunity from suits for money damages. The only question which the Supreme Court addressed is whether the state of Texas, by accepting money from the federal government, waived its sovereign immunity for money damages. The Supreme Court ruled:

> We conclude that States, in accepting federal funding, do not consent to waive their sovereign immunity to private suits for money damages under RLUIPA because no statute expressly and unequivocally includes such a waiver.

It is expected that RLUIPA will continue to generate litigation about how correctional agencies must accommodate the religious rights of prisoners. These issues include questions as to when a prisoner's religious rights have been substantially burdened, whether the government's interest in restricting the rights is a compelling one, and if so, did the government choose the least restrictive means of furthering that governmental interest which is involved in the circumstances.

■ Other Free Exercise Issues in Prisons

Many kinds of religious activities and special provisions for religious exercise have been requested by prison inmates. When denied or restricted, lawsuits (usually under 42 U.S.C. § 1983) have been brought. We will discuss just a few of these. It should be noted that earlier court decisions (those decided before RLUIPA) may receive a different analysis and holding, in light of RLUIPA.

Diet

Both Muslim and Jewish inmates have asked that they be provided specially prepared foods, based on the religious dietary laws of their faiths. The dietary requirements of the two religions are similar in that adherents of both religions refrain from eating pork or anything that comes into contact with pork. Muslims would ask that the meat that they eat be slaughtered in special rites, with a prayer being said at the time of slaughter (Hallal). Strict Jewish diets are called kosher and follow religious laws for the preparation and serving of food (kashruth laws).

Some courts held that special meals did not have to be prepared for Muslim inmates, as long as they could nutritionally sustain themselves by eating what was served to all inmates, while refraining from eating pork or pork products. To assist them in doing this, some prisons mark (with an asterisk, for example) those items on the menu board that contain any pork.[8]

Jewish dietary requirements are complex, requiring not only specially prepared foods but also the separation of pots, pans, and eating utensils (milk and meat products must be strictly separated), and the inspection of food storage, preparation, and serving areas by rabbinical authorities. Courts have divided on whether prisons must meet these dietary requirements for observant Jews, but one court held that "prison authorities must accommodate the right of prisoners to receive diets consistent with their religious scruples." *Kahane v. Carlson*, 527 F.2d 492 (2nd Cir. 1975). That court brushed aside objections that such special food preparation would be extremely burdensome and expensive for prison authorities, saying that this problem would be surmountable "in view of the small number of practicing orthodox Jews in federal prisons," which would not exceed approximately 12 persons. The problem with this estimate made by the *Kahane* court was that following the laws of Kashruth is not limited to orthodox Jews; any Jew, as an individual matter, may choose to follow these laws. When kosher foods were made available, scores of Jewish inmates requested that diet. (Whether this was as a consequence of individual religious conviction, a desire to create administrative headaches for authorities, or a perception that the kosher diet would be better than the regular inmate dining room fare was not clear.)

What is virtually impossible for prison officials to do is to base the provision of such special religious items as diet on the sincerity or the "orthodoxy" of the inmate's beliefs. The courts have shown reluctance to inquire into the sincerity of religious beliefs, and as a practical matter, testing "sincerity" is an administrative nightmare. Having said that, individual sincerity is challenged by some prison authorities and examined by some courts. If it can be shown that the inmate's dietary request is not religiously motivated, then there is no First Amendment issue.

The courts have considered a few factors to determine religious sincerity: whether the inmate participates in other religious observances at the prison, whether the inmate eats food that is not consistent with his religious beliefs, and whether she purchases commissary items contrary to her religious views. What is not acceptable is for prison officials to make their finding based on a determination that the beliefs fall outside the main or customary tenets of the stated religion.

An example of religious diet for a different religion is *DeHart v. Horn*, 227 F.3d 47 (3rd Cir. 2000), where a state prison inmate taught himself Buddhism during his confinement. From his readings of Buddhist religious texts (Sutras), DeHart became a vegetarian, based on a precept in Buddhism that prohibits the killing of any living thing. DeHart went through the state grievance process and was denied special food. The state's position was that a vegetarian diet is not mandated by any recognized Buddhist sect. In denying preliminary injunctive relief, the circuit court said the court's task was to decide if the beliefs were sincerely held and religious in nature in the individual's "scheme of things." The case was remanded for an analysis under the *Turner* standards in order to decide whether the prison restrictions were reasonably related to a legitimate prison objective.

In *Jackson v. Mann*, 196 F.3d 316 (2nd Cir. 1999), an inmate was denied a kosher diet following a determination by the prison chaplain that the inmate failed to meet the requirement to be a Jew (either being born Jewish or completing a formal conversion process). The inmate filed suit under 42 U.S.C. § 1983. The district court granted summary judgment to the prison officials, saying the inmate had provided no proof that he was Jewish "according to the practices of the Jewish religion." The circuit court reversed and remanded, saying the focus must be on whether the inmate's belief is religious and sincerely held, not whether it follows ecclesiastical law.

Where challenged, most corrections facilities have made some accommodation to Jewish inmates' dietary requests. Like the *Kahane* court, most judges would require "the provision of a diet sufficient to sustain the prisoner in good health without violating the Jewish dietary laws." How to accomplish this is left to prison officials. Although some have attempted to set up a kosher kitchen, doing this within a prison is very difficult. Some institutions have ordered frozen or prepared foods from the outside, which are certified as being kosher. Others have tried to provide a selection of food items that are regularly prepared for all inmates, such as raw fruits and vegetables, boiled eggs, and canned fish, so that the Jewish inmates can have a kosher diet by selecting those permissible items from the food line.

In *Beerheide v. Suthers*, 286 F.3d 1179 (10th Cir. 2002), the department of corrections (DOC) in Colorado appealed a district court decision, holding not only that the DOC had to provide inmates a kosher diet, but must provide the diet without requiring a contribution from the inmates. The court also found no acceptable alternative means for the inmates to exercise the right to maintain a kosher diet. The court rejected the department's suggestion that the inmates could purchase such meals in the commissary because the evidence showed the inmate–plaintiffs were not financially able to do this. It rejected the suggestion that kosher food could be provided by members of the community, saying the Jewish community could not be expected or required to provide food to the inmates. The court also rejected the offering of the prison common fare program (which served vegetarian meals or meals prepared with no pork or pork by-products). The court held that this program did not meet such factors required by kosher rules as the storage, source, and preparation of the ingredients and the service of meals.

This federal court also rejected the DOC's proposal that inmates taking part in the kosher meal program be required to make a co-payment of no more than 25% of the additional cost of providing the meals. The district court found that under this proposal an inmate maintaining a kosher diet would be expected to pay $90 per month, incurring a debt to his prison account if unable to pay. The court determined that an inmate living solely on earnings from prison work received a maximum of approximately $57 per month, thus incurring a debt of $30 each month. While some inmates might have more than the minimal income earned from work, the court noted, "Forcing prisoners to decide between communicating with family and legal representatives, seeking medical treatment, and following religious tenets constitutes a Hobson's choice rather than a true alternative."[9]

The Colorado DOC also argued that there was an adverse impact on financial resources and staff and administrative resources. The court held that there was insufficient information provided by the department in support of its position. Finally, the district court found that providing inmates with kosher meals free of charge, coupled with a selective screening process unrelated to money,[10] was an alternative with only a slight impact on the department's food budget. The federal appeals court affirmed these holdings of the district court.

In another case concerning religious diet, a federal inmate at Texarkana, Texas asked to be provided with a diet consistent with his religious beliefs, which were not of any widely known religious group but were based on his interpretations of certain Biblical texts. The inmate insisted on only organically grown produce, which was to be washed in distilled water. A lower court held that meeting the inmate's demands would put an undue burden on the prison system. In *Udey v. Kastner*, 805 F.2d 1218 (5th Cir. 1986), the appeals court held that providing such special dietary requests would lead to a probable proliferation of claims for special food. Having to process such multiple dietary claims, and trying to meet them, would pose "undue costs and administrative burdens" to the government. On this ground, the inmate's requests for the special diet were denied.

A similar concern was the basis for a federal court ruling in New York in *Benjamin v. Coughlin*, 708 F.Supp. 570 (S.D. NY 1989). There, Rastafarians asked for a special diet, based on their religious teachings. The diet involved no meat, foods raised only with organic fertilizers, and food cooked in natural materials, such as clay pots. The court in the *Benjamin* case ruled that prison authorities did not have to supply those food items, because they were too complex, and providing them would present too heavy a financial and administrative burden.

The number of different religions with special dietary needs can pose a large burden on a corrections facility that tries to accommodate all the various demands. (This would seem to be especially true in facilities in large cities or large corrections systems.) With demands on staff for supervising the preparation and serving of special foods and the increased costs of providing special religious diets, the administrative burdens can become immense. Verifying the true dietary requirements of religious groups and making sure the special food supplies from outside the prison, as well as those separated and prepared inside the prison, meet religious requirements, add to the burden. While most administrators would like to respect religious beliefs and teachings and see inmates adhere to and strengthen their religious ties to the community, doing this equitably and respectfully in response to numerous religious requests for special diets can become an overwhelming task.

In a special dietary request that was well publicized at the time, members of the Church of the New Song (CONS, the inmate-founded religion that we discussed earlier in this chapter) requested that filet mignon and sherry be provided for a special sacramental meal. By this time, the federal court in northern Georgia had held that the inmates in CONS were entitled to First Amendment (free exercise) protection. That court, in *Theriault v. Carlson*, 339 F.Supp. 375 (N.D. GA 1973) had ordered authorities at the Atlanta Penitentiary to permit group meetings, religious instruction by the CONS leaders, and religious writings to be mailed and received. However, the request for steak and wine went too far and was not approved. Later, a different court in Texas (where Theriault was then confined) ruled that the Church of the New Song was a "masquerade," a philosophy seeking to cause disruption in prisons, and was not a religion at all. *Theriault v. Silber*, 391 F.Supp. 578 (W.D. TX 1975). We should note that federal courts in Iowa ruled that the Church of the New Song was a religion and was entitled to the protections of the First Amendment. Based on that finding, the authorities at the Iowa State Penitentiary were ordered to allow CONS to exercise their religion equally with other religions in *Remmers v. Brewer*, 494 F.2d 1277 (8th Cir. 1974).

Levitan v. Ashcroft, 281 F.3d 1313 (DC Cir. 2002) was a case involving Federal Bureau of Prisons inmates who were practicing Catholic Christians. The inmates challenged the Bureau's rule barring their drinking of small amounts of wine as part of Communion (a Catholic sacrament). Under that rule, only the supervising chaplain was allowed to consume the wine. The inmates argued that the prohibition violated the free exercise clause of the First Amendment. The district court ruled in favor of the prison officials, saying that under the First Amendment a religious practice must be mandated by the inmate's religion. The Court of Appeals for the DC Circuit disagreed and held that the proper approach was to use the *Turner* and *O'Lone* balancing standard. Because this was not done by the district court, the decision of the lower court was reversed and the case remanded for fact finding under a *Turner* and *O'Lone* analysis. (The decision in *Levitan* was handed down in March 2002; in August of that year, the Bureau of Prisons revised its policy to allow inmates to receive, under the supervision of clergy, a small amount of wine as part of a religious ritual.)

Application of the requirements of RFRA or RLUIPA in the area of religious dietary practices requires additional analysis. In the first instance, a prisoner must demonstrate that his or her religious beliefs were substantially burdened. While the Supreme Court has not addressed what constitutes a "substantial burden," the lower courts have generally ruled that a "substantial burden" occurs when the government, through act or omission, puts substantial pressure on individuals to modify their behavior and violate their religious beliefs.

In *Lovelace v. Lee*, 472 F.3d 174 (4th Cir. 2006), the court held that a substantial burden under RLUIPA is imposed by a prison's practice of removing an inmate from what was called the Ramadan Observance pass list, as this removal precludes the inmate from not only the special pre-dawn and post-sunset Ramadan meals, but also from taking part in his religion's group prayers or services held before or after the special breakfast meal. The court said the prison's policy works "to restrict the religious exercise of any [Nation of Islam] inmate who cannot or does not fast, but who still wishes to participate in group services or prayers."

In a case involving a denial of a *halal* diet to a Muslim inmate, the court of appeals defined "substantial burden" as one which (1) requires participation in an activity prohibited by a sincerely held religious belief; (2) prevents participation in conduct motivated by sincerely held religious belief; or (3) places substantial pressure on a prisoner not to engage in, or engage in conduct contrary to, sincerely held religious beliefs. *Abdulhaseeb v. Calbone*, 600 F.3d 1301 (10th Cir. 2010).

Once the prisoner demonstrates that his or her religious beliefs were substantially burdened, the government must come forward with credible evidence to demonstrate that the restriction was the least restrictive means of furthering a compelling governmental interest. The

Supreme Court, in *Cutter v. Wilkinson*, discussed above, concluded that prison security and order were compelling governmental interests. The Fifth Circuit Court of Appeals has concluded that budgetary and administrative considerations can be "compelling governmental interests." *Baranowski v. Hart*, 486 F.3d 112 (5th Cir. 2007). The court said that:

> [t]he uncontroverted summary judgment evidence submitted by Defendants establishes that TDCJ's [Texas Department of Criminal Justice] budget is not adequate to cover the increased expense of either providing a separate kosher kitchen or bringing in kosher food from the outside; that TDCJ's ability to provide a nutritionally appropriate meal to other offenders would be jeopardized ... that such a policy would breed resentment among other inmates; and that there would be an increased demand by other religious groups for similar diets.

Once the government establishes that the restriction furthers a compelling governmental interest, it must also demonstrate that it is using the "least restrictive means" to further that compelling governmental interest. The "least restrictive means" also has been interpreted differently by appeals courts. One court of appeals has ruled that the "least restrictive alternatives" are used when the department of corrections actually considered and rejected less restrictive measures as not satisfactorily accommodating the compelling governmental interest. *Jova v. Smith*, 582 F.3d 410 (2nd Cir. 2009).

Like the issue raised in the *Levitan* case discussed above, some correctional organizations have attempted to apply a "religiously required" test by requiring that a prisoner's desired practice must be "compelled by" or be "central to" the prisoner's faith. In *Koger v. Bryan*, 523 F.3d 789 (7th Cir. 2008), the court of appeals disagreed with prison officials who had denied a prisoner the opportunity to eat a nonmeat diet because the prisoner had been unable to establish that his faith group required the nonmeat diet.

Grooming

Inmates have claimed that their religious teachings require certain grooming, or personal appearance, standards. One of the most common is that men are not allowed to cut their facial hair, or any hair on their heads, resulting in beards and long hair.

For many years, most correctional agencies had required men to cut their hair and to be clean shaven. One of the reasons for this was, no doubt, a desire for a standard, military-like appearance. Also, sanitation was raised as a concern. When challenged, the best argument of officials was that there was a security concern, because inmates had to be readily identified (by means of photo IDs, among other things). Allowing beards, mustaches, or long hair changed the appearance and made identification more difficult. With the 1960s, beards and longer hair became more common for men, and confrontation on this issue was inevitable.

Some inmates claimed the long hair was required by their religion, and a free exercise claim was generated. In *Goings v. Aaron*, 350 F.Supp. 1 (D. MN 1972), a Native American inmate claimed that he made a religious vow at his father's funeral that he would return to old traditions and would not cut his hair. He was punished in prison for refusing to have his hair cut. The federal district court, although expressing some doubt about the inmate's sincerity, ruled that he could be required to cut his hair while confined, even if not cutting it was a religious claim.

A different result was reached in *Benjamin v. Coughlin*, 905 F.2d 571 (2nd Cir. 1990), when the New York State Department of Correctional Services (DOCS) appealed a district court order that prohibited the DOCS from requiring newly admitted Rastafarian inmates to cut their hair for the taking of initial photographs. The state argued that requiring inmates to cut their hair for photographs was a legitimate governmental interest related to identifying prisoners who escape. The court of appeals agreed with the district court that the state could obtain suitable photographs by having the prisoners pull their hair back for the photographs. While giving great deference to the state's security interests, the court relied upon *Turner v. Safley* to conclude the state had failed to demonstrate that this accommodation would have more than a minimal effect on the state's legitimate penological interest.

In *Moskowitz v. Wilkinson*, 432 F.Supp. 947 (D. CT 1977), an Orthodox Jewish inmate at the Danbury Federal Correctional Institution filed suit when authorities ordered him to remove his beard, which he had grown based on his religious teachings. The government asserted its interest in requiring no beards, based on prison security, because growing a beard and shaving it would make identification of the inmate more difficult (both within the prison, and outside in case identification had to be made to facilitate apprehension in the event of escape). The court found this argument weakened by experiences in other states. A survey had shown that about half the states operated without a no-beard rule. The court held that the no-beard rule was an impermissible infringement on the inmate's sincerely held religious beliefs and that punishing him for refusing to shave his beard was unconstitutional. (See also *Fromer v. Scully*, 874 F.2d 69 (2nd Cir. 1989).)

In *Pollock v. Marshall*, 845 F.2d 656 (6th Cir. 1988), inmate Pollock claimed his religious beliefs in the teachings of the Lakota American Indians taught him that hair was sacred and that it should not be cut. Marshall, the superintendent of the Southern Ohio Correctional Facility, required Pollock to cut his hair, and Pollock sued under 42 U.S.C. § 1983. Although Marshall asserted that Pollock was not truly a believer—because he was not born a Lakota Indian and couldn't just become one by professing to be—the courts assumed, for purposes of deciding the case, that Pollock did believe in the religion of the Lakota Indians. They used the test of *Turner v. Safley*, maintaining that the regulation impinging on the inmate's constitutional rights would be valid if it was reasonably related to legitimate penological interests. The Sixth Circuit found that there were legitimate interests supporting the Ohio regulation: "Quick identification, removal of a place to hide small contraband, prevention of sanitation problems and homosexuality [prisoners with long hair were alleged by the superintendent to provide homosexual attraction to other inmates], and reduction of [physical] contact between prisoners and guards are all legitimate penological interests that are furthered by requiring inmates to keep their hair short."[11]

The impact of correctional grooming policies under the heightened standards of RFRA and RLUIPA has been mixed. The Ohio grooming policy discussed in *Pollock* above was found not to violate a Native American prisoner's religious rights under RLUIPA. In *Hoevenaar v. Lazaroff*, 422 F.3d 366 (6th Cir. 2005), the court of appeals agreed with the district court that the prison system's ban on long hair promoted security by preventing inmates from hiding contraband in their hair and preventing prisoners from quickly changing their appearance by cutting their hair after an escape. After finding that these governmental interests were present, the court of appeals reversed the district court's order allowing the prisoner to wear a kouplock (described as a 2-inch square of hair at the base of the skull) because the district court failed to afford appropriate deference to the views and expertise of correctional officials in addressing security matters.

■ Unusual Religious Groups

We have already referred to the Church of the New Song, certainly one of the most unusual nonmainstream organizations that have sought First Amendment protection for their activities. This was also a brilliant effort by an inmate (who undoubtedly had too much time on his hands!) to achieve free exercise rights for his group of inmates. We have also noted inmate Udey, who was in a group of worshipers numbering only a few people, who held somewhat unusual beliefs. The small number of believers was not the ground for turning down his requests for special diet, however; administrative burden to the government was the ground for that ruling.

In *Jones v. Bradley*, 590 F.2d 294 (9th Cir. 1979), an inmate at the Washington State Penitentiary asked to use the chapel and to perform marriages, claiming he was a pastor of the Universal Life Church (ULC). The district court dismissed his complaint, holding that the ULC is not a religion and not entitled to First Amendment protections. The court of appeals held that it was improper to inquire into the "truth" of religious beliefs or to discredit them because of their unusual nature. Rather, it decided the case on the assumption that the ULC is a religion. Given that assumption, it concluded that inmate Jones was not entitled to the activities he requested; he could not use the chapel, because he did not intend to use it for the ceremonial purposes for which it was provided. (He said he wanted to have "study groups," and the court suggested that another room might be made available for that purpose.) He was not entitled to perform marriages, because that was a matter regulated by state licensing requirements, and it did not require free exercise protection.

Another group claiming First Amendment free exercise rights has been the Metropolitan Community Church (MCC). The MCC is a group of Christian churches that ministers primarily to the spiritual and religious needs of homosexuals. In Michigan, the court of appeals upheld a ban on the activities within prisons of inmates affiliated with the MCC. *Brown v. Johnson*, 743 F.2d 408 (6th Cir. 1984). Prison officials had testified that there was a strong correlation between inmate homosexuality and prison violence. Also, they asserted that attending MCC worship services (or being involved in other MCC activities) would identify the participating inmates as homosexuals, which would increase the risks for confrontation or disruptive behavior. The court accepted those concerns as a basis for concluding that there was a strong interest in maintaining internal security within the prison, which justified the ban on MCC services and activities.

In a California case, a three-judge U.S. district court was convened to review a constitutional attack on a state ban on worship services and counseling conducted by ministers of the MCC. *Lipp v. Procunier*, 395 F.Supp. 871 (N.D. CA 1975). The state first argued that the MCC was not a bona fide religion, but rather "a self-proclaimed religious and social group," without standing to assert a constitutional claim of denial of religious rights to free exercise. The court rejected this argument, finding that "the Church's ministry and work and the religion espoused by the Church … possess the cardinal characteristics associated with traditional 'recognized' religions in that it teaches and preaches a belief in a Supreme Being, a religious discipline, and tenets to guide one's daily existence." The court dismissed any consideration of the sexual orientation of the Church's adherents, noting that "the mere fact of one having homosexual proclivities does not per se deprive him of legal entitlements and constitutional immunities."

However, the court held that there could be a security concern that would justify restrictions on the activities of the MCC. "Whether the proclivities, habits or inclinations of an individual or group of prison inmates to act present a clear and present danger to prison discipline and control of prison safety to persons and property" is the question to be answered. The court deferred its final decision pending the presentation of evidence on that question. (State officials, after this court decision, withdrew the ban and allowed some activities of the MCC. Thus, there is not a ruling in this case that the MCC is entitled to engage in its activities within prisons, only a statement of what standards would have to be met, under the First Amendment, in order to justify a restriction or ban of the MCC activities.)

In *McCorkle v. Johnson*, 881 F.2d 993 (11th Cir. 1989), an inmate (McCorkle) at the Holman, Alabama prison had filed a Section 1983 suit, claiming that authorities were violating his constitutional rights by restricting his exercise of his Satanic religion. The court of appeals affirmed a district court ruling that officials had not violated McCorkle's First Amendment rights. The state had first argued that Satanism was not a religion and McCorkle was not a sincere believer in that "religion." The courts refused to get embroiled in those difficult questions. (As we have already noted, proving what is or is not a religion and deciding the sincerity of religious beliefs are issues that courts prefer to avoid.) The courts said that, even if Satanism is a religion and McCorkle was a sincere believer, the Alabama policy was valid, because it was reasonably related to a legitimate penological interest.

Johnson (the Alabama warden) had testified that he was concerned about the Satanic teachings and actions being a threat to the security and orderly running of the prison. He noted that he had seen phrases in the Satanic "bible" that taught hatred of enemies and revenge as a top priority. McCorkle himself had testified that he wanted to practice sacrifices, draw (human) blood for initiation (he had, in fact, cut his own wrists in connection with his Satanic rituals), and eat human flesh. Desecration of Christian symbols and mockery of traditional religious morals and teachings were also taught. (The courts noted that McCorkle had been able to perform some alternative Satanic actions, such as wearing a medallion and being able to recount Satanic texts that he had memorized. It is not clear that those things had any impact at all on the courts' rulings.) Applying the standards of the Supreme Court rulings in *O'Lone v. Shabazz* and *Turner v. Safley*, these courts held that the restrictions placed on Satanic activities were a permissible response to a valid penological concern.

> **It [the ban on Satanic written materials and Satanic worship] is an informed and measured response to the violence inherent in Satanic worship, and to the potential disorder that it might cause in prison.[12]**

Are prison officials required to treat atheism as a religion? A Wisconsin inmate argued that he was denied the opportunity to create a group within the prison to study and discuss atheism. Prison officials concluded there was no religious basis for the group, so the application was treated as a request to form an "inmate activity group." As such, the request was denied. The inmate sued prison officials, claiming his rights of free exercise were violated by the prison's action as well as giving favored treatment to religious groups, which was a violation of the establishment clause of the First Amendment. In *Kaufman v. McCaughtry*, 419 F. 3d 678 (7th Cir. 2005), the court of appeals affirmed the dismissal of the free exercise claim. The court ruled that the term *religion* has been interpreted broadly to include "non-theistic and atheistic beliefs, as well as theistic ones." However, the prisoner had failed to demonstrate any burden that the state had placed on his practice of atheism, and the prisoner was not prohibited from other means of practicing atheism, including individual study, informal discussion with other atheist inmates, and correspondence with atheist groups in the community.

The dismissal of the prisoner's establishment clause claim was reversed. Because atheism may be considered a religion for First Amendment purposes, the appellate court ruled that prison officials and the district court erred when concluding the request to form an atheist study group was not a request to form a religious group. Other religious groups within the prison, including Christians, Muslims, Buddhists, and Wiccans, were authorized to conduct formal group meetings to study religious beliefs, creeds, dogma, tenets, and rituals. Accommodation of those religious groups, while denying similar privileges to an atheist group, results in promoting certain religious faiths over others, a violation of the establishment clause. In the absence of evidence demonstrating that a group meeting of atheist inmates posed a greater threat to institution security and order than those of other religious groups, dismissal of the prisoner's complaint was in error, this court of appeals said.[13]

SUMMARY

- The First Amendment's freedom of religion provisions contain two parts: the establishment clause and the free exercise clause.
- There are few issues from prisons that have been litigated under the establishment clause, which forbids any action by the government to "establish religion." Most religion cases from prisons arise under the "free exercise" clause.
- Under the establishment clause, federal courts have upheld the use of federal money to pay prison chaplains, build chapels, and purchase religious materials (*Theriault v. Carlson*).
- Both President Bush and President Obama have issued executive orders providing for faith-based initiatives. Program supporters believe such initiatives will help an inmate prepare for a successful return to the community. Governmental funding for such programs may be used only for purposes which are secular in nature and may not be used to advance or endorse religion (*Americans United for Separation of Church and State v. Prison Fellowship Ministries, Inc.*).
- The Supreme Court ruled that a Buddhist inmate would have to be given the opportunity to pursue his faith, comparable to the opportunity given to prisoners of other faiths (*Cruz v. Beto*).
- Litigation brought by Black Muslim inmates in the early 1960s can be credited with opening up federal courts to civil rights claims by prisoners, not only on religious freedom claims, but more broadly on claims of constitutional violations.

- The Supreme Court held that New Jersey prison officials were justified in restricting the movement of inmates in and out of the prison, which prevented Muslim inmates from coming back into the institution on Friday at noon for Jumu'ah prayers. The Court said that officials met the standard of acting reasonably, in pursuit of a valid correctional purpose, which was maintaining prison security and order (*O'Lone v. Shabazz*).

- The standard of *O'Lone* (bearing a reasonable relationship to a legitimate governmental objective) was called into question by the action of Congress in passing the Religious Freedom Restoration Act (RFRA). That act says that government may substantially burden a person's free exercise of religion only if it is necessary to further a compelling governmental interest and is the least restrictive means of achieving that interest. That law applied to state and federal prison administrators.

- In *City of Boerne v. Flores*, the Supreme Court held that RFRA was unconstitutional. The federal government interpreted the Court's ruling as applying only to the states, so RFRA is still considered to be applicable to the federal government.

- In 2000, Congress passed the Religious Land Use and Institutionalized Persons Act of 2000 (RLUIPA). This act re-established the compelling government interest and least restrictive means test of RFRA in certain cases, including for the protection of religious exercise by institutionalized persons. RLUIPA is applicable to state programs which use federal funding. RLUIPA was applicable to states receiving federal funds. In *Cutter v. Wilkinson* (2005), the United States Supreme Court upheld the constitutionality of this statute. The court also noted that prison security and good order remain a compelling governmental interest.

- Some religious groups have strict dietary requirements. In the 1960s and 1970s, some courts required prisons to provide special religious diets, such as pork-free diets for Muslims and kosher diets for Jewish inmates. In more recent cases, some requests for religious diets by individuals or groups with only a few members have been disapproved, primarily on the basis of administrative and financial burdens.

- Grooming cases (especially by male inmates who want to grow beards or long hair, based on religious teachings) have also gone both ways. As with religious diet cases, the Supreme Court has not ruled on these inmate complaints. Some lower federal courts have ruled in favor of inmates, saying that prison officials did not have a sufficient justification for requiring clean-shaven or short-haired inmates. Other courts have upheld prison policies that required inmates to shave or cut their hair against claims of First Amendment protections.

- Claims for free exercise of religious beliefs have been made by many inmates who adhere to teachings that are not in the mainstream of religious groups. Courts generally are loath to become embroiled in the question of whether religious beliefs are held by adherents of a "true religion." More often, courts will concede, or assume for the purposes of deciding a case, that an individual's or a group's beliefs are religious. The courts will then decide claims for religious protections and activities based on whether the exercise of those teachings in a prison setting would pose a threat to prison order or security or would pose a significant burden on prison administration.

THINKING ABOUT IT

Inmates in the custody of the New York Department of Corrections (NYDOC) advised prison officials that they belonged to a religion called Tulukeesh. The religious requirements of Tulukeesh were set forth in the book, "Holy Blackness," and included various dietary requirements (followers are required to eat only a complex, highly regimented, non-soybean-based vegan diet); a mandate that members engage in sparring; and a rule prohibiting members from appearing nude in front of nonmembers. The prisoners also desired to engage in group religious activities. The DOC advised the inmates they could conduct religious practices in their cells, but to conduct group services the group should attempt to have an outside member of the clergy volunteer to administer such services. As to the religious diet, the state offered a religious alternative meal which Tulukeesh members could request. The prisoners were also administratively disciplined for practicing martial arts and engaging in sparring. Do you think the actions of the prison officials violate the First Amendment free exercise rights of the prisoners, and did prison officials comply with RLUIPA? See *Jova v. Smith*, 582 F.3d 410 (2nd Cir. 2009).

KEY TERMS

facial challenge: A claim that a statute is unconstitutional on its face. A facial challenge does not get into the consideration of any specific facts but is limited to the issue of whether the statute itself, as written, is unconstitutional.

ENDNOTES

1. Please try to make your own identification of these cases, which have actually been decided under the First Amendment. Numbers 1, 2, 4, and 6 are free exercise cases. In them, U.S. citizens of different religious backgrounds claimed the right to engage in certain protected, religion-dictated activity without government interference or regulation. Numbers 3 and 5 are establishment cases, where persons objected to government activity that seemed to give preference to or endorse a particular religious group or function (with government funding). Number 7, school prayer, perhaps the most famous constitutional religious issue in recent years, actually involves both freedoms. It is decided primarily on the basis of the establishment clause, with the assertion that the public school system, a government function, cannot endorse a prayer or Bible reading that is presented to all children. Competing with it is a free exercise claim of students and parents, who want school children to be able to participate in some kind of religious observance in the classroom.
2. In December 2002, President Bush issued Executive Order 13279, Equal Protection of the Laws for Faith-based and Community Organizations. This order specifically states that the "Federal government must implement Federal programs in accordance with the

Establishment Clause and the Free Exercise Clause of the First Amendment to the Constitution." In December 2008, the White House issued *Innovations in Compassion: The Faith Based and Community Initiative: A Final Report to the Armies of Compassion.* (Accessed March 4, 2011, http://georgewbush-whitehouse.archives.gov/government/fbci/pdf/innovation-in-compassion.pdf.) Among the areas discussed in this document are prisoner reentry and the Mentoring Children of Prisoners program. In February 2009, President Obama amended Executive Order 13199 (January 29, 2001). See Executive Order No. 13498, 74 Fed. Reg. 6533-6535 (2009). The new Executive Order changed the Office's name from "White House Office of Faith-Based and Community Initiatives" to the new name, "White House Office of Faith-Based and Neighborhood Partnerships."

3. The court held that the private religious program, Interchange Freedom Initiative (IFI), had to return to the state the funds IFI had received after the district court decision was issued, but not the funds received prior to that date.

   Faith-based initiatives continue to be used in some prison systems, with the use of government funding limited to nonreligious purposes (for example, supervision of inmates). One example of a faith-based initiative is the Florida Department of Corrections' Faith- and Character-Based Correctional Initiative, (Accessed March 4, 2011, http://www.dc.state.fl.us/oth/faith/index.html). The program is described as an "innovative effort to reduce recidivism and disciplinary infractions... by offering character-based programming in a positive environment to inmates committed to inner transformation...Without additional cost to the state, this program employs residential clustering to encourage a sense of community among enrolled inmates." The program uses citizen volunteers to mentor inmates and volunteers use an open public forum to teach inmates. The inmate's religious preference is not a criterion for inmate participation.

4. Cripe, C. "Religious Freedom in Institutions" (paper presented at the American Correctional Association Annual Congress, Denver, CO, 1976).

5. *Fulwood v. Clemmer,* 206 F.Supp. 370 (D.D.C. 1962). The court tied a "religion" to "a belief in the existence of a supreme being controlling the destiny of man." Activities showing support of that belief would also be important in deciding this question.

6. In the year 2000, Public Law 106-274 (RLUIPA) amended provisions of RFRA to remove any reference that RFRA applied to the states.

7. The Court, referring to the Prison Litigation Reform Act (PLRA), says that "[s]tate prison officials make the first judgment about whether to provide a particular accommodation, for a prisoner may not sue under RLUIPA without first exhausting all available administrative remedies." Further, RLUIPA section 2000cc-2(e) specifically states that RLUIPA is not to be interpreted as amending or repealing the PLRA.

8. Cases dealing with Muslim dietary requirements include *Abernathy v. Cunningham*, 393 F.2d 775 (4th Cir. 1968), and *Barnett v. Rodgers*, 410 F.2d 995 (DC Cir. 1969).

9. The phrase *Hobson's choice* is defined as an apparently free choice when there is no really good alternative.

10. The screening process provides guidelines for the loss of the religious diet privilege. These include being observed violating the religious dietary requirements; providing all or a portion of the specially prepared meal to other offenders; eating both the specially prepared

meal and the general diet meal that is offered to the general population; and discovering that an inmate no longer practices the religion.

11. As a point of interest, prior to the Supreme Court ruling in *City of Boerne*, the case of *Abordo v. Hawaii*, 938 F.Supp. 656 (D. HI 1996) involved a RFRA challenge to a grooming regulation at a state maximum security prison. The district court held in favor of the state, citing contraband and safety concerns and the absence of reasonable, less restrictive alternatives.

12. The issue of prison officials asking about the doctrinal beliefs of religious service providers was looked at in an April 2004 report issued by the U.S. Department of Justice's Office of the Inspector General (OIG). Based on its initial review, OIG suggests that the law allows Bureau of Prisons officials "for security purposes, to ascertain from chaplain, contractor, and volunteer applicants information to determine whether their religious beliefs include: 1) endorsement of violence, 2) support of terrorism or other anti-U.S. activities, or 3) discrimination against other inmates or exclusion of other inmates from their services, whether based on race, religion, or other discriminatory factors." See Office of the Inspector General. *A Review of the Federal Bureau of Prisons' Selection of Muslim Religious Service Providers.* Washington, DC: U.S. Department of Justice, 2004. Available from http://www.usdoj.gov/oig. The report also includes a concern over inmates functioning as surrogate chaplains, and supports the need for greater staff supervision of inmate-led services, saying this is "essential to deterring and preventing inmate radicalism."

This report also cited a concern relating to chapel libraries, recommending that the Bureau of Prisons "undertake an inventory of chapel books and videos to confirm that they are permissible under BOP security policies." The report notes that inmates "may be predisposed to violence, feel disenfranchised from society ... or cling to a radical or extremist religious 'family.'"

Citing this information and section 214 of the Second Chance Act recognizing that the Bureau may restrict inmate access to materials in a chapel library that "seek to incite, promote, or otherwise suggest the commission of violence or criminal activity," the Bureau of Prisons, on January 16, 2009, published a proposed amendment to its religious beliefs and practices regulations. The proposed regulation adds a new section authorizing the Bureau to exclude material from a chapel library upon determining that such material "could incite, promote, or otherwise suggest the commission of violence or criminal activity." This can include material that advocates or fosters violence, vengeance, or hatred toward particular religious, racial, or ethnic groups or urges the overthrow or destruction of the United States. This proposed rule has received significant public comment.

13. After the court of appeals remanded this case back to the district court, the state revised its policy in light of the court of appeals opinion and now considers atheism a religion. The district court also ruled that the prison officials were entitled to qualified immunity for money damages as the law was not clearly established at the time of the complained about action. *Kaufman v. McCaughtry*, 422 F.Supp.2d 1016 (W.D. WI 2006).

10 Fourth Amendment: Search and Seizure, and Privacy

A right of privacy in traditional Fourth Amendment terms is fundamentally incompatible with the close and continual surveillance of inmates and their cells required to ensure institutional security and internal order. We are satisfied that society would insist that the prisoner's expectation of privacy always yield to what must be considered the paramount interest in institutional security.

U.S. Supreme Court, *Hudson v. Palmer*

Chapter Outline

- Searches in Prisons
- *Hudson v. Palmer*
- *Bell v. Wolfish*
- *Lanza v. New York*
- *United States v. Hearst*
- Attorney Visits, Communications
- Strip Searches
- Pat Searches and Other Inmate Searches
- DNA Collection
- Searches of Non-Inmates
    - Searches of Employees; *City of Ontario, CA. v. Quon*
    - Visitor Searches

The Fourth Amendment to the Constitution provides:

> **The right of the people to be secure in their persons, houses, papers, and effects, against unreasonable searches and seizures, shall not be violated.**

In this chapter, we will look at the question of whether and to what extent this provision applies within prisons and jails. As you can see, the exact language of the amendment protects "persons, houses, papers, and effects." Does this include inmates in their prison cells? The amendment does not forbid all searches of persons and their homes and property, but only "unreasonable" searches. The job of the courts, in looking at claims of illegal searches, is to decide two questions: Is the area of the search protected under the Constitution? If so, has a search been conducted in a reasonable or an unreasonable manner? There are, as we will see, special limitations on both of these concepts in a prison setting.

■ Searches in Prisons

There are two principal kinds of searches in prisons: searches of an inmate's cell or living quarters and searches of the person. As to searches of the person, there are several kinds of inmate searches: pat or frisk searches, visual or strip searches, digital or simple instrument searches, urine testing, X-ray examinations, and blood tests. Besides those principal kinds of searches, there are searches of all other physical areas within the facility, such as work and recreation areas and the grounds surrounding the buildings, as well as the obvious searches of inmates' living quarters (whether in cells, rooms, or dormitories). Also, there are questions of searches of visitors and employees.

On the part of inmates, some are looking for ways to escape, some are assaultive, and some are looking for ways to introduce **contraband**. Corrections officials, on the other hand, are looking for ways to stop these illegal occurrences. Searches are commonly used for this purpose. They are conducted by looking for escape implements, weapons that might be used in assaults, and all other kinds of contraband, such as drugs and money.

A relatively new and serious form of contraband is cell phones. These may be used by inmates to avoid staff monitoring of their telephone calls. Cell phones may be used to plan escapes and other crimes, threaten persons in the community, or otherwise facilitate criminal activity. A legal challenge to the ban on cell phones in prisons or jails could involve inmates arguing that cell phone usage is a less expensive and more efficient way to maintain contact with family members and others. It is doubtful that such claims would prevail, as prison officials should be able to effectively show that a ban against cell phone or other wireless device usage is reasonably related to legitimate penological interests.[1]

As to searches of prisoners' cells, the Supreme Court has given guidance in two leading cases.

■ *Hudson v. Palmer*

Palmer was an inmate at the Bland Correctional Center in Virginia. Hudson, a correctional officer, and another officer conducted a **shakedown** search of Palmer's cell and locker, looking for contraband. During the search, they found a ripped pillowcase in a trash can in the cell. They filed charges against Palmer for destroying state property, and he was found guilty of that offense in a disciplinary hearing. Palmer filed a lawsuit under 42 U.S.C. § 1983, claiming that Hudson had violated his Fourth Amendment right not to be subjected to unreasonable searches and seizures.

Palmer also claimed that Hudson, during the search, destroyed some of Palmer's personal property, just to harass him. Although the matter of this loss of property was treated as a due process claim, which is not the issue under discussion here, we will note here the outcome of that claim. The Supreme Court held that, because the state had a remedy that Palmer could file to seek compensation for his lost property, there was no due process violation, even if (as alleged) the property was destroyed intentionally and without authorization. (*Parratt v. Taylor*, 451 U.S. 527 (1981), *Daniels v. Williams*, 474 U.S. 327 (1986), and *Davidson v. Cannon*, 474 U.S. 344 (1986), provide a full picture of the Supreme Court's current treatment of this kind of due process claim by inmates.)

The main question in *Hudson v. Palmer*, 468 U.S. 517 (1984), was "whether [Palmer] has a right of privacy in his prison cell entitling him to the protection of the Fourth Amendment against unreasonable searches." The Fourth Circuit Court of Appeals held that an inmate had a limited privacy right in his cell. The Supreme Court reversed that ruling:

> **[T]he Fourth Amendment proscription against unreasonable searches does not apply within the confines of the prison cell.**

After discussing the volatile and often violent nature of prisons, the Court emphasized that prison officials "must be ever alert to attempts to introduce drugs and other contraband into the premises which, we can judicially note, is one of the most perplexing problems of prisons today." Officials must also prevent the flow of weapons into the prisons, look for escape plots or tools, and try to maintain as sanitary an environment as possible. Because of these concerns and the fact that contraband may often be hidden in cells, the Supreme Court recognized the need for cell access:

> **Unfettered access to these cells by prison officials, thus, is imperative if drugs and contraband are to be ferreted out and sanitary surroundings are to be maintained.**

As with many constitutional claims of prisoners, the Court noted that the question of privacy in prison is based on a balancing of interests: the interest of society in the security of prisons and the interest of prisoners in having privacy in their cells. The Court came down firmly on the side of prison security:

> **A right of privacy in traditional Fourth Amendment terms is fundamentally incompatible with the close and continual surveillance of inmates and their cells required to ensure institutional security and internal order ... We believe that it is accepted by our society that "[l]oss of freedom of choice and privacy are inherent incidents of confinement."**

Palmer had also claimed a Fourth Amendment violation, because Hudson had seized and destroyed some of his property during the search. The Court said, albeit in a footnote, that the Fourth Amendment's proscription of unreasonable seizures was also inapplicable in a prison cell:

> **Prison officials must be free to seize from cells any articles which, in their view, disserve legitimate institutional interests.**

The Supreme Court tersely but sweepingly held:

> **[T]he Fourth Amendment has no applicability to a prison cell.**

■ *Bell v. Wolfish*

In *Bell v. Wolfish*, 441 U.S. 520 (1979), which dealt with several constitutional claims raised by inmates at the Metropolitan Correctional Center (MCC, a federal detention center in New York City), the Court addressed two search issues: searches of living quarters (inmates' cells) and visual strip searches. (Strip searches will be discussed later in this chapter.)

The MCC, like most jails and detention centers, held both pretrial detainees and convicted prisoners. Most inmates were unconvicted persons who were confined while awaiting trial. The convicted persons at MCC included those who were being held after their convictions, while awaiting sentencing and then transfer to a regular prison, and those who were serving short sentences. Other convicted persons were brought back to the jail from prison where they were serving sentences, for purposes of post-trial hearings on their cases, to consult with counsel on appeals, or perhaps to testify in another person's case. (The major part of the *Wolfish* opinion deals with a discussion of the issue of double-bunking pretrial detainees in a detention facility, which is discussed elsewhere in an examination of the conditions of confinement.)

Staff at the MCC conducted randomly timed, unannounced searches of inmate living quarters. During these "shakedowns," all inmates would usually be cleared out of the particular living unit and a team of correctional officers would search each room in that unit. Inmates complained that during these searches items in the cells were left in needless disarray, and sometimes they were damaged or destroyed. They asked for permission to be present during the searches of their cells to watch the searches (and presumably to serve as a deterrent to overzealous or wrongful searching by the staff). The district court had ordered that inmates would have to be present during searches, in order to have "reasonable" searches and seizures. Prison officials said that permitting inmates to observe room inspections would lead to friction between the inmates and the security guards and would allow the inmates to attempt to frustrate the search by distracting personnel and moving contraband from one room to another ahead of the search team.

The Second Circuit Court of Appeals agreed with the district court and held the room-search policy of the MCC to be unconstitutional. (The Supreme Court complained that the court of appeals had not identified the constitutional provision on which it relied when it set aside the prison's room-search rule. The district court had said that the pretrial detainees retained a right of privacy, which was found in the Fourth Amendment.) The Supreme Court disagreed and reversed the lower courts' rulings.

For both unsentenced (pretrial) detainees and persons serving sentences, the Supreme Court said that an inmate has no privacy right with respect to his room or cell. The MCC's room-search rule was found *not* to violate the Fourth Amendment.

> **[R]oom searches represent an appropriate security measure ... [E]ven the most zealous advocate of prisoners' rights would not suggest that a warrant is required to conduct such a search[2] ... The room search rule simply facilitates the safe and effective performance of the search which all concede may be conducted. The rule itself, then, does not render the searches "unreasonable" within the meaning of the Fourth Amendment.**

The question of whether an inmate has a right to be present during a search of his cell was raised again in the case of *Block v. Rutherford*, 468 U.S. 576 (1984), even though it had been recently decided in *Wolfish*. (*Block* also concerned pretrial detainees at the Los Angeles County Jail and dealt mainly with the issue of contact visiting.) The Supreme Court in *Block* reiterated its stand on the cell-search rule and held (again) that prisoners have no constitutional right to be present to observe a search of their cells.

■ *Lanza v. New York*

Although *Hudson* and *Wolfish* constitute the definitive word from the Supreme Court on room searches in prison, some other cases gave forewarning of the *Hudson* approach and cast some light on other types of prison searches.

In *Lanza v. New York*, 370 U.S. 139 (1962), Lanza had a visit from his brother in a local jail. The two conversed in the visiting room. Unknown to them, there was an electronic device hidden in the room that picked up their conversation and a transcript was made of what was said. A state legislative committee, which was investigating possible corruption in the state parole system, called Lanza to testify, based on the content of the transcript of the jail conversation. Lanza refused to testify and was convicted for that refusal. He claimed that it was improper for the jail officials to electronically intercept and record his visiting room conversation. He further claimed that it was a violation of his constitutional rights when he was punished for refusing to talk about the contents of that intercepted conversation.

The Supreme Court disagreed with Lanza and upheld his conviction. The Court first pointed out that Lanza's claim that the officials' action was a violation of the Fourth Amendment was based necessarily on the assumption that the visiting room of the jail was a constitutionally protected area and that the surreptitious eavesdropping in that room was an unreasonable search and seizure.

> **But to say that a public jail is the equivalent of a man's "house" or that it is a place where he can claim constitutional immunity from search or seizure of his person, his papers, or his effects, is at best a novel argument … [I]t is obvious that a jail shares none of the attributes of privacy of a home,[3] an automobile, an office, or a hotel room. In prison, official surveillance has traditionally been the order of the day.**

The Supreme Court observed, however, that the legislative committee had other grounds to question Lanza. Therefore, his prosecution for refusing to testify (even when given immunity from prosecution) was permissible, even if there had been a constitutional problem with the intercepted conversation. Thus, there is not a clear holding that there was no Fourth Amendment protection in the visiting situation at the jail. But the language quoted previously shows the predilection of the Supreme Court to find no privacy in a prison or jail, even in a conversation with a person from the outside community. (In an aside, the Court did note that relationships that have special legal protection, such as attorney–client relationships, would have at least as much protection in a jail as in the outside world. In effect, the Court found no fault with the jail intercepting a conversation with a social, family member visitor but warned that "special relationships" must be carefully protected in jail.)

■ *United States v. Hearst*

Of similar import is the case involving the prosecution of Patty Hearst. In *United States v. Hearst*, 563 F.2d 1331 (9th Cir. 1977), cert. denied, 435 U.S. 1000 (1978), the court of appeals upheld Hearst's conviction over an objection that it was obtained using evidence of an intercepted conversation Hearst had in jail. While she was held in the San Mateo County (California) Jail shortly after her arrest, Hearst had a visit from a friend. They communicated over a phone, while viewing each other through a glass window (typical noncontact visiting). The conversation was monitored and recorded by jail staff, which was often done in that jail. The tape of this conversation was delivered to the Federal Bureau of Investigation (FBI), and the tape was later used against Hearst at trial; some portions were read to the jury and other parts of the tape were used by the prosecution in the cross-examination of Hearst.

The question raised on appeal of Hearst's conviction was whether making that tape and using it at her trial was a violation of the Fourth Amendment. The court of appeals noted the *Lanza* decision and the fact that *Lanza* was still a valid statement of the law. In the *Hearst* case, jail officials had a justifiable security purpose in monitoring and recording conversations of inmates with their visitors, the court said. Once the government established a justifiable purpose for its intrusion on individuals' rights, the question of the constitutionality of the jail's actions was to be resolved in its favor. This was because courts should show a deference to the needs of prison (and jail) administration and because there were obviously "traditional notions regarding surveillance of prisoners." The court further noted the Supreme Court decision in *Procunier v. Martinez*, 416 U.S. 396 (1974), which allowed the reading of prisoner correspondence when justified on grounds of institutional security and order. "It would be anomalous indeed to permit prison officials to intercept written correspondence … while prohibiting the interception of oral communications between prisoners and visitors conducted for essentially the same purposes: prison security and order." The court further noted that it was permissible for the jail to turn the tapes over to law enforcement personnel (the FBI). Once the tapes were legitimately in government control, they could be used as evidence by the government.

In *United States v. Paul*, 614 F.2d 115 (6th Cir. 1980), cert. denied, 446 U.S. 941 (1980), correctional officers at a federal prison monitored a telephone call in which inmate Pierce was telling an unidentified woman to "bring the material" and that he would "have the money." The following day, Pierce, prior to going to a visit, was searched and found to have an unauthorized $5.00 bill on his person. Susan Paul, who came to visit Pierce, was taken to the warden's office and strip-searched, but nothing was found. Through subsequent monitoring of a telephone conversation between another inmate and a woman identified as Susan, the staff heard the woman say she had "ditched the stuff" under the chair. With that lead, hashish was located, and Pierce and Paul were prosecuted for introducing drugs into a federal prison.

During the trial process, the defendants argued that the testimony regarding the monitored telephone conversations should have been suppressed and that the taping was in violation of the federal wiretapping statute, under Title 18, U.S. Code, Sections 2510 et seq. The district court refused to suppress testimony regarding the monitored telephone conversations and held that the facts of this case fell under Section 2510(5)(a) of the law, which permits interception of wire communications when done by a law enforcement officer in the ordinary course of his duties. The circuit court agreed, referring to *Lanza* and *Hearst*.

Section 2511(2)(c) is another provision of this act (the "wiretap" law) that is used to uphold the monitoring of prison telephone conversations. This section allows monitoring where "one of the parties to the communication has given prior consent to such interception." As part of the rules in many prisons and jails, and supported by a notice posted in the telephone area, every inmate is advised of the potential for monitoring and that the inmate's use of the telephone constitutes her consent for this monitoring. In *United States v. Amen*, 831 F.2d 373 (2nd Cir. 1987), cert. denied, 485 U.S. 1021 (1988) the court approved this policy:

> **If security concerns can justify strip and body-cavity searches … and wholly random cell searches … then surely it is reasonable to monitor prisoners' telephone conversations, particularly where they are told that the conversations are being monitored.**

■ Attorney Visits, Communications

To protect the privacy of attorney–client communications, most prisons and jails have special areas where attorneys can meet with their clients without prison officials being in a position to hear the conversations. Prison officials must take appropriate steps to ensure the privacy of these conversations. In *Lonegan v. Hasty*, 436 F. Supp. 2d 419 (E.D. NY 2006), the court refused to grant qualified immunity protection to prison officials who secretly audio-taped communications between detainees and their attorneys. The court noted that while prisons are not usually places where a person expects privacy, the Fourth Amendment protects communications between attorneys and clients in prison, especially those communications taking place in an area designated for attorney–client meetings.

In *United States v. Hatcher*, 323 F.3d 666 (8th Cir. 2003), the prisoners and attorneys were aware their conversations were being recorded by prison officials. However, the district court ruled that the tapes were protected by the attorney–client privilege and refused to order their disclosure. The court of appeals disagreed, ruling that carrying on a conversation knowing it was being monitored by a third party was a waiver of any attorney–client privilege.

A variation of this is *United States v. Novak*, 531 F.3d 99 (1st Cir. 2008). Inmate Holyoke contacted attorney Novak through telephone calls made from the Barnstable County Jail in Massachusetts. The jail randomly recorded and monitored inmate phone calls. Pursuant to state and federal regulations, attorney–inmate calls may not be monitored; however, the procedures in place to prevent such monitoring failed in this instance, and the law enforcement officer hearing the inmate–attorney call learned of planned criminal activity. Government officials asked Holyoke for his cooperation in an investigation of attorney Novak. Holyoke agreed, and in later conversations Novak agreed to launder what he believed were the proceeds of drug trafficking. Novak was subsequently arrested for endeavoring to obstruct justice and money laundering. He filed a motion to suppress the recordings, claiming that the first instance of monitoring violated the Fourth Amendment. While the district court agreed and suppressed the evidence, the First Circuit reversed, saying Novak had limited his suppression arguments to a Fourth Amendment claim. (The Sixth Amendment would protect the defendant's right to the assistance of counsel.) The court said that the monitoring posed a "significant Sixth Amendment issue," but since this was not raised by Novak, it would not be considered by the court. As to the Fourth Amendment, the court observed that a "telephone call can be monitored and recorded without violating the Fourth Amendment so long as one participant in the call consents to the monitoring."

■ Strip Searches

The appellate court, in *Forts v. Ward*, 621 F.2d 1210 (2nd Cir. 1980), said, "the modern sensitivity to the significance of gender in American life and law has made it inevitable that cases will arise where gender-based legal contentions conflict." This case arose out of the Bedford Hills Correctional Facility in New York, a women's prison. In 1977, there was a change of policy whereby, for the first time, male corrections officers were assigned to duty in the facility's sleeping quarters. Female inmates filed suit under 42 U.S.C. § 1983, claiming that their constitutional rights to privacy were violated when male officers were able to routinely view them while partially or completely unclothed. The union representing the corrections officers joined administrators in opposing the lawsuit. The officers' argument was based primarily on their equal employment opportunity rights. They claimed that excluding them from certain positions violated Title VII of the Civil Rights law and (in this situation) disadvantaged male officers.

One part of the solution, developed earlier in the case by the administration, was to remove men from night-shift duties, when they would encounter female inmates disrobed more frequently, as the inmates prepared for bed or were in bed. The cells at Bedford Hills had solid doors, with a clear glass window (6"x9"). The inmates were allowed to close their doors and to cover their door windows for 15-minute intervals (for privacy, presumably when changing their clothes or preparing for bed). Taking the men off night-shift duty not only reduced the job-assignment opportunities for men but also for women, because the women would have to cover all night-shift posts and would therefore have reduced opportunities to work the day shift, which most staff preferred.

The district court in *Forts* had found that female inmates were entitled to be protected from being viewed by male officers when they were partially or completely unclothed. This included while they were sleeping (inmates also complained that male officers would view them unnecessarily while they were sleeping), while they were receiving medical treatment in the hospital, while showering, and while using toilet facilities. That court (the trial court) upheld the nighttime ban on male officers in the housing quarters but allowed men to work the daytime shifts, because women inmates could cover their cell windows when they needed privacy.

The court of appeals was concerned about the district court's order because the officers' Title VII equal employment rights still seemed to be infringed. Without describing just where in the Constitution the inmates' privacy rights were found, the appeals court worried that there was a direct conflict here between the privacy rights of inmates in their cells and the employment rights of the officers. The court of appeals tried to accommodate both concerns by endorsing a plan that changed the supervision and living arrangements. The state had agreed to allow inmates to cover their windows when they were changing their clothes or using the toilet. The court approved this change, which would cover nighttime hours as well as daytime. Prison officials proposed to solve the problem of inmates complaining that they could be viewed while sleeping by issuing to anyone who wanted them one-piece pajamas (the "Doctor Denton" solution—if you don't know what Doctor Dentons are, ask your parents!). The district court had rejected this offer because the pajamas were unattractive and uncomfortably warm, but the court of appeals said those concerns were not sufficient to outweigh equal employment rights. The court directed the parties to explore what kind of sleepwear could be agreed on to achieve the privacy protection desired by inmates. That privacy protection covered only the involuntary viewing of private parts of the body by male officers and did not extend (as inmates argued) to a protection against being viewed at all while asleep. These two concessions by the state satisfied the appellate court by achieving some accommodation of the competing rights of the parties.[4]

As noted earlier in this chapter, the Supreme Court decision in *Bell v. Wolfish*, 441 U.S. 520 (1979) dealt with two search issues. The one we discussed earlier dealt with cell searches. The second one involved body cavity searches during strip searches. At all Federal Bureau of Prisons facilities, inmates were required to undergo a strip search (by an officer of the same sex) after every contact visit with a person from outside the institution. As part of these searches, the inmates were required to expose their body cavities for visual inspection. Prison officials testified that these were necessary to find and to deter the introduction of contraband into the institution. The district court had allowed the strip searches but had banned the body cavity searches, unless there was probable cause that the inmate was, in fact, concealing contraband. The court of appeals affirmed, finding that this "gross violation of personal privacy" was not justified by the government's security interest in conducting the search.

The Supreme Court commenced its discussion on the legality of body cavity searches by noting that "this practice instinctively gives us the most pause." On this one issue, an additional justice dissented, making this a five-to-four decision on the body cavity searches, while all other issues in *Bell* were decided in favor of the government by a six-to-three vote.[5] The Court's decision was specifically stated to apply both to the convicted prisoners and to the pretrial detainees, both of whom were housed at the New York MCC and were subject to these searches after visiting.

The Supreme Court assumed, for the purpose of making its constitutional analysis, that the inmates retained some Fourth Amendment rights while in the jail facility. It pointedly did not decide that they did have any such rights; it only assumed so for purposes of deciding the case and pointing out what searches could be conducted. Searches under the Fourth Amendment, the Court said, would be impermissible only if they were unreasonable. "The Fourth Amendment prohibits only unreasonable searches, and under the circumstances, we do not believe that these searches are unreasonable." The Court further explained this point:

> **The test of reasonableness under the Fourth Amendment is not capable of precise definition or mechanical application. In each case it requires a balancing of the need for the particular search against the invasion of personal rights that the search entails…A detention facility is a unique place fraught with serious security dangers…[I]nmate attempts to secrete [contraband] items…by concealing them in body cavities are documented in this record, and in other cases.**

Stating further that they did not underestimate "the degree to which these searches may invade the personal privacy of inmates," the Court held that such searches, conducted in a reasonable manner (and not abusively), could be conducted at the conclusion of visits, without a necessary finding of probable cause or **reasonable suspicion** (which some others, including dissenting justices, would require) before a body cavity search could be conducted.

Courts have also shown great reluctance to approve strip searches of persons immediately after their arrest or upon being taken into jail. In general, courts, until recently (see the discussion in the case of *Bull v. City and County of San Francisco* below), have said that reasonable suspicion (of having secreted improper materials, such as drugs or weapons) is required to justify a strip search upon arrest. Across the board, courts disapprove of strip searching persons arrested for minor offenses. Arrest for a felony alone may not justify a strip search; the Ninth Circuit Court of Appeals held, in *Kennedy v. Los Angeles Police Department*, 901 F.2d 702 (9th Cir. 1989), that a strip search of a person arrested on a property offense, even though a felony, was unreasonable. However, earlier that year, in *Thompson v. Los Angeles*, 885 F.2d 1439 (9th Cir. 1989), that court held that a felony arrest for auto theft carried sufficient risk of violence to justify a strip search.

Recently, some courts have reconsidered whether strip searching all persons admitted into a jail's general population for custodial housing, regardless of the charged offense, violates the arrestee's Fourth Amendment rights. *Bull v. City and County of San Francisco*, 595 F.3d 964 (9th Cir. 2010) (en banc), addressed whether the county's policy of strip searching all persons placed in the jails' (San Francisco County operated six jails) general population for custodial housing violated the Fourth Amendment. The county justified its procedures as an effort to control the introduction of drugs, weapons, and other contraband. Records maintained by the sheriff established that in the almost four years the policy was in effect, 1,574 items of contraband (for example, drugs, homemade knives, and jail-made handcuff keys) were uncovered during the searches. The searches were required to be performed in a professional manner by an officer of the same sex in an area affording privacy to the arrestee.

The district court held the policy violated the Fourth Amendment rights of those persons who were searched. The court of appeals focus was on the inmate's challenge to the jail's blanket policy and practice of searching prearraignment arrestees; it did not consider individual cases.

The court of appeals first determined that the searches conducted by the Sheriff's Department did not differ in scope, manner, or justification from the searches approved by the Supreme Court in *Bell v. Wolfish*. In addition, the record of contraband intercepted in the San Francisco searches far exceeded what had been used to justify the searches in *Bell v. Wolfish*.

The court of appeals in *Bull* also considered the strip search policy under the standards established in *Turner v. Safley*, 482 U.S. 78 (1987), and concluded that the policy was reasonably related to legitimate penological interests. The court of appeals found that the strip search policy furthered a legitimate governmental purpose of restricting the introduction of contraband. Without the policy, the jail would experience increased contraband introduction, leading to utilization of greater resources in order to detect and confiscate the contraband, this court said. The court also noted the plaintiffs had not shown that the policy was an exaggerated response to the prison's concerns over contraband introduction. The court held that the policy requiring strip searches of all arrestees placed into the jail's general custodial population was reasonable under the Fourth Amendment.[6]

Similar blanket policies of strip searching all detainees admitted into the general population of a jail were upheld in *Powell v. Barrett*, 541 F.3d 1298 (11th Cir. 2008) and *Florence v. Board of Chosen Freeholders*, 621 F.3d 296 (3rd Cir. 2010). Cases in other circuits, however, have held that strip searches are unreasonable, unless there is reasonable suspicion that an individual arrestee is smuggling contraband. See *Roberts v. Rhode Island*, 239 F.3d 107 (1st Cir. 2001),

Masters v. Crouch, 872 F.2d 1248 (6th Cir. 1989), and *Shain v. Ellison*, 273 F.3d 56 (2nd Cir. 2001). The Supreme Court addressed this split among the circuits and upheld a policy of conducting strip searches on all inmates admitted into a jail's general population in *Florence v. Board of Chosen Freeholders*, 566 U.S. __ (2012). In affirming the court of appeals, the Supreme Court ruled: **"It is not surprising that correctional officials have sought to perform thorough searches at intake for disease, gang affiliation, and contraband....There is a substantial interest in preventing any new inmate, either of his own will or as a result of coercion, from putting all who live or work at these institutions at even greater risk when he is admitted to the general population."** The Court, however, did not go so far as to issue an all-encompassing rule, recognizing, for example, that under a fact pattern different from the one in *Florence* there **"may be legitimate concerns about the invasiveness of searches that involve the touching of detainees."** [In *Florence,* there were no allegations that the detainees were touched as part of the searches.]

Another point, which was already mentioned, but must be emphasized, is that searches must be performed professionally. This means they must be conducted in as private a place as possible, not within view of other inmates or even of other staff who do not need to see them (and certainly never within view of outsiders, such as visitors). They must also be performed as calmly and as matter-of-factly as possible.

In *Goff v. Nix*, 803 F.2d 358 (8th Cir. 1986), inmates at the Iowa State Penitentiary complained of the strip searches that were conducted before and after their contact visits (including visits with lawyers and clergy) and before and after going to medical facilities, to court, and to exercise areas. The district court banned the strip searches in relation to lawyer and medical care visits, finding that some inmates were discouraged from engaging in these constitutionally protected visits because of their dislike of the strip searches. The court of appeals reversed and upheld the necessity for the searches in all of these cases, noting that inmates could smuggle contraband in body cavities if the searches were not conducted.[7] (For an example of contraband found in body cavities, see **Figure 10-1**.) The court of appeals strictly prohibited one aspect of the searches: those that involved situations in which officers, during strip searches, made "rude and offensive" comments or otherwise verbally harassed the inmates. Such verbal misconduct was found to be demeaning, bearing no relationship to the prison's need to conduct the searches.

■ Pat Searches and Other Inmate Searches

Another type of search is the pat search. Pat searches (or frisks) are commonly done as inmates move from one place to another in an institution, as they work or engage in other activities in a variety of places within the prison or jail, or as they enter or exit the institution. All staff members are trained to conduct pat searches. (These involve running the hands over all parts of the inmate's body on top of the clothes. In addition, contents of pockets and anything being carried are examined separately, and hats, gloves, and jackets are removed for visual and tactile examination.) It is assumed that female officers can pat-search male inmates, and male officers can pat-search female inmates (just as police officers conduct cross-gender pat searches). A court may place some restrictions on such searches, such as saying a cross-gender search is permissible as long as it does not involve touching of genital areas or breasts. (For example, see *Grummett v. Rushen*, 779 F.2d 491 (9th Cir. 1985) and *Smith v. Fairman*, 678 F.2d 52 (7th Cir. 1982).)

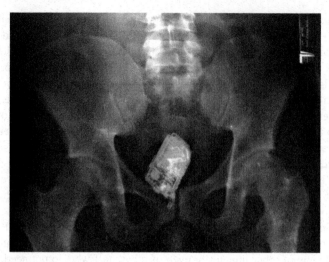

Figure 10-1 This image shows an x-ray of a prisoner taken in a maximum security prison, showing a cell phone in the inmate's intestines.
Source: © Centros Penales/AP Photos

In *Watson v. Jones*, 980 F.2d 1165 (8th Cir. 1992), two male inmates complained that a female officer fondled their genitals and anuses when she conducted pat searches. This officer, they said, conducted almost daily pat searches of them, and, during her searches, she engaged in "prolonged rubbing and fondling of the genitals and anus area." They claimed, in a Section 1983 action, that this was a violation of the Fourth Amendment. The trial court had dismissed the claim, granting summary judgment to the officer, mainly because she stated that she never did such crotch searches, except when she knew "something was there." The appeals court agreed that it was constitutionally permissible for a female officer to conduct pat searches of male inmates. *Timm v. Gunter*, 917 F.2d 1093 (8th Cir. 1990), had approved that practice. The appeals court in *Watson* distinguished *Timm*, on the grounds that the *Timm* case involved a claim by male inmates that it was in all situations a violation of their rights to be pat-searched by female officers. The court in *Timm* held that it was not a per se violation for female officers to pat-search male inmates.

However, the allegations by the inmates in *Watson* went beyond the basic issue of cross-gender pat searches. The court said that summary judgment in the lower court had been improper, because that court had not looked into the allegations that the officer had subjected the inmates to "sexually harassing and physically intrusive pat-down searches." The case was returned for further inquiry into whether the searches were unreasonable, and therefore unconstitutional, because they were excessively intrusive or sexually harassing. (That is, it was remanded in order to determine whether the searches had occurred in the crotch area more than was necessary for a routine tactile search for contraband.)

Perhaps the extreme ruling was in *Jordan v. Gardner*, 986 F.2d 1521 (9th Cir. 1993), where the court held that cross-gender pat searches of female inmates could not be conducted in prison.

This holding was arrived at, not based on an analysis of the Fourth Amendment, but based on a finding that many women had been physically and sexually abused before they came into prison, which would cause them to be traumatized by being pat-searched by male officers. This was held to be a violation of their Eighth Amendment rights, constituting cruel and unusual punishment of the female inmates.

In addition to the searches already mentioned, inmates may also be subject to searches by simple instruments or X-rays. These would occur when staff have a reasonable belief that an inmate is concealing contraband inside or upon his person and when a visual search is either not possible or would not be sufficient to reveal the hidden contraband. In those instances, medically trained staff may be allowed by policy (and provided that the local courts have not disapproved of the practice) to use a medical instrument or an X-ray to look for the contraband. X-rays, of course, must be handled by medical staff in order to ensure that excessive exposure to radiation is avoided and proper procedures are followed. (See Figure 10-1.) In some cases, blood or urine tests may be used to detect drug use, and breathalyzer or other on-the-spot tests may be used to detect alcohol use.

What must be emphasized is that the staff in any location must check with and receive legal advice from counsel to make sure what the position of local courts may be on any of these kinds of searches of the person. What we know from experience is that courts in many places are very sensitive about these search situations and have awarded money damages against staff members who performed unreasonable searches, particularly searches of the opposite gender and searches that were physically intrusive.

■ DNA Collection

On almost any day of the week, a person can watch a crime program on television where law enforcement solves the case through analysis of DNA (deoxyribonucleic acid). While the current science of DNA testing and identification is more complex than depicted in the media, the use of DNA to identify perpetrators and as evidence of criminal involvement cannot be underestimated. Because each person's DNA is unique (with the exception of identical twins), collecting this evidence from a crime scene can implicate or eliminate a suspect. DNA evidence also can be used in analyzing unidentified remains, and can help solve cases that may be many years old.[8]

In 1994, Congress first instructed the Federal Bureau of Investigation to initiate a data bank for collecting, storing, and analyzing DNA samples to assist in the solving of crime. Many states passed similar legislation directing state officials to gather DNA specimens for analysis. In 2000, Congress passed the DNA Analysis Backlog Elimination Act (42 U.S.C. § 14135, et seq), which directed that all persons convicted of specified federal felonies be compelled to provide a specimen for DNA analysis. Four years later, Congress passed the Justice for All Act (42 U.S.C. § 14135a(d)), which required that all persons convicted of *any* federal felony provide a DNA specimen. The effect of this legislation resulted in prison, parole, and probation officials requiring persons under their supervision to provide specimens of bodily fluids, usually a blood sample, for delivery to the FBI for inclusion in its Combined DNA Index System (CODIS).[9] As of April 2011, the FBI's National DNA Index (NDIS) contained 9,635,757 offender profiles.[10]

Prison officials were then tasked with developing procedures to collect specimens from inmates and forward the specimens of bodily fluid for DNA analysis. Early testing required the collection of a sample of blood (the current collection method is a swab of the mouth), a process which required a trained medical professional to extract the blood using a needle. One legal question posed by a number of prisoner lawsuits was whether the collection of blood for DNA analysis without warrant, probable cause, or reasonable suspicion violated the Fourth Amendment rights of the prisoners.

While the U.S. Supreme Court has not ruled on whether collection of DNA exemplars violates an inmate's Fourth Amendment rights, some federal courts of appeals have. Shortly after the enactment of the DNA Analysis Backlog Elimination Act, two prisoners filed a *Bivens* lawsuit against prison officials claiming that collection of bodily fluid pursuant to the statute violated their right to be free from unreasonable search and seizure under the Fourth Amendment. In *Groceman v. U.S. Department of Justice*, 354 F.3d 411 (5th Cir. 2004), the Fifth Circuit held that the Fourth Amendment is implicated by the extraction of blood from a prisoner to collect a DNA sample. In upholding the statute against Fourth Amendment challenge, the court concluded that collection of DNA specimens from a prisoner is reasonable in light of (1) a prisoner's diminished expectation of privacy, (2) the minimal intrusion involved in collecting the specimen, and (3) the legitimate governmental interest furthered by having DNA to investigate and prosecute crimes.

A similar analysis was used by federal courts of appeals in *Shaffer v. Saffle*, 148 F.3d 1180 (10th Cir. 1998), analyzing a state DNA collection statute, and in *United States v. Sczubelek*, 402 F.3d 175 (3rd Cir. 2005), holding that "[t]he government's interest in building a DNA database for identification purposes, similar to its interest in maintaining fingerprint records, outweighs the minimal intrusion into a criminal offender's diminished expectation of privacy."

Other courts have upheld the collection of DNA exemplars from prisoners under a "special needs" analysis, referring to a need beyond the ordinary law enforcement need.[11] In *Nicholas v. Goord*, 430 F.3d 652 (2nd Cir. 2005), several inmates in New York state custody challenged New York's DNA collection statute, seeking money damages and injunctive relief in a suit under 42 U.S.C. § 1983. The Second Circuit concluded that the extraction of DNA from a prisoner implicated the Fourth Amendment and served a special need. The court said, "Because the state's purpose in conducting DNA indexing is distinct from the ordinary 'crime detection' activities associated with normal law enforcement concerns, it meets the special needs threshold." The special needs analysis is discussed below in more detail.

■ Searches of Non-Inmates

[WARNING.] THIS IS A STATE CORRECTIONAL INSTITUTION. ALL PERSONS, VEHICLES AND PERSONAL PROPERTY ENTERING OR BROUGHT ON THESE GROUNDS ARE SUBJECT TO SEARCH. DRUG DETECTION DOGS AND ELECTRONIC DEVICES MAY BE USED FOR THIS PURPOSE.[12]

Persons in custody share the correctional environment with prison staff and visitors (e.g., inmate visitors, attorneys, government and community representatives, volunteers, and vendors). Courts have long taken notice that correctional institutions are unique places "fraught with serious security dangers" (*Bell v. Wolfish*). Prison security and good order are central objectives of correctional staff and administration. In order to promote prison security and good order, correctional administrators have the responsibility to prevent the introduction of contraband into the prison. In some cases, sources of contraband introduction are prison staff and visitors to the institution. Several important questions are raised in this context: What expectations of privacy do prison employees and visitors have? And, how do prison administrators accommodate these privacy interests, if any, with the interest in maintaining security by prohibiting the introduction of contraband? A sign, similar to the one at the beginning of this section often is found at the entranceways to prisons and serves to put on notice those persons entering prison property that they, their vehicles, and their personal property are subject to search.

Searches of Employees; *City of Ontario, CA. v. Quon*

Staff searches are very sensitive and generally are conducted only on a finding of reasonable suspicion. For visitors and staff, the suspicion often is founded upon confidential information, sometimes provided by an inmate. This requires assessing the reliability of the informant and determining whether there is any corroborating information or circumstance.

Staff members should be advised, throughout their training, that their persons and anything they bring into an institution are subject to search. (Signs, as noted above, also are posted to warn visitors that they are not to bring in contraband and that they may be subject to search to ensure that contraband is not brought in.) It would be good if we could believe that staff are always trustworthy and would never bring in contraband, but we know from experience that some staff, albeit a small number, can be corrupted, and have been used to bring all sorts of contraband into prisons and jails.[13]

Security is the prime concern of correctional facilities. Some correctional systems limit the amount of personal property that staff members may bring into the institution; others may subject staff to a routine metal detector and pat search. If the propriety of a search is in doubt, turning the employee away (just as the visitor can be turned away) while the matter is investigated may sometimes be the best solution. But to collect evidence and to be certain that allegations or suspicions are well-founded, searches of employee lockers, cars, clothes, purses and wallets, and searches of their persons, may be necessary.

In 2001, a police department in California acquired alphanumeric pagers to be used to contact SWAT members in the event of an emergency. The contract for service was with the city, and the city paid the monthly fees. When the pagers were issued, the officers were advised that use of the pagers could be monitored by the city, and that the officers should have no expectation of privacy or confidentiality during such usage. The city's contract with the service provider permitted a limited number of characters for each pager each month, and any overage was billed at an additional cost. The city noted that some officers were exceeding their monthly character limits and initially offered the officers the opportunity to reimburse the city for the overage rather than have an audit done of the messages. After the overages continued, the city conducted an audit of the usage of those officers to determine if the contracted limits were sufficient for city business. After transcripts of the messages were collected and reviewed, it was determined that at least one officer was using the pager for personal messages and was conducting personal business while on duty. After the city initiated disciplinary action against the officer, litigation began. One of the issues was the privacy interest that a public employee maintains when using city-owned electronic communication devices.

In *City of Ontario, CA v. Quon*, 560 U.S. __ (2010), the Supreme Court addressed the issue of whether a public employee had an expectation of privacy protected by the Fourth Amendment in personal communications made using a government-owned communications device, and if so, did the city's action of reviewing such communications amount to a "reasonable" search. The Court first noted that the Fourth Amendment applies to conduct by officers of the government in situations other than investigations of criminal activity. The Fourth Amendment also applies to the government in its capacity as an employer. Public employees do not lose the protections of the Fourth Amendment merely because they work for the government, rather than a private employer. The Court also noted that the function and operation of the government create "special needs" beyond normal law enforcement needs that make the usual requirements of a warrant or probable cause impractical in the government workplace.

To answer the first question, whether the police officer had an expectation of privacy protected by the Fourth Amendment, the Court first considered the non-law enforcement case of *O'Connor v. Ortega*, 480 U.S. 709 (1987). *O'Connor* dealt with the warrantless search of an office and files of a state hospital employee. The Court noted that *O'Connor* held that workplace conditions in the public sector can vary significantly and that there may be certain circumstances in public sector employment where an employee will have no reasonable expectation of privacy. However, these instances must be determined on a case-by-case basis. To decide the *Quon* case, the Supreme Court presumed that the officer had a reasonable expectation of privacy in the communications—that obtaining and reviewing a transcript of the communications constituted a search under the Fourth Amendment and that principles of law applicable to searches of physical office space apply with at least the same force to electronic communications.

The last issue for the Court to decide was whether the search was reasonable. While the Fourth Amendment usually requires a warrant to be reasonable, there are exceptions, including "special needs of the workplace." A warrantless search by a government employer which is conducted for a:

> **noninvestigatory, work-related purpos[e] or for the investigatio[n] of work-related misconduct…is reasonable if it is justified at its inception and if the measures adopted are reasonably related to the objectives of the search and not excessively intrusive in light of the circumstances giving rise to the search [internal quotations omitted].**

In this case, the search was "valid at its inception" because its purpose was to determine if the city's contract provided a sufficient amount of coverage to carry out public business and to ensure that the city was not using public funds to pay for an employee's extensive personal communications. The scope of the search was also reasonable because only two of several months of communications were reviewed, and only communications made while the officer was on duty were reviewed. The Court also concluded that the extent of the expectation of privacy is important. In this case, the officer was advised that the communications were subject to audit.

As a law enforcement officer, he would or should have known that his actions were likely to come under legal scrutiny, and that might entail an analysis of his on-the-job communications.

The precise impact and application of *Quon* in the correctional setting are unclear. The "special needs of the workplace," as applied to the public sector work environment, certainly may impact the status of the law in the areas of prison employee and visitor searches. One example is whether the "special needs of the workplace" standard justifies warrantless and suspicionless searches of prison employees' vehicles parked on prison grounds. In *True v. Nebraska*, 612 F.3d 676 (8th Cir. 2010), the state had a policy which authorized prison personnel, without warrant, probable cause, or reasonable suspicion, to search employee vehicles parked on prison grounds. The vehicles that were searched were chosen randomly by location. Before a search was made, the employee was asked to consent to the search, and if consent was refused, no search would be done, but the employee could be disciplined. In *True*, the employee refused to consent, no search was made, and the employee was disciplined. The court of appeals first noted that while correctional workers retain certain expectations of privacy, the fact that the employee works in a prison diminishes any subjective expectation of privacy. The next questions were whether the search was justified by "special needs of the workplace" and if the search was reasonable. In upholding the policy, the court ruled that search of a vehicle is less intrusive than a search of a person. The court also ruled that conducting random searches of vehicles parked on prison grounds where inmates might have access to the vehicle was a reasonable practice to prevent the introduction of contraband. The court's decision held that prison security and order are factors to consider in determining whether "special needs of the workplace" exist. In deciding this case, factual determinations such as whether vehicles are in an area accessible to inmates, and whether the selection of vehicles to be searched was based on a uniform or systematic random selection, were important.[14]

Earlier in this chapter we noted that the issue of when prison officials may conduct strip searches of inmates caused the Supreme Court in *Bell v. Wolfish* "the greatest pause." The Court concluded that a reasonable response to the security needs of the prison was to conduct strip searches of inmates who had access to persons or places where contraband could be obtained. One issue that was not addressed by *Bell v. Wolfish* is under what conditions, if any, can prison employees be subjected to strip searches. This is a question the Supreme Court has not yet answered, but several lower courts have provided guidance to prison officials. Jurisdictions that have addressed the issue have generally held that correctional workers may be strip searched without a warrant only when there is reasonable suspicion the employee is transporting contraband. *McDonell v. Hunter*, 809 F.2d 1302 (8th Cir. 1987). Reasonable suspicion requires that the search be based on "specific objective facts and rational inferences they [officials] are entitled to draw from those facts in light of their experience. It requires individualized suspicion, specifically directed to the person who is targeted for the strip search." *Hunter v. Auger*, 672 F.2d 668 (8th Cir. 1982). The courts have applied a balancing test: weighing privacy interest of employees (which are diminished because of their workplace) with the legitimate governmental interest of promoting institution security and good order by preventing the introduction of contraband. Again, law enforcement officials and counsel should be consulted and local court rulings on searches must be carefully followed. As a rule of thumb, reasonable suspicion that an employee is carrying contraband is the minimum standard for conducting a search, but a search warrant is always the safest way to go.

Visitor Searches

Visitors to prisons or jails no doubt retain some degree of Fourth Amendment protection, and they have a greater expectation of privacy than inmates have. Nonetheless, once they enter the jail or prison, security concerns are pervasive, and prison and jail staff can take necessary steps to protect the security and good order of the facility. This means that, in all facilities, visitors may be constantly monitored, which may include camera surveillance; they may be asked to check their possessions, such as bags and purses, in lockers at the entrance; and they may be asked to walk through a metal-detecting device. Some places require, and courts have approved, routine pat downs (conducted by a staff member of the same sex) and searches of bags and briefcases before entering a corrections facility. If a person refuses, the visitor may be permitted to turn around and leave. (This practice of allowing a visitor to leave, which, of course, is not an option for an inmate, prevails simply because the prime interest of prison or jail officials is to prevent the introduction of contraband into the institution. When the visitor leaves, the introduction of contraband has probably been prevented, at least for that visit.) Not all correctional systems offer the departure option, and one court has refused to suppress evidence found in a search of a vehicle on prison grounds after the visitor refused to give express consent for the search. *United States v. Prevo*, 435 F.3d 1343 (11th Cir. 2006). In that case, the court relied on the fact that this visitor had driven her car onto prison grounds several times and was aware that her vehicle could be subject to search. The court of appeals concluded that implicit consent could not be withdrawn once law enforcement officers determined to search the vehicle. The search of the vehicle produced a loaded firearm, drugs and drug paraphernalia, and over $20,000 in cash.[15]

In another instance, a court used a balancing test to conclude that the "special needs" of a prison in preventing the introduction of contraband outweighed the minor inconvenience of a search of a prison visitor's vehicle without warrant or probable cause. *Neumeyer v. Beard*, 421 F.3d 210 (3rd Cir. 2005). Like the facts in *United States v. Prevo*, a notice that vehicles were subject to search was prominently posted, and the visitors had parked in the visitor parking lot several times before the search. The court did question the absence of any written standards by the state directing how vehicles were to be randomly selected and how the searches were to be conducted, but in the absence of any evidence of abuse of discretion, this was not sufficient to warrant finding the search unreasonable.

Other searches, such as strip searches and holding (detaining) a visitor to conduct a thorough search of personal property, require reasonable suspicion (that the visitor is, in fact, carrying contraband or illicit property) to justify a search being conducted. When time allows, it may be best to contact local law enforcement officials, because these circumstances generate concern about the possibility of a criminal prosecution as much as they do about introduction of contraband. The best option, when time allows (which often is not the case), is to go to court and obtain a **search warrant** for a strip search of a visitor, or even for a pat search or search of a visitor's possessions (including a car).

SUMMARY

- Conducting searches of persons and of property and places in prisons and jails is essential to maintain security.
- The Supreme Court held that the Fourth Amendment does not apply to a prison cell. An inmate has no protected right of privacy in prison. Officers may conduct searches of cells to the extent they believe it is necessary in order to maintain security and order. They may also seize articles that are found during searches and that are deemed to be contraband (*Hudson v. Palmer*). An inmate has no right to be present during the search of his cell (*Bell v. Wolfish*).
- There is also no right to privacy in other areas of a jail. It was held to be permissible for authorities to eavesdrop, and record, a conversation in the visiting room between an inmate and his brother (*Lanza v. New York*). A recording made in such a visiting situation may be turned over to law enforcement officials and used in prosecution of the inmate (*United States v. Hearst*).
- Under the federal statute on wiretapping (interception of communications, 18 U.S.C. § 2510 et seq.), prison officials, within the ordinary course of business, may monitor inmate telephone conversations without obtaining judicial approval. Monitoring may also occur with the consent of one party to the conversation (*United States v. Paul; United States v. Amen*).
- There is no Fourth Amendment protection when a party consents to his conversation with an attorney being recorded and monitored by others (*United States v. Novak*). When attorneys and their clients carry on communications knowing their communications are being recorded and monitored by third parties, there can be no claim to attorney–client privilege in the communication (*United States v. Hatcher*).
- Strip searches of inmates cause special concerns to the courts. The Supreme Court upheld a policy of conducting body cavity searches after all contact visits in a jail (*Bell v. Wolfish*). Cross-gender pat searches are widely performed, but strip searches are usually performed by officers of the same sex as the inmates, except, perhaps, in emergency situations.
- A federal court in New York required prison authorities to make arrangements to ensure the privacy of female inmates, so male officers who were working in their living units would not be able to observe them unclothed (*Forts v. Ward*).
- In most cases, courts have disapproved of strip searches being conducted of arrestees when the arrests were for minor offenses. A federal appeals court even disapproved of a strip search for a felony offense because the circumstances did not indicate a risk of violence (*Kennedy v. Los Angeles Police Department*). Strip searches tend to make the courts very nervous and cautious. Recently, however, the U.S. Supreme Court upheld strip searches of detainees admitted to a jail's general population, citing the government's substantial

interest in preventing any new inmate from putting those who live or work at these institutions at even greater risk. The Court did not consider its ruling all-encompassing, recognizing that under a different set of facts, for example, involving the touching of detainees, there may be legitimate concerns over the invasiveness of searches *(Florence v. Board of Chosen Freeholders).*

- Pat searches of inmates are commonly done as inmates move about the institution. While cross-gender pat searches may occur, restrictions may be placed on such searches. Another type of search is by simple instruments or X-rays, with these performed by medical personnel.

- Appellate courts have held that the collection of DNA specimens from a prisoner is reasonable (and not a violation of the Fourth Amendment) in light of a prisoner's diminished expectation of privacy; the minimal intrusion involved in collecting the specimen; and the legitimate governmental interest furthered by having DNA to investigate.

- In most jurisdictions, visitors and employees may be subject to searches when prison or jail staff have reasonable suspicion that they may be carrying contraband. Most facilities post warnings, advising visitors that they are not to bring any contraband into the facilities and that they may be subject to searches of their persons or property. The application of the "special needs" test may permit the government to conduct warrantless searches, without reasonable suspicion, of the vehicles of visitors and employees. In this area of searches, because the Supreme Court has not ruled and there is clearly a constitutional right involved, prison or jail administrators must make certain what the local state of the law is. If there is doubt about the propriety of a search and if no search warrant has been obtained, it is usually better to turn the visitor (or employee) away and refuse entry into the facility, rather than risk an unlawful search.

- The Supreme Court has held that a warrantless search of a government employee by his employer conducted for a noninvestigatory, work-related purpose or to investigate work-related misconduct is reasonable. The search must be justified at its inception and the adopted measures must be reasonably related to the search objectives and not excessively intrusive in light of the circumstances that gave rise to the search *(City of Ontario, CA v. Quon).*

THINKING ABOUT IT

Prison officials have received information that Lisa Boren, during previous visits with her husband, wore white denim jeans with a hole in her crotch, and that she and her husband became involved in inappropriate conduct during visiting hours. This information came from other prison visitors, and a correctional officer had seen the hole in the pants. On her next visit, she was wearing white denim jeans and was told she had to submit to a strip search in order to receive the visit. She did. No hole was found in the jeans, and the visit was allowed. She sued, claiming that the search violated her Fourth Amendment rights. Was she successful? This case is reported in *Boren v. Deland,* 958 F.2d 987 (10th Cir. 1992).

KEY TERMS

contraband (corrections): Material which is prohibited, either by law or regulation. It includes material which can reasonably be expected to cause physical injury or adversely affect the security, safety, or good order of a prison or jail.

reasonable suspicion: A set of facts (used as the standard, for example, to stop a suspected offender in a public place) that would lead a prudent person under the circumstances to believe criminal activity is present.

search warrant: A written order, issued by a judicial officer, authorizing the search and seizure of property, for evidence of criminal activity, including illicit goods and the fruits of crime.

shakedown (corrections): Vernacular in correctional facilities for the search of a person or place.

ENDNOTES

1. Burke, T. and Owen, S. "Cell Phones as Prison Contraband," *FBI Law Enforcement Bulletin*, July (2010): 10–15. On August 10, 2010, President Obama signed the Cell Phone Contraband Act of 2010 (Public Law 111-225). In part, this legislation amends 18 U.S.C. § 1791, "Providing or possessing contraband in prison," by expanding the term prohibited object to include a phone or other device used by a user of commercial mobile service." The punishment for providing or attempting to provide an inmate this prohibited object, or for an inmate to make, possess or obtain, or attempt to make or obtain this prohibited object, is up to one year in prison, a fine, or both.

2. The authors are not convinced of that statement. We note that zealous advocates, including some courts, asserted that inmates had full privacy protection in their cells, their "home away from home," and such advocates would therefore require a warrant to search a cell, especially of a pretrial detainee. An interesting example of this stance was seen in the trial of John Hinckley in U.S. District Court in the District of Columbia for the attempt to assassinate President Ronald Reagan. At one point in the trial, an extremely important piece of prosecution evidence was excluded on the grounds of invasion of the defendant's privacy in his cell. An officer had found, in a regular search of Hinckley's cell, a diary that Hinckley was keeping. He noted some entries in that diary, copied them, and turned them over to authorities. A government witness, a psychiatrist, was ready to testify about Hinckley's mental state—his "sanity"—based on the writings in that diary. However, the witness was not allowed to do so on the grounds that the diary writings were protected by a privacy right and that they had been taken and copied in an "unreasonable seizure" under the Fourth Amendment. It is possible to speculate that, had the *Hudson* ruling been available, the ruling of that trial court would have been different, and the psychiatrist would have been allowed to testify, using Hinckley's diary entries, perhaps leading to a different outcome on Hinckley's sanity. Hinckley, you may recall, was found not guilty by reason of

insanity and has been committed, for many years, to St. Elizabeth's Hospital, the psychiatric hospital of the District of Columbia.

3. The authors recall a situation many years ago that is somewhat contrary to the statement that a cell is not a home. Specifically, an inmate claimed that he could not practice his orthodox religious faith outside of his own residence; his religious leaders confirmed this concept. The solution: prison officials allowed him to "rent" his cell for a nominal amount, thus affirming it as his residence.

4. The concessions made by the state would be of concern to some correctional administrators. While inmates were showering, the court had required and the state had agreed to provide screens that would prevent viewing of the naked inmates by staff. As we have noted, the state also agreed to allow windows in the cell doors to be covered at the inmate's request for 15-minute intervals. It is a truism in prison security that there cannot be any areas that are off-limits to staff supervision. The same kind of concern has arisen in the religious area, where Black Muslims objected to any white staff being present during their meetings and where Native Americans, who disrobe during the ceremonies, objected to staff being present in their sweat lodges. Courts rejected both claims, noting the security concerns of the supervision of the prison that overrode inmates' concerns about staff presence. In the same way here, there would be a concern on the part of prison staff about any accommodation of inmate privacy that would place an area off-limits to any staff supervision (the shower and the inmate's cell). Those areas, as much as any other, are of concern, because they can be used for improper activities, to the detriment of institution security.

5. It has been our observation that these issues of nudity and exposure of body parts give the courts great discomfort. In some cases, the courts have flat out said so (as the Supreme Court does here, in its muffled comment about "giving us pause"). At presentations in court, some judges are barely able to contain their displeasure about the government insisting on having staff view nude bodies of inmates.

   This does not seem to provoke such an emotional response in the health care (hospital) setting, where viewing of the opposite sex has come to be commonly accepted. It has been our assertion in prison cases that the same kind of professional approach must be taken, because occasional viewing and (more seldom) touching of the bodies of the inmates must be done as part of correctional officers' jobs. It will no doubt be many years before the courts come to view this opposite-sex viewing and occasional touching as a necessary part of the correctional setting, to be handled, of course, in as straight-forward and professional a manner as possible.

6. The court in *Bull* stated that it was overruling its own panel opinion in *Thompson* (previously discussed in this section), which held "that a blanket policy of stripping arrestees was per se unconstitutional." The court also made it clear that it was not disturbing its prior opinions dealing with "searches of arrestees who were not classified for housing in the general jail or prison population." An example of this is an intoxicated person who is released upon becoming sober.

   Surprisingly, the issue of strip searches recently arose within the context of a middle school. In *Safford Unified School District v. Redding*, 557 U.S. __ (2009), the Supreme Court said,

[t]he issue here is whether a 13-year-old student's Fourth Amendment right was violated when she was subjected to a search of her bra and underpants by school officials acting on reasonable suspicion that she had brought forbidden prescription and over-the-counter drugs to school. Because there were no reasons to suspect the drugs presented a danger or were concealed in her underwear, we hold that the search did violate the Constitution, but because there is reason to question the clarity with which the right was established, the official who ordered the unconstitutional search is entitled to qualified immunity from liability.

7. Inmates can be clever in finding ways to introduce contraband. For example, see Figure 10-1. In addition, the authors have seen an X-ray of an inmate's rectal cavity that contained both a handcuff key and a loaded gun.
8. DNA Initiative. "Advancing Criminal Justice Through DNA Technology." Accessed January 14, 2011. http://www.dna.gov/basics/biology
9. For a more complete description of the collection process and CODIS, see *United States v. Kincade*, 379 F.3d 813 (9th Cir. 2004) (en banc).
10. Federal Bureau of Investigation. "CODIS-NDIS Statistics." Accessed June 15, 2011. http://www/fbi.gov/about-us/labs/codis/ndis-statistics
11. The Supreme Court has ruled that the Fourth Amendment prohibits only unreasonable searches and seizures and that usually a search without "reasonable suspicion" is per se unreasonable. When the search is done for the purpose of collecting evidence of criminal wrongdoing, usually a warrant is required. In several non-law enforcement cases, the Supreme Court ruled that searches on less than "reasonable suspicion" may not violate the Fourth Amendment if the search serves "special needs beyond the normal need for law enforcement."
12. *Neumeyer v. Beard*, 421 F.3d 210 (3rd Cir. 2005). This particular sign was posted at the prison entranceways and in front of the visitor parking lot at the Pennsylvania Department of Corrections' State Correctional Institute at Huntingdon. Such signs are common at prisons and serve to put people coming to the prison on notice that their person, vehicle, and personal property are subject to search to prevent the introduction of contraband and to help ensure prison security and good order.
13. An unfortunate example of this is shown in a June 16, 2010, U.S. Department of Justice press release. The press release discussed the sentencing of two prison staff members and an inmate for smuggling drugs and contraband into a federal prison. The staff members supplied an inmate with marijuana, cell phones, and other contraband and, in return, received money. The two staff received 21 months and 18 months sentences. The inmate also received 21 months, with this to begin following completion of his original sentence.
14. Appellant True also alleged that by conducting random searches of employees' cars, but not the cars of visitors, there was an equal protection violation. The appeals court disagreed, affirming the lower court's grant of summary judgment for the defendants. The appeals court held the differential treatment was "rationally related to a legitimate state interest." Those interests were institutional security, contraband interdiction, and administrative efficiency. The court noted that employee cars are at the prison daily, conceivably making it easier to smuggle contraband. The court held there was no violation of the equal protection clause.

15. In *Prevo*, one argument raised by the defendant was that searches of cars in the parking lot of a work release center generally will be ineffective. The court spoke to the deference that is to be provided to prison administrators. In a humorous commentary, the court then added, "Whatever else may be said about the effectiveness of the search policy, it did work in this case…For Prevo, who was caught, to complain that the search policy is ineffective is like a law school graduate who flunked the Bar complaining that the exam is too easy to do any good."

11 Fifth and Fourteenth Amendments: Due Process—Inmate Discipline

There is no iron curtain drawn between the Constitution and the prisons of this country. Prisoners may also claim the protections of the Due Process Clause. They may not be deprived of life, liberty, or property without due process of law.

U.S. Supreme Court, *Wolff v. McDonnell*

Chapter Outline

- The Fifth and Fourteenth Amendments
- The Importance of Inmate Discipline
- How Prison Discipline Works
- *Wolff v. McDonnell*
- *Sandin v. Conner*
- *Baxter v. Palmigiano*
- Double Jeopardy
- *Superintendent v. Hill*
- *Hewitt v. Helms*
- Confidential Informants

Due process is found at two places in the U.S. Constitution: the Fifth Amendment and the Fourteenth Amendment.

The Fourteenth Amendment, Section 1, says:

No State shall ... deprive any person of life, liberty, or property without due process of law; nor deny to any person within its jurisdiction the equal protection of the laws.

This amendment was adopted after the Civil War and guarantees protections against state actions (which also include local government actions) that would take away the life, liberty, or property of its citizens.

There is also a due process clause in the Fifth Amendment, which protects citizens against federal government actions that would take away life, liberty, or property:

No person shall be ... deprived of life, liberty, or property, without due process of law.

We will see in this chapter how these due process provisions of the Constitution protect inmates against unfair actions of the government (state and local inmates are protected by the Fourteenth Amendment, federal inmates by the Fifth Amendment). This chapter discusses due process in the context of inmate discipline. A separate chapter discusses due process with respect to classification, transfers, personal injuries, and property loss.

◼ The Fifth and Fourteenth Amendments

As you can see from the language of the due process clauses, there are two inquiries to be made in any claim of constitutional protection against state action. The first question is, has there been any deprivation of life, liberty, or property? Not every type of government action that offends a person raises a due process question. A person claiming violation of the due process clause must show that life, liberty, or property has been taken or is adversely affected. The second question (once it is decided that there has been a deprivation of constitutional concern, that is, of life, liberty, or property) is, what process is due to the person who has been deprived? This is a matter that the courts have called "fundamental fairness." The purpose of due process is to ensure that the government has taken action that it is justified to take or that it has taken the action with procedural steps that ensure fairness. What makes an action fair? Generally speaking, the courts have said that fairness means providing steps that ensure that the facts are as the government claims they are, and the action taken is authorized by law (that is, the government agency or official taking the action has been given the legal authority to act). Beyond those general statements, the exact procedure that must be followed—the "process that is due" to the individual affected—varies greatly from one situation to another.

Courts tend to say that the more serious the loss is to the individual, the more procedural protections (due process) must be provided by the government. For example, what is the most serious kind of deprivation that the government can take? We would probably agree that taking a convicted offender's life as punishment for a capital offense is the highest kind of deprivation. In response to that analysis, beyond the stringent procedural requirements for criminal trials in general (probably the most stringent evidentiary and procedural requirements in any courts in the world), even more detailed procedural protections are established before capital punishment can be imposed. At the other extreme would probably be a minor loss of property, in which a person is entitled to a claim procedure that is handled administratively (informally) to reimburse the citizen for her loss. We will see that some actions in prison carry a high degree of procedural protection, and others carry low degrees of due process entitlement—or none at all (even though the offended person claims there has been a "deprivation" by the government).

◼ The Importance of Inmate Discipline

This chapter deals with the most frequently contested and litigated type of action involving inmates: inmate **discipline.** Why is disciplinary action against inmates so often contested? There are a number of reasons. The action taken can be very serious to the individual inmate, affecting his sentence (as when good time is taken away, or his parole date is moved back) and thus his liberty in getting to the streets. Or disciplinary action may take away his property, confiscating some item he has in his cell or ordering him to pay for damage he has done to someone else's property. The disciplinary action may adversely affect the conditions under which he is held; for instance, he may be placed in highly restricted **disciplinary confinement** (which is variously called detention, segregation, isolation, or "the hole" and can be thought of as a jail within the prison). His privileges may also be taken away, such as recreation, visiting, or commissary purchases.

The persons who are disciplined typically are those who have trouble adjusting to the regimen and rules of prison life and are contesting or trying to circumvent those rules almost every day of their incarceration. It should not be surprising that convicted criminals get into trouble inside the prison as well as outside.[1] A large number of inmates are sociopathic, to one degree or another. They not only get into trouble, but they reject any personal responsibility for violating the rules (whether inside or outside the prison). They search to place the blame on others, so when they are charged with violating the prison's rules, they dispute the charges or the authority of prison officials to place any sanctions upon them. Appealing disciplinary action by any means that are available is commonplace. In grievance procedures (in those jurisdictions that allow administrative appeals of the disciplinary actions), complaints about disciplinary actions are the most common type of complaints filed by inmates. The ultimate appeal (through legitimate channels) is to file an action in court, challenging the disciplinary sanction that was taken. In lawsuits in which inmates have raised due process questions about the fairness of the actions taken by prison staff, disciplinary actions are frequently cited complaints.

It is probably immediately evident to those of us who have worked in prisons or jails that a disciplinary process that punishes inmates for infractions of the rules is vitally necessary. But some who are not familiar with corrections institutions may wonder why additional punishment is necessary when the inmates are already locked up and are thereby being punished severely for their criminal activity. The answer is complex and is open to discussion, but the main reasons are these: most prisons today are surprisingly (to an outsider) free-flowing and tolerant of a wide variety of activities, and inmates, in large numbers, move from living quarters to dining hall, to work, to recreation, to visiting, to school. Long gone are the days when inmates moved from place to place in the institution in lockstep and without speaking or even while chained together.

The large varieties of activities and programs that are offered today, even in a highly regimented prison or jail environment (there are, of course, fewer programs and much less inmate movement in jails than in prisons), provide many benefits. These include a greater normalization of the living environment, which reduces tensions for inmates and thereby also for staff; a greater variety of programs, which assist the inmates in rehabilitation efforts and in preparing them for return to the community; and greater opportunities for interaction with others, both inmates and staff, which assist inmates in having more positive interpersonal relationships. Although there are many benefits to such activities, there are also increased risks, the most important of which is increased risk to security. Flowing numbers of inmates moving from place to place in the institution increase the opportunities for misconduct, such as planning escapes, assaults (on other inmates and on staff), and traffic in contraband. In high security institutions and in antiquated facilities in which the supervision of inmate movement and programs is difficult, there will be much less flow of inmate traffic within the institution and less variety in programs.

Because the majority of inmates want to adjust as well as they can to the requirements of prison life (doing their time quietly and with as few confrontations as possible), it is the goal of the staff to help those inmates by providing a safe and secure environment. To accomplish this, those who create trouble must be punished, either by coercing them into conforming their behavior to expected prison norms or by removing them from the population where they disrupt and intimidate others. As a side benefit, staff are hoping to instill better self-control skills and the ability to adjust to societal norms of behavior, producing inmates who respect authority and the rules that protect the safety and the rights of all.

■ How Prison Discipline Works

There is a need for an internal disciplinary system in every corrections facility, a system that must be firm and fair. Every inmate upon admission to the facility, in the orientation procedure, should be given notification (preferably both written and oral) of the contents of the system. Central to this orientation procedure, and underlying inmate discipline, is a purpose of instilling in inmates a sense of responsibilities, which go along with freedoms and liberties that they may have while confined. (Obviously, these freedoms and rights are much reduced compared to those of persons on the outside, but it is important to emphasize the ones that inmates do retain.) **Box 11-1** provides a model set of rights and responsibilities addressed to inmates.

Staff must also be trained in disciplinary procedures (because an offense may be committed in the presence of any staff member, everyone must be taught the requirements of the system and how misconduct by inmates is handled). The most basic training starts with the "criminal code" for the prison—that is, the list of offenses inside the institution and also the list of sanctions that may be imposed. There is a large list of offenses on the misconduct list (some things, such as murder, assault, and theft, are just like offenses on the outside, while others, such as escape, riot, and offenses involving contraband, are peculiar to prisons). At the end of this text is Appendix 6, which presents a model misconduct code for a prison. It sets out a list of typical prison offenses, shows their degree of seriousness, and gives the types of sanctions that may be imposed when an inmate commits a particular offense. (It must be emphasized—this is a model code and not one that is legally required or judicially approved.)[2]

Typically, as is shown in Appendix 6, offenses are of different categories of severity, and sanctions may be imposed in a range, according to the severity of the offense that has been committed. Sanctions are of many kinds. In those jurisdictions with parole, serious misconduct is usually reported to the parole board, and serious problems with misconduct in the prison may adversely affect parole decisions. Most jurisdictions have some sort of good time. This is time taken off the full length of the sentence, so that an inmate can be released early (if she is not paroled first) with the accumulation of good time credits. (Good time in some places is also applied to the parole eligibility or parole grant date, so that earning good conduct time can also advance a parole release date.) Most often, good time is given for good conduct for each month the sentence is served (or for working in a factory or in the fields, or for an unusually meritorious event, such as assisting staff in a riotous situation). In some states, it is given at the beginning of the sentence, according to the number of years in the sentence, and the inmate retains that "lump sum" of good time unless there is reason to take it away. Taking good time

Box 11-1 Inmate Rights and Responsibilities

Bureau of Prisons, Justice
§ 541.12 Inmate rights and responsibilities.

Rights		Responsibilities	
1.	You have the right to expect that as a human being you will be treated respectfully, impartially, and fairly by all personnel.	1.	You have the responsibility to treat others, both employees and inmates, in the same manner.
2.	You have the right to be informed of the rules, procedures, and schedules concerning the operation of the institution.	2.	You have the responsibility to know and abide by them.
3.	You have the right to freedom of religious affiliation, and voluntary religious worship.	3.	You have the responsibility to recognize and respect the rights of others in this regard.
4.	You have the right to health care, which includes nutritious meals, proper bedding and clothing, and a laundry schedule for cleanliness of the same, an opportunity to shower regularly, proper ventilation for warmth and fresh air, a regular exercise period, toilet articles and medical and dental treatment.	4.	It is your responsibility not to waste food, to follow the laundry and shower schedule, to maintain neat and clean living quarters, to keep your area free of contraband, and to seek medical and dental care as you may need it.
5.	You have the right to visit and correspond with family members, and friends, and correspond with members of the news media in keeping with Bureau rules and institution guidelines.	5.	It is your responsibility to conduct yourself properly during visits, not to accept or pass contraband, and not to violate the law or Bureau rules or institution guidelines through your correspondence.
6.	You have the right to unrestricted and confidential access to the courts by correspondence (on matters such as the legality of your conviction, civil matters, pending criminal cases, and conditions of your imprisonment).	6.	You have the responsibility to present honestly and fairly your petitions, questions, and problems to the court.
7.	You have the right to legal counsel from an attorney of your choice by interviews and correspondence.	7.	It is your responsibility to use the services of an attorney honestly and fairly.

(*continued*)

Box 11-1 (*continued*)

Rights		Responsibilities	
8.	You have the right to participate in the use of law library reference materials to assist you in resolving legal problems. You also have the right to receive help when it is available through a legal assistance program.	8.	It is your responsibility to use these resources in keeping with the procedures and schedule prescribed and to respect the rights of other inmates to the use of the materials and assistance.
9.	You have the right to a wide range of reading materials for educational purposes and for your own enjoyment. These materials may include magazines and newspapers sent from the community, with certain restrictions.	9.	It is your responsibility to seek and utilize such materials for your personal benefit, without depriving others of their equal rights to the use of this material.
10.	You have the right to participate in education, vocational training and employment as far as resources are available, and in keeping with your interests, needs, and abilities.	10.	You have the responsibility to take advantage of activities, which may help you live a successful and law-abiding life within the institution and in the community. You will be expected to abide by the regulations governing the use of such activities.
11.	You have the right to use your funds for commissary and other purchases, consistent with institution security and good order, for opening bank and/or savings accounts, and for assisting your family.	11.	You have the responsibility to meet your financial and legal obligations, including, but not limited to, court-imposed assessments, fines, and restitution. You also have the responsibility to make use of your funds in a manner consistent with your release plans, your family needs, and for other obligations that you may have.

Source: Reprinted from the Federal Bureau of Prisons, published in Title 28 CFR, § 541.12 (Revised as of July 1, 2010).

from an inmate is, thus, a significant sanction, especially in some circumstances in which many months can be taken from the inmate (good time **forfeiture**).

A common type of punishment, which was already referred to, is placing the inmate for a certain length of time in disciplinary confinement inside the prison (disciplinary segregation or detention). Property may also be taken away or privileges revoked. Assignments to a preferred job or preferred housing may be changed. The inmate may be ordered to be transferred to a higher level institution. For some offenses, only one or two types of sanction are available; for others, there may be a whole range and combination of sanctions that may be applied for the individual offender and his offenses (just as in sentencing in criminal court).

There is also a specific procedure established for deciding the "guilt" or "innocence" of the inmate and deciding the sanctions that are appropriate. (We place the terms *guilt* and *innocence* in quotes, because, technically, these terms are tied to criminal prosecutions, and it is more accurate to say that the inmate is found to have committed the offense or not. In common parlance, staff and inmates often use the criminal court terminology, and that should be no surprise. We have long recommended that corrections staff avoid using the criminal terms in inmate disciplinary actions. For one thing, to do so invites courts, when reviewing administrative discipline matters, to use their well-understood standards of criminal law proceedings, rather than to focus on the very different nature of the prison hearing.) The inmate is brought before a disciplinary authority, which may be a single individual or a committee. These are staff members who are experienced in prison matters and have been trained to conduct such hearings. (A few states have tried using a hearing officer, who has a greater degree of independence and is from outside the prison.)

The inmate receives a written copy of the charges before the hearing (we will look at the constitutional requirements for the different elements of the proceedings later in this chapter). At the hearing, the inmate may have someone assist him (ordinarily not an attorney or someone from the outside) or may appear without assistance. The inmate may present his version of what happened. The hearing officer or committee examines the evidence and decides whether or not the inmate did the prohibited act, as charged. If the officer or committee concludes that he did, the same authority decides what sanction to impose (again, as with the terms *guilty* and *innocent*, inmates and staff may use the term *sentence* taken from criminal court terminology). Often, the decisions regarding whether the inmate committed the prohibited act and which sanction is to be imposed may be reviewed by a reviewing authority, at the institution or at a higher level of the agency. Some jurisdictions allow the inmate to appeal an adverse decision through the inmate grievance procedure, and some provide for automatic review of all disciplinary actions, at least when they are of a higher degree of severity.

■ *Wolff v. McDonnell*

Wolff v. McDonnell, 418 U.S. 539 (1974), is the "granddaddy" of inmate discipline decisions. As in many other prison cases dealing with all sorts of prison operations, lower courts had diverged widely on the disciplinary issues regarding whether inmates were entitled to any due process protections at all, and if so, what the constitutional due process requirements were. With *Wolff*, the Supreme Court gave us the constitutional standards. Later cases decided subsidiary issues or refined the holdings in *Wolff*, but this case remains our leading, landmark decision on due process in prison hearings.

McDonnell was a Nebraska inmate who filed a Section 1983 action, claiming that disciplinary proceedings did not comply with the due process clause. (The *Wolff* decision also addressed the issue of attorney mail, and there was a question about the adequacy of the legal assistance program provided to inmates. But *Wolff* is known principally as the "inmate discipline case.") McDonnell was found guilty of serious misconduct. Under Nebraska rules, infractions that were less than serious could be punished only by loss of privileges. For "flagrant or serious misconduct," the inmate could have his good time credits taken away, and he also could be placed in a disciplinary cell. Loss of good time not only potentially lengthened the time to be held in prison, but it also had to be reported to and considered by parole authorities. Nebraska argued that the procedure for disciplining inmates was a matter of internal policy that raised no constitutional issues. McDonnell argued that his liberty was seriously affected by the state's actions in taking his good time credits, which required due process protections.

First, the Supreme Court rejected the contention that prisoners had no due process rights:

Prisoners may ... claim the protections of the Due Process Clause. They may not be deprived of life, liberty, or property without due process of law.

The Court also held that 42 U.S.C. Section 1983 was a proper way for the prisoner to raise this question in federal courts. The Court recognized that there are special problems in prison administration that must be balanced with any rights claimed by the prisoner.

[T]here must be mutual accommodation between institutional needs and objectives and the provisions of the Constitution that are of general application ... But here the State itself has not only provided a statutory right to good-time but also specifies that it is to be forfeited only for serious misbehavior ... Since prisoners in Nebraska can only lose good-time credits if they are guilty of serious misconduct, the determination of whether such behavior has occurred becomes critical, and the minimum requirements of procedural due process appropriate for the circumstances must be observed.

Determining when action taken against a prisoner is so serious that it triggers due process is, as pointed out previously, the entry question in any due process analysis. The kinds of actions that trigger due process requirements had been discussed and developed in many Supreme Court decisions that dealt with nonprison matters. That discussion is mainly now of interest only to lawyers in their historical analysis of due process rights in prisons. It has been put to rest, at least for now, in the decision of *Sandin v. Conner*, which follows in this chapter. *Sandin* gave us the answer about how to evaluate entitlement to due process rights in prisons.

What *Wolff* gave us are the procedural requirements that must be followed by prison officials in those cases where due process is required. The Court said that what is required in some other kinds of actions affecting inmates, such as revocation of probation or parole, is not required in a prison disciplinary hearing. The Court reviewed the background of prison proceedings, which "take place in a closed, tightly controlled environment peopled by those who have chosen to violate the criminal law and who have been lawfully incarcerated for doing so." The Court noted the argument that disciplinary proceedings further "the institutional goal of modifying the behavior and value systems of prison inmates sufficiently to permit them to live within the law when they are released." Because of the nature of prisons, "there would be great unwisdom in encasing the disciplinary procedures in an inflexible constitutional straitjacket that would necessarily call for adversary proceedings typical of the criminal trial."

The Court then specified the minimal due process standards for a prison disciplinary hearing, which are far short of criminal trial proceedings.

> **[There must be, in a prison hearing] advance written notice of the claimed violation and a written statement of the fact findings as to the evidence relied upon and the reasons for the disciplinary action taken…At least a brief period of time after the notice, no less than 24 hours, should be allowed to the inmate to prepare for the appearance before the [Disciplinary] Committee…[T]he inmate facing disciplinary proceedings should be allowed to call witnesses and present documentary evidence in his defense when permitting him to do so will not be unduly hazardous to institutional safety or correctional goals…Where an illiterate inmate is involved…or where the complexity of the issue makes it unlikely that the inmate will be able to collect and present the evidence necessary for an adequate comprehension of the case, he should be free to seek the aid of a fellow inmate, or if that is forbidden, to have adequate substitute aid in the form of help from the staff or from a sufficiently competent inmate designated by the staff.**

The Court also suggested that impartiality of the disciplinary committee was necessary when it ruled that the Nebraska Adjustment Committee was sufficiently impartial to satisfy the due process clause.

There we have the minimum procedural requirements for a prison hearing. In a footnote, the Court noted that these requirements are set for a serious sanction, such as the loss of good time, and are not required for "lesser penalties such as the loss of privileges." Also very important in the decision is what the Court did *not* require. There is no requirement that the inmate must be given the right to appeal to a higher authority. Although the inmate is given the right to call witnesses, the court noted the potential for disruption that this could cause and said that "[p]rison officials must have the necessary discretion to keep the hearing within reasonable limits and to refuse to call witnesses that may create a risk of reprisal or undermine authority." Also, if the committee did not call the witnesses the inmate asked for, the Court said it would be good to give its reasons for not calling the witnesses. Confrontation and cross-examination also were recognized to present special hazards in a prison setting. The Court declined to require them, saying, "the Constitution should not be read to impose the procedure at the present time and…adequate bases for decision in prison disciplinary cases can be arrived at without cross-examination."

A major due process concern was the right to counsel at prison hearings. Although a few states had allowed attorneys or outside representatives at hearings, most did not. The Court noted that allowing counsel would "inevitably give the proceedings a more adversary cast and tend to reduce their utility as a means to further correctional goals." The Court said that "we are not prepared to hold that inmates have a right to either retained or appointed counsel in disciplinary proceedings."

The Court also noted that the procedures specified were "not graven in stone. As the nature of the prison disciplinary process changes in future years, circumstances may then exist which will require further consideration and reflection of this Court." Although this statement fairly invites challenges to its decision "at some future time," the ruling about the procedural requirements still stands and is our guidance until the Court does reconsider prison disciplinary circumstances. (**Box 11-2** provides an example of some aspects of one state's inmate discipline policy, including its coverage of the *Wolff* requirements.)

Box 11-2 Inmate Discipline

POLICY:

A. The NMCD shall provide a safe and secure environment for both staff and inmates. In order to implement this policy, it is essential that reasonable standards of control and discipline are established and maintained. Staff and inmates will be provided access to copies of this policy and procedure and additions/revisions as they are implemented. This policy and procedure shall be reviewed at least annually and updated as necessary.

B. There are written rules of inmate conduct that specifies acts prohibited within the institutions and the penalties that can be imposed for various degrees of violation. [4-4226]

C. A rulebook containing chargeable offenses, ranges of penalties, and disciplinary procedures shall be given to each inmate and staff member and shall be translated into those languages spoken by significant numbers of inmates. Signed acknowledgement of receipt of the rulebook shall be maintained in the inmate's file. When a literacy or language problem prevents an inmate from reading the rulebook, a staff member or translator shall assist the inmate in reading the rules. [2-CO-3C-Ol] [4-4228]

D. All personnel that work with inmates shall receive sufficient training so that they are thoroughly familiar with the rules of inmate conduct, the rationale for the rules, and the sanctions available. [4-4229]

E. This policy includes written guidelines for resolving minor inmate infractions, which includes a written statement of the rule violated, and a hearing and decision within seven days, excluding weekends and holidays, by a person not involved in the rule violation; inmates may waive their appearance at the hearing. [4-4230] [2-CI-5A-6]

F. When an inmate allegedly commits an act covered by criminal law, the case shall be referred to the appropriate court or law enforcement officials for consideration for prosecution. [4-4231]

G. The disciplinary process of the industry program shall be in accordance with this policy. [2-CI-5A-5]

H. When a rule violation requires a formal resolution, staff members shall prepare a disciplinary report and forward it to the designated supervisor. [4-4232]

I. Disciplinary reports by staff members should include at a minimum: [4-4233]

- specific rule(s) violated;
- a formal statement of the charge;
- any unusual inmate behavior;
- any staff witnesses;

Box 11-2 (*continued*)

- any physical evidence and its disposition;
- any immediate action taken, including the use of force; and,
- reporting staff member's signature and date and time of report.

J. When an alleged rule violation is reported, an appropriate investigation shall begin within twenty-four (24) hours of the time the violation is reported and shall be completed without reasonable delay, unless there are exceptional circumstances for delaying the investigation. [4-4234]

K. An inmate charged with rule violations that is placed on prehearing detention status shall be reviewed by the Warden or designee within seventy-two (72) hours, including weekends and holidays. [4-4235]

L. An inmate charged with a rule violation shall receive a copy of the disciplinary report which includes the written statement of the charge(s), a description of the incident, and specific rules violated. The inmate shall be given the copy of the report prior to the report being forwarded to the Hearing Officer and no less than twenty-four (24) hours prior to the disciplinary hearing. The hearing may be held within the twenty-four (24) hours with the inmate's written consent. [4-4236]

M. An inmate may waive his/her right to a hearing provided that the waiver is documented and reviewed by a Deputy Warden. [4-4237]

N. An inmate charged with rule violations shall be scheduled for a hearing as soon as practicable but no later than seven days, excluding weekends and holidays, after being charged with a violation. Inmates are notified of the time and place of the hearing at least twenty-four (24) hours in advance of the hearing. [4-4238]

O. Continuances of the disciplinary hearing shall be for a reasonable period of time and for good cause. [4-4239]

P. Disciplinary hearings on rule violations shall be conducted by an impartial person. A written record of the proceedings shall be made and maintained in accordance with state archive rules; a taped record of all major level proceedings shall be made and maintained for at least one year. [4-4240]

Q. An inmate charged with rule violations shall be present at the hearing unless they waive that right in writing or through their behavior. Inmates may be excluded during the testimony of any inmate whose testimony must be given in confidence; the reason for the inmate's absence or exclusion shall be documented. [4-4241]

R. An inmate shall have an opportunity to make a statement and present documentary evidence at the hearing and can request witnesses on their behalf; the reasons for denying such a request shall be stated in writing. [4-4242]

(continued)

Box 11-2 (*continued*)

    S. A staff member or an agency representative may assist an inmate at disciplinary hearings if requested. A representative shall be appointed when it is apparent that an inmate is not capable of collecting and presenting evidence effectively on his or her own behalf. [4-4243]

    T. The hearing officer's decision shall be based solely on information obtained in the hearing process, including staff reports, the statements of the inmate charged, and evidence derived from witnesses and documents. [4-4244]

    U. A written record shall be made of the decision and the supporting reasons and a copy shall be given to the inmate. The hearing record and supporting documents shall be kept in the inmate's file and in the disciplinary archive file. [4-4245]

    V. If an inmate is found not guilty of an alleged rule violation, the disciplinary report shall be removed from the inmate's file. [4-4246]

    W. A Deputy Warden shall review all disciplinary hearings and dispositions to assure conformity with policy and procedures. [4-4247]

    X. All inmate disciplinary infraction data shall be entered into Criminal Management Information System (CMIS).

    Y. Data on disciplinary infractions shall be utilized to determine assault rates on NMCD staff and inmates.

    Z. Inmates have the right to appeal any decision of the hearing officer to the Warden. Inmates shall have up to fifteen (15) days of receipt of the decision to submit an appeal. The appeal shall be decided within thirty (30) days of its receipt by the Warden's office and the inmate shall be promptly notified in writing of the results. [4-4248]

Source: New Mexico Department of Corrections. Inmate Discipline (CD-090100). 09/04/85, reviewed/revised 02/23/11. Pages 5-7. Available from <http://www.corrections.state.nm.us/policies/current/CD-090100English.pdf>. [20 May 2011.]

Note: The numerical references at the end of some paragraphs refer to the Commission on Accreditation for Corrections Standards.

■ *Sandin v. Conner*

The Supreme Court *did* reconsider its ruling on the first part of our due process analysis in *Sandin v. Conner*, 515 U.S. 472 (1995). You will recall that the first question to be answered in any due process case is: Has there been a deprivation of life, liberty, or property that triggers activation of the clause, requiring some due process protection? The *Sandin* case revisits the issue of "the circumstances under which state prison regulations afford inmates a liberty interest protected by the Due Process Clause."

Conner, a Hawaii inmate, was charged with serious misconduct, found guilty of the charges before an adjustment committee, and "sentenced" to 30 days in disciplinary segregation. He was not allowed to call witnesses to testify at his hearing before the committee. The Ninth Circuit Court of Appeals held that Conner had a liberty interest in remaining free from disciplinary segregation and that he had not received the due process required by *Wolff* when he was not allowed to present any witnesses. The Supreme Court reversed that judgment.

There is an excellent discussion of the history of prison due process decisions in *Sandin*, if you are interested in reading it. The Court noted that its analysis of due process entitlement in prison had culminated in the decisions of *Greenholtz v. Inmates*, 442 U.S. 1 (1979), and *Hewitt v. Helms*, 459 U.S. 460 (1983). Essentially, those decisions held that due process turned on whether state action was mandatory or discretionary. That is, if officials were required (mandated) to reach a certain result if certain facts existed, then some due process was required. A clue to whether an action is mandatory is use of the word "shall" in regulations or policy. From the opposite perspective, if the official action was totally discretionary (for example, when policy used the word "may"), then no due process was required. The Court in *Sandin* abandoned that standard, finding it too mechanical and cumbersome. It found two major problems with that standard: it encouraged states to avoid due process by always writing discretionary language ("officials may" do this or that) into their rules, and it led to over-involvement of the courts in the day-to-day management of the prisons. Further, it encouraged inmates to comb through regulations, looking for mandatory language on which they could bring a due process challenge.

Finally, the Court said that the legalistic search for mandatory language in prison rules "strayed from the real concerns undergirding the liberty protected by the Due Process Clause." The purpose of prison discipline is to effectuate prison management and prisoner rehabilitative goals, according to the Supreme Court. Prison discipline does not ordinarily impose any sanction or retribution beyond that contained in the sentence being served. As long as it does not add on to that sentence or go beyond the conditions contemplated in the sentence, the disciplinary action does not create a liberty interest.

> **We hold that Conner's discipline in segregated confinement did not present the type of atypical, significant deprivation in which a state might conceivably create a liberty interest ... Conner's confinement did not exceed similar, but totally discretionary confinement in either duration or degree of restriction ... The regime to which he was subjected as a result of the misconduct hearing was within the range of confinement to be normally expected for one serving an indeterminate sentence of 30 years to life.**

Thus, the question is not whether the inmate is punished, or even punished (in his view) severely. The question is whether the punishment is within the range of conditions, restrictions, and sanctions that are contemplated while serving such a sentence of confinement. If punishment extends the duration of the sentence, some due process would be required. In Hawaii, although the parole board must consider prison misconduct, it is not required to deny parole for the misconduct record of an inmate. The parole board itself has procedural protections at its hearings that allow the inmate to explain his misconduct record. That process protects the parole decision making so far as due process is concerned, and no additional protection is needed at the prison's disciplinary hearing.

We hold, therefore, that neither the Hawaii prison regulation in question nor the Due Process Clause itself afforded Conner a protected liberty interest that would entitle him to the procedural protections set forth in *Wolff*.

Sandin, of course, has led to a flurry of court decisions interpreting disciplinary procedures in light of the new standard (and it has also triggered reexaminations by corrections agencies of their rules). This process will continue, as adjustment is made to the starker (and somewhat simpler) standard, in deciding whether due process applies to prison hearings.

■ *Baxter v. Palmigiano*

In *Baxter v. Palmigiano,* 425 U.S. 308 (1976), the Supreme Court considered several disciplinary issues. One was whether inmates were entitled to counsel at discipline hearings. Two courts of appeals had held that counsel must be provided if the misconduct charges involved crimes punishable under state criminal statutes. (Both of those cases were considered together in this opinion under the name of *Baxter v. Palmigiano. Baxter v. Palmigiano* was a Rhode Island case on writ of certiorari from the Court of Appeals for the First Circuit. *Enomoto v. Clutchette,* on certiorari from the Ninth Circuit, involved California prison hearings and was decided as a companion case with *Baxter.*) The Supreme Court disagreed with the two courts of appeals and reaffirmed its holding in *Wolff:*

[W]e are not prepared to hold that inmates have a right to either retained or appointed counsel in disciplinary proceedings.

Another issue that was already considered in *Wolff* was raised again in *Baxter.* The Ninth Circuit Court of Appeals had required reasons in writing to an inmate if he was denied the right to cross-examine or confront witnesses against him at the hearing. The Supreme Court reversed this requirement also. It pointed out that, in *Wolff,* it recommended but did not require written reasons for denying inmates the right to call witnesses on their own behalf, but it made no such requirement for confrontation and cross-examination. In the prison setting, those hearing steps carry inherent dangers, the Court said, and there is no due process requirement for prison officials to allow confrontation and cross-examination.

A new issue raised in *Baxter* was the right of the inmate to remain silent at his disciplinary hearing. Inmate Palmigiano was told that he was not required to testify at his hearing, that he could remain silent, but that his silence could be used against him. The First Circuit Court of Appeals held that this violated the self-incrimination privilege of the Fifth Amendment, made applicable to the States by reason of the Fourteenth Amendment, and that adverse inferences could *not* be drawn from an inmate's failure to testify. The Supreme Court disagreed:

[A]n inmate's silence in and of itself is insufficient to support an adverse decision by the Disciplinary Board...[P]ermitting an adverse inference to be drawn from an inmate's silence at his disciplinary proceedings is not, on its face, an invalid practice.

Further, the Court noted that if an inmate was compelled to furnish evidence that might incriminate him in a later criminal proceeding (that is, he was ordered to testify), he would have to be given immunity regarding the use of that testimony in the criminal proceedings. Thus, we know from *Baxter* that an inmate in a disciplinary proceeding can be advised that his silence can be used against him, but that the silence is not enough by itself to convict him (there must be other evidence); if he is ordered to testify, he must be given immunity from use of that testimony in a criminal proceeding.

Finally, the Ninth Circuit (in the companion case of *Enomoto v. Clutchette*) had ruled that minimum due process was necessary even when inmates were deprived of privileges. The Supreme Court rejected that ruling. We know now, with even more certainty from *Sandin*, that loss of privileges is certainly not the type of disciplinary sanction that would require due process.

■ Double Jeopardy

The discussion of the rights of inmates in *Baxter* raises a question about **double jeopardy**, when inmates are subject to both disciplinary sanctions for misconduct in prison and also criminal prosecution in criminal court for the same misconduct. The Double Jeopardy Clause is found in the Fifth Amendment:

> **[N]or shall any person be subject for the same offence to be twice put in jeopardy of life or limb.**

The Supreme Court has not ruled specifically on this issue. But lower courts have consistently held that it is not a constitutional violation to proceed against a prisoner in both forums—in a prison disciplinary action and in a criminal prosecution. These courts have ruled it is permissible to have both institutional sanctions and a criminal sentence imposed for the same misconduct.

For example, see the case of *Porter v. Coughlin,* 421 F.3d 141 (2nd Cir. 2005). Porter had participated in a riot at his New York prison. He was ordered to be confined for three years in a Special Housing Unit, following a disciplinary hearing. He was additionally convicted for that same offense in state court and sentenced to an additional three to six years of incarceration. This court notes that the Supreme Court has said (but it was not in a prison discipline case) that the Double Jeopardy Clause "protects only against the imposition of multiple *criminal* punishments for the same offense." *Hudson v. United States,* 522 U.S. 93 (1997). Criminal prosecution and prison disciplinary proceedings based on the same offense do not implicate double jeopardy concerns.

In *United States v. Simpson,* 546 F.3d 394 (6th Cir. 2008), inmate Simpson had escaped from a Tennessee jail where he was held as a federal prisoner following conviction on several federal crimes. He was charged for the escape in a disciplinary hearing and was given 60 days in disciplinary segregation, 40 days of good time disallowed, and a 6-month loss of visitation privileges. Simpson was then indicted in federal court for escape. He received an additional 18-month consecutive sentence for the escape. He challenged that federal prosecution for the same escape. This court said that action did not constitute double jeopardy, noting that he was twice put in jeopardy only if he was at risk for *criminal* punishments for the same offense.

"Every circuit court of appeals to consider this question has given the same answer. The Double Jeopardy Clause was not intended to inhibit prison discipline, and disciplinary changes in prison conditions do not preclude subsequent criminal punishment for the same misconduct."

■ *Superintendent v. Hill*

The question in *Superintendent (of the Massachusetts Correctional Institution at Walpole) v. Hill*, 472 U.S. 445 (1985), concerned the degree of evidence that must be present to support a finding of guilt in a prison disciplinary hearing. Inmate Hill was found guilty of assault based on testimony from a prison guard (officer) that he heard some commotion, went to investigate, and found an assaulted inmate. He saw Hill (and two other inmates) running away and no other inmates in the area. He charged the three inmates with the assault. The disciplinary board also considered the guard's written report. They found the charged inmates guilty of the assault. Hill lost 100 days of good time and was placed in isolation for 15 days. He filed suit in state court, which found insufficient evidence to support the finding of guilt. The Massachusetts Supreme Judicial Court affirmed that ruling. The U.S. Supreme Court reversed the Massachusetts courts.

> [R]evocation of good time does not comport with "the minimum requirements of procedural due process," unless the findings of the prison disciplinary board are supported by some evidence in the record ... [D]ue process in this context requires only that there be some evidence to support the findings made in the disciplinary hearing.

The Court found that the minimal evidence in this case—testimony from the prison guard and copies of his written report—was "some evidence" and thus was sufficient to meet due process requirements.

What this case does point out is that courts in many situations are unaccustomed to dealing with the obviously lessened levels of procedure that are constitutionally required in prison hearings. The evidence in *Superintendent v. Hill* was minimal, but sufficient, the Supreme Court said, to satisfy the low levels of protection required in prison hearings. This same understandable predilection of courts (as in the Massachusetts courts here) to apply court-hearing standards to prison administrative hearings can be found in many situations, especially in the lower courts.

■ *Hewitt v. Helms*

Hewitt v. Helms, 459 U.S. 460 (1983), involved the placement of inmate Helms in administrative segregation status at the Huntingdon, Pennsylvania State Correctional Institution. There was a major disruption at the institution involving several assaults on prison officers and the destruction of property. Helms was removed from his cell after order was restored and placed in restrictive confinement for questioning during the investigation of the riot. He was given a minimal hearing some five days later. The question was whether moving Helms from his regular cell in the general population to administrative segregation required due process, and, if so, what amount of process was required.

> **[T]he transfer of an inmate to less amenable and more restrictive quarters for nonpunitive reasons is well within the terms of punishment ordinarily contemplated by a prison sentence.**

The Court then concluded that placement in more restrictive, segregated confinement did not create any liberty interest. So Helms did not have any due process entitlement found in the Constitution itself.

However, this is the case that spelled out that there was another source of liberty interest in the Fourteenth Amendment—namely, state rules that mandated certain actions if certain facts were found. The Court found that Pennsylvania had used explicit mandatory language in its rules for placement in prison segregation, and, thereby, a right to due process was created. This is the analysis that *Sandin* later specifically rejected (overruled), so, in the *Sandin* analysis, Helms was not entitled under the Constitution to any due process whatsoever for his placement in administrative segregation.

In *Hewitt*, the Supreme Court went on to hold that the small amount of procedural protection used by Pennsylvania was sufficient. All that was required was "some notice of the charges against him and an opportunity to present his views to the prison official charged with deciding whether to transfer him to administrative segregation." That decision maker would then review the charges and the evidence (including the inmate's statement). This very minimal procedure was all that would be required to satisfy due process requirements.

A case of similar concerns is *United States v. Gouveia*, 467 U.S. 180 (1984). Gouveia, a federal inmate, was placed in administrative detention[3] while authorities investigated the murder of an inmate. He remained in administrative detention for 19 months, until he was indicted and arraigned in federal court. During the time he was in detention, he had no counsel. He claimed this was a violation of his Sixth Amendment right to counsel, but the trial court denied that claim. He was convicted of murder.

The Ninth Circuit Court of Appeals reversed his conviction on the ground that Gouveia had to be given counsel after 90 days in prison detention or else be released back into the general prison population. The Supreme Court reversed, holding that inmates were not constitutionally entitled to the appointment of counsel while they were in administrative segregation and before any judicial proceedings had been initiated against them. Neither is an inmate, during this investigation period, entitled to someone who will investigate the case on his behalf.

> **The right to counsel attaches only at or after the initiation of adverse judicial proceedings against the defendant.**

■ Confidential Informants

Another issue that is of continuing concern in prison discipline cases is the use of confidential informant evidence. The Supreme Court has not addressed this issue. We must use what guidance we have, primarily from federal courts of appeals.

In the prison setting, staff receive information from a variety of sources, which assists them in maintaining security and control of the facility. As inmates have become more sophisticated, as gangs in prisons present a threat to the safety of inmates and staff, and as drugs and other contraband are continuing, if not increasing, problems, prison staff must use any information they can acquire to make institutions as safe and secure as possible. One of the oldest and most common sources of information is the inmate **informant** (in prison jargon, a "snitch" or a "rat").

Often, information from these informants leads to prison disciplinary action, bringing charges against the inmate based on the informant evidence. The question is, how is this information to be used in disciplinary hearings? The Supreme Court at least tacitly recognized the difficulty of this problem when, in *Wolff* and in *Baxter,* it held that, in a prison, there was no right to confrontation and cross-examination of adverse witnesses. This allows prison staff to protect the identity of the informants. The confidentiality of the informants protects both their own safety and the opportunity to continue to use their information in the future.

But how does one ensure the fairness of the prison proceeding based on informant evidence? How can one protect against an inmate fabricating information or pointing a finger at a person with whom he just wants to get even? Corrections officials and courts have struggled with this issue, and, in general, they have come up with the conclusion that there must be some way that officials ascertain the reliability of the informant's story. Often, the hearing officer or committee is required to make a statement in the record that informant information has been used as evidence in the case and that the officer or committee is satisfied that that information is reliable. Such a conclusion about reliability may be based on a review of the background and the circumstances that support reliability by the hearing officer himself, or it may be based on a report from an investigative officer who presents to the committee his reasons for believing the inmate. All of this consideration about the inmate informant is discussed out of the presence of the inmate who is charged, of course. This protects the inmate "snitch" against reprisals. The informant's reliability may be shown by reliability established in other situations, by detailed accounts that could only be known by someone who was there, or by corroborative evidence developed in the case.

For an example of a case in which the court of appeals required such an inquiry into the reliability of the informant to be placed into a confidential record of the proceedings, see *McCollum v. Williford*, 793 F.2d 903 (7th Cir. 1986). This is one of several areas in which different courts have arrived at different requirements for prison officials to follow. Until the Supreme Court addresses these questions, prison staff will have to ascertain what courts in their jurisdiction have said and follow those rulings regarding legal requirements in inmate disciplinary hearings. With *Sandin*, however, lower court reviews of these disciplinary questions should be reduced, and a Supreme Court review (of the confidential informant issue, for example) may be a long time in coming.[4]

SUMMARY

- Due process is a concept that is guaranteed in two places in the Constitution: the Fifth Amendment (for federal actions) and the Fourteenth Amendment (for state actions).

- There are two inquiries in due process cases: (1) whether a person has been deprived of life, liberty, or property and (2) if there was such deprivation, whether procedural protections (due process) were provided.

- The disciplining of inmates is an important part of prison and jail administration. It is essential for the safety and orderly running of a corrections facility. It must be done fairly and evenhandedly, in accordance with written rules.

- The Supreme Court held, in the leading case on inmate discipline, that inmates are entitled to the protection of the due process clause. In cases of serious sanctions, inmates must be given these procedural rights: advance written notice of the charges; some time to prepare for the hearing; the right to call witnesses and present documentary evidence (unless to do so would be hazardous); a right to assistance, for illiterate inmates or in complex cases; and a written statement of the findings, including the evidence relied on and the reasons for the action taken. There is no need to provide an appeal process or to provide legal counsel (*Wolff v. McDonnell*).

- More recently, the Supreme Court has said that prison disciplinary action does not deprive an inmate of liberty and does not require due process, unless the sanction adds on to the sentence or goes beyond the conditions contemplated in the sentence. In that case, the Supreme Court held that the inmate's placement in disciplinary segregation (a common sanction in prison cases) did not create a liberty deprivation that required a due process hearing. It was a punishment "within the range of confinement to be normally expected" (*Sandin v. Conner*).

- The Supreme Court (disagreeing with some appellate courts) held that counsel did not have to be provided at prison disciplinary hearings, even when the misconduct amounted to criminal misconduct. Also, the Court ruled that an inmate could be advised at a disciplinary hearing that he had the right to remain silent, but that if he did, his silence could be used against him. The silence by itself could not support an adverse decision. If the inmate was ordered to give evidence that could incriminate him in a later criminal proceeding, he would have to be given immunity as to the use of that testimony in a criminal trial (*Baxter v. Palmigiano*).

- An inmate may receive disciplinary sanctions for misconduct committed inside the prison (or jail) where he is confined. In addition, he may be prosecuted and sentenced in criminal court for the same misconduct. This is not a constitutional violation under the Double Jeopardy Clause. Several courts of appeals (but not the Supreme Court) have adopted this ruling.

- At a prison disciplinary hearing, the amount of evidence required to support a finding that an inmate committed misconduct is "some evidence" (*Superintendent v. Hill*).

- The holding of *Hewitt v. Helms,* that in some cases staff would have to provide a minimal due process hearing before placing an inmate into restrictive confinement within the prison, has been overruled by the due process analysis of *Sandin v. Conner.*

- Confidential informants are often used in prison security investigations and disciplinary matters. The Supreme Court has not ruled on the standards for using evidence from confidential informants. Lower courts have held that hearing officials must, at a minimum, satisfy themselves of the reliability of the information that has been provided by any inmate informants.

THINKING ABOUT IT

Phillips was an inmate confined in an Arkansas prison. In June 2000, he was charged by the staff with carrying contraband (smoking products). Pending a hearing, he was transferred from general housing to an isolation area. In the isolation area, he was without (1) the privileges of contact visits, (2) yard and gym access, and (3) chapel privileges. Although the contraband charge was never acted on, Phillips was not returned to his original housing unit. Upset, he refused to return to his assigned housing area. He received disciplinary action, was found guilty, and lost, among other things, good time. He was released from isolation near the end of July. Phillips filed a Section 1983 action, claiming, in part, constitutional violations of his due process rights, specifically citing the atypical hardships necessitated by his placement in isolation for 37 days. He argued that the Fourteenth Amendment prohibited violation of his liberty interests without due process of law. What Supreme Court decision should be applied in the ruling on this case? What do you feel should be the decision of the appeals court? This case was reported as *Phillips v. Norris*, 320 F.3d 844 (8th Cir. 2003).

KEY TERMS

disciplinary confinement: The act (and the place) of confining inmates separately because of their institutional misconduct. Segregation for disciplinary reasons. (Variously called disciplinary detention, disciplinary segregation, punitive segregation, and isolation.)

discipline (corrections): The program in a corrections agency or facility of punishing inmates who violate the internal code of conduct adopted for that agency or facility.

double jeopardy: a prohibition against a person being prosecuted after there was a first trial for the same offense. The Fifth Amendment of the U.S. Constitution provides that no person shall "be subject for the same offence to be twice put in jeopardy of life or limb."

forfeiture: The loss of something by way of penalty. (An example in corrections is good time forfeiture. See good time.)

informant: A person, usually undisclosed to the accused, who provides information or accusations against another person. (Also called an informer.)

ENDNOTES

1. In its 2010 Annual Report, the Ohio Department of Rehabilitation and Correction reported over 223,000 conduct violations in fiscal year 2010, with over 20% of the conduct violations being for violation of Ohio Rule 21: Disobedience of a direct order. Its inmate population in fiscal year 2010 was 50,944. Ohio Department of Rehabilitation and Correction. *"Transformation and Change"—2010 Annual Report*, 18, 31. Accessed June 15, 2011. http://www.drc.ohio.gov/web/Reports/Annual/Annual%20Report%202010.pdf.

2. This appendix identifies major and minor disciplinary offenses and sanctions (see the "Low moderate" category). Examples of minor offenses include single incidents of using obscene language, or malingering (feigning illness). Sanctions for such one-time offenses do not involve a substantive loss of "liberty" (such as a recommendation for parole date rescission or retardation or the imposition of disciplinary segregation). Instead, lesser sanctions may consist of a change in housing, a reprimand and warning, or extra duty. Offenses warranting the more serious sanctions are handled by an institution's discipline authority (typically a committee or a hearing officer).

3. There are several different names for this same kind of prison cell—in *Hewitt* it was called administrative segregation, and in *Gouveia* it was called administrative detention, but it is the same kind of cell. It is a jail within the prison where people are held when, for security reasons, they cannot be kept in the general population, and they are not being punished by being placed in isolation or disciplinary confinement. While in administrative status, the inmate may receive the same general privileges given to an inmate in the general prison population, such as access to education programs, counseling, commissary, visiting, and use of a radio. Although the inmate cannot move about the prison in the same way as a regular inmate, he experiences better conditions and privileges than a disciplinary status inmate.

4. In *Kansas v. Ventris*, 556 U.S. __ (2009), the state prior to trial, "planted an informant in Ventris's holding cell, instructing him to 'keep [his] ear open and listen' for incriminating statements ... According to the informant, in response to his statement that Ventris appeared to have 'something more serious weighing in on his mind,' Ventris divulged that '[h]e'd shot this man in his head and in his chest' and taken 'his keys, his wallet, about $350.00, and ... a vehicle.'" The state acknowledged "that there was "probably a violation" of Ventris's Sixth Amendment right to counsel but nonetheless argued that the statement was admissible for impeachment purposes because the violation 'doesn't give the Defendant ... a license to just get on the stand and lie.'" The Supreme Court held the informant's testimony was admissible solely for impeachment purposes.

12 | Fifth and Fourteenth Amendments: Due Process— Classification, Transfers, Personal Injuries, and Property Loss

Confinement in any of the State's institutions is within the normal limits or range of custody which the conviction has authorized the State to impose. That life in one prison is much more disagreeable than in another does not in itself signify that a Fourteenth Amendment liberty interest is implicated when a prisoner is transferred to the institution with the more severe rules.

U.S. Supreme Court, *Meachum v. Fano*

Chapter Outline

- The Nature of Classification
- *Meachum v. Fano; Montanye v. Haymes*
- *McKune v. Lile*
- *Howe v. Smith*
- *Olim v. Wakinekona*
- *Vitek v. Jones*
- *Wilkinson v. Austin*
- *Young v. Harper*
- *Kansas v. Hendricks; Kansas v. Crane*
- *Farmer v. Brennan*
- International Transfers
- Loss of Property and Personal Injuries
  - *Parratt v. Taylor*
  - *Hudson v. Palmer*
  - *Daniels v. Williams*
  - *Davidson v. Cannon*
- Use of Excessive Force

We have seen the claims of due process that are raised in connection with inmate disciplinary hearings. That is very important and probably the central issue of due process protection that is encountered in prison administration.

In this chapter, we will look at a wide range of other actions, primarily in prisons, where due process claims have been made. Under the due process clauses of the Fifth and the Fourteenth Amendments, no person may be "deprived of life, liberty, or property, without due process of law." Action is not taken in prisons to deprive persons of their lives, except in death penalty cases, though property and liberty deprivation claims are common. We will discuss in this chapter cases in which inmates raise due process claims because of the loss of their property, and some cases (other than discipline), in which claims have been made that the liberty of inmates has been taken away by the actions of prison officials.

■ The Nature of Classification

One of the most important functions in running prisons is the classification of prisoners. Classification involves several decisions about the individual inmate, including where (to what institution) he should be sent to serve his sentence and where he should be assigned (within an institution) for housing, special programs, and work. There are, in every corrections agency, staff members who are specially trained to make those decisions about the classification of inmates. Written policies in the agency set the rules for classification.

Procedures for classifying inmates take into account numerous factors, including: (1) the age and sex of the offender; (2) the criminal sophistication of the offender; (3) geographic concerns (such as where the offender's home has been, where his family are located, from what location he is likely to get visitors, and to what area he is likely to be released); (4) special needs, focusing first on any medical or psychiatric problems and then on other special needs, such as education and vocational training; (5) special security problems, such as other offenders from whom this inmate should be separated (whether codefendants, members of gangs, persons with whom he has been confined before, informants, law enforcement or public officials, etc.) and whether the inmate is known to be an escape risk; (6) special factors, such as recommendations from the sentencing court; and (7) the availability of space in appropriate facilities.

The last factor (7) involves another classification process—the classification of facilities. Institutions in the corrections department are classified according to security level, the types of inmates they receive, and the programs they offer. Obviously, each institution has a geographic location, which often enters into classification decision making. Classification officials must know well the different types of institutions and what kinds of inmates go to each one.

Institutions are typically classified as *minimum*, *medium*, and *maximum* security. Other titles may also be used. The level of security is decided by physical factors, such as the type of perimeter security (such as a wall, fencing, or no fencing at all) and type of housing inside (single cells are most desirable for high-security inmates, and open housing, as in dormitories, is best for low-security inmates), and levels of staffing. The old-style penitentiary or state prison, with high walls and towers spaced around the walls where armed guards keep watch, is thought of as high security. More recent prison architecture does not include walls (mainly because of expense), although high-security features can be built on the perimeter of the institution, which, it is claimed, give just as high a degree of security. Those features typically include a double fence, with barbed (now usually razor) wire on the top and coils of razor wire laid between the fences and on the ground next to the fences. Inside a prison, security features are many: gates to the institution, typically a double set at each entry point, which are operated from a remote, protected location; grilled doors located on corridors into the main part of the institution and at strategic points in the facility where there is inmate movement; security cameras, which allow surveillance of most areas of the institution and enable correctional staff to watch remote locations; heavily secured gates and doors, which may be operated electronically or by keys; and alarm systems, which are triggered by improper movement or other breaches of security. The most important security feature is trained staff, who are alert to possible problems and move through an assigned area to make sure all is well. Communication between staff, whether by phone, radio, or electronic means, is also a vital security feature. From these many factors, a security assessment is made of the facility, so that classification and assignment to the right institution may be made for the individual inmate.

Institutions are also classified according to the kinds of programs they offer. Some have highly specialized medical or psychiatric units. Some have vocational or educational programs of a specialized nature. Some have more internal security units, so they can take more people who may need separation for protection, detention, or disciplinary housing. Of course, some facilities are for women and others for men. (Nationwide, there are a few institutions that take both male and female inmates into the same facility.) Some institutions specialize in programs for younger offenders. By sheer numbers, a very large prison system will have a larger variety of institutions and a greater number of classification choices for the individual. A very small system will have very few choices—perhaps only one male institution and a much smaller one for women.

As a basic rule of classification (or at least a desirable rule of institution assignment), an inmate will be sent to an institution as close to his home as possible. All of the other classification factors will enter into the decision: he must be sent to a facility that is appropriate for his security level and that has special features or programs that he needs (including medical and psychiatric care, educational programs, and separation from certain other people). In order to make these decisions, the staff needs as much reliable information about the offender as possible. At initial classification, this information will usually come from the defendant's presentence report and from law enforcement or court authorities (who will provide his criminal history, rap sheet, and special information, such as escape or suicide attempts). If the inmate has been confined in the system before, his records from the previous incarceration will be used. The classification officer (or team), on the basis of review of the records (sometimes, with a face-to-face interview, especially in those states that have an initial diagnostic and reception center, one of the main purposes of which is to make a better-informed classification decision for each inmate), then makes a decision to send the inmate to a certain facility. Later, there may be a decision to reclassify the inmate, based on factors that come to light after he is serving his sentence. These factors for reclassifying the inmate may include information in any of the areas mentioned previously, such as moving the inmate to a place of higher security (because of discipline or escape problems), relieving crowding in the inmate's present facility, moving the

Figure 12-1 A hearing at the Community Corrections Center in Lincoln, Nebraska.
Source: © Mikael Karlsson/Alamy Images

inmate closer to home as he approaches release, or moving him to a facility where special programs he may need are available (see **Figure 12-1**).

Here is what two states say about classification:

The NMCD [New Mexico Corrections Department] shall establish procedures to implement and monitor an inmate's status relating to [the inmate's] risk assessment, program assignment, good time and release preparation. This will include consideration of any special needs of the inmate. The NMCD shall ensure that all inmates are classified into the most appropriate custody level based on security and custody considerations with the intent of balancing the inmate's program and treatment needs....The NMCD utilizes an objective rating process to assign inmates to the most appropriate custody level consistent with the safety of the general public, staff and other inmates.[1]

In Alaska, the following policy has been established:

The Department will classify and assign each prisoner to the appropriate security level facility and custody status guided by the principles of placement in the least restrictive setting consistent with maintaining the security and order of the institution, the special needs of the prisoner, and resources available to the Department....Classification includes: 1. assigning prisoners to the proper security and custody levels; 2. furthering the Department's goals for humane treatment, public safety and effective correctional administration; 3. providing information for prisoner population management and planning; 4. distributing correctional resources to meet the Department's and the prisoners' needs; and 5. identifying prisoner programs and services for budgetary purposes.[2]

We will next look at some decisions that raise constitutional issues in classification decision making. The main concern is due process: Is the inmate entitled to any process or any kind of hearing before he is classified to a particular institution or before he is moved to a particular place?

▮ *Meachum v. Fano; Montanye v. Haymes*

Meachum v. Fano and *Montanye v. Haymes*, both Supreme Court cases and both decided on June 25, 1976, address the due process question for inmate classification and transfers. They involve just slightly different aspects of transfers of prisoners.

Meachum v. Fano, 427 U.S. 215 (1976), involved the transfer of inmate Fano and five others from the Massachusetts Correctional Institution at Norfolk, a medium security facility, to a maximum security prison. The transfer was based on information that authorities received, indicating the inmates were involved in criminal conduct—namely, the possession of weapons or ammunition during a time when the institution was caught up in several disturbances. None of the inmates were punished by the loss of good time or by disciplinary confinement; they were transferred to a place where living conditions were "substantially less favorable than those at Norfolk." The question to be decided, as stated by the Supreme Court, was "whether the Due Process Clause of the Fourteenth Amendment entitles a state prisoner to a hearing when he is transferred to a prison the conditions of which are substantially less favorable to the prisoner."

The Supreme Court held that there was no due process entitlement in such a transfer.

> **We reject at the outset the notion that *any* grievous loss visited upon a person by the State is sufficient to invoke the procedural protections of the Due Process Clause....Similarly, we cannot agree that *any* change in the conditions of confinement having a substantial adverse impact on the prisoner involved is sufficient to invoke the protections of the Due Process Clause....[G]iven a valid conviction, the criminal defendant has been constitutionally deprived of his liberty to the extent that the State may confine him and subject him to the rules of its prison system so long as the conditions of confinement do not otherwise violate the Constitution. The Constitution does not require that the State have more than one prison for convicted felons; nor does it guarantee that the convicted prisoner will be placed in any particular prison if, as is likely, the State has more than one correctional institution. The initial decision to assign the convict to a particular institution is not subject to audit under the Due Process Clause, although the degree of confinement in one prison may be quite different from that in another. The conviction has sufficiently extinguished the defendant's liberty interest to empower the State to confine him in *any* of its prisons.**

This Supreme Court decision is full of language of the same sort, emphasizing that a liberty interest was not created by placing an inmate in a particular kind of confinement that is more disagreeable than another might be. Many federal courts previously had held that if an inmate suffered a "grievous loss" or if there was a "substantial deprivation" imposed by prison officials, then there would have to be a due process hearing before that transfer action was taken, in order to protect the constitutional rights of the inmate. The Supreme Court rejected those standards and said specifically that they did not trigger due process entitlements.

> **Transfers between institutions, for example, are made for a variety of reasons and often involve no more than informed predictions as to what would best serve institutional security or the safety and welfare of the inmate....That an inmate's conduct, in general or in specific instances, may often be a major factor in the decision of prison officials to transfer him is to be expected unless it be assumed that transfers are mindless events. A prisoner's past and anticipated future behavior will very likely be taken into account in selecting a prison in which he will be initially incarcerated or to which he will be transferred to best serve the State's penological goals....Massachusetts prison officials have the discretion to transfer prisoners for any number of reasons....Holding that arrangements like this are within reach of the procedural protections of the Due Process Clause would place the Clause astride the day-to-day functioning of state prisons and involve the judiciary in issues and discretionary decisions that are not the business of federal judges....Our holding is that the Due Process Clause does not impose a nation-wide rule mandating transfer hearings.**

The language of the *Meachum* opinion is mostly in terms of the "transfer" of prisoners, but you can see that the language also covers what we would call classification decisions. From *Meachum*, we know that an agency's classification and transfer actions, as a general principle, are not subject to due process requirements.

The companion case of *Montanye v. Haymes*, 427 U.S. 236 (1976), followed the same track as *Meachum*, with just slightly altered facts. Inmate Haymes was transferred from the Attica Correctional Facility in New York to Clinton Correctional Facility, both of them maximum-security prisons. Haymes claimed that Superintendent Montanye transferred him for disciplinary reasons, because Haymes was circulating a petition among inmates complaining of Haymes being removed from his work assignment as an inmate clerk in the law library. As a clerk, Haymes had been providing legal assistance to other inmates. Those inmates also claimed that they were deprived of that assistance as a result of Haymes's work reassignment. When Haymes filed suit, complaining of the prison actions against him, the district court ruled that there had been no violation of his constitutional rights. The court of appeals reversed and sent the case back for further consideration on the ground that Haymes's transfer was a disciplinary action, not an administrative one. That court reasoned that the transfer, like other serious disciplinary action, could not be taken without certain procedural protections; that is, the consequences of the transfer were so burdensome that they probably triggered due process clause protections, necessitating a hearing.

The Supreme Court disagreed with the reasoning of the court of appeals and reversed.

> **We held in *Meachum v. Fano*, that no Due Process Clause liberty interest of a duly convicted prison inmate is infringed when he is transferred from one prison to another within the State, whether with or without a hearing....As long as the conditions or degree of confinement to which the prisoner is subjected are within the sentence imposed upon him and are not otherwise violative of the Constitution, the Due Process Clause does not in itself subject an inmate's treatment by prison authorities to judicial oversight. The Clause does not require hearings in connection with transfers whether or not they are the result of the inmate's misbehavior or may be labeled as disciplinary or punitive.**

That language used in *Montanye*, "as long as the conditions...are within the sentence imposed upon him," is especially noteworthy, because it anticipates the standards for due process entitlement adopted in *Sandin v. Conner*, 515 U.S. 472 (1995). In *Sandin*, the Court rejected and overruled a due process analysis that had been adopted in another type of special transfer, namely, the transfer of a prisoner from the general population of a prison into administrative segregation. In *Hewitt v. Helms*, 459 U.S. 460 (1983), the Court had said that placement in segregated confinement did not, in and of itself, create a liberty interest, which would necessitate a due process hearing. However, the Court noted that the state had used mandatory language in its rules, and that kind of language triggered due process entitlement for that kind of transfer. The *Sandin* decision rejected that analysis, saying that due process is not required when action is taken against the inmate "within the range of confinement to be normally expected for one serving" a sentence of confinement. Therefore, we can add the transfers of inmates from the regular population to administrative detention or segregation to those transfers that will not require due process hearings.

■ *McKune v. Lile*

In *McKune v. Lile*, 536 U.S. 24 (2002), Kansas inmate Lile refused to participate in the prison's mandatory Sexual Abuse Treatment Program (SATP). Part of SATP required the inmate to sign an "Admission of Responsibility" form, accepting responsibility for the crimes for which he had been sentenced and detailing all prior sexual activities, even those not charged. No legal immunity was provided. Failure to comply would result in the reduction of prison privileges and transfer to a potentially more dangerous unit. The inmate refused to cooperate with the SATP requirements and sued for injunctive relief, claiming a violation of his Fifth Amendment right against self-incrimination. The district and appeals courts held in favor of the inmate. The Supreme Court reversed. Citing *Meachum*, the Court held that no transfer hearing was required. Although *McKune* deals with the privilege against compelled self-incrimination, not due process, the Court saw *Meachum* as controlling authority for its position that, by the fact of their convictions, inmates must expect significant restrictions on rights and privileges that free citizens take for granted. No liberty interests (such as eligibility for good time credits or parole, which would affect an inmate's release date) were implicated.

> **No one contends...that the transfer is intended to punish prisoners for exercising their Fifth Amendment rights. Rather, the limitation on these rights is incidental to Kansas' legitimate penological reason for the transfer: Due to limited space, inmates who do not participate in their respective programs will be moved out of the facility where the programs are held to make room for other inmates....It is well settled that the decision where to house inmates is at the core of prison administrators' expertise....For this reason the Court has not required administrators to conduct a hearing before transferring a prisoner to a bed in a different prison, even if "life in one prison is much more disagreeable than in another."...This logic has equal force in analyzing respondent's self-incrimination claim.**

The *McKune* decision was not unanimous. The opinion of the Court, including one concurring opinion, was divided in a five-to-four split. The dissenting justices noted that, although Kansas's goal of reducing **recidivism** among sex offenders was admirable, an inmate should not be compelled to forfeit the privilege against self-incrimination simply because the ends are legitimate or because the conviction is for a sex offense. The dissenting justices asked the question, "[W]hat if this is one of those rare cases in which the jury made a mistake and he is actually innocent?"

■ *Howe v. Smith*

This case flowed from the decision of officials in Vermont to "get out of the prison business." In December 1974, the Vermont commissioner of corrections announced that he would close the state prison at Windsor, the only high-security facility in the state. This would leave only community correctional centers (for minimum security inmates) and the diagnostic treatment facility at St. Albans as state corrections facilities for adult inmates, inside the state. Howe was serving a life sentence for first-degree murder. The Department of Corrections Classification Committee decided that he should be kept in a maximum security facility. When the decision was made to close Windsor, it was proposed that Howe should be transferred to a federal prison. The Federal Bureau of Prisons had agreed to take up to 40 Vermont prisoners. This was done pursuant to Title 18, U.S. Code, Section 5003(a), which allowed the director of the Bureau of Prisons to take state prisoners upon certification that there were federal facilities that could accommodate them (such a certificate was made). Howe was given a hearing in Vermont, with advance notice of the proposal and the reasons for it. The hearing officer recommended that Howe be transferred to a federal institution, because Howe was dangerous and could not be placed in a community-based program. The hearing officer also found that Howe was an escape risk (he had previously escaped from the maximum security wing at St. Albans) and that he needed long-term maximum-security supervision.

In *Howe v. Smith*, 452 U.S. 473 (1981), the Supreme Court upheld the validity of the transfer. The legal analysis turned principally on the federal statute that authorized the Bureau of Prisons to take state prisoners, 18 U.S.C. § 5003, and not on constitutional protections. "The plain language, the legislative history, and the longstanding administrative interpretation of [Sec.] 5003(a) clearly demonstrate that the provision is a broad charter authorizing the transfer of state prisoners to federal custody. There is no basis in [Sec.] 5003(a) for the petitioner's challenge to his transfer to federal custody."

■ *Olim v. Wakinekona*

Olim v. Wakinekona, 461 U.S. 238 (1983), involved another type of prisoner transfer. Wakinekona was serving a life sentence in the Hawaii State Prison. Because he was a serious troublemaker, a "Program Committee" recommended his transfer to a prison on the mainland. He was later transferred to Folsom State Prison in California. Wakinekona filed a Section 1983 action against state officials, claiming that he had been denied procedural due process, because he had not been given a hearing before he was transferred. The Supreme Court reviewed the case because it presented the new question of whether the due process clause protects inmates in cases of interstate transfers.

The Court noted that Hawaii, like many other states, had statutes that allowed it to transfer inmates to other states or to federal prisons. It also noted that "[o]vercrowding and the need to separate particular prisoners may necessitate interstate transfers." Another frequent reason for interstate transfer would be the one in Wakinekona's case: for the orderly running of an institution, it may be very desirable to transfer a troublemaker out of the system to another state. Thus, an inmate "has no justifiable expectation that he will be incarcerated in any particular State," just as he has no justifiable expectation that he will be placed into a particular prison within a state.

The reasoning of *Meachum* and *Montanye* compels the conclusion that an interstate prison transfer, including one from Hawaii to California, does not deprive an inmate of any liberty interest protected by the Due Process Clause in and of itself.

■ *Vitek v. Jones*

The prior cases on inmate transfers identify situations in which no due process rights are implicated. The Court, however, has set some limits to transfer actions. *Vitek v. Jones*, 445 U.S. 480 (1980), is a case that can best be interpreted, in contrast to the other transfer cases we have just discussed, as a transfer made outside the range of conditions normally to be expected by one serving a sentence of confinement. Jones was serving a sentence of three to nine years in the Nebraska state prison. Jones was placed in the penitentiary hospital, apparently for displaying psychiatric and behavioral problems. Two days later he was placed in solitary confinement, where he set his mattress on fire, burning himself. He was treated for the burns in a nearby private hospital. Then, based on reports that he was suffering from a mental illness or defect and a finding that he could not receive proper treatment for that condition in the penal complex, he was transferred to the Lincoln Regional Center, a state mental hospital. Jones and other inmates challenged the Nebraska procedures, claiming that they were not given due process protections when they were transferred from the prison complex to the mental hospital. A three-judge U.S. district court, convened to consider the constitutionality of the state law and procedure, agreed with the inmates that their transfer, without adequate advance notice and opportunity for a hearing, deprived them of liberty without due process of law in violation of the Fourteenth Amendment.

The Supreme Court agreed to review the case, to decide whether the involuntary transfer of a state prisoner to a mental hospital affected a liberty interest that is protected by the due process clause. The Court first reviewed the recent prison cases that involved due process (*Meachum, Montanye, Greenholtz v. Inmates,* 442 U.S. 1 (1979), [a parole case], and *Wolff v. McDonnell,* 418 U.S. 539 (1974) [an inmate discipline case]). After this review, the Court concluded that Jones was entitled to due process because Nebraska had set up a procedure that created the expectation that action would not be taken against him unless he demonstrated specified behavior. These would be the factual substantive predicates, under the "mandatory language" analysis, which the Supreme Court later rejected in *Sandin v. Conner.*

However, apart from that reliance on mandatory language in the state statute, the Supreme Court also found that, by the very nature of the transfer, "the transfer of a prisoner from a prison to a mental hospital must be accompanied by appropriate procedural protections." The transfer of a prisoner from a regular prison facility to a mental hospital, the Court found, implicated a liberty interest that is protected under the due process clause. The Court noted that an ordinary citizen would be entitled to due process before he could be involuntarily sent to a mental health facility.

We conclude that a convicted felon also is entitled to the benefit of procedures appropriate in the circumstances before he is found to have a mental disease and transferred to a mental hospital....A criminal conviction and sentence of imprisonment extinguish an individual's right to freedom from confinement for the term of his sentence, but they do not authorize the State to classify him as mentally ill and to subject him to involuntary psychiatric treatment without affording him additional due process protections.

The Court concluded that there were stigmatizing consequences of a transfer to a mental hospital for involuntary psychiatric treatment (which could involve subjecting the patient to mandatory behavior modification treatments). Those consequences constituted the kinds of deprivation of liberty that due process was established to protect. Although the state had an interest in placing the inmate in a specialized psychiatric facility for treatment, the inmate still had a strong interest in not being arbitrarily or wrongly classified as mentally ill and then being subjected to unwanted treatment.

The Supreme Court identified the amount of due process—that is, the hearing requirements—which would have to be observed before transferring a prisoner to a mental hospital. The process would have to include: (1) advance written notice to the prisoner that a transfer was being considered; (2) a hearing, with disclosure of the evidence that officials were relying on and an opportunity for the prisoner to be heard in person and present documentary evidence; (3) an opportunity at the hearing to present witnesses and confront and cross-examine state witnesses, unless there was a finding of good reason not to permit witnesses or confrontation and cross-examination; (4) an independent decision maker; (5) a written statement by the factfinder as to the evidence relied on and the reasons for the action that was recommended; (6) availability of counsel, furnished by the state, if the inmate was not able to provide his own; and (7) effective and timely notice of all these hearing rights. It must be noted that item 6 in the procedures, providing counsel to the prisoner, was not agreed to by a majority of the Court. A five-to-four decision settled all other aspects of the case. Justice Powell departed from the majority on the right-to-counsel issue. He voted to require only some "competent help" at the hearing and disagreed that the state would have to provide legal counsel. Therefore, item 6 cannot be considered to be part of the majority decision of the Court, and the right to legal counsel cannot be considered to be a constitutional due process requirement in these hearings.

▦ *Wilkinson v. Austin*

Since the 1980s, partly in response to increased violence in prisons, many states and the federal government have established increased high security or "supermax" prisons. The state of Ohio did this at the Ohio State Penitentiary (OSP). This facility was designed to house 504 inmates in single cells. The conditions were more restrictive than anywhere else in the state system, with prisoners confined to their 7x14-foot cells for 23 hours a day (with one hour a day allowed for exercise at an indoor recreation cell), a light (dimmed at night) burning in each cell at all times, meals provided and eaten in the cells, and "inmates being deprived of almost any environmental or sensory stimuli and of almost all human contact." Further, placement at the OSP was indefinite, and prisoners at the OSP were ineligible for parole. The purpose was to "separate the most predatory and dangerous prisoners from the rest of the ... general [prison] population."

In *Wilkinson v. Austin*, 545 U.S. 209 (2005), the Supreme Court determined "what process the Fourteenth Amendment to the United States Constitution requires Ohio to afford to inmates before assigning them to Supermax." Noting the severe conditions at the OSP, the Court concluded:

> **While any of these conditions standing alone might not be sufficient to create a liberty interest, taken together they impose an atypical and significant hardship within the correctional context. It follows that respondents [the prisoners] have a liberty interest in avoiding assignment to OSP.**

Having determined that placement at the OSP deprived inmates of a protected liberty interest, it follows that they were entitled to due process protection before that action was taken. What procedure were they entitled to? Looking at standards established in other due process cases, the Court said that the Ohio policy met constitutional standards for procedural protections. That policy provided for a prison official to conduct a classification review, a three-tiered further review process if there was a recommendation that the inmate be placed in OSP, notice to the inmate of the factual basis leading to the OSP placement recommendation, and an opportunity for the inmate to submit objections prior to final determination, including a fair opportunity for rebuttal at a hearing (but without the opportunity to call witnesses). These procedures met the factors that had to be considered in satisfying due process: the inmate's interest in avoiding erroneous placement in OSP, minimizing the risk of making an erroneous placement in OSP, and satisfying the concerns of prison management to ensure the safety of prison personnel, the public, and the prisoners themselves. The Court specifically refrained from saying just what procedural steps would be required to meet the due process concerns in any such placement decision, but said Ohio's policy was satisfactory, providing sufficient procedural protection to the inmate.

◼ *Young v. Harper*

In *Young v. Harper*, 520 U.S. 143 (1997), the Court considered whether *Meachum* applied in a situation in which an inmate was removed from a preparole program. In *Young*, Oklahoma's Preparole Program became effective whenever state prisons became overcrowded (when the prison population exceeded 95% of capacity). The program authorized the release by administrative action of inmates before their sentences expired. This was called conditional release. Harper had served 15 years of a life sentence for two murders. Following a review by state officials, he was released, spending five months in the community. Subsequently, the governor, pursuant to his authority under this program, denied Harper parole and Harper was returned to prison. He then filed a petition for a writ of habeas corpus, claiming deprivation of his liberty without due process. The state argued that *Meachum* was controlling, claiming that reincarceration of a preparolee was nothing more than a "transfer to a higher degree of confinement." The Supreme Court disagreed, supporting the appeals court holding that preparole "more closely resembles parole or probation than even the more permissive forms of institutional confinement.... [D]ue process therefore mandates that program participants receive at least the procedural protections described in *Morrissey*." The Supreme Court said the "conditional release" was just like parole and that due process requirements for parole actions applied.

■ *Kansas v. Hendricks; Kansas v. Crane*

These two Supreme Court decisions dealt with Kansas's Sexually Violent Predator Act. In 1994, Kansas passed this act, which set procedures for civilly committing persons who, due to a "mental abnormality" or "personality disorder," are likely to become involved in "predatory acts of sexual violence." The statute was used for Hendricks, an inmate with a long history of sexually molesting children. In 1984, he was convicted for taking "indecent liberties" with two 13-year-old boys. After serving nearly 10 years for those offenses, he was due for release from prison shortly after the law became effective. The state filed a petition, seeking his confinement under the new law. Hendricks challenged the law on various points, alleging a lack of due process and also that he was subjected to double jeopardy and **ex post facto** statutory punishment.

At a hearing on his commitment, Hendricks admitted he had repeatedly abused children when not confined; that this occurs whenever he "get[s] stressed out"; that he "can't control the urge"; and that the "only sure way he could keep from sexually abusing children in the future was 'to die.'" He did not object to the diagnosis that he suffered from pedophilia.

The Kansas Supreme Court invalidated the act, holding that the pre-commitment condition of a "mental abnormality" did not meet what the court saw as the due process requirement that involuntary civil commitment must be based on a finding of "mental illness." Kansas petitioned the U.S. Supreme Court for a writ of certiorari and Hendricks filed a cross petition, reasserting his claims of double jeopardy and ex post facto violations.

The Supreme Court, in *Kansas v. Hendricks*, 521 U.S. 346 (1997), upheld the Kansas act, likening it to state civil commitment procedures for mental patients that it had previously approved.

> The challenged Act unambiguously requires a finding of dangerousness either to one's self or to others as a prerequisite to involuntary confinement. Commitment proceedings can be initiated only when a person "has been convicted of or charged with a sexually violent offense," and "suffers from a mental abnormality or personality disorder which makes the person likely to engage in the predatory acts of sexual violence." ... The [Kansas] statute thus requires proof of more than a mere predisposition to violence.... The precommitment requirement of a "mental abnormality" or "personality disorder" is consistent with the requirements of ... other statutes that we have upheld in that it narrows the class of persons eligible for confinement to those who are unable to control their dangerousness.

> Indeed, we have never required State legislatures to adopt any particular nomenclature in drafting civil commitment statutes. Rather, we have traditionally left to legislators the task of defining terms of a medical nature that have legal significance.

The Supreme Court also looked at Hendricks's claims of double jeopardy and ex post facto, rejecting each of them:

> **Where the State has "disavowed any punitive intent"; limited confinement to a small segment of particularly dangerous individuals; provided strict procedural safeguards; directed that confined persons be segregated from the general prison population and afforded the same status as others who have been civilly committed; recommended treatment if such is possible; and permitted immediate release upon a showing that the individual is no longer dangerous or mentally impaired, we cannot say that it acted with punitive intent. We therefore hold that the Act does not establish criminal proceedings and that involuntary confinement pursuant to the Act is not punitive. Our conclusion that the Act is nonpunitive thus removes an essential prerequisite for both Hendricks' double jeopardy and ex post facto claims.**

The Supreme Court in *Hendricks* found no indication on the face of the statute to suggest that the intent of the legislature was anything other than an action, using civil commitment proceedings, intended to protect the public from harm.

Several years later, in *Kansas v. Crane*, 534 U.S. 407 (2002), the Supreme Court looked again at the Kansas procedure for committing sexual predators. The Court examined the question of whether *Hendricks* required a finding that the person is "*completely* unable to control his [dangerous] behavior." Crane was a previously convicted sexual offender who was diagnosed as suffering from exhibitionism and antisocial personality disorder. After a hearing before a jury, the district court ordered his civil commitment. The Kansas Supreme Court reversed, holding that the district court did not meet the *Hendricks* requirement of finding that Crane could not control his dangerous behavior.

The Supreme Court held that *Hendricks* established no requirement of *total* or *complete* lack of control but disagreed with the state's position that *Hendricks* allows commitment without *any* determination at all of lack of control.

> **[W]e recognize that in cases where lack of control is at issue, "inability to control behavior" will not be demonstrable with mathematical precision. It is enough to say that there must be proof of serious difficulty in controlling behavior. And this, when viewed in light of such features of the case as the nature of the psychiatric diagnosis, and the severity of the mental abnormality itself, must be sufficient to distinguish the dangerous sexual offender whose serious mental illness, abnormality, or disorder subjects him to civil commitment from the dangerous but typical recidivist convicted in an ordinary criminal case.[3]**

■ *Farmer v. Brennan*

Farmer v. Brennan, 511 U.S. 825 (1994), raised serious questions about the proper classification of an inmate. The inmate, Farmer, was a transsexual. He was medically identified as a male, because he possessed male sex organs. (He would have much preferred being treated and classified as a female; he thought of himself as a female and had taken steps before his incarceration to physically change to a female.) The case was decided as an Eighth Amendment case in order to consider Farmer's claim that he had been subjected to cruel and unusual punishment when he was placed in a male penitentiary, where he was sexually assaulted and injured.

We mention the case here to emphasize the difficult problems that can be encountered in properly classifying an inmate. Farmer was an inmate who presented complex questions about how best he could be placed and treated inside the prison system. Providing for inmate safety, according to the Supreme Court and many lower courts, is a requirement demanded by the Eighth Amendment. Prison officials, however, are not guarantors of the safety of inmates, courts have said. But the officials must take steps to protect inmates, particularly when the officials are on notice that a risk is presented by a particular inmate's behavior.

There are two possible types of liabilities in such circumstances: common law tort liability and liability for violating the inmate's constitutional rights. If officials are negligent in taking protective steps (when they have received some notice of danger to the inmate and the inmate is then assaulted because of officials' inaction), their liability would fall under traditional, common law tort standards. An official could also be held constitutionally liable, as the Supreme Court said in *Farmer,* if he knows that an inmate faces a substantial risk of serious harm and the official disregards that risk and fails to take reasonable steps to avoid it.

To be sure, some responsibility is also placed on the inmate: if he knows he is in danger, he has some obligation to let prison officials know that. If officials are proposing to place him into the regular prison population, and he fears for his safety if that happens, he should let prison staff know of his fears and the basis for them. But the decision in *Farmer* emphasizes that, even though the standards for constitutional liability under the Eighth Amendment are rigorous, the mistaken classification of an inmate may expose staff to constitutional (Section 1983) liability in cases of "unnecessary and wanton infliction of pain." If that high standard is not proved, there may still be regular, common law tort liability for classifying an inmate mistakenly, particularly when decisions were not made according to commonly accepted correctional guidelines.

Would inmate Farmer have a constitutional claim against prison officials for "wrongly" classifying him? Does a prisoner have a liberty interest, protected by the due process clause, in prison classification? The Supreme Court in *Moody v. Daggett,* 429 U.S. 78 (1976) ruled that prisoners (at least federal prisoners) have no liberty interest, protected by the due process clause, in prison classification:

> **We have rejected the notion that every state action carrying adverse consequences for prison inmates automatically activates a due process right. In *Meachum v. Fano* ... for example, no due process protections were required upon the discretionary transfer of state prisoners to a substantially less agreeable prison, even where that transfer visited a "grievous loss" upon the inmate. The same is true of prisoner classification and eligibility for rehabilitative programs in the federal system. Congress has given federal officials full discretion to control these conditions of confinement.**

In those jurisdictions where prisoner classification is vested in the discretion of prison officials, a prisoner would not have a constitutionally protected liberty interest in any particular classification.

■ International Transfers

Another type of transfer, of more recent vintage, is the transfer of an inmate from one country to another. For the United States, these transfers were initiated by discussions with Canada in 1975.[4] There is, of course, heavy and fairly free movement of persons between Canada and the United States. This large volume of traffic results in the prosecution and conviction of many persons who commit crimes in the neighboring country. The main concern underlying the initial discussion regarding the international transfer of inmates was a humanitarian and practical one: to get the offenders closer to home and under the supervision of the laws and customs of their home country. At first, the discussion focused on setting up legal arrangements to transfer the supervision of parolees from one country to the other. But this soon expanded to the consideration of all types of sentences—probation, imprisonment, parole, and even juvenile dispositions.

It must be understood that issues of sovereignty are involved in such transfers.[5] Considerations of the principles of international law are necessarily present. The enforcement of criminal laws is an essential part of a nation's sovereignty. When a person is transferred out of a country, that sovereign nation is giving up a degree of control in a central aspect of its sovereignty. There are also extremely practical, and sometimes troublesome, questions of differences between the criminal laws of the two nations. No two nations have identical laws. (The criminal approaches of Canada and the United States are quite similar, so this was helpful in working out transfers between those two countries. But some things are different. For example, all sentences—for any crimes—of greater than two years in Canada are served in federal institutions and not provincial ones. Of course, in the United States, every state plus the federal government administers its own criminal sanctions, of all lengths and of every type, and every state as well as the federal government has institutions for different lengths of sentences.) Attributes of sentences are often different. Such things as parole eligibility, good-conduct allowances, and inmate discipline vary (after all, as we have mentioned, these things even vary greatly from jurisdiction to jurisdiction within the United States). Also, there may be some serious differences regarding how each nation views the seriousness of particular offenses. The question then is, when a prisoner is transferred, does the exact length of the sentence he has to serve become the sentence in the receiving country (his home country), and do all the other aspects of his sentence (such as parole, probation, good time, disciplinary sanctions) apply after his transfer?

Shortly after the discussions were held with Canada, the same kind of talks took place between the United States and Mexico. There was somewhat more urgency with Mexico, because the numbers of prisoners were greater on both sides of the border. Concerns of families of U.S. citizens who were arrested in Mexico (and then of the members of Congress with whom those families talked) and of the State Department over conditions in Mexican jails and prisons and about Mexican criminal procedures encouraged the talks. There were more differences between the Mexican and American systems, so the talks with Mexico presented more practical problems than did those with Canada. With the election of President Carter in 1976, there was a decisive push to finalize the discussions on prisoner transfers, because he was meeting with the president of Mexico soon after his election, and an issue was sought that could be held out as an example of goodwill and cooperation between the two countries. Ultimately, an announcement was made at that meeting that the two nations were signing a treaty to allow for sentenced offenders to be sent from one country to the other.

From the talks with Canada, and as an accommodation for the concerns of sovereignty and the differences between the criminal justice systems in the two countries, the following principles were agreed on: (1) Transfers would occur only for those who were convicted of offenses that were recognized as criminal violations in both countries. For example, if there is an offense in Country A of impersonating the president, which is not a crime in Country B, the offender in Country A convicted of that offense would not be a candidate for transfer to Country B. Otherwise, the offender would be imprisoned in Country B for activity that is not considered criminal in Country B. (2) The transfer would always be based on a tripartite agreement. This meant that the holding country (where the offender was tried and sentenced), the receiving country (his home country), and the offender would have to agree to the transfer. Because the main purpose of the program was humanitarian, if the offender did not want to return to his home country to serve his sentence, he should not have to go. (3) The fact of the conviction and the sentence would be given full recognition in the receiving country. The length of sentence would be transferred intact from one nation to the other. The other attributes of the sentence, such as the eligibility for parole on the length of a sentence, the requirements for parole supervision, remission (good time) credits, disciplinary procedures, and all kinds of programs that might be offered, would be governed by the law and procedures of the receiving country. (4) All appeals of the conviction or sentence would have to be completed before the transfer. A prisoner would not be considered "legally ready" for transfer consideration if appeals were still pending. (5) For sheer administrative convenience, a prisoner should have a certain length of time still remaining on his sentence in order to be eligible for a request for transfer. At the beginning, this was one year; later, it was reduced to six months. It takes some length of time just to process the transfer papers through diplomatic and corrections channels. If an inmate is very close—less than six months, for example—to release, there are often ways to reduce the remaining time to be served in confinement or under supervision and effect the release without having to go through the international transfer process. (6) The transfer of probation and parole, including both supervision and revocation authority, was authorized.

These principles became the foundation for the treaties entered into with Mexico on November 25, 1976, and with Canada on March 2, 1977. You will recall that only the federal government in the United States can enter treaties or any kind of agreements or transactions with foreign nations. (Article II, Section 2 of the Constitution gives the power to make treaties to the president. Two-thirds of the Senate must vote to ratify a treaty.) To achieve the international transfer of prisoners, treaties had to be negotiated and signed with each country and then sent to the Senate for ratification. Besides the treaties, it was recognized that, in the United States, implementing legislation would be needed. In 1977, a federal statute was passed (it is codified in Title 18, U.S. Code, Sections 4100 and following). It sets up the mechanics for transfers from and to the United States, primarily through the Department of Justice. The Department of State must also be involved in every case. States (in the United States) are authorized to send offenders who are foreign nationals to their home countries through this mechanism, and they can also receive back (to their home states in the United States) offenders from foreign countries.

Through the intervening years, treaties have been negotiated and signed with many countries. As of 2009, the United States had treaties with more than 90 countries and territories. In 2009, there were, pursuant to these treaties, 231 inmates transferred, with 57 American citizens coming to the United States and 174 foreign nationals from Bureau of Prisons facilities leaving the United States.[6]

It should have been a surprise to no one that prisoners who were returned under the transfer treaty would bring lawsuits challenging their custody after they were back in the United States. The leading case considering challenges to the treaty process and the authority to hold prisoners under sentences imposed in foreign countries is *Rosado v. Civiletti*, 621 F.2d 1179 (2nd Cir. 1980). In that case, Rosado and three other U.S. citizens had been arrested in Mexico and charged with narcotics offenses. After their arrests, they claimed that they were stripped, bound, beaten, and tortured with electric prods. They had no access to attorneys or family members, they said. They refused to sign confessions that were prepared by authorities. They were transferred into a regular prison, where they alleged that they were told the charge for a cell (and other amenities) would be $2,000. After a month, they were taken to court and were asked to confirm the statements that prosecutors had prepared for them. They denied them and were returned to prison. Some time later, they were advised that the judge in their cases had convicted each of them for the drug offenses and had sentenced each one to nine years of imprisonment. At no time did they see the judge, an attorney, or any of the witnesses against them. These were the allegations of the plaintiffs in *Rosado*. (Similar allegations had been made by many other Americans who were arrested and convicted in Mexico. Suffice it to say, conditions in Mexican jails and prisons were very different from those in the United States, and the criminal process was a far cry from the procedures in American courts. But, lest we be too smug, it may be noted that Canadians regarded the conditions their citizens were facing in U.S. jails and prisons to be barbaric, from the stories they had heard, in comparison to Canadian facilities. These comments are made from one author's own recollections, based on information provided by State Department officials and other sources at that time in the 1970s.)

The appeals court in *Rosado* noted that, at the Senate hearings on the transfer treaties, complaints had been heard from many U.S. citizens who had been held in Mexican jails and prisons. Those stories provided compelling arguments to approve a transfer process. The prisoners in *Rosado* had been advised, while confined in Mexico, that the treaty had been approved in 1977, and they were informed of the necessary procedures to initiate a transfer. One of the conditions of the transfer, which had to be agreed to by the prisoners, was that there would be no legal remedy available to challenge their convictions or sentences once in the United States. This was part of the established principle that any appeals or challenges to the underlying conviction and sentence had to be brought and completed in the sending country. Also, as part of the process and the protection given to inmates, on the part of the United States, all prisoners (in this case, all of those who were in Mexican custody) were interviewed and advised by a U.S. public defender, who explained to them in detail the workings of the transfer treaty. Also, as a part of the transfer process, a U.S. magistrate went to the foreign country (or met the inmates at the border) and made certain that the inmates understood the consequences of the transfer. The inmates were also advised that nothing in the treaty prevented them from challenging their custody status, the legality of the treaty, or the manner in which their sentences were being executed once they returned to the United States. Any such challenge would have to be by means of petition for habeas corpus.

That was what the *Rosado* plaintiffs did: they challenged the constitutionality of their detention by habeas corpus action. A U.S. district court ordered their release, finding that their consents to be transferred were not voluntarily given (in view of the coercive nature of the conditions under which they were held in Mexico). The court of appeals disagreed and upheld the constitutionality of the transfer procedure.

First, the court noted that the law was clear that the U.S. Constitution only applied to actions taken in the United States or to actions taken by U.S. agents working in a foreign country. The Bill of Rights does not protect U.S. citizens against any actions that might be taken by a foreign nation's officials. A major concern in the litigation was the voluntariness of the prisoners' consent to be returned to the United States. The court applied the same standards used to test voluntariness of pleas of guilty in U.S. criminal cases: whether it was a deliberate, intelligent choice. The court concluded that the inmates' decisions were voluntarily and intelligently made.

[B]ecause the statutory procedures governing transfers of these prisoners to United States custody are carefully structured to ensure that each of them voluntarily and intelligently agreed to forego his right to challenge the validity of his Mexican conviction, and because we must not ignore the interests of those citizens still imprisoned abroad, we hold that the present petitioners are estopped from receiving the relief they now seek.

In other words, this appeals court approved the concept and the legality of the international transfer process. The court recognized the desirability of having the transfer procedure available and did not want to jeopardize the chances of other prisoners to transfer out of Mexico. (After all, if a court had found that Mexican procedures and conditions were so bad that these prisoners in *Rosado* had to be released, it would probably eliminate the chances for others to transfer back to the United States. The U.S. government, in effect, would have been blocked from trying to assist its citizens to transfer, because an essential element of the treaty was that a transferred prisoner would be held in custody under the sentence that had been imposed in the sending country.) There was also concern about the impact, if such a ruling were made, on the relations between the two countries: Mexico would no doubt be offended and might itself abandon the treaty or any efforts to assist U.S. citizens if American courts intensively reviewed conditions in Mexico, based on the prisoners' assertions about what happened, and found the conditions and procedures so bad that they were serious violations of U.S. constitutional requirements.

In any event, the international transfer program has withstood constitutional attack in the courts. Inmates in the United States, however, are allowed to challenge any conditions or actions of U.S. officials after they are returned to U.S. custody. These challenges are brought, as for any American prisoner, using habeas corpus or Section 1983 actions to challenge the legality of their custody or the conditions under which they are held.

Another aspect of the treaty transfer program was challenged in *Marquez-Ramos v. Reno*, 69 F.3d 477 (10th Cir. 1995). Marquez-Ramos was a Mexican national serving a sentence in a federal prison. He sought a writ of **mandamus** (under Title 28, U.S. Code, Section 1361), asking the court to require the U.S. Attorney General to transfer him to Mexico. The court noted that, under the Treaty on the Exercise of Penal Sentences between the United States and Mexico, a request for transfer by an inmate is to be transmitted by the Transferring State (in this case, the

United States) to the Receiving State (Mexico) only if the authority of the Transferring State "finds the transfer of an offender appropriate." The treaty, and its implementing statute in the United States, gave the authority to review such requests to the U.S. Attorney General. The treaty also set out the factors to be considered in reviewing a request for transfer. Those factors include whether the transfer will contribute to the social rehabilitation of the offender, the nature and severity of his offense and previous criminal record, and the strength of his family relationships and of his other connections of residence (whether in the United States or in his native country). In this case, the attorney general denied Marquez-Ramos's transfer request, mainly because of his serious offense and his ties to the United States. The district court and the court of appeals ruled that Marquez-Ramos had no entitlement to mandamus relief, because the attorney general had total discretion to make the transfer decision within the framework of the treaty. Mandamus was not available to challenge the discretionary authority of the attorney general, the courts said.

■ Loss of Property and Personal Injuries

You will recall that the due process clause also protects against the unlawful deprivation of property. We will consider two cases in the Supreme Court (*Parratt* and *Hudson*) that dealt with property deprivation. The remaining cases in this chapter deal with the loss of liberty that may be caused by personal injury.

Parratt v. Taylor

Historically, we must consider *Parratt v. Taylor*, 451 U.S. 527 (1981), although it was later overruled. Taylor was an inmate at the Nebraska Penal and Correctional Complex. He ordered some hobby materials, for which he paid $23.50. Somehow, the materials were lost after they had arrived at the prison and before they got to Taylor. Taylor brought suit under Section 1983, claiming that his property had been taken (*deprived*, to use the constitutional language) without due process of law. The Supreme Court noted that his claim was that the property was negligently lost and that the court analysis would have to focus on whether the essential elements of a Section 1983 claim were present: (1) whether the loss was caused by a person who was acting under color of state law and (2) whether that state official's conduct deprived Taylor of a right given him under the Constitution.

The Court found that Taylor had been deprived of his property under color of state law. Thus, the first question was answered in the affirmative. To answer the second question, the Court had to look to the constitutional provision invoked, which was the due process clause. Taylor's claim did involve an alleged loss of his property. That part of the due process clause (a deprivation of life, liberty, or property) was met. However, the second part of the clause, that he was deprived of his property without due process of law, was not met. This was because the state of Nebraska provided a remedy to persons who suffered a loss of property at the hands of the state because of state negligence. This tort claims procedure was available to inmates. "The remedies provided could have fully compensated [Taylor] for the property loss he suffered, and we hold that they are sufficient to satisfy the requirements of due process."

Thus, the Supreme Court held that a loss of property could be the basis of a claim for the deprivation of constitutional rights under Section 1983, if the state did not have an adequate remedy (due process) to compensate the inmate for that deprivation. In this case, though, Nebraska had a process for compensation to the inmate, and the existence of that tort claim procedure allowed the state to have the Section 1983 action dismissed for failure to state a claim under the statute (Section 1983) and under the Constitution.

Hudson v. Palmer

Hudson v. Palmer, 468 U.S. 517 (1984), is a case that involves both a Fourth Amendment cell search (and whether there is any privacy right in prisons) and a claimed deprivation of property without due process. Palmer claimed that the officers destroyed some of his personal property in the cell just to harass him. The Supreme Court extended its holding in *Parratt*, saying that even though there was a claim of intentional destruction of Palmer's property, the requirements of due process had been met in this case, because the state (Virginia) gave Palmer a remedy. He could file a claim for compensation for his lost or damaged property, and that remedy precluded bringing a claim for constitutional deprivation under Section 1983. Thus, even intentional damage to property is not the basis for a constitutional claim, as long as the state has a remedy for the inmate to use to be compensated for his loss.

Daniels v. Williams

Daniels sued under 42 U.S.C. § 1983, seeking damages for back and ankle injuries he sustained when he fell on a stairway at the city jail in Richmond, Virginia. He claimed that a jail officer had negligently left a pillow on the stairs, which caused his fall. This, he claimed, deprived him of his liberty interest to be free from bodily injury. The Supreme Court, in *Daniels v. Williams*, 474 U.S. 327 (1986), said that the due process clause was intended to secure individuals from abuse of power by government officials. The Constitution does not say one way or the other whether ordinary negligence is enough to state a constitutional claim. Therefore, the Court had to address that issue.

The word *deprive* in the Constitution connotes more than a negligent act, according to the Supreme Court.

> [We] overrule *Parratt* to the extent that it states that mere lack of due care by a state official may "deprive" an individual of life, liberty, or property under the Fourteenth Amendment....Far from an abuse of power, lack of due care suggests no more than a failure to measure up to the conduct of a reasonable person. To hold that injury caused by such conduct is a deprivation within the meaning of the Fourteenth Amendment would trivialize the centuries-old principle of due process of law.

The Court held that a state official's negligent act that caused unintended loss of life, liberty, or property did not implicate the due process clause. There was no constitutional claim made by Daniels when he alleged he was injured by the negligent act of the jail officer.

Davidson v. Cannon

Davidson v. Cannon, 474 U.S. 344 (1986), was a companion case to *Daniels* and was decided by the Supreme Court on the same day. Davidson was an inmate in the New Jersey State Prison. He sent a note, saying that he had been threatened by another inmate, to the assistant superintendent of the prison, who, in turn, sent it on to a corrections sergeant. The sergeant failed to read the note right away and left the prison. Later, Davidson was assaulted and injured by the inmate he had identified in his note. Davidson brought suit under Section 1983, alleging that his constitutional rights had been violated under the Eighth and Fourteenth Amendments. The U.S. district court ruled that prison officials had failed to take reasonable steps to protect Davidson and that, for this reason, he was injured. Using *Parratt* standards, that court found that Davidson was deprived of his liberty interest in his own personal security and that New Jersey did not have a law or procedure that would compensate him for his injury. Therefore, the trial court said, he had been deprived of his liberty without due process of law, and he was awarded damages of $2,000 against the prison officials.

The court of appeals reversed the lower court's judgment. The Supreme Court agreed to review the matter. Applying its reasoning in *Daniels*, the Supreme Court agreed with the court of appeals:

> **[W]here a government official is merely negligent in causing the injury, no procedure for compensation is constitutionally required ....[The officials'] lack of due care in this case led to serious injury, but that lack of care simply does not approach the sort of abusive government conduct that the Due Process Clause was designed to prevent.**

Here, rather than abuse of power, the officials mistakenly believed that the situation was not too serious, and the sergeant simply forgot about the note from Davidson. The government—in this case, prison officials—is not required by the Constitution to use due care in all situations, the Court ruled; the Constitution does not guarantee against officials making mistakes or being unintentionally negligent.

Davidson had indicated that he just wanted some kind of remedy. New Jersey did not have one for him for this kind of injury, and he wanted some compensation, such as Nebraska had for inmate Taylor (for his lost hobby materials) or Virginia had for Daniels (for his injuries sustained in the fall on the jail stairs). But the Supreme Court held that the Constitution does not require that the state provide a remedy in situations in which there has been no deprivation of a protected interest (life, liberty, or property). The Court said that it might indeed be good for the state to have a means of compensating for such injuries, but the Constitution does not require it, and federal courts cannot require it as a constitutional matter.

■ Use of Excessive Force

Because we are considering here prisoners' claims of injury, we should briefly discuss here the use of force. This topic is covered in more detail when we discuss conditions of confinement. The cases of *Whitley v. Albers,* 475 U.S. 312 (1986), and *Hudson v. McMillian,* 503 U.S. 1 (1992), particularly involve questions of inmates being injured as a result of force and whether those actions were excessive, creating constitutional liability. Those cases were brought and analyzed by the courts as Eighth Amendment cases, because the inmates claimed that they had been punished cruelly and unusually by staff actions. Claims of staff abuse, or of overreaction by staff in certain circumstances, certainly could also be brought or considered under the Fourteenth or Fifth Amendments. If action by staff was taken maliciously and sadistically, so as to be an Eighth Amendment violation, that would seem to show an abusive use of government power or authority, which the Court in *Daniels* and *Davidson* said the due process clause was meant to protect against. Then, the question would be whether the state had an adequate remedy under some claim procedure for such injuries to compensate inmates for injuries that they suffered as a result of abusive use of government authority. If not, the inmate so injured and left without a state remedy would have a claim to be made under Section 1983 for violation of his due process rights. The Supreme Court has not yet decided that exact case. Our analysis is based on what the Supreme Court has said in other due process cases (*Daniels* and *Davidson*) and excessive force cases (*Whitley* and *Hudson*).

SUMMARY

- Classification—assigning each inmate to the proper institution within the prison system and to the proper housing and programs within that institution—is a central part of good prison management.

- The Supreme Court has ruled that a corrections agency may assign an inmate to any institution within the agency, without implicating any due process concerns under the Constitution (*Meachum v. Fano; Montanye v. Haymes; McKune v. Lile*).

- A state inmate may be transferred to any institution in the federal system (*Howe v. Smith*) or out of the state without a hearing (*Olim v. Wakinekona*).

- The transfer of an inmate from a prison to a mental hospital, however, involves a protected liberty interest and requires a hearing. The requirements include advance written notice to the prisoner; a hearing, with disclosure of evidence relied on to support the transfer; the opportunity to present witnesses and to confront and cross-examine official witnesses; an independent decision maker; a written statement of the evidence relied on and the reasons for the action taken; and assistance by someone at the hearing (*Vitek v. Jones*).

- A prisoner has a liberty interest in avoiding transfer to a prison (such as a supermax) where the conditions of confinement at the new facility pose "an atypical and significant hardship on the inmate in relation to the ordinary incidents of prison life" (*Wilkinson v. Austin*). The procedures provided by the state, including advance written notice, an opportunity to object, and a right to receive a written statement as to why placement was made, satisfied due process for such a transfer to a supermax facility.

- The Court has held that due process considerations are required with respect to the reconfinement of an inmate participating in a preparole program (*Young v. Harper*).

- Committing dangerous sex offenders, beyond their confinement for sex crimes, was found in Kansas to be permissible, comparable to civilly committing dangerous mental patients (*Kansas v. Hendricks; Kansas v. Crane*).

- While prison officials are not guarantors of inmate safety, the mistaken classification of an inmate may expose staff to liability when that mistake results in "unnecessary and wanton infliction of pain" to the inmate (*Farmer v. Brennan*).

- There is now, by treaty, a procedure for transfers of prisoners between the United States and many other countries. This procedure requires the application and approval of the transfer by both countries and the inmate. The procedure has been upheld in federal courts against claims that criminal proceedings in the foreign country violated due process standards (*Rosado v. Civiletti*), and claims by a U.S. prisoner that he should be returned to his native country even though the U.S. government did not approve of the transfer (*Marquez-Ramos v. Reno*).

- Property claims—inmate claims that property has been lost, damaged, or destroyed by government officials—at first found support as stating constitutional violations (because of deprivation of property) in *Parratt v. Taylor. Parratt* was overruled by later Supreme Court decisions, which held that mere claims of government negligence would not support a constitutional claim under 42 U.S.C. § 1983. To state a constitutional claim, there must be abusive conduct by government officials (*Daniels v. Williams; Davidson v. Cannon*). For such claims of property loss or personal injury as a result of negligence on the part of government employees, the remedy in most states is a tort claims procedure.

THINKING ABOUT IT

In *McKune v. Lile*, the Supreme Court upheld a state policy requiring an inmate, as part of a mandatory treatment program, to provide information about his sexual history. Failure to do so could lead to various, less favorable actions, including transfer to another institution. Do you believe that this decision will stand the test of time and future court challenges? How significant is it that the state does not offer legal immunity from prosecution based on statements the inmate makes within the context of the program?

KEY TERMS

ex post facto: Literally, after the act is committed. Used to signify something done after the fact, which is intended to affect something that was done before. An ex post facto law refers to a law that is enacted to impose a penalty for doing something that was lawful when it was done or to increase the punishment for a crime, making the sanction greater than when the crime was committed.

mandamus: A writ (order) requiring a person to do what he should do. Sometimes called a mandatory injunction. See also injunction (court order).

recidivist (recidivism): A repeat offender. One who habitually commits crimes.

ENDNOTES

1. New Mexico Corrections Department. *Institutional Classification, Inmate Risk Assessment and Central Office Classification.* Available from http://corrections.state.nm.us/policies/current/CD-080100.pdf. Accessed June 15, 2011.

2. Alaska Department of Corrections. *Classification Mission Statement.* Available from http://www.correct.state.ak.us/corrections/pnp/pdf/701.02.pdf. Accessed June 15, 2011.

3. Congress enacted a sexual predator commitment statute (18 U.S.C. § 4248) similar to the Kansas statutes discussed in the text. The statute was challenged by persons whom the United States sought to commit, and one basis of the challenges was that Congress lacked constitutional authority to enact such a statute. After several lower courts had declared the statute unconstitutional, concluding that Congress lacked authority under the "necessary and proper" clause to enact such a statute, the issue was addressed by the Supreme Court. In *United States v. Comstock*, 560 U.S. __ (2010) the Supreme Court ruled that enactment of 18 U.S.C. § 4248 did not exceed Congress's authority under the necessary and proper clause of the Constitution.

4. One of the authors was a member of the U.S. group that discussed and set the standards for international transfers, first with Canada and later with Mexico.

5. Please note that these are called *international* or *foreign transfers* of prisoners. Sometimes this process has been called *prisoner exchange*, but that is an improper and misleading term, because there is no requirement that one prisoner must be exchanged for another or that there must be any kind of equality or balancing of numbers when prisoners are transferred. It is true that supervision over the criminal sentence is being "exchanged" between the two sovereign countries, but *transfer* is the preferred term for this program.

6. Federal Bureau of Prisons. *State Of The Bureau 2009 – The Bureau's Core Values.* Page 3. (Washington, DC: Federal Bureau of Prisons, U.S. Department of Justice). Also see Federal Bureau of Prisons Program Statement 5140.39, Transfer of Offenders to or from Foreign Countries.

13 Fourteenth Amendment: Equal Protection—Female Offenders and Others

To withstand constitutional challenge, classifications by gender must serve important governmental objectives and must be substantially related to achievement of those objectives.

U.S. Supreme Court, *Craig v. Boren*

Chapter Outline

- Female Offenders
- *Pargo v. Elliott*
- Noncitizens (Foreign Offenders)
- Other Equal Protection Cases
- Racial Discrimination
- *Johnson v. California*

The Fourteenth Amendment, which we have just examined in many correctional practices that have been raised in the courts under the due process clause, also contains the equal protection clause:

No State shall ... deny to any person within its jurisdiction the equal protection of the laws.

The Supreme Court may use an equal protection analysis to protect the rights of inmates, even in cases in which there may be another constitutional provision, which one would think might be applicable. For instance, in the case of *Cruz v. Beto*, 405 U.S. 319 (1972), the Supreme Court said that if the Buddhist inmate who brought that lawsuit was being denied opportunity to pursue his faith comparable to the opportunity given to other prisoners of other faiths, then there was impermissible discrimination by the state of Texas against him. One may have thought there would have been more analysis under the First Amendment (freedom of religion), but "equal protection" seemed to be the basis of the Court's reasoning. It can also be called, as in that ruling about religious activities in prisons, the "non-discrimination" requirement of the Constitution.

■ Female Offenders

The most striking (albeit recent) application of the equal protection clause is in the realm of female offenders. As of December 31, 2009, there were 105,197 sentenced female inmates under the jurisdiction of state or federal correctional authorities. This number represents 6.8% of all sentenced prisoners.[1] Because of the smaller number of female offenders (even though the number of female offenders is markedly higher than 20 or 30 years ago), most states have only one corrections facility for women (see **Figure 13-1**). Even in the larger states, where there are larger numbers of both male and female offenders, there are many more male institutions than female. These basic differences in numbers (along with old-fashioned ideas about the way women offenders should be treated) lead to many of the complaints about disparity in treatment, which we will examine in the following court decisions.

One early reference to the constitutional requirement of comparable treatment for women was in the case of *Bounds v. Smith,* 430 U.S. 817 (1977). In *Bounds*, a district court had required North Carolina to come up with a plan for law libraries in its prison system to enable inmates to do legal research and prepare legal papers in order for them to have access to the courts. The state drew up a plan, which provided for a sizable collection of law books to be placed in several facilities throughout the state. Inmates who were not located in one of those facilities would be transported to a facility with a law library, upon request, to do their legal research. This plan was approved by the district court and the Fourth Circuit Court of Appeals, except that the latter court required the state to modify its plan to ensure that female inmates had access to similar legal research facilities. The Supreme Court approved the North Carolina plan (without a specific discussion of the availability of lawbooks to female inmates).

Figure 13-1 A corrections office address a group of inmates in the female unit of the Santa Ana, California, City Jail.
Source: © Spencer Grant/Alamy Images

In the case of *Bukhari v. Hutto*, 487 F.Supp. 1162 (E.D. VA 1980), the court had complaints from female inmates in Virginia that they were treated differently—and more poorly—than men. The court noted in its opinion that, for many centuries (in Anglo-American practice), there had not been separate facilities for male and female inmates: all were confined together. It was considered a great improvement when reformers insisted on separate institutions for men and women. The court observed that in Virginia (and the same is true in many states) the women's institution was more campuslike, smaller, and more relaxed than the men's institutions. There was just one state facility, the Virginia Correctional Center for Women, which took most of the women offenders. Although there was a better staff-to-inmate ratio there, there were also fewer programs than were available for men. The court set down the principles for further considera- tion of women's claims: the state would have to justify its reasons for treating female inmates separately and differently from men. The equal protection clause requires parity of treatment for women, the court said, but not identical treatment. Further hearings were ordered to look into the justifications for the disparate treatment.

In *Batton v. State Government of North Carolina*, 501 F.Supp. 1173 (E.D. NC 1980), female inmates claimed they were sent from all over the state to one institution, the North Carolina Correctional Center for Women in Raleigh. This resulted in many of them being farther from their homes than male inmates were. Also, it meant that there was no classification of female offenders according to their ages, the seriousness of their offenses, and their custody requirements. The female inmates also claimed that they had fewer opportunities for programs and activities than men had; they had fewer work-release placements, less vocational training, lower wages for their prison work, less access to medical and psychiatric care, and a less adequate law library. The court noted that only 4% of the 15,000 North Carolina inmates at that time were women. To evaluate, under the Constitution, the women's claims of unconstitutional, disparate treatment, the court took the standard from the Supreme Court decision in *Craig v. Boren*, 429 U.S. 190 (1976):

To withstand constitutional challenge ... classifications by gender must serve important gov- ernmental objectives and must be substantially related to achievement of those objectives.

Although not a prison case, the *Craig* language has been widely quoted as the constitutional statement of equal protection to be used in assessing equal protection claims by women offenders. (*Craig* was a Supreme Court case reviewing an Oklahoma statute, which prohibited sales of 3.2% beer to males under 21 and to females under 18. The Court said that the gender-based differential in Oklahoma law constituted a denial of equal protection to males who were between 18 and 20 years of age. Oklahoma had not shown, the Court said in *Craig*, that the different treatment was necessary to further the legitimate objective of the statute, which was traffic safety.)

The federal court in *Batton* said that it would defer to state officials' judgment whenever possible in assessing the treatment of female offenders. Applying the *Craig v. Boren* standard, quoted above, the court found that, with respect to medical and psychiatric care, disparate wage rates, and the law library, the state had shown its justification for different treatment of females. Summary judgment was granted to state officials for those issues. On other issues (parole, work- release and vocational training opportunities, education, recreation, classification, and the housing of offenders), the court said that further evidence would have to be developed to see whether there was a substantial relationship between the reasons for those female programs being dis- parate and the achievement of legitimate government objectives.

A federal court, in *Glover v. Johnson*, 478 F.Supp. 1075 (E.D. MI 1979), held that educational and vocational programs offered by Michigan to female inmates were markedly poorer than those offered to male inmates. The court ruled that this lack of parity denied equal protection to the women. The court ordered that there be an evaluation and report made of the educational and vocational interests and capabilities of female inmates. Then, with those facts in hand, the state would be required to establish a program substantially equivalent to the one offered throughout the state to male inmates.

Another issue addressed by the courts has been the difference in the treatment of women in their transfers, especially outside the state of their residence and conviction. A federal court, in *Park v. Thompson*, 356 F.Supp. 783 (D. HI 1973), held that it was unconstitutional for Hawaii not to have any long-term facilities for women in the state. Inmate Park challenged, by habeas corpus, her transfer to a federal prison in California to serve her sentence. (The court first ruled that habeas corpus could be used to test the validity of the place of confinement, as well as the underlying validity of the confinement—the traditional purpose of the habeas corpus writ.) The court ruled that it was an equal protection violation to transfer women outside the state, when men could remain in the state in similar circumstances. (One would have to speculate about whether this case would have been decided differently after the Supreme Court's ruling in *Olim v. Wakinekona*, 461 U.S. 238 (1983), where the Court found no constitutional violation in the transfer of inmates to facilities in other states, specifically from Hawaii to California. That decision was based on a due process analysis. The decision in *Park* was based on disparate treatment for women under the equal protection clause. The *Olim* decision would take care of the due process arguments, but the equal protection concerns, as they existed in 1973, still would remain on the facts of *Park v. Thompson*.)

A very different result on out-of-state transfers of female inmates was reached in *Pitts v. Thornburgh*, 866 F.2d 1450 (DC Cir. 1989). Women complained that they were transferred some 260 miles to a federal facility for women in rural West Virginia, whereas male inmates, in most cases, stayed in facilities close to home (the District of Columbia). The trial court had ruled that these transfers caused no violation of constitutional rights, because there was no evidence to show that facilities or programs at the female facility were inferior to those for men in the District of Columbia. The court of appeals affirmed that ruling, finding no "invidious discrimination" against women and no violation of equal protection rights, because the government had an important objective to achieve: the relief of severe overcrowding in the DC facilities.

A similar ruling occurred in *Jackson v. Thornburgh*, 907 F.2d 194 (DC Cir. 1990). In *Jackson*, the District of Columbia Good Time Credits Act of 1986 granted early release to inmates serving sentences in DC prison facilities. The purpose was to reduce overcrowding. Female DC inmates housed in a federal prison, and thus not covered by the law, challenged its constitutionality on the basis of equal protection, claiming, in part, unlawful gender discrimination. The court denied the claim, holding that the act's distinction was not based on gender, either overtly or covertly.

With respect to inmate visiting rights, there have been opinions both supporting and rejecting (for constitutional violations) jail programs that are different for male and female inmates. In *Molar v. Gates*, 159 Cal. Rptr. 239 (1979), a county jail's practice of providing minimum security status and facilities for male inmates when they were not provided for female inmates was found to be unconstitutional, violating the equal protection clauses of both the federal and the state constitutions. Because of the much larger numbers of male inmates, a greater variety of living units and programs, with differing levels of security, was provided for the male inmates. Female inmates were all treated alike. Consequently, there were no minimum security privileges for females. Importantly for this case, minimum security for male inmates meant they could have contact visits. No females were allowed to have contact visits. The court found this disparate treatment to be unsupportable.

But in *Morrow v. Harwell*, 768 F.2d 619 (5th Cir. 1985), the federal appeals court upheld a visiting program in a county jail that allowed more visitation time for males than for females. In the jail, more than 90% of the inmates were male. Female inmates complained, because on visiting days more time was set aside for male visits than for female visits. This amounted to one more hour of visiting time overall for all males. A magistrate at the trial level had ruled that this visiting disparity violated the equal protection standards of the Fourteenth Amendment. However, no inmate, because of the large number of inmates, was allowed more than 15 minutes for a visit. The appellate court held that allowing more overall time for males was justified, because a greater percentage of the population was male. No violation of equal protection was found on the appeals level. (Note: in *Morrow*, the appeals court also looked at the county's legal assistance program for inmates. The court held that the county's bookmobile check-out system, combined with restricted assistance from law students, did not meet the *Bounds* requirement that all inmates must be given meaningful access to the courts; today, this would likely not be the case, as *Morrow* had no showing of actual injury to the inmates, as required by the Supreme Court's post-*Bounds* decision in *Lewis v. Casey*, 518 U.S. 343 (1996).)

■ *Pargo v. Elliott*

A major lawsuit, which has an involved history in the courts, is *Pargo v. Elliott*, 49 F.3d 1355, 69 F.3d 280 (8th Cir. 1995). Inmates at the Iowa Correctional Institution for Women (ICIW) filed a Section 1983 action, claiming that their equal protection rights were violated because prison programs and services at the ICIW differed substantially from those provided to male inmates in Iowa institutions. The U.S. district court had initially used the case of *Klinger v. Department of Corrections*, 31 F.3d 727 (8th Cir. 1994), as its guide.[2] The court of appeals in *Klinger* had held that there was no equal protection violation in Nebraska, where women were treated differently from men, because the two groups of inmates were not sufficiently similar. In that case, male inmates in the state penitentiary were not similarly situated to women because of the size of the institution used for comparison, the length of sentences being served, and the custody classification levels of the two groups of inmates.

The Eighth Circuit, in its first opinion in *Pargo*, observed that the ruling in *Klinger* does not stand for the proposition that male and female inmates can never be similarly situated. In *Pargo*, female inmates argued that men and women with the same custody levels and sentence length had very different programs and services available to them. This, they argued, made *Pargo* very different from *Klinger*. The court of appeals (in its first ruling, reported at 49 F.3d 1355) said that there were not enough facts in the record (even though it was a long one, based on lengthy hearings and much documentation) to allow the court to make a determination of whether the men and women inmates in Iowa were similarly situated. The case was sent back (remanded) to the district court, with instructions to make detailed findings and conclusions, on the issue of the similar or dissimilar situation of the Iowa inmates.

The district court, on the remand of the case, prepared 115 pages of findings and conclusions. The findings spelled out the custody levels Iowa used for classifying men and women and the programs that were available, in each custody level, to women as compared to men. The district court concluded that there was no evidence of "invidious discrimination" (a term given by the Supreme Court in *Personnel Administrator of Massachusetts v. Feeney*, 442 U.S. 256 (1979), to test discrimination allegations). The programs and services to men and women, the court said, taken as a whole or compared by custody level, were substantially similar. Any differences in programs and services had been justified by state prison officials. The court of appeals, in its second opinion (reported at 69 F.3d 280), affirmed the district court's judgment. The major focus left in the case was whether female inmates who were classified as "minimum live-out" (MLO) were disparately and unconstitutionally treated, compared to their male counterparts.

Female inmates in MLO status claimed that they lived in more confined housing, with fewer furloughs, fewer off-grounds work opportunities, less library and yard time, different substance abuse programs, and more restrictive settings for their visits. The courts found that the differences in these programs were not because of "invidious discrimination." Female plaintiffs who were in other security levels also complained that, compared to men in the same security classification, they had fewer legal assistance programs, less work-release time, fewer therapy programs, and fewer yard and library privileges. The district court found, and the appeals court approved, that any differences in these programs were "rationally related to legitimate penological interests, such as security and rehabilitation." The Iowa prison officials prevailed in this large-scale challenge to practices in their institutions.

In *Archer v. Reno*, 877 F.Supp. 372 (E.D. KY 1995), 13 female inmates at the Federal Medical Center at Lexington, Kentucky had been enrolled in a dental education course or had worked in the dental lab there. They brought a Bivens action (the federal equivalent of Section 1983), seeking an injunction against their transfers out of Lexington. They complained that their transfers would deny them the opportunity to complete their dental training program and to become certified dental technicians. (There were five dental labs in the federal prison system, all of which were located in male institutions once the Lexington institution became an all-male institution.) The Bureau of Prisons had decided to convert Lexington to a male institution because of population pressures and consideration of the types of facilities that were available for men and women. (A new medical facility was then being opened in Fort Worth, Texas, and that facility would, in effect, replace Lexington for female inmates with medical needs, including medical training needs.)

The federal district court ruled that the female inmates had no right to specific educational or vocational programs; there was no constitutional right to be rehabilitated (citing *Rhodes v. Chapman*, 452 U.S. 337 (1981) and *Garza v. Miller*, 688 F.2d 480 (7th Cir. 1982)). The court further noted that inmates had no constitutional right to be assigned to a particular job (citing *Flittie v. Solem*, 827 F.2d 276 (8th Cir. 1987) and *Twyman v. Crisp*, 584 F.2d 352 (10th Cir. 1978)). In addition, the inmates had no constitutional right to remain in a particular institution (citing the Supreme Court transfer cases *Meachum v. Fano*, 427 U.S. 215 (1976), *Montanye v. Haymes*, 427 U.S. 236 (1976), and *Olim v. Wakinekona*, 461 U.S. 238 (1983)). The court found that the Bureau of Prisons had presented justification for its decisions about the classification of institutions and of inmates, which were related to its legitimate security and penological interests. It is noteworthy that the court did not undertake any discussion of equal protection rights of the female inmates or of the Supreme Court standard in *Craig v. Boren*, which other courts have used in disparate treatment cases. One must assume that it was not raised by the plaintiff-inmates and did not occur to the court.

■ Noncitizens (Foreign Offenders)

The number of noncitizens in the United States is increasing, both in general and in the country's jails and prisons. On June 30, 2009, state and federal prisons housed 94,498 non-U.S. citizens. The Federal Bureau of Prisons held 30,445 of these noncitizen inmates. The highest state number was in California, which housed 18,705 inmates who were non-U.S. citizens (defined as inmates held by U.S. Immigration and Customs Enforcement).[3] In fiscal year 2009, non-U.S. citizens made up 44.7% of persons sentenced in U.S. district courts under the U.S. sentencing commission guidelines. By far, for these defendants, the largest number of offenses was for drug trafficking (19.5%) and immigration offenses (68.2%).[4]

Does the equal protection clause protect only citizens of the United States? If you look at the language of the Fourteenth Amendment, you see that it protects "persons" and not just citizens. And yet, there are court rulings that state that persons who have entered the United States illegally are not protected by some constitutional provisions. This is based on the theory that, if persons are taken into custody at the border or at any place (such as an airport terminal or a dock) where they are trying to enter the country without authorization, they are "excludable aliens." In that status, they are legally considered not to have entered the country. (No matter where they are subsequently confined, they are considered to have been caught "at the border.") Consequently, they are not entitled to all the rights of persons who are legally within the jurisdiction of the United States and under the protection of the Constitution.

Despite these legal distinctions of immigration law, courts have given protections to noncitizen, foreign-born inmates. In the case of *Thongvanh v. Thalacker*, 17 F.3d 256 (8th Cir. 1994), for example, dealing with inmate mail that was written in a foreign language (Lao), the court applied an equal protection analysis to conclude that, because translations were already being made for Spanish speaking inmates, an effort had to be made to provide translators who could review mail written in Lao. Noncitizen inmates may also be more likely to request religious activities or materials that are related to religions that are outside the "mainstream" of religious observances in the United States. The Supreme Court decision in *Cruz v. Beto*, in particular, relied on equal protection analysis to conclude that if prison authorities provided religious privileges to other religious groups, they would have to show why they could not do the same for Buddhist inmates. (Technically, that is a First Amendment, freedom of religion case, but the reasoning of the court was couched very much in equal protection terms.)

■ Other Equal Protection Cases

Equal protection can also be raised on the other side (in a claim of reverse discrimination) by men claiming disparate treatment, with more favorable treatment being given to women. In *Hill v. Estelle*, 537 F.2d 214 (5th Cir. 1976), six Texas male inmates brought a Section 1983 action, claiming violation of their constitutional (equal protection) rights because female inmates were not held to the same grooming standards (they were allowed to have long hair of different styles); females, unlike men, could make telephone calls to their families; and females, unlike men, were allowed to decorate their cells. The court of appeals conceded that there was some disparate treatment between the men and the women, but it held that the state's policies on these matters did not amount to constitutional violations. The court found that no fundamental right was infringed and that the disparity was not of an unreasonable or egregious level.

■ Racial Discrimination

Racial discrimination can also be raised by inmates as an equal protection violation. The Supreme Court, in *Lee v. Washington*, 390 U.S. 333 (1968), held that prisoners are protected against discrimination based on race. Inmates in Alabama had challenged the segregation of prisoners in the Alabama system. Officials claimed that segregation was necessary to protect institutional security. The federal district court had conceded that, in isolated instances, it might be necessary to separate races for a limited period of time, but held that complete and permanent segregation of the races in all Alabama penal facilities was unconstitutional. The Supreme Court, in a per curiam opinion, supported that decision.

In *Woods v. Edwards*, 51 F.3d 577 (5th Cir. 1995), an inmate in the Louisiana State Penitentiary at Angola filed a Section 1983 action, claiming that his extended lockdown (for nearly four years) was because of his race and was therefore a violation of his equal protection rights. (The court stated that his race was presumed to be black; apparently that was not specified in the pleadings or the record!) The inmate claimed that similarly situated white inmates had been released from lockdown status much earlier than he had been released. The court of appeals noted that, to prove his case, the inmate would have to show that prison officials acted with a discriminatory purpose. According to the court in *United States v. Galloway*, 951 F.2d 64 (5th Cir. 1992), "Discriminatory purpose in an Equal Protection context implies that the decisionmaker selected a particular course of action at least in part because of, and not simply in spite of, the adverse impact it would have on an identifiable group." The defendants had shown that the inmate's lockdown had been extended because of the repeated seriousness of his behavior, including writing threatening letters and forging another inmate's name on letters. The court said the inmate had provided no proof of discriminatory intent on the part of officials. Lacking any evidence of discriminatory intent, and, to the contrary, finding officials had a non-discriminatory reason for their actions, the action of the district court, granting summary judgment to the prison-official defendants, was affirmed.

■ *Johnson v. California*

Because of concerns over violence that might occur between prison racial gangs, California had an unwritten policy of segregating by race all inmates housed in two-person cells at the state's reception centers. These centers housed, for up to 60 days, all newly admitted male inmates and those male inmates transferred from other state facilities. Other areas within the institution, such as recreation and dining, were not subject to the segregation rule. The separation practice was challenged by an African American inmate who had been placed in segregated housing several times during his incarceration in the state. The inmate argued that such segregation violated his right under the equal protection clause of the Fourteenth Amendment. The district court granted the prison officials qualified immunity, and the court of appeals affirmed. The court of appeals had reviewed the racial discrimination issue using the deferential standard of *Turner v. Safley*, 482 U.S. 78 (1987), and ruled that there was a "'common sense connection' between the policy and prison violence."

In *Johnson v. California*, 543 U.S. 499 (2005), the Supreme Court applied its earlier decision in *Lee v. Washington* to reaffirm that all governmental classifications which use race are viewed with "strict scrutiny." The use of race as a factor in classification presents serious concerns.

> **Racial classifications raise special fears that they are motivated by an invidious purpose. Thus, we have admonished time and again that, "[a]bsent searching judicial inquiry into the justification for such race-based measures, there is simply no way of determining ... what classifications are in fact motivated by illegitimate notions of racial inferiority or simple racial politics."**

Strict scrutiny generally applies to "suspect" classifications (such as race) and requires that the government establish that its classification furthers a *compelling* governmental objective and is narrowly tailored to further that objective. This is a different, and higher, standard than that applied in *Craig v. Boren*, discussed above, which required that gender-based classification serve an *important* governmental objective, and the classification must be substantially related to the achievement of the objective. The least stringent level of review is called a "rational basis" and requires the government demonstrate only that classification bears a rational relationship to a legitimate purpose.

The Court also noted that racial classification has led to stigmatization and increased racial hostility, and that virtually all states and the Federal Bureau of Prisons are able to safely manage prison populations without using racial segregation. The state had argued that the more relaxed standard of review was appropriate because the state's policy was based on its need to maintain the safety and security of prisons, an area in which prison officials are provided significant discretion. In rejecting the use of the *Turner v. Safley* deference standard given to prison administrators, the Court ruled:

> **The right not to be discriminated against based on one's race is not susceptible to the logic of *Turner*. It is not a right that need necessarily be compromised for the sake of proper prison administration. On the contrary, compliance with the Fourteenth Amendment's ban on racial discrimination is not only consistent with proper prison administration, but also bolsters the legitimacy of the entire criminal justice system. Race discrimination is "especially pernicious in the administration of justice." ... Granting the CDC an exemption from the rule that strict scrutiny applies to all racial classifications would undermine our "unceasing efforts to eradicate racial prejudice from our criminal justice system."**

The Court's decision did not prohibit all race-based classifications in a correctional setting, but only directed that race-based classifications further a compelling governmental interest and be narrowly drafted to further that purpose. The case was remanded back to the lower courts to determine, under the strict scrutiny standard, if the state could demonstrate that these conditions were met.

SUMMARY

- The controlling principle for the treatment of female offenders is that there must be parity of treatment for male and female inmates. This means that there must be substantially equivalent facilities and treatment programs for men and women. Because of the difference in numbers and needs, there cannot be total equivalency. Identical treatment is not required for men and women (*Pargo v. Elliott*).

- The equal protection clause requires that any disparity in treatment between male and female inmates must be justified by important government objectives and must be substantially related to advancing those objectives (*Craig v. Boren*).

- Equal protection also serves to protect other classes of inmates from discrimination. When considering programs and services, in order to justify different treatment for racial and ethnic minorities, the elderly and youths, noncitizen inmates, and other groups (persons with disabilities are now covered by their own protective statute, the Americans with Disabilities Act), there must be a substantial government (correctional) reason for the difference. Absent that, corrections officials can expect courts to examine closely, and perhaps reject, any significant difference in treatment.

- The Supreme Court has not yet addressed equal protection rights for inmates, except in the case of racial discrimination, which it has forbidden (*Lee v. Washington*).

- While prison officials may consider race in making classifications, such classifications must further a compelling governmental interest and be narrowly tailored to further that purpose (*Johnson v. California*).

THINKING ABOUT IT

An inmate claims that Virginia prison officials do not allow gay, male inmates (like himself) to double-bunk, that is, to have a cellmate, allegedly because of his sexual preference. The inmate files a complaint, alleging equal protection violations in making cell assignments on account of his sexual preference and his gender, because the same policy does not apply to heterosexual males and homosexual females who are housed at the same facility. Will the inmate prevail? (Note: Virginia denies having such a policy; however, for the purpose of the constitutional analysis, the court took the inmate's allegations as true.) This case is reported as *Veney v. Wyche*, 293 F.3d 726 (4th Cir. 2002).

ENDNOTES

1. West, H. , Sabol, W., and Greeman, S. *Prisoners in 2009*. Appendix Table 7. (Washington, DC: Bureau of Justice Statistics, U.S. Department of Justice. 2010).

2. After remand and on reconsideration in a further appeal, the court of appeals held that the comparison of educational opportunities available to female inmates at the Nebraska Center for Women with educational opportunities for male inmates at the state penitentiary was not sufficient to prove violation of Title IX. Further, the court, in *Klinger v. Department of Corrections*, 107 F.3d 609 (8th Cir. 1997), held that the inmates failed to establish that they were denied meaningful access to the courts, based on their failure to show actual injury or prejudice as a result of their denial of access to a law library or legal assistance.

3. West, H. *Prison Inmates at Midyear 2009—Statistical Tables*. Table 20. (Washington, DC: Bureau of Justice Statistics, U.S. Department of Justice. 2010).

4. United States Sentencing Commission. *Overview of Federal Criminal Cases Fiscal Year 2009*. Page 2. December 2010. Available from http://www.ussc.gov/Research/Research_Publications/2010/20101230_FY09_Overview_Federal_Criminal_Cases.pdf. Accessed June 16, 2011.

14 Eighth Amendment: The Death Penalty and Other Sentencing Issues

The basic concept underlying the Eighth Amendment is nothing less than the dignity of man. While the State has the power to punish, the Amendment stands to assure that this power be exercised within the limits of civilized standards.

U.S. Supreme Court, *Trop v. Dulles*

Chapter Outline

- Sentencing
- Death Penalty Sentences
- Death Row Conditions
- Legal Challenges to the Method of Execution
- Cruel and Unusual Punishment in Noncapital Sentencing Cases

▨ Sentencing

The whole of the Eighth Amendment reads as follows:

> **Excessive bail shall not be required, nor excessive fines imposed, nor cruel and unusual punishments inflicted.**

All of these components of the Eighth Amendment refer to criminal processes and sanctions. The first two clauses do not concern us too much, in a study of corrections, because the excessive bail clause deals primarily with the pretrial release of arrestees, and the excessive fines clause deals with a particular type of criminal sentencing (imposing fines).

If we realign the wording of the amendment, the language that is of direct and frequent importance to corrections is, "cruel and unusual punishments shall not be inflicted." The Supreme Court has used the **cruel and unusual punishment** clause to weigh sentencing. That is one of the main uses of the clause. Criminal sentences have been challenged as being too harsh and, thus, in violation of the Constitution. In *Trop v. Dulles*, 356 U.S. 86 (1958), the Court found that the sanction of loss of nationality following conviction by military court martial of desertion during wartime was too severe and, therefore, was cruel and unusual punishment. Perhaps more important, the *Trop* case gave us some of the standards for judging what "cruel and unusual" means. The Court said that the Eighth Amendment is tied to a concern for "the dignity of man."

The Amendment must draw its meaning from the evolving standards of decency that mark the progress of a maturing society.

This is a frequently quoted phrase, used to help in interpreting the amendment's language. But does it really help? Where does a court find the currently evolved "standards of decency"? The statement clearly says that "cruel and unusual punishment" is an evolving standard. In some way, a court must "test the waters" of our society and decide whether certain punishment exceeds the current "standards of decency." This invites courts to use some subjective evaluation to determine the "evolving standards," does it not? Is there any place where we can find an objective assessment of what those words mean? But then again, is not *cruel and unusual* a term that is itself inherently subjective?

Another sentencing case that gives us some guidelines about what *cruel and unusual* means is *Weems v. United States*, 217 U.S. 349 (1909). There, the sentence given was 12 to 20 years at hard labor, with ankle and wrist chains to be worn during the entire service of sentence and perpetual loss of civil rights. The crime for which that sentence was imposed was being an accessory to falsification of a government document. The Supreme Court overturned the sentence as being too harsh. Again, more important than the specific holding regarding that particular "excessive" sentence is the language the Supreme Court used to analyze when punishment is cruel and unusual. The Court noted that a punishment is cruel and unusual if (1) it is greatly disproportionate to the offense for which it has been imposed or (2) it goes far beyond what is necessary to achieve a sentencing aim, even if that aim is justified. The second guideline may be taken to say that a punishment is cruel and unusual if it is unnecessarily severe for whatever sentencing purpose a court is using.

Over 50 years after *Trop* and 100 years after *Weems*, the Supreme Court continues to look at the issues of "evolving standards of decency" and "proportionality" in regard to punishments. In *Atkins v. Virginia*, 536 U.S. 304 (2002), the Court said:

A claim that punishment is excessive [and therefore disproportionate to the offense] is judged not by the standards that prevailed in 1685 when Lord Jeffreys presided over the "Bloody Assizes" or when the Bill of Rights was adopted, but rather by those that currently prevail.

Our independent evaluation of the issue reveals no reason to disagree with the judgment of "the legislatures that have recently addressed the matter" and concluded that death is not a suitable punishment for a mentally retarded criminal. We are not persuaded that the execution of mentally retarded criminals will measurably advance the deterrent or the retributive purpose of the death penalty. Construing and applying the Eighth Amendment in the light of our "evolving standards of decency," we therefore conclude that such punishment is excessive.

We will review *Atkins* in greater detail in the next section on death penalty sentences.

■ Death Penalty Sentences

The constitutionality of the death penalty has been analyzed under the cruel and unusual pro-scription of the Eighth Amendment. This analysis has been overlaid with concerns under the due process clause. Starting with *Furman v. Georgia*, 408 U.S. 238 (1972), the Supreme Court examined closely the use of the death penalty itself, and it considered in what circumstances or with what procedural protections it *could* be used. In earlier days, the Court had assumed that the death penalty was a permissible sanction. Cases only looked at whether the particular means of executing the defendant was cruel and unusual or constitutional. For example, in *Wilkerson v. Utah*, 99 U.S. 130 (1878), the Supreme Court upheld the constitutionality of execution by firing squad against an Eighth Amendment challenge.[1]

In the *Furman* case, the Supreme Court called a halt to the prior (some would say wide-spread, although a number of states had already repealed capital punishment) use of the death penalty. The Court found that it was imposed, like other sentences, at the complete discretion of the judge or jury, and it held that this practice was a violation of the Eighth Amendment. The practice led to such arbitrary and varied results that the Court found "no meaningful basis for distinguishing the few cases in which it is imposed from the many cases in which it is not."

The states (at least those that wanted to use the death penalty) scrambled to find procedures that would satisfy the Supreme Court's concerns. These procedures were found in *Gregg v. Georgia*, 428 U.S. 153 (1976), where the Court again looked at the constitutionality of the death penalty.

> **It is apparent from the text of the Constitution itself that the existence of capital punishment was accepted by the Framers. At the time the Eighth Amendment was ratified, capital punishment was a common sanction in every State. Indeed, the First Congress of the United States enacted legislation providing death as the penalty for specified crimes.... The Fifth Amendment, adopted at the same time as the Eighth, contemplated the continued existence of the capital sanction by imposing certain limits on the prosecution of capital cases: "No person shall be held to answer for a capital, or otherwise infamous crime, unless on a pre-sentment or indictment of a Grand Jury... nor shall any person be subject for the same offense to be twice put in jeopardy of life or limb... nor be deprived of life, liberty, or property, without due process of law..."**

> **And the Fourteenth Amendment, adopted over three-quarters of a century later, similarly contemplates the existence of the capital sanction in providing that no State shall deprive any person of "life, liberty, or property" without due process of law.**

As mentioned, in *Gregg*, a formula for sentencing that would meet Eighth (and Fourteenth) Amendment standards was found. (The Court noted that, after the *Furman* ruling, 35 states and the federal government had enacted new statutes for death penalty sentencing.) Under the Georgia scheme, at least one aggravating factor had to be found by the jury to exist beyond a reasonable doubt before a death sentence could be imposed. This was intended to meet the Supreme Court's concern in *Furman* that death sentences were imposed in an arbitrary or capri-cious manner. Besides the minimum of one aggravating factor, the jury in death penalty cases could consider other relevant aggravating and mitigating factors. Also, Georgia provided that there would be an automatic appeal of all death sentences to the Georgia Supreme Court. Besides reviewing all the procedural proprieties for such cases, the state supreme court was charged with comparing the death sentence with those sentences imposed on all similarly situated defendants in the state. These procedures satisfied the U.S. Supreme Court.

> **No longer can a jury wantonly and freakishly impose the death sentence; it is always circumscribed by the legislative guidelines....[T]he statutory system under which Gregg was sentenced to death does not violate the Constitution.**

In the course of its opinion, the Supreme Court also looked at the history of the Eighth Amendment and reviewed those standards that reflect "standards of decency" and make punishments constitutionally acceptable. At its simplest, the "cruel and unusual punishment" clause means that punishments must not be excessive, but what does *excessive* mean?

> **First, the punishment must not involve the unnecessary and wanton infliction of pain. Second, the punishment must not be grossly out of proportion to the severity of the crime.**

Is the death penalty, in all cases, excessive and, therefore, cruel and unusual? Two justices gave their opinions that it is. They would vote to ban all capital punishment as cruel and unusual. But the majority of the Supreme Court held that it is not an unconstitutional punishment per se.

> **[T]he decision that capital punishment may be the appropriate sanction in extreme cases is an expression of the community's belief that certain crimes are themselves so grievous an affront to humanity that the only adequate response may be the penalty of death....[In this case,] we are concerned...only with the imposition of capital punishment for the crime of murder, and when a life has been taken deliberately by the offender, we cannot say that the punishment is invariably disproportionate to the crime. It is an extreme sanction, suitable to the most extreme of crimes. We hold that the death penalty is not a form of punishment that may never be imposed.**

This is a somewhat indirect (and possibly wavering) statement by the Supreme Court, in which it found that the death penalty is not per se unconstitutional.

Along with and following *Gregg,* numerous other death penalty sentencing formulas have been reviewed in the Supreme Court. Most have been approved. The Supreme Court in *Maynard v. Cartwright*, 486 U.S. 356 (1988), however, rejected a death penalty imposed in a case in which Oklahoma required the jury to find an aggravating circumstance to support a death sentence. One egregious circumstance, which the Oklahoma law specified could be used to support a death sentence, was that a murder was "especially heinous, atrocious, or cruel." The Supreme Court said that language was too vague and could result in arbitrary results; a person might believe, for example, that "every unjustified, intentional taking of human life is 'especially heinous.'"

The standards that Georgia adopted, which the Court approved in *Gregg,* need not always be strictly followed as the only permissible sentencing scheme. The Georgia sentencing scheme is not the only scheme that will produce a constitutional result. This is shown, for example, in *Pulley v. Harris*, 465 U.S. 37 (1984). In this case, the Court upheld the California sentencing scheme, which did not include a review of the death penalty in comparison to other similar cases in the state, even though Georgia required such a review by its supreme court on mandatory appeal, as approved by the U.S. Supreme Court in *Gregg*. (In other words, the Supreme Court ruled that the comparative proportionality review of sentences, as Georgia had established, is not required in every state's review of death sentences.) What is required is a system of procedural checks and precautions that prevents arbitrariness, according to the Court in *Pulley*.

Is it permissible to have a death penalty system that mandates the death penalty for all offenses of a certain kind? Does this avoid arbitrariness? North Carolina passed a law that mandated the death sentence for all convictions of first-degree murder. In *Woodson v. North Carolina*, 428 U.S. 280 (1976), the Supreme Court rejected that statute as unconstitutional. Besides the two justices who would find all death sentences unconstitutional, three other justices voted against this statute on the grounds that it did not meet "civilized standards" and that it was contrary to "contemporary values," being "unduly harsh and unworkably rigid." The Court was also concerned that this mandatory kind of sentencing eliminated consideration of the individual defendant, which the Court stated was an important (and apparently necessary) sentencing requirement, at least for death penalty cases. The North Carolina scheme (and others that tried to cure *Furman* problems with mandatory sentencing) was rejected.

A sentencing statute in Nevada, which mandated the death penalty in all cases of murder by an inmate who was serving a life sentence without parole, was also rejected in *Sumner v. Shuman*, 483 U.S. 66 (1987). But in *Blystone v. Pennsylvania*, 494 U.S. 299 (1990), the Supreme Court upheld a death penalty statute that required the jury to impose the death sentence in a murder case if the jury found that aggravating circumstances outweighed any mitigating circumstances. The Pennsylvania death penalty statute required a jury to impose a death sentence when at least one aggravating circumstance and no mitigating circumstances were found. Blystone's death sentence was upheld.

In *Kansas v. Marsh*, 548 U.S. 163 (2006), the Supreme Court held that a state statute which required a jury to impose a death sentence when it found an equal number of aggravating and mitigating circumstances was constitutional. The Court ruled that the state did not create an unconstitutional presumption in favor of the death penalty. In explaining the differences between state statutes and what the Constitution requires in this regard, the Court noted that a state capital sentencing system is constitutional when it (1) "rationally narrows the class of death-eligible defendants" and (2) "permits a jury to consider any mitigating evidence relevant to its sentencing determination."

The Court has clearly indicated that its concern for individualizing the sentence requires the jury to consider mitigating circumstances in all death penalty cases. This is supported in *Hitchcock v. Dugger*, 481 U.S. 393 (1987); *Eddings v. Oklahoma*, 455 U.S. 104 (1982); and *Lockett v. Ohio*, 438 U.S 586 (1978). From *Eddings*, we have the guidance that what the Court is looking for is a death penalty system that is "at once consistent and principled but also humane and sensible to the uniqueness of the individual." The Court in *Eddings* applied the following rule from its earlier decision in *Lockett*:

[W]e conclude that the Eighth and Fourteenth Amendments require that the sentencer ... not be precluded from considering, as a mitigating factor, any aspect of a defendant's character or record and any of the circumstances of the offense that the defendant proffers as a basis for a sentence less than death.

In *Coker v. Georgia*, 433 U.S. 584 (1977), the Supreme Court held that the death penalty for the crime of rape of an adult woman is unconstitutional on the ground that it is disproportionate to the offense. In *Kennedy v. Louisiana*, 554 U.S. 407 (2008), the Supreme Court ruled that imposition of the death penalty for the rape of a child under 12 was disproportionate to the offense and violated the Eighth Amendment. When death did not occur or was not intended, the Court said its determination of the constitutionality of the death penalty has been guided by "objective indicia of society's standards, as expressed in legislative enactments and state practice with respect to executions."

After reviewing the authorities informed by contemporary norms, including the history of the death penalty for this and other non-homicide crimes, current state statutes and new enactments, and the number of executions since 1964 [none for child rape], we conclude there is a national consensus against capital punishment for the crime of child rape.

While noting both the devastating impact of rape on its victims and the general public abhorrence of the crime of rape of a child, the Court ruled:

Consistent with evolving standards of decency and the teachings of our precedents we conclude that, in determining whether the death penalty is excessive, there is a distinction between intentional first-degree murder on the one hand and nonhomicide crimes against individual persons, even including child rape, on the other. The latter crimes may be devastating in their harm, as here, but "in terms of moral depravity and of the injury to the person and to the public," ... they cannot be compared to murder in their "severity and irrevocability."

However, the death sentence is not reserved solely for the offense of committing murder. In *Tison v. Arizona*, 481 U.S. 137 (1987), for example, the Court ruled that it was not cruel and unusual to impose the death penalty on a defendant who did not commit the murder himself, but who was a significant accomplice. In that case, the defendant, Tison, by assisting his father and another inmate to escape from prison and then to commandeer a car in which all four passengers were killed, showed "reckless indifference to human life." The Court further noted that Tison "knowingly engaged in activities known to carry a grave risk of death."

In *Thompson v. Oklahoma*, 487 U.S. 815 (1988), a statute that allowed the death penalty for persons aged 15 or younger was held to be unconstitutional. But the Court held, in *Stanford v. Kentucky*, 492 U.S. 361 (1989), that death sentences imposed on persons aged 16 and 17 were constitutional. In 2005, the Supreme Court in *Roper v. Simmons*, 543 U.S. 551 (2005), declared that the execution of a person for a crime committed as a juvenile violates the Eighth and Fourteenth Amendments.

All states forbid the execution of persons who are (or have become) insane. The Supreme Court approved, in *Ford v. Wainwright*, 477 U.S. 399 (1986), the rule that the Eighth Amendment prohibits the execution of a person who is presently insane.

The Court, in *Penry v. Lynaugh*, 492 U.S. 302 (1989), upheld the death penalty of a person who was, as described by the court, "mentally retarded." *Penry* was abrogated by the Court's decision in *Atkins v. Virginia*, 536 U.S. 304 (2002). Atkins was convicted of abduction, armed robbery, and capital murder. In assessing punishment, a forensic psychologist testified that Atkins was "mildly mentally retarded." The U.S. Supreme Court reviewed the death sentence, saying it was doing so, in part, "in light of the dramatic shift in the state legislative landscape that has occurred in the past 13 years." Holding the executions of mentally retarded criminals as cruel and unusual punishment in violation of the Eighth Amendment, the Court said in 1986:

> [T]he public reaction to the execution of a mentally retarded murderer in Georgia apparently led to the enactment of the first state statute prohibiting such executions. In 1988, when Congress enacted legislation reinstating the federal death penalty, it expressly provided that a "sentence of death shall not be carried out upon a person who is mentally retarded." In 1989, Maryland enacted a similar prohibition. It was in that year that we decided Penry, and concluded that those two state enactments, "even when added to the 14 States that have rejected capital punishment completely, do not provide sufficient evidence at present of a national consensus."

The Court noted that much had changed over the intervening years. State legislatures, responding to the national attention received by the Bowden[2] execution and the *Penry* decision, began to address the issue. The Court identified 16 additional states since 1990 that prohibited the execution of the mentally retarded.

> It is not so much the number of these States that is significant, but the consistency of the direction of change. Given the well-known fact that anticrime legislation is far more popular than legislation providing protections for persons guilty of violent crime, the large number of States prohibiting the execution of mentally retarded persons (and the complete absence of States passing legislation reinstating the power to conduct such executions) provides powerful evidence that today our society views mentally retarded offenders as categorically less culpable than the average criminal....And it appears that even among those States that regularly execute offenders and that have no prohibition with regard to the mentally retarded, only five have executed offenders possessing a known IQ less than 70 since we decided *Penry*. The practice, therefore, has become truly unusual, and it is fair to say that a national consensus has developed against it.

What is the current status of the death penalty in the United States? At yearend 2009, 36 states and the federal government had statutes authorizing the death penalty. There were 3,173 persons confined by these jurisdictions under a sentence of death. In 2010, there were 46 executions in the United States. Forty-four were carried out by lethal injection, one by electrocution, and one by firing squad. One of the persons executed in 2010 was female.[3]

Death Row Conditions

Another aspect of the death penalty is a consideration of the conditions under which persons who have been sentenced to that penalty are held. In those states (and the federal government) where the death penalty is authorized, it has long been the practice to have a separate prison area called "death row." All those with a death sentence are assigned to it (there are separate facilities for women who may receive a death sentence), and they are held there, in a segregated unit from other inmates, for as long as they are in custody with the death penalty in place. Security conditions are high, and program opportunities are few, though there are often recreation facilities inside the unit or attached to it. Prisoners are allowed out of their cells to shower and to receive visitors. Food is brought to the unit to be eaten there, and medical staff visit the unit to check on medical complaints and to take care of as many problems as possible inside the unit. If the inmate is taken out of the unit, for example to a community medical facility, a court, or even a clinic or visiting area inside the prison, he is usually handcuffed and shackled. These conditions, of course, typically go on for many years. (In 2009, the average elapsed time from sentence to the date of execution was 169 months,[4] because there are lengthy appeals and other legal proceedings in connection with the death sentence.) This separate, often harsh confinement, like so many other aspects of corrections, can be traced historically to English law, which required solitary confinement as "a further terror and peculiar mark of infamy" attached to the death penalty. This language is quoted in *In re Medley*, 134 U.S. 160 (1890).

The *Medley* case was the first taken to the Supreme Court to complain of death row conditions. Medley, under death sentence in Colorado for killing his wife, challenged his solitary confinement conditions while awaiting execution. He brought a habeas corpus action directly into the Supreme Court, which held that Medley's solitary confinement was "additional punishment" and, in the circumstances of his case, was unconstitutional. (This was because Colorado's law that required the solitary confinement was enacted after the offense and was therefore an ex post facto law—increasing the penalty for the offense after the offense had been committed. There was not a ruling that the conditions were themselves unconstitutional.)

The Supreme Court has not subsequently set any constitutional requirements for death row conditions of confinement. It has given some indication that the question of whether many years spent on death row, in and of themselves, raises a question of cruel and unusual punishment. On March 27, 1995, the Supreme Court denied certiorari in the case of *Lackey v. Texas*, 514 U.S. 1045 (1995). Lackey sought review of the question of whether the 17 years he had spent on death row violated the Eighth Amendment. Although the Court refused to issue a ruling on that question, Justice Stevens noted that it was, for several reasons, a significant question, which would have to be addressed eventually. He suggested that the issue would best be considered in the Supreme Court after it had been addressed by some additional lower courts.[5]

As we observed in the preceding section, the Supreme Court has given much attention and many opinions in the last 25 years on constitutional requirements for imposing the death penalty. Conditions on death row have been challenged in lower courts, and we have some guidance from those courts. In short, they show us that death row inmates cannot be held in "barbarous and torturous" conditions. But they can be held in segregated confinement—that is, in units segregated from inmates serving regular terms of imprisonment—for the many years which death sentence appeals take.

Inmate Sinclair complained of many conditions on Louisiana's death row in *Sinclair v. Henderson*, 331 F.Supp. 1123 (E.D. LA 1971). Among other conditions, Sinclair complained of unsanitary food; inadequate plumbing, ventilation, bedding, and medical attention; the use of inmate guards; and a lack of physical exercise. All of the complaints were rejected, except the last one. The court supported the need for regular exercise:

Confinement for long periods of time without the opportunity for regular outdoor exercise does, as a matter of law, constitute cruel and unusual punishment....[I]t is feasible both economically and from a security standpoint for the defendant to make arrangements for all prisoners on Death Row to have regular outdoor exercise opportunity.

Although confinement without exercise for short periods might be tolerable (for Eighth Amendment assessment), because of the long periods of time that death row inmates are held, regular out-of-cell exercise is viewed as a necessity. This is true of other conditions on death row as well. What might be constitutionally permissible over a short time may become unconstitutional when it continues over a long period of time.

In *Gates v. Cook*, 376 F.3d 323 (5th Cir. 2004), Mississippi death row inmates complained about their conditions of confinement. The court of appeals affirmed the district court's order directing the Department of Corrections to ensure death row cells were adequately cleaned before assigning an inmate to that cell; provide adequate cleaning materials; develop a plan to control insects, including use of screens; improve plumbing, lighting and ventilation on the death row unit; and improve the process for dealing with mental health issues.[6]

A prison policy in Oklahoma that prohibited contact visits by death row inmates (or other "high-maximum" security inmates) with their attorneys was struck down by a federal appeals court in *Mann v. Reynolds*, 46 F.3d 1055 (10th Cir. 1995). The principal problem for the state was that prison officials allowed these same inmates to have contact during visiting with other persons, but they singled out attorneys for the special ban. The state did not provide "an explanation why they have singled out attorneys for the restricted contact." Apparently, there had not been any particular problems with attorney visits, except for "isolated occasions when cigarettes, chewing gum, pens, and paper clips have been unwittingly passed by uninitiated lawyers to inmates." Absent such a showing that the ban on contact visiting with attorneys was necessitated by prison security concerns, the court said it was not rational to enforce such a ban.

We saw in the case of *Smith v. Coughlin*, 748 F.2d 783 (1984), that the Second Circuit Court of Appeals ruled that it was permissible for prison authorities in New York to restrict the visits made to death row inmates. There, visits were limited to members of the inmate's immediate family, and the court said that policy, based on security and administrative concerns, was justified and not unconstitutional.

▨ Legal Challenges to the Method of Execution

In *Wilkerson v. Utah*, mentioned earlier in this chapter, the Court ruled that the method of carrying out the sentence of death by firing squad was governed by the Constitution and could not be cruel or unusual. Twelve years later in *In re Kemmler*, 136 U.S. 436 (1890), the Court ruled that execution by the newly developed electric chair did not violate the Constitution, since the method was enacted by the state legislature and designed to reduce the suffering which might occur when a death penalty is carried out.[7]

By the 1980s, most states that authorized the use of capital punishment had adopted lethal injection as the method of execution. Lethal injection uses one or more commonly available drugs to cause death. In the last several years, the Supreme Court decided several cases related to both procedural and substantive aspects of carrying out capital punishment. The distinction between prisoner litigation as habeas corpus or Section 1983 is not always clear. In *Nelson v. Campbell*, 541 U.S. 637 (2004), without deciding the difficult legal question of what the appropriate legal procedure is—habeas or Section 1983—for challenging a method of execution, the Court ruled that because the prisoner was claiming that a procedure in the execution process to be used by prison officials would cause unnecessary pain and suffering, the prisoner could use Section 1983 to obtain injunctive relief. Two years later, in *Hill v. McDonough*, 547 U.S. 573 (2006), the Court did rule that a prisoner under sentence of death may use Section 1983 to challenge particular execution procedures.

In *Baze v. Rees,* 553 U.S. 35 (2008), death-sentenced inmates in Kentucky claimed the state's protocol (procedure) for carrying out executions by lethal injection violated the Eighth Amendment ban against cruel and unusual punishment. The Supreme Court affirmed the state supreme court's ruling that the procedures used by Kentucky, including its use of a three chemical combination to cause death, did not violate the Constitution.[8]

The federal Constitution is not the only resource to challenge methods of execution. In 2008, the Nebraska Supreme Court ruled that the state statute authorizing execution by electrocution violated the state constitution's ban against cruel and unusual punishment. *State v. Mata*, 745 N.W. 229 (Nebraska 2008). The court said its holding that a method of execution (electrocution) was cruel and usual punishment was not directed to the validity of the sentence, but only to the legality of the execution of the sentence.

State law also may require that execution procedures be promulgated using the state's administrative procedure act, which may require public notice, comment, and even public hearings before adopting the procedures to be used in executions.[9]

■ Cruel and Unusual Punishment in Noncapital Sentencing Cases

The Supreme Court also has considered the cruel and unusual punishment clause in cases in which the sentence was less than the death penalty. (We noted early in this chapter the historic cases of *Weems v. United States* (1909) and *Trop v. Dulles* (1958), in which the Supreme Court found the sentences (having to wear ankle and wrist chains throughout the service of a 20-year sentence in *Weems* and the loss of nationality for military desertion in *Trop*) unconstitutional, because they were too severe.)

In sentencing cases since *Weems* and *Trop*, the Supreme Court considered the heavy sanctions imposed for repeat offenders. (No, the recent "three-strikes-and-you're-out" laws are not new legislative ideas!) In *Rummel v. Estelle*, 445 U.S. 263 (1980), Texas had enacted a law that required life imprisonment for a person who was convicted the third time for a felony. Rummel was charged with felony theft for obtaining $120.75 by false pretenses. The jury convicted him of that offense and also found that he had two prior felonies (fraudulent use of a credit card, by which he obtained $80 in goods and passing a forged check, which was $28.68 in value). A life sentence was imposed, as required by the state statute. (The Supreme Court noted that, at that time, Washington and West Virginia also had mandatory life sentences for the commission of a third felony. Several other states had mandatory life sentences upon conviction of a fourth felony.

Others required at least one of the felonies to be of a violent nature to support a life sentence.) The Court observed that the purpose of the recidivist statute was to deter repeat offenders and to segregate the recidivist from society for a lengthy period of time. The mandatory life sentence was upheld, and it was not found to be cruel and unusual or unconstitutional.

Three years later, in *Solem v. Helm*, 463 U.S. 277 (1983), the Supreme Court found a South Dakota recidivist sentence to be unconstitutional. The sentencing statute required that a person convicted of a felony who had at least three prior felony convictions was to be sentenced as a Class 1 felon, which meant life imprisonment without parole. Helm had been convicted of six prior nonviolent felonies. He then was convicted of writing a "no account" check for $100. The ordinary penalty for that offense alone would have been a maximum of five years imprisonment. Noting that the Eighth Amendment cases had established that a sentence must be proportionate to the crime the defendant has committed, the Court examined the gravity of Helm's current offense and the harshness of his sentence and held that his sentence was "significantly disproportionate to his crime" and therefore was in violation of the Eighth Amendment.

The *Solem* decision is very hard to reconcile with the Court's ruling in *Rummel*. But the Court specifically did not overrule the *Rummel* decision. It said that the South Dakota (*Solem*) sentence was "far more severe" than the life sentence in *Rummel*. Why? Apparently, the key factor for the Court was that Rummel was eligible, under Texas law, for parole on his sentence, whereas Helm was not eligible for parole. The only way for Helm to be released was by commutation of his sentence by the Governor; that relief had been granted very rarely on life sentences. Also, the Court noted that only one other state had such a severe recidivist statute with a nonparolable life sentence as punishment.

In *Ewing v. California*, 538 U.S. 11 (2003), the Supreme Court examined the constitutionality of California's three-strikes law. Under the law, a defendant who is convicted of a felony and has previously been convicted of at least two serious or violent felonies must receive an indeterminate life-imprisonment term. Ewing, on parole from a nine-year term for first-degree robbery and residential burglary, tried to walk out of a golf club's pro shop with three golf clubs, valued at $399 each, concealed in his pants leg. He was convicted of felony grand theft. Ewing was sentenced under the three-strikes law to a term of 25 years to life. The Supreme Court affirmed the California sentence, with four justices dissenting. The Court's opinion held that the punishment was not grossly disproportionate to the severity of the crimes committed and did not violate the Eighth Amendment ban on cruel and unusual punishment.[10]

Throughout the States, legislatures enacting three strikes laws made a deliberate policy choice that individuals who have repeatedly engaged in serious or violent criminal behavior, and whose conduct has not been deterred by more conventional approaches to punishment, must be isolated from society in order to protect the public safety....Our traditional deference to legislative policy choices finds a corollary in the principle that the Constitution "does not mandate adoption of any one penological theory."...A sentence can have a variety of justifications, such as incapacitation, deterrence, retribution, or rehabilitation....Some or all of these justifications may play a role in a State's sentencing scheme. Selecting the sentencing rationales is generally a policy choice to be made by state legislatures, not federal courts.[11]

> **Ewing's sentence is justified by the State's public-safety interest in incapacitating and deter-
> ring recidivist felons, and amply supported by his own long, serious criminal record .... To
> be sure, Ewing's sentence is a long one. But it reflects a rational legislative judgment,
> entitled to deference, that offenders who have committed serious or violent felonies and
> who continue to commit felonies must be incapacitated.**

The dissenting justices concluded that Ewing's sentence was grossly disproportionate to the "triggering offense conduct"—stealing three golf clubs—that led to the sentence.

In *Lockyer v. Andrade*, 538 U.S. 63 (2003), a companion case (also from California) to *Ewing*, the Court declined to accept the argument that two consecutive terms of 25 years to life for stealing about $150 in video tapes were grossly disproportionate to the offense committed and in violation of the Eighth Amendment. Andrade, like Ewing, had a long criminal history and was therefore subject to the three-strikes penalty. The Supreme Court again held that the three-strikes sentences were not grossly disproportionate and not a violation of the Eighth Amendment.

The Supreme Court, in *United States v. DiFrancesco*, 449 U.S. 117 (1980), upheld an imposition of a greater sentence by an appellate court (as that court was authorized by statute to do). Such an increase was not considered unconstitutional, but rather a variety of a "two-stage" sentencing procedure.

What of the sentencing that requires a convicted sex offender to be castrated or allows the defendant to choose castration to avoid many years of imprisonment? The Supreme Court has not ruled on the constitutionality of such statutes, and the lower court opinions have split. For cases that seem to go in both directions, see *State v. Brown*, 326 S.E.2d 410 (SC 1985) (holding that castration, a form of mutilation, violates the South Carolina state Constitution, which prohibits cruel and unusual punishment; thus, castration as a condition to suspension of sentence and placement on probation was void); and *People v. Foster*, 124 Cal.Rptr.2d 22 (CA App. 4 Dist. 2002) (upholding a plea agreement where Foster, "having bargained for a 30-year sentence that included the possible imposition of hormone suppression treatment in exchange for the dismissal of myriad serious felony charges ... cannot then maintain on appeal that such treatment cannot be imposed because it would violate prohibitions against cruel and unusual punishment. To do so would be to have his cake and eat it too.")

What can be seen in these cases, and in those involving conditions of confinement, is that the Supreme Court and the lower courts, in dealing with the Eighth Amendment, come up with paraphrases, or interpretive yardsticks, to define what "cruel and unusual" means. How easy it would be to say that "this sentence" or "this condition in prison" is cruel and unusual and is therefore unconstitutional. That would entail an entire decision of only one or two paragraphs, of no more than 10 sentences. But there is no such simple court opinion. Is *cruel and unusual* too difficult a phrase to understand? The Court has never said so. It has never ducked away from giving us an interpretation of what the phrase means in a sentencing or prison situation merely because the concept of *cruel and unusual* is too complex to understand. The words are not uncommon, and they are certainly not legalistic, but they apparently require some degree of judicial translation to turn them into an understandable concept. At least the courts seem to believe that we readers of the opinions need such help in understanding and applying what *cruel and unusual* means as a constitutional concept.

SUMMARY

- The Eighth Amendment's proscription of cruel and unusual punishments has been interpreted and applied by using many other phrases and definitions, supposedly to make it easier to understand what "cruel and unusual punishments" means.

- In sentencing, a sanction is cruel and unusual if it is disproportionate to the offense for which it is imposed or if it goes far beyond what is necessary to achieve a justified sentencing goal (*Weems v. United States*). The Supreme Court has recognized that "cruel and unusual" is an evolving standard, tied to "the progress of a maturing society" (*Trop v. Dulles*).

- With respect to the death penalty, the Supreme Court, in 1972 (*Furman v. Georgia*), struck down sentencing that was "arbitrary" and "unprincipled."

- The death penalty, the Supreme Court has ruled, is not per se cruel and unusual punishment (*Gregg v. Georgia*). The Court has reviewed cases from many states and has approved death sentences when there are procedural protections that ensure consideration of the individual's background and situation and when there are adequate review procedures. The death penalty was disapproved in cases in which the result was "unduly harsh and rigid," such as requiring the death penalty in all cases of murder and in cases in which the penalty was found to be disproportionate or excessive. The death penalty was also disapproved when used for the crime of rape of an adult woman (*Coker v. Georgia*), the rape of a child under age 12 (*Kennedy v. Louisiana*), and when imposed on persons who were not yet 18 when they committed their capital offense (*Roper v. Simmons*). The Supreme Court has also ruled that executing a person who is currently insane (*Ford v. Wainwright*), or who is mentally retarded (*Atkins v. Virginia*), violates the Eighth Amendment.

- The conditions of confinement on death row have not been considered by the Supreme Court regarding the constitutional standards that apply there. Lower courts have acknowledged that death row inmates may need to be confined in housing that is segregated from other prisoners. Confining inmates for long periods of time without the opportunity to have outdoor exercise was held to be cruel and unusual by one court. One court has required that death row conditions not violate the Eighth Amendment in such areas as the ventilation that is provided, pest control, and adequate plumbing and lighting. Visiting for death row inmates may need to be limited, but restrictions must be justified by significant administrative or security considerations.

- The method that is used to carry out an execution is governed by the Constitution and may not be cruel and unusual (*Wilkerson v. Utah*). It is legislatures that provide for the method of execution in each jurisdiction (*In re Kemmler*).

- An inmate who is sentenced to death may use Section 1983 to challenge the specific procedures (claiming they will cause unnecessary pain and suffering) that will be used to carry out the execution (*Nelson v. Campbell* and *Hill v. McDonough*).

- The Supreme Court approved Kentucky's three-drug execution protocol, holding that a method of execution violates the Eighth Amendment only if the method creates an objectively intolerable risk of unnecessary pain and suffering (*Baze v. Rees*).

- The Supreme Court upheld a severe recidivist sentencing statute in one case (*Rummel v. Estelle*), in which a mandatory life sentence was required for a third-time felony conviction. However, it disapproved of a similar law (*Solem v. Helm*), apparently because the life sentence, imposed for a fourth-time felony conviction, did not carry any opportunity for parole release and was, therefore, too harsh and excessive. More recently, the Court upheld California's three-strikes law (*Ewing v. California; Lockyer v. Andrade*), holding that the punishment was not grossly disproportionate to the severity of the crimes committed.

THINKING ABOUT IT

Gregory Thompson was convicted of capital murder in Tennessee and sentenced to death. While in prison he exhibited symptoms of mental illness and was treated with psychotropic medication to reduce the effects of his mental illness. After the state sought to set an execution date, Thompson initiated a suit arguing that under *Ford v. Wainwright* he was presently insane and could not be executed. Thompson's symptoms of mental illness were controlled through medication, and without the medication, he would arguably be incompetent to be executed. Should the state involuntarily medicate Thompson to render him sufficiently sane to be executed, and if so, would the state's action violate his rights under the Eighth Amendment? Compare *Thompson v. Bell*, 580 F.3d 423 (6th Cir. 2009) with *Singleton v. Norris*, 319 F.3d 1018 (8th Cir. 2003).

KEY TERMS

cruel and unusual punishment: Excessive, inhumane penalties or correctional treatment, prohibited by the Eighth Amendment to the U.S. Constitution.

ENDNOTES

1. A federal court in the state of Washington ruled in 1994 that a man on death row (inmate Rupe), who had gained weight while confined to the point that he weighed 410 pounds, could not be executed by hanging because he would risk decapitation. Under state law, inmates could be executed by hanging or by lethal injection. If an inmate failed to choose, which was inmate Rupe's situation, by law, he would be hanged. After hearing expert testimony as to the physical impact of the hanging, the federal judge concluded that hanging Rupe would risk decapitating him. The court ruled that placing Rupe on the gallows would offend "basic human dignity" and "public perceptions of standards of decency." Fowler, R. "Inmate Ruled Too Heavy to be Hanged." Page A3. *Washington Post.* September 21, 1994.
2. Jerome Bowden, a person identified as suffering from mental retardation, was scheduled for execution in Georgia in June 1986. The Georgia Board of Pardons and Paroles granted a stay, following public protests over his execution. A psychologist selected by the state

evaluated Bowden and determined he had an I.Q. of 65, which is consistent with mental retardation. Nevertheless, the board lifted the stay and Bowden was executed the next day. The board concluded that Bowden understood the nature of his crime and his punishment, and, therefore the execution, despite his mental deficiencies, was permissible. See footnote 8 in the opinion in *Atkins v. Virginia*, 536 U.S. 304 (2002).

3. Snell, T. *Capital Punishment, 2009—Statistical Tables.* Page 1 and Table 21. (Washington, DC: Bureau of Justice Statistics, U.S. Department of Justice. 2010).

4. See endnote 3, Table 12.

5. Since *Lackey*, three federal courts of appeal have held that long confinement on death row awaiting execution does not violate the Constitution. *Thompson v. Secretary for the Department of Corrections*, 517 F.3d 1279 (11th Cir. 2008); *Allen v. Ornoski*, 435 F.3d 946 (9th Cir. 2006) cert. denied 546 U.S. 1136 (2006); and *Chambers v. Bowersox*, 157 F.3d 560 (8th Cir. 1998). In *Knight v. Florida* and *Moore v. Nebraska*, 528 U.S. 990 (1999) (two cases considered at the same time), the Supreme Court was asked to consider whether the Eighth Amendment prohibits as "cruel and unusual punishment," the execution of persons who have spent nearly 20 years or more on death row. The Supreme Court declined to review those cases. In a dissenting opinion, Justice Breyer argued for consideration of the Eighth Amendment claim, stating that both of the cases involved "astonishingly long delays flowing in significant part from constitutionally defective death penalty procedures." Justice Breyer also noted, "A growing number of courts outside the United States—*courts that accept or assume the lawfulness of the death penalty*—have held that lengthy delay in administering a *lawful* death penalty renders ultimate execution inhuman, degrading, or unusually cruel." It is anticipated that the Supreme Court, at some point, will review this Eighth Amendment issue in detail. Until then, the Justices of the Supreme Court continue to discuss this issue in concurring or dissenting opinions related to denial of petitions for certiorari. A recent example is *Thompson v. McNeil*, 556 U.S. ___ (2009). In addressing the denial of the petition for writ of certiorari, Justice Stevens noted that "[t]hirty-two years have passed since petitioner was first sentenced to death." Further, he said, "our experience during the past three decades has demonstrated that delays in state-sponsored killings are inescapable and that executing defendants after such delays is unacceptably cruel. This inevitable cruelty, coupled with the diminished justification for carrying out an execution after the lapse of so much time, reinforces my opinion that contemporary decisions to 'retain the death penalty as a part of our law are the product of habit and inattenton rather than an acceptable deliberative process.'"

6. The concerns identified in *Gates* occurred in a death row unit, and this case could easily be considered as a discussion on the conditions of confinement. For example, the trial court in *Gates* found that some cells were "extremely filthy" with crusted fecal matter, urine, dried ejaculate, peeling and chipping paint, and old food particles on the walls. The court of appeals agreed with the trial court that such conditions would present a substantial risk of serious harm to the inmates, and therefore violated the Eighth Amendment. The court also required plumbing problems to be addressed, including fixing a problem resulting in inmates being exposed "to each others' feces for over a decade."

7. In its opinion, the Court noted that Section 505 of New York's Code of Criminal Procedure was amended in 1888 to read as follows: "§ 505. The punishment of death must, in every

case, be inflicted by causing to pass through the body of the convict a current of electricity of sufficient intensity to cause death, and the application of such current must be continued until such convict is dead."

8. The three drugs commonly used by the states are sodium thiopental, which induces unconsciousness; pancuronium bromide, which is a paralytic that causes breathing to cease; and potassium chloride, which interrupts electrical activity of the heart.

9. Compare *Bowling v. Kentucky Department of Corrections*, 301 S.W. 3d 478 (KY 2009) (corrected 2010) and *Morales v. California Department of Corrections and Rehabilitation*, 168 CA App. 4th 729 (2008) (requiring adoption pursuant to state Administrative Procedures Act, APA) with *Porter v. Commonwealth*, 661 SE 2d 415 (VA 2008) (state APA not applicable to state execution procedures) and *Middleton v. Missouri DOC*, 278 S.W. 3d 193 (MO 2009). (Missouri execution protocol is not a rule and is not subject to promulgation under state APA).

10. In reaching its decision, the Supreme Court stated that it was being guided by Justice Kennedy's concurrence in *Harmelin v. Michigan*, 501 U.S. 957 (1991). Harmelin was convicted under Michigan law of having in his possession over 650 grams of cocaine. He received a mandatory life sentence with no possibility of parole. The Supreme Court rejected Harmelin's claim that his sentence was cruel and unusual because it was "significantly disproportionate" to his crime. Justice Kennedy's concurrence identified four considerations of a proportionality review: substantial deference to legislative determinations; the variety of legitimate penological schemes; the nature of our federal system, which recognizes that differing attitudes and perceptions of local conditions could result in different, yet rational conclusions on the length of prison terms; and proportionality guided by objective factors to the fullest extent possible. Justice Kennedy also stated that the Eighth Amendment does not require strict proportionality between crime and sentence, but rather forbids only extreme sentences that are grossly disproportionate to the crime.

11. In an interesting discussion, the Supreme Court commented on three strikes and its relationship to recidivism. Citing a U.S. Department of Justice, Bureau of Justice Statistics study (June 2002) entitled *Recidivism of Prisoners Released in 1994* (prepared by P. Langan and D. Levin), the Court noted that approximately 67% of former inmates released from state prisons had new charges for serious crimes within three years of release; for property offenders like Ewing, the rate was 73%. In contrast, a 1998 California report on its three-strikes law stated that four years after the passage of this law, the recidivism rate of parolees returned to prisons for new offenses dropped by nearly 25%. See *Three Strikes and You're Out"—Its Impact on the California Criminal Justice System After Four Years*. California Department of Justice, Office of the Attorney General. 1998.

15 | Eighth Amendment: Conditions of Confinement— Cruel and Unusual Punishment

No static "test" can exist by which courts determine whether conditions of confinement are cruel and unusual, for the Eighth Amendment must draw its meaning from the evolving standards of decency that mark the progress of a maturing society. But the Constitution does not mandate comfortable prisons.

U.S. Supreme Court, *Rhodes v. Chapman*

Chapter Outline

- Conditions in Prisons
- Opening the Gates
- Crowding in Prisons and Jails
- Effect of the Prison Litigation Reform Act
- *Bell v. Wolfish*
- *Rhodes v. Chapman*
- *Brown v. Plata*
- *Whitley v. Albers*
- *Wilson v. Seiter*
- *Hudson v. McMillian; Wilkins v. Gaddy*
- *Farmer v. Brennan*
- *Helling v. McKinney*
- Qualified Immunity

As a reminder, the Eighth Amendment reads as follows:

Excessive bail shall not be required, nor excessive fines imposed, nor cruel and unusual punishments inflicted.

In this chapter, we continue to examine the phrase "cruel and unusual punishments." It is this language that is used, constitutionally, to weigh the variety of conditions under which prisoners are held. We will review the conditions that have been addressed by the courts, particularly by the Supreme Court, using the Eighth Amendment as the yardstick. At what point do punishments become "cruel and unusual" and, therefore, unconstitutional? How does a correctional worker (or a judge, lawyer, or inmate) tell whether certain actions or conditions amount to cruel and unusual punishment?

◼ Conditions in Prisons

Prior to the 1960s, the courts took a "hands-off" attitude toward prisons and did not give any constitutional guidelines for the management of correctional facilities. This was certainly true, and especially noticeable, with respect to the conditions under which individual prisoners were held. Courts, including the Supreme Court, involved themselves very little, if at all, in looking at the circumstances in which prisoners were held. The prison wall was a barrier behind which the courts were loath to look. To be sure, there were some things going on that deserved scrutiny from the outside, but the courts in those days were saying that the Constitution did not give them the keys to unlock the doors and look into conditions behind the prison and jail walls. From the 1960s to the 1980s, how that did change!

◼ Opening the Gates

One of the cases (and there were many of them) that started the opening of the prison gates for court examination under the Eighth Amendment was *Wright v. McMann*, 387 F.2d 519 (2d Cir. 1967). A prisoner at Clinton State Prison in New York alleged that the conditions under which he was held in the solitary confinement unit of that prison (where he had been placed for violating prison rules) were deplorable. To name just a few of those conditions, the cell was dirty, without means of cleaning it; the toilet and sink were encrusted with slime and human excrement residue; the prisoner was left nude for several days, after which he was given only a pair of underwear to wear; he had no hygiene items—no soap, towel, toilet paper, toothbrush, or comb; he was not permitted to sleep during daytime hours, between 7:30 A.M. and 10:00 P.M.; the windows in his cell were left open, causing exposure to the cold winter air during subfreezing temperatures; the cell had no furniture except the toilet and sink, so he had to sleep on the cold concrete floor without bedding; and his food was served in bowls that were placed on the floor of his cell. Wright claimed he was kept in this cell for 33 days beginning in February 1965 and for another 21 days the following year.

These were the allegations made by Wright without the assistance of any counsel. The district court dismissed the complaint on the grounds that it did not make a showing of a denial of constitutional rights. If Wright did have a remedy, the court said, it was in the New York state courts. On appeal of this kind of dismissal, because there had been no hearing, the appeals court took the inmate's allegations as being the facts of the case.

The case was brought under Section 1983 of the Civil Rights Act. The court of appeals noted that, for many years, federal courts failed to review prisoner complaints about disciplinary proceedings in state prisons. One reason for this had been that the courts thought the Eighth Amendment did not apply to state prisoners. Also, courts were reluctant to interfere in the internal operations of state prisons and preferred to see the state courts look at such complaints. Those views, by the time of the *Wright* case, had been set aside. First, there was no question that the Eighth Amendment applied to the states, which had been demonstrated in *Robinson v. State of California*, 370 U.S. 660 (1962). Further, a state prisoner could bring an action under the Civil Rights Act, as held in *Cooper v. Pate*, 378 U.S. 546 (1964). Also, the Supreme Court made it clear in *Monroe v. Pape*, 365 U.S. 167 (1961), that the Civil Rights Act could be used for relief (in that case, against city police officers) without having to exhaust state remedies first. Finally, noting a number of recent cases (many of them involving Black Muslim claims), this court drew the following conclusion:

> **[W]hile federal courts are sensitive to the problems created by judicial interference in the internal discipline of state prisons, in appropriate cases they will not hesitate to intervene.**

The court of appeals in *Wright* then gave a brief overview of the history of the Eighth Amendment. What was its purpose? The writers of the amendment had in mind the abuses of certain English monarchs, the court said, and primarily intended to prevent "torture and barbarous punishments, such as pillorying, disemboweling, decapitation, and drawing and quartering." By the 1800s, the cruel and unusual punishment clause was thought to be dead, because those historic punishments had disappeared. The Supreme Court, however, revitalized the amendment in *Weems v. United States*, 217 U.S. 349 (1910), saying that a constitutional principle "must be capable of wider application than the mischief which gave it birth." The Court in *Weems* noted that the Constitution:

> **... is not fastened to the obsolete, but may acquire meaning as public opinion becomes enlightened by a humane justice.**

Thus was born the concept that what "cruel and unusual punishment" means is found in an evolving, ever-changing state of public opinion—that is, in the views of American society. In *Wright*, the court of appeals applied these broad standards of justice and decency to arrive at these conclusions:

> **[T]he debasing conditions to which Wright claims to have been subjected would, if established, constitute cruel and unusual punishment in violation of the Eighth Amendment .... We are of the view that civilized standards of humane decency simply do not permit a man for a substantial period of time to be denuded and exposed to the bitter cold of winter in northern New York State and to be deprived of the basic elements of hygiene such as soap and toilet paper .... The Eighth Amendment forbids treatment so foul, so inhuman, and so violative of basic concepts of decency.**

The case was returned to the trial court. That court was required to conduct a hearing on Wright's charges to see if they were true. If they were proved, Wright had been subjected to cruel and unusual punishment and would be entitled to relief under Section 1983. A concurring judge, while agreeing that the case had to be returned for a hearing, warned that there was a flood of complaints waiting to be released by opening the gates with an approval of closer examination by federal judges of Section 1983 complaints. That judge noted that "the great majority of prisoners are prone to make whatever charge they have reason to believe will get them a hearing, with little or no regard for the truth of their allegations." Whether that cynical viewpoint is accurate might be debated; what is clearly accurate is that judge's prediction of letting loose a flood of prisoner petitions and the greatly increased burden that flood would produce in the workload of the federal courts. The number of prisoner petitions filed in federal courts grew from approximately 23,000 in 1980 to a peak of over 68,000 in 1996.[1]

■ Crowding in Prisons and Jails

There have been many things written on the topic of crowding, and it is universally agreed that the prisons and jails in the United States are crowded, in many jurisdictions, beyond their most desirable **capacity**.[2] It is also generally agreed that this crowding leads to other problems in corrections facilities by straining budgets, diluting programs, and creating tensions in everyday living conditions. (Most people refer to this problem as "overcrowding," but the authors find the frequent and loose use of that word objectionable. Use of the term *overcrowded* implies that the level of prison population is bad. Typically, whenever a prison's population exceeds its designed or planned capacity, the prison is said to be overcrowded and carries the judgment with it that it is therefore bad. In fact, prisons and jails can be decently run at something over design or ideal capacity. Adequate funding and staffing, along with many other factors, contribute to a well-run, though crowded, facility. The term *overcrowding* should be reserved for those conditions in which the population has reached a truly risky or unmanageable level. Otherwise, the term *crowding* should be used when a facility's population rises above "normal" or planned levels.)

Crowding in prisons and jails, with its companion problems, has led to huge numbers of lawsuits, most of them under Section 1983, with many of them leading to court orders or consent decrees requiring corrective action.[3] At least 40 states, plus the District of Columbia, Puerto Rico, and the Virgin Islands, have been under such orders or decrees. About 500 jails have been under such orders. In many cases, the corrections administrators entered into the consent decrees (that is, they agreed to the decrees and signed them). **Consent decrees** are agreements by the parties, and approved by the court handling the case, that certain steps will be taken to improve conditions. Historically, they were often entered into, sometimes at the poor advice of attorneys, who were eager to avoid the extensive time and effort that go into such large-scale cases on conditions of confinement. In such cases, attorneys were also often brow-beaten by judges who had their own notions from the outset about what changes were needed and who were also eager to avoid time-consuming trials. With an attorney who seemed glum about the prospects of the case and a judge who was anything but sympathetic in her preliminary views about the case, the government was often willing to settle a case. Later in this chapter, we discuss legislative enactments, such as the Prison Litigation Reform Act (PLRA), which directly impact existing and new consent decrees.

It is an unfortunate fact of life that in many states the administrators of corrections systems (or the sheriffs or superintendents of jails) are political appointees, whose tenures are, on average, painfully short. (As of October 2001, the average tenure of adult correctional agency directors was 3.3 years.[4]) Besides other problems that are created by this too-frequent turnover of top administrators, the presence of a consent decree is an albatross that is passed from one administrator to the next. Many an administrator has come into a new job expecting to be able to manage things with changes or methods of his or her own choosing, only to find that the playing field is already severely restricted by the requirements of a consent decree.

There are myriad other problems created by these court orders or consent decrees in conditions cases. One pervasive problem is that changes usually require outlays of money—in some cases, very large outlays, which a court has no authority to appropriate. The moneys have to come from legislative appropriations. Although some initial funding may be obtained (at the request of and with the support of the current governor, county executive, mayor, or sheriff), the funding ordinarily must be continued over a period of time. Subsequent executives or legislatures may have differing views about appropriating money or using limited resources for prison or jail problems. It makes no difference: the order or decree is still there, hanging over the head of the corrections administrator, who can be found in contempt and be punished for failing to carry out its terms, even though it may be a decree with which he disagrees and that he might never have signed himself. The enactment of the PLRA provides corrections administrators with a means to address these concerns.

Some Section 1983 cases have involved individual inmate–plaintiffs who seek relief in the form of money damages. In addition, you will recall that Section 1983 actions can provide for injunctive relief, and this is sought in many cases. When cases are expanded to be class actions on behalf of all inmates in a particular facility, or even in an entire corrections system, injunctive relief is the principal remedy sought. In many of these cases that govern conditions of prisons or jails, the courts may appoint a master to assist in the administration of the relief that is granted. In the past, these masters, although theoretically limited to be assistants to the judges who appoint them, had in fact been given such wide authority by judges in some cases that they became involved in the day-to-day running of the prisons or were authorized to look over the shoulders of administrators in many different aspects of their jobs.

It should be noted that many defendant–administrators willingly signed consent decrees because they agreed with their provisions and wanted to see the changes made that were demanded by inmates (or by the attorneys for inmates' rights groups). The administrators knew that an agreement for better prisons or jails would result in additional or new facilities, more staff, expanded programs, better health care, and better food service. This leads to a very complex public administration problem: What right does an administrator have to sign an agreement that requires the government of the state (or county or city) to expend large sums of taxpayer money for programs or changes that he decides are desirable? What authority does that administrator have to bind future legislatures or governors to that course of expensive changes? The same questions can be asked of a federal judge for her part in such an agreement. The short and somewhat too-easy answer is that the administrator (or the judge) has no such right or authority, because the power to raise money for the government and to decide where it is spent is first and foremost with the political arm of government, which is directly answerable to the people—namely, the legislature.

■ Effect of the Prison Litigation Reform Act

Although a consent decree is not the same as a court order entered after trial, it is binding and enforceable by the court. Until recently, it could go on indefinitely. However, changes occurred with passage of the Prison Litigation Reform Act (PLRA). The PLRA was enacted by Congress in 1996 in response to concerns over inmate-related litigation. While the PLRA does not change an inmate's substantive rights, it does establish guidelines (such as requiring exhaustion of grievances). It also focuses on the use of consent decrees by federal judges.[5]

The PLRA defines *consent decree* as "any relief entered by the court that is based in whole or in part upon the consent or acquiescence of the parties but does not include private settlements." *Relief* is defined as all relief that may be granted or approved by the court and includes consent decrees. Under the PLRA, the court may not grant or approve prospective relief in any civil action with respect to prison conditions unless it finds the relief is narrowly drawn, extends no further than necessary to correct the violation of a federal right, and is the least intrusive means necessary to correct that violation. The court is also required to give substantial weight to any adverse impact that the proposed relief has on public safety or the operation of a criminal justice system. As noted in the prior section, historically, consent decrees had not met these guidelines. This statute places strong constraints on consent decrees in prisoner suits.

The PLRA also addresses existing consent decrees. It provides for termination of a decree, upon the motion of any party or intervener, no later than two years after the date the court granted or approved the prospective relief; one year after the court has entered an order denying termination of prospective relief; or, for orders issued on or before the date of enactment of the PLRA, two years from the date of the law's enactment. A party can move for immediate termination of the prospective relief if the conditions mandated by the statute are not met. A different section of the PLRA concerns special masters and includes limitations on their powers and duties, including a prohibition against their making findings or communications *ex parte* (on one side only). These provisions reflect Congress's intent to limit judicial management of prisons.

The case of *Miller v. French*, 530 U.S. 327 (2000), dates back to 1975, when inmates at the Pendleton (Indiana) Correctional Facility brought a class action lawsuit under 42 U.S.C. Section 1983. The district court found constitutional violations of the Eighth Amendment, and the appeals court affirmed in part. Injunctive relief was ordered, remaining in effect through the current litigation, with the last modification occurring in 1988. In 1997, the state, citing the PLRA, filed a motion to end the relief and the continuing oversight of the federal courts. Inmates sued, asking the district court to stop implementation of the PLRA's automatic stay provision[6] (here, involving temporary suspension of the court-ordered injunctive relief), saying it violated the separation of powers doctrine. The lower courts held that the statutory stay provision impermissibly limited the courts' powers. The Supreme Court disagreed and reversed, with the language:

> **The entry of the stay does not reopen or 'suspend' the previous judgment....[T]he stay merely reflects the changed legal circumstances—that prospective relief under the existing decree is no longer enforceable, and remains unenforceable unless and until the court makes the findings required by [18 U.S.C.] § 3626(b)(3).**

Gilmore v. People of the State of California, 220 F.3d 987 (9th Cir. 2000), examined the constitutionality of the provisions of the PLRA that require termination of prospective relief in prison condition cases. Pursuant to the PLRA, state officials filed for the termination of court orders (dating back to 1972) and consent decrees (dating back to 1980). The federal appeals court noted the following: "No circuit court has found the PLRA to violate due process or the Equal Protection Clause .... We decline to stray from these precedents."

The court in *Inmates of Suffolk County Jail v. Rouse*, 129 F.3d 649 (1st Cir. 1997), also rejected the inmates' attack on the PLRA's termination provisions. The case dated back to 1971 and involved conditions of confinement, primarily the double-bunking of pretrial detainees. A 1979 consent decree ratified an architectural plan for a new facility with single-occupancy cells and a phasing out of the old jail. For various reasons, the new facility was not completed until mid-1990, and there was difficulty from the start in providing single occupancy in its cells. Modifications of the consent decree occurred in 1985, 1990, and 1994. Passage of the PLRA was followed by an action by the state government to terminate the consent decree. The district court upheld the PLRA's constitutionality and said it would not order enforcement of the consent decree's provisions. The court, however, refused to vacate the decree or terminate its obligations because these were undertaken by agreement of the parties and with court approval. An appeal was filed by both parties.

The appeals court ordered termination of the consent decree. This appeals court found the PLRA legislation to be rational, and upheld its provisions against the constitutional objections that inmates had brought. The court drew the following conclusion:

Under the PLRA, the courthouse doors remain open and the withdrawal of prospective relief—above and beyond what is necessary to correct the violation of federally protected rights—does not diminish the right of access .... [W]hile there is a constitutional right to court access, there is no complementary constitutional right to receive or be eligible for a particular form of relief.

A statute that neither abridges a fundamental right nor operates against a suspect class receives rational basis review when it is challenged under the Equal Protection Clause .... The PLRA is such a statute: ... it does not impair a fundamental right.

In *Imprisoned Citizens v. Ridge*, 169 F.3d 178 (3rd Cir. 1999), an appellate court reached a similar conclusion:

The termination provision [of the PLRA] does not deny prisoners "a reasonably adequate opportunity to present claimed violations of fundamental constitutional rights to the courts." *Lewis v. Casey*, 518 U.S. 343, 351 (1996) .... The provision therefore does not infringe any identified fundamental right, and is subject to only rational basis review.

While [18 U.S.C.] § 3626(b)(2) [providing for immediate termination of prospective relief] admittedly singles out certain prisoner rights cases for special treatment, it does so only to advance unquestionably legitimate purposes—to minimize prison micro-management by

federal courts and to conserve judicial resources.... "[I]t is not the role of courts, but that of the political branches, to shape the institutions of government in such fashion as to comply with the laws and the Constitution."

At this point, you may think that the PLRA's termination provisions provide almost a sure way for prison administrators to end obligations previously agreed to (either by themselves or their predecessors). Keeping in mind that pre-PLRA consent decrees were likely to be broader in scope, this may be a fair assumption. However, as shown in *Benjamin v. Fraser*, 264 F.3d 175 (2nd Cir. 2001), this is not always the case.

The plaintiffs in *Benjamin* and several related cases were pretrial detainees. Suit was first brought in 1975, alleging that conditions in New York City jails violated the inmates' constitutional rights. The original consent decrees dated to 1978 and 1979. The New York City Department of Correction attempted to terminate operation of the decrees, pursuant to PLRA provisions. The district court granted relief, terminating consent decrees that called for judicial supervision over restrictive housing, inmate correspondence, and law libraries. But the court denied termination of the decrees that involved attorney visitation and the proper use of restraints on inmates.

The district court's action was appealed. Looking just at the issue of attorney visitation, the appeals court supported the lower court's retention of this part of the earlier decrees. The court observed that the corrections department offered no justification for allowing family visits, but not attorney visits, during counts; no reasons why the process of bringing detainees to the counsel rooms could not begin upon the attorney's arrival at the prison, rather than his arrival at the visiting area[7]; and no reasons why a space reservation policy could not be used in those institutions with limited visiting areas. The appeals court found the measures ordered to be reasonable to safeguard the detainees' constitutional rights at minimal cost to the department and without impairing institutional concerns. The appeals court affirmed the "continuing need for prospective relief to correct an ongoing denial of a federal right, and that the relief ordered was sufficiently narrow to satisfy the requirements of the PLRA." When there are good, historic reasons, the provisions of a consent decree (even though it is many years old) may be continued, even though the PLRA facilitates the termination of many decrees.

The PLRA does not inhibit a federal court from ensuring that prisons are operated in a constitutional manner when challenged under Section 1983. When it comes to the constitutional requirements of running government, the courts must have some means of ensuring that constitutional standards are met. The government (theoretically) does not have to run prisons. (In the 1970s, Vermont, because of increasing prison problems, tried to get out of the prison business altogether by closing its prisons and sending all people who were sentenced in Vermont courts to places outside the state, which were willing to contract to take them. See *Howe v. Smith*, 452 U.S. 473 (1981).) But, if a state is going to run a prison, it must meet the minimum constitutional standards set for prisons. (Vermont had to see that its prisoners were properly cared for—court action by inmates transferred out of the state saw to that.) The courts have the challenge of enforcing the orders to bring prison or jail conditions up to those minimum constitutional standards. Prior to the PLRA, one widespread problem was that court orders and consent decrees of the 1970s and 1980s (their heyday) dealt with literally hundreds of items that inmates (and judges and even administrators) wanted to see changed but that had no relationship to a constitutional requirement. The PLRA has addressed this concern about court orders and consent decrees that cover multiple issues for unlimited amounts of time. We will, however, see more on judicial intervention in prison conditions later; in particular, see the Supreme Court's discussion in *Wilson v. Seiter* that appears later in this chapter.

■ *Bell v. Wolfish*

The first Supreme Court case dealing with conditions of confinement and interpreting the Eighth Amendment was *Bell v. Wolfish*, 441 U.S. 520 (1979). You will recall that we have already discussed the *Wolfish* opinion as it dealt with important but collateral issues: the publisher-only rule for incoming publications and the inspection of personal packages, as well as the requirement for inmates to be present during searches of their rooms and the issue of searches of body cavities during strip searches. *Wolfish* arose as a class action by the inmates of the Metropolitan Correctional Center (MCC) in New York City, operated by the Federal Bureau of Prisons. The MCC housed pretrial detainees who were awaiting trial in federal court, along with some inmates who were already convicted and serving sentences. It was opened in 1975. That same year, inmates filed the suit, challenging the conditions in the MCC on almost every front.

The planned capacity for the MCC was 449 inmates, who were to be housed primarily in rooms designed for single occupancy. About 60 inmates were to be housed in dormitories, large open rooms with bunks and minimal physical separations for privacy. Because of rapid increases in the numbers of commitments from the local courts, the number of persons confined at the MCC rose quickly. The MCC's planned capacity was exceeded shortly after it opened. To provide sleeping space, the single bunks in the dormitories and in the single rooms were replaced with double bunks. Often, new arrivals had to sleep on cots in the common areas (used for watching television or other recreation purposes) until space became available in the regular rooms. While the complaints of the inmates, and the orders of the lower court in this case, dealt with many issues, we will address the principal issue and holding of the case, the so-called double-bunking issue. The constitutional question was, is it permissible to place two (or more) inmates in a space planned or designed for one person? Is it a constitutional violation to "overcrowd"—that is, to place many more people into a jail than it was designed to hold?

In *Wolfish*, the Supreme Court addressed overcrowding, or double-bunking, with respect to pretrial detainees. The lower courts had started (as most federal courts had done in other jail cases) with the premise that these people were to be treated as innocent until they were proved guilty. This was not the same as requiring compliance with "contemporary standards of decency," which would be required by the cruel and unusual punishment clause of the Eighth Amendment. Rather, pretrial detainees, according to those lower courts, could be subjected only to those "restrictions and privations" that were inherent in the confinement itself (restriction of their freedom to come and go as they pleased), which were justified by compelling necessities of jail administration. The insistence on showing "compelling necessity" was central to the rulings for the inmates in the lower courts, which had found double-bunking unconstitutional. It was a prevalent approach among federal courts before *Wolfish*.

The Supreme Court rejected the "compelling necessity" test, finding no source for it in the Constitution. The Court also dismissed the "presumption of innocence" analysis, pointing out that that presumption is only a doctrine that governs the burden of proof in criminal trials and that it has no application to a determination of the rights of an accused person who is being confined before trial.

It is the due process clause of the Constitution, not the Eighth Amendment, which protects a pretrial detainee from certain conditions and restrictions. (The Eighth Amendment deals with punishments, which cannot be cruel and unusual. A pretrial detainee, having not been convicted, cannot be punished at all. Therefore, the "cruel and unusual" proscriptions of that amendment do not apply.)

> **[W]hat is at issue when an aspect of pretrial detention that is not alleged to violate any express guarantee of the Constitution [such as a free speech, religion, or search question] is challenged, is the detainee's right to be free from punishment....In evaluating the constitutionality of conditions or restrictions of pretrial detention...we think that the proper inquiry is whether those conditions amount to punishment of the detainee.**

Under the due process clause, the detainee is entitled to be protected against deprivation of his liberty without due process of law. That is the standard for evaluating conditions of his confinement in general and, in particular, whether double-bunking is permissible:

> **For under the Due Process Clause, a detainee may not be punished prior to an adjudication of guilt in accordance with due process of law.**

Therefore, to ascertain whether there has been a due process—a constitutional—violation, we must look to see whether the detainee has been punished. How do we ascertain that?

> **Not every disability imposed during pretrial detention amounts to "punishment" in the constitutional sense....[The government, everyone agrees, can detain a person awaiting trial, and it must be able to use the devices necessary to achieve detention.] Loss of freedom of choice and privacy are inherent incidents of confinement in such a facility. And the fact that such detention interferes with the detainee's understandable desire to live as comfortably as possible and with as little restraint as possible during confinement does not convert the conditions or restrictions of detention into "punishment."**

But how do we tell whether the conditions amount to "punishment"?

> **A court must decide whether the disability is imposed for the purpose of punishment or whether it is but an incident of some other legitimate governmental purpose. Absent a showing of an expressed intent to punish on the part of detention facility officials, that determination generally will turn on "whether an alternative purpose to which [the restriction] may rationally be connected is assignable for it, and whether it appears excessive in relation to the alternative purpose assigned [to it]."**

The Court summarizes as follows:

[I]f a particular condition or restriction of pretrial detention is reasonably related to a legitimate governmental objective, it does not, without more, amount to "punishment."

On the other hand,

[I]f a restriction or condition is not reasonably related to a legitimate goal—if it is arbitrary or purposeless—a court permissibly may infer that the purpose of the governmental action is punishment that may not constitutionally be inflicted upon detainees.

With these holdings, we have the yardstick to measure whether conditions in a jail are unconstitutional. Now, let's get down to applying that yardstick to specific jail conditions.

[T]he Government must be able to take steps to maintain security and order at the institution.... Restraints that are reasonably related to the institution's interest in maintaining jail security do not, without more, constitute unconstitutional punishment.... On this record, we are convinced as a matter of law that "double-bunking" as practiced at the MCC did not amount to punishment and did not, therefore, violate [inmates'] rights under the Due Process Clause.... While confining a given number of people in a given amount of space in such a manner as to cause them to endure genuine privations and hardship over an extended period of time might raise serious questions under the Due Process Clause as to whether those conditions amounted to punishment, nothing even approaching such hardship is shown by this record.

Wolfish is important on two critical points: it gave us the standard for measuring the constitutionality of conditions for pretrial detainees, and it ruled that double-bunking is not per se unconstitutional. (Many courts had ruled that double-bunking was per se unconstitutional and that putting more inmates into a living space than the number it was designed for was always impermissible. The Court in *Wolfish* said that crowding, at least under the conditions at the MCC, was permissible and not a constitutional violation.[8]) What this invites, of course, are challenges to other jail conditions on the grounds that the conditions are far worse than those spelled out at the New York MCC. (This is called "distinguishing the case." If you are a lawyer for jail inmates who are claiming crowded conditions, you point out to the court how different the conditions are in your jail, distinguishing it from the MCC and the "double-bunking is okay" ruling of *Wolfish*.) The *Wolfish* decision has allowed jails to be double-bunked and otherwise crowded, so long as conditions do not become "genuine privations and hardship over an extended period of time." The prevention of such privations and hardships is a challenge for jail administrators, one that can often be met by sound correctional management and the effective use of those resources that are available, even though they may be less than ideal.

The *Wolfish* opinion also establishes the necessity for identifying the precise constitutional source of the right sought to be protected. Pretrial detainees are not protected by the prohibition against "cruel and unusual punishment" in the Eighth Amendment. Instead, protection is found in the due process clauses of the Fifth and Fourteenth Amendments. When analyzing a claim that would fall under the Eighth Amendment if made by a convicted and sentenced prisoner, it is imperative to identify the precise status of the prisoner making that claim so the proper constitutional analysis can be considered and applied.

■ *Rhodes v. Chapman*

Because of the way the *Wolfish* case developed, the double-bunking issue was decided in *Wolfish* only for pretrial detainees. (The other issues, concerning searches and mail, were decided for both the pretrial detainees and the sentenced inmates.) This left double-bunking in prisons for sentenced inmates as an issue to be decided in another case, which the Supreme Court did very soon thereafter in *Rhodes v. Chapman*, 452 U.S. 337 (1981). The single issue in that case was "whether the housing of two inmates in a single cell at the Southern Ohio Correctional Facility is cruel and unusual punishment prohibited by the Eighth and Fourteenth Amendments."

Ohio inmates brought this Section 1983 action, claiming that double celling in the maximum security state prison at Lucasville resulted in inmates having to live too closely together and further claiming that this crowding strained the prison's facilities and staff. Like the MCC, in *Wolfish*, the Lucasville prison was new. It opened in the early 1970s and contained 1,620 cells, with each cell measuring 63 square feet. (The number of square feet in a cell, or per inmate, was very important in prison standards and guidelines, which were published by professional organizations and others and had been relied on in a number of court decisions in deciding whether conditions were unconstitutional.) Each cell at Lucasville had a bed, a nightstand, a sink, and a toilet. When commitments to Ohio prisons rose, double-tiered bunks were placed in the cells. Like most prisons, there were also "day rooms," which were adjacent to the cell block areas and were furnished with television sets, card tables, and chairs. At the time of the lawsuit, Lucasville held 2,300 inmates, most of whom were serving life or long-term sentences. Most inmates had to spend about 25% of their time in their cells; they were allowed to spend the rest of the time at work, at meals, in the showers, in the day rooms, at school, in the library, or other recreation areas. Some inmates were restricted to their cells for longer hours for security and control purposes.

The district court (trial court) had concluded that double celling at Lucasville was cruel and unusual punishment. This decision was based on five factors: (1) inmates were serving long terms of imprisonment there; (2) the institution was 38% over its "design capacity," and this led to limitation of movement as well as "physical and mental injury from long exposure"; (3) the court relied on studies that recommended that each person in a prison should have 50 to 55 square feet of living-quarters space; (4) a prisoner who was double celled had to spend most of his time in his cell with a cellmate; and (5) double celling had become the long-term practice at Lucasville— it was not temporary.

The Supreme Court rejected the district court's reliance on those five factors as showing constitutional violation of the cruel and unusual punishment clause: "These general considerations fall far short in themselves of proving cruel and unusual punishment….At most, these considerations amount to a theory that double celling inflicts pain."

The Court presented a brief review of the standards that have been used to interpret those three words—cruel and unusual. The Court noted that it is not a static test but one that has been interpreted "in a flexible and dynamic manner." Clearly, the Eighth Amendment goes beyond the original concern over barbarous physical punishments:

Conditions must not involve the wanton and unnecessary infliction of pain, nor may they be grossly disproportionate to the severity of the crime warranting imprisonment.

That is the current "standard of decency" that must be used to measure whether conditions amount to cruel and unusual punishment.

In an interesting observation in a footnote, the Court brushed aside reliance on experts or the standards adopted by various organizations as pointing the way to "contemporary standards of decency." Regarding an organization's standards, "they simply do not establish the constitutional minima; rather, they establish goals recommended by the organization in question." As to the opinions of experts, the Court said that they cannot weigh as heavily in determining contemporary standards of decency as "the public attitude toward a given sanction" (citing *Gregg v. Georgia*, 428 U.S. 153 (1976), a death penalty case). The Court observed, "We could agree that double celling is not desirable, especially in view of the size of these cells. But there is no evidence in this case that double celling is viewed generally as violating decency." (We have pointed out before that corrections administrators would much prefer to run prisons and jails that are not crowded. We have never known an administrator who would prefer to manage a double-bunked institution rather than one that is single celled.)

Applying these "contemporary standards of decency," the Supreme Court found no cruel and unusual punishment in double-bunking per se, or in the conditions that prevailed at the Lucasville prison.

[T]here is no evidence that double celling under these circumstances either inflicts unnecessary or wanton pain or is grossly disproportionate to the severity of crimes warranting imprisonment.

Along the way, the Court also made some interesting observations:

[T]he Constitution does not mandate comfortable prisons.

Indeed, prisons of necessity produce some discomfort, the Court said. It is up to prison administrators and legislators, rather than courts, to weigh the conditions and decide how best to resolve problems of prison population pressures. Inquiries in lawsuits into prison conditions "spring from constitutional requirements...rather than a court's idea of how best to operate a...facility."

Courts certainly have a responsibility to scrutinize claims of cruel and unusual confinement, and conditions in a number of prisons, especially older ones, have justly been described as "deplorable" and "sordid" [citing *Wolfish*]. When conditions of confinement amount to cruel and unusual punishment, "federal courts will discharge their duty to protect constitutional rights" [citing *Procunier v. Martinez*, 416 U.S. 396 (1974)].

■ Brown v. Plata

A major decision on overcrowding—a decision with huge impact on statewide prison operations—was *Brown v. Plata*, 563 U.S. __ (2011). California prisons had been under class-action litigation in two cases (one case involving inmates with serious mental disorders and the second involving inmates with serious medical conditions) for many years. Each district court determined that to correct the constitutional violation, a reduction in the California Department of Corrections' prison population was needed. Pursuant to 18 U.S.C. § 3626(a) of the Prison Litigation Reform Act (PLRA), the district court judges in each case independently requested a three-judge court be convened. The Chief Judge of the Court of Appeals for the Ninth Circuit agreed, and the two cases were consolidated. The three-judge court found deplorable conditions which amounted to impermissible, unconstitutional treatment of inmates. After other attempts to correct the problems failed, the lower (three-judge) court concluded that the only way to achieve that result was to require reduction of the overall prison population in the state. An order to that effect was entered and was appealed by the state to the Supreme Court. (A direct appeal to the Supreme Court was authorized from a finding of unconstitutional action by a three-judge court.)

The Supreme Court first had to determine whether the case was properly handled in the courts by the stringent requirements of the PLRA. The Court found that, pursuant to the PLRA, the three-judge court was a proper way to review the sweeping allegations of unconstitutional state actions. Only a three-judge district court could order release of prisoners to cure systemic violations of constitutional rights; a single-judge court could not. Further, the lower courts had given the state several years to remedy the conditions, including actions beyond simply reducing the prison population. The unconstitutional, Eighth Amendment violations continued.

The Court found that the procedural requirements of the PLRA were met and that the case was ripe for Supreme Court review. But what was the violation of the Constitution? We know, from the earlier cases on prison crowding we have reviewed, that having prison populations over (even considerably over) planned capacity does not in itself create a constitutional violation. There must be a separate violation (or several violations) found, to warrant court intervention. Remedies taken must be designed to remedy those specific violations.

Here, the constitutional violations centered on two factors: the failure to provide minimal, basic care to inmates with serious mental illnesses and deficiencies in adequate medical care (the state had even conceded that medical care was so deficient as to be in violation of inmates' Eight Amendment rights). Attempts to provide good medical and mental health care had failed. The basic cause of this system-wide deficiency was found to be the overcrowded state of the prisons.

California's prisons were designed to hold about 80,000 inmates. At the time of trial, the population was about 156,000. For many years, the prisons had operated with almost double the numbers they were designed for, which resulted in exceptionally severely crowded conditions. See **Figure 15-1**. (In an unusual step in a Court opinion, photographs of some living conditions were included in the opinion. They show, for example, where "as many as 200 prisoners may live in a gymnasium, monitored by as few as two or three correctional officers.") How does this become a constitutional violation? Because, as the lower court concluded, and the Supreme Court agreed,

Figure 15-1 Inmates at the California Institute for Men in Chino, CA, sit in crowded conditions.
Source: © California Department Of Corrections/AP Photos

there is an overwhelming demand placed on the medical and mental health staff and facilities that are available. (The situation was exacerbated by the fact that there were high vacancy rates for medical and mental health staff.) It was noted, for example, that there could be backlogs of up to 700 prisoners who were waiting to see a doctor, a suicide rate "approaching an average of one per week," and urgent specialty referrals "pending for six months to a year." The crowding was found to create unsanitary living conditions and increased violence, which are problems by themselves, but which could also aggravate mental health problems in prisoners with latent illnesses.

The Court concluded that overcrowding was the "primary cause" (the required finding under 18 U.S.C. § 3626(a)(3)(E)) of the violations of prisoners' constitutional rights. The Eighth Amendment violation, the cruel and unusual punishment of the prisoners, was found in their "severe and unlawful mistreatment... through grossly inadequate provision of medical and mental health care."

The Court concluded:

For years the medical and mental health care provided by California's prisons has fallen short of minimum constitutional requirements and has failed to meet prisoners' basic health needs. Needless suffering and death have been the well-documented result. Over the whole course of years during which this litigation has been pending, no other remedies have been found to be sufficient. Efforts to remedy the violation have been frustrated by severe overcrowding in California's prison system.

The lower court's order for relief, requiring reduction of the prison population by about 46,000 inmates, was affirmed. (It had been found that, to achieve proper conditions, the population would have to be capped at 137.5% of design capacity.) The Court recognized that the required release of large numbers of prisoners was an exceptional step and a matter of "grave concern."[9] It was emphasized that the release was to be carefully monitored and that the "three-judge court must remain open to a showing or demonstration by either party that the injunction should be altered to ensure that the rights and interests of the parties are given all due and necessary protection." While new construction and out-of-state transfers might accomplish some population reduction, releasing some prisoners before their sentences were fully served would undoubtedly be required. The state could propose other measures (diverting lower-risk offenders might be one way) to mitigate the severe impact of the order.

The population reduction potentially required is nevertheless of unprecedented sweep and extent.

The reduction of population ordered by the district court was to occur within two years. The Supreme Court noted though that the state should be given latitude to adjust its efforts to correct the constitutional violations, consistent with concerns for public safety, which might allow for extending the time for remedial action up to five years. However:

Without a reduction in overcrowding, there will be no efficacious remedy for the unconstitutional care of the sick and mentally ill in California's prisons.

◼ *Whitley v. Albers*

As we have seen, *Wolfish* and *Rhodes* take care of the broad question of general conditions in a prison facility and the specific questions of double-bunking and crowding. Those cases give us the constitutional standards (the paraphrasing of the Eighth Amendment language) for evaluating conditions cases. Now we will turn to cases that consider cruel and unusual punishment claims by an individual inmate, based on the way he was treated.

In *Whitley v. Albers*, 475 U.S. 312 (1986), the Supreme Court considered the claim of an inmate who was shot and seriously injured inside the Oregon State Penitentiary. The shooting occurred during a riot at that prison. Inmates took control of a two-tiered cell block where inmate Albers lived. An officer was taken hostage on the upper tier. Officers formed an assault squad to regain control of the cell block. The security manager, Captain Whitley, led the assault and proceeded to the second tier himself to try to free the hostage. Three officers who were armed with shotguns followed Whitley into the cell block and were given instructions to shoot low at any prisoners who tried to climb the stairs, because they would be a threat to Whitley or the hostage. When Albers started up the stairs, after Whitley had run up, an officer fired a shot that struck Albers in the left knee. (A warning shot had been fired into the wall when the officers first entered the barricaded cell block. Another inmate was shot on the stairs, and several others on the lower tier were also wounded by gunshots.) The hostage was rescued, and the cell block was retaken. Albers filed a Section 1983 claim, alleging Eighth Amendment deprivations because of the physical damage to his knee and mental and emotional distress.

The Supreme Court noted that it is "the unnecessary and wanton infliction of pain" that constitutes cruel and unusual punishment. (This language is cited from *Estelle v. Gamble*, 429 U.S. 97 (1976). The four dissenting justices would limit the standard to those words, "unnecessary and wanton infliction of pain." They objected to the extension of that standard, which the majority adopted.) The Court elaborated further:

> **It is obduracy and wantonness, not inadvertence or error in good faith, that characterize the conduct prohibited by the Cruel and Unusual Punishments Clause.**

Thus, an inmate would have to prove that the injury suffered was caused by an unnecessary and wanton infliction of pain to support a cruel and unusual claim. To some extent, the *Whitley* decision turns on the unusual circumstances that prison authorities faced. Those circumstances posed substantial risks to the safety of prison staff and inmates. In any event, to ascertain whether there was a constitutional violation, the Court identified the following standard:

> **[W]hether the measure taken inflicted unnecessary and wanton pain and suffering ultimately turns on "whether force was applied in a good faith effort to maintain or restore discipline or maliciously and sadistically for the very purpose of causing harm"** [citing a Second Circuit case, *Johnson v. Glick*, 481 F.2d 1028 (2nd Cir. 1973)].

The Court then reviewed and analyzed the factual situation at the Oregon State Penitentiary that led to the shooting and injury of inmate Albers. The Court said that the situation was "dangerous and volatile.... Under these circumstances, the actual shooting was part and parcel of a good-faith effort to restore prison security. As such, it did not violate [Albers'] Eighth Amendment right to be free from cruel and unusual punishments."

Albers also claimed that his rights were violated by taking away his liberty under the Fourteenth Amendment without due process of law. The Court quickly disposed of this claim:

> **We think the Eighth Amendment, which is specifically concerned with the unnecessary and wanton infliction of pain in penal institutions, serves as the primary source of substantive protection to convicted prisoners in cases such as this one, where the deliberate use of force is challenged as excessive and unjustified.**

Thus, a due process claim under the Fourteenth Amendment was summarily dismissed.

While we are discussing the use of excessive force, we should note the holding of *Tennessee v. Garner*, 471 U.S. 1 (1985). Although that case involved the shooting of a fleeing suspect by a police officer, its language substantially changed the assumption about when **deadly force** can be used. The Supreme Court established three standards to be met for the use of deadly force: (1) the force must be necessary to prevent the escape of the suspect; (2) there must be probable cause for the officer to believe that the suspect poses "a significant threat of death or serious physical injury to the officer or others"; and (3) if possible, there must be some kind of warning given to the fleeing person before deadly force is used. Especially notable is the fact that there is no reliance on the previous "fleeing felon" rule, which had been used by U.S. police.

These guidelines must also be kept in mind in correctional situations, because we must assume the Supreme Court (and lower courts) would use the same kind of analysis in looking at the use of force in a prison or jail. The first element would be implicit in using force to stop an escapee (or a would-be escapee). In a prison disturbance or in an escape, elements 2 and 3 should also be followed: to use deadly force, there must be a significant threat to the safety of the staff or others, and some warning must be given if possible before force is used. In an institution that houses convicted felons or even those accused of violent crimes, the second element would appear to be met: staff members should be able to assume that the escape of such a person poses a threat of serious bodily injury to the public. To require staff in a prison or jail to identify a person who is scaling a wall or fleeing from the institution, before shots can be fired, would be unreasonable in most circumstances. Every corrections facility should establish a policy on the use of force and especially should define those limited circumstances when deadly force may be used. All staff should be fully trained on those policy guidelines. Failure to follow the facility's use of force procedures could result in the staff member facing criminal prosecution.[10]

■ *Wilson v. Seiter*

The meaning of the cruel and unusual punishment clause as applied to an individual inmate is rounded out in the decision of the Supreme Court in *Wilson v. Seiter*, 501 U.S. 294 (1991). Wilson, an inmate at the Hocking Correctional Facility in Ohio, claimed under Section 1983 that his Eighth Amendment rights were infringed by his treatment, which involved "overcrowding, excessive noise, insufficient locker storage space, inadequate heating and cooling, improper ventilation, unclean and inadequate restrooms, unsanitary dining facilities and food preparation, and housing with mentally and physically ill inmates."

After reviewing the line of cases that had developed the guidance for interpreting the Eighth Amendment, the Supreme Court particularly qualified the *Whitley* decision, which we have just discussed as applying to circumstances in which officials were reacting to an emergency situation. Wanton misconduct would have to be shown by actions taken "maliciously and sadistically for the very purpose of causing harm." All agreed that the very high state of mind required by *Whitley* does not apply to general prison conditions cases, such as in *Wilson*. But, the Court said, whether the conduct is wanton depends on the state of mind of the prison official. Using the standard of *Estelle v. Gamble*, which relates to health care, the Court said that "deliberate indifference" to the needs of the inmate was the state of mind of the prison official that must be found to constitute cruel and unusual punishment.

> **Whether one characterizes the treatment received…as inhumane conditions of confinement, failure to attend to his medical needs, or a combination of both, it is appropriate to apply the "deliberate indifference" standard articulated in *Estelle*.**
>
> **The source of the intent requirement is…the Eighth Amendment itself, which bans only cruel and unusual punishment. If the pain inflicted is not formally meted out as punishment**

by the statute or the sentencing judge, some mental element must be attributed to the inflicting officer before it can qualify.

This statement increases the burden on inmates to show deliberate indifference by prison officials to support a claim of cruel and unusual punishment. In many instances, the conditions complained about may be a result of such factors as older facilities or a lack of funds. When these are the cause, there is no "mental element," no adverse intent, and thus no "deliberate indifference" to the needs of the inmate.

Another important component of the *Wilson* decision is the Court's consideration of the inmate's claim that a court must look at the overall conditions to decide whether there was cruel and unusual punishment. This approach had been followed by many federal courts in deciding that a prison's conditions were unconstitutional. The Supreme Court rejected that approach.

Nothing so amorphous as "overall conditions" can rise to the level of cruel and unusual punishment when no specific deprivation of a single human need exists.

It is true that some conditions may be viewed in combination with others, the Court said, when they have a "mutually enforcing effect," such as when cells are at a low temperature at night and there are no blankets issued to keep warm. Other cases cited with approval involved the provision of outdoor exercise, which was required in *Spain v. Procunier*, 600 F.2d 189 (9th Cir. 1979), when prisoners were confined in small cells for almost 24 hours a day, but which was not required in *Clay v. Miller*, 626 F.2d 345 (4th Cir. 1980), when prisoners had access to a day room for 18 hours per day.

The Supreme Court, in this part of its decision, is endorsing the approach of *Wright v. Rushen*, 642 F.2d 1129 (9th Cir. 1981), which said that, in examining the constitutionality of conditions of confinement,

> a court should examine each challenged condition of confinement, such as the adequacy of the quarters, food, medical care, etc., and determine whether that condition is compatible with "the evolving standards of decency that mark the progress of a maturing society." Any condition of confinement which passes this test is immune from federal intervention. If no challenged condition fails to meet the test, the entire facility and its administration are immune from Eighth Amendment attack.

Flowing from this approach, if a court finds a violation with respect to a specific condition, the court should order relief with respect to that condition. It does not entitle the court to adopt remedies to bring all aspects of the prison into accord with the court's ideas of what is right and proper for a prison.

In the *Wilson* decision, the case was remanded to the lower courts to determine whether any individual condition violated the "deliberate indifference" standard.

■ *Hudson v. McMillian; Wilkins v. Gaddy*

The *Hudson* case considered the question of what degree of injury is required before an inmate can claim an Eighth Amendment—cruel and unusual punishment—violation. Hudson, a Louisiana inmate, claimed that he was beaten by guards while he was handcuffed and shackled. He said he sustained minor bruises, some facial swelling, loosened teeth, and a cracked dental plate. The court of appeals set aside an award of damages to Hudson, ruling that to constitute an injury recoverable under the Eighth Amendment there must have been "significant injury," whereas Hudson only showed minor injuries that required no medical attention. The Supreme Court reversed in *Hudson v. McMillian*, 503 U.S. 1 (1992), giving the following reasons:

> [W]henever prison officials stand accused of using excessive physical force in violation of the Cruel and Unusual Punishments Clause, the core judicial inquiry is that set out in *Whitley*: whether force was applied in a good-faith effort to maintain or restore discipline, or maliciously and sadistically to cause harm....[T]he extent of injury suffered by an inmate is one factor that may suggest "whether the use of force could plausibly have been thought necessary" in a particular situation....Thus, courts considering a prisoner's claim must ask both if "the officials act[ed] with a sufficiently culpable state of mind" and if the alleged wrongdoing was objectively "harmful enough" to establish a constitutional violation.

Regarding the specific question raised by this case, the Court held that a serious injury was not necessary for an inmate to pursue a cruel and unusual punishment claim. A court must look at the particular circumstances of the case. The Court stated that the unjustified striking of an inmate would raise a serious question about the "concepts of dignity, civilized standards, humanity, and decency" that lie behind the Eighth Amendment. This is true, without regard to how severe the inmate's injuries are. Hudson had a claim about cruel and unusual punishment, the Supreme Court said, which had to be looked into by the courts.

In *Wilkins v. Gaddy*, 559 U.S. __ (2010) (per curiam), Wilkins, the prisoner, stated that the officer had entered his cell and without provocation assaulted him by slamming him to the concrete floor and punching, kicking, kneeing, and choking him. The prisoner stated that as a result of the beating, he suffered a bruised heel, lower back pain, increased blood pressure, migraine headaches, and dizziness, as well as psychological trauma and mental anguish. The district court dismissed the suit, ruling that Wilkins' injuries were minimal (de minimis) and did not state a claim under the Eighth Amendment. The dismissal was affirmed on appeal. The Supreme Court rejected the lower courts' interpretation that prisoners alleging the use of excessive force must demonstrate a "significant injury" to state an Eighth Amendment claim.

> Injury and force, however, are only imperfectly correlated, and it is the latter that ultimately counts. An inmate who is gratuitously beaten by guards does not lose his ability to pursue an excessive force claim merely because he has the good fortune to escape without serious injury.

The court further explained that the ruling in *Hudson v. McMillian* intended to

> **... shift the "core judicial inquiry" from the extent of the injury to the nature of the force—specifically, whether it was nontrivial and "was applied ... maliciously and sadistically to cause harm** [citing *Hudson v. McMillian*].

A case further developing the standard of *Hudson* is *Smith v. Mensinger*, 293 F.3d 641 (3rd Cir. 2002). Smith, an inmate in the Pennsylvania prison system, received prison misconduct reports, including one for punching an officer in the eye. Smith alleged he was later handcuffed behind his back. Shortly thereafter, he claimed several officers rammed his head into walls and cabinets and knocked him to the floor, where one officer kicked and punched him. While this was occurring, Smith claimed that another officer saw the beating but made no effort to intervene or restore order. Smith filed suit, alleging constitutional violations of his rights under 42 U.S.C § 1983. The lawsuit named several officers as defendants, including the officer who only saw the beating. The federal court of appeals held that the officer who observed, but did not intervene, could be held liable, provided he had a reasonable opportunity to intervene and simply refused to do so.

> **The approving silence emanating from the officer who stands by and watches as others unleash an unjustified assault contributes to the actual use of excessive force, and we cannot ignore the tacit support such silence lends to those who are actually striking the blows. Such silence is an endorsement of the constitutional violation resulting from the illegal use of force.**

The court cited *Hudson,* where the supervisor allegedly stood by and told officers who were beating the inmate "not to have too much fun." The court in *Smith* did acknowledge that there could be an even greater degree of "dereliction of duty" for a supervisor than for an officer of lower rank.

An issue not addressed in the above cases is whether a person who has been convicted, but not yet sentenced, is more like a convicted prisoner or a pretrial detainee. As discussed above, the Eighth Amendment does not apply to the use of force against pretrial detainees. For those offenders, analysis must be done under the Due Process Clause of the Fourteenth Amendment. In *Lewis v. Downey*, 581 F.3d 467 (7th Cir. 2009), the court of appeals was faced with a plaintiff (inmate) who had been found guilty but was awaiting sentencing and the entry of final judgment. The inmate stated that while he was in his cell, correctional staff had ordered him to stand up, but due to illness (he had been on a hunger strike), he was unable to promptly comply. Correctional staff then tasered the inmate. The district court had granted summary judgment to the correctional personnel, in part because the district court concluded that use of the taser was a minimal use of force. The court of appeals reversed the district court's grant of summary judgment for the officer who fired the taser. In its decision, the court noted that the Supreme Court has not decided what precise constitutional provision protects a detainee from excessive force. The court of appeals ruled that conduct which would violate the Eighth Amendment "cruel and unusual punishment" clause would also violate the due process rights of the detainee under the Fourteenth Amendment. The court of appeals also ruled that a legal analysis of excessive force claims must assess the pain suffered, not necessarily the injury caused. The court concluded that the use of a taser against a prisoner is more than a minimal use of force. The court noted this conclusion shifted the focus "away from the act and to the actor, away from the objective to the subjective....What matters—and what will generally be the decisive factor in cases such as this—is the mindset of the individual applying the force."

■ *Farmer v. Brennan*

Farmer was a biological male who was medically diagnosed as a transsexual. Before being committed to prison, he had undergone estrogen therapy, received silicone breast implants, and undergone unsuccessful testicular surgery. He was placed in the Federal Penitentiary at Terre Haute, Indiana. He wore clothes in a feminine manner and took hormonal drugs (he said) that were smuggled to him in prison. He was usually segregated from the general prison population because of his own misconduct and also for his safety. (He was in a male institution, because doctors said he was still biologically a male.) He was released into regular population at the Terre Haute prison, without any objection by him. Within two weeks, he said he was beaten and raped by another inmate.

Farmer filed a Bivens suit (the equivalent of a Section 1983 action) against federal officials, claiming that he had been cruelly and unusually punished when he was transferred to the prison where officials knew there were assaultive inmates and where Farmer would be particularly vulnerable to sexual attack. He claimed that this was deliberate indifference to his personal safety, and he sought damages and an injunction that he not be placed in a penitentiary (a high-security institution) in the future. The lower courts granted summary judgment to the prison officials on the grounds that they could be held liable only if they had actual knowledge of a potential danger to Farmer, which had not been shown. In *Farmer v. Brennan*, 511 U.S. 825, (1994), the Supreme Court vacated the judgment of the lower courts and remanded the case for further consideration based on the guidelines that it laid down.

The Court made these observations and holdings:

> The [Eighth] Amendment imposes duties on [prison] officials, who must provide humane conditions of confinement; prison officials must ensure that inmates receive adequate food, clothing, shelter and medical care, and must "take reasonable measures to guarantee the safety of the inmates" [citing *Hudson v. Palmer*, 468 U.S. 517 (1984)]....[P]rison officials have a duty...to protect prisoners from violence at the hands of other prisoners.

This does not mean, however, that every injury suffered by an inmate at the hands of another leads to constitutional liability for the prison officials.

> [A] prison official violates the Eighth Amendment only when two requirements are met. First, the deprivation alleged must be, objectively, "sufficiently serious" [citing *Wilson v. Seiter*]....The second requirement follows from the principle that "only the unnecessary and wanton infliction of pain implicates the Eighth Amendment." To violate the Cruel and

Unusual Punishments Clause, a prison official must have a "sufficiently culpable state of mind." In prison-conditions cases that state of mind is one of "deliberate indifference" to inmate health or safety.

Taking those principles from *Wilson*, the Court held:

[A] prison official may be held liable under the Eighth Amendment for denying humane conditions of confinement only if he knows that inmates face a substantial risk of serious harm and disregards that risk by failing to take reasonable measures to abate it.

In *Farmer*, the case was remanded to see whether the conditions met these standards laid down by the Court. The district court had given great weight to the fact that Farmer had not given officials notice of the risk of harm that he feared. That fact, the Court said, was not enough to dispose of the case. The lower court would have to examine the evidence, the Supreme Court said, to see if officials had other reason to know that the inmate faced "substantial risk of serious harm" and failed to take reasonable steps to avoid that risk.

■ *Helling v. McKinney*

Finally, we will look at a Supreme Court opinion that could be placed in a discussion of inmate health care. However, we will look at it here as a cruel and unusual punishment case dealing with conditions of confinement.

McKinney, a Nevada inmate, filed suit under 42 U.S.C. § 1983. He claimed that his involuntary exposure to environmental tobacco smoke (ETS) posed an unreasonable risk to his health in violation of the Eighth Amendment. In *Helling v. McKinney*, 509 U.S. 25 (1993), the Supreme Court agreed that he had a good constitutional claim.

McKinney complained that he was assigned to a cell with an inmate who smoked several packs of cigarettes a day. He also said that cigarettes were sold in the prison without warning of the health hazards they posed to nonsmoking inmates and that some cigarettes were burning continuously, releasing chemicals into the prison air. Finally, he claimed to suffer from health problems that were caused by exposure to ETS.

The first court that considered McKinney's claims granted a directed verdict to the defendant prison officials, ruling that the inmate had no constitutional right to be free from tobacco smoke. The Ninth Circuit Court of Appeals reversed that ruling, saying that the inmate had stated a valid claim under the Eighth Amendment by alleging that he had been exposed to levels of ETS that posed an unreasonable risk of harm to his future health. The Supreme Court sent that ruling back to the court of appeals, to reconsider its decision in light of the intervening decision in *Wilson v. Seiter* (in other words, to apply the standard of that case). The court of appeals reinstated its previous ruling, using the *Wilson* standard.

In its *Helling* decision, the Supreme Court restated the basic rule that, under the Eighth Amendment, prison authorities may not be deliberately indifferent to an inmate's health problems. Does this apply only to current health problems, or does it also apply to the risk of future problems?

> The Amendment…requires that inmates be furnished with the basic human needs, one of which is "reasonable safety." It is "cruel and unusual punishment to hold convicted criminals in unsafe conditions." It would be odd to deny an injunction to inmates who plainly proved an unsafe, life-threatening condition in their prison on the ground that nothing yet had happened to them.

In an amicus brief (a brief filed by an interested person who is not a party in the case before the court), the United States (the federal government) agreed that there might be situations in which exposure to toxic or dangerous substances would pose a risk of sufficient likelihood and magnitude that the protection of the Eighth Amendment should be given, even though the effects might not be shown for some time. But the government argued that exposure to ETS was not a sufficiently grave and certain risk to pose a "serious medical need" (the preliminary standard for examining health claims), keeping in mind that the amendment is to be used to protect "current standards of decency." The Supreme Court did not agree with this argument but approved the approach of the court of appeals, which said that McKinney's claim alleged ETS exposure, which posed an unreasonable danger to his future health.

McKinney also argued that current standards of decency do not support such involuntary exposure as he was required to encounter in the prison and that prison officials were deliberately indifferent to his concerns. The case was returned for the lower court to inquire into his allegations (by trial or by discovery), to see whether he could prove an Eighth Amendment violation based on ETS exposure.

> McKinney states a cause of action under the Eighth Amendment by alleging that [prison officials] have, with deliberate indifference, exposed him to levels of ETS that pose an unreasonable risk of serious damage to his future health.

The Court ended by pointing out things that McKinney would have to prove: (1) that he was being exposed to unreasonably high levels of ETS; (2) that the intervening adoption of a smoking policy in the prisons, including the establishment of a number of nonsmoking areas, did not sufficiently reduce risks to McKinney; (3) that the risks he complained of violated "contemporary standards of decency," as opposed to risks that today's society chooses to tolerate; and (4) that the prison officials had shown "deliberate indifference" to substantial risks to McKinney's future health by their attitudes and conduct. The first two elements are difficult enough for the inmate to prove, but the last two—proving society's current attitudes and proving officials' indifference to ETS risks—would likely be extremely difficult. Indeed, the Supreme Court concluded its opinion by noting that the adoption by Nevada officials, while the case was being litigated, of a smoking policy that offered protections to nonsmokers (and how it was in fact enforced) might indeed make it very difficult to show that officials were ignoring the dangers of ETS.

The third and fourth elements outlined by the Court were later addressed in another case, *Atkinson v. Taylor*, 316 F.3d 257 (3rd Cir. 2003). Atkinson was a blind, diabetic prisoner in Delaware and was a former pack-a-day smoker. He shared a cell with constant smokers. One of his complaints was that he was exposed, with deliberate indifference, to constant smoking (ETS) in his cell for more than seven months, leading to nausea, the inability to eat, headaches, chest pains, difficulty breathing, and other symptoms. Atkinson's requests to prison officials to change these conditions essentially went unanswered. He filed suit under 42 U.S.C. § 1983, claiming prison officials violated his Eighth Amendment rights by exposing him to ETS that created a serious medical need and posed unreasonable risk of harm.

As to "contemporary standards of decency," the court of appeals noted that, since 1993, "almost every Court of Appeals that has addressed this issue has recognized that a prisoner's right to be free from levels of ETS that pose an unreasonable risk of future harm was clearly established by *Helling*." Also, the court noted that Atkinson had presented evidence that "society has become unwilling to tolerate the imposition on anyone of continuous unwanted risks of second-hand smoke."

As to whether officials were deliberately indifferent, the court observed that a prisoner cannot simply walk out of his cell whenever he wishes. "When a susceptible prisoner is confined to a cell, a small and confined space, with a 'constant' smoker for an extended period of time, such symptoms may transform what would otherwise be a passing annoyance into a serious ongoing medical need." Atkinson produced evidence that, after telling prison officials about his sensitivity to ETS, no change was made in his housing conditions. This evidence, the court concluded, demonstrated deliberate indifference on the part of prison officials.

In *Reilly v. Grayson*, 310 F.3d 519 (6th Cir. 2002), an asthmatic inmate, Reilly, charged state prison officials in Michigan with violation of his Eighth Amendment right to be free from cruel and unusual punishment. Reilly said he complained repeatedly to prison officials that his medical problems were made worse by failure to house him in an area free of second-hand smoke (ETS). He claimed that this exposed him to an unreasonable risk of harm to his health and constituted deliberate indifference to his serious medical needs. In the district (trial) court, he was awarded $36,500 in compensatory damages and $18,250 in punitive damages against the officials, plus attorney fees in the amount of $51,786.

The federal appeals court for the Sixth Circuit followed the Supreme Court's decision in *Helling* and one of its own circuit cases, both of which emphasized the right to be free from exposure to second-hand smoke. This court emphasized the defendants' failure to respond to the repeated medical staff recommendations that Reilly be moved to a smoke-free environment. The court found sufficient evidence in the record to show that the inmate suffered both an increase in the severity of his asthma and the risk of future damage to his health as a result of his exposure to ETS. Punitive damages were seen as appropriate based on the defendants' "reckless ... disregard of Reilly's rights." Indicative of the potential impact of an adverse ruling in a Section 1983 action, the *Reilly* holding required that all compensatory and punitive damages and attorney fees be paid by the warden and two deputy wardens who were found liable in their personal capacities for the harm caused and for the constitutional violations of Reilly's rights.[11]

■ Qualified Immunity

This is a good time to look again at the issue of immunity for prison officials. *Immunity* is a legal concept that you have probably more often encountered in the criminal setting—persons are given immunity when they are in a protected status and cannot be sued (prosecuted). This may be because they have cooperated with law enforcement personnel or have given testimony to assist prosecutors. This kind of immunity from criminal prosecution is similar to our interest in this discussion, which is immunity from liability in civil cases. Specifically, we are concerned with immunity in Section 1983 actions, in which officials may be personally sued because of alleged violations of the constitutional rights of others.

In the civil area, the broadest kind of immunity is called absolute immunity. Under the status of absolute immunity, persons cannot be sued because their actions are protected in the interest of public policy, so long as the actions are taken as part of their official duties. This immunity is available to legislators, judges, prosecutors, and jury members. Absolute immunity is not granted to government officials in the executive branch (except the president). Prison staff members are considered to be executive branch officials.

Lawyers for prison staff members did try to claim absolute immunity for their clients in the case of *Cleavinger v. Saxner*, 474 U.S. 193 (1985). They argued that the purpose of giving immunity is to protect the independence of decision makers and that persons who acted like judges in their government roles should be protected, as judges are. This kind of protection (absolute immunity) had been given to people in government who acted like judges, such as hearing examiners and administrative judges who heard evidence and ruled on controversies (for example, the Federal Trade Commission). The *Cleavinger* case involved a suit against prison disciplinary committee members who had "tried" a case involving an inmate's misconduct, found the inmate "guilty" of that conduct, and imposed punishment for that offense.

The Supreme Court rejected the argument and held that prison officials, even in disciplinary hearings, were not the same as judges and did not have absolute immunity. The Court found that the disciplinary committee members were not independent enough, were not professional hearing officers, and were not bound to procedural requirements that are imposed on judicial officers. The Court compared the prison committee membership to a school board disciplinary process, for which it was decided in *Wood v. Strickland*, 420 U.S. 308 (1975), that members were protected by only qualified immunity and not absolute immunity.

Therefore, qualified immunity, rather than absolute immunity, is available to prison officials. Claiming qualified immunity is a common defense used by prison staff in Section 1983 lawsuits. How does this immunity work? In a Section 1983 action, the plaintiffs (inmates) must show that the conduct complained about was in violation of a constitutional right. (Where in the Constitution is protection given against this kind of action?) If this can be shown, it must further be shown that that right was clearly established at the time of the action that is complained about. (What evidence exists to show that the action taken by prison staff members was already prohibited by court decisions prior to the occurrence of that action?) If officials can show that either of these requirements is not met, then they are entitled to qualified immunity—protection against being sued for constitutional violations, under Section 1983. Typically, this argument is made by filing motions on behalf of the defendants (prison officials). If the judge is convinced by the arguments, she will dismiss the lawsuit.[12]

An example of the immunity defense is demonstrated in the case of *Hope v. Pelzer,* 536 U.S. 730 (2002). Hope, who was an inmate in Alabama, had been handcuffed to a hitching post at the prison because of his disruptive conduct. He was cuffed with his hands above the height of his shoulders, and he alleged that this was painful. The first time he was cuffed to the post, he was offered drinking water and was given a bathroom break every fifteen minutes. On a second occasion, he was involved in an altercation with an officer at his chain gang's worksite. Hope was sent back inside the prison, ordered to take off his shirt, and forced to spend the next seven hours attached to the post. This time, he was given one or two water breaks but no bathroom breaks. He filed a Section 1983 action against prison officials, alleging violation of his Eighth Amendment rights. Lower courts granted the officials qualified immunity, with the court of appeals concluding that, although the hitching-post punishment was cruel and unusual, it was not an action that was clearly established as being unconstitutional at the time the officers acted in that way.

The Supreme Court in *Hope* disagreed with the lower courts. At the first stage of analysis, the Court concluded that there had been an Eighth Amendment violation. This was found in the officers' actions of tying Hope to the hitching post when there was no emergency situation that mandated that action, resulting in serious discomfort, including the deprivation of bathroom breaks. Citing *Trop v. Dulles,* 356 U.S. 86 (1958), the Court found that this conduct was a violation of the "basic concept underlying the Eighth Amendment, [which] is nothing less than the dignity of man."

On the second element of qualified immunity analysis, the Court said that the constitutional law was clearly established at the time of the officials' actions. The Court cited the cases of *Gates v. Collier,* 501 F.2d 1291 (5th Cir. 1974), which held that it was unconstitutional to handcuff inmates to the fence or to cells for a long period of time, and *Ort v. White,* 813 F.2d 318 (11th Cir. 1987). In Ort, an inmate had been denied water after he refused to do his assigned work on a farm. That court noted that "physical abuse directed at the prisoner *after* he terminated his resistance to authority would constitute an actionable eighth amendment violation." As a further consideration, the Department of Justice had studied the use of the hitching post in Alabama and had advised the state to discontinue its use of the post in order to meet constitutional standards. In the *Hope* case, the Supreme Court drew the following conclusion:

> **[The prison officials] violated clearly established law .... Hope was treated in a way antithetical to human dignity—he was hitched to a post for an extended period of time in a position that was painful, and under circumstances that were both degrading and dangerous. This wanton treatment was not done of necessity, but as punishment for prior conduct. Even if there might once have been a question regarding the constitutionality of this practice, the [court rulings, buttressed by the Department of Justice report] put a reasonable officer on notice that the use of the hitching post under the circumstances alleged by Hope was unlawful.**

As we have previously observed, it is essential that prison policy be kept up-to-date with developing law that establishes the standards for constitutional conduct. Then, it is essential that prison staff carefully follow the policy of the agency. Staff members should be able to rely on written policy as being a correct reflection of current constitutional requirements. As you can see, if these two steps are taken, prison officials should be able to assert the defense of qualified immunity in any Section 1983 action.

SUMMARY

- With respect to prison conditions, an early case (*Wright v. McMann*) showed that the courts, starting in the 1960s, were willing to use the Eighth Amendment to prohibit "debasing conditions" in prisons that violated "civilized standards of humane decency."

- The Prison Litigation Reform Act (PLRA) was enacted by Congress to address concerns over the burgeoning amount of inmate litigation in federal courts. One part of the PLRA was directed toward the widespread use of consent decrees in prison and jail cases.

- The PLRA provided for the termination of long-standing decrees and has been used by numerous federal courts to end court supervision of prison and jail conditions.

- As prisons and jails became more and more crowded, a major issue was whether cells could be double-bunked—that is, whether two inmates could be placed into a cell that was designed for one person. In two leading cases, the Supreme Court held that it was not unconstitutional to practice double-bunking. As to pretrial detainees, the Court in *Bell v. Wolfish* held that, under the Constitution, inmates could not be punished before they were convicted. (This was decided by application of the due process clause, not the cruel and unusual punishment clause of the Eighth Amendment.) The crowded jail conditions were found not to amount to punishment, because they were incidental to a legitimate government purpose and were not done with an intent to punish. With respect to sentenced inmates, the Supreme Court in *Rhodes v. Chapman* held that the standard for applying the Eighth Amendment was whether the conditions involved the wanton and unnecessary infliction of pain. The Court found that double celling did not inflict unnecessary or wanton pain and therefore was not unconstitutional.

- The Supreme Court, in a sweeping order requiring California to eliminate constitutional violations in its prison population, said that large-scale reduction of the prison population in the state would be required. The violations were a serious and longstanding deprivation of basic health care for the sick and mentally ill inmates in the system. That was the constitutional, Eighth Amendment violation. To correct it (along with other steps that might be taken), the state would have to comply with a lower court order to reduce its prison population to 137.5% of its designed capacity within two years (*Brown v. Plata*).

- The standard used in *Rhodes* ("unnecessary and wanton infliction of pain") was applied to a case in which an inmate was shot during a prison disturbance. The Supreme Court held that "obduracy and wantonness, not inadvertence or error in good faith" would show cruel and unusual punishment. Because force (the shooting) was used in a good-faith effort to restore order, and not "maliciously and sadistically for the very purpose of causing harm," there was no Eighth Amendment violation (*Whitley v. Albers*).

- In *Wilson v. Seiter*, the Supreme Court noted that the very high standard noted in *Whitley* ("maliciously and sadistically for the very purpose of causing harm") applied only to officials who were handling emergency situations. In the more general poor-conditions cases, such as *Wilson,* the state of mind of prison officials was determinative, but what would have to be shown to sustain a finding of cruel and unusual punishment was deliberate indifference on the part of officials to the basic needs of inmates. Each need of inmates or each claimed violation of constitutional standards would have to be examined individually to determine whether officials had been deliberately indifferent to that need. It was found to be improper to look at "overall conditions" to decide whether there was cruel and unusual punishment.

- The Supreme Court ruled that when there were allegations of the use of excessive physical force against an inmate, the deciding factor would be whether force was used in a good-faith effort to maintain discipline or, to the contrary, maliciously and sadistically to cause harm. Injury to the inmate does not have to be severe or even "significant." If malicious or sadistic wrongdoing was involved, any amount of harm inflicted on the inmate could sustain a finding of constitutional violation (*Hudson v. McMillian*; *Wilkins v. Gaddy*).

- Claims by an inmate that he was placed in a prison population in which he was known to be at high risk for being assaulted and where he was later, in fact, beaten and raped, raised possible findings of cruel and unusual punishment. The Supreme Court said that prison officials must take reasonable steps to protect the safety of inmates. In the case of this inmate (who was a transsexual), an official would be liable if he knew that the inmate faced a substantial risk of serious harm and then disregarded that risk by failing to take precautions to protect the inmate (*Farmer v. Brennan*).

- An inmate's claim of being treated cruelly and unusually by being exposed to environmental tobacco smoke was held by the Supreme Court to raise a possible Eighth Amendment violation. Much like other situations we have discussed, this could be proved if the inmate could show that the officials were deliberately indifferent to significant risks to the inmate's future health. The inmate, in order to show deliberate indifference, would have to prove that the officials exposed him to unreasonably high levels of smoke and failed to take sufficient steps to reduce the levels of smoke, that the exposure to the smoke violated "contemporary standards of decency," and that officials showed deliberate indifference to the inmate's health by their attitudes and conduct (*Helling v. McKinney*).

- Prison officials have a defense of qualified immunity against Section 1983 (constitutional violations) lawsuits. To obtain this immunity, officials must show that their actions were taken in accord with clearly established constitutional law, as of the time of their actions (*Cleavinger v. Saxner; Hope v. Pelzer*).

THINKING ABOUT IT

Inmate Treats was instructed by a correctional officer to take a copy of the form Treats had just signed, acknowledging that his radio had been confiscated. Treats refused. Twice more, he was told to take the form. When Treats turned to go back and talk with the lieutenant about this situation, the officer, without warning, sprayed Treats with capstun pepper spray. The lieutenant ran out of his office and threw Treats to the floor, where he was handcuffed. Treats was taken to the infirmary, where his eyes and skin were flushed with water. He later filed a lawsuit under

Section 1983, alleging that his Eighth Amendment constitutional rights were violated when "he was unnecessarily and unreasonably sprayed with capstun, slammed down, and handcuffed."

In response to the lawsuit, the officers moved for summary judgment, arguing that Treats had failed to state a constitutional violation and that they were entitled to qualified immunity because their use of force had been reasonable and that any harm to Treats was minimal. Do you think the officers are entitled to qualified immunity? This case was reported in *Treats v. Morgan*, 308 F.3d 868 (8th Cir. 2002).

KEY TERMS

capacity (corrections): The number of inmates or residents that a correctional facility can house.

consent decree: A decree (judgment or order of a court) that is agreed to by both parties in a lawsuit and, when approved by the court, is binding on them both.

deadly force: Force intended or likely to cause death or serious bodily harm.

ENDNOTES

1. With respect to civil rights (including prison conditions) petitions, in 1995, there were 41,679 civil rights petitions filed in U.S. district courts by state and federal prison inmates. Congress, in 1996, passed the Prison Litigation Reform Act (PLRA) in an effort to reduce the number of prisoner civil rights lawsuits. The PLRA requires an inmate to exhaust administrative remedies prior to filing suit. This act appears to have resulted in a decrease in such filings; 25,504 civil rights petitions were filed in 2000. The filing rate—the number of civil rights petitions filed per one thousand inmates—fell from 37 to 19. Scalia, J. *Prisoner Petitions Filed in U.S. District Courts, 2000, with Trends 1980-2000*. Page 1. (Washington, DC: Bureau of Justice Statistics, U.S. Department of Justice, 2002).

2. Every five years, the Bureau of Justice Statistics (BJS) compiles a census of state and federal correctional facilities. In 2005, adult correctional facilities were operating at 11% above rated capacity, an increase from 2% in 2000. Federal facilities were operating at a rate of 37% above capacity, state facilities at a rate of 8% above rated capacity, and private facilities were operating at 5% under rated capacity. Stephan, J. *Census of State and Federal Correctional Facilities, 2005*. Pages 1–3. (Washington, DC: Bureau of Justice Statistics, U.S. Department of Justice, 2008).

   One problem in approaching these figures is that there is not a universally accepted way of defining or measuring rated capacity. This is true among corrections agencies, and it is certainly a problem in court definitions of what amounts to acceptable "capacity" for prisons or jails.

3. As of December 30, 2005, 44 correctional facilities under state or federal authority were under court order to limit the size of their inmate population, with 27 of these facilities restricted to housing fewer than 250 inmates. Two hundred eighteen correctional facilities

were under court orders or consent decrees for specific conditions of confinement. Crowding, along with the lawsuits and court rulings that have accompanied it, has led to large expansions in prison and jail facilities. Between 2000 and 2005, the number of state and federal correctional facilities increased by 9%, while the number of offenders confined increased by 10%. Maximum security facilities increased by 12% (332 to 372), medium security facilities decreased by 8% (522 to 480), and minimum security facilities increased by 19% (814 to 969). Stephan, J.—see endnote 2.

4. Camp, C. G., ed. *The 2002 Corrections Yearbook—Adult Corrections.* Page 150. (Middletown, CT: Criminal Justice Institute, 2003).

5. The PLRA does not apply to relief entered by a state court that is based only upon claims arising under state law.

6. The PLRA provides for an automatic stay to begin 30 days after a motion is made to modify or terminate prospective relief under the PLRA; courts can postpone the entry of the automatic stay for up to 60 days for "good cause," which cannot include general congestion of the court's docket.

7. The district court found that attorneys were forced to wait 45 minutes to 2 hours, or longer, after arriving. The reasons given by the department involved a scarcity of meeting rooms, a need for escort officers to accompany some of the detainees, and the fact that inmates were not brought to meetings during prison counts, although they could be taken for regular visiting.

8. During an oral argument in the Supreme Court, we recall one justice asking the inmates' counsel, "Are bunk beds punishment? Because if they are, I am going to apologize to my sons." (This is confirmed in the transcript of the hearing.)

9. We do not, as a rule, comment on dissents (or the number of votes in a case decision) in discussing a ruling. In this case, however, we note that there were four dissenting justices, and two dissenting opinions written. They expressed unusually strong opinions in opposition to the majority opinion. Justice Scalia said:

> Today the Court affirms what is perhaps the most radical injunction issued by a court in our Nation's history: an order requiring California to release the staggering number of 46,000 convicted criminals.

> There comes before us, now and then, a case whose proper outcome is so clearly indicated by tradition and common sense, that its decision ought to shape the law, rather than vice versa. One would think that, before allowing the decree of a federal district court to release 46,000 convicted felons, this Court would bend every effort to read the law in such a way as to avoid that outrageous result. Today, quite to the contrary, the Court disregards stringently drawn provisions of the governing statute [the PLRA], and traditional constitutional limitations upon the power of a federal judge, in order to uphold the absurd.

> The proceedings that led to this result were a judicial travesty. I dissent because the institutional reform the District Court has undertaken violates the terms of the governing statute, ignores bedrock limitations on the power of Article III judges, and takes federal courts wildly beyond their institutional capacity.

In his dissenting opinion, Justice Alito wrote:

> The decree in this case is a perfect example of what the Prison Litigation Reform Act...was enacted to prevent. The Constitution does not give federal judges the authority to run state penal systems. Decisions regarding state prisons have profound public safety and financial implications, and the States are generally free to make these decisions as they choose." [Citing *Turner v. Safley*, 482 U.S. 78 (1987)]

> In this case, a three-judge court exceeded its authority under the Constitution and the PLRA. The court ordered a radical reduction in the California prison population without finding that the current population level violates the Constitution.

10. In some instances, actions by correctional personnel which violate the rights of persons in their custody have resulted in criminal prosecution of the staff. Title 18, U.S.C. § 242 permits prosecution of persons, including law enforcement officers and correctional officers, for willfully violating the civil rights of an individual. One such example came out of the arrest of Rodney King in California and the allegations of excessive force, which were documented on video. After the officers were acquitted on state criminal charges, the United States prosecuted some of the officers, alleging their conduct violated King's constitutional rights. *Koon v. United States,* 518 U.S. 81 (1996). Recent examples of similar civil rights prosecutions of correctional staff include *United States v. LaVallee*, 439 F.3d 670 (10th Cir. 2006), involving charges of conspiracy to violate and violating the rights of inmates at a federal penitentiary by 10 federal correctional officers. One of the officers received a federal prison term of 30 months, and two others each received terms of 41 months. In another case, a former correctional worker received a life sentence after being convicted of conspiracy to violate the rights of a detainee, which led to the detainee's death from the injuries suffered in an assault and subsequent denial of medical care (*United States v. Conatser*, 514 F.3d 508 (6th Cir. 2008)).

11. In *Grass v. Sargent*, 903 F.2d 1206 (8th Cir. 1990), the court of appeals held there was no constitutional right to smoke in prison. Perhaps as a result of the *Helling* opinion and related litigation, many prisons have gone smoke-free, both for inmates and staff.

12. See *Saucier v. Katz*, 533 U.S. 194 (2001). In *Saucier*, the Court noted that, where a defendant seeks qualified immunity, a ruling on the request should be made early in the proceedings. A favorable judicial determination of qualified immunity is an entitlement for the person not to stand trial or to face the other burdens of litigation. This rationale was again emphasized in *Pearson v. Callahan*, 555 U.S. 223 (2009).

16 | Eighth Amendment: Health Care

The government [has an] obligation to provide medical care for those whom it is punishing by incarceration. An inmate must rely on prison authorities to treat his medical needs.

It is but just that the public be required to care for the prisoner, who cannot, by reason of the deprivation of his liberty, care for himself.

U.S. Supreme Court, *Estelle v. Gamble*

Chapter Outline

- *Estelle v. Gamble*
- *West v. Atkins*
- *Washington v. Harper; Sell v. United States*
- Other Involuntary Treatment Cases
- Inmate Suicides
- *Logue v. United States*
- Special Health Care Needs of Female Prisoners
- HIV and AIDS
- Tuberculosis in Prisons
- An Aging Prison Population

It is probably evident that correctional facilities must provide inmates with health care. Health care is one of the basic needs of prisoners that the courts have recognized.[1] As a consequence of being incarcerated by the government, inmates are obviously cut off from ordinary sources of health care that they might have in the community. The Supreme Court, in the quotation from *Estelle v. Gamble* set out at the beginning of this chapter, recognized that basic requirement: for prisons to give health care to inmates. In some states, statutes or even the state constitution may specify that health care is to be provided to inmates. The statutes may be detailed, or they may just require generally that at least the emergency health needs of detainees and the necessary health care of prisoners should be provided by the government.

A few facilities in this country allow inmates to obtain their own health care in the community. This may be more prevalent in jails, and it is especially more common for inmates who have already commenced treatment for a condition and wish to continue treatment with the same provider. And, of course, it is a more likely circumstance for an inmate who has resources (health insurance or cash) to pay for his own medical care. Most prisons, as a matter of principle, do not allow inmates to obtain their own health care from a provider of their choice in the community after they are incarcerated. It is generally accepted that, as another equalizing factor whereby all inmates are treated the same, health care will be provided at a minimum for the treatment of injuries, for the diagnosis and treatment of medical conditions that require ongoing care, and for a serious medical problem that must be looked after before the inmate's release.

A development over the last 20 years has been the introduction of charges to inmates for routine health care. In 1995, only nine corrections agencies imposed such charges. In 2006, over 35 agencies reported using medical co-pay plans. Most states charged five dollars or less, and no state charged more than $10.00 (to remain consistent with other dollar amounts in chapter).[2] In the year 2000, the Federal Prisoner Health Care Copayment Act of 2000 was enacted.[3] This legislation authorized charging inmates confined in an institution under the Bureau of Prisons' jurisdiction, and those charged with or convicted of an offense against the United States, a fee for health care services. The legislation specifies that an inmate may not be refused treatment for financial reasons and also identifies a number of areas where fees may not be charged, such as for preventative health care services and mental health care. **Box 16-1** shows the Bureau of Prisons rule (published in Title 28, Code of Federal Regulations—CFR) relating to Fees for Health Care Services.

This move toward charging inmates for services rendered was initiated for a variety of reasons. The soaring cost of providing health care was one factor—charging for the care would make a small dent in those costs, but it was hoped that it would make a greater impact by reducing unnecessary inmate visits to medical services. Charging for visits and services would also bring the prison experience closer to the community one—after all, is it fair for inmates to have totally free care at the government's expense when citizens in the outside world often cannot obtain proper health care?

Setting the policy is one thing; carrying it out may be a very different and difficult thing. For example, how are the funds collected? (Inmates don't walk around with lots of cash, or checkbooks, in their pockets—at least, not in most corrections facilities.) Most prisons and jails have a "canteen" or "commissary" where an inmate may purchase some desirable items that are not provided by the government, such as snacks, toiletries, and stationery items. Purchases there are paid for by the use of a revolving account; the inmate or his family makes deposits to his account, and purchases are debited against that account. Charges for health services may be debited against that same account. What if an inmate is covered by health insurance? Collecting from insurers for small items may be more costly than it is worth, but using that insurance (including even Medicare) may be attempted for more costly procedures.

Court cases have upheld the concept of charging an inmate a fee. In *Gardner v. Wilson*, 959 F. Supp. 1224 (C.D. CA 1997), the court said there was no Eighth Amendment violation for requiring an inmate to pay a $5.00 copayment for medical care. The court noted that assuring that inmates do not abuse their access to limited medical resources is a legitimate government purpose. An appellate court, in *Reynolds v. Wagner*, 128 F.3d 166 (3rd Cir. 1997), similarly said that charging inmates modest fees for medical services is not per se unconstitutional. That court said this practice teaches prisoners financial responsibility and deters the abuse of sick call— goals that are within the scope of legitimate penological objectives. In the same context, a federal

Box 16-1 Subpart F-Fees for Health Care Services

§ 549.70 Purpose and scope.

(a) The Bureau of Prisons (Bureau) may, under certain circumstances, charge you, an inmate under our care and custody, a fee for providing you with health care services.

(b) Generally, if you are an inmate as described in § 549.71, you must pay a fee for health care services of $2.00 per health care visit if you:

   (1) Receive health care services in connection with a health care visit that you requested, (except for services described in § 549.72); or

   (2) Are found responsible through the Disciplinary Hearing Process to have injured an inmate who, as a result of the injury, requires a health care visit.

§ 549.71 Inmates affected.
This subpart applies to:

(a) Any individual incarcerated in an institution under the Bureau's jurisdiction; or

(b) Any other individual, as designated by the Director, who has been charged with or convicted of an offense against the United States.

§ 549.72 Services provided without fees.
We will not charge a fee for:

(a) Health care services based on staff referrals;

(b) Staff-approved follow-up treatment for a chronic condition;

(c) Preventive health care services;

(d) Emergency services;

(e) Prenatal care;

(f) Diagnosis or treatment of chronic infectious diseases;

(g) Mental health care; or

(h) Substance abuse treatment.

§ 549.73 Appealing the fee.
You may seek review of issues related to health service fees through the Bureau's Administrative Remedy Program (see 28 CFR part 542).

§ 549.74 Inmates without funds.
You will not be charged a health care service fee if you are considered indigent and unable to pay the health care service fee. The Warden may establish procedures to prevent abuse of this provision.

Source: Reprinted from the Federal Bureau of Prisons, published in Title 28 CFR, Subpart F - Fees for Health Care Services (Revised as of July 1, 2010).

court, in *Hutchinson v. Belt*, 957 F.Supp. 97 (W.D. LA 1996), said there was no constitutional right to *free* medical care.

We first will look here at what the constitutional requirements are. Is a prisoner entitled to medical treatment and care for any health problems she may have? How much health care does the state have to provide? In what circumstances will a prison official be liable, under the U.S. Constitution, for failing to provide health care? These questions, as far as defining constitutional violations and the requirements under 42 U.S.C. § 1983, are decided under the Eighth Amendment. (For pretrial detainees, as pointed out in *Bell v. Wolfish*, 441 U.S. 520 (1979), they are decided under the Fourteenth Amendment on the basis of the due process clause. As a practical matter, the standards for providing care are virtually the same for pretrial detainees and for sentenced inmates. The two constitutional provisions do not result in much difference as to the kind of care that must be provided. There may, of course, be different standards established locally by state or local legislation or by court rulings about what is required for detainees.)

■ *Estelle v. Gamble*

The governing constitutional case on providing health care in prisons is *Estelle v. Gamble*, 429 U.S. 97 (1976). As we have noted, the Supreme Court started with the principle that the government must provide medical care to those whom it has imprisoned.

Gamble was an inmate in the Texas Department of Corrections. He was injured at work when a bale of cotton fell on him. When he complained, he was sent to the hospital. From there, he was sent to his cell to rest. When he returned to the hospital with increased pain, he was given pain pills. The next day, he saw a doctor, who prescribed a pain reliever and a muscle relaxant. He was placed on medical orders on "cell-pass," meaning he stayed in his cell except for showers. After a week, the doctor prescribed another pain reliever. Despite continuing pain, the doctor said Gamble could return to light work. When Gamble refused to work, he was taken before a prison disciplinary committee, which ordered him to be seen by another doctor. This second doctor ran tests and prescribed additional medication. Gamble was ordered several times to go to work, but he continued to refuse, saying he was in too much pain. He eventually was placed in solitary confinement as a disciplinary sanction for refusing to work. He then claimed chest pains and "blank outs." He was seen one time in the hospital for these complaints. When he reported continuing pains to guards in administrative segregation, he was twice refused permission to see a doctor. He filed his complaint in court, under Section 1983, claiming cruel and unusual punishment in his medical care.

The core of the Supreme Court's opinion is based on a concern over denial of medical care to prisoners, which leads to unnecessary pain and suffering. Such unnecessary suffering would be inconsistent with "contemporary standards of decency," which of course is the concern of the "evolving" Eighth Amendment proscription against cruel and unusual punishments.

> **We therefore conclude that deliberate indifference to serious medical needs of prisoners constitutes the "unnecessary and wanton infliction of pain" proscribed by the Eighth Amendment. This is true whether the indifference is manifested by prison doctors in their**

response to the prisoner's needs or by prison guards in intentionally denying or delaying access to medical care or intentionally interfering with the treatment once prescribed. Regardless of how evidenced, deliberate indifference to a prisoner's serious illness or injury states a cause of action under Section 1983.

The Court then went on to note that "an inadvertent failure to provide adequate medical care" would not be a "wanton infliction of unnecessary pain" so as to constitute a constitutional violation. More to the point,

> **[A] complaint that a physician has been negligent in diagnosing or treating a medical condition does not state a valid claim of medical mistreatment under the Eighth Amendment. Medical malpractice does not become a constitutional violation merely because the victim is a prisoner. In order to state a cognizable claim, a prisoner must allege acts or omissions sufficiently harmful to evidence deliberate indifference to serious medical needs. It is only such indifference that can offend "evolving standards of decency" in violation of the Eighth Amendment.**

Applying these standards to the claims written and filed by inmate Gamble, the Court concluded that he had not shown that there was deliberate indifference to his medical complaints. He was seen by medical personnel on 17 occasions during a three-month period. He was treated for three conditions that they identified after examining and testing him. Although Gamble claimed more testing should have been done, especially regarding his lower-back complaints (and the court of appeals had agreed with him on that), the patient complaining of that particular problem points to "a classic example of a matter for medical judgment," the Court said. Failure to order certain tests or medications does not constitute cruel and unusual punishment. At most, it would suggest negligence, or medical malpractice, and that is not a constitutional level of concern. (It would be properly considered, the Court indicated, under the Texas Tort Claims Act.)

West v. Atkins

Having decided the constitutional standard to assess health care in prisons, other litigation explores the reach of the "deliberate indifference" standard of *Estelle v. Gamble* or looks at how it may apply in different kinds of circumstances. One question is whether the Eighth Amendment (and its application by Section 1983) applies to private physicians and other health care providers who offer services to prison or jail inmates. Corrections is turning more and more frequently to the private sector to provide services in different areas of prison and jail operations. Some jurisdictions have contracted with private companies to build and run complete institutions for the state or local government. Others have contracted to provide one area of services for an institution or for an entire state. The two most commonly contracted services are food services and health care. (There are companies that specialize in providing food or health services just for corrections agencies.)

In *West v. Atkins,* 487 U.S. 42 (1988), the Supreme Court addressed the question of "whether a physician who is under contract with the State to provide medical services to inmates at a state-prison hospital on a part-time basis acts 'under color of state law' within the meaning of 42 U.S.C. § 1983, when he treats an inmate." West, an inmate at a North Carolina prison, tore his Achilles tendon while playing volleyball. He was sent to the Central Prison Hospital in Raleigh, the principal medical facility for state inmates. There, Dr. Atkins, a private physician who worked under contract with the state, provided orthopedic services and treated West. West was not allowed, as a prisoner, to see a physician of his own choosing. Atkins placed West's leg in a series of casts. West alleged in his lawsuit that Atkins said surgery would be necessary but that the doctor refused to schedule it. West sued under Section 1983, claiming violation of his constitutional right to be free from cruel and unusual punishments. He alleged that Dr. Atkins was deliberately indifferent to his serious medical needs when he failed to provide adequate treatment (the surgery the doctor himself had recommended).

Lower courts took different positions on the claim (as to whether Section 1983 would apply to the contract physician), but the Fourth Circuit ended up affirming and applying the position it had taken in *Calvert v. Sharp,* 748 F.2d 861 (4th Cir. 1984), where it held that a contract physician who provided services to Maryland inmates did not act "under color of state law," which was required to pursue a Section 1983 action. The Supreme Court reversed.

Acting under color of state law is an essential element of pursuing a Section 1983 action, and it is an implicit element of pursuing a claim of violation of the Fourteenth Amendment (which applies to "State" actions). The Eighth Amendment also requires state action, or inaction, because cruel and unusual punishments can only be inflicted by the states—not by private parties (who have no authority to punish at all). The Court in *West* relied on the guidance of other Section 1983 decisions that:

> [A]cting under color of state law requires that the defendant in a [Section] 1983 action have exercised power "possessed by virtue of state law and made possible only because the wrongdoer is clothed with the authority of state law." ... It is firmly established that a defendant in a [Section] 1983 suit acts under color of state law when he abuses the position given to him by the State.

This requirement is comparatively easy to apply when the action is taken by a government official, because a state employee acts under color of state law whenever he acts in his official capacity, exercising his responsibilities under the law. (One type of government employee is exempted from Section 1983 by a Supreme Court decision: a public defender. The defender has been shielded from Section 1983 liability on the grounds that he retains the attributes of a private attorney, keeping especially his independence from state interference, indeed, operating often in opposition to the state. The Court in *West* distinguished the role of a prison doctor from that of the public defender.)

The Supreme Court said that it is the physician's function for the prison system, not the nature of his employment, which determines whether his actions are attributable to the state.

> Contracting out prison medical care does not relieve the State of its constitutional duty to provide adequate medical treatment to those in its custody, and it does not deprive the

State's prisoners of the means to vindicate their Eighth Amendment rights.... It is the physician's function while working for the State, not the amount of time he spends in performance of those duties or the fact that he may be employed by others to perform similar duties, that determines whether he is acting under color of state law. In the State's employ, [Dr. Atkins] worked as a physician at the prison hospital fully vested with state authority to fulfill essential aspects of the duty, placed on the State by the Eighth Amendment and state law, to provide essential medical care to those the State had incarcerated. Doctor Atkins must be considered to be a state actor.

The case was remanded to pursue the Section 1983 action in trial court—that is, to determine whether Dr. Atkins acted with deliberate indifference to West's serious medical needs and, thus, violated his constitutional right to be free from cruel and unusual punishment.

■ *Washington v. Harper; Sell v. United States*

Another important aspect of medical treatment, and one that is as pressing an issue in prison health care as it is in private community medical treatment, is the question of involuntary treatment of the patient. This becomes especially important in the care of mentally ill patients, where staff must know when they are permitted to intervene without the patient's consent to provide treatment. The Supreme Court, in *Washington v. Harper*, 494 U.S. 210 (1990), addressed this question.

Sometimes, medical staff must make the decision to provide treatment when the patient cannot decide for himself—for example, when he is unconscious or mentally incompetent. For the unconscious prison patient, the decision would be made on the same grounds as it would be in the outside community: if care must be given to avoid or ameliorate a life-threatening situation, or if circumstances, which if left untreated, could result in serious, long-term adverse consequences, then the medical staff are justified in taking those emergency steps to assist the patient.[4] For the incompetent patient, there may be a guardian who has been given authority to make decisions regarding medical care on behalf of the patient. In some jurisdictions, courts have said that wardens or jail superintendents stand in the place of guardians, and if medical care is needed for the benefit of the inmate patient, in a serious, health-threatening situation, the warden or superintendent may make that decision on behalf of the inmate. If there is no guardian who is known or who is available to give the necessary consent, application may need to be made to a court to appoint a guardian. Advice of counsel should always be sought to determine what the local judicial view is on the authority of the warden or superintendent to act and whether the appointment of a guardian should be sought.

The second situation for providing involuntary medical care arises when the patient does not wish to be treated. The question then becomes, when do inmates have the right to refuse medical treatment? Unfortunately, the decision in *Harper* does not give us definitive guidance about the constitutional standards to be used in assessing circumstances that may require treatment over the patient's objections. Harper was an inmate in the state of Washington who was given antipsychotic medication despite his refusal to take it. Although the case would seem to have some Eighth Amendment concerns embedded in it, it was decided as a due process case under the Fourteenth Amendment. The Court held that the decision to involuntarily medicate the inmate did involve his liberty interest—his desire to make his own decisions to remain unmedicated. Therefore, due process protections would apply to the decision-making process. In other words, the patient did have a constitutional right to refuse medication.

That right of the inmate to refuse treatment (medication) could be overcome by the state, the Court said, based on the context of his status of confinement.

> **The State has undertaken the obligation to provide prisoners with medical treatment consistent not only with their own medical interests, but also with the needs of the institution. Prison administrators have not only an interest in ensuring the safety of prison staffs and administrative personnel ... but the duty to take reasonable measures for the prisoner's own safety.... Where an inmate's mental disability is the root cause of the threat he poses to the prison population, the State's interest in decreasing the danger to others necessarily encompasses an interest in providing him with medical treatment for his illness.**

Washington authorities had well-established, nonjudicial administrative procedures that had to be followed prior to involuntarily medicating a prisoner, and the Supreme Court approved the state's approach. (Just how much less than Washington's procedures might also be acceptable is not made clear.) The Court did specify that treatment could not be given just to control or improve the inmate's disruptive or difficult behavior.

The state policy was approved, because:

> **[I]ts exclusive application is to inmates who are mentally ill and who, as a result of their illness, are gravely disabled or represent a significant danger to themselves or others. The drugs may be administered for no purpose other than treatment, and only under the direction of a licensed psychiatrist.**

The Court rejected the inmate's argument that, rather than forced administration of the drugs, alternative means of treatment, such as physical restraints or seclusion, should have been used. The Court said that it had not been shown that those alternatives would be as effective as medication.

> **We hold that, given the requirements of the prison environment, the Due Process Clause permits the State to treat a prison inmate who has a serious mental illness with antipsychotic drugs against his will, if the inmate is dangerous to himself or others and the treatment is in the inmate's medical interest.**

The concept of *Harper* was carried further in the Supreme Court decision in *Sell v. United States*, 539 U.S. 166 (2003). The case involved the issue of whether the government could administer antipsychotic medication against the defendant–inmate's will, solely to render him competent to stand trial for serious, but nonviolent offenses. Sell, a dentist, was charged with making false representations in connection with health care payments. An initial mental health assessment determined that he was competent to stand trial, but there existed potential for a psychotic episode. While on bail, he was accused of attempting to intimidate a witness and was brought before a magistrate judge. His behavior in the judge's words was "totally out of control" at this hearing and included his spitting in the judge's face. Sell's bail was subsequently revoked, and he was detained. A new indictment was later brought against him, charging him with an attempt to kill a witness and an FBI agent.

Sell was sent to the Medical Center for Federal Prisoners in Springfield, Missouri. He was determined by two clinicians to need antipsychotic medication to restore him to competency, so that he could stand trial. Sell said he did not want to take the medication. Lower federal court rulings held that Sell could be forcibly medicated in order to make him competent to stand trial. The case was taken to the Supreme Court, which followed the guidelines it had set forth in *Harper*.

> In *Harper*, this Court recognized that an individual has a "significant" constitutionally protected "liberty interest" in "avoiding the unwanted administration of antipsychotic drugs."

> [T]he Constitution permits the Government involuntarily to administer antipsychotic drugs to a mentally ill defendant facing serious criminal charges in order to render that defendant competent to stand trial, but only if the treatment is medically appropriate, is substantially unlikely to have side effects that may undermine the fairness of the trial, and, taking account of less intrusive alternatives, is necessary significantly to further important governmental trial-related interests.

The Court in *Sell* further noted that in *Riggins v. Nevada*, 504 U.S. 127 (1992), it had again stated that a person has a "constitutionally protected liberty 'interest in avoiding involuntary administration of antipsychotic drugs'—an interest that only an 'essential' or 'overriding' state interest might overcome."

The Court in *Sell* continued by providing detailed directions. The Court stated that a court must find that there are important governmental interests at stake; that administration of the drugs is substantially likely to make the defendant competent to stand trial; that involuntary medication is necessary to further those interests; that there are no alternative, less intrusive treatments; and that administration of the drugs is in the patient's best medical interests. With these detailed directions for a trial court to use, the case was remanded (returned) for consideration as to whether the guidelines were met in Sell's case and would support a continuing order for forced medication.

We emphasize that *Sell* applies to persons awaiting trial. It is of interest, therefore, primarily to trial courts and to the lawyers (prosecutors and defense counsel) who handle criminal cases in which the mental competency of the defendant is at issue. These concerns are often of interest to prison and jail staff, because those pretrial inmates are usually held in prison or jail hospitals (as Sell was).

■ Other Involuntary Treatment Cases

Medical treatment can come in many forms, including testing and treatment for communicable diseases; providing nutrition and hydration necessary to maintain life; or receiving other medical interventions, such as insulin for diabetes or kidney dialysis treatment. While the interests of the state also are diverse, lower federal courts and the highest appellate courts of some states have identified several important governmental interests that might outweigh the individual's right to refuse medical treatment: (1) preservation of life; (2) protection of innocent third parties; (3) the prevention of suicide; and (4) the maintenance of the ethical integrity of the medical profession. With the addition of the incarcerated individual, a fifth interest—maintaining prison security and orderly administration—can be added. *McNabb v. Department of Corrections*, 180 P.3d 1257 (Wash. 2008).

In *Commissioner of Corrections v. Myers*, 399 N.E.2d 452 (MA 1979), the prisoner refused to continue with kidney dialysis treatment as a form of protest over his placement in a medium, rather than a minimum security prison. The court specifically noted that the inmate's refusal had "little to do with his disease," was unrelated to any religious objections, nor did he wish to die. After the court weighed the factors of preservation of life, protection of third parties, prevention of suicide, the ethical integrity of the medical profession, and the integrity of the correctional system, it ruled the state's interest in prison operation justified intervention:

> [T]he State's interest in upholding orderly prison administration tips the balance in favor of authorizing treatment without consent. Our evaluation of this interest takes account of the threat posed to prison order, security and discipline by a failure to prevent the death of an inmate who attempts to manipulate his placement within the prison by refusing life-saving treatment.[5]

A similar situation existed in *Singletary v. Costello*, 665 So.2d 1099 (Fla. Ct. App. 1996). Costello fasted to protest his punitive transfer to another institution and also to protest what he said was a false disciplinary report. Medical staff determined that failure to intervene in his case would result in his death (in effect, his suicide). The issue was whether the inmate had the legal right to refuse medical treatment and intervention. As in *Myers*, this inmate did not actually want to die; rather, his fast was done as a form of protest, with the object of resolving his complaints.

The Florida court held that the inmate (so long as he was competent) had the fundamental right to refuse medical treatment. The task was balancing this right against the state's interest. This court held that the state's interest in the preservation of life was not sufficient to overcome the inmate's fundamental right to refuse life-sustaining medical treatment. Refusing medical treatment would not endanger public health, the court said. Further, the interest in the protection of innocent third parties did not apply in this case, as there was no evidence of minor children depending on the inmate. Thus, this inmate could refuse medical treatment and pursue his self-induced hunger strike.

There we have it: similar fact patterns with apparently different holdings. The word "apparently" is used because the court in *Singletary* noted that the state had not produced any evidence that Costello's hunger strike had posed any security risk to the correctional facility.

In *Thor v. Superior Court*, 855 P.2d 375 (CA 1996), an inmate who was serving a life sentence fractured a cervical vertebra while in prison and became paraplegic as a result. The inmate refused to be fed and refused medication and other treatment. Psychiatrists said he was depressed, but he was mentally competent to understand his medical condition and the consequences of his actions, which were leading to his severe deterioration and ultimate death. Health staff members went to court to get permission to forcibly medicate and feed the inmate. The Supreme Court of California ruled that, under California law, the competent inmate had a right to refuse unwanted medical treatment, even though it would certainly result in his death. Unlike the prisoner in *Myers* discussed above, the prisoner's refusal to eat and receive treatment was not an attempt to manipulate prison officials or to undermine prison integrity or public safety. In denying the petition, and allowing the prisoner to refuse treatment, the court said:

> [A] competent, informed adult has a fundamental right of self-determination to refuse or demand the withdrawal of medical treatment of any form irrespective of the personal consequences…[I]n the absence of evidence demonstrating a threat to institutional security or public safety, prison officials, including medical personnel, have no affirmative duty to administer such treatment and may not deny a person incarcerated in state prison this freedom of choice.

There are many peripheral questions that spin off this basic question of involuntary medical treatment. One is the administration of drugs for the purpose of the rehabilitation of the inmate. In *Knecht v. Gillman*, 488 F.2d 1136 (8th Cir. 1973), inmates complained that they had been injected with the drug apomorphine without their consent. Prison staff members testified that the drug was used for its negative, adverse effects; it was used for inmates who had disruptive behavioral problems. A physician said that the drug was used when inmates did not get out of bed or when they swore or lied to the staff. The drug induced vomiting for 15 minutes to an hour. Although the drug was prescribed and administered in a medical facility of the prison system where patients were sent for treatment of mental incompetency and mental illnesses, its use, as shown in this case, was for the behavior modification of disorderly inmates. The Eighth Circuit Court of Appeals disapproved this practice:

> **[T]he act of forcing someone to vomit for a fifteen minute period for committing some minor breach of the rules can only be regarded as cruel and unusual unless the treatment is being administered to a patient who knowingly and intelligently has consented to it….The use of this unproven drug for this purpose on an involuntary basis, is, in our opinion, cruel and unusual punishment prohibited by the Eighth Amendment.**

A case of the same sort, which does not deal with health care at all but is an interesting case of involuntary treatment for the good of the inmate, is *Rutherford v. Hutto*, 377 F.Supp. 268 (E.D. AR 1974). Rutherford, an inmate at the Cummins Unit in Arkansas, complained that he was being forced to attend school against his will. He said that this constituted cruel and unusual punishment in violation of the Eighth and Fourteenth Amendments.

Rutherford was 43 years old and illiterate. He had very little formal education, because, he said, his parents took him out of school in the first or second grade when he had typhoid fever, and he never returned to school. He testified that sitting in a classroom made him extremely nervous. He claimed that he had a constitutional right to remain ignorant and illiterate. Prison officials said that he had to attend classes eight hours a day, one day each week. The prison (like most prisons) offered the equivalent of a 12-grade school, with academic and vocational courses. Inmates were required to attend classes until they reached the fourth-grade level in their education. (That has been a commonly used standard to measure literacy.) Participation in school programs was voluntary beyond the fourth grade. Rutherford had even made some progress in school, despite his objections, because he was reading at the second-grade level when the lawsuit was filed, and he had shown some improvement in arithmetic skills. The federal district court supported the program.

> [A] State clearly has a right to undertake to rehabilitate its convicts....Granting the right of a State to try to rehabilitate the inmates of its penal institutions, the Court does not think that it should necessarily be left up to an individual convict to determine whether or not he is to participate in a rehabilitative program such as the one involved here....[T]he Court does not consider that a convict has any more right to refuse to be given a chance to benefit from a rehabilitative program than he has to refuse to work or to obey other lawful orders that may be given him by prison personnel.

Finally, and emphatically, this district court stated:

> The "constitutional right to be ignorant" or the "constitutional right to remain uneducated," which petitioner postulates, simply does not exist....[T]he Court holds that a State has a sufficient interest in eliminating illiteracy among its convicts to justify it in requiring illiterate convicts, including adults, to attend classes designed to bring them up to at least the fourth grade educational level.[6]

If the inmate refused to attend classes, he could be disciplined by prison officials, the court said.

Although the term "involuntary treatment" is ordinarily used to refer to medical or mental health care, *Rutherford* is a case that shows that courts will also support prison officials in pursuing other programs "for the good of the inmate." Sensitivity to requiring attendance at school is probably not as strong as forcing unwanted medication or other medical treatment, but the principle is very similar.

■ Inmate Suicides

It is an unfortunate fact that suicides are a significant problem that corrections administrators have to face. In 2007, 6.3% of the 3,388 deaths of state prisoners and 25.9% of the 1,102 deaths of persons in local jails were caused by suicide.[7] Many persons committed to jails and prisons have mental problems, and the stress of confinement adds to the concerns of those people. Depression, no doubt, is as prevalent among inmates as it is among the general citizenry. Staff members must always be on the lookout for suicidal tendencies among inmates and should be trained to look for the symptoms of a suicidal inmate. Suicide prevention programs have been instituted in many facilities and are recommended for all types of institutions. A review of available records about an inmate should always include looking for signs of suicidal inclinations. The screening of an inmate at admission should also involve an attempt to spot the suicide problem case. Courts have emphasized this concern that correctional officials must address.

A psychological or psychiatric condition can be as serious as any physical pathology or injury, especially when it results in suicidal tendencies. And just as a failure to act to save a detainee from suffering from gangrene might violate the duty to provide reasonable medical care absent an intervening legitimate government objective, failure to take any steps to save a suicidal detainee from injuring himself may also constitute a due process violation under *Bell v. Wolfish*.

This quotation is from *Partridge v. Two Unknown Police Officers*, 791 F.2d 1182 (5th Cir. 1986). Although corrections staff must always be on the alert for the suicidal inmate in their facility, the fact that an inmate has killed himself does not necessarily mean that officials are constitutionally liable for the death. Deliberate indifference to the suicidal tendencies of the inmate must be shown in the circumstances of each case. It has been observed in *Freedman v. City of Allentown*, 853 F.2d 1111 (3rd Cir. 1988), that jail officials cannot guarantee the safety of inmates and that inmates who are truly intent on killing themselves will probably be able to do so eventually. Deliberate indifference requires a "strong likelihood" rather than a "mere possibility" that self-inflicted harm will occur. *Gish v. Thomas,* 516 F.3d 952 (11th Cir. 2008).

In the case of *Heflin v. Stewart County*, 958 F.2d 709 (6th Cir. 1992), the court upheld a jury award to the family of a jail inmate who hanged himself. Inmate Heflin was found hanging in his cell, but the deputy sheriff ordered that his body should remain hanging until a doctor or emergency medical staff arrived. When medical staff did arrive (after some 20 minutes), Heflin was cut down, but he died soon thereafter. The appeals court noted a basic principle:

[P]retrial detainees have a constitutional right to the same protection afforded convicted prisoners who have serious medical needs.

While the Supreme Court has not yet affirmed this same principle, it appears to be a sound holding, based on the language and concerns of *Bell v. Wolfish*. Applying that principle to the facts of this case, the court of appeals agreed with the result in the lower (trial) court, finding that the deputy sheriff should have immediately cut down the inmate and administered CPR, because he was trained in that procedure. In these circumstances, "the unlawfulness of doing nothing to attempt to save Heflin's life would have been apparent to a reasonable official in [the deputy's] position." Thus, there was a finding of negligence on the part of the deputy. There was also apparently deliberate indifference (the constitutional standard) toward the condition of the inmate. These facts and findings would support both a common law tort claim, and a claim of constitutional violation of the inmate's rights.

Reed v. Woodruff County, 7 F.3d 808 (8th Cir. 1993), another case of a jail suicide, had similar facts but a very different result. A trustee prisoner was found hanging in a shower stall, where it was determined that he had died (apparently unintentionally) while engaging in "autoerotic asphyxiation"—using hanging to bring about sexual gratification. Staff had been aware that the inmate was not in his cell. They had not found him until he had hanged himself, and he was dead when he was found. His family claimed that his death was the result of negligence and that there was also a violation of his constitutional rights. Under Arkansas law, the county was immune from a negligence suit. The family said that the jailer who found the inmate (the jailer was a trained emergency medical technician) should have attempted to resuscitate him and that his failure to do so showed deliberate indifference, a constitutional violation. The federal court of appeals disagreed (and reversed a lower court), holding that there was no obligation to try to revive the prisoner when the trained jailer determined that he was dead. There was no evidence that an attempt to resuscitate could have succeeded, and, therefore, there was no constitutional violation.

Myers v. County of Lake, 30 F.3d 847 (7th Cir. 1994), involved an attempted suicide by a juvenile detainee. The 16-year-old tried to hang himself in a county facility but was unsuccessful. However, he suffered permanent brain damage and was awarded $600,000 in a suit alleging negligence against the county officials. (A claim for a constitutional violation had been dismissed by a magistrate, who found there was no evidence of deliberate indifference to support a constitutional-level claim.) Applying Indiana state law, a jury had found that the detention facility was negligent in not taking adequate precautions against suicide attempts. The federal appeals court upheld this judgment, concluding that state law required institutions to use reasonable care to prevent suicides by their wards. The court acknowledged that all suicides could not be prevented but said that taking reasonable measures to prevent them was required. The county argued that it was severely "starved" for funds and that the facility in question was shorthanded, so appropriate steps could not be taken to identify and protect those who were suicide risks. The court rejected this as a defense. Although the lack of funds and adequate staffing might have meant that no individuals were negligent, the county could not use lack of funds to defend against a claim that it had failed to perform its legally required functions.

There are a number of cases in which courts held that the circumstances were not sufficient to show deliberate indifference because there was not enough evidence to make officials aware of the suicidal risk. In *Freedman v. City of Allentown*, 853 F.2d 1111 (3rd Cir. 1988), officers were not liable because they did not realize that scars on the inmate's wrists and neck were from previous suicide attempts. In *State Bank v. Camic,* 712 F.2d 1140 (7th Cir. 1983), signs that an arrestee was intoxicated, unruly, and violent were not enough to conclude that there was a high risk of suicide. In *Boyd v. Harper*, 702 F.Supp. 578 (E.D. VA 1988), an arrestee who was crying continuously in his cell just before he committed suicide did not show a strong likelihood of being suicidal.

In *Collins v. Seeman*, 462 F.3d 757 (7th Cir. 2006), the court of appeals affirmed a grant of summary judgment to prison officials, even though the prisoner, after telling staff he was suicidal, successfully committed suicide. The prisoner advised a correctional officer that he wanted to see a counselor because he was feeling "suicidal." The officer immediately initiated suicide prevention procedures, including advising his supervisors. Supervisory staff implemented other procedures, including notifying the institution's "crisis counselor" who located the inmate's file and began to review it. The officer who reported the inmate was suicidal also returned to the prisoner's cell and advised him the crisis counselor would be there "as soon as she could." This officer and another, who was made aware of the threat, also looked in on the inmate. These contacts did not reflect the inmate was in distress and the inmate told staff he was all right. Less than one hour after first telling the officer he felt suicidal, the inmate was found hanging in his cell (using a bed sheet).

The court of appeals ruled in this case that the subjective component of an Eighth Amendment claim requires a showing the defendant both "subjectively knew the prisoner was at substantial risk of committing suicide," and the defendant intentionally disregarded the risk. It is not enough to demonstrate that the defendant "should have been aware" of the risk. The court said that the official must be aware of facts from which an inference of substantial risk of serious harm exists, and the official must also draw that inference. "In other words, the defendant must be cognizant of the significant likelihood that an inmate may imminently seek to take his own life." Because prison officials responded in a reasonable manner to the risk of inmate suicide, they were entitled to qualified immunity even though the inmate committed suicide.

Logue v. United States

In *Logue v. United States*, 412 U.S. 521 (1973), the Supreme Court dealt with the death of a jail inmate. Logue was arrested by U.S. marshals on charges of smuggling marijuana into the United States. He was placed in the Nueces County Jail in Texas to await trial. (Most federal detainees awaiting trial were, and are placed in state and local jails, which contract with the federal government to hold a certain number of inmates. This is because, in most localities, there are so few federal defendants being held that it is not economically feasible to build a separate federal jail. The federal government has built jails in some large cities, such as the Metropolitan Correctional Center in New York City, which was discussed in *Bell v. Wolfish*.) Logue committed suicide in the jail by hanging himself. His parents sued the United States for his wrongful death under the Federal Tort Claims Act.

The Supreme Court held that, even though Logue was placed in the jail as a federal prisoner by a deputy U.S. marshal, he was under the control of the local sheriff and his staff and not that of the marshal. To be liable under the Tort Claims Act, any negligent action had to be done by a "federal agency." The jail was a contractor with the federal government, not a federal agency. The Tort Claims Act specifically excluded a contractor with the United States from the definition of a federal agency. This insulated the United States from liability for the negligent acts or omissions of the jail's employees. However, there was a question whether the deputy U.S. marshal, knowing that Logue had some suicidal tendencies, should have alerted the jail officials to that problem and should have made sure there were arrangements to place Logue under constant surveillance. The Supreme Court said that knowing that there was a serious suicidal risk and failing to take steps to avoid the suicide could have amounted to negligence, the standard for liability under the Tort Claims Act. The case was sent back for the lower courts to ascertain whether the federal employee was negligent regarding that one aspect of the inmate's death.

Special Health Care Needs of Female Prisoners

At times, it may become necessary for prisoners to be hospitalized for necessary medical care. During these hospitalizations, correctional personnel supervise and, when necessary, apply appropriate restraints, including shackling the offender to minimize the risk of escape. In *Nelson v. Correctional Medical Services*, 583 F.3d 522 (8th Cir. 2009), the court of appeals addressed the issue of whether the application of restraints (shackling both legs to the opposite side rails of a hospital bed) to a female prisoner who was in active labor constituted deliberate indifference to a serious medical need. The prisoner argued that the shackling had caused "extreme mental anguish and pain, permanent hip injury, torn stomach muscles, and an umbilical hernia [that required] surgical repair." Prison policy authorized the use of shackles "only when circumstances require the protection of inmates, staff, or other individuals from potential harm or to deter the possibility of escape."

The court of appeals upheld the denial of qualified immunity to the escorting officer who was responsible for applying the restraints. The court ruled that based upon medical evidence presented to the trial court, shackling a prisoner in active labor posed a danger both to the prisoner and the fetus. The court also ruled a fact finder could conclude the officer was subjectively aware of the prisoner's pain and that the officer was aware that it would be unnecessary to shackle a very sick inmate or pregnant inmate in active labor.

The medical needs of female prisoners must also be considered when the female prisoner elects to terminate a pregnancy. In *Victoria W. v. Larpenter*, 369 F.3d 474 (5th Cir. 2004), a female prisoner serving a short sentence learned she was pregnant. She advised officials she wished to have an elective abortion. The facility had a policy requiring all prisoners seeking any elective medical treatment to obtain a court order. Officials met with the inmate and explained the policy to both her and her attorney. The prisoner's attorney filed a motion with the local court to have the prisoner released from her sentence but did not seek a court order authorizing her release and transport to receive an abortion. By the time of her release, the month following her hearing, it was too late to have an abortion. She sued various correctional officials and the political subdivision (a Louisiana parish), claiming her rights to obtain an elective abortion and to be free from cruel and unusual punishment were violated. The district court granted summary judgment in favor of the defendants, and the court of appeals affirmed. The court of appeals used the factors set forth in *Turner v. Safley*, 482 U.S. 78 (1987), to rule that the policy was constitutional. Because prison officials in *Victoria W.* presented evidence the policy was based on legitimate penological grounds, including security, the policy was found to be reasonable: "The policy's aim is to maximize inmate security and avoid liability. Nothing suggests that its purpose or effect was to deter abortions.... To the contrary, because the policy is reasonably related to legitimate penological interests, we find that it was constitutionally permissible."[8]

Another case dealing with a female prisoner's right to choose to have an elective abortion is *Roe v. Crawford*, 514 F.3d 789 (8th Cir. 2008). In 2005, the Missouri Department of Corrections (MDC) changed its policy from one of providing transportation for inmates wanting to terminate their pregnancies to one of allowing such transportation only where the abortion is indicated "due to threat to the mother's life or health, and if approved by the Medical Director in consultation with the Regional Medical Director." In *Roe,* a female prisoner requested transportation to obtain an elective abortion and was denied. She sued, challenging the policy as a violation of her rights under the Fourteenth and Eighth Amendments. After the case was certified as a class action (on behalf of all female prisoners in the custody of the department of corrections), the district court struck down the new policy as violating the inmates' rights under both the Fourteenth and Eighth Amendments. The appeals court affirmed the lower court's judgment but did find that the district court erred in its Eighth Amendment analysis and on one part of its *Turner* analysis.

In holding the new policy unconstitutional, the district court applied the four-factor analysis used in *Turner v. Safley*. The appeals court determined that the state did provide a valid, rational security concern (the first *Turner* factor) by its reference to "the existence of protesters and the configuration of the clinic result[ing] in higher risks to the guards and inmates, as well as a greater potential for inmates to escape." The appeals court, citing the deference owed prison officials, held that the district court erred in finding the MDC policy irrational because there had been no prior problems.

Examining the other three *Turner* factors, the courts found these were not met in *Roe*. The second factor, alternative means of obtaining an elective abortion, did not exist. Once incarcerated in the MDC, an elective abortion, which the Supreme Court determined is a liberty interest protected under the Fourteenth Amendment, is *entirely* unavailable. (Emphasis in original.) By completely eliminating any alternative means of obtaining an elective abortion, the MDC policy represents precisely the "exaggerated response to... security objectives" that *Turner* forbids.

In similar manner, the third and fourth factors of *Turner* were found not to be in favor of the MDC. On the third *Turner* factor, impact on other inmates and prison resources, the court found "the policy does not logically reduce the overall number of [trips]" and that cost savings would be minimal. Finally, the court ruled that the correctional department's previous policy of permitting elective abortions "represents a ready alternative." Following its analysis, the court of appeals held the new policy violated the Fourteenth Amendment rights of female prisoners.

The court of appeals, however, reversed the district court's finding that the policy violated the Eighth Amendment rights of prisoners. The state had argued that an elective abortion was by definition not necessary and therefore could not be a serious medical need. The court of appeals ruled:

> We hold an elective, non-therapeutic abortion does not constitute a serious medical need, and a prison institution's refusal to provide an inmate with access to an elective, non-therapeutic abortion does not rise to the level of deliberate indifference to constitute an Eighth Amendment violation.

Readers are reminded that the *Roe v. Crawford* opinion is binding only within the Eighth Circuit and that the policy was found not to violate a prisoner's Eighth Amendment rights. This part of the ruling must be read in conjunction with its earlier portion that found that the state's policy which prohibited all elective abortions violated the prisoner's rights under the Fourteenth Amendment.

■ HIV and AIDS

In recent years, corrections administrators, in addition to the challenges of managing prisons and jails that were crowded and providing health care with scant resources, have had to confront the outbreak of a particularly deadly (and costly) disease—HIV/AIDS. Identified in the U.S. population in 1981, and not taken very seriously until the mid-1980s, AIDS is now recognized as a serious health threat in the U.S. general population and even more so in prisons and jails.

The most recent figures show that at the end of 2008, there were 21,987 inmates in state and federal prisons in the United States who were HIV-positive or had confirmed AIDS. At year-end 2008, 1.5% of all male and 1.9% of all female inmates held in state or federal prisons were HIV-positive or had confirmed AIDS. There were a reported 5,174 inmates in custody of state and federal prison authorities who had confirmed AIDS at the end of 2008. These inmates accounted for about 0.5% of inmates in state prisons and 0.3% of inmates in federal prisons. For 2007, the overall rate of estimated confirmed AIDS cases in the state and federal prison population was over two times the rate in the United States general population. There were 130 AIDS-related deaths of state and federal prisoners in 2007. From a historical perspective, the number of AIDS-related deaths in state prisons is declining, dropping from 1,010 in 1995 to 256 in 2001 to 120 in 2007.

The AIDS cases were concentrated in the prisons of certain states and were virtually unknown in others. Four states—Florida (3,626), New York (3,500), Texas (2,450), and California (1,402)—accounted for almost half of all confirmed AIDS or HIV-positive cases. Four states reported fewer than 10 confirmed AIDS cases at the end of 2008.[9]

This bleak statement of the extent of HIV/AIDS in American prisons is the setting for numerous questions for corrections administrators: Should the corrections agency adopt a testing policy to detect HIV-positive cases, and, if so, who should be tested and when? Should inmates who test positive be segregated from the rest of the population? If they are left in the general population, should they be placed in the same work assignments and other programs as all other inmates? Who should be notified of HIV test results? Do all corrections staff have a right to know which inmates are HIV-positive? Once AIDS symptoms develop, where should the inmates be placed? How should disciplinary cases be handled? Are there special concerns for the assaultive (especially sexually assaultive) and drug-using offenders? If so, how should these special offenders be handled? Should AIDS patients be returned early to the community? When they are released, should any special efforts be made to arrange for their care? When HIV-positive inmates are released, should persons in the community with whom they will have contact be notified of their HIV status?

These are just some of the perplexing questions with which corrections administrators have had to deal. They are matters primarily of health policy and corrections management; courts have ruled on few of these questions, and most rulings have been at the local level. There are no universally correct or accepted answers to the questions, and this is not the place to settle or advise on matters of correctional and health policy. (As an example, on the issue of testing inmates, all 50 states and the federal system report that they will conduct HIV tests if there are clinical indications of HIV infection or upon an inmate's request, and 42 states and the federal system will do so on the occurrence of an incident that prompts concern. Twenty-three jurisdictions test all incoming inmates, and 18 states and the federal system test members of specific high-risk groups. Only six test inmates at the time of their release, and only three conduct random tests of inmates.)[10] However, these questions, which raise some of the troublesome issues about the management of HIV/AIDS inmates, all have legal implications. Some have been the subject of court decisions—there has been considerable litigation over AIDS issues in prisons and jails. We will discuss just a few of those court cases.

The Supreme Court has issued two opinions that have some impact on dealing with HIV/AIDS within the prison setting. In *Pennsylvania Department of Corrections v. Yeskey*, 524 U.S.

206 (1998), inmate Yeskey was denied placement in a motivational boot camp due to his hypertension. He sued, alleging a violation of the Americans with Disabilities Act (ADA). The Supreme Court agreed, holding that the ADA applied to inmates in state institutions.

During the same term, the Court decided *Bragdon v. Abbott*, 524 U.S. 624 (1998). Although this case deals with a private citizen, not an inmate, its holding, which interprets the ADA, gives guidance to prison and jail officials. In 1994, Abbott, who was infected with HIV, went for a dental appointment. In completing the registration form she mentioned her HIV infection. Upon discovering a cavity, Dr. Bragdon told Abbott that he would fill the cavity at a hospital at no added cost for his services, as his policy was not to fill cavities of HIV-infected persons in his office. Abbott was told, however, she would have to pay costs for using the hospital facilities. Abbott sued, in part, under Section 302 of the ADA, which provides the following:

No individual shall be discriminated against on the basis of disability in the full and equal enjoyment of the goods, services, facilities, privileges, advantages, or accommodations of any place of public accommodation by any person who....operates a place of public accommodation.

Within the context of this discussion, disability is defined in the statute as "a physical or mental impairment that substantially limits one or more of the major life activities of such individual." The district and appeals courts held that Abbott's HIV infection satisfied the definition of "disability." The Supreme Court agreed. Thus, the protections of the ADA apply to persons with HIV infections.

One of the most sweeping decisions on AIDS in prisons was made in *Harris v. Thigpen*, 941 F.2d 1495 (11th Cir. 1991); 727 F.Supp. 1564 (M.D. AL 1990). Alabama had a program for the mandatory testing of all inmates and for the segregation of those found to be HIV-positive. There was a broad attack on the state's approach, supported by outside organizations. The district court held that the mandatory testing program, conducted for all inmates at admission, was a reasonable means of trying to address the threat of AIDS to the inmate population. It was upheld, against challenges of unreasonable search and seizure, cruel and unusual punishment, and due process violations. Both the district and appellate courts held that the placement of HIV-positive inmates in segregated confinement was not cruel and unusual and that no due process hearing was required before they were placed there. Inmates challenged the state's lack of medical care, particularly when AZT (a commonly used drug to try to prevent HIV infection from developing into full-blown AIDS) was not used for the treatment of HIV-positive inmates to the extent that it was recommended in the outside community (or in some other state prison systems). These courts found that there were no constitutional violations (no deliberate indifference to health needs) by Alabama and that the failure to provide the AZT treatment was permissible (justifying its conclusion in large part on the high cost of the drug treatments).

In a somewhat unusual twist, a number of non-HIV-infected inmates joined the *Harris* case in support of the state officials and asked the court to approve the testing and segregation program, so that they would be protected from the spread of HIV infection. The district court acknowledged their concerns but refused to say that they were entitled to the testing and segregation program as a matter of constitutional right and protection. In other words, the court refused to order the state to provide its program of segregating HIV-positive inmates as a constitutional entitlement for the inmates. (But the court did uphold the decision of the state to adopt the program as a justifiable policy for the good of the corrections system and its inmates.)

Inmates who were HIV-positive also objected to the fact that they were not eligible for placement into programs, such as vocational training and work release, which would help them upon release. The courts held that they were not entitled to such programs as a matter of law and that the decision to limit their access to such programs was one for the prison officials to make on the basis of their informed correctional judgment. The appeals court did send the case back for further fact-finding by the district court on the issue of whether the segregated HIV-positive inmates were excluded from programs that were available to other inmates and whether this was a violation of the Rehabilitation Act of 1973 (Title 29, U.S. Code, Section 794). The court indicated particular concern over the complaints of inmates that they did not have access to the law library materials and that this denied them equal access rights to the courts. Thus, on virtually all fronts, the concerns of the inmates were turned aside by these courts, in a big showing of deference to the policies and approaches of the corrections managers.

Eight years later, the Eleventh Circuit Court of Appeals issued its opinion on whether Alabama's policies were in violation of Section 504 of the Rehabilitation Act. In *Onishea v. Hopper*, 171 F.3d 1289 (11th Cir. 1999), cert. denied, 528 U.S. 1114 (2000), HIV-positive inmates sued the Alabama Department of Corrections under that act to force integration (mixing HIV-positive and HIV-negative inmates) in prison recreational, religious, and educational programs.

The district court denied relief, finding that sexual conduct, intravenous drug use, and blood-shed were always a possibility in prison when staff are not watching; that prison life is unpredictable; and that because HIV is transmitted by the previously listed actions, HIV transmission in prison is more than a "theoretical possibility." Since such conduct can occur within a prison and because of the catastrophic severity that would result if it did, the court held that integrating the programs would present a significant risk of transmitting the HIV virus and that HIV-positive inmates were not "otherwise qualified" for the benefits provided in the federal statute. On appeal, the circuit court, in an en banc decision, agreed with the district court. In framing the issue of the case, the court cited *School Board of Nassau County v. Arline*, 480 U.S. 273 (1987):

A person who poses a significant risk of communicating an infectious disease to others in the workplace will not be otherwise qualified for his or her job if reasonable accommodation will not eliminate that risk.

As to the element of risk in AIDS management, this appeals court joined three other circuits in holding:

[S]aying a risk of an event is small does not mean that it will not happen. And each time the event occurs, it is real people . . . that suffer the consequences. Saying that only one in 42,000 persons will die if exposed to a risk does not make that one's death insignificant.

The facts that prisons have violence, intravenous drug use, and sexual conduct and that these acts may cause blood-to-blood contact, providing the opportunity for transmission of the virus, was sufficient to conclude there was significant risk. This risk removed the inmates from the protective benefits of the Rehabilitation Act.

The court also held that there was a legitimate penal concern here. Security concerns and costs were identified as such legitimate government concerns. The appeals court affirmed the decision of the district court, denying relief to the inmates. A writ of certiorari was filed with the U.S. Supreme Court in this case and was denied in *Davis v. Hopper,* 528 U.S. 1114 (2000).

Although the above decisions remain good caselaw, at the current time it appears that Alabama is one of only two states (along with South Carolina) that segregate HIV-infected inmates from other prisoners, and those states are now being challenged on their policy, with specific reference to claimed violations of Title II of the Americans with Disabilities Act.[11]

As to the right of an HIV-positive inmate to be involved in programs alongside other inmates, in *Gates v. Rowland,* 39 F.3d 1439 (9th Cir. 1994), the court of appeals held that California officials did not have to place the HIV-infected inmates into work assignments in food service. A lower court had enjoined the prison officials from denying those regular work assignments to any HIV-positive inmates. The appeals court, although recognizing that there was little risk of spreading the virus through the food service work, upheld the rationale of the prison officials for their decision. The government's argument had been that other inmates would perceive a threat, even if medically there was little or none there, and that maintaining positive attitudes among the inmates about the safety and sanitation of their food was particularly important in the prison setting. The court ruled that these were legitimate penological concerns and that the state would not be required to assign HIV-positive inmates to food service jobs.

There is some basis for asserting that the HIV (positive) test results and AIDS diagnosis are matters of particular sensitivity to individuals. It may be argued that inmates may have privacy rights, so that those facts should not be revealed to persons outside the immediate health care staff who have an obvious need to know about them. The court in *Harris v. Thigpen* did not find much in the way of privacy protections for HIV/AIDS inmates. But the federal court in *Doe v. Coughlin,* 697 F.Supp. 1234 (N.D. NY 1988), did find that there was a privacy interest retained by the inmate patient, who should have control over who has access to information about his medical status.

In *Doe v. Delie,* 357 F.3d 309 (3rd Cir. 2001), the court of appeals ruled that prisoners do have a right to medical privacy, subject to legitimate penological interests, protected by the Fourteenth Amendment. Doe alleged that prison officials did not maintain the privacy of his HIV status in the following ways: (1) advised escorting officers of his status; (2) during physician visits, maintained an open-door policy, allowing others to hear his communications with the physician; and (3) when administering medication, the staff loudly announced the name of the medication, permitting others (inmates) to know his status. The court of appeals ruled that a person's HIV status is entitled to privacy protection because disclosure may result in stigma, harassment, and other risks of harm.

The court also held that while a prisoner lacks an expectation of privacy in his cell (*Hudson v. Palmer*, 468 U.S. 517 (1984)), "the right to nondisclosure of one's medical information emanates from a different source and protects different interests than the right to be free from unreasonable searches and seizures." The court said that a right to privacy in medical information for a prisoner is necessarily limited by correctional necessity, and the right against disclosure of confidential medical information does not mean that Doe may expect to "conceal this diagnosed medical condition from everyone in the corrections system."

The interest of staff in knowing who is HIV-positive relates to inmates' privacy concerns. There are at least two potential areas of staff interest. The first is one of wanting to know who in a prison's general population is HIV-infected so that staff may take appropriate safety precautions. Another, more problematic issue concerns the assault upon a staff member by an inmate in which there may be exposure to blood. Should the staff member be notified if the inmate is HIV-positive? To provide this information could raise the privacy concerns mentioned before, although the employee's interest in knowing is certainly understandable.[12] One approach in such an instance is to offer the employee periodic testing, with pretest and posttest counseling. Costs in this situation would be absorbed by the agency, and if the employee elects to go to a private physician, a claim for reimbursement might be made through workman's compensation.

Each correctional facility should check the state and local requirements for reporting HIV/AIDS cases to the local health authorities. Most jurisdictions have requirements for reporting these cases. Especially on an inmate's release, requirements of state, county, and city departments of health must be followed regarding the notification that must be made.

With respect to providing medical care for the HIV-infected inmate and the AIDS patient, staff should apply the same standards in adopting policy and procedures that they would apply for other health care. Regarding constitutional challenges, they must not be deliberately indifferent to the (obviously serious) medical needs of the inmate. With regard to any possible tort claims about inadequate or negligent care, they must stay informed about the current level of accepted care and precautionary treatments that are followed in the community, and they must try to follow those guidelines (especially the ones periodically issued for correctional institutions by the Centers for Disease Control and Prevention [CDC]) to the extent possible.[13]

■ Tuberculosis in Prisons

It is important to comment on the prevalence of tuberculosis infection and disease (TB) in our prisons and jails. It is now well known that there was a resurgence of tuberculosis in the United States in the 1980s. The spread of TB is a special concern in corrections institutions because of the close living environment, which can facilitate the spread of the disease, and the interaction that has been identified between TB and HIV infection, which is also prevalent in many corrections institutions.

The close and often crowded conditions in jails and prisons create an environment of increased risk for the spread of TB. Compounding this problem is the discovery of drug-resistant strains of TB, which further increase the risk of spreading the disease. It has been found that the presence of immunosuppressions in an individual (the presence of HIV, for example) may cause the individual not to be reactive to a TB skin test. This means, of course, that that person can elude detection for a long period of time and continue to spread the disease, while receiving no treatment for himself because of his negative test results.

The prevalence of TB remains much higher among prison inmates than the U.S. general population. In midyear 2003, less than 1% of the U.S. population was in jail or prison, but this confined population contained 3.2% of all TB cases nationwide. Three factors have been cited as contributing to this high rate. First, a significant number of persons in prison pose a high risk for TB (for example, drug users; persons with HIV; and persons who, prior to confinement, often did not receive standard public health interventions or non-emergency medical care). Second, as noted above, there is the institution's physical structure (close living quarters, crowded conditions, and ventilation). The third factor is the movement of inmates in and out of "overcrowded and inadequately ventilated facilities," joined with the existing inmate risk factors for TB.[14]

Most state and federal prison systems follow the recommendations of the Centers for Disease Control and Prevention on the screening of inmates. In a 2005 survey, 94% of the 47 responding state and federal prison systems require mandatory skin testing for TB within two weeks of prison admission. More than 90% of the state/federal systems conduct annual TB screening of all inmates.[15] Those who are diagnosed as infectious should be isolated from other inmates. The preferred method of isolation is placement in a negative-pressure isolation room (a room with ventilation that does not flow into the general ventilation system). Treatment for active cases is a combination of drugs. Inmates who show positive test results but are asymptomatic should be given preventive drug therapy and should be directly and periodically observed by health staff to detect any TB symptoms. When infected inmates are scheduled for release, it is important that they are referred to local health departments, and, if possible, arrangements for continued treatments and follow-up checks should be made.

With respect to legal issues, the main concerns have been lawsuits brought alleging failures to take adequate steps to prevent the spread of the disease, thereby placing other inmates (and staff, for that matter) at increased risk. One court of appeals, in *DeGidio v. Pung*, 920 F.2d 525 (8th Cir. 1990), held that an agency's failure to take adequate steps to detect and fight the disease could show a pattern that would amount to deliberate indifference to the serious medical needs of inmates (the constitutional standard for liability under *Estelle v. Gamble*). In *Blumhagen v. Sabes*, 834 F.Supp. 1347 (D. WY 1993), an inmate in Wyoming alleged that officials had screened all inmates for TB but had failed, after testing, to isolate the infectious TB cases. In this case, the federal district court held that the allegations showed only differences of opinion about how TB cases should be treated, and the court concluded that the actions of Wyoming officials did not amount to indifference to the prisoners' medical needs. The court did note, however, that the inmate might have a claim for malpractice under Wyoming tort law and suggested that the inmate look into that as a possible remedy.

Those two cases point out the standards that would be recommended for corrections officials: (1) Because of the prevalence of the disease and its highly dangerous nature in prisons, corrections officials should regularly consult with health officials about the adoption of detection and treatment programs according to current guidelines (from the CDC and others) about TB care in corrections facilities. To fail to do so could expose officials to a claim of indifference to the medical needs of inmates and thus expose those officials to personal liability under 42 U.S.C. § 1983, pursuant to constitutional standards. (2) Even if programs are implemented, officials are well-advised to update them and make sure that staff members follow through with all recommended testing and treatments to avoid tort claims of medical malpractice.

A second legal issue involves inmates' objections to being tested when there is a mandatory, universal testing program in an institution or agency. The Massachusetts Appeals Court, in *Langton v. Commissioner of Corrections*, 614 N.E.2d 1002 (1993), upheld the state's policy (required by a state law) that inmates had to be tested for TB. That court noted that the commissioner had a responsibility to protect the health of all inmates and staff. Because of the legitimate concerns for inmate security and safety, the court said that the policy for mandatory testing was lawful and justified and that the inmate could be disciplined for refusing to take the TB test.

Also on this issue, there is a case that appears to come down on the other side. In *Jolly v. Coughlin*, 894 F.Supp. 734 (S.D. NY 1995), aff'd., 76 F.3d 468 (2nd Cir. 1996), Jolly, a New York inmate who was also a Rastafarian, refused to take the TB screening test based on his religious beliefs. Pursuant to the corrections department's TB control program, inmates who refused the test were put in "medical keeplock," meaning they had to stay in their cells at all times, except for showering. (They were not placed in respiratory [negative pressure] isolation, as active cases were.) Inmate Jolly was in keeplock status for more than three and a half years. He never displayed any symptoms of TB, and his three X-ray tests were negative.

Applying the standards of the Religious Freedom Restoration Act, the court found that officials were substantially burdening Jolly's exercise of his religious beliefs and that there was not a compelling governmental interest in doing so. Although conceding that there was a compelling interest in preventing the spread of TB (and that interest would support universal testing programs, one might note, even against religious objections), the defendant prison officials did not convince the court that their means of dealing with this inmate (placing him in indefinite keeplock) was the least restrictive means of furthering their interest in fighting the spread of TB. Officials, in fact, conceded that Jolly was not contagious. The court ordered Jolly released from keeplock status and enjoined prison officials from placing him there.

From these cases on TB testing, we can conclude that, in most circumstances, mandatory and universal testing is a wise medical and correctional decision, and it can be defended in court. Cases of religious objections to the testing program must be evaluated on an individual basis and reviewed with legal counsel. The merits of individual cases should be explored, along with what alternatives there may be to handle the conscientious religious objector.

■ An Aging Prison Population

We know that an increase in the elderly population has occurred, and continues to occur, across America. This increase is reflected in the nation's prisons. As of December 31, 2009, it was estimated that over 10% of the nation's 1.5 million sentenced prisoners under state or federal jurisdiction were age 50 or older[16] (this is the age commonly used to report on, or count the elderly). What can surely be expected is that this elderly inmate population will continue to increase because of two principal factors: the increased number of elderly in the general population produces an increased pool of older offenders (although crime slows down with aging, it does not disappear); and longer sentences (including three-strikes statutes), many without parole, in many jurisdictions ensure that the existing inmate population will age while in prison and become part of that elderly group of inmates.

The increased number of elderly inmates presents several management problems that are more or less unique to this age group. While different correctional systems define elderly in different terms, either by chronological age or assessment of needs, the group as a whole possesses special needs in such areas as programming, housing, and treatment. For example, physical ailments and the general deterioration of energy levels and muscles produce problems in the classification of elderly inmates regarding housing units, job assignments, and other programs. Nutritional needs are different for aging inmates and may require the consideration of different dietary planning. Some activities, such as practicing religion, watching television, and participating in prison organizations, may be more attractive to the elderly than to younger inmates. The elderly can become easier targets for other inmates to prey on.

Because many persons in prison come from poor backgrounds, many failed to receive suitable health care treatment in the community. This lack of adequate health care, when coupled with use of tobacco, alcohol, and illegal drugs, and high risk sexual activities, increases the risk that the elderly prisoner will suffer from a chronic or serious disease, violence, or some other condition that will impact bodily function or mobility. The health care needs of the elderly are usually greater than those of younger inmates, as the elderly inmate may suffer more frequently from physical ailments such as hypertension, diabetes, and heart disease. The older inmate more often has chronic ailments, such as hearing or vision loss, incontinence, confusion, and digestive system ailments. As a result of these conditions, it is more common to see the use of canes, wheel chairs, hearing aids, and special clothing by elderly inmates.[17]

How prison administrators react to these special problems varies. There is no set approach or agreed-upon response. Prison administrators do agree that the special situation of the aging is present and that some coordinated response must be adopted in each agency. In some agencies, the elderly (especially those needing special attention or care) are placed in certain institutions where staff members are trained to look after their needs. At some facilities, the elderly are housed together. Those with significant physical disabilities (such as those in wheelchairs or those who can walk only with a cane) are likely to be assigned to first-floor living quarters. (A federal statute that has impact on corrections is the Americans with Disabilities Act (ADA), enacted in 1990. The Act was amended in 2010. Among its provisions are standards for accessible design. These standards have the objective of making prison facilities readily accessible to and usable by persons with disabilities. In addition, the ADA also has new provisions on "discrimination prohibited." See Title 28, Code of Federal Regulations, Section 35.152, paragraph (b).) Some institutions have jobs that are largely sedentary and easy to get to, which are set aside for assignment to the elderly (and disabled) inmates. There is no agreement, among staff or among inmates, about whether elderly inmates should be totally segregated or should be mixed with younger inmates as long and as far as possible. Many of the elderly prefer separate, quieter quarters and generally find living with their own age group less stressful.

The legal problems of dealing with the elderly are essentially the same as dealing with the general prison population, but the terms "aging" or "elderly" are placed in front of the issues and the legal answers. For example, prisons obviously have a basic requirement to look after the health needs of all inmates, including the elderly. Constitutionally, the standard is the same as for all: prison officials must not show deliberate indifference to the serious medical needs of the inmates, and in this case, the increased medical needs of elderly inmates. In a similar way, common law tort (malpractice) standards are the same as those for the general population, with modification needed to reflect the recognized degree of care that must be provided to the special needs of the elderly population. As part of those broad concerns for the well-being of the elderly inmates, decisions on food service, special accommodations for visiting and other contacts with family and friends, and assignments to special housing or special programs must all reflect some sensitivity to their specialized needs. (Ignoring these problems completely could result in claims of indifference to the needs of the elderly inmates and, thus, possible exposure to individual constitutional liability under Section 1983.)

The growth in this segment of the inmate population has been gradual, but it is demonstrable. Standards of the American Correctional Association call for prison and jail administrators to take this group's special needs into account in their planning, and in the facilities and activities that are provided. Although there is no universal or easy answer to the issues presented, it is clear that corrections administrators are aware of the problem and have taken some steps to address it.

Several jurisdictions have attempted to address this issue by enacting legislation to permit release of prisoners who reach a certain age. Persons in federal custody can be recommended for early release when they have reached the age of 70 and have served more than 30 years of their sentence. This so called "safety valve" legislation is found in Title 18, U.S.C. § 3582. The statute requires that a reduction may be considered by the sentencing court only upon recommendation of the Director of the Bureau of Prisons. There are several lower court opinions which have denied consideration of an inmate's petition to be released earlier because there was no such recommendation. *Morales v. U.S.,* 353 F.Supp. 2d 204 (D. MA 2005). In another case, while noting the court lacked jurisdiction because there was no recommendation, the court ruled that the decision not to recommend early release had been reviewed by several levels of prison officials and was not arbitrary or capricious because the prisoner suffered only from chronic ailments. *Leja v. Sabol,* 487 F.Supp. 2d 201 (D. MA 2007)[18]

Two additional special medical concerns, not discussed in this chapter on health care, are covered in the discussion of the Fifth and Fourteenth Amendments: Due Process. The cases are *Vitek v. Jones,* 445 U.S. 480 (1980), which considers the due process rights of a prisoner when he is transferred from a regular prison to a psychiatric hospital, and *Farmer v. Brennan,* 511 U.S. 825 (1994), which discusses the problems presented in properly classifying a transsexual inmate in a prison. Although those cases have definite health care aspects and could have been discussed in this chapter, they are included in the discussion of due process, which addresses the classification of inmates and the transfers of inmates from one institution to another.

SUMMARY

- Prisons and jails must provide health care to inmates, because the inmates are not in a position to obtain health care for themselves. Under certain circumstances, an inmate may be charged a fee (medical co-pay) for health care services.

- The governing case for prison health care is *Estelle v. Gamble.* In that case, the Supreme Court held that prison staff (whether doctors or officers or any others) violated the Eighth Amendment if they were deliberately indifferent to the serious medical needs of prisoners. Such deliberate indifference shows the unnecessary and wanton infliction of pain that the cruel and unusual punishment clause prohibits.

- Instances of medical malpractice, mistaken judgments in providing medical care, and differing opinions about what care should be provided, do not amount to "deliberate indifference." They are not constitutional violations but may state claims under tort claims procedures, where negligence is the standard.

- In *West v. Atkins*, a private physician, who was under contract to provide health care to inmates, was found to be acting "under color of state law" and was therefore potentially liable for constitutional violation on an inmate's claim that he was deliberately indifferent to the inmate's serious medical needs.

- The Supreme Court ruled that an inmate could be given involuntary treatment (against his wishes) when he had a serious mental illness and treatment was necessary to alleviate a significant danger that the inmate posed to himself or to others. The treatment also had to be in the best medical interest of the inmate (*Washington v. Harper*). In another case, it was held that the government may medicate a mentally ill inmate against his will to render him competent to stand trial when the criminal charges are serious and with other precautions for his treatment (*Sell v. United States*).

- Lower federal courts and the highest appellate courts of some states have identified several important governmental interests that might outweigh the incarcerated individual's right to refuse medical treatment: preservation of life; protection of innocent third parties; the prevention of suicide; the maintenance of the ethical integrity of the medical profession; and maintaining prison security and orderly administration (*McNabb v. Department of Corrections*).

- In other involuntary treatment cases, lower federal courts held that aversive treatment to control disruptive behavior was cruel and unusual and therefore impermissible (*Knecht v. Gillman*) and that an inmate could be required to attend classes, against his will, in order to achieve a justifiable rehabilitative goal of the state to attain literacy among inmates (*Rutherford v. Hutto*).

- Inmate suicides present challenges to prison and jail officials. Staff members must be on the lookout for signals of suicidal tendencies and must take steps to try to prevent suicides in order to provide for the safety and medical well-being of inmates and to avoid showing deliberate indifference to inmates' serious needs.

- Prison officials need to ensure that appropriate procedures are in place to meet the particularized needs of female prisoners. The needs of pregnant female offenders require careful consideration of restraint policies (*Nelson v. Correctional Medical Services*). Correctional policies that prevent a female prisoner from obtaining an elective abortion may violate the prisoner's rights under the Fourteenth Amendment (*Victoria W. v. Larpenter* and *Roe v. Crawford*).

- HIV/AIDS presents additional serious medical and management problems to corrections administrators. The protections of the Americans with Disabilities Act (ADA) apply to persons with HIV infections (*Bragdon v. Abbott*). A leading case on the treatment of HIV/AIDS inmates is *Harris v. Thigpen*. Alabama had instituted universal, mandatory HIV testing for all inmates at admission and placed all HIV-positive inmates in separate housing. The components of this program, to which the segregated inmates objected, were approved in most aspects against the inmates' constitutional and statutory claims. Other claims about HIV/AIDS programs are being litigated in federal and state courts. In *Doe v. Delie*, the court ruled that prisoners have a right to privacy in their HIV status, and prison officials should take appropriate steps to prevent the unnecessary disclosure of the prisoner's condition.

- Corrections officials must be aware of the risks presented by the presence of TB in prisons and jails. For the protection of inmates (and to avoid a showing of deliberate indifference), jail and prison staff should take steps to test for and treat the disease, in accordance with currently recommended standards of control and care.

- Care for the elderly is another area that administrators must be aware of and appropriately respond to. The special needs of these offenders, who have been identified as a constantly increasing component of expanding corrections populations, must be met.

THINKING ABOUT IT

Joel Caulk was a 36-year-old inmate in the New Hampshire State Prison system. He was serving a 10- to 20-year sentence for aggravated felonious sexual assault, and he had a separate 5- to 10-year sentence for burglary, which would begin when Caulk completed the 10- to 20-year sentence. In addition, Caulk had other charges pending in New Hampshire, as well as in California, and he claimed that he had a 20- to 30-year sentence in Massachusetts. Not wishing to spend the rest of his life in prison, Caulk stopped eating solid food, and he drank certain liquids as his only nourishment. He said that he chose this method of dying so that he could remain competent. He stated that he was not committing suicide, but rather allowing himself to die. He had no life-threatening or terminal illness, and he did not make any demands or ask for anything in return. The prison administration filed in court, seeking court authorization to "feed and nourish Joel Caulk over his objection[s]." How do you think the court ruled? This case is reported in *In re Caulk*, 480 A.2d 93 (NH 1984).

ENDNOTES

1. For example, several courts have referred to the basic needs of inmates, which the government must look after, and they have included medical needs in that list. *Lewis v. Casey*, 518 U.S. 343 (1996); *Wilson V. Seiter*, 501 U.S. 294 (1991); and *Newman v. State of Alabama*, 559 F.2d 283 (5th Cir. 1977).
2. Camp, C. G., ed. *The 2002 Corrections Yearbook—Adult Corrections*. Pages 106–107. (Middletown, CT: Criminal Justice Institute, 2003). Also, *Medical Co-Pay Plans/Release Provisions/Telemedicine*. *Corrections Compendium*. 2006. 31:5:32–34.
3. Federal Prisoner Health Care Copayment Act of 2000 (Pub. L. 106-294, October 12, 2000, 114 Stat. 1038). The language is codified in 18 U.S.C. § 4048.
4. These matters, as they apply in U.S. hospitals and other medical facilities, are discussed in Pozgar, G. *Legal Aspects of Health Care Administration*. Pages 273–280 and 301–320. (Gaithersburg, MD: Aspen Publishers, 1993). As Pozgar points out (p. 314), "exceptions (to consent requirements) do exist with respect to emergency situations. Implied consent generally exists when immediate action is required to save a patient's life or to prevent permanent impairment of the patient's health. If it is impossible in an emergency to obtain

the consent of the patient or someone legally authorized to give consent, the required procedure may be undertaken without any liability for failure to procure consent. An emergency situation removes the need for consent."

5. The *Myers* decision includes, as an appendix, portions from an affidavit done by the commissioner of corrections at that time. Describing the situation, the commissioner stated: "In dealing with a prisoner such as Myers, he [commissioner] had only two options if the law gave him no right to compel submission to treatment: 'One would be to simply grant the demands. There would be great pressure for me to do this since the only other option is to let the man die. Nevertheless, submitting to the demands would be intolerable, because it would violate my legal responsibilities (particularly, in this case, my duty to protect the public) and greatly undermine my ability to effectively and fairly manage the Department of Correction.... [T]o allow Myers, or other inmates in similar situations, to destroy themselves while in prison would create very serious practical problems in prison administration. One very serious practical problem is that it would be very difficult to make the prisoners, their families and the correction department staff understand that I had done everything legally possible to prevent a death of a prisoner in my charge. Faith in the correctional system's ability to protect inmates would be seriously undermined. More immediately, one could expect an explosive reaction by other inmates to the death and to the failure of the commissioner to prevent it by simply releasing Myers to minimum security. In my opinion, such a reaction is much more likely in a situation where Myers is permitted to die, than where he is subjected to involuntary treatment to keep him alive."

6. With respect to federal offenders, the rehabilitative aspect of prison was recently addressed in *Tapia v. U.S.*, 564 U.S. __ (2011). Tapia was convicted of alien smuggling. She was sentenced to 51 months, with the district court judge saying, "[t]he sentence has to be sufficient to provide needed correctional treatment, and here I think the needed correctional treatment is the 500 hour drug program." Tapia argued that the lengthening of her prison term was contrary to the provisions of 18 U.S.C. § 3582(a), which specifically states that the federal court in imposing or determining the length of a prison term shall recognize that imprisonment is not an appropriate means of promoting correction and rehabilitation.

   The appeals court upheld the district court decision. In reversing, the Supreme Court pointed to the clear statutory language—"what Congress said was that when sentencing an offender to prison, the court shall consider all the purposes of punishment except rehabilitation—because imprisonment is not an appropriate means of pursuing that goal." The Supreme Court noted that a sentencing court is without decision making authority as to where the federal offender serves her sentence or in what program she becomes involved. The court can recommend, but not order, a particular facility placement or program involvement, with this authority resting with the Federal Bureau of Prisons. [As an aside, Tapia was encouraged by Bureau of Prisons staff to enroll in the drug program, but said she was not interested.]

7. Noonan, M. *Deaths in Custody: State Prison Deaths, 2001–2007—Statistical Tables*. Table 1. (Washington, DC: Bureau of Justice Statistics, U.S. Department of Justice, 2010). Also, Noonan, M. *Mortality in Local Jails, 2000–2007*. Appendix Table 2. (Washington, DC: Bureau of Justice Statistics, U.S. Department of Justice, 2010) (Revised October 26, 2010).

8. In *Victoria W.*, the court, noting her attorney's delay both in filing for the court order and in requesting an early release, rather than release or transport to receive an abortion, said, "…regardless of the policy's requirements, it functioned properly in this case. Her attorney's action, not the policy, denied Victoria an abortion."

9. The information in the preceding two paragraphs of the text was taken from Maruschak, L. *HIV in Prisons, 2007–2008.* Pages 1–3, Appendix Table 1. (Washington, DC: Bureau of Justice Statistics, U.S. Department of Justice, 2009) (revised January 28, 2010). Also see Maruschak, L. *HIV in Prisons, 2001.* Page 1. (Washington, DC: Bureau of Justice Statistics, U.S. Department of Justice, 2004).

10. See endnote 9. Maruschak, L. *HIV in Prisons, 2007–2008.* Appendix Table 5.

11. On March 28, 2011, a class action complaint for Declaratory and Injunctive Relief was filed in the United States District Court for the Middle District of Alabama (Northern Division). An amended complaint was filed May 11, 2011. The case filing is *Henderson, et al. v. Bentley, et al.* (Civil Case No. 2:11cv224-MHT). The complaint says that a majority of state correctional systems in the 1980s, reflective of "a tidal wave of public fear over the HIV/AIDS epidemic" adopted policies "requiring the segregation of prisoners with HIV." The complaint says that as new medications developed, the methods of HIV transmission were more clearly identified and the myths "debunked. Until today only two states continue to segregate inmates with HIV "in separate, specially designated housing units." The litigation, in part, is requesting a declaration that the state be enjoined (stopped) "from engaging in discriminatory policies and practices" on the basis of the inmates' HIV status and a declaration that the Alabama Department of Corrections HIV segregation policy violates Title II of the Americans with Disabilities Act and Section 504 of the Rehabilitation Act. In response to the filing, the state commissioner of corrections, in late March 2011, issued a statement saying that the Department of Corrections will "zealously" defend against the "false and misinformed allegations that regrettably ignore this Department's important obligations to provide health care, prevent the transmission of sexually transmitted diseases, and manage the prison population in such a way to ensure the safety of that population, Departmental staff, and the public at large."

12. For an approach addressing an employee's concern, see 18 U.S.C. § 4014, Testing for human immunodeficiency virus. Paragraph (b) states, "If the Attorney General has a well-founded reason to believe that a person sentenced to a term of imprisonment for a Federal offense, or ordered detained before trial … may have intentionally or unintentionally transmitted the [HIV] virus to any officer or employee of the United States, or to any person lawfully present in a correctional facility who is not incarcerated there, the Attorney General shall … [have] the person who may have transmitted the virus to be tested … and communicate the test results to the person tested [and also "… inform any person … who may have been exposed to such virus of the potential risk involved and, if warranted by the circumstances, that prophylactic or other treatment should be considered."]."

13. Centers for Disease Control and Prevention. *HIV Testing Implementation Guidance for Correctional Settings.* January 2009: Pages 1–38. Available from http://www.cdc.gov/hiv/topics/testing/resources/guidelines/correctional-settings. This document provides information on HIV/AIDS in correctional settings and covers such topics as screening, privacy, testing, medical care, and reporting.

14. Centers for Disease Control and Prevention. *Prevention and Control of Tuberculosis in Correctional and Detention Facilities: Recommendations from CDC.* Pages 1–3. MMWR 2006; 55 (No. RR-9).

15. Hammett, T., Kennedy, S., and Kuck, S. *10th NIJ/CDC National Survey of Infectious Diseases in Correctional Facilities: Tuberculosis Screening, Treatment and Education. Final Report.* Pages 1, 9–10. November 9, 2006.

16. West, H., Sabol, W., and Greenman, S. *Prisoners in 2009.* Appendix Table 13. (Washington, DC: Bureau of Justice Statistics, U.S. Department of Justice, 2010).

17. Anno, B., Graham, C., Lawrence, J., and Shansky, R. *Correctional Health Care: Addressing the Needs of Elderly, Chronically Ill, and Terminally Ill Inmates.* Washington, DC: National Institute of Corrections, U.S. Department of Justice, 2004.

18. A more direct approach is H.R. 223—Federal Prison Bureau Nonviolent Offender Relief Act of 2011—introduced in the U.S. House of Representatives on January 7, 2011. This proposed legislation would require the Federal Bureau of Prisons, pursuant to a good time policy, to release from confinement an inmate who has served at least one-half of her prison term if that inmate is at least 45 years of age, has never been convicted of a crime of violence, and has not had a violation of prison disciplinary regulations involving violent conduct. At the time this book was prepared, the legislation had been referred to the House Committee on the Judiciary, Subcommittee on Crime, Terrorism, and Homeland Security.

17 Probation and Parole, Community Corrections, and Fines

Due process is not so rigid as to require that the significant interests in informality, flexibility, and economy must always be sacrificed.

U.S. Supreme Court, *Gagnon v. Scarpelli*

Chapter Outline

- How Probation and Parole Work
- *Jones v. Cunningham*
- *Morrissey v. Brewer*
- *Gagnon v. Scarpelli; Mempa v. Rhay*
- *Griffin v. Wisconsin; United States v. Knights; Samson v. California; Pennsylvania Board of Probation and Parole v. Scott*
- *Martinez v. California*
- *Payne v. Tennessee; Greenholtz v. Inmates; Swarthout v. Cooke; Board of Pardons v. Allen*
- *Connecticut Board of Pardons v. Dumschat; Ohio Adult Parole Authority v. Woodard*
- *United States v. Addonizio; California Department of Corrections v. Morales; Garner v. Jones; Lynce v. Mathis*
- *Jago v. Van Curen*
- *Moody v. Daggett*
- *Smith v. Doe; Connecticut Department of Public Safety v. Doe*
- Community Corrections
- Use of Fines
- *Williams v. Illinois; Tate v. Short*
- *Bearden v. Georgia*

In this chapter, we will examine the constitutional decisions that affect the work of probation and parole officers. This is the part of corrections that is nonincarcerative. It is therefore sometimes called "alternative sentencing" or **community corrections.** We examine in this chapter the various aspects of community corrections. Besides probation and parole, this includes the use of fines and other types of community corrections. We include fines here because, although they are not a large part of corrections administration, they are widely used as sentencing options for many offenses (particularly less serious ones). In addition, technically, a fine may be considered a community corrections alternative, because the offender remains in the community, whether the fine is used as the only sanction or in combination with probation (a common sentencing combination).

First, it is important to clearly distinguish between probation and parole. Although they have many similarities, they are very different in their functions from a sentencing standpoint.

■ How Probation and Parole Work

Probation and parole are both parts of the sentencing phase of criminal justice. They are further similar in that persons who are placed on probation or parole live in the community, rather than in corrections facilities. The essence of their status is that they (probationers and parolees) are under the supervision of trained officers, and they are legally placed under conditions or restrictions on their release status. A key distinction is that probation is a judicial function (under court auspices), while parole is administrative (under executive authority).

Probation is a form of sentencing, so it is imposed by a court. In one type of probation, a court will impose a sentence of jail time, imprisonment, or even a fine or restitution and then **suspend** that sentence while the defendant is placed on probation. This kind of probation is called a suspended execution of sentence. In another type of probation, the court suspends the imposition of the sentence and places the defendant on a term of probation. In this kind of probation (called a suspended imposition), no set term of imprisonment hangs over the probationer's head; if he violates probation, the court may impose any sentence that might originally have been imposed. In both types of probation, a specified length of time is set for the probation to last, and, during that time, the probationer is typically assigned to a supervising officer, to whom he must report at regular intervals. Reporting may be in person—the probationer goes to see the probation officer at her office, or, less frequently, the officer meets the probationer at home or at work—or reporting may be done by telephone or even by mail. The degree of supervision may range greatly, from minimal contact with the probation officer to intensive probation, where the probationer is frequently seen and talked to by the officer to make sure he is doing well. Probation is by far the most common correctional supervision, with an estimated 4.2 million people on probation at year's end 2009.[1]

Parole, on the other hand, is release to the community after serving time in prison. There is a paroling authority, often called a parole board or a parole commission, which is usually staffed by full-time board members who are appointed, for certain length terms, by the governor of the state. (At one time, parole board members were mostly part-time appointees.) Usually, a hearing is conducted with each eligible inmate at the prison where she is confined. In some states, the board members themselves conduct the hearings; in others, hearing examiners or parole officers conduct the hearings, and they make their reports to the members, who vote to parole or not to parole. Eligibility for parole is determined by law. The parole statute for the state will indicate when parole may be considered.

Let's look at some of the ways parole eligibility is set. In some states, sentencing statutes provide that the court at sentencing may set the parole eligibility date for the defendant, within ranges specified by the legislature. In such states, the court may impose, for example, a sentence of one year to five years. The one-year date is the parole eligibility date—the earliest the defendant can be released on parole. Or the sentence may be eighteen months to five years, which means parole eligibility occurs at eighteen months. In other states, courts only impose the full-term date of the sentence (five years, in the examples just given). Parole eligibility is then set at a date that is figured by a formula (such as one-third of the sentence), which is set by the parole law. Also, there may be so-called indeterminate parole sentences, whereby the court imposes a single term (for example, five years), and the defendant is immediately eligible for parole and may be paroled at any time during the sentence at the total discretion of the parole board. For a life sentence, the parole eligibility date may be set by state statute or specified as part of the sentence imposed by the court. (For example, in a sentence of 15 years to life, the "15 years" may be a statutory date or may be chosen by the sentencing judge, depending on the law.) The legislature may make some offenses nonparolable or may even eliminate parole altogether.

By the end of 2000, 16 states had abolished discretionary parole for all inmates; four additional states had abolished it for certain violent offenses or other crimes against a person. The federal government also has abolished parole. See **Table 17-1** for a list of those agencies. Please keep in mind that the abolition of parole does not mean that parole boards and paroling

Table 17-1 States that Have Abolished Discretionary Parole as of 2000

All offenders		Certain violent offenders
Arizona	Minnesota	Alaska
California[1]	Mississippi	Louisiana
Delaware	North Carolina	New York
Florida[2]	Ohio[4]	Tennessee
Illinois	Oregon	
Indiana	Virginia	
Kansas[3]	Washington	
Maine	Wisconsin	

Source: Hughes, T., Wilson, D., and Beck, A. *Trends in State Parole, 1990–2000* (Washington, DC: Bureau of Justice Statistics, U.S. Department of Justice), October 2001.

[1] In 1976, the Uniform Determinate Sentencing Act abolished discretionary parole for all offenses except some violent crimes with a long sentence or a sentence to life.

[2] In 1995, parole eligibility was abolished for offenses with a life sentence and a twenty-five-year mandatory term.

[3] Excludes a few offenses, primarily first-degree murder and intentional second-degree murder.

[4] Excludes murder and aggravated murder.

authorities no longer exist. These entities continue to function for those offenders who were sentenced prior to the abolition of parole. What it does mean is that, over time, there should be fewer people released by way of discretionary parole (released based on parole board decision). In 2009, there were approximately 147,000 discretionary releases, representing about 27% of adults entering parole. In 1990, discretionary parole represented 59% of persons released to parole supervision.[2]

Besides the possibility of being paroled, inmates also usually earn good conduct allowances, which are subtracted from the full-term date of the sentence and, in some cases, from the parole eligibility date as well. In other words, good conduct may (if so established by state law) reduce the time the prisoner has to wait for her first parole hearing. In other states, good time is only subtracted from the full-term date of the sentence; if the inmate is not paroled, she will be released, by operation of the law, when that good time date is reached. In 2009, more than 250,000 prisoners were released under mandatory provisions—releases from prison were not decided by a parole board (46% of releases).[3]

Besides the persons who are released on parole by favorable action of the parole board, in most places persons who are released with good conduct allowances are also treated as if they were released on parole, and the releasee is under some degree of community supervision. The parolee is supervised, much like a probationer, in the community, with the conditions and restrictions of the release set by the parole board, rather than by a court. In some jurisdictions, a separate office handles the supervision of parolees; in other states, parolees are supervised by probation officers.

The essence of the probation or parole release is supervision. To enforce supervision, revocation of the probation or parole is a necessary component. Revocation occurs when the supervising officer makes a negative report, which may recommend revocation. For a probationer, this report goes to the court, which reviews it and decides whether the actions of the probationer are serious enough to terminate probation by a revocation action. When probation is revoked, the court may impose the original sentence (or any part of it) that was imposed and suspended. Or, if the court suspended the imposition of any prison term at the original sentencing and placed the offender on probation, then, upon revocation, any length of sentence to imprisonment that could have originally been imposed may be imposed. If probation is revoked, the probationer is sent to jail or prison to serve the term specified by the court (which, as we have pointed out, can be the original prison term that was imposed and suspended or a lesser amount). In some places, but not in all jurisdictions, the court may also add more supervision time onto the sentence as another option at the revocation hearing.

To enforce parole, a similar revocation process for a parolee may occur, except that a negative report from the supervising officer goes to the parole board, which is given the power to revoke parole. The case is then reviewed (we will look more closely at the review process in revocation cases for probationers or for parolees later in this chapter). If a decision is made to revoke parole, the person is returned to prison to serve out the balance of the sentence, computed in accordance with the laws of the state. (These rules of computation of sentences are fairly complex and vary from state to state.) In most places, the person returned from parole can earn good time again on the balance of the sentence to be served and may be paroled again. As you can imagine, this will happen more often on longer sentences, where an inmate may be paroled and returned to prison two, three, or more times on a single sentence.

In 2009, some 2.14 million people were reported to have been placed on probation in the United States, and just over one million successfully completed their terms of probation. However, 271,000 probationers were incarcerated (under their current sentence, with a new sentence, for treatment, or for other reasons). Twenty-four percent of persons on probation in 2009 were females. As to parole, more than 277,000 persons completed their term of parole in 2009, and more than 185,000 parolees were returned to incarceration with either a new sentence, a parole revocation, to receive treatment, or for other, unknown reasons.[4]

▨ *Jones v. Cunningham*

In this case, a Virginia parolee raised the question of whether he could go into federal court and challenge his state sentence under the federal habeas corpus statute, 28 U.S.C. § 2241. Jones originally filed his challenge to his sentence, while he was in the state penitentiary, against Cunningham, the penitentiary superintendent. (Habeas corpus actions are always brought against the custodian.) Before his case was decided in the court of appeals, Jones was paroled. Jones tried to add or substitute the parole board members as respondents in the habeas corpus action, but the court refused, saying that he was no longer in custody but rather was "at large." In *Jones v. Cunningham*, 371 U.S. 236 (1963), the Supreme Court agreed to decide the question of whether a parolee is "in custody" within the meaning of the federal habeas corpus statute and the Constitution.

The Court reviewed the history of the Writ of Habeas Corpus in the Constitution and in English law, from where it was historically and legally derived. The Court concluded that the writ could be used for more than just physical incarceration.

> **History, usage, and precedent can leave no doubt that, besides physical imprisonment, there are other restraints on a man's liberty, restraints not shared by the public generally, which have been thought sufficient in the English-speaking world to support the issuance of habeas corpus.**

Habeas, for example, has been used by an alien seeking entry into the United States after being detained at the border. It has been used to question the legality of induction into the military service. It has even been used to test child custody when there is a dispute between the parents. Here, when Jones was paroled, his habeas corpus case against the penitentiary superintendent was ended (it "became moot"), because the superintendent's custody of Jones had ended. But can the parole board be considered to have Jones in its custody so that he can use habeas corpus to challenge the parole restraints on his liberty?

The Court noted that the Virginia parole restraints were significant: Jones was limited to a particular community, house, and job, unless it was changed by his parole officer. He had to report to the parole officer and allow the parole officer to visit his home and job to check on him. He had to "keep good company and good hours, work regularly, keep away from undesirable places, and live a clean, honest, and temperate life." He could be rearrested, at any time, at the order of the board or his parole officer, and he could be required to serve the balance of his sentence (the sentence that he claimed was illegal). (These conditions, although using language that may sound a little dated, are fairly typical of the restraints placed on parolees.

Therefore, the *Jones* case is not unique or distinguishable on the grounds that the conditions were more strenuous or very unusual.) Based on these factors, the Court recognized Jones's right to pursue a habeas corpus action.

> [The parole conditions and restrictions] significantly restrain petitioner's liberty to do those things which in this country free men are entitled to do. Such restraints are enough to invoke the help of the Great Writ.... While petitioner's parole releases him from immediate physical imprisonment, it imposes conditions which significantly confine and restrain his freedom; this is enough to keep him in the "custody" of the members of the Virginia Parole Board within the meaning of the habeas corpus statute.

From this ruling, we know that parolees may use the habeas corpus statute to challenge the conditions of their custody, just as prisoners do. (As an aside, it is clear that probationers and parolees may use 42 U.S.C. § 1983 to challenge anything they claim is a constitutional violation, because all citizens are allowed to do that.)

■ *Morrissey v. Brewer*

Morrissey had been paroled from serving his sentence at the Iowa State Penitentiary. Seven months later, he was arrested and charged with being a parole violator. After review of his parole officer's report, the board of parole revoked Morrissey's parole and ordered that he be returned to prison. He challenged the revocation action, using habeas corpus, on the grounds that he was given no hearing. The Supreme Court, in *Morrissey v. Brewer*, 408 U.S. 471 (1972), addressed the question of whether a parolee is entitled to due process—that is, to some kind of hearing—before being returned to prison by revocation of his parole status.

The Court first examined the nature of parole, noting that it was "an established variation on imprisonment of convicted criminals. Its purpose is to help individuals reintegrate into society as constructive individuals as soon as they are able, without being confined for the full term of the sentence imposed." The Court further noted that "the parolee is entitled to retain his liberty as long as he substantially abides by the conditions of his parole." The Court also noted that "the revocation of parole is not part of a criminal prosecution and thus the full panoply of rights due a defendant in such a [prosecution] proceeding does not apply to parole revocations." Whether the person is entitled to due process rights under the Constitution turns on whether the person's interest in remaining on parole is a liberty interest, within the meaning of the Fourteenth Amendment. The Court concluded that it was such an interest.

> [T]he liberty of a parolee, although indeterminate, includes many of the core values of unqualified liberty and its termination inflicts a "grievous loss" on the parolee and often on others.

Therefore, some process is due to the parolee, and the Court described what was needed: "an informal hearing structured to assure that the finding of a parole violation will be based on verified facts and that the exercise of discretion will be informed by an accurate knowledge of the parolee's behavior."

With that guidance in mind, the Court defined the precise minimal requirements needed for parole revocation. These are the requirements of an informal, due process hearing:

> **[D]ue process [requires] that some minimal inquiry be conducted at or reasonably near the place of the alleged parole violation or arrest and as promptly as convenient after arrest....Such an inquiry should be seen as in the nature of a "preliminary hearing" to determine whether there is probable cause or reasonable ground to believe that the arrested parolee has committed acts that would constitute a violation of parole conditions.**

This "preliminary hearing" requires determination by an impartial party—someone not directly involved in the case (that is, never the supervising parole officer). The parolee must be given notice that the hearing will take place and must be informed of the parole violations that have been alleged. The parolee must be allowed to "appear and speak in his own behalf; he may bring letters, documents, or individuals who can give relevant information to the hearing officer." A person who has given adverse information on which the revocation may be based must be available, at the parolee's request, for questioning in the parolee's presence. The hearing officer must make a summary or digest of the hearing and should determine whether there is probable cause to hold the parolee for a final decision. The officer should also state the reasons for his determination and the evidence on which he relied.

After this preliminary hearing and within a reasonable time (the Court indicated that two months was a reasonable amount of time, even though the parolee may have been delivered to prison within that time), there must be a "final hearing." Rather than determining whether there is probable cause to hold the parolee on revocation charges (which is the purpose of the preliminary hearing), the final hearing determines whether the facts warrant revocation. "The parolee must have an opportunity to be heard and to show, if he can, that he did not violate the conditions, or, if he did, that circumstances in mitigation suggest that the violation does not warrant revocation." The Court emphasized that each state must write its own procedures to cover parole revocation hearings, but these are the minimum requirements to satisfy due process:

> **[The state must provide:] (a) written notice of the claimed violations of parole; (b) disclosure to the parolee of evidence against him; (c) opportunity to be heard in person and to present witnesses and documentary evidence; (d) the right to confront and cross-examine adverse witnesses (unless the hearing officer specifically finds good cause for not allowing confrontation); (e) a "neutral and detached" hearing body such as a traditional parole board, members of which need not be judicial officers or lawyers; and (f) a written statement by the factfinders as to the evidence relied on and reasons for revoking parole.**

The Court specifically noted that it did not "reach or decide the question whether the parolee is entitled to the assistance of retained counsel or to appointed counsel if he is indigent." That question was reached in the following case, *Gagnon v. Scarpelli.*

■ *Gagnon v. Scarpelli; Mempa v. Rhay*

Scarpelli pleaded guilty to armed robbery in Wisconsin. He was sentenced to 15 years imprisonment, but the judge suspended that sentence and placed him on probation for 7 years. He was allowed to reside in Illinois, where he was under supervision under the interstate compact for probation.[5] He was later arrested during the course of a house burglary by Illinois police. His probation was revoked by Wisconsin without any hearing. He was later sent to the State Reformatory at Green Bay to serve the 15 years that had originally been imposed. He challenged the revocation of his probation by petitioning for a writ of habeas corpus. Before that was decided, he was placed on parole, but the court held that his petition was not moot because he was still under the restraints of his parole.

The Supreme Court, in *Gagnon v. Scarpelli*, 411 U.S. 778 (1973), addressed the question of due process at probation revocation proceedings. The Court noted first its decision in *Mempa v. Rhay*, 389 U.S. 128 (1967), which involved an unusual sentencing procedure in the state of Washington. Mempa, with appointed counsel assisting him, had been convicted on a guilty plea. He was placed on probation for two years on condition that he spend 30 days in the county jail (just a "taste" of jail!), and the imposition of further sentence was deferred. Four months later, he was brought into court on charges of a burglary. He was not represented by counsel, nor was he asked whether he wanted counsel. The court revoked his probation and imposed the maximum sentence of 10 years (but with a recommendation to the parole board that he serve only one year and then be paroled). Six years later, Mempa filed for a writ of habeas corpus, claiming due process violation in the denial of counsel at his sentencing and probation revocation proceeding. The "deferred sentencing" procedure in Washington was held by the Supreme Court to have been such an important proceeding that due process required the presence of counsel. In effect, it was a combination of probation revocation and sentencing.

In *Gideon v. Wainwright*, 372 U.S. 335 (1963), the right to counsel had been established as a basic right in felony cases. This was done by application of the Sixth and the Fourteenth Amendments. The right was extended by the Court to a defendant in a deferred sentencing and probation revocation proceeding in *Mempa*. As the Court said in *Mempa*, there is a constitutional right to counsel in felony cases "at every stage of a criminal proceeding where substantial rights of a criminal accused may be affected." At his sentencing, albeit "deferred," Mempa was entitled to the appointment of counsel, the Supreme Court said, because his rights (his liberty interest) were so substantially affected.

The second decision heavily relied on by the Court in *Gagnon* was *Morrissey v. Brewer,* the parole revocation case that we just discussed.

> **Even though the revocation of parole is not a part of the criminal prosecution, we held [in *Morrissey*] that the loss of liberty entailed is a serious deprivation requiring that the parolee be accorded due process.**

The Court held that the revocation of probation and the revocation of parole are so similar that the right to due process is the same for each one. Therefore, for revocation of probation, the Supreme Court held that:

[A] probationer, like a parolee, is entitled to a preliminary and a final revocation hearing, under the conditions specified in *Morrissey v. Brewer*.

At the preliminary hearing for probation revocation (just as for parole revocation), there must be advance notice of the alleged violations, an opportunity to appear and to present evidence, a conditional right to confront adverse witnesses, an independent decision maker, and a written report of the hearing. (The condition on the right to confront adverse witnesses is that the hearing judge or officer may decline confrontation of a witness in cases in which it is determined to pose a risk to the safety of the witness.) The minimum requirements at a final hearing are very similar; the one additional requirement for final hearings is that the parolee (or probationer) should be advised of what evidence there is against him.

The Court then went on in *Gagnon* to decide the issue left undecided in *Morrissey*: whether there is also a right to counsel (either retained or, for indigents, appointed) at revocation hearings. The Court accepted neither the argument that counsel should be provided in all hearings nor the argument that there is no due process requirement to provide counsel at all. In many cases, the Supreme Court said, the probationer or parolee has been convicted of committing another crime or has admitted those charges against him. In those cases, there is no need to provide counsel in order to relitigate those criminal charges as a basis for revocation. The probationer or parolee may want to present mitigating reasons why (even if there has been criminal or other violative conduct) revocation is not appropriate. Those reasons, however, are not usually so complicated that they necessitate counsel, according to the Court.

The Court also expressed concern that the introduction of counsel into revocation proceedings would change the nature of those proceedings and make them more adversarial and confrontational.

It is neither possible nor prudent to attempt to formulate a precise and detailed set of guidelines to be followed in determining when the providing of counsel is necessary....[C]onsiderable discretion must be allowed the responsible agency in making the decision. Presumptively, it may be said that counsel should be provided in cases where, after being informed of his right to request counsel, the probationer or parolee makes such a request, based on a timely and colorable claim (i) that he has not committed the alleged violation of the conditions upon which he is at liberty; or (ii) that, even if the violation is a matter of public record or is uncontested, there are substantial reasons which justified or mitigated the violation and make revocation inappropriate, and that the reasons are complex or otherwise difficult to develop or present.

Thus, for probation or parole revocation proceedings, there is a right to counsel but only in limited circumstances: when the charges are contested, or when there are substantial mitigating reasons for the violative conduct and those reasons are complex or difficult to present. Well, that is all very good for the Supreme Court to proclaim, and it is (by reason of that proclamation) the law for entitlement to counsel in revocation proceedings. But the guidance is so complex to pursue in practice that, rather than risk mistakes in its application, it should be no surprise that, as a matter of reasonable precaution, courts at probation revocation proceedings and parole boards at most parole revocation proceedings typically allow counsel to appear.

Courts, of course, have the authority to appoint counsel (or obtain representation from a local defender's office). Parole boards typically do not have such authority, so they must set up some procedure to obtain counsel for indigents when the need exists, based on the Supreme Court standard, or perhaps in all revocation hearings.

▪ *Griffin v. Wisconsin; United States v. Knights; Samson v. California; Pennsylvania Board of Probation and Parole v. Scott*

When they are under supervision, it is clear that the rights of probationers and parolees are significantly limited, mainly by the conditions and restrictions that are placed upon them in the terms of their probation or parole. Their constitutional rights may also be limited in comparison to ordinary citizens, as was shown in *Griffin v. Wisconsin*, 483 U.S. 868 (1987). Probation officers went to Griffin's apartment and searched it without a warrant after the police advised them that he might have guns there. Police officers went along during the search, and a gun was found. Griffin was convicted of possession of a firearm by a convicted felon.

The Supreme Court, in its opinion, noted the very practical problems that obtaining a search warrant would present, as opposed to the need for efficiently supervising a probationer. There could be delays in obtaining a warrant, and the court deciding upon issuing a search warrant would have the authority to decide whether this degree of supervision was necessary. The burden of having to show probable cause, as a basis for issuance of the search warrant, would probably not have been met in this case. Although searching without probable cause and without a warrant clearly can operate to the detriment of the probationer, his situation as a person under close supervision by his probation officer overrides his personal protections, the Court said, which are otherwise guaranteed to him by the Constitution.

> **[T]he probation agency must be able to act based upon a lesser degree of certainty than the Fourth Amendment would otherwise require in order to intervene [by conducting a search] before a probationer does damage to himself or society.**

Thus, the Supreme Court held that the warrantless search of the probationer's home did not violate the constitutional rights of the probationer.

In *Griffin*, the right to search was granted to probation officers by a state regulation that gave them permission to search a probationer's residence when there were "reasonable grounds" to believe there was something illegal or impermissible in his home. Other states may also have statutes that provide such authority to search. Alternatively, state authorities may have probationers sign a consent that permits searches of their homes or possessions (such as a car) when they are placed on probation. This practice—having the probationer agree in writing to the searches, and the searches conducted under it—has been declared constitutional in *United States v. Giannetta*, 711 F. Supp. 1144 (D. ME 1989). This agreement, in effect, becomes part of the order that places the probationer on probation. Similarly, the search authority may be incorporated into the standard conditions of probation that are given to (and should be explained to) the probationer when he is ordered into probation status.

In *United States v. Knights*, 534 U.S. 112 (2001), the Supreme Court discussed the breadth of this concept. As a condition of placing Knights on probation, a California court's order provided that Knights's person, property, vehicle, residence, and personal effects would be subject "to search at anytime, with or without a search warrant, warrant of arrest or reasonable cause by any probation officer or law enforcement officer." Knights signed the order, acknowledging this condition.

Shortly after being placed on probation, Knights was suspected of being involved in criminal activity. Police surveillance was set up. Based on reasonable suspicion, but without a warrant and pursuant to Knights's probation condition, police searched his apartment, where they found, among other items, a detonation cord, ammunition, and liquid chemicals. Knights was arrested and subsequently indicted. Knights moved to suppress the evidence found during the search of his apartment. The district court, with the court of appeals affirming, held that the search was impermissible. The appeals court held that the search condition in Knights's probation order had to be seen as limited to probation searches and did not extend to those for investigation purposes. The Supreme Court reversed, holding that the Fourth Amendment did not limit searches pursuant to this probation condition to those with a probationary purpose.

When an officer has reasonable suspicion [rather than probable cause, which is a higher standard ordinarily required by the Fourth Amendment] that a probationer subject to a search condition is engaged in criminal activity, there is enough likelihood that criminal conduct is occurring that an intrusion on the probationer's significantly diminished privacy interests is reasonable.

Griffin and *Knights* concerned probationers, but similar rules apply to persons released on parole and generally to the authority of supervising parole officers, because parolees also are clearly under sanction of a sentence; therefore, the rationale for restrictions on their rights (even constitutional ones) as spelled out in *Griffin* and *Knights* would equally apply.

A question left unresolved by *Griffin* and *Knights* was "whether a condition of release can so diminish or eliminate a released prisoner's reasonable expectation of privacy that a suspicion-less search by a law enforcement officer would not offend the Fourth Amendment." It was this question that the Supreme Court answered in *Samson v. California*, 547 U.S. 843 (2006).

California passed a law requiring that persons released on state parole had to agree in writing to searches of their person by a parole officer or other law enforcement officer at any time without warrant or cause. Samson was released on parole after expressly agreeing to the search condition, as well as other conditions of parole. His status as a parolee was known by local police, and acting under the belief there was a parole warrant for Samson, local police stopped him. After learning there was no warrant, local police, pursuant to the state statute authorizing the search of a person on parole, conducted a search of Samson's person. During the search, illegal drugs were found on Samson. After the state courts concluded the search was constitutional, Samson appealed to the Supreme Court.

Relying heavily on its previous *Griffin* and *Knights* opinions, the Court first noted that on the continuum of criminal punishment, a parolee has "fewer expectations of privacy than probationers, because parole is more akin to imprisonment than probation is to imprisonment." A person placed on parole remained under the custody of the state Department of Corrections and was subject to a number of mandatory restrictions, such as drug testing, limitations on travel and association, and requirements for reporting to a parole officer. The nature and extent of these restrictions "demonstrate that parolees...have severely diminished expectations of privacy by virtue of their status alone." As a condition of being allowed to serve the parole term in the community, Samson had to agree to suspicionless searches by a parole officer or other law enforcement officer; his agreement "significantly diminished" his reasonable expectation of privacy.

The Court next ruled that the state has "an 'overwhelming interest' in supervising parolees because 'parolees...are more likely to commit future criminal offenses.'" The state has an interest in reducing recidivism, and promoting both reintegration into the community and the positive citizenship of offenders. These substantial governmental interests justify "privacy intrusions that would not otherwise be tolerated under the Fourth Amendment." The Court agreed with the state that the "ability to conduct suspicionless searches of parolees serves [the state's] interest in reducing recidivism, in a manner that aids, rather than hinders, the reintegration of parolees into productive society."

The Court concluded that the search by law enforcement officers of a parolee like Samson was reasonable under the totality of circumstances. The Court considered, but rejected, the argument that most other states and the federal government are able to safely monitor the behavior of offenders on community supervision, and both reduce recidivism and promote reintegration while mandating that searches of parolees be based on some degree of individualized suspicion.

> **That some States and the federal government require a level of individualized suspicion is of little relevance to our determination whether California's supervisory system is drawn to meet its needs and is reasonable, taking into account a parolee's substantially diminished expectation of privacy.**

In *Pennsylvania Board of Probation and Parole v. Scott*, 524 U.S. 357 (1998), Scott, as a condition of his release, agreed not to own or possess any firearms or other weapons. His parole agreement, which he signed, allowed state probation and parole authorities to search his person, property, and residence, without warrant, and to seize and use as evidence in revocation proceedings any violative items found.

Five months into his parole, an arrest warrant was issued. Three parole officers arrested Scott. Prior to being transferred to a correctional facility, Scott gave the officers the keys to his residence. The officers went to his house and conducted a search without warrant. There they discovered five firearms, a compound bow, and three arrows. This discovery was a contributory factor, along with alcohol consumption charges, to the decision to revoke Scott's parole and recommit him to prison.

Scott filed suit in the Commonwealth Court of Pennsylvania—both that court and, later, the Pennsylvania Supreme Court found a violation of Scott's Fourth Amendment right against unreasonable searches, regardless of Scott's signing of the parole agreement. The United States Supreme Court disagreed and held that the search was permissible and the revocation action taken was proper.

> **The costs of allowing a parolee to avoid the consequences of his violation are compounded by the fact that parolees...are more likely to commit future criminal offenses than are average citizens....Indeed, this is the very premise behind the system of close parole supervision.**

Because parole revocation deprives the parolee not "of the absolute liberty to which every citizen is entitled, but only of the conditional liberty properly dependent on observance of special parole restrictions,"...States have wide latitude under the Constitution to structure parole revocation proceedings.[6]

The Supreme Court, in these holdings, is clearly distinguishing the rights (and the conditional liberty) of probationers and parolees from the liberty afforded to regular, law-abiding citizens.

■ Martinez v. California

An interesting sidelight of parole status is presented in *Martinez v. California*, 444 U.S. 277 (1980). Thomas was convicted of attempted rape and sentenced to 20 years, with a recommendation that he not be paroled. Nevertheless, after five years in prison he was paroled. Five months later, Thomas tortured and killed a 15-year-old girl. Her family brought suit in state court against California and its parole authorities, alleging that her life had been taken without due process of law and claiming that the parole authorities were therefore liable for the wrong decision made in releasing Thomas.

According to the record (allegations by the plaintiffs), it was more than a poor decision. The parole was made despite Thomas's record and the warning in his record that he was likely to commit another violent crime. Also, it was alleged that Thomas was not properly supervised while on parole. The actions of officials were called, in the plaintiffs' pleadings, "reckless, willful, wanton, and malicious." The key to the outcome of the case, however, was a California statute that provided that government officials were not liable for any injury resulting from a decision to release a prisoner on parole, from determining the conditions of his parole, or whether to revoke his parole. This was held to be a complete defense for the defendants in the case, giving them absolute immunity from a suit for damages.

Noting that the availability of the statutory defense might have encouraged the parole board to take greater risks in their decision making than they would otherwise have done, the Supreme Court upheld the legality of the immunity statute and the dismissal of the case that was brought by the victim's family.

This [immunity] statute merely provides a defense to potential state tort law liability....Whether one agrees or disagrees with California's decision to provide absolute immunity for parole officials in a case of this kind, one cannot deny that it rationally furthers a policy that reasonable lawmakers may favor....We therefore find no merit in the contention that the State's immunity statute is unconstitutional.

Martinez (the deceased's family) had also filed action under 42 U.S.C. § 1983, claiming a constitutional violation of the victim's rights in depriving her of her life without due process of law. The statute granting immunity did not apply to this claim, because the California immunity statute only protected defendant officials in state tort law actions. The Section 1983 action, although a federal law, was accepted for adjudication in the state courts under precedent, in

Testa v. Katt, 330 U.S. 386 (1947), that allowed states to entertain claims under federal statutes for enforcement in state courts.

The Supreme Court reasoned as follows: Section 1983 protects persons from injuries suffered because of violations of rights that are secured by the U.S. Constitution. The plaintiffs here claimed a constitutional violation when the victim's life was taken from her without due process of law. "But the Fourteenth Amendment protected her only from deprivation by the 'State of life without due process of law.'" The Court explained further:

> **Although the decision to release Thomas from prison was action by the State, the action of Thomas five months later cannot be fairly characterized as state action....Her life was taken by the parolee five months after his release. He was in no sense an agent of the parole board....[The victim's] death is too remote a consequence of the parole officers' action to hold them responsible under the federal civil rights law.**

The action by a court placing a defendant on probation is even more clearly immunized from suits for damages, such as those claiming a poor or even reckless decision, because judges have long been held to be immune from lawsuit arising from their judicial decisions, and the same applies broadly to judicial officers. See *Stump v. Sparkman*, 435 U.S. 349 (1978). Judges enjoy a sweeping kind of immunity, which bars any money-damages suit whenever the judge is performing a judicial act.

But that does not mean that a judge is immune from all lawsuits and can never be held liable. In *Forrester v. White,* 484 U.S. 219 (1988), Judge White had hired Forrester as an adult and juvenile probation officer. The Supreme Court in the *Forrester* case observed that judicial immunity is an accepted principle in this country:

> **[T]his Court [has] found that judicial immunity was "the settled doctrine of the English courts for many centuries, and has never been denied, that we are aware of, in the courts of this country."**

[The authors observe: Judges repeatedly holding that they are immune from lawsuits somehow is not too surprising.] Nonetheless, such immunity only applies to the court's adjudicative functions and not employment or other administrative functions. When the judge fired the probation officer, he was acting in an administrative capacity, the Court held, and the judge in that situation was not entitled to absolute immunity. (The Court did note that qualified immunity, similar to that enjoyed by officials in the executive branch of government, would be available to judges in their employment decisions, such as this one.)

■ *Payne v. Tennessee; Greenholtz v. Inmates; Swarthout v. Cooke; Board of Pardons v. Allen*

An essential area of probation and parole that we have not yet considered is the initial decision to place the defendant on probation or the inmate on parole. As to probation, the law is clear that, because placing the defendant on probation is an imposition of a sentence, the due process protections of a criminal trial apply; this entitles the defendant to the opportunity to be present and to present evidence for mitigation of the sentence and to be heard himself (the right of **allocution**). Procedures at sentencing are somewhat more relaxed, and due process requirements are not as strict as they are in the main part of the trial, when the court or jury is considering the defendant's guilt or innocence. This is because the main inquiry at sentencing is to find the most appropriate sanction for the particular defendant in light of his past behavior and (at least in some courts) his rehabilitative needs. Individualization of the sentence has been recognized by the Supreme Court as an important sentencing objective, as emphasized in *Williams v. New York*, 337 U.S. 241 (1949).

As we saw, in *Mempa v. Rhay,* even in the case of deferred sentencing there is a right to counsel at every significant stage of the proceedings, which includes any sentencing hearing or procedure. There are many rules that are developed locally regarding sentencing requirements. For example, there has been a strong movement recently to afford more rights to victims and their families at sentencing, and, in some jurisdictions, a "victim impact statement" (VIS) must be presented to the court. The Supreme Court has noted this procedure and approved it in *Payne v. Tennessee,* 501 U.S. 808 (1991).

> **We thus hold that if the State chooses to permit the admission of victim impact evidence and prosecutorial argument on that subject, the Eighth Amendment erects no per se bar. A State may legitimately conclude that evidence about the victim and about the impact of the murder on the victim's family is relevant to the jury's decision as to whether or not the death penalty should be imposed. There is no reason to treat such evidence differently than other relevant evidence is treated.**

This is consistent with *Williams v. New York*, cited previously, which encourages sentencing courts to gather all kinds of information about the defendant in order to individualize the sentence. The *Williams* case has never been overruled, but it has been cited in later years in numerous cases as a guiding Supreme Court ruling with regard to sentencing standards. In any event, we know that some basic due process rights apply at sentencing when the defendant is placed on probation. These are the same rights that any defendant has at the sentencing stage of his criminal prosecution.

The more contentious question is whether due process is required at the time the decision is made whether to place an inmate on parole—that is, at the hearing on his parole release. In *Greenholtz v. Inmates*, 442 U.S. 1 (1979), the Supreme Court noted that "parole *release* and parole *revocation* are quite different. There is a crucial distinction between being deprived of a liberty one has, as in parole [revocation], and being denied a conditional liberty that one desires." (The Court notes a wonderful quote from Judge Henry Friendly: "There is a human difference between losing what one has and not getting what one wants.") The Court in *Greenholtz* applied this concept:

> **That the state holds out the possibility of parole provides no more than a mere hope that the benefit will be obtained. [That is] a hope which is not protected by due process.**

Thus, the Court in *Greenholtz* held that the paroling process—the review and decision making on whether an inmate should be paroled—involves subjective and discretionary assessments.

There is no liberty interest inherent in the parole-release procedures and, therefore, no constitutional right to due process inherent in those procedures.

However, the Court found that there was another possible source of a liberty interest, which was in the language of the parole statute. The Nebraska statute provided that the parole board "shall order" the release of an inmate unless it found that one of four conditions prevailed. The Court concluded that this language created an expectation of release that entitled an inmate to some due process during the consideration of his parole. How much due process?

Merely because a statutory expectation exists cannot mean that in addition to the full panoply of due process required to convict and confine there must also be repeated, adversary hearings in order to continue the confinement.... The Nebraska procedure affords an opportunity to be heard, and when parole is denied it informs the inmate in what respects he falls short of qualifying for parole; this affords the process that is due under these circumstances.

Those seem to be the minimal due process steps that the Court would require when the state statutes or rules have mandatory, nondiscretionary language that governs parole board actions. Nebraska, in fact, had some additional procedural protections, but those were not required in the Court's holding just quoted. The more formal hearing, which included more procedures, that the court of appeals had ordered was found to be too heavy and was not endorsed by the Supreme Court. The appellate court had ordered advance written notice, the right to appear and present documentary evidence (but not witnesses), a written record of the proceedings, and a written explanation of the facts relied on and the reasons for the board's actions. As a result of the Court's rejection of these requirements, due process entitlement at parole release hearings is limited to the few requirements referred to in the previous quotation.

The Court reaffirmed this position in *Swarthout v. Cooke*, 562 U.S. ___, (2011). In *Swarthout* (and the companion case *Cate v. Clay*), the Ninth Circuit Court of Appeals had held that California's parole statute created a liberty interest protected by the due process clause and that the state's statutory language of "some evidence" was a component of the federally protected liberty interest. The Supreme Court disagreed. The Supreme Court said the proper analysis under the due process clause has two steps: "We first ask whether there exists a liberty or property interest of which a person has been deprived, and if so we ask whether the procedures followed by the State were constitutionally permissible." On the first point, the Court held that whatever liberty interest did exist, it was created by state law, adding that, "no opinion of ours supports converting California's 'some evidence' rule into a substantive federal requirement." The Court continued, saying when such an interest is created, "the minimum procedures adequate for due process protection of that interest are those set forth in *Greenholtz*."

In *Board of Pardons v. Allen*, 482 U.S. 369 (1987), the Court underscored the holding of *Greenholtz*. This was a case brought by Montana inmates who claimed, under 42 U.S.C. Section 1983, that they had been denied due process rights in parole release procedures. The Montana statute stated that "the Board shall release on parole [an inmate] ... when in its opinion there is reasonable probability that the prisoner can be released without detriment to the prisoner or to the community." The Court held that this language created a liberty interest in parole release under the due process clause, because it used mandatory ("shall") language that created a presumption that parole release would occur when the designated findings were made.[7]

■ Connecticut Board of Pardons v. Dumschat; Ohio Adult Parole Authority v. Woodard

In *Connecticut Board of Pardons v. Dumschat*, 452 U.S. 458 (1981), the Supreme Court dealt with a challenge to the actions of the Connecticut Board of Pardons. Dumschat was serving a life sentence and applied for a **commutation** of sentence.[8] When his application for commutation of sentence was summarily denied, Dumschat claimed that he should have been given a hearing by the pardons board. The Connecticut law gave total discretion to the board to grant or deny pardons or commutations. Dumschat, however, contended that he had some expectation of receiving a commutation, because 85–90% of life sentences in the state were commuted. The Supreme Court denied his contention.

> [A] Connecticut felon's expectation that a lawfully imposed sentence will be commuted or that he will be pardoned is no more substantial than an inmate's expectation, for example, that he will not be transferred to another prison; it is simply a unilateral hope.... No matter how frequently a particular form of clemency has been granted, the statistical probabilities standing alone generate no constitutional protections; a contrary conclusion would trivialize the Constitution. The ground for a constitutional claim, if any, must be found in statutes or other rules defining the obligations of the authority charged with exercising clemency.

The Court relied on both *Greenholtz* and *Dumschat* in *Ohio Adult Parole Authority v. Woodard*, 523 U.S. 272 (1998). The Ohio constitution gives the governor the power to grant clemency as he believes proper. The legislature may regulate the application and investigation process (which it has delegated largely to the Ohio Adult Parole Authority), but it may not curtail the governor's discretionary authority.

Woodard was sentenced to death for aggravated murder, which he committed in the course of a carjacking. His conviction was affirmed, and the Supreme Court declined to review the conviction. As his date for execution approached, the Ohio Adult Parole Authority, as required, notified Woodard that he could have a clemency interview on September 9, 1994, if he wished, and that his clemency hearing would be on September 16, 1994. Woodard objected to the short notice for the interview and requested counsel be allowed to participate. Ohio did not allow counsel at this interview. The Supreme Court held that there was no due process violation in these procedures.

> Despite the Authority's mandatory procedures, the ultimate decisionmaker, the Governor, retains broad discretion. Under any analysis, the Governor's executive discretion need not be fettered by the types of procedural protections sought by respondent [Woodard]....There is thus no substantive expectation of clemency. Moreover....the availability of clemency, or the manner in which the State conducts clemency proceedings, does not impose "atypical and significant hardship on the inmate in relation to the ordinary incidents of prison life."...A denial of clemency merely means that the inmate must serve the sentence originally imposed.

Nor did the Court see a violation of Woodard's right under the Fifth Amendment to be free from self-incrimination.

> It is difficult to see how a voluntary interview could "compel" respondent to speak. He merely
> faces a choice quite similar to the sorts of choices that a criminal defendant must make in the
> course of criminal proceedings, none of which has ever been held to violate the Fifth
> Amendment.

■ *United States v. Addonizio; California Department of Corrections v. Morales; Garner v. Jones; Lynce v. Mathis*

These cases look at the question of whether the parole rules may be changed after the defendant has been sentenced. In *United States v. Addonizio*, 442 U.S. 178 (1979), Addonizio complained that the U.S. Parole Commission had changed its rules while he was confined and that the change of rules resulted in his being imprisoned longer than the sentencing judge intended. The action brought was a collateral attack on Addonizio's sentence under a federal statute (Title 28, U.S. Code, Section 2255) that permits a challenge when a prisoner contends that his sentence is constitutionally or legally invalid. (All jurisdictions have procedures for such a post-sentencing attack on the validity of the sentence. In common law, the procedure was called petitioning for a writ of **coram nobis**. Most U.S. jurisdictions have abandoned that old nomenclature but provide for the same type of judicial review by some statutory or procedural authorization.) Addonizio had been sentenced to 10 years imprisonment, but the judge had indicated that he expected, with good institutional behavior, Addonizio would be released when he became eligible for parole after serving one-third of his sentence. The U.S. Parole Commission adopted new policies three years after Addonizio was sentenced, giving much heavier weight to the seriousness of the offense in determining parole release and resulting in the postponement of Addonizio's consideration for parole. When he applied to his sentencing court, that court found that its sentencing expectations had been frustrated by the commission's actions and ordered Addonizio released, reducing his sentence to "time served."

The Supreme Court held that that action by the sentencing court was invalid. In effect, it said that frustrating the desires of the sentencing judge was not a basis for setting aside the sentence.

> [T]he sentence was and is a lawful one .... Congress has decided that the [Parole] Commission
> is in the best position to determine when release is appropriate, and in doing so, to moderate
> the disparities in the sentencing practices of individual judges .... The import of this statutory
> scheme is clear: the judge has no enforceable expectations with respect to the actual release
> of a sentenced defendant short of his statutory term .... [T]he actual [parole] decision is not
> his to make, either at the time of sentencing or later if his expectations are not met.

Which is to say, when there are parole statutes, the parole decision is to be made by the parole board and not by the court (much as many judges dislike this limitation on their sentencing power and discretion).

In *California Department of Corrections v. Morales*, 514 U.S. 499 (1995), Morales was serving a sentence of 15 years to life and became eligible for parole in 1990. He was given his first parole hearing in 1989, and parole was denied. Under rules in effect at the time he committed his offense, Morales would have been entitled to subsequent hearings every year on his suitability to be paroled. The law was then amended to allow the Board of Prison Terms to defer suitability hearings for up to three years if the inmate had been convicted of more than one offense involving the taking of life (Morales had been convicted twice of murder). Pursuant to this change in the law, the board rescheduled Morales for a hearing in three years; that is, he would be heard in 1992 rather than in 1990. Morales filed a habeas corpus petition, claiming the amendment constituted an ex post facto law in violation of the Constitution.

The Constitution forbids (in Article I, Section 10) passing any "ex post facto Law." This phrase has been interpreted to mean that laws may not be enacted that alter the definition of a crime after it has been committed, or that increase the punishment for criminal acts after their commission. The California statute clearly did not change the definition of Morales' crime, so the question is whether the amendment of the parole law increased the punishment for his crime. The Supreme Court held that it did not. It did allow the board to change the times when it would hold parole hearings, but this was only a procedural change. Here, the change only applied to a class of inmates for whom the likelihood of release on parole was fairly remote (inmates who had taken more than one life). The Court held that the California amendment did not violate the ex post facto clause, because it created "only the most speculative and attenuated risk of increasing the measure of punishment attached to the covered crimes."

The *Morales* decision led to *Garner v. Jones*, 529 U.S. 244 (2000). Jones was serving a life sentence in Georgia for murder. After five years, he escaped, during which time he committed a second murder, receiving a second life term. Under Georgia law, the Georgia Parole Board was required to consider parole for inmates serving life sentences after seven years. At the time Jones was convicted of his second murder, the board's rules required reconsideration every three years. In 1985, after Jones began serving his second life sentence, the board amended its rules to provide reconsideration hearings for inmates serving life sentences at least every eight years.

At his 1989 hearing, Jones was told he would be next considered for parole in 1997. In 1991, the Court of Appeals for the Eleventh Circuit, in a separate case, held that the retroactive application of the eight-year rule violated the ex post facto clause. The Georgia Parole Board therefore returned to its three-year rule. Accordingly, Jones appeared before the board in 1992 and 1995, being denied on both occasions.

Following the Supreme Court's 1995 *Morales* ruling, the board again began to schedule eight-year reconsiderations. The board had the option to make the period shorter, but chose not to do so for Jones because of his multiple offenses and the circumstances and nature of the second offense. Jones sued, alleging violation of the ex post facto clause. The Supreme Court saw the Georgia law as reasonable, allowing it to put its resources to better use, stating that "By concentrating its efforts on those cases identified as having a good possibility of early release, the Board's Rules might result in the release of some prisoners earlier than would have been the case otherwise."

The Court found that, based on the record in this case, it could not conclude that the change lengthened Jones's period of actual confinement, noting that the Georgia rule allowed for earlier consideration when warranted.

In *Morales*, we relied upon the State's representation that its parole board had a practice of granting inmates' requests for early review....The policy statement here, by contrast, is a formal, published statement as to how the Board intends to enforce its Rule....Absent

any demonstration to the contrary from respondent [Jones], we respect the Board's representation that inmates, upon making a showing of a "change in their circumstance(s)" or
upon the Board's receipt of "new information," may request expedited consideration.

The Court thus gave deference to the Georgia Parole Board and, by extension, to other
correctional professionals, allowing them to retain the flexibility needed to manage the parole
process for the benefit of all. Experience has shown that, where officials fail to follow through
on this trust, the courts will step forward.

Lynce v. Mathis, 519 U.S. 433 (1997), is a prison case in which the Supreme Court held
there was an ex post facto violation. In 1986, Lynce received a 22-year (8,030 days) sentence
for attempted murder. In 1992, he was released from prison after the Florida Department of
Corrections determined he had earned five different types of early-release credits, totaling 5,668
days. In addition, 1,860 of those days (called provisional credits) were awarded as a result of
the state's plan to reduce overcrowding in its prisons. Shortly after being released, the Florida
attorney general issued an opinion interpreting a 1992 statute as having retroactively canceled
all provisional credits awarded to inmates who had been convicted of murder or attempted
murder. Lynce was one of the 164 offenders Florida released who suddenly had an arrest warrant
issued because of this change in the law providing provisional release credits. He was returned
to custody with a new release date in 1998.

In his petition for a writ of habeas corpus, Lynce claimed the retroactive cancellation of
provisional credits violated the ex post facto clause. The Supreme Court agreed. To be ex post
facto, the Court said the law had to be retrospective—it would have to apply to events occurring
before its enactment—and it must disadvantage the affected offender. The Court held that the
operation of the 1992 statute, which canceled the overcrowding credits and required Lynce's
reconfinement, was clearly retroactive. On the issue of whether Lynce had been "disadvantaged,"
the Court stated the following:

> The 1992 statute has unquestionably disadvantaged the petitioner because it resulted in his
> rearrest and prolonged his imprisonment. Unlike the California amendment at issue in
> *Morales*, the 1992 Florida statute did more than simply remove a mechanism that created
> an opportunity for early release for a class of prisoners whose release was unlikely; rather
> it made ineligible for early release a class of prisoners who were previously eligible—
> including some, like petitioner, who had actually been released.

A key distinction between *Morales* and *Lynce* is that *Morales* did not affect the length of
punishment being served; *Lynce* did, by canceling provisional credits the inmates had previously
earned and, as in Lynce's case, resulting in pulling some people back into prison.

■ *Jago v. Van Curen*

What if officials give an inmate a break, but then change their minds? Van Curen was sentenced
to a term of 6 to 100 years in prison. He would have been eligible for parole in 1976. Ohio
passed a "shock parole" statute, which allowed earlier parole of first offenders who had served

at least six months in prison for nonviolent crimes. Under this statute, Van Curen was evaluated by the Ohio Adult Parole Authority (OAPA), which approved his early release in 1974. He attended prerelease classes and was measured for civilian clothes. But then, soon after his parole interview, the Parole Authority learned that Van Curen had not been truthful in the interview or in the parole plan he had submitted for his release. He said he had embezzled $1 million when, in fact, he had embezzled $6 million; he said that he was planning to live with his half-brother if paroled, when, in fact, he intended to live with his homosexual lover. Because of these revelations, OAPA rescinded its earlier action and continued his case to a later date. Van Curen received no hearing with regard to the parole rescission action.

The court of appeals ruled that, once the decision to release Van Curen on shock parole was made, he was entitled to a hearing to explain the false statements that became the basis for the rescission decision. In *Jago v. Van Curen*, 454 U.S. 14 (1981), the Supreme Court disagreed and reversed.

> **We do not doubt that respondent suffered "grievous loss" upon OAPA's rescission of his parole. But we have previously "reject[ed]...the notion that any grievous loss visited upon a person by the State is sufficient to invoke the procedural protections of the Due Process Clause." *Meachum v. Fano*....We hold that the Court of Appeals erred in finding a constitutionally protected liberty interest...We think that the reasoning of *Greenholtz...Dumschat*...and the Court of Appeals' own concession that Ohio law creates no protected "liberty" interest, require reversal of the holding of the Court of Appeals that respondent was entitled to a hearing prior to denial of his parole.**

■ Moody v. Daggett

Moody was on parole from a federal rape conviction and was sentenced to new 10-year sentences for manslaughter and second-degree murder. He was serving those sentences when the U.S. Board of Parole issued a warrant that charged him with violating the terms of his parole release. This warrant was lodged (as is frequently done) with prison authorities as a detainer. Moody asked that the warrant be executed at once, so any prison time he had to serve for violation of the terms of his parole could run concurrently with his homicide sentences. The parole board denied his request and ordered the warrant to be held until his release on the homicide sentences, at which time the board intended to execute its warrant and take Moody into custody for his parole violation. (This meant that any term for parole violation would be served consecutively to his new prison terms—not concurrently, as Moody would have liked.) Moody filed a habeas corpus petition, claiming primarily that he had been denied a prompt parole revocation hearing.

In *Moody v. Daggett*, 429 U.S. 78 (1976), the Supreme Court held that there had not been an illegal loss of liberty caused by the lodging of the warrant against Moody and that he was not entitled to an immediate parole revocation hearing. The Court noted that the loss of liberty that Moody was suffering came from his sentences on his two homicide convictions. Even though Moody claimed that the existence of the warrant was a heavy cloud over his head and might adversely affect his eligibility for some privileges while confined, the Court said that there were good reasons for the board to defer its decision and consider Moody for release or revocation of his parole when he finished his current sentences.

> **With only a prospect of future incarceration which is far from certain, we cannot say that the parole violator warrant has any present or inevitable effect upon the liberty interests which *Morrissey* [that is, the decision in *Morrissey v. Brewer*, discussed earlier in this chapter] sought to protect. [*Morrissey*] established execution of the warrant and custody under that warrant as the operative event triggering any loss of liberty attendant upon parole revocation....[T]he loss of liberty as a parole violator does not occur until the parolee is taken into custody under the warrant....[W]e hold that he has been deprived of no constitutionally protected rights simply by issuance of a parole violator warrant.**

Thus, the practice of lodging warrants for violations of parole or probation against inmates who are in custody on new charges continues. A **detainer** is often held on file until the inmate is released from the sentence(s) he is serving on his new (more recently committed) offenses. The *Moody* decision tells us that there is no constitutional violation in that practice. Indeed, the Supreme Court pointed out that there may be very good reasons for the parole or probation authorities to wait until the new sentence is served, allowing them to make a more informed judgment about whether the probation or parole status of the inmate should be revoked. (Not infrequently, the revocation authority may decide that the new sentence is punishment enough and that the inmate may be released to the street after that sentence is served, usually returning to supervision under the earlier probation or parole status.)

■ *Smith v. Doe; Connecticut Department of Public Safety v. Doe*

Are there crimes that are thought to be so reprehensible as to require continuing governmental oversight even after the criminal has paid his debt to society? *Kansas v. Hendricks*, 521 U.S. 346 (1997), discussed the Court's upholding civil commitment for persons who complete their criminal sentences and who, due to "mental abnormality" or "personality disorder," are likely to become involved in "predatory acts of sexual violence." But are there other steps that may be taken, short of confinement? The answer is yes. In *Smith v. Doe*, 538 U.S. 84 (2003), and its companion case, *Connecticut Department of Public Safety v. Doe*, 538 U.S. 1 (2003), the Supreme Court upheld the constitutionality of sex offender registration. In *Smith*, the challenge was made based on ex post facto arguments. In *Connecticut,* the challenge was based on allegations of due process violation.

    Smith concerned the Alaska Sex Offender Registration Act. That Act required every sex offender or child kidnapper in the state to register with the department of corrections within 30 days prior to release from custody. If the offender was not confined, registration with local law enforcement agencies had to occur within a working day of the conviction or of the offender's entrance into the state. Periodic verification of the submitted information (which included name, address, and other specified information) was required, with the frequency (quarterly or annually) determined by the individual's type of criminal behavior. Similarly, the criminal behavior determined whether the verification was to continue for 15 years or for life. Nonconfidential information about the offender (such as name, address, photograph, place of employment, and nature of conviction) would also be made available to the public. The Act allowed the state to choose the means for making the public aware of the nonconfidential information, and the state chose to do this through the Internet. The Act's registration and notification requirements were to be retroactive.

The Doe respondents (two anonymous offenders) in *Smith* were convicted sex offenders. They had been released from prison and had completed sex offender treatment programs. Their convictions occurred before the act's passage, but pursuant to the Act they were required to register as sex offenders.

Doe I and Doe II and the wife of Doe I brought suit under 42 U.S.C. § 1983, asking that the Act be declared inapplicable to them under the ex post facto clause (of Article I of the Constitution) and the due process clause (of the Fourteenth Amendment). The district court ruled for the State; however, the appeals court held that the registration requirements were violations of the ex post facto clause because of the act's punitive and retroactive effects.

The Supreme Court, as it did in *Hendricks*, saw the threshold question as being whether the legislature meant to establish civil proceedings. If the Act was civil in nature, then the question would be whether the statutory scheme was so punitive in purpose or effect as to negate the state's intent (that is, to turn the procedure into criminal proceedings, despite what the legislature said).

In considering the first question, the Court examined what the state legislature identified as the law's objective—protection of the public. To assist in this process, the legislature believed it was beneficial to release certain information about sex offenders to public agencies and the general public. The Act mandated no specific procedures, leaving this to the Department of Public Safety, an agency responsible for enforcing both criminal and civil regulatory laws. The Court found this to be persuasive in determining the legislative intent of the law to be civil and not criminal.

In considering the second question, the Court did not see the Act's statutory scheme as being punitive.

> **Our system does not treat dissemination of truthful information in furtherance of a legitimate governmental objective as punishment.**

> **Although the public availability of the information may have a lasting and painful impact on the convicted sex offender, these consequences flow not from the Act's registration and dissemination provisions, but from the fact of conviction, already a matter of public record. The State makes the facts underlying the offenses and the resulting convictions accessible so members of the public can take the precautions they deem necessary before dealing with the registrant.**

> **[T]he Act has a legitimate nonpunitive purpose of "public safety, which is advanced by alerting the public to the risk of sex offenders in their community."**

The Court rejected the appeals court's view that the registration requirement was parallel to probation or supervised release (parole), as to the degree of restraint imposed. The Court pointed out that probation and supervised release have a number of mandatory conditions.[9] A person's failure to abide by these conditions can result in the person's return to prison. By contrast, sex offenders who are subject to the Act's registration requirements do not have such constraints.

The Court also said that features of the Act, such as its application to all convicted sex offenders without regard to their future dangerousness, the duration of the reporting requirements, and the wide dissemination of the information, did not make the law punitive.

> **The excessiveness inquiry of our ex post facto jurisprudence is not an exercise in determining whether the legislature has made the best choice possible to address the problem it seeks to remedy. The question is whether the regulatory means chosen are reasonable in light of the nonpunitive objective. The Act meets this standard.**

The Supreme Court looked at another challenge to sex offender registration, based on a due process complaint, in *Connecticut Department of Public Safety v. Doe*. This Doe filed on behalf of himself and other similarly situated sex offenders, claiming he was not a dangerous sex offender and that his being listed without a hearing deprived him of a liberty interest—his reputation combined with the alteration of his status under state law—and was violative of his due process rights. The district court enjoined the law's public disclosure provisions, and the appeals court affirmed.

In reversing the lower courts' decisions, the Supreme Court relied on Connecticut's legislative intent in passing the act. The Court said the state's intent was to facilitate access to publicly-available information about persons convicted of sexual offenses. There was no assessment of the specific risk of reoffending or of current dangerousness. Persons included on the registry were listed because of their conviction record and state law, and the main purpose of providing this information on the Internet was to make it more easily available, not to warn about any specific person. The Court held that the state's legislative scheme would govern.

> **[E]ven if respondent [Doe] could prove that he is not likely to be currently dangerous, Connecticut has decided that the registry information of all sex offenders—currently dangerous or not—must be publicly disclosed. Unless respondent can show that that substantive rule of law is defective (by conflicting with a provision of the Constitution), any hearing on current dangerousness is a bootless exercise.**

■ Community Corrections

In this section, we address a variety of correctional approaches, which, as a group, are somewhat difficult to define. Community corrections includes a diverse group of programs that are based in the community and offer sentencing alternatives to incarceration. Probation and parole fall under this broad category. Also included are facilities with such titles as prerelease centers, group homes, halfway houses, residential reentry centers, and community treatment centers (see **Figure 17-1**). The degree of security and staff supervision in these facilities may vary greatly, but, for our purposes, they all belong to the field of community corrections, because their security features are less restrictive than the traditional jail or prison. (This distinction tends to blur at the upper end of community facilities and the lower end of confinement facilities. Some community facilities enforce strict restrictions on residents' movements, allowing them to leave the "house" or "center" only for work, job interviews, or school, while some low security corrections facilities enforce very few restrictions.) The distinguishing feature is that in community corrections, the offender has some degree of freedom to move around in the surrounding community and also some gradual freedom to visit home and family.

Another kind of community corrections is the sentencing alternative, which avoids placing the defendant in a prison or jail. Probation is obviously one such type of sentencing alternative.

Figure 17-1 Front entrance of the Community Corrections Center in Omaha, Nebraska.
Source: © Mikael Karlsson/Alamy Images

Restitution and fines, strictly speaking, are sentencing alternatives because they are often used in place of a jail term, but they are not considered community corrections because they do not involve any supervisory action, other than the passive one of collecting the fine or the restitution payment from the offender.

Use of Fines

Fines are one of the oldest kinds of sentences. They are also the most common sanction used for minor offenses. For some serious offenses—particularly those involving financial gain, such as embezzlement, tax evasion, and drug offenses—they may be imposed in combination with other sanctions, including imprisonment. The Supreme Court has considered constitutional questions in connection with fines in a few instances.

Williams v. Illinois; Tate v. Short

In *Williams v. Illinois*, 399 U.S. 235 (1970), Williams had been sentenced to one year in jail and a $500 fine for petty theft. He did not have the money to pay the fine. Under an Illinois law, Williams was to be kept in jail until he "worked off" his fine at the rate of $5 a day. This meant that he would be kept in jail 100 days longer than he would have been had he been able to pay the fine. This extended sentence also was 100 days longer than the maximum jail sentence authorized for the crime he committed. The Supreme Court held that it was a violation of the equal protection clause to require an indigent defendant to serve longer than the most that could be served by a nonindigent defendant.

In the case of *Tate v. Short*, 401 U.S. 395 (1971), the Court extended its protection of indigents in fine cases. In this case, the defendant was convicted of several traffic offenses, none of which authorized sentences of incarceration. He was given a fine, which he was unable to pay. The court ordered him to the prison farm, where he was to "work off" his fine at the rate of $5 a day. The Supreme Court held that this too was impermissible discrimination against an indigent defendant in violation of the Fourteenth Amendment. Here, confinement was ordered "solely because of his indigency." This was an equal protection violation, which could not stand. Through these rulings, the old practices of "working off" fines have been abolished; the sentence of "$100 or 10 days," as well as its many variations, is no longer allowed.

■ *Bearden v. Georgia*

In *Bearden v. Georgia*, 461 U.S. 660 (1983), Bearden had been placed on probation, with a condition that he pay a fine of $500 and $250 in restitution. He paid $200 toward his fine, but he lost his job and was unable to pay more. When the balance of his fine and restitution came due (the court had given him four months to make the payments), Bearden told the probation office that he was going to be late with his payments because he could not find a job. He was taken before the trial court for a revocation hearing. Based on his failure to pay the fine and restitution, the court revoked probation and sentenced him to serve the balance of his probationary term (nearly three years) in prison. The Georgia Court of Appeals and the Georgia Supreme Court rejected Bearden's claim that imprisoning him for inability to pay his fine violated the equal protection clause. Courts in other states had held that revoking the probation of indigents for failure to pay their fines did violate the equal protection clause. The U.S. Supreme Court agreed to review this question to resolve the differences in the rulings of lower courts.

Which side did the Supreme Court come down on, the Georgia position (that it was permissible to revoke probation for an indigent's failure to pay a fine) or the opposing position (that it was unconstitutional to revoke probation because of an indigent's inability to pay)? Well, the Court chose neither side. As in a number of other cases, the Supreme Court refused to answer with a simple yes or no. They forged a new (somewhat complex) rule, trying to take the competing interests into account. They recognized that an indigent should not be excused from punishment if he willfully refused to pay the fine (or restitution). But if the indigent probationer had made good efforts to pay the fine and could not do so, the Court held that "it is fundamentally unfair to revoke probation automatically without considering whether adequate alternative methods of punishing the defendant are available." All of these considerations were influenced by the Court's earlier decisions in *Williams v. Illinois* and *Tate v. Short*. There, the Supreme Court noted, it had ruled that a state cannot "impose a fine as a sentence and then automatically convert it into a jail term solely because the defendant is indigent and cannot forthwith pay the fine in full." Here, the Court held:

> **[I]n revocation proceedings for failure to pay a fine or restitution, a sentencing court must inquire into the reasons for the failure to pay. If the probationer willfully refused to pay or failed to make sufficient bona fide efforts legally to acquire the resources to pay, the court may revoke probation and sentence the defendant to imprisonment within the authorized**

range of its sentencing authority. If the probationer could not pay despite sufficient bona fide efforts to acquire the resources to do so, the court must consider alternative measures of punishment other than imprisonment. Only if alternative measures are not adequate to meet the State's interests in punishment and deterrence may the court imprison a probationer who has made sufficient bona fide efforts to pay.

Here, the case was sent back for the trial court to consider the new rule for revoking probation, taking into account the indigency of the probationer.

Other sentences that avoid confinement are orders for community service and other creative orders, which require certain activities or contributions by the defendant in lieu of sentencing to confinement. Electronic monitoring is a recent technological innovation, which allows offenders to remain in the community when, in some cases, they would otherwise be sent to prison. Such monitoring, which keeps track of the offender's location, verifying that he is at home, work, or other approved place or, to the contrary, indicating that he has gone outside his permitted areas, is often used in conjunction with probation (or parole) supervision. It can also be structured to work outside of regular probation supervision, such as when it is administered by a private company, under court specifications, to monitor the whereabouts and activities of offenders. In 2009, more than 8,000 probationers (including approximately 3,400 sex offenders) and almost 16,600 parolees (including approximately 10,500 sex offenders) were being tracked by a global positioning system (GPS). GPS is a more detailed and location-specific type of monitoring than the older technology of electronic monitoring (radio frequency devices).[10]

Drug testing is a similar tool. It is usually used as a condition of probation, but it may be used as an independent kind of sentencing, operated by a private company, a drug treatment clinic, or other facility, to monitor the drug-free status of the defendant, when that is specifically ordered by the sentencing court.

Also included within community corrections are those programs that release the offender from a confinement facility into the community under special conditions, while the constraints of the term of imprisonment still hang over his head. Parole is, under this definition, the most common type of such release into the community. Other community programs, which are used in many jurisdictions, are furloughs and work (or study) releases. These are available to prison and jail officials in jurisdictions where they have been specifically authorized by statute. **Furloughs** are releases of inmates for short periods of time, usually for participation in or attendance at important functions, such as a hospital visit to a very sick relative, attendance at a child's wedding, or attending a school graduation. Inmates must meet eligibility requirements for furloughs, which usually include establishing trustworthiness, having good conduct, and having no criminal record of violence, sex offenses, or escape. Sometimes, furloughs are authorized for offenders of higher security risk to attend a very important event, such as the funeral of a parent, to which the inmate is escorted by officers. (The cost of these escorts may have to be paid for by the inmate or his family.)

Work release is a program that allows low-risk inmates to leave the prison or jail during the day to go to a job and to return to the institution at night and on weekends. Study release is a similar program, which allows inmates to go out during limited hours to attend school and then to return to sleep and eat at the corrections facility. In 2005, there were approximately

54,200 inmates in community-based facilities. These are facilities where at least 50% of the residents were allowed to leave on a regular basis, without staff escort, to work or study in the community. The term includes such categories as halfway houses, residential treatment centers, restitution centers, and prerelease centers.[11]

The legal questions that are raised by such community corrections activities are few compared to those of prisoners' rights.[12] There have been no Supreme Court decisions or significant constitutional rulings on such programs, except the body of probation and parole cases that we discussed earlier in this chapter. Because most kinds of community corrections are tied to sentencing, and because judges have great discretion in sentencing (and also because those who are placed into alternative community sentences are usually so grateful for the opportunity to avoid confinement that they do not raise legal objections), there has been very little litigation involving such programs. What little there is comes from the disgruntled—those who are denied the alternative of participating in community programs or those who are terminated from program participation because of some failure on their part. Complaints of this type can be handled rather summarily, as matters of judicial discretion. The only significant concern would seem to be to ensure that such programs are available to all offenders, without regard to race, gender, disability status, or other unjustifiable distinctions. Otherwise, the guidelines of the probation and parole law discussed earlier are the rules for community placement.

The same concerns apply to prison and jail programs involving community activities: placing inmates into work or study release, on furlough, or on parole is a discretionary function, in which conditions for consideration must be tied to the criminal history and past behavior of the offenders, along with their prospects for successful involvement in community programs or supervision. Apart from impermissible factors of discrimination, the decisions for such releases into the community should be based on eligibility and risk criteria, along with correctional judgment, which are virtually impervious to legal attack. Inmates who are denied community programs are, understandably, unhappy and frequently file administrative grievances about those denials. For a well-managed program (in those places that have community-release or furlough programs), those grievances should be the extent of claims about selections for community releases.

Parole law is a separate and fairly well-defined area, which specifies the legal constraints on parole releases and parole supervision and revocation. In addition to court rulings, specific state and local statutes and policies govern these types of releases into the community, and they provide the answers to most legal questions about community programs for parolees.

SUMMARY

- Probation and parole are similar in that they allow offenders to go into the community, under supervision, rather than be confined. Probationers are under the supervision and control of sentencing judges, and parolees are under the supervision and control of parole boards.

- Persons released on parole are under such restraints on their liberty that they may challenge their custody by using the writ of habeas corpus (*Jones v. Cunningham*).

- When it comes to revoking parole (and the rules for revocation are virtually identical for probationers), there is a liberty interest in remaining on parole. Therefore, a parolee must be given two hearings when his parole is revoked and he is returned to prison. At the first hearing, near the place of arrest, the parolee must be given notice of the hearing and of the charges; he must be allowed to appear and present evidence; there must be a neutral decision maker; there should ordinarily be opportunity for the questioning of adverse witnesses; and a decision must be made with written reasons for the determination and a statement of evidence relied on. Later, there will be a final hearing, often at the prison where the sentence is to be served, and there are, again, due process steps to be followed. These are similar to the procedural requirements at the first hearing (*Morrissey v. Brewer*).

- The Supreme Court held that probationers who faced revocation of their probation were entitled to the same due process protections the Court had required at a minimum for parole revocations (*Gagnon v. Scarpelli*).

- As to the right to have counsel at revocation hearings, the Supreme Court said that counsel should be provided when the probationer (or parolee) contests the charges or when he contends there are substantial, complex reasons to support mitigation of the action being considered (*Mempa v. Rhay*).

- Searches of the homes, property, or persons of probationers and parolees may be performed by supervising probation or parole officers without obtaining search warrants (*Griffin v. Wisconsin*; *United States v. Knights*; *Samson v. California*; *Pennsylvania Board of Probation and Parole v. Scott*).

- It is permissible for states to immunize parole board members from liability for their decision making regarding parole release (*Martinez v. California*). In the same case, the Court also held that such decisions do not expose parole board members to liability under 42 U.S.C. § 1983 for mistaken decisions when persons released on parole commit offenses and the victims of those offenses sue. The criminal actions are those of the offender, not of the state. They are not the direct fault of the parole decision makers. The same immunity from liability also applies to probation decision making, because judges are absolutely immune for their judicial actions.

- The decision to place a defendant on probation is part of the sentencing process. It therefore is covered by the same due process protections that apply to sentencing, which include the right to be present, the right to counsel, and the right to allocution. Sentencing procedures, however, are much more informal, and are not bound by such strict due process protections as the criminal trial itself. The State may choose to permit victim impact evidence as part of the sentencing consideration (*Payne v. Tennessee*).

- The Supreme Court has ruled that the decision to place an inmate on parole is a discretionary one and does not, by the nature of the action itself, require due process protections. No constitutional standards apply to such decision making (*Greenholtz v. Inmates*). State created liberty interests do not become federally protected liberty interests (*Swarthout v. Cooke*). However, if the state statute for parole requires the release of an inmate if certain conditions are found to exist (mandatory decision making), minimal due process is required. An opportunity for the inmate to appear and be heard at the parole hearing and a notification to the inmate of why parole is denied, if denial occurs, are the only steps required (*Greenholtz v. Inmates; Board of Pardons v. Allen*).

- Where total discretion is given to a board or governor to grant or deny pardons or commutations or clemency (or paroles), no due process hearing is constitutionally required (*Connecticut Board of Pardons v. Dumschat; Ohio Adult Parole Authority v. Woodard*).

- The Supreme Court held that it was constitutionally permissible (causing no ex post facto violation) for the rules of parole to be changed while the offender is confined, awaiting parole (*United States v. Addonizio; California Department of Corrections v. Morales; Garner v. Jones*). However, there is an ex post facto violation when a law is retroactive and disadvantages the affected offender, for example, when an entitlement is taken away that leads to the offender being returned to custody (*Lynce v. Mathis*).

- When a parole board decides to release a parolee, but then changes its mind and says the inmate must stay in prison (rescinding its action), there is no requirement of a hearing before the change is made (*Jago v. Van Curen*).

- It is also permissible, the Supreme Court said, for parole authorities to place a warrant for parole violation (as a "detainer") against a prisoner when he has been imprisoned on a new offense and to hold that warrant against him without any action on it until he completes service of his new sentence (*Moody v. Daggett*).

- In considering whether sex offender registries violate due process or the ex post facto clause, it is necessary to look at the state's statutory scheme. Registries intended to protect the public by providing information about convicted sex offenders have been held not to be punitive and, therefore, not violative of ex post facto or due process limitations (*Smith v. Doe; Connecticut Department of Public Safety v. Doe*).

- "Community corrections" is a broad concept, encompassing all kinds of sanctions and sentencing arrangements that permit offenders to remain principally in the community and not be confined in regular prison facilities. This concept includes probation, parole, prerelease centers, halfway houses, community service, fines, restitution, furloughs, work and study releases, and electronic monitoring.

- Fines (and orders for restitution payments) are frequently used sentences. The Supreme Court held that an indigent defendant cannot be held in jail because of his inability to pay the fine because of lack of funds (*Williams v. Illinois; Tate v. Short*). When an offender's probation was revoked because he did not have the money to continue making payments on his fine (which was one of the conditions of his probation), the Supreme Court said that a revocation action was too hasty. In such a case, the sentencing court would have to make an inquiry into the individual case, and if the probationer had made good-faith efforts to pay but could not, the court should first consider whether alternative methods of punishment would suffice; if they would not, only then could revocation of probation be ordered (*Bearden v. Georgia*).

THINKING ABOUT IT

Randy Spencer filed a petition for a writ of habeas corpus, seeking to invalidate his September 1992 order revoking parole. Because he had completed the entire term of imprisonment underlying the parole revocation, the court had to decide whether his petition was moot. That is, was there no longer any live issue for the court to consider since his sentence was completely served? From his perspective, Spencer identified four continuing "injuries": the parole revocation could be used to his detriment in a future parole proceeding; the Order of Revocation could be used to increase his sentence in a future sentencing proceeding; the revocation could be used to impeach him should he appear as a witness or litigant in a future judicial proceeding; and the revocation could be used directly against him should he appear as a defendant in a criminal proceeding. What do you think? This case was reported as *Spencer v. Kemna*, 523 U.S. 1 (1998).

KEY TERMS

allocution: Inquiry made by a judge directly to a defendant who has been convicted as to whether there is any legal reason why judgment should not be rendered. More frequently today, asking the defendant at the sentencing phase of the criminal proceeding for any statement in mitigation of the sentence.

community corrections: All of those organizations, facilities, and programs that operate in a locality outside of traditional confinement facilities.

commutation: The act of clemency, reducing a sentence. Changing a sentence to one that is less severe.

coram nobis: Technically, a writ of error coram nobis. An order at common law to correct a judgment in the same court in which it was entered.

detainer: A notice that informs prison authorities that charges (or sometimes an unserved sentence, as for an escapee) are pending elsewhere against an inmate, and asks that the custodian notify the requesting jurisdiction before the inmate is released.

furlough: A temporary leave of absence, authorizing an inmate to depart from a correctional facility for a specified purpose, to a specific place, and with strict time limitations. These actions must be authorized by statute, or, in rare cases, by judicial order.

suspend: To postpone, delay, or discontinue. A suspended sentence is one that is imposed, but not executed.

ENDNOTES

1. Glaze, L., Bonczar, T., and Zhang, F. *Probation and Parole in the United States, 2009.* Page 2. (Washington, DC: Bureau of Justice Statistics, U.S. Department of Justice, 2010.)
2. See endnote 1. Appendix Table 13. The 1990 information came from Glaze, L. *Probation and Parole in the United States, 2001.* Page 6. Washington, DC: Bureau of Justice Statistics, U.S. Department of Justice. August 2002 (revised February 9, 2004).
3. See endnote 1. Appendix Table 13.
4. See endnote 1. Appendix Tables 2, 4, 5, and 14.

5. Compacts are laws that are written so that states may cooperate with each other on matters of common interest.

6. The question before the Supreme Court was "whether the exclusionary rule, which generally prohibits the introduction at criminal trial of evidence obtained in violation of a defendant's Fourth Amendment rights, applies in parole revocation hearings." The Court held it did not, specifically declining to apply the exclusionary rule to proceedings other than criminal trials. The Court then noted, "Application of the exclusionary rule would both hinder the functioning of state parole systems and alter the traditionally flexible, administrative nature of parole revocation proceedings."

7. This reliance on the mandatory language standard has been called into question by the Supreme Court decision in *Sandin v. Conner*, 515 U.S. 472 (1995). The Court in *Sandin* gave reasons for abandoning the "mandatory language" standard in inmate discipline cases, and it did so, overruling *Hewitt v. Helms*. The *Hewitt* case, like the *Greenholtz* and *Allen* parole cases, was founded on an analysis of due process entitlement generated by a state statute that used mandatory language. This invites states to question and litigate the use of that standard in corrections-related matters such as parole.

8. A commutation is a reduction or melioration of the sentence, meaning either a reduction in the amount of time to be served or a change in some attribute of the sentence, such as making the inmate eligible for parole when he had not been. A pardon is the full-fledged wiping out of the conviction and sentence of the inmate, resulting in his total release, although the pardoning authority typically has the authority to place restrictions, such as supervision requirements, on the releasee. Pardoning power is given by the U.S. Constitution to the president, and most states grant such power to the governor. In Connecticut, a board was established to consider pardon and commutation actions.

9. The Court observed that, unlike probation or supervised release, offenders subject to the registration system were free to move where they wished and to live and work as other citizens, with no supervision. For example, the registration system could not impose on the registrant any curfew restrictions or ban against alcohol consumption, as probation or parole could.

10. See endnote 1. Appendix Tables 11 and 22.

11. Stephan, J. *Census of State and Federal Correctional Facilities, 2005*. Table 3 and page 8. (Washington, DC: Bureau of Justice Statistics, U.S. Department of Justice, 2008.)

12. Often, a more significant problem is establishing the location of community facilities and trying to counter the "NIMBY" ("not in my back yard") philosophy of many communities. Opponents use a variety of arguments to oppose the location of community facilities for offenders, raising such issues as proximity to schools, property value effects, and zoning rules.

Statutory and Administrative Law, Jails, Juveniles, Privatization, and Other Special Issues in Corrections

In Part II, we examined the constitutional rights of prisoners. The U.S. Constitution is the primary source of prisoners' rights, and, in the past 40 years, most litigation that contested the conditions, programs, and activities in prisons has flowed out of the federal Constitution. Specifically, litigation has been filed by inmates under 42 U.S.C. § 1983 (or with Bivens actions, for federal prisoners), alleging violations of prisoners' constitutional rights and demanding monetary damages or injunctive relief, or both.

But there are other sources of prisoners' rights, and there are other legal issues (besides prisoners' rights) that corrections administrators must be concerned about. In Part III, we will look at some of these other issues and at the sources of law that most affect them.

Note: The information in Part III often covers cases first discussed in Part II, the Constitutional Law of Corrections. Readers may locate these earlier discussions by referring to either the Table of Contents or to the Table of Cases (located at the end of this text).

18 Statutory and Administrative Law

This Constitution, and the Laws of the United States which shall be made in Pursuance thereof; and all Treaties made, or which shall be made, under the Authority of the United States, shall be the supreme Law of the Land.

U.S. Constitution, Article VI, Clause 2

Chapter Outline

- The Hierarchy of Laws in the United States
- Interstate Compacts and Uniform Laws
  - The Interstate Agreement on Detainers
  - The Uniform Criminal Extradition Act
  - Interstate Compacts for Transfer of Prisoners
  - Interstate Compact for Adult Offender Supervision
  - Interstate Compact for Juveniles
- State and Local Laws; Regulations, Rules, and Policies
- The Federal Bureau of Prisons
- State and Local Corrections
- Accreditation

In this chapter, we will look at non-constitutional sources of law (that is, those outside the U.S. Constitution) that will be of most concern to corrections workers and to offenders who are in the corrections system.

▓ The Hierarchy of Laws in the United States

The U.S. Constitution is the supreme law of the country. According to the terms of the Constitution (specifically, Article VI, Clause 2), which had to be subscribed to by every state when it joined

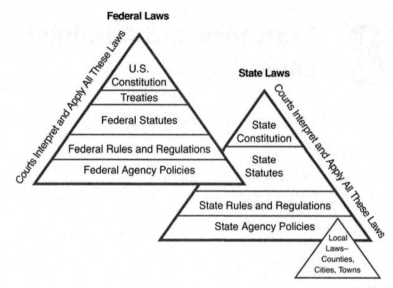

Figure 18-1 Hierarchy of Laws in the United States.

the Union of states, the Constitution, federal laws, and federal treaties (which can only be made by the federal government) are the "supreme Law of the Land." By that provision, federal laws take precedence over state laws when they conflict. **Figure 18-1** shows the hierarchy of laws in the United States. It depicts the different levels of government and the kinds of laws that are enacted at each level—federal, state, and local.

There are some areas in which the federal government and state governments may pass laws that govern the same matters, and therefore the two kinds of laws may come into conflict. In other areas, such as foreign affairs and treaties, which we just mentioned, only the federal government has authority to act. But we should note that Congress only has authority to act by powers given to it by the Constitution in Article I. All other matters are left to the authority of the states, as provided by the U.S. Constitution in Amendment 10. For example, see *United States v. Lopez*, 514 U.S. 549 (1995), where a high school student was arrested and charged under the Gun-Free School Zones Act of 1990 (18 U.S.C. § 922(q)) for possession on school premises of a concealed handgun and five bullets. The district court denied the student's motion to dismiss his indictment holding that § 922 fell within Congress' power to "regulate activities in and affecting commerce, and the 'business' of elementary, middle and high schools ... affects interstate commerce." Following conviction, the defendant (student) appealed to the Fifth Circuit Court of Appeals. The Fifth Circuit reversed, holding that Congress exceeded its authority to legislate under the Commerce Clause. The Supreme Court agreed, stating that Congress had overstepped its constitutional authority, that the "possession of a gun in a local school zone is in no sense an economic activity that might, through repetition elsewhere, substantially affect any sort of interstate commerce." Texas did have criminal statutes covering the same activity. Legislatures (both the U.S. Congress and state legislatures) have become much more active in the last 100 years, and legislation has come to embrace and affect myriad areas of our lives.

■ Interstate Compacts and Uniform Laws

While we are discussing state statutes, it would be helpful to take a look at a special kind of statute, the interstate compact. The U.S. Constitution specifically forbids states to enter agreements or compacts with other states without the consent of Congress (U.S. Constitution, Article I, Section 10). Congress has given consent for states to enter compacts in certain areas. One of those areas includes a consent to enter compacts between states for cooperative efforts in the prevention of crime and the enforcement of criminal laws and policies (which is authorized under 4 U.S.C. § 112).

> The consent of Congress is hereby given to any two or more States to enter into agreements or compacts for cooperative effort and mutual assistance in the prevention of crime and in the enforcement of their respective criminal laws and policies, and to establish such agencies, joint or otherwise, as they may deem desirable for making effective such agreements and compacts.

With this consent and authority, there have been interstate agreements and compacts drawn up in several areas of criminal justice to allow for such cooperation on criminal matters of mutual concern. Some of those compacts are discussed below.

The Interstate Agreement on Detainers

The provisions of the Interstate Agreement on Detainers (IAD) allow a prosecutor to obtain an individual from another state for prosecution. (You can find the provisions of this agreement in Title 18, U.S. Code, Appendix 2, Section 2, Articles I–IX.) The detainer, an official notice to prison authorities that charges are pending elsewhere against an inmate, requests that the custodian notify the requesting state before the inmate is released. Under the terms of this agreement, once the detainer is filed, not only is the holding state (the custodian) obliged to notify the requesting state before the inmate's release, there is also a provision for an inmate to request prompt production for disposition of the pending charges. If such a request is made, the requesting state sends officers to take temporary custody of the inmate and to transport him to the jurisdiction where the charges are pending. Thus, under the agreement, either the prosecutor or the inmate may make a request for transfer to the jurisdiction where charges are pending and from which the detainer has been filed.

The inmate, while being produced on the charges in the receiving state, remains legally in the custody of the original, sending state. His sentence continues to run in the sending state, just as if he were still confined there. The inmate must be brought to trial within 180 days of his request; charges are dismissed (by effect of the statute) if the inmate is not tried within that time. There is no hearing required (specifically, no extradition or rendition hearing) before the inmate is transferred to the requesting state. (See the Supreme Court decision in *Cuyler v. Adams*, discussed later in this chapter, for a ruling on that provision of the agreement, which does not provide for a hearing.) At the conclusion of the prosecution (or other disposition of the charges), the inmate must be returned to the state where he was serving sentence.

As you can see, these provisions allow for pending charges to be expeditiously disposed of. This may be an advantageous process for the prosecution to use to obtain a defendant who is in custody in another state. But it also may be a definite benefit to inmates, who want to get rid of detainers that are hanging over their heads and that may adversely affect their opportunities for some programs and benefits (such as a reduction in custody, better housing or job assignments, and consideration for community programs). In many cases, the provisions speed up the procedure for trying inmates on charges in different jurisdictions. They may also force a state to drop charges that have been lodged as a detainer, for example, when there is some weakness in a case or in those cases in which prosecution was never fully intended to occur but in which the detainer was lodged merely for notification (or even harassment) purposes.

In *Alabama v. Bozeman*, 533 U.S. 146 (2001), there is an example of the absolute language of a statute controlling the outcome of the case, here, to the inmate's benefit. Bozeman was in a federal prison on a federal sentence. He also had a nonfederal charge in Alabama. State officials sought state custody of him for the purpose of arraignment and appointment of counsel. Bozeman was transferred to Covington County, Alabama, where he spent the night in the county jail, appeared in local court the next day, and was returned to the federal prison. The following month, he was brought back to Covington County for trial. Bozeman's counsel filed a motion for dismissal based on the IAD, specifically, Article IV(e). This section states that if a trial is not held on any indictment, information, or complaint prior to the inmate returning to the original place of confinement (in this case to federal custody) the indictment, information, or complaint "shall not be of any further force or effect, and the court shall enter an order dismissing the same with prejudice."

Bozeman was convicted in Covington County, and the court then denied his motion for dismissal of the charges. A state appeals court affirmed. The state supreme court reversed, holding that the literal language of the statute controlled. The U.S. Supreme Court agreed. It dismissed the state's claim that the statutory violation was "de minimis," that it did not really violate the statutory intent "to protect the prisoner against endless interruption of the rehabilitation programs because of criminal proceedings in other jurisdictions." The Court said the statutory language was absolute; however, even if it were to accept the "de minimis" argument, the Court did not necessarily see the current violation as "trivial."

> **[T]o call such a violation "technical," because it means fewer days spent away from the sending State, is to call virtually *every* conceivable anti-shuttling violation "technical"—a circumstance which, like the 13th chime of the clock, shows that Alabama's conception of the provision's purpose is seriously flawed.**

Another case, *New York v. Hill*, 528 U.S. 110 (2000), shows that absolute language may be waived. Article III(a) of the IAD provides that an inmate must be brought to trial within 180 days following his request for disposition of the detainer. At a court hearing to set the trial date, Hill's counsel agreed to a trial date outside the 180-day period. Prior to trial and after lapse of the statutory 180-day period, Hill filed for dismissal. The court denied the motion, saying the defense counsel's agreement to the trial date constituted a waiver or abandonment of Hill's rights under the IAD. Hill was convicted. On appeal, he argued that the indictment should have been dismissed. Appeals courts first upheld the conviction and then (in a higher court) reversed it.

The Supreme Court noted that the IAD does not specifically address the effect of a defendant's consent to delay the applicable time limits. The Court had previously recognized that the most basic rights of criminal defendants are subject to waiver.

What suffices for waiver depends on the nature of the right at issue....For certain fundamental rights, the defendant must personally make an informed waiver....For other rights, however, waiver may be effected by action of counsel. "Although there are basic rights that the attorney cannot waive without the fully informed and publicly acknowledged consent of the client, the lawyer has—and must have—full authority to manage the conduct of the trial."

Hill's prosecution and conviction beyond the 180-day limit were upheld.[1]

The Uniform Criminal Extradition Act

The cooperation required between states is first based on the U.S. Constitution, Article IV, Section 2, Clause 2. This "Extradition Clause" provides that a person who is charged with a crime, and who flees to another state, must, on demand of the executive authority of the state from which he has fled, be delivered to the state having jurisdiction over the crime which it is alleged he has committed. The federal government further sets rules for extradition in Title 18, U.S. Code, Sections 3181–3196. This law specifies the procedure to be followed when a fugitive's return is sought.

Most states have adopted the Uniform Criminal Extradition Act, which provides for more detailed procedures by states that are parties to the act and that are under the umbrella of the federal constitutional law and statute. Requests for the return of a fugitive who has fled to a foreign country must be handled through the federal government (specifically, the Department of State and the Department of Justice). This is because a sovereign country is under no obligation to surrender a person to another country just because that person is wanted on criminal charges. To accomplish such a transfer (also called a "rendition"), there must be a treaty between the two nations. By such means, through specific diplomatic and legal procedures, a person can be returned from a foreign country for prosecution. (Such a treaty and the corresponding rendition procedures, of course, operate for transfers in both directions, between both countries.)[2]

The Supreme Court considered the somewhat competing provisions of these two compacts— the Interstate Agreement on Detainers and the Uniform Criminal Extradition Act—in the case of *Cuyler v. Adams*, 449 U.S. 433 (1981). Adams was serving a sentence of 30 years in Pennsylvania. A prosecutor in New Jersey lodged a detainer against Adams and moved to bring him to trial on armed robbery charges. This was done pursuant to the IAD. Adams objected to his transfer to New Jersey, claiming that he was entitled to a hearing before his transfer under the provisions of the Extradition Act. (Both states were parties to both compacts.) After examining the provisions and the history of the IAD and the Extradition Act, the Supreme Court held that the rights and protections of the Extradition Act, specifically the right to a hearing before transfer, were reserved for the prisoner.

This was the holding, even though the IAD did not require a hearing by its terms and even though the prosecutor moved to bring the inmate to trial in New Jersey under the IAD. The main difference hinges on who makes the request to be taken to court on the detainer. If the prisoner makes the request, as provided by Article III of the IAD (and, as mentioned previously, there are often reasons why the prisoner wants to request production, such as to get the charges disposed of so they do not remain on file against him for a long period of time), he is deemed to have waived extradition rights, and there is no need for a hearing. But if the prosecutor requests the transfer, as provided by Article IV of the IAD, then the prisoner retains any right that he may have to contest the legality of his transfer to the requesting state. The Supreme Court agreed with lower courts that had held that this provision meant that, upon the prosecutors' requests for transfer, inmates had the rights given them in the Extradition Act to contest the transfers. (If the states are not parties to the Extradition Act, then the inmates would have the right to contest the transfers that they would have under existing extradition law in the holding state.)

The case of *New Mexico ex rel. Ortiz v. Reed*, 524 U.S. 151 (1998), involved interstate extradition of a parole violator. In 1993, Ortiz, who had been paroled in 1992, was told by Ohio prison officials that his parole was going to be revoked. Ortiz fled to New Mexico. Ohio sought his extradition, and New Mexico issued the appropriate warrant. After being arrested in 1994, Ortiz sought a writ of habeas corpus from a New Mexico district court. His claim was that he was not a fugitive for purposes of extradition, because he fled under duress. He alleged that Ohio authorities planned to revoke his parole and to "cause him physical harm" if he was returned to an Ohio prison. The New Mexico district court granted the writ, and the state supreme court affirmed. In making its determination, the court said the extradition did not comply with one of the four considerations announced by the U.S. Supreme Court in *Michigan v. Doran*, 439 U.S. 282 (1978). Specifically, the New Mexico court held that Ortiz was not a fugitive, instead referring to him as a "refugee from injustice." The court held that he fled to avoid the threat of bodily harm and that this "duress" negated his fugitive status.

The U.S. Supreme Court disagreed. Noting Ohio was not a party to the New Mexico proceeding, the Court rejected the New Mexico courts' actions:

> **In case after case we have held that claims relating to what actually happened in the demanding State, the law of the demanding State, and what may be expected to happen in the demanding State when the fugitive returns are issues that must be tried in the courts of that State, and not in those of the asylum State.**

The Court also cited practical reasons for its decision, saying that it would be a great burden on the demanding state (Ohio) to provide witnesses and records in the asylum state (New Mexico) to counter the allegations made. New Mexico had made determinations it was not entitled to make on an extradition matter, the Supreme Court said, and Ortiz would have to be returned to Ohio.

Interstate Compacts for Transfer of Prisoners

Three interstate compacts address the interstate transfer of prison inmates. The national Interstate Compact for Corrections, with 40 states as parties, provides for uniform procedures and treatment of prisoners transferred from the supervisory agency of one state to that of a second state. The statutory language, as enacted in most states, covers such areas as purpose, authority, procedures and rights, and choice of law (which state's decisions are conclusive and when).

In addition to the national compact, there is the Western Corrections Compact, with 11 signatory states, providing "for the joint use of corrections facilities in the West." The New England Corrections Compact, adopted by six states, "provides for cooperation in the confinement, treatment, and rehabilitation of offenders." Additional authority for inmate transfers may be found in state statutes, agency policy, judicial action, intergovernmental agreements, memoranda of understanding, and contracts. In 2005, there were 1,587 inmates transferred under interstate compacts, with another 502 inmates transferred through non-compact methods. Transfers to federal prison facilities (345 inmates) and to private prisons (2,466 inmates) were done by means other than interstate compacts. Most inmate transfers were because of facility crowding. Other reasons for transfers were security issues ("poses danger"; "needs protection"), and "other" reasons (special program needs, pending adjudication, and post-incident cool down).[3]

Interstate Compact for Adult Offender Supervision

The Interstate Compact for Adult Offender Supervision (ICAOS) became effective in June 2002, replacing the Interstate Compact for the Supervision of Probation and Parolees. ICAOS, which has been adopted by all 50 states, is a "formal agreement between member states that seeks to promote public safety by systematically controlling the interstate movement of certain adult offenders." (ICAOS addresses the interstate supervision of offenders on some type of community release.) Responsibility for overseeing this compact is vested in the Interstate Commission for Adult Offender Supervision, a quasi-governmental administrative body. The states have provided the Commission with broad regulatory authority:

> [T]he Commission seeks to achieve the goals of the compact by creating a regulatory system applicable to the interstate movement of adult offenders, provide an opportunity for input and timely notice to victims of crime and to the jurisdictions where offenders are authorized to travel or to relocate, establish a system of uniform data collection, provide access to information on active cases to authorized criminal justice officials, and coordinate regular reporting of Compact activities to heads of state councils, state executive, judicial, and legislative branches and criminal justice administrators. The Commission is also empowered to monitor compliance with the interstate compact and its duly promulgated rules, and where warranted to initiate interventions to address and correct noncompliance. The Commission will coordinate training and education regarding regulations of interstate movement of offenders for state officials involved in such activity.[4]

Figure 18-2 provides an overview of the Interstate Compact Process for the interstate transfer of adult offender supervision. It is worth noting that the flow chart starts with a statement that there is no constitutional right that allows an offender to relocate.

Interstate Compact for Juveniles

The Interstate Compact for Juveniles (ICJ) has an interesting developmental background, and serves as a good example of how the news media can effect change. In the early 1950s, *Parade* magazine published a series of articles called "Nobody's Children." These articles showed the plight of

Overview of the Interstate Compact Process

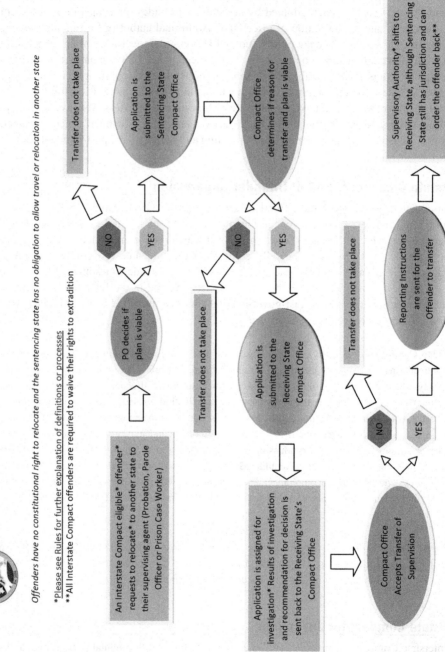

Offenders have no constitutional right to relocate and the sentencing state has no obligation to allow travel or relocation in another state

*Please see Rules for further explanation of definitions or processes
**All Interstate Compact offenders are required to waive their rights to extradition

An Interstate Compact eligible* offender* requests to relocate* to another state to their supervising agent (Probation, Parole Officer or Prison Case Worker)

PO decides if plan is viable

NO → Transfer does not take place
YES

Application is submitted to the Sentencing State Compact Office

Compact Office determines if reason for transfer and plan is viable

NO → Transfer does not take place
YES

Application is submitted to the Receiving State Compact Office

Application is assigned for investigation* Results of investigation and recommendation for decision is sent back to the Receiving State's Compact Office

Compact Office Accepts Transfer of Supervision

NO → Transfer does not take place
YES

Reporting Instructions are sent for the Offender to transfer

Supervisory Authority* shifts to Receiving State, although Sentencing State still has jurisdiction and can order the offender back**

Figure 18-2 Overview of the Interstate Compact Process for the Interstate Transfer of Adult Offender Supervision.
Source: Courtesy of Interstate Commission for Adult Offender Supervision (ICAOS)

runaways in the United States. Inspired by the articles and recognizing the need to do something, a group of organizations met "to develop a uniform set of procedures to facilitate the return of juveniles who ran away to other States and to create a system in which juvenile offenders could be supervised in other States." The involved organizations—the Council of State Governments, National Council on Crime and Delinquency, National Council of Juvenile and Family Court Judges, American Public Welfare Association, National Association of Attorneys General, and Adult Parole and Probation Compact Administrators Association—drafted the Interstate Compact on Juveniles. The compact was approved by these organizations in 1955 and was subsequently ratified by all 50 states, plus the District of Columbia, the Virgin Islands, and Guam.[5]

Based on the successful revision of the Interstate Compact for the Supervision of Probation and Parolees (now ICAOS), the Office of Juvenile Justice and Delinquency Prevention began a similar process for the ICJ. The new compact language was finalized in 2002, became available for introduction to the states in 2003, and became active in 2008. The compact currently has 41 member states. Its governing body is the Interstate Commission for Juveniles, whose mission statement provides:

> The Interstate Commission for Juveniles, the governing body of the Interstate Compact for Juveniles, through means of joint and cooperative action among the compacting states, preserves child welfare and promotes public safety interests of citizens, including victims of juvenile offenders, by providing enhanced accountability, enforcement, visibility, and communication in the return of juveniles who have left their state of residence without permission and in the cooperative supervision of delinquent juveniles who travel or relocate across state lines.[6]

■ State and Local Laws; Regulations, Rules, and Policies

Legal sources do not stop with enactments of Congress and state statutes. In the states, lower subdivisions of government have been established, and these subdivisions are given authority, both to enact laws in certain limited areas and to enforce the laws. These lower subdivisions are, in most places, called counties (parishes, in Louisiana), cities, and towns or townships.

In counties and cities, all three branches of government typically are established. There are judges who interpret the law, who rule on disputes in civil cases, and who preside in criminal cases. There are legislative bodies (ranging from the pure democracy of town meetings in New England to city councils and county boards of commissioners or supervisors, with different titles in some places, of course). These legislative bodies are authorized to enact laws governing just their local community, and usually only in very limited areas, such as zoning details, local (minor) offenses, and appropriations for local activities, usually including schools and police.

There is an executive authority, in all levels of government, to enforce the laws. This includes sheriffs in the counties and mayors in the cities. (Sheriffs have broad authority in law enforcement, especially in the South and West, but often much less so in the North. Sheriffs also typically administer the jails in all parts of the country.) Sheriffs and mayors are, in most places, elected to their offices. Some counties have elected county executives. Some cities, towns, and counties appoint nonpolitical executives; such officials are usually appointed by the legislative body or sometimes by the executive (mayor or other elected executive) with the agreement of the legislative body. These appointees are city managers, county managers, and the like. Typically, the mayor or manager in a city appoints executive officials in different posts, including police and fire chiefs, jail superintendents, and administrators of social services.

These various types and positions of government overlap and interact in a huge variety of complex ways. It is impossible to say that there is one system of state and local government in the United States. In fact, it is safe to say that there are no two states that share an identical setup of local government authorities. Therefore, we must talk in generalities and consider the most common way of doing things, realizing that there are bound to be variations in each state and locality.

Besides the laws (usually called **ordinances** in the localities) enacted by the legislature, there are regulations, rules, and policies that are adopted by different levels of government. At the federal level, agencies may be given the authority to adopt rules and regulations. (They cannot do so unless they are given the authority by statute.) The authority to issue rules and regulations may be very broad or specifically limited. Federal agencies, of course, cover an extensive range of affairs. Some regulatory agencies, such as the Federal Communications Commission and the Federal Trade Commission, were established for the primary purpose of issuing rules that regulate their particular area of responsibility. Those regulatory agencies also act to investigate violations of their rules, and they sit in judgment on persons who are accused of violating the rules that they have issued. Congress typically has given each regulatory agency some power of enforcement, including the power to issue penalties (such as revoking a television station's license) for violations. Federal rules are found in a large set of volumes, called the Code of Federal Regulations (CFR). These rules comprise the detailed laws (they are considered to have the authority and effect of the statutory law that authorized the agency to issue them) of most agencies.

But that is still not the end of it. Many agencies have internal policies, which govern their day-to-day operations. What is the difference between internal policies and rules? Under the Administrative Procedure Act (this entire area of the law is called "administrative law"), rules should be issued when they affect the conduct of private citizens, when they require certain actions to be taken, or when they incorporate penalties and other enforcement procedures for citizen actions or inactions. If it is a federal rule, it must be published in the Federal Register (a daily compendium of all kinds of new or changed federal rules) for everyone to see. Citizens are invited to comment on the proposed rules. After a period of consideration, the agency may adopt and publish its final rules. Only these final rules are collected in the CFR.

Agencies also need to have rules that govern their internal affairs, but that do not directly regulate or affect the private community. These are called policy issuances, and every agency has a set of them. They cover such matters as personnel policies, business operations, transportation, communications (including computers and other record-keeping systems), and day-to-day operations (such as places and hours of work).

■ The Federal Bureau of Prisons

Let's look at one federal agency, the one most involved in corrections, to put all those general descriptions we have just made into a practical framework. The Federal Bureau of Prisons, created by Congress and placed in the Department of Justice (the Director of the Bureau of Prisons is appointed by and reports to the U.S. Attorney General), is charged with the "safekeeping, care, and subsistence of all persons charged with or convicted of offenses against the United States, or held as witnesses or otherwise." That mandate is in Title 18, U.S. Code, Section 4042. (The U.S. Marshals Service has responsibility for holding prisoners awaiting trial; most of these prisoners are held in contract jail facilities—local jails with which the Marshals Service negotiates a contract to hold federal, mainly pretrial, prisoners. The U.S. Probation Service, which is part of the federal court system, is responsible for supervising those offenders who are placed on probation by federal courts, as well as those who are released on parole. The U.S. Parole Commission makes parole decisions for federal prisoners; parole was abolished for federal offenses committed on or after November 1, 1987, but parole release and revocation decisions still have to be made for those who committed their offenses before that date and who are still serving those older sentences, for which parole is available.)

In some large cities, especially those with a large number of federal criminal prosecutions, the Bureau of Prisons has built detention facilities, primarily to hold pretrial inmates. There are detention centers in Brooklyn, Chicago, Honolulu, Houston, Los Angeles, Miami, New York City, Philadelphia, Puerto Rico, San Diego, and Seattle, and there is a specialized one for immigration detainees in Oakdale, Louisiana. Several of the regular federal prisons have units that are set aside for federal detainees awaiting trial in nearby cities (for example, the Milan, Michigan, Correctional Institution for Detroit and the Englewood, Colorado, Correctional Institution for Denver). Some 116 federal prisons, spread all over the country, hold approximately 180,000 inmates. The institution security level ranges from minimum security in several prison camps to high security in penitentiaries. There are also administrative institutions (such as medical centers), detention facilities (as noted above), and, as it is sometimes called, a "supermax," in Florence, Colorado.

The legal authority of the Bureau of Prisons flows first from its congressional mandate, which established it as a federal agency. That set of laws is contained in Title 18 of the U.S. Code. Congress has also, by statute, provided for the federal sentencing schemes, which authorize federal courts to impose different types of federal sentences. The Bureau of Prisons operates under federal statutes that legislate such matters as good-time allowances for prisoners, parole eligibility, the establishment of prison industries, the provision of medical care (which is accomplished in conjunction with support from the U.S. Public Health Service), and the provision of other programs, such as education, vocational training, and rehabilitative services. Perhaps most important of all, at least as a practical matter, is the appropriation of funds by Congress for the Bureau of Prisons to operate. As in many states, there has been a building program of new prisons, and the money for all of those federal facilities comes from Congress. Just as important, Congress provides for the staffing of those facilities, authorizing each year certain numbers of staff to be employed by the Bureau of Prisons, and appropriating each year the money to pay for those staff members, along with all the other expenses of running the prisons.

Under that umbrella of legal authority, the Bureau of Prisons issues many regulations and policies. Its regulations are published as federal rules in the Federal Register, allowing the public (including inmates and other interested persons and organizations) to comment on them. After reviewing those comments, final rules are published in the CFR under Title 28.

The Administrative Procedure Act (APA) requires that a reviewing court "hold unlawful and set aside agency action, findings, and conclusions found to be—arbitrary, capricious, an abuse of discretion, or otherwise not in accordance with law." This was the issue in *Arrington v. Daniels,* 516 F.3d (9th Cir. 2008). Eighteen inmates filed habeas corpus petitions challenging a Bureau of Prisons final rule categorically excluding from early release consideration inmates whose crimes involved the carrying, possession, or use of a firearm or other dangerous weapon or explosives. The lawsuit did not focus on the categorical exclusion; instead, the inmates argued the absence of a rationale for the decision, in violation of the Administrative Procedure Act, Section 706(2)(A). The court agreed.

> Although agencies enjoy wide discretion in fashioning regulations governing the statutes that they are charged with administering, section 706 of the APA requires that they articulate a rationale when they exercise that discretion. This is not an empty requirement. Because we may not substitute our own rationales for those of the agency ... when an agency fails to provide an explanation for its actions we are left with no means of reviewing the reasonableness of that action. Here, the Bureau failed to set forth a rationale for its decision to categorically exclude prisoners convicted of offenses involving the carrying, possession, or use of firearms from eligibility for a sentence reduction under § 3621(e). This failure renders the Bureau's final rule invalid under the APA.[7]

Bureau of Prisons rules fill approximately 180 pages of the published CFR. They cover the "core" policies and procedures, those that most directly affect inmates and also persons on the outside. Some key rules deal with inmate classification and transfers, contacts with people in the community (correspondence rules, visiting, telephone contacts, and news media), inmate discipline, medical care, education programs, community programs (furloughs and other releases into the community), inmate property rules, and drug programs.

Beyond these "core" regulations, which are written in very precise terminology, there are implementing policies and background instructions to staff and to others for running the agency. These are called "program statements," and they are all issued out of the headquarters office of the Federal Bureau of Prisons in Washington, DC, where they are signed by the director of the bureau. Many of the program statements are now available on the Internet (http://www.bop.gov). Program statements govern the affairs of the agency nationwide and cover every type of institution in every locality. Locally, wardens and superintendents of institutions are authorized to issue "institution supplements," which establish the local procedures for running the facility. They cannot establish policy or deviate from national policy, but they give necessary local instructions (for example, the details for when telephones may be used and how telephone calls are paid for, and the details of the local visiting program, including the days and hours of operation of the visiting room).

Box 18-1 shows how law is contained in three levels—statutes, rules, and internal policy (program statements). The specific area addressed in this box is the goal of ensuring safe prisons and ensuring that unauthorized items (contraband) are not introduced into or possessed within the prison.

Box 18-1 Example of a Statute to Rule to Policy Directive

Statutory provision

Title 18, United States Code, Section 4042. Duties of Bureau of Prisons

(a) IN GENERAL.—The Bureau of Prisons, under the direction of the Attorney General, shall—

   (1) have charge of the management and regulation of all Federal penal and correctional institutions;

   (2) … provide for the safekeeping, care, and subsistence of all persons charged with or convicted of offenses against the United States, or held as witnesses or otherwise;

   [Comment: This statute sets the broad framework for the operation of the prison system.]

Statutory provision

Title 18, United States Code, Section 1791. Providing or possessing contraband in prison

(a) OFFENSE.—Whoever—

   (1) in violation of a statute or a rule or order issued under a statute, provides to an inmate of a prison a prohibited object, or attempts to do so; or

   (2) being an inmate of a prison, makes, possesses, or obtains, or attempts to make or obtain, a prohibited object;

   shall be punished as provided in subsection (b) of this section.

   [Comment: This statute recognizes that contraband can endanger institution security and establishes as a criminal act the distribution or possession of contraband.]

Agency rule

Title 28, Code of Federal Regulations, Section 552.10. Purpose and Scope.
In order to further the safe, secure, and orderly running of its institutions, the Bureau of Prisons conducts searches of inmates and of inmate housing and work areas to locate contraband and to deter its introduction and movement. Staff shall employ the least intrusive method of search practicable, as indicated by the type of contraband and the method of suspected introduction.

   [Comment: This rule, adopted by the Bureau of Prisons, is intended to show one of the approaches used by the prison officials to provide for the safekeeping of prisoners and to prevent contraband from being introduced into the prison.]

(continues)

Box 18-1 (*continued*)

Agency program statement: internal instructions

Program Statement 5521.05. Searches of Housing Units, Inmates, and Inmate Work Areas.

Non-intrusive sensors should be used whenever feasible. When searches are required, staff shall avoid unnecessary force and strive to preserve the dignity of the individual being searched.

[Comment: This program statement language relates to the management of the prison and provides staff with additional guidance on how searches are to be conducted. This represents internal language that is provided to staff and placed in a program statement immediately after Section 552.10.]

Note: An institution supplement would apply the agency program statement on searches to the individual institution.

Another example of an agency rule would be a disciplinary act and sanction for possession of contraband. In the event of a legal challenge to the agency rule or policy, a question can arise on the agency's statutory authority to issue its policy. The Supreme Court addressed this in *Chevron U.S.A. v. National Resources Defense Council*, 467 U.S. 837 (1984). In a judicial review of an agency's construction and implementation of a statute, the court is to examine the statute itself to see if Congress has "spoken to" the precise question under focus; if not, the court is to examine whether the agency's action is premised on a permissible construction of that statute.

■ State and Local Corrections

State and local corrections departments will have the same sort of legal framework, similar to the one just described in some detail for the Bureau of Prisons. They will have (at the state level) a statute (some have authorizing language in the state constitution) that establishes the department, division of corrections, or whatever it is named. Statutes, some in considerable detail but most in general terms, authorize programs, activities, and services in the corrections department. The state legislature must appropriate the money for the operation of the corrections department. A major task for each administrator of a department is to appear before the legislative committee that oversees the corrections area and to answer questions about the goals, plans, and shortcomings of the department. Appropriations committees oversee the department's finances and, in many ways, make its operations effective or not, as they give money to pay for prison necessities (such as food, clothes, and medical care) and staffing. When prison populations swell (usually, in response to get-tough enactments in the legislature on criminal law and sentencing statutes), the legislature is the place where new facilities or the expansion of existing ones are authorized and funded—it is hoped in advance of the population crisis, but in practice it is seldom so. The legislature may also consider, authorize, and provide funding for private companies to provide corrections services for the state. Departments of corrections issue policies for all components of the agency to follow. (A number of correctional agencies now place some of their policies on the Internet.) Local administrators usually have the authority to issue local rules to govern local operations.

As corrections agencies get smaller, down to the city, county, and town level, the complexity of rules diminishes, and the sheer volume of regulations and policies also gets smaller. Of course, courts may also get involved in rule writing or policy making, at all levels. For example, a local city judge may contact the city jailer, asking what the rules are for inmate misconduct in the jail and whether an inmate may be punished at the jail for misbehavior in the courthouse. If the jailer does not have written rules on inmate discipline or if the rules do not cover the concerns of the judge, that judge may suggest (using one of many different kinds of messages, with different degrees of pressure) that rules should be adopted. Such a suggestion from a judge will usually lead to the drafting and issuance of rules. This is because the jail is holding persons awaiting trial who are under the jurisdiction of the local court; to a considerable degree, the jail is an arm of the criminal court, and local judges usually have a strong interest in how the jail is being run. The local jailer, it is hoped, receives the advice of legal counsel who is knowledgeable about both the practical and the legal (constitutional and statutory) requirements of jail administration. (If not, there may be some office at the state level, or in a professional association, that can help with making proper rules.) The same process may also occur in connection with litigation, when the policies of a local, state, or federal facility come under attack and when a judge requests or orders changes in the rules. The process may be as informal as a phone call from the judge's office to the jail or prison facility or may be as formal as a court order.

One of the best pieces of advice for corrections facilities, at every level, is to invite local and nearby judges to tour the facility. It is always good for a judge to see what the facility is really like and not rely solely on newspaper accounts or on the complaints of inmates and their lawyers about problems and conditions at the facility. It is almost a truism that judges (and most people) have misconceptions about how jails and prisons are run and what the conditions inside are really like. A tour is a good way to educate people and to set aside some of the misconceptions.[8] Of course, it is always better to conduct such a tour when things are quiet and not when there is a lawsuit that causes the spotlight to shine on the institution. If the judge herself will not come to a tour, it is good to extend the invitation to the judge's law clerks or any other staff members in the courthouse. (It is perhaps surprising, perhaps not, how many people are reluctant to enter a jail or prison to see its operations, probably based on fear. Judges are not exceptions to this observation.) During a tour, of course, not only will the judge (or other visitor) have an opportunity to ask questions, but there is opportunity for the warden (or whoever is escorting the visitor) to point out problems that are encountered at the facility and describe what noteworthy things are being done or are planned. It is always best when the judge is able to place the complaints regarding a jail or prison, which she is almost certain to hear from many possible sources (back at the courthouse, media reports, letters from inmates, friends' conversations at social events, etc.), in the context of what her personal observations have been.

■ Accreditation

Although, strictly speaking, it is not statute or law, there is another level of authority in corrections that should be mentioned. That is the **accreditation** of corrections facilities and agencies under professional standards. The leading professional association in the corrections field is the American Correctional Association (ACA). Founded in 1870, the association, headquartered in Alexandria, Virginia, serves as an "umbrella" organization for the entire corrections profession, with affiliate organizations serving the many components of corrections, including jails, community corrections, probation and parole authorities, adult corrections administrators, juvenile and youth agencies, and state corrections associations from virtually all the states. (The ACA also has international affiliations.)

In 1977, the first set of accreditation standards was issued. They were published in the *Manual of Standards for Adult Correctional Institutions*. The standards contained in that volume served as the yardstick for the accreditation procedure, administered by the Commission on Accreditation for Corrections (CAC). The CAC, in partnership with ACA, administers the only national program of accreditation for all components of adult and juvenile corrections.

> The mission of the Commission on Accreditation for Corrections is to upgrade and improve practices and conditions in adult and juvenile correctional facilities and programs through an accreditation process which is founded on a commitment to accountability, professionalism and respect for basic human rights and which recognizes sound and effective correctional practices, while striving towards excellence in the field of corrections.

The movement toward professional accreditation was a gradual one, dating back to the 1960s and even earlier. There were a number of factors that pushed the ACA toward a process of accreditation. These included an understanding that, to be recognized as a profession, corrections needed stronger steps to proclaim and enforce agreed-upon standards; a realization that outside groups were pushing for reforms of all kinds and that corrections itself was the best place for standards to be set; a recognition of the constantly growing involvement (in the 1970s) of the courts in corrections matters, with a corresponding recognition that it was best for corrections to "set its own house in order," and that most courts would appreciate, and perhaps even defer to, those efforts; and a hope that the standards and the auditing process would provide corrections managers with comprehensive and convincing reports and guidelines to inform governmental authorities (legislators and governors, as well as judges) about the needs of the correctional agencies.

It was decided by the ACA that a separate commission was needed to administer the accreditation functions. A process was established to set the standards, and, just as important, a process was also established to modify and amplify them. After the original standards were published and the first institutions pursued them, it was found that some standards were hard to understand, some were hard to implement, and some were hard to measure. There were also gaps in certain areas. All of these findings pointed to the need for a constant revision process; such a process was adopted and continues today. There is an ACA Standards Committee, which constantly reviews standards alongside the review process of the CAC. Standards are revised based on changing practices, current case law, and agency experiences. The approved standards reflect the views of correctional practitioners, architects, and medical and legal experts. Input and recommendations are sought from agencies that have been through the accreditation process, those who serve on accreditation audit teams, those who work in the field at all levels, and any interested organizations or persons outside the ACA. The ACA describes its own operation as follows:

> The American Correctional Association and the Commission on Accreditation for Corrections are private, non-profit organizations which administer the only national accreditation program for all components of adult and juvenile corrections. The purpose of these organizations is to promote improvement in the management of correctional agencies through the administration of a voluntary accreditation program and the ongoing development and revision of relevant, useful standards.[9]

Different sets of standards have been established for different types of programs, covering both adults and juveniles. These programs include the administration of correctional agencies and institutions, community residential services, boot camp programs, detention facilities, probation and parole, health care, correctional industries, training, electronic monitoring, day treatment, aftercare services, and food service programs.

Early on, it was realized that there was a need for the prioritization of standards. Not all standards were of the same degree of importance. For many years, there were three levels of ACA standards: (1) essential standards, which dealt with conditions that could adversely affect the life, health, or safety of offenders, staff, or the public (all of which had to be met to achieve accreditation); (2) important standards (90% of which had to be met to achieve accreditation); and (3) desirable standards (80% of which had to be met to achieve accreditation). Currently, only two categories are used: mandatory, requiring 100% compliance, and nonmandatory, requiring at least 90% compliance. Provided below are examples of mandatory and nonmandatory standards:

4-4206—(Mandatory): Written policy, procedure, and practice restrict the use of physical force to instances of justifiable self-defense, protection of others, protection of property, prevention of escapes, and to maintain or regain control, and then only as a last resort and in accordance with appropriate statutory authority. In no event is physical force justifiable as punishment. A written report is prepared following all uses of force and is submitted to administrative staff for review.

4-4457—(Nonmandatory): Written policy, procedure, and practice provide that the security and program determinations necessary for any individual to be eligible for industries work are made by the classification committee.

The ACA unveiled its first set of performance-based standards in August 2000. These standards improve the delivery of care to offenders within the correctional environment and enable administrators to not only monitor activities, but to also measure, over time, the outcomes of their efforts.[10]

In 2010, ACA unveiled Core Jail Standards (CJS) for adult local detention facilities of all sizes. The CJS are a comprehensive set of minimum jail standards. These standards allow jails of all sizes to improve operational effectiveness and efficiency. ACA offers an independent audit of the standards to these facilities, similar to accreditation, though not as rigorous. Successful adherence to the CJS results in certification.

The accreditation process, in brief, involves these steps: A manager within an institution (or facility or agency) that wishes to become accredited (the program is voluntary) contacts the Standards and Accreditation Department which conducts an initial review of eligibility and sends papers for the process to begin. The agency may request a preaudit assessment, in which case an ACA auditor spends one or two days visiting the facility, reviewing various data, interviewing staff and offenders, and answering questions on the agency's readiness for a full audit. This process helps staff members determine their level of compliance prior to the actual audit and identify in advance possible problem areas. The institution conducts its own self-evaluation to determine compliance with the standards, attaches documentation (internal policies, reports, etc.) to support its record of compliance, and drafts plans to correct any deficiencies.

Once the required levels of compliance have been achieved, the institution (agency) can request an audit to verify compliance. Upon such a request, an audit team, composed of trained specialists for the specific type of institution, visits the institution. During the audit, records are reviewed further, all operations are observed first-hand, and staff and inmates are interviewed. These are all accomplished at different times of the day, to get a better overview of the facility at different work times. Individual team members talk with staff in all departments as they proceed. At the end of the audit visit, team members sit down with the warden (or chief administrator) and go over accomplishments, commendations about specific matters, and any deficiencies found. Audit reports are prepared by the audit team and submitted by the audit chairperson in what is called the Visiting Committee Report (VCR).

Regular meetings of the CAC are scheduled to publicly review audit results. Institutions and agencies that have been successful in meeting standards are awarded certificates of accreditation. Those with deficiencies may work to correct them and then may apply for reconsideration. Accreditation lasts for three years, after which time the accredited facility must go through a reaccreditation process. During the three-year accreditation period, accredited agencies submit annual certification statements confirming continued compliance with the accreditation standards, progress on completing plans of action, events which may affect its accreditation, and "written responses to public criticism, notoriety, or complaints about agency activity that suggest a failure to maintain standards compliance."

More than 1,500 correctional facilities and programs are involved in accreditation. Approximately 80% of all state correctional agencies and youth services are active participants, as well as the Federal Bureau of Prisons and elements of the private sector in corrections.

Early on, most corrections officials realized that legal standards, especially constitutional requirements, were not the same as professional standards. Although it was hoped that accreditation would be helpful in defending against claims of violations of prisoners' rights, it was never (or it should never have been) assured that accreditation would be such a sure defense. What must be emphasized is that the two processes are very different and serve to meet different goals and expectations. Courts review prison (or other agency) conditions to see whether they meet constitutional standards that have been set. If a constitutional standard has not yet been established, then the court can address the particular constitutional provision and specify how it should be applied in prison situations. Professional (ACA) standards are based on commonly accepted levels of performance in every area of institutional management and operation. They are not tied to specific constitutional language.

Court rulings may be very instructive to those in the field, especially those who are working constantly on the language of the professional standards. As court standards are set, corrections specialists must make sure that existing ACA standards incorporate the requirements pronounced in court decisions. ACA standards must never fall below the court standards, but, in most areas, they go beyond what the courts have required. As the Supreme Court pointed out in *Rhodes v. Chapman*, 452 U.S. 337 (1981), courts should not rely on the standards for prisons that have been adopted by various organizations (and there are a number of other organizational standards besides the ACA's[11]). In looking at conditions of confinement, the Court said in *Rhodes*, judges are looking at "contemporary standards of decency" as the yardstick to determine violations of the Eighth Amendment. Organization standards set goals adopted or recommended by the organization, but these goals do not tell the courts what the current constitutional "standard of decency" is. Such judgment, according to the Supreme Court, depends much more on public attitudes than on what organizations publish as their individual and specialized goals.

This is not to say that accreditation is of no legal use to corrections managers. First of all, if the ACA specialists and experts working on the content of the standards are doing their jobs well, standards will always incorporate at least the minimums set by court rulings. Thus, compliance with the standards should give some assurance that court expectations will be met.

Administrators and individual staff have reported that, when they are sued or when they are testifying, the fact that a facility or program has been accredited, and the specific steps that were followed in order to achieve that accreditation, have assisted in convincing courts that the particular facility or program is run professionally and is in good order regarding the specific concerns of the court. Further, research and surveys conducted by the ACA have revealed that courts have frequently looked at the ACA standards in order to learn the current expectations for managing particular areas of corrections. In this way, the standards can serve as an educational tool for the courts, which usually approach a case with little good information about corrections management. Less frequently, courts have incorporated ACA standards as guidance for what the courts will require (contrary to the *Rhodes* warnings of the Supreme Court), or (more justifiably) the courts will adopt ACA standards as part of a court order or consent decree (with the concurrence of corrections officials, who would probably like to gain accreditation anyway), to correct specific violations after the court has found certain conditions or programs to be independently deficient under legal standards of review.

SUMMARY

- The U.S. Constitution is the supreme law of the country. Treaties, which can only be made by the federal government, and federal statutes are also supreme laws, which take precedence over state laws. Federal powers, however, are limited by the Constitution. Sometimes, federal authorities go beyond the limited powers that are given to them in the Constitution, as Congress did when it made drug activities within local schools a federal crime. Such a matter, the Supreme Court said, should be left to the states to regulate (*United States v. Lopez*).

- Under the Constitution, states may enter into compacts when authorized to do so by Congress. In the criminal justice area, there are several compacts that have been authorized by Congress, which many states have joined. These include compacts on detainers, extradition, transfer of prisoners, adult offender supervision, and juveniles.

- Failure to comply with the literal language of the Interstate Agreement on Detainers (IAD) may bar further criminal proceedings by the requesting state (*Alabama v. Bozeman*). However, the time limits of the IAD may be waived by action of the defendant or his counsel (*New York v. Hill*).

- An inmate has the statutory right to a hearing under Article IV(d) of the IAD before being transferred to another jurisdiction (*Cuyler v. Adams*). Claims relating to conditions in the demanding state are issues that must be tried in the courts of that state (*New Mexico ex rel. Ortiz v. Reed*).

- At all levels of government (federal, state, and local), there are three branches of government (legislative, executive, and judicial). There are also prioritized levels of laws enacted at the different levels of government. At the highest level is a constitution (federal and state); then come the enactments of the legislature (federal, state, and local); next, most levels of government issue published rules and regulations; and most agencies (corrections included) have internal policies governing their operation.

- We looked at one corrections agency, the Federal Bureau of Prisons, to see how these various levels of laws (statutes, rules, and policies) are issued and how they impact the operations of the agency. State and local corrections agencies operate under similar levels of governing laws, but each agency has its own unique set of laws. (And these, of course, at all levels, are impacted by constitutional requirements and the rulings of courts that interpret and apply them.)

- Professional accreditation is a relatively recent development in corrections. The American Correctional Association (ACA) first issued standards for accrediting adult correctional facilities in 1977. Today, all kinds of corrections operations (probation, parole, community corrections, juveniles, and so on) are covered by different sets of accreditation standards. These are administered by the Commission on Accreditation for Corrections (CAC). More than 1,500 correctional facilities and programs are involved in the accreditation process. Accreditation, once achieved, lasts for three years, after which the agency or facility must go through a reaccreditation process.

THINKING ABOUT IT

Kenneth Gregory is confined in a federal prison. His sister, Lisa Lockhart, is on his approved visiting list. Before one of her visits, the prison staff receives information that Lisa might attempt to bring her brother some sort of contraband. The introduction of contraband into a federal institution is a crime, as set forth in Title 18, U.S. Code, Section 1791.

During the visit, officials observe Lisa spitting something into a cup and her brother taking the cup and swallowing its contents. After the visit, Gregory is placed in a dry cell (which contains no water, to prevent the flushing of any contraband). Eventually, he passes two balloons filled with drugs (cocaine and methamphetamine). Gregory and his sister are convicted for violation of 18 U.S.C. § 1791.

In appealing her conviction, Lisa argues "legal impossibility," that she cannot be guilty of the underlying offense, because prison officials knew she was bringing in contraband and allowed it to occur. As a result of their knowledge, she claims she committed no crime under Title 28, Code of Federal Regulations, Section 6.1, which states, "The introduction or attempt to introduce into or upon the grounds of any Federal penal or correctional institution or the taking or attempt to take or send therefrom anything whatsoever without the knowledge and consent of the warden … is prohibited." Did the appeals court agree? This case is reported as *United States v. Gregory*, 315 F. 3d 637 (6th Cir. 2003).

KEY TERMS

accreditation: Recognition by an authority that an organization, program, or facility has achieved high professional standards. (In corrections, there is an accreditation program administered by a commission associated with the American Correctional Association.)

ordinance: Broadly, the same as a law or a statute. Most often used to refer to a municipal statute, the enactment of the legislative body of a municipality.

ENDNOTES

1. In a non-correctional context, there are two other examples of the reading of statutory language. In *Gonzalez v. United States*, 553 U.S. 242 (2008), the Supreme Court, citing *Hill*, held that express consent by counsel, without a specific waiver by the defendant, is sufficient to allow a magistrate judge to preside over jury selection in a felony trial. In *Zedner v. United States*, 547 U.S. 489 (2006), the Supreme Court held that a defendant may not prospectively waive the application of the Speedy Trial Act of 1974, 18 U.S.C. §§ 3161-3174.
2. On February 1, 2010, the Office of Public Affairs, U.S. Department of Justice issued a press release announcing the implementation of a new extradition agreement between the European Union and the United States. Negotiations for the agreement began following the September 11, 2001 terrorist attacks in an effort to improve cooperation in criminal matters among the parties. "The agreement on extradition, among other things: replaces lists of offenses that are deemed extraditable with a modern dual criminality standard; contains measures to streamline the exchange of information and transmission of documents; sets rules for determining priority in competing requests for surrender of a fugitive." The agreement has a provision allowing extradition to be conditioned on non-application of the death penalty.
3. Lis, Inc. *Interstate Transfer of Prison Inmates in the United States.* Longmont, Colorado: National Institute of Corrections Information Center, U.S. Department of Justice, 2006.
4. Interstate Commission for Adult Offender Supervision. *ICAOS Rules.* March 1, 2011. Accessed June 20, 2011 from http://www.interstatecompact.org/.

5. Holloway, C. *Interstate Compact on Juveniles*. Washington, DC: Office of Justice Programs, Department of Justice, 2000.

6. Interstate Commission for Juveniles. *ICJ Rules—Interstate Commission for Juveniles—Serving Juveniles While Protecting Communities*. February 2011. Accessed February 13, 2011 from http://juvenilecompact.org/home.aspx.

7. The court said its ruling was not based on the agency's decision to exclude a category of inmates, saying this likely would have withstood judicial scrutiny. It was the agency's lack of an explanation, with this absence rendering the decision arbitrary and capricious. As an aside, *Arrington* is cited for how a court will review administrative rule making, not necessarily that the outcome is one to which all courts agree. In fact, a number of circuit courts have rejected the reasoning in *Arrington*. See *Gatewood v. Outlaw*, 560 F.3d 843 (8th Cir. 2009), cert. denied 130 S.Ct. 490 (2009), declined to follow, finding public safety rationale despite absence in formal administrative record; *Gardner v. Grandolsky*, 585 F.3d 786 (3rd Cir. 2009); and *Handley v. Chapman*, 587 F.3d 273 (5th Cir. 2009), cert. denied, 131 S.Ct. 71 (2010).

8. We would note, from one author's experience, that visitors touring a facility often fail to fully recognize the impact of a prison on the inmate and inmate's family. Some visitors, after touring the prison and observing inmate activities, have commented that prison is not that bad and that inmates are seemingly not being punished. These visitors do not recognize that no matter what amenities are provided within the prison confines, the inmate does not have her freedom—for example, the ability to go where she desires, to be with family, to choose where and how to live.

9. Much of the current information for this section comes from publications of the ACA and the CAC, and communication with Kathy Black-Dennis, Director of Standards, Accreditation and Professional Development, American Correctional Association (http://www.aca.org). The publications include *Facts about The Accreditation Process*; *Standards for Adult Correctional Institutions—4th Edition*. January 2003; and *Accreditation Guidelines—Blueprint for Corrections*. Lanham, MD: American Correctional Association, Standards and Accreditation.

10. The ACA is continuing to develop new standards by using a performance-based model. For example, Health Care Performance Standard 1A states that offenders are to have unimpeded access to a continuum of health care services so that their health care needs are met in a timely and efficient manner. Listed under this performance standard are more than 30 expected practices, both mandatory and nonmandatory, covering such topic areas as access to care, communicable disease and infection control programs, health appraisal, mental health appraisal, and pharmaceuticals. Performance standard 1A has 36 outcome measures, such as, the "[n]umber of offender grievances related to the quality of health care found in favor of offenders in the past 12 months divided by the number of offender grievances related to the quality of health care in the past 12 months."

11. For example, The Joint Commission (formerly the Joint Commission on Accreditation of Healthcare Organizations) has standards that are used to accredit medical and mental health facilities and organizations. These are used for the accreditation of correctional health facilities, as well as those outside corrections.

19 | Federal Statutes: Equal Employment, Disabilities, and Tort Claims

In enacting Title VII, Congress required the removal of artificial, arbitrary, and unnecessary barriers to employment when the barriers operate invidiously to discriminate on the basis of racial or other impermissible classification.

U.S. Supreme Court, *Dothard v. Rawlinson*

Chapter Outline

- Employment Law
  - Failure to Train
  - Standards of Employee Conduct
  - Fair Labor Standards Act, Portal-to-Portal Act
- Equal Employment
- *Dothard v. Rawlinson*
- Title VII and Inmate-Created Hostile Work Environment
- Tort Claims
- The Americans with Disabilities Act (ADA)
  - 2010 ADA Standards for Accessible Design
  - Employment under the ADA
  - Inmate Programs and Services under the ADA
- Other Federal Statutory Laws
  - Prison Rape Elimination Act of 2003
  - Adam Walsh Child Protection and Safety Act of 2006
  - Second Chance Act of 2007

In this chapter, we will look at some examples of statutory and administrative laws. More specifically, we will look at federal statutes that have a direct impact on prisons and jails at all levels. We must also keep in mind that many states and localities have laws on these same topics. The corrections administrator must deal with the complexity of following those statutes and regulations that affect correctional operations, whether their source is federal, state, or local.

We have already observed some federal statutes that have a direct and considerable effect on corrections. They include those that are related to constitutional rights. The Civil Rights Act, 42 U.S.C. § 1983, authorizes persons to bring actions in federal courts when they believe their constitutional rights have been denied by state officials (persons acting under color of state law). The federal habeas corpus statute, at 28 U.S.C. § 2254, authorizes the filing of habeas corpus actions by state prisoners in federal courts. In the Religious Freedom Restoration Act, Congress tried to redefine the standard to be used when courts examine religious rights guaranteed under the First Amendment; because of the Supreme Court's decision in *City of Boerne v. Flores*, 521 U.S. 507 (1997), that act now applies only to federal prisoners' claims of interference with the exercise of religious beliefs. After the *Boerne* decision, Congress passed the Religious Land Use and Institutionalized Persons Act of 2000 (RLUIPA), a renewed effort to achieve the protection of religious activities by institutionalized persons in the states. The Supreme Court upheld RLUIPA in *Cutter v. Wilkinson*, 544 U.S. 709 (2005).

In this chapter, we will discuss statutes that particularly affect corrections management. The civil rights laws and the Americans with Disabilities Act have a significant impact on the rights of minority groups, including persons with disabilities. We will look at the federal laws that govern these areas, remembering that many states also have laws on the same topics, which affect employment decisions and, in some cases, also the treatment of offenders. In a similar way, tort claims statutes, at federal and state levels, waive sovereign immunity, allowing persons to bring suits on common law tort injuries against federal, state, and local governments. However, because of the sovereign immunity doctrine, those governments may only be sued to the exact extent allowed by the tort statutes. We also will discuss some recent federal legislation, covering such issues as prisoner rape, sex offender registration, and prisoner reentry into the community following incarceration.

■ Employment Law

In every state, there are laws that govern personnel matters, which we will call employment law. This includes, as a body, the employment statutes, the regulations that implement them, and the court decisions that interpret them. These laws set the guidelines, requirements, and standards for the entire range of staffing decisions in a corrections agency. They cover advertising vacancies; eligibility, recruiting, interviewing, testing, and hiring staff members; training the staff; setting standards of job performance, evaluations of work, pay, hours, places of work, and promotions; maintaining relationships with employee bargaining or representation groups (in states in which union activities by state employees are allowed); providing retirement and other special benefits, such as health plans; and handling disciplinary matters, such as demotions, suspensions, and terminations. Typically, a specialist or a separate department (depending on the size of the agency or the facility) handles the details of these employment laws. Each administrator obviously must rely on the expertise and the efficiency of that personnel department or human resources specialist to advise him on the intricacies of the employment laws and to keep the agency running as smoothly as possible by adhering to those legal requirements.

It has been observed, and it may safely be asserted, that there is no area of management that is more vital to the smooth operation of the organization than human resource management.

Certainly, the quality of staff is the key to effective operations of corrections or any agency. Dedicated, highly motivated staff members are essential to the professionalism and excellence associated with the prison, jail, probation office, or corrections department. Within the correctional environment, staff—the entire staff—are the critical component.

All correctional employees are to be considered "correctional workers" first, and then workers at their specialty. Because a corrections facility is a community comprised of many specialized activities, staff represent a wide variety of backgrounds and occupational specialties—plumbers, electricians, landscapers, factory foremen, doctors, teachers, clergy, police officers, private security officers, military personnel, social workers, and many others. Inside the facility where they all work, they are interdependent. They not only must depend on each other for their safety and the orderly running of the facility, but they must be able to work with one another, and with inmates, to achieve what is in the ultimate best interest of all: the security, good order, and discipline of the institution. Two of the more important skills for all correctional workers are the ability to effectively communicate (both among themselves and with inmates) and to show respect for other persons.[1]

Recruiting and retaining good staff are challenges that involve hard work and creative steps, which are geared to the job market and the employment pool in the particular state or region. Training the staff is of prime importance; more and more resources have been devoted to this area in recent years. At one time, not too long ago, new staff almost exclusively learned on the job. A new recruit was placed in a work area and "learned the ropes" from an experienced worker in that department, who, along the way, was expected to point out the differences between working in a corrections facility and working in the outside community. Security concerns must always be emphasized in corrections work.

Over time, more formal training was developed, including classroom work and even training in a separate "corrections academy" for the state or locality. In addition to initial training, refresher training for all staff, especially in such areas as firearms proficiency; first aid (including CPR and handling injured inmates); self-defense; emergency procedures (hostage-taking, disturbances, etc.); and, yes, even developments in the law are wise additions to the training schedules at corrections facilities. Virtually all areas of a corrections facility, certainly all areas in which staff work directly with inmates, involve exposure to liability (tort liability and, in some cases, even constitutional liability), particularly if proper training has not been provided. For example, deliberate indifference to an inmate's medical or psychiatric needs (such as when there are indications of suicidal intent, injuries sustained in a fight or work accident, or difficulty in breathing at any time or any place) can be grounds for individual liability under Section 1983 (a violation of the Eighth Amendment, amounting to cruel and unusual punishment).

Failure to Train

Providing good staff training is more than just good management practice. Exposures to legal liability are heightened if staff members are not properly trained in the use of firearms or other use of force, how to behave on escape hunts, how to supervise legal and other visits, and a host of other procedures in the corrections facility. Apart from suits against the individual staff member for shortcomings in his performance, which may have been caused by inadequate or improper training, there have also been suits brought against managers for not providing the proper training for staff members.

A leading case showing the hazards of failure to train is *Davis v. Mason County*, 927 F.2d 1473 (9th Cir. 1991). In Mason County, Washington, there had been four separate incidents in which citizens were arrested by deputies of the sheriff's office. In each incident, there was evidence that the persons arrested were beaten and charged with offenses that were later dropped. In a Section 1983 suit, a jury found the county, the sheriff, and the deputies liable for constitutional violations. The appeals court affirmed the jury verdicts. It found that, in addition to the violations of the constitutional rights of the citizens that were committed by the deputies, the sheriff and the county were properly held liable for failure to provide adequate and proper training to the officers.

The county was liable in *Davis* because it was responsible for setting the policy for the types of action involved. According to the decision in *Monell v. New York City Department of Social Services*, 436 U.S. 658 (1978), a municipality or a county may be held liable under Section 1983, not because of improper actions by its employees, but only when the execution of a government policy that was established by the municipality or county leads to the injury. In *Davis,* the county's failure to train showed "reckless disregard for" or "deliberate indifference to" the safety of its citizens, the court said. This conclusion was based on the standards set in the Supreme Court decision in *City of Canton v. Harris*, 489 U.S. 378 (1989). In *Harris*, the court held that city or county liability in failure-to-train cases is proper when "the failure to train amounts to deliberate indifference to the rights of persons with whom the police come into contact."[2]

The sheriff was held liable in the *Davis* case because he was a policy-making official, a chief executive officer for the county. He had ultimate authority to train persons in his department, and his actions "constituted county policy" on the matter of training. (This was the holding against the sheriff's argument that the state's civil service commission was responsible for all personnel matters. The court said that the commission was responsible for policy on such matters as hiring, promotions, transfers, and discipline but had no power with respect to law enforcement training.) The court pointed out that the training of deputies in this county was "woefully inadequate." Deputies had not been sent to the State Training Academy, but had received "field training," which the sheriff devised. In fact, most deputies did not even receive that training and were sent out without any training whatsoever. Deputies were not given adequate training on arrest and search procedures. There was no training at all on the legal limits to the use of force, and this fact constituted "deliberate indifference" to the rights of citizens, as a matter of law, the court said.

In *Blankenhorn v. City of Orange,* 485 F.3d 463 (9th Cir. 2007), Blankenhorn filed suit to hold the city liable for the arresting officers' alleged use of excessive force. To show that the city failed to train its officers in the use of excessive force, Blankenhorn focused exclusively on the actions of one officer. The Ninth Circuit ruled that "evidence of the failure to train a single officer is insufficient to establish a municipality's deliberate policy." The court held that absent a showing of a "program-wide inadequacy in training," a shortfall in one officer's training may be considered negligence on the part of the municipality but that this is a much lower fault standard than deliberate indifference.

In *Brumfield v. Hollins,* 551 F.3d 332 (5th Cir. 2008), inmate Smith hanged himself while in a jail "drunk tank" (holding cell). His daughter sued, alleging, in part, that the sheriff had failed to promulgate policies concerning inmate supervision and medical care and that the "Old Jail," as it was known, did not have written policies and procedures to cover such activities, similar to ones existing at a nearby facility (known as the "New Jail"). The court said the validity of prison policies does not depend on whether such policies are written or verbal. Rather, an official policy is "either a policy statement, ordinance, regulation…that has been officially adopted…or a persistent widespread practice of officials or employees, which although not authorized by officially adopted and promulgated policy, is so common and well settled as to constitute a custom that fairly represents the municipality's policy." The court in *Brumfield* ruled that verbal policies did exist for inmate supervision and medical care.

The Supreme Court considered the injurious action of a sheriff's deputy during a traffic stop in the case of *Board of the County Commissioners of Bryan County, Oklahoma v. Brown,* 520 U.S. 397 (1997). Reserve Deputy Burns grabbed passenger Jill Brown's arm and pulled her from her car, severely injuring her knees. She sued Burns, the county sheriff, and the county, claiming, in part that by hiring Burns the county was liable for what she alleged was his use of excessive force. The district court, following a jury trial, found the county liable based on its "hiring policy" and "training policy" with respect to Burns. The decision was affirmed by the court of appeals on the basis of the hiring claim alone. The Supreme Court said it did not find the analogy between failure to train and inadequate screening of persons newly hired to be persuasive.

> **Unlike the risk from a particular glaring omission in a training regimen, the risk from a single instance of inadequate screening of an applicant's background is not "obvious" in the abstract; rather, it depends upon the background of the applicant.**

The Court found that what was lacking in the district court's instructions on culpability and, thus, the jury's finding of liability, was a determination on "whether Burns' background made his use of excessive force in making an arrest a plainly obvious consequence of the hiring decision." The lower court's decision was vacated and remanded.

Thus, we have clear word from the courts that government entities and managers can be held liable for failing to set up adequate training programs. At a minimum, to avoid liability for constitutional violations under Section 1983, agencies should be sure that staff are trained in the basics of job performance in any areas where the work they do may implicate constitutional requirements. For example, security personnel must be trained in the proper use of force to subdue or restrain unruly inmates. Mailroom staff must understand the rules for the proper handling of mail, especially the mail sent to and from attorneys and the courts. The implications of constitutional requirements reach into many departments of a prison or jail, and they affect a wide variety of actions by corrections workers. Corrections staff do not have to memorize all kinds of corrections law. What they must know is the policy that affects their work, and managers must make sure that the policy of the agency reflects the constitutional requirements. (It may be helpful for staff to know which policies are based on constitutional mandates to be extra careful that there is no deviation below the minimum standards established in those policy areas.)

Standards of Employee Conduct

> It is the policy of the [Colorado] Department of Corrections (DOC) that DOC employees, contract workers, and volunteers are to have honesty, integrity, and respect for the worth and individuality of human beings, as well as a strong commitment to professional and ethical correctional service....This administrative regulation and "Code of Ethics" provide DOC employees, contract workers, and volunteers with rules and standards governing their conduct as correcional professionals.[3]

> All [Minnesota] department employees, when on and off duty, will conduct themselves in a manner that will not bring discredit or criticism to the department. Common sense, good judgment, consistency and the department's mission will be the guiding principles for the expected employee standard of conduct. Workplace violence is strictly prohibited.[4]

As shown by the above examples, correctional organizations have developed "standards of employee conduct." These standards set out what the employer expects from the employee, and, within the policy, advise the employee of limitations or restrictions on their on-duty or off-duty behavior. Standards of employee conduct can provide very specific guidance as to prohibited conduct, such as not to give or accept a gift, directly or indirectly, from an inmate or an inmate's family and to prohibit the use, or being under the influence, of alcohol while on duty or immediately prior to reporting for duty. Some prohibitions are less specific, such as "conduct unbecoming," which prohibits on- or off-duty conduct that negatively impacts job performance, not specifically mentioned in administrative regulations: "The act or conduct tends to bring the DOC into disrepute or reflects discredit upon the individual as a DOC employee, contract worker, or volunteer."[5]

The significance of these kinds of standards is so important that agencies often require each employee to receive (and sign for) a copy of the standards upon beginning employment and a new copy any time the standards are modified. In addition to providing guidance on prohibited conduct, agencies may have internal investigatory procedures for determining if prohibited conduct by an employee has occurred. In order to fully carry out this investigatory role, two important rules require employees to report violations of the standards of employee conduct to appropriate officials and that every employee is required to cooperate fully and truthfully in official investigations. Employees have important rights during an investigation, established by law and policy. Some correctional workers have been disciplined, including terminated from employment, for not cooperating with these investigations or providing false or misleading statements to investigators. When an employee has been found to have violated the standards, available sanctions can range from an oral reprimand to termination. Some cases of serious misconduct can also result in criminal prosecution.[6]

The case of *City of San Diego v. Roe*, 543 U.S. 77 (2004), concerns a police officer but is informative for its holding regarding a government employee's right of free speech. Roe was a city police officer who sold videotapes of himself engaging in sexually explicit acts. The video was sold on the adults-only section of eBay. Aspects relating to this activity suggested a law enforcement connection (e.g., his code name, clothing clearly identifiable as a police uniform, and a user profile identifying himself as working in law enforcement). Following being discovered, the police department ordered Roe to "cease displaying, manufacturing, distributing, or selling any sexually explicit materials or engaging in any similar behaviors, via the internet, U.S. Mail ... or any other medium available to the public."

Although Roe reduced his activity, he did not stop, nor did he change his seller's profile. Upon discovering this, the police department began termination proceedings, resulting in his dismissal from the department. Roe brought a Section 1983 suit, claiming that the loss of his job violated his First Amendment right to free speech. The district court dismissed the suit, holding that Roe had not shown that his activities qualified as an expression relating to a matter of "public concern" under the Supreme Court's decision in *Connick v. Myers*, 461 U.S. 138 (1983). The appeals court reversed, stating that Roe's conduct did fall within the protected category of citizen commentary on matters of public concern. The appeals court noted that Roe's expression was not an internal workplace grievance, that he was off-duty and away from the work site during the time, and that his actions were unrelated to his employment.

The Supreme Court reversed, holding that the police department showed "legitimate and substantial interests of its own that were compromised by his [Roe's] speech."

> **The use of the uniform, the law enforcement reference in the Web site, the listing of the speaker as "in the field of law enforcement," and the debased parody of an officer performing indecent acts while in the course of official duties brought the mission of the employer and the professionalism of its officers into serious disrepute.**

Citing its earlier cases, the Court described "public concern" as something that is a subject of legitimate news interest—that is, it is a "subject of general interest and of value and concern to the public at the time of publication." The Court held that Roe's expression did not meet this standard, negating any need to balance his interest against those of the police department.[7]

Fair Labor Standards Act, Portal-to-Portal Act

The Fair Labor Standards Act of 1938, 29 U.S.C. § 201 *et seq.*, was intended to ensure that employees covered by the act were compensated for the work they performed. The act was amended by the Portal-to-Portal Act of 1947, 29 U.S.C. § 251 *et seq.*, to describe work as compensable if it relates to the principal activity or activities that the employee is expected to perform. Not compensable are activities that are preliminary or postliminary to the principal activity.

IBP, Inc. v. Alvarez, 546 U.S. 21 (2005), is not a prison case but is important to us in its holding. IBP is a producer of fresh meat and related products. Some IBP employees, for example, those in the slaughter and processing areas, must wear outer garments and protective equipment. Production workers' pay, however, was based on the time spent cutting and bagging meat. IBP employees filed a class action to recover compensation for preproduction and postproduction work, including time spent putting on and taking off protective gear and walking between the locker rooms and the production floor before and after their assigned shifts. The district court held that these activities were unique to the jobs and were compensable, saying that they were "integral and indispensable to the work of the employees who wore such equipment." The court also held that the walking time was compensable as it occurs during the workday. The court of appeals affirmed, although in part for different reasons. IBP did not challenge before the Supreme Court the finding that the putting on and taking off unique protective gear are "principal activities" under the

Portal-to-Portal Act. The question that the Court had to decide was whether the walking between the locker rooms and the production areas was compensable. The Court held it was.

> **[A]ny activity that is "integral and indispensable" to a "principal activity" is itself a "principal activity" under § 4(a) of the Portal-to-Portal Act. Moreover, during a continuous workday, any walking time that occurs after the beginning of the employee's first principal activity and before the end of the employee's last principal activity is ... covered by the FLSA.**

You may wonder how this relates to a prison environment. The nature of prison work requires some staff to perform specific functions prior to reporting to their assigned post. For example, security staff may need to pick up keys or equipment; inmate work supervisors may need to report early to prepare for the arrival of the inmate crews. The issue is whether such activities, and the time it then takes the employees to walk to their duty posts, are compensable. The Supreme Court has not ruled under these facts. However, in 2006, the Federal Labor Relations Authority, in a case involving a prison facility and a local prison union, upheld an arbitrator's ruling that certain employees were entitled to overtime for a specified period.

> The Arbitrator ... considered each of the departments ... concerning which the Union had presented evidence. Beginning with the Custody Department, the Arbitrator found that employees ... were entitled to overtime pay because there was "a sufficient showing that staff in this department do work in excess of eight hours and that their excess time worked is more than *de minimis*" .... [T]he Arbitrator found that, although shifts did not officially begin until the time employees reported to their assigned post, a change in shift at the post required an exchange of equipment, an inventory of equipment, and an exchange of information. The Arbitrator found that these activities are "integral to the job[.]" ... The Arbitrator concluded that "it still takes at least 15 minutes or more to make a relief at a 24-hour duty post even with the equipment placed at the post." ... As to [the Industries] and the Facilities Department, both of which employ inmates, the Arbitrator found that, in order to ensure that equipment and materials were ready for the inmates to begin work when they reported, the staff checks in at the Control Center well before the scheduled beginning of the shift. Based on the evidence presented, the Arbitrator concluded that staff in those departments "have worked more than eight hours with the knowledge of the Agency."[8]

The task for prison officials is to have procedures in place to help ensure that "principal activities" begin and end within the employee's work shift. This could mean that schedules would need to be adjusted and shifts overlap for posts requiring relief (this refers to one staff member replacing another staff member at a specific work position).

■ Equal Employment

In every jurisdiction, there are laws and rules that outlaw discrimination in employment. These laws generally prohibit any kind of decision making (hiring, promotion, conditions of work, disciplining) that is based on race, creed, or color. These are the very broad terms of equal employment law. In practice, and in detail, the laws vary from place to place regarding the exact employment decisions that are covered and the types of discrimination that are banned.

Embracing all discrimination laws in this country is the federal civil rights law, especially the Civil Rights Act of 1964. Title VII of that act (Title 42, U.S. Code, Section 2000e-2) provides the following:

> **It shall be an unlawful employment practice for an employer—(1) to fail or refuse to hire or to discharge any individual, or otherwise to discriminate against any individual with respect to his compensation, terms, conditions, or privileges of employment, because of such individual's race, color, religion, sex, or national origin; or (2) to limit, segregate, or classify his employees or applicants for employment in any way which would deprive or tend to deprive any individual of employment opportunities or otherwise adversely affect his status as an employee, because of such individual's race, color, religion, sex, or national origin.**

In the Equal Employment Opportunity Act of 1972, the coverage of Title VII was extended to state governments. Thus, any state administrator (and any local administrator, by derivation of authority from the state) is considered an employer under the Civil Rights Act and is barred from the discriminatory actions specified in that act.

A survey of corrections agencies asked for the numbers of corrections officers of one sex who were working in opposite-sex institutions. (The corrections officer positions are the most instructive and sensitive, because (1) corrections officers make up the largest single group of employees in correctional institutions (66%, including line staff and supervisors)[9], and (2) these are the positions where staff come into the most frequent, direct contact with inmates.) Among 46 states and the Federal Bureau of Prisons, 41,220 female officers were assigned to male institutions on September 30, 2009. Among 45 states and the Federal Bureau of Prisons, 7,499 male officers were assigned to female institutions.[10]

■ *Dothard v. Rawlinson*

Rawlinson applied to be a correctional counselor (prison guard) in Alabama. She was rejected because she failed to meet the minimum height and weight requirements that had been set for the job: five feet, two inches was the minimum height and 120 pounds was the minimum weight. (An interesting companion plaintiff was Brenda Mieth, who challenged the five feet, nine inches and 160 pounds height and weight requirements for the position of state trooper. The district court upheld her complaint, and Alabama did not appeal the ruling, effectively abandoning those height and weight requirements.) Rawlinson filed a complaint with the Equal Employment Opportunity Commission (EEOC), the agency established to administratively review challenges brought under the federal law, claiming sex discrimination. Besides her complaint based on the discrimination inherent in the height and weight requirements for the job, Rawlinson also complained of the prison rule that barred correctional counselors from working in direct contact with inmates of the opposite sex. The EEOC gave Rawlinson a right-to-sue letter, in effect transferring her case to the federal courts.

A three-judge U.S. district court decided in Rawlinson's favor, finding that the height and weight requirements would exclude more than 40% of the female population but less than 1% of the males who might apply. This was found to show a **prima facie** case of sex discrimination (that is, a claim presumed to be true unless overcome by other evidence), which would be unlawful under Title VII of the 1964 Civil Rights Act. The district court ruled that being male was not a necessary qualification for being a correctional counselor in Alabama, even in the maximum security penitentiary for which she applied.

The Supreme Court, in *Dothard v. Rawlinson*, 433 U.S. 321 (1977), reversed the judgment of the lower court, at least in part. The Court found and agreed that the facts did show a prima facie case of sex discrimination, because the height and weight requirements served to select applicants in a significantly discriminatory manner. The fact that Rawlinson relied on national statistics to show the pattern of sexual discrimination, rather than statistics of actual applicants in Alabama, was satisfactory, the Court said. However, finding a prima facie pattern of discrimination did not end the matter. The employer could, under employment law and Title VII precedents, show that the discrimination was justified, legally rebutting the sexual discrimination showing. In this case, the Board of Corrections (the agency employer) argued that there was a job-related requirement for the minimum height and weight requirements, because those requirements were necessary to obtain persons who had the strength essential to the performance of the correctional counselor job. This justification was rejected, because Alabama had provided no evidence to support their argument that a certain amount of strength was necessary to perform the job well.

On another basis, however, the Supreme Court decided that Alabama had shown a bona fide occupational qualification (BFOQ) that exempted females from consideration. The evidence showed that the prison system was rife with violent behavior by the inmates; that inmates had frequent contact with the officers in the prison living arrangements (which involved dormitory-style living rather than single cells); that correctional institutions were understaffed; and that a substantial portion of the inmate population (about 20%) was composed of sex offenders, who were mixed in with the general population. Because of these factors, the Court said, the use of female guards in the maximum security institutions would pose a substantial security problem, directly linked to the sex of the guards. Based on this, the Court found that there was a BFOQ that justified the exclusion of females from the Alabama guard force (at least in the maximum security facilities).

> **The likelihood that inmates would assault a woman because she was a woman would pose a real threat not only to the victim of the assault but also to the basic control of the penitentiary and protection of its inmates and the other security personnel. The employee's very womanhood would thus directly undermine her capacity to provide the security that is the essence of a correctional counselor's responsibility....On the basis of that evidence, we conclude that the District Court was in error in ruling that being male is not a bona fide occupational qualification for the job of correctional counselor in a "contact" position in an Alabama male maximum security penitentiary.**

It was a strange sort of victory for the Alabama corrections system, because the decision was based on a finding that the work environment was "a peculiarly inhospitable one," an environment of violence and disorganization. The decision does shed some light on the nature of the BFOQ, especially in the prison workplace. It is hard to imagine that other correctional agencies would rush to justify male-only hiring of corrections officers on the grounds that their institutions were, in effect, out of control. The decision does, however, show a legal justification for insisting on same-sex job assignments, particularly in positions in which close physical contact is required and where sex offenders are present in the population. (We doubt that the presence of sex offenders in the population is a decisive factor, because the Supreme Court itself observed, "There would also be a real risk that other inmates, deprived of a normal heterosexual environment, would assault women guards because they were women." This observation, of course, is relevant whether or not there are many sex offenders in the population.)

There is still a difference of opinion among correctional administrators about whether it is best to require corrections officers to be the same sex as the inmate population. Can this not be handled by assigning the opposite sex to noncontact positions—that is, by placing them in work in which they do not come into direct physical contact with inmates? Why is that not a good solution? It is somewhat analogous to the debate about the role of women in combat positions in the military. In most corrections agencies, officers are expected to rotate among the different types of jobs (usually called "posts") in the prisons or jails. In fact, promotion opportunities are often based on the ability to handle well a variety of post assignments. Some places have handled opposite-sex hiring by placing these correctional officers in positions where they do not come into contact with inmates, particularly when the inmates are naked, as in the living quarters or during visual (strip) searches. Making the decision more complicated is the fact that some inmates object to being observed without clothes or while scantily clad by a member of the opposite sex. This has been claimed by inmates to be an unwarranted invasion of their privacy. (Cross-gender strip searches present practical problems and raise serious questions about equal employment opportunities under Title VII.)

■ Title VII and Inmate-Created Hostile Work Environment

The courts have held that employers can be held liable under Title VII for the third-party harassment of its employees when such conduct creates a hostile work environment. But does this standard apply when the third parties are inmates?

This question was addressed in *Beckford v. Department of Corrections*, 605 F.3d 951 (11th Cir. 2010). In *Beckford*, 14 non-security prison employees sued the Florida Department of Corrections (DOC), claiming the DOC failed to "remedy a sexually hostile work environment" established by male inmates for female employees. The women worked in the prison's "close management" housing dorms, consisting of inmates found unsuitable for the general prison population. These inmates were said to have abused staff, especially female staff, including using gender-specific abusive language and openly masturbating towards female staff (a practice referred to as "gunning"). Suggestions offered by staff to address their concerns were not adopted, nor were complaints to prison management successful. At trial, the DOC's Equal Employment Opportunity investigator said that the department's sexual harassment policy, as explained to the female employees, did not cover harassment by inmates, but if it had, the employees "had fully satisfied the reporting requirements of the policy by complaining to prison management, the Florida Commission on Human Relations, and the Equal Employment Opportunity Commission."

In instructing the jury, the district court asked the jury to decide, after looking at all the circumstances, whether the "preponderance of the evidence" showed a "hostile or abusive" employment environment. The jury ruled against the department, awarding $45,000 to each employee.

In affirming, the appeals court held that neither inmates nor prisons should be treated differently from other third-party harassers or employers under Title VII. The court recognized that not all harassment by inmates may be reasonably avoided but said the department was required to adopt reasonable measures to curtail inmate harassment. In this instance, the court cited several examples of such reasonable measures, including enforcing the inmate dress policy (inmates were required to wear pants when female staff were in the unit); having male staff accompany female staff while they were in the unit; requiring security staff to write appropriate disciplinary reports; referring for prosecution incidents of masturbation directed towards female staff; and putting in place a specific anti-gunning policy. (Note: the court rejected the DOC's claim that the close management unit inmates were "equal opportunity harassers" and that the women chose to work in that environment. The court held there was sufficient evidence to show the harassment was sex-based and that the jury was entitled to find the DOC made "almost no effort to protect its employees from this sex-based harassment.")

Other circuits have made similar rulings. In *Freitag v. Ayers,* 468 F.3d 528 (9th Cir. 2006), the California Department of Corrections was held liable for its failure to correct a hostile work environment resulting from sexual harassment by male inmates of female staff. Also see *Erickson v. Wisconsin Department of Corrections*, 469 F.3d 600 (7th Cir. 2006). Erickson, a female payroll and benefits specialist at a Wisconsin correctional center, had informed her supervisor and others (including the warden) that she had been "freaked and scared" by the unexpected presence of an inmate in her work area after hours. She was assured that action would be taken to prevent a reoccurrence. It was not, and eight days later, she was raped by the same inmate. Erickson sued under Title VII's hostile work environment provision. The district and appeals court found for Erickson, with the appeals court holding that a reasonable jury could have determined that the department of corrections had sufficient information to recognize the probability that Erickson was being subjected to sexual harassment but "took no remedial action as it was obligated to do under Title VII."

To prevent such holdings based on sexual harassment by inmates, correctional agencies should have clear policy recognizing its obligation to prevent the sexual harassment (and harassment in general) of its employees by inmates, and the steps that are to be taken to prevent this. These steps, at a minimum, should include written policy and directives (covering expectations for both staff and inmate); staff training, including a specific focus on supervisory responsibilities; and taking actions, up to and referring for prosecution where warranted, for inmate misconduct in this area.

■ Tort Claims

When speaking of "torts," there is one type of claim for violations of persons' rights—constitutional torts. These lawsuits involve rights protected under the Constitution and are authorized by federal statute. 42 U.S.C. § 1983. When lawyers talk of tort actions, however, they are usually speaking of common law torts. Common law torts are injuries caused by one person to another, based on some duty owed. They are called "common law" torts because they were developed and defined in English courts and then later adopted by American courts and statutes. The most common torts at common law are assault and battery. These cover all kinds of injuries, from automobile accidents, to fistfights, to medical malpractice.

Regarding torts, there is something called sovereign immunity, which applies to all kinds of lawsuits. *Immunity* means protection against being sued or, if sued, against being held liable. *Sovereign* refers to the government (originally, it referred to the king of England; in our country, it was carried over and refers to the government). So, *sovereign immunity* means that the king (or, in our country, the government) cannot be sued unless he (or it) agrees to be sued. Therefore, to bring a suit against the government in the United States, the government (the legislature) must have passed a law that says that persons are allowed to sue the government. In such laws, there are usually precise limitations and conditions; the sovereign is allowed to place any restrictions it wants on the authority to sue it—after all, if no law was passed, the sovereign could not be sued at all.

An example is *Ali v. Federal Bureau of Prisons*, 552 U.S. 214 (2008). Ali, a federal inmate, sued the Bureau of Prisons (BOP), claiming that he did not receive all his personal property following his transfer from one federal institution to another. His administrative tort claim was denied, with prison officials saying that Ali's signature on the receipt form certified the accuracy of the inventory listed, and he had thus relinquished any future claims relating to missing or damaged property. Ali sued, alleging violations of the Federal Torts Claims Act, 28 U.S.C. §§ 1346, 2671 et seq. The BOP argued that Ali's claim was barred by the exception in Section 2680(c) for property claims against law enforcement officers. The district court agreed and dismissed Ali's claim for lack of subject matter jurisdiction. The appeals court affirmed, holding that Section 2680(c)'s statutory language "or any other law enforcement officer" included the Bureau of Prisons. Ali's argument was that this phrase reflects what precedes it, that it includes only law enforcement officers acting in the customs or excise capacity that preceded the language of "any other law enforcement officer."

The Supreme Court affirmed the lower courts, saying that the phrase "any other law enforcement officer" suggests a broad meaning.

> **In the end, we are unpersuaded by petitioner's [the inmate's] attempt to create ambiguity where the statute's text and structure suggest none. Had Congress intended to limit §2680(c)'s reach as petitioner contends, it easily could have written "any other law enforcement officer** *acting in a customs or excise capacity.*" **Instead, it used the unmodified, all-encompassing phrase "any other law enforcement officer." Nothing in the statutory context requires a narrowing construction—indeed, as we have explained, the statute is most consistent and coherent when "any other law enforcement officer" is read to mean what it literally says.**

This brings us to tort claims acts, or statutes. In virtually all states and in the federal government there are laws that allow persons to sue over injuries committed (torts done) by the government or its agents. In any case where a tort has been committed, there are typically administrative procedures established for the victim to use to file a claim against the government. Such claims may involve injuries to the person or to the person's property (such as a negligent government driver hitting a car). Usually, a claim form must be submitted first to allow the government to investigate and consider the claim, before it goes into court. This is true no matter what the size of the claim (whether it concerns a few dollars for property damage or millions of dollars for severe injuries). If the claim is not settled to the claimant's satisfaction, then he typically may proceed to court and file a tort suit.

What are the typical kinds of common law torts in prison? Loss of or damage to property is probably the most common type of tort claim that is filed. The claim, to be successful, must show that the injury was caused by the negligence of the government official or agent—that is, the official did not exercise the degree of care that is required by the law (or by the government's own policies or regulations) in such circumstances. In *Parratt v. Taylor*, 451 U.S. 527 (1981), an inmate sued for the loss of his hobby materials, which he had ordered by mail and which prison staff had apparently lost. The Supreme Court originally said this was a constitutional tort, stating a "deprivation of property" under the Fourteenth Amendment, but, because the state had a tort claim procedure, the inmate did have process of law to cover his loss. Later, in *Daniels v. Williams*, 474 U.S. 327 (1986), the Supreme Court rejected that analysis, saying that mere negligent action by an official was not enough to trigger the due process clause of the Fourteenth Amendment. States also usually have tort claims procedures available for inmates to use. In any event, for negligent action causing loss of property or minor injury, the remedy for an inmate would be a tort claims procedure, not a claim under the Constitution.

Besides property loss, the most frequently encountered torts in corrections work are assaults (claims against staff members for physical injuries and claims against the government that an inmate was injured in an assault by another inmate, due to the negligence of the staff in not providing proper protection) and medical malpractice. Claims over improper medical care can cover the full range of claims that may be presented in the outside community, and, indeed, the standards used to evaluate tort claims by prisoners are typically the standards of care that prevail in the surrounding community. Medical claims can include allegations of failing to provide care when symptoms or complaints would warrant a certain course of care; taking medical steps against the wishes of the inmate-patient or plain old mistakes in health care, such as amputating the wrong foot, leaving sponges inside the patient during surgery, or making a bad diagnosis.

Tort claims are made against the government. If liability is found (that is, if there was negligence on behalf of the government official or agent), the relief given is money damages, and that money is paid by the government. (This contrasts with constitutional tort claims, where the claims are made against the individual actors, and money damages are typically assessed against the individual officials who are found at fault. Also, injunctive relief is available in constitutional tort actions, but it is not available in common law tort suits or claims.)

Government employees can be subject to constitutional tort liability for conduct, and their employer may be subject to common law tort liability for similar activity. For example, the use of force against a person in custody can generate an "excessive use of force" constitutional claim against the individual officer as well as a common law tort claim for assault and battery against the officer's employer. Although the two types of claims have different elements, different levels of proof, and different remedies, would it be possible for Congress or a state legislature to limit a prisoner's choice as to the type of law suit the prisoner can bring? In some cases, the answer is yes. In *Hui v. Castaneda*, 559 U.S. __ (2010), a prisoner in federal custody alleged that

United States Public Health Service (USPHS) medical staff assigned to provide medical services to inmates in immigration detention were deliberately indifferent to the detainee's serious medical needs. The complaint alleged that following his March 2006 detainment at the San Diego Correctional Facility, the prisoner sought medical care and treatment and that medical staff failed to provide this care in a timely manner. Castaneda was eventually diagnosed with penile cancer and died in 2008.

Prior to his death, Castaneda sued various officials, alleging they were deliberately indifferent to his serious medical needs. The defendant USPHS officials claimed that a provision of federal law, Title 42 U.S.C. § 233(a), made the Federal Torts Claims Act (FTCA) the exclusive remedy for any personal injury caused by a USPHS officer performing a medical or related function within the scope of his office or employment. After the lower courts denied immunity to the defendant medical officers, they sought review in the U.S. Supreme Court. The Court reversed the lower courts, holding that Congress had intended that the FTCA should be the exclusive remedy for such injuries:

> **Section 233(a) makes the FTCA remedy against the United States "exclusive of any other civil action or proceeding" for any personal injury caused by a PHS officer or employee performing a medical or related function "while acting within the scope of his office or employment." Based on the plain language of § 233(a), we conclude that PHS officers and employees are not personally subject to *Bivens* [constitutional tort] actions for harms arising out of such conduct.**

Thus, in *Hui*, the Supreme Court concluded that Congress could and did limit the remedy that persons may seek against particular persons, in this case, USPHS employees who provide medical care and who are acting within the scope of their duties.

To the extent that a state has a tort claims procedure that covers negligent actions in all kinds of common law tort situations, the individual official of the government is protected as far as individual liability is concerned. In most places, the question asked by the government is whether the official was acting "in the course of duty." If so, he will be covered by the government defending the suit, as a common law tort claim. The central advice to all staff, therefore, is always to act in accordance with agency policy, procedures, and training. If this is done, there is some assurance that the actions taken, which may occasionally lead to injuries to inmates or others, will be covered by the government, because the employee will have acted "in the course of his duties." For this reason, it may not be necessary for government officials to carry liability insurance for protection against tort suits. As a matter of extreme caution, some employees (especially doctors and other health care workers) do choose to carry liability (or malpractice) insurance.

In these common law tort situations, when a tort claim or a tort suit is filed against a corrections agency, the case will be defended by a government attorney, so it is not necessary for the individual employee to obtain counsel. In those rare situations in which it is found that the employee was acting outside his instructions or in violation of policy and practice, he will have to obtain his own representation, which will have to be paid for out of his own pocket (or by his insurance company, if he carries liability insurance).

■ The Americans with Disabilities Act

Another federal statute that has considerable impact on corrections is the Americans with Disabilities Act (ADA), which was enacted in 1990. Titles I, II, and III of the Act are codified in Title 42, chapter 126 of the U.S. Code. (A previous law, the Rehabilitation Act of 1973, requires that there be no discrimination against persons with disabilities in federal agencies and programs; the 1973 act applies also to those receiving federal funds or working under federal contracts.) These laws prohibiting discrimination on the basis of disability thus apply to all governmental agencies—federal, state, and local. Attempts to exclude law enforcement and corrections agencies from the ADA's coverage were rejected in Congress. There are three aspects of the law that are of direct importance to corrections: (1) 2010 ADA Standards for Accessible Design, (2) employment, and (3) inmate programs and services.

2010 ADA Standards for Accessible Design

On September 15, 2010, the Department of Justice published revised regulations for Title II (Public Services) of the Americans with Disabilities Act.[11] Among the changes, Subpart D—Program Accessibility added paragraphs (e) and (k) to Title 28, Code of Federal Regulations (CFR) § 35.151 (New construction and alterations) and a new Section 35.152 (Jails, detention and correctional facilities, and community correctional facilities). In Section 35.151, new paragraph (e), *Social service center establishments,* states that halfway houses may fall within the provisions of the 2010 standards relating to residential facilities. New paragraph (k), *Detention and correctional facilities,* discusses the requirements for the new construction of jails, prisons, and other detention and correctional facilities and for alterations to detention and correctional facilities. The Department discussed new paragraph (k) in its comments accompanying publication of the final regulations.

> Based on complaints received by the Department, investigations, and compliance reviews of jails, prisons, and other detention and correctional facilities, the Department has determined that many detention and correctional facilities do not have enough accessible cells, toilets, and shower facilities to meet the needs of their inmates with mobility disabilities and some do not have any at all. Inmates are sometimes housed in medical units or infirmaries separate from the general population simply because there are no accessible cells. In addition, some inmates have alleged that they are housed at a more restrictive classification level simply because no accessible housing exists at the appropriate classification level. The Department's compliance reviews and investigations have substantiated certain of these allegations.
>
> The Department believes that the insufficient number of accessible cells is, in part, due to the fact that most jails and prisons were built long before the ADA became law and, since then, have undergone few alterations that would trigger the obligation to provide accessible features in accordance with UFAS [Uniform Federal Accessibility Standards] or the 1991 Standards. In addition, the Department has found that even some new correctional facilities lack accessible features. The Department believes that the unmet demand for accessible cells is also due to the changing demographics of the inmate population. With thousands of prisoners serving life

sentences without eligibility for parole, prisoners are aging, and the prison population of individuals with disabilities and elderly individuals is growing. A Bureau of Justice Statistics study of State and Federal sentenced inmates (those sentenced to more than one year) shows the total estimated count of State and Federal prisoners aged 55 and older grew by 36,000 inmates from 2000 (44,200) to 2006 (80,200).... This jump constitutes an increase of 81 percent in prisoners aged 55 and older during this period.

The final rule requires that both the new construction and the alterations of jails, prisons, and other detention and correctional facilities comply with the 2010 ADA Standards for Accessible Design (also issued by the Department September 15, 2010, with an effective date of March 2012), with the objective of making such facilities readily accessible to and usable by persons with disabilities. New Section 35.151, paragraph (k), further specifies that public entities shall provide such accessible mobility features for at least 3%, but no less than one, of the total number of cells being constructed or altered.

Section 35.152, Jails, detention and correctional facilities, and the community correctional facilities, is shown in **Figure 19-1**. In that Figure, paragraph (a), *General,* identifies those areas affected by this section. Paragraph (b), *Discrimination prohibited,* requires public entities (prisons) to ensure that qualified inmates or detainees with disabilities are not excluded from programs, services or activities of a public entity because a facility is not accessible or usable by a person with disabilities; are housed in the most integrated setting appropriate to the person's needs; and have access to safe and appropriate housing.

It is anticipated that litigation will arise from these new rules. For example, litigation is likely to occur around the discrimination-prohibited language of Section 35.152, covering such areas as program participation and physical location (the section says inmates or detainees with disabilities shall not be deprived of visitation with family members arising from placement in distant facilities where, except for their disability, they would not otherwise be housed). Correctional personnel should work closely with staff in the appropriate areas to effectively meet the new ADA provisions. Specific attention should be given to the training of program staff to make them familiar with the program and location accessibility requirements.

In *United States v. Georgia,* 546 U.S. 151 (2006), inmate Goodman sued under Title II of the ADA and also 42 U.S.C. § 1983, challenging the conditions of his confinement. He made numerous claims, some of which were described as trivial. The district court, adopting the magistrate judge's recommendation that the complaint allegations were vague and constituted insufficient notice, dismissed the Section 1983 claims, as well as the Title II claims against all individual defendants. Later, the court granted summary judgment to the state defendants on the inmate's Title II claims asking for money damages. The court held those claims were barred by state sovereign immunity. Goodman appealed.

The appeals court ruled that Goodman's lower court filings alleged sufficient facts to support some Eighth Amendment claims under Section 1983. The appeals court identified three such claims, including one where Goodman "claimed that he was confined for 23-to-24 hours per day in a 12-by-3-foot cell in which he could not turn his wheelchair around." (This, if true, appears to be an example of a cell that is without the mobility features called for in the new ADA regulations discussed above.)

---

§ 35.152 Jails, detention and correctional facilities, and community correctional facilities.

(a) *General.* This section applies to public entities that are responsible for the operation or management of adult and juvenile justice jails, detention and correctional facilities, and community correctional facilities, either directly or through contractual, licensing, or other arrangements with public or private entities, in whole or in part, including private correctional facilities.

(b) *Discrimination prohibited.*

  (1) Public entities shall ensure that qualified inmates or detainees with disabilities shall not, because a facility is inaccessible to or unusable by individuals with disabilities, be excluded from participation in, or be denied the benefits of, the services, programs, or activities of a public entity, or be subjected to discrimination by any public entity.

  (2) Public entities shall ensure that inmates or detainees with disabilities are housed in the most integrated setting appropriate to the needs of the individuals. Unless it is appropriate to make an exception, a public entity—

    (i) Shall not place inmates or detainees with disabilities in inappropriate security classifications because no accessible cells or beds are available;

    (ii) Shall not place inmates or detainees with disabilities in designated medical areas unless they are actually receiving medical care or treatment;

    (iii) Shall not place inmates or detainees with disabilities in facilities that do not offer the same programs as the facilities where they would otherwise be housed; and

    (iv) Shall not deprive inmates or detainees with disabilities of visitation with family members by placing them in distant facilities where they would not otherwise be housed.

  (3) Public entities shall implement reasonable policies, including physical modifications to additional cells in accordance with the 2010 Standards, so as to ensure that each inmate with a disability is housed in a cell with the accessible elements necessary to afford the inmate access to safe, appropriate housing.

Source: 75 Fed. Reg. 56164 (2010) (codified at 28 CFR 35.152). The quoted material in this section is found on page 56183.

Figure 19-1 Jails, Detention and Correctional Facilities, and Community Correctional Facilities, from the 2010 ADA Standards for Accessible Design.

The appeals court returned the case to the district court to allow Goodman to amend his complaint. The appeals court also held that the state's sovereign immunity barred Title II claims for money damages. The Supreme Court agreed to hear only the issue of whether Title II of the ADA nullifies state sovereign immunity. In its opinion, the Court said the inmate's Title II claims for money damages from the state were "evidently based ... on conduct that independently violated ... § 1 of the Fourteenth Amendment." [The alleged denial of the benefits of prison services and programs without due process of law.]

> **[I]nsofar as Title II creates a private cause of action for damages against the States for conduct that *actually* violates the Fourteenth Amendment, Title II validly abrogates state sovereign immunity.**

In *Armstrong v. Schwarzenegger*, 622 F.3d 1058 (9th Cir. 2010), the state of California claimed it was not responsible for providing reasonable accommodations to state prison inmates and parolees with certain disabilities that the state chooses to house in county jails. The inmate-plaintiffs had asked the court to issue "an order requiring Defendants to develop and implement effective policies and procedures ensuring all prisoners and parolees with mobility, vision, hearing, developmental, kidney, and learning disabilities housed in county jails receive the accommodations they need." In denying responsibility, California said that while Title III (on public accommodations and services operated by private entities) barred the affected entities from discriminating either "directly, or through contractual, licensing, or other arrangements," this same language is not in Title II (dealing with public services). According to the State, "Congress unambiguously intended that public entities not be subject to liability for violations of the ADA when they provide programs or services through arrangements with third parties." The district court disagreed, and ordered the state to provide the counties housing the affected inmates with a plan to comply with the ADA, to include improving the tracking of inmates (including parolees) the state houses in county jails; notifying jails when the state sends the county a class member with a disability; and ensuring an adequate ADA grievance procedure is available to the inmate class members confined in the jails.

The appeals court affirmed, holding that the state was responsible for ensuring reasonable accommodations to disabled prisoners and parolees that the state houses in county jails. Both courts pointed to a regulation promulgated by the U.S. Attorney General, 28 C.F.R. § 35.130(b)(1), that specifically barred discrimination by public entities, either directly or through contractual, licensing, or other arrangements from discriminating against persons with disabilities. The appeals court said that this regulation was developed pursuant to Congressional direction that regulations implementing Title II be consistent with Section 504 of the Rehabilitation Act. The lower courts ruled that although Congress omitted from Title II the language that was used in Title III, this omission did not clearly indicate Congress' intent that public entities would not be liable for violations of the ADA committed by third parties contracting with the public entity. The court noted that Section 504 of the Rehabilitation Act states that a party receiving federal financial aid may not discriminate "directly or through contractual, licensing, or other arrangements, on the basis of handicap."

Another part of *Armstrong* dealt with the Prison Litigation Reform Act (PLRA) and its provision that courts "shall not grant or approve any prospective relief [for prison conditions] unless the court finds that such relief is narrowly drawn, extends no further than necessary to correct the violation of the Federal right, and is the least intrusive means necessary to correct the violation of the Federal right." California argued that this requirement was not met, that the court did not make the requisite findings for correcting ADA violations (on a provision-by-provision basis), and that the plan was not narrowly drawn or minimally intrusive. In rejecting the first argument, the court held that absent a clear statement of Congressional intent for the statutory language, it was appropriate for the court to make a broad (as opposed to provision-by-provision) finding that it found the requisite need, narrowness, and lack of intrusiveness. To do otherwise could lead to unwarranted challenges to the findings and unnecessarily delay resolution.

On the second argument, the court held that the state failed to provide alternatives that were more narrow or less intrusive. "Allowing defendants to develop policies and procedures to meet the ADA's requirements is precisely the type of process that the Supreme Court has indicated is appropriate for devising a suitable remedial plan in a prison litigation case....A demonstration that an order is burdensome does nothing to prove that it was overly intrusive." The court rejected the state's claim that a more narrowly drawn provision would be for the state to provide information to the county jails to help the counties "enhance" their own ADA compliance. The court saw this suggestion as an effort by the state to pass its responsibility on to the counties; further, that "enhanced" ADA compliance may not be the same as actual compliance. Nor did the court see the state's suggested alternative that the inmate should be allowed to sue for non-compliance as being more narrowly drawn or less intrusive.[12]

Employment under the ADA

The employment section of the law (Title I of the act) bars employment discrimination in hiring and in other employment opportunities against qualified persons with disabilities. The legal definition of a disability is given in Title 42, U.S. Code, Section 12102:

> **The term "disability" means, with respect to an individual—(A) a physical or mental impairment that substantially limits one or more major life activities of such individual; (B) a record of such an impairment; or (C) being regarded as having such an impairment.**

Because the thrust of the act is to provide equal opportunity to disabled persons, the employment section of the law is written to provide an additional type of protection, similar to those protections covered in Title VII of the Civil Rights Act. What kinds of discriminatory actions are prohibited? The law (42 U.S.C. § 12112) says that "no covered entity [defined as an employer, employment agency, labor organization, or joint labor-management committee] shall discriminate against a qualified individual on the basis of disability in regard to job application procedures, the hiring, advancement, or discharge of employees, employee compensation, job training, and other terms, conditions, and privileges of employment." Similar to the protections given in other antidiscrimination laws, some exceptions are allowed. Although an employer is expected to make "reasonable accommodation" for a disabled person to perform a job, in broader terms, the disabled person must be "otherwise qualified" to perform the job.

Looking at the exact language of the law (Section 12113), there is a defense to discrimination charges that is allowed when the employer can show that "qualification standards, tests, or selection criteria that screen out or tend to screen out or otherwise deny a job or benefit to an individual with a disability [have] been shown to be job-related and consistent with business necessity, and such performance cannot be accomplished by reasonable accommodation." This, of course, is similar to the bona fide occupational qualification (BFOQ), which we saw as an exception in the Civil Rights law.

When hiring, the law says that an employer may not make a medical examination or medical inquiries (related to any disability) before the employee is hired. What can be done at the hiring or interview stage is to inquire into the specific ability of the applicant to perform functions that are necessary to the job. After an offer of employment has been made, the employer may condition an offer on the results of a medical exam, but only if all entering employees are subjected to such exams.

Some have heard of the ADA primarily in terms of requiring physical alterations to building entrances, work spaces, or restrooms. But the law has a much broader impact than that. Employers are expected to make efforts to make a job possible for a disabled person to perform, unless doing so will create an "undue hardship." Interpretation of these key terms in the law—"undue hardship," "reasonable accommodation," and "qualified individual"—will, no doubt, be litigated for many years.[13]

It is safe to say that, as in other areas of balancing interests, corrections administrators can most readily show "undue hardship" if an accommodation would adversely affect the security operations of the agency. Accommodations that cost extra money or create some readjustment of duties between jobs will likely have to be made, up to the point that they would be unduly expensive or disruptive. "Undue hardship" is defined in Section 12111 as "an action requiring significant difficulty or expense." In determining whether an accommodation would impose an undue hardship, factors to be considered "include the nature and cost of the accommodation" and such factors as the size, resources, and structure of the employer's operation.

A person who is a "qualified individual with a disability" is a person "who meets legitimate skill, experience, education, or other requirements of an employment position that s/he holds or seeks, and who can perform the essential functions of the position with or without reasonable accommodation.... If the individual is qualified to perform essential job functions except for limitations caused by a disability, the employer must consider whether the individual could perform these functions with a reasonable accommodation."[14] In correctional facilities, just where those boundaries are will have to be explored for different work situations, involving such factors as the degree of contact with inmates, the security levels of different institutions, and the degrees of physical or mental abilities required in specific jobs. In tough cases, or legal challenges by persons with disabilities to the agency's employment practices, the history of the agency in making efforts to accommodate disabled persons in various types of jobs can also become very important.

In *Hennagir v. Utah Department of Corrections* (DOC), 581 F.3d 1256 (10th Cir. 2009), Hennagir had been working for several years as a prison physician assistant (PA) when the DOC made arrangements to enroll its prison medical personnel in the Utah Public Safety Retirement System. This enrollment necessitated that these staff achieve Peace Officer Standards and Training Certification (POST). The certification encompassed an assessment of physical strength, flexibility, and endurance.

Due to her physical disability (which did not appear to be questioned), Hennagir did not complete the training and was determined by the DOC as being unable to meet the new job requirements. She declined several DOC-offered job alternatives, and the DOC notified her that her employment was being terminated. Hennagir sued, alleging, in part, discrimination and denial of reasonable accommodation in violation of the ADA and the Rehabilitation Act.

The district court granted the DOC's motion for summary judgment, finding Hennagir not qualified for the PA position and that her proposed accommodations were not reasonable. The appeals court affirmed, finding that Hennagir did not meet the "qualified individual" standard set forth in the ADA. The court found the safety training requirement an essential job function. In making this determination, the court said it "weigh[s] heavily the employer's judgment regarding whether a job function is essential." The court spoke to the risks involved in "direct inmate contact," noted a prior incident where a DOC medical technician was attacked by an inmate (and the victim's lawsuit), and the subsequent recommendation of the State Risk Management Division that a POST certification requirement be implemented.

The court found insufficient Hennagir's argument that in her work career, prior to the certification requirement, she never had to employ emergency training. The court said that the ADA imposes no limitation on the employer's ability to establish or change aspects of a job and that "We must look instead to whether a job function was essential at the time it was imposed on Hennagir." The court further commented, "Although a deputy [sheriff] may be required physically to restrain inmates only infrequently, the potential for physical confrontation with inmates exists on a daily basis, and the consequence of failing to require a deputy to perform this function when the occasion arises could be a serious threat to security." [citing *Hoskins v. Oakland County Sheriff's Department*, 227 F.3d 719, 727 (6th Cir. 2000)]

With respect to reasonable accommodation, the court held that Hennagir's proposed accommodations—a waiver of the requirement; to "grandfather" her in the position; and a change of job title (without a change in job)—were not reasonable, that each proposal was in effect a request that an essential job function be eliminated.

It is highly desirable, if not essential, for administrators to adopt policies and procedures to show that the administration is aware of the requirements of the ADA and is trying to accommodate them. Personnel policies should be revised to show that the goals of the ADA are understood. For example, statements that the agency does not discriminate in hiring or in other personnel matters should include references to persons with disabilities. Of course, the exceptions allowed by the Act may also be referred to (provided the person does "not pose a direct threat to the health or safety of other individuals in the workplace," or "does not pose a threat to the secure and orderly running of the institution" are phrases that may be considered). Such references are desirable in personnel policies, and they also apply in the area of inmate programs and services.

One goal of the ADA is to integrate persons with disabilities into the mainstream. This should be kept in mind when policies in either area of concern (employment or inmate programs) are considered. To the extent possible, disabled persons should be included in activities along with others. Sometimes, in order to provide access to benefits or services, adaptations may be necessary to accommodate the disabled. A second principle that should be kept in mind in adopting employment policies and procedures is that corrections facilities are not required to accommodate disabled persons if to do so would present a "direct threat." This term is defined in 42 U.S.C. § 12111 as "a significant risk to the health or safety of others that cannot be eliminated by reasonable accommodation." The regulatory definition for "direct threat" is in Title 29, Code of Federal Regulations, Section 1630.2(r). The regulation requires an individualized assessment "of the individual's present ability to safely perform the essential functions of the job." The assessment is to be based on reasonable medical judgment "that relies on the most current medical knowledge and/or the best available objective evidence." The regulation identifies factors to be considered in determining if a person would pose a direct threat. These factors include "(1) The duration of the risk; (2) The nature and severity of the potential harm; (3) The

likelihood that the potential harm will occur; and (4) The imminence of the potential harm."
The ADA does not confer a right to any particular accommodation.

Inmate Programs and Services under the ADA

[The reader is reminded that new regulations in this area were finalized in September 2010, with
some becoming effective in March 2011 and others (the 2010 Standards for Accessible Design)
in March 2012. Some of the discussion that follows reflects language from earlier editions of this
text. While we believe it continues to apply, the true test must await potential litigation challenges.]

Title II of the ADA does require compliance for state and local correctional agencies with
respect to programs, services, and activities that are offered to inmates, and also to their visitors,
which includes family members, attorneys, religious visitors, and volunteer workers. Not to be for-
gotten are accommodations for other government workers who may be visiting the facilities, such
as parole or probation officers and law enforcement officers (from federal, state, or local levels).

The first, and perhaps most noteworthy, aspect of accommodation is physical access.
Correctional activities and services may not be denied to persons with disabilities because the
facilities are inaccessible. The ADA does not require, however, that existing facilities be drastically remodeled to meet ADA standards. The requirement for fuller physical accessibility applies
to new construction and alterations made to existing structures. Providing program access is not
required if it would result in significant difficulty or expense—for example, undue financial or
administrative burdens.

Sometimes, ensuring program accessibility may involve changing the location where the
activities are conducted, rather than making changes to existing physical structures. In making
such changes, however, it is important to keep in mind another new provision in Section 35.151,
"New construction and alterations," discussed earlier in this chapter. Section 35.151(a)(2)(i)
allows for an exception to the design standards for "structural impracticability," but defines this
term as applicable "only in those rare circumstances when the unique characteristics of terrain
prevent the incorporation of accessibility features." It also is important that corrections officials
become familiar with the provisions of new Section 35.152(b), "*Discrimination prohibited*," also
discussed earlier in this chapter (see Figure 19-1).

Another requirement under the act involves communication. Basically, an agency or facility
must make sure that its communications with disabled persons are as effective as its communications with others. As with all other types of accommodation, this requirement does not apply
when doing so would require significant difficulty or expense—for example, an undue financial
and/or administrative burden. The most obvious example in this area is the use of telecommu-
nication devices for the deaf (TDDs) for persons who are deaf or hard of hearing. Qualified
readers or recorded texts are examples of auxiliary aids for persons who are blind or visually
impaired. It may be that, in classes or in administrative hearings in prisons (such as disciplinary
or parole hearings), sign language interpretation will have to be supplied to deaf prisoners or to
those with severe speech impairments. Accommodations must also be sought for inmates who
are mentally disabled. It is acceptable to provide special housing units or facilities for inmates
with mental disabilities, as long as those inmates are not excluded from the same kinds of programs and services that are available to other inmates. However, they may be excluded when
they are not eligible or capable of participating in programs or activities without changing the

essential nature of the programs or when including them would pose a threat to the health or safety of others. New Section 35.139, "Direct threat," states the public entity (prison) is not required to allow a person to take part in, or benefit from the public entity's services, programs, or activities when that person "poses a direct threat to the health or safety of others." Similar to the employment provisions discussed earlier (29 CFR § 1630.2(r)), the determination of a direct threat set out in Section 35.139(b) involves the public entity making an individualized assessment, using current medical knowledge or "the best available" objective evidence to determine "the nature, duration, and severity of the risk; the probability that the potential injury will actually occur; and whether reasonable modifications of policies, practices, or procedures or the provision of auxiliary aids or services will mitigate the risk."

The new ADA provisions set out what are likely to be more stringent requirements with respect to persons with disabilities. This makes it even more important for corrections officials to review their written policies and procedures in all areas in which inmates and visitors to the facility are directly affected. Those policies and procedures should be revised as necessary to show the accommodations that will be made as the need arises. That latter statement points out the critical issue of the classification of inmates (and their visitors): at intake screenings, the needs of any incoming inmate who is disabled must be identified. (With due consideration and sensitivity to privacy issues, it should be remembered that inquiries should be made to the incoming inmate about whether any prospective visitor to that inmate has special needs due to disability.) From this intake assessment, proper classification can be made to accommodate any immediate needs. Such needs may include medical or psychiatric attention, special programming (such as counseling and educational opportunities), special assignment (because the disabled inmate may pose some risk to himself or to others), proper housing and work assignments, and contacts with persons on the outside (by mail, by telephone, or in the visiting room).

During this classification process, and at all times in dealing with the disabled inmate, staff should keep in mind that persons should not be segregated solely on the grounds of their disability; a major goal is to include all disabled persons (mainstreaming) in existing activities. For example, it may be necessary to assign a disabled person to first-floor housing, but that person should be mixed in with other inmates on that floor. To the extent feasible, staff should avoid placing all persons with a particular disability, or all disabled inmates, together in the same housing area. It is important to remember that new Section 35.152(b) establishes an expectation that "inmates or detainees with disabilities are housed in the most integrated setting appropriate to the needs of the individuals." If it becomes necessary to place disabled inmates together in the same housing area, it is important for written documentation, both for setting forth the basis for this approach and to show that it was done with an awareness of the ADA regulations. Failure to do this provides a basis for inmate litigation.

Special program assignments present special challenges. To the extent possible, inmates with disabilities should be assigned to classes, vocational training, drug or alcohol counseling, work programs, work-release programs, and religious programs. Eligibility requirements for such programs are not allowed to exclude disabled inmates unless it can be shown that the requirements are necessary for the service to be provided or for the activity to take place. A program such as a **boot camp** presents a clear dilemma: It is typically for younger offenders with minimal criminal histories, and it offers earlier release than regular incarceration in return for strenuous physical exercise and work. For certain physical disabilities, involvement in the customary military drills, calisthenics, and hard labor would be impossible.

This was the situation facing inmate Ronald Yeskey. His sentencing court imposed a term of 18 to 36 months but recommended he serve the sentence in Pennsylvania's Motivational Boot Camp for first-time offenders. Successful completion of this program could lead to his parole in just six months. Because of Yeskey's hypertension, corrections officials denied him participation in the program. He sued, alleging an ADA violation. The district court dismissed for failure to state a claim; the appeals court reversed. The U.S. Supreme Court reviewed the case.

In *Pennsylvania Department of Corrections v. Yeskey,* 524 U.S. 206 (1998), the Court held that the ADA clearly applies to state prisons. Title II of the ADA provides the following:

> **Subject to the provisions of this subchapter, no qualified individual with a disability shall, by reason of such disability, be excluded from participation in or be denied the benefits of the services, programs, or activities of a public entity, or be subjected to discrimination by any such entity.**

"Public entity" includes "any department, agency, special purpose district, or other instrumentality of a State or States or local government."

The state argued that the ADA language was ambiguous as applied to state prisons and state prisoners. The state claimed that the law was not intended to benefit inmates and the fact that the inmate was held against his will, in effect, removed him from the coverage of the act.

The Supreme Court disagreed. Prisons offer many programs, from recreational to medical to educational, the Court said, all of which are at least "theoretically" beneficial. To bring the point home, the enabling statute in Pennsylvania calls the Motivational Boot Camp a "program." The Court pointed out that some programs are mandatory for all eligible inmates, giving as an example a drug addict for whom the court orders drug program participation. Also, the Court asserted that even if the words did suggest voluntary participation, all prison programs still would not be excluded: the Court pointed out that participation in the Motivational Boot Camp program and in the services offered by the inmate law library are voluntary.

Yeskey makes it clear that the ADA applies to state prisons. Prison administrators are thus challenged either to adapt existing programs or to create alternatives to provide comparable programs to disabled individuals so that they can obtain the benefits of such programs. This is particularly true where there are reductions in terms to be served (as is typically provided in a boot camp program).

Very similar challenges are presented in prison work programs that may require physical abilities the disabled do not have, but that also offer special benefits for those who participate, such as early release, extra good-time credits, or wages. As time goes by, administrators will continue to be called on to show why inclusion of the disabled in such programs, perhaps with special accommodations, cannot be made without "undue burdens."

Some additional observations about the ADA are as follows:

- Some accommodations would clearly cost too much and would therefore be an undue financial burden—for example, providing duplicate law books for blind inmates in braille. However, providing readers for the blind or providing recorded books from the general library for recreational reading may be an effective approach.

- The ADA does not give inmate workers in prison industries the legal status of employees for the benefits of the nondiscrimination portions of the act that protect employees; at least, the regulations implementing the act would indicate this, and no court has yet required such added protection. It remains to be seen how the ADA's new provisions will be interpreted in this area.

- Auxiliary aids of some kind will ordinarily be required to assist disabled inmates so that they can participate in education and special support programs (such as Alcoholics Anonymous). These aids need not be of a particular kind, so long as they are effective. Inmates cannot be required to pay for such special assistance.

- It is permissible at the classification or intake stages of an inmate's incarceration to ask the inmate about his disabilities. Asking about HIV or AIDS status may be permissible, because that status legally qualifies the person as disabled, so long as it is done to ascertain the ability of the individual to participate in regular programs and activities and to determine whether special accommodations will have to be made. Because HIV or AIDS is ordinarily addressed as a medical issue, and would be covered in medical screening at intake or classification, it may be best to leave that particular type of disability to the medical staff to review, rather than to handle it by routine classification inquiries (especially because there are special confidentiality concerns that apply).

- The Act applies to all types of state and local facilities, including jails and other short-term institutions. It does not cover the executive branch of the federal government (covered by Title V of the Rehabilitation Act of 1973) but does cover Congress and other entities in the legislative branch of the federal government.

Title II of the ADA does not apply to private prison corporations. In *Edison v. Douberly*, 604 F.3d 1307(11th Cir. 2010), a Florida state prison inmate (Edison) sued several employees (in their official capacities) of GEO Care Group, Inc. GEO is a private prison corporation. Edison claimed the defendants discriminated against him because of his disabilities, in violation of the ADA, Title II.

Saying that GEO is not a public entity, the district court held the ADA did not apply and granted summary judgment to the defendants. The appeals court affirmed. That court looked at the statutory language (42 U.S.C. § 12131), which defines public entity as "an instrumentality of a State."

> We ... have long recognized that our authority to interpret statutory language is constrained by the plain meaning of the statutory language in the context of the entire statute .... We have affirmed many times that we do not look at one word or term in isolation but rather look to the entire statute and its context .... Our job ... is to interpret the ADA's use of the words "instrumentality of a State" in a manner consistent with their plain meaning and context ... [T]he term "instrumentality of a State" refers to governmental units or units created by them.[15]

■ Other Federal Statutory Laws

This section discusses three recently enacted federal statutes that may have considerable future impact on corrections. It is important for correctional officials to be aware of the requirements of each statute and to take appropriate action to address those requirements. Whenever possible, it also is valuable for correctional officials to review proposed legislative enactments, both to assess the impact of the legislation on the correctional organization, and, where appropriate, to make recommendations on revising the legislation.

Prison Rape Elimination Act of 2003

Public Law 108-79, the Prison Rape Elimination Act (PREA) of 2003, is codified at 42 U.S.C. §§ 15601-15609. The law's introductory language says the PREA is "[t]o provide for the analysis of the incidence and effects of prison rape in Federal, State, and local institutions and to provide information, resources, recommendations, and funding to protect individuals from prison rape." Among the Act's nine cited purposes are having each prison system make the prevention of prison rape a top priority; putting in place national standards for the detection, prevention, reduction, and punishment of prison rape; and protecting federal, state, and local prisoners' Eighth Amendment rights.

The Bureau of Justice Statistics has collected, since 2003, data on the incidence and prevalence of sexual assault within correctional facilities. In addition, the National Prison Rape Elimination Commission was established and, as set forth in the public law, given the responsibility to develop national standards. The Commission's approach included public hearings, expert committees, a needs assessment that involved site visits to diverse correctional facilities, and a thorough review of the relevant literature. In 2009, the commission released its report, the "National Prison Rape Elimination Commission Report." On March 10, 2010, the United States Department of Justice published in the Federal Register an advance notice of proposed rulemaking (ANPRM) to invite public comment on the commission's proposed national standards and to solicit information useful to the department in publishing a final rule. On February 3, 2011, the department published its proposed rules on the National Standards to Prevent, Detect, and Respond to Prison Rape. This document proposes a set of national standards and provides responses to the approximately 650 public comments received on the ANPRM.[16]

The commission's 2009 Report refers to the Eighth Amendment's prohibition against cruel and unusual punishment, describing it as "a ban that requires corrections staff to take reasonable steps to protect individuals in their custody from sexual abuse whenever the threat is known or should have been apparent." It may well be that courts, in considering inmate allegations of cruel and unusual punishment under the Eighth Amendment, may look to these standards for guidance on sexual assaults in prison.

Adam Walsh Child Protection and Safety Act of 2006

The introductory language of the Adam Walsh Child Protection and Safety Act of 2006 (AWA, Public Law 109-248) says the Act is "[t]o protect children from sexual exploitation and violent crime, to prevent child abuse and child pornography, to promote Internet safety, and to honor the memory of Adam Walsh and other child victims." Several provisions of the AWA impact on corrections. Title I, codified at 42 U.S.C. 16901 et seq., requires sex offender registration. For the initial registration, a sex offender is required to register "before completing a sentence of imprisonment with respect to the offense giving rise to the registration requirement." An appropriate official is required to notify the sex offender of the registration requirement and to ensure that the registration occurs. The sex offender is expected to provide specific information for inclusion in the registry: name and social security number, residence, employment, school, and vehicle identification, as well as other information required by the U.S. Attorney General. The jurisdiction where the sex offender registers is to provide additional information, for example, a physical description of the offender, current photo, criminal history, and DNA sample. The AWA also amends 18 U.S.C. § 3621, adding a new subsection (f), requiring the Bureau of Prisons to establish sex offender management programs and residential sex offender treatment programs.

The AWA also provides for civil commitment programs for sexually dangerous persons. For example, 42 U.S.C. § 16971 provides for the U.S. Attorney General to make "grants to jurisdictions [defined in the Act to include states, the District of Columbia, Guam, and several other areas] for the purpose of establishing, enhancing, or operating effective civil commitment programs for sexually dangerous persons." The Act also provides, in 18 U.S.C. § 4248, for the civil commitment of a sexually dangerous person in federal custody. The term "sexually dangerous person" is defined in 18 U.S.C. § 4247(a)(5) as "a person who has engaged or attempted to engage in sexually violent conduct or child molestation and who is sexually dangerous to others."[17]

The Supreme Court has upheld the constitutionality of the civil commitment of a sexually dangerous person, most recently in *U.S. v. Comstock*, 560 U.S. __ (2010), ruling that enactment of 18 U.S.C. § 4248 did not exceed Congress' authority under the necessary and proper clause of the Constitution.

Second Chance Act of 2007

The Second Chance Act of 2007 (Public Law 110-199), codified primarily in 42 U.S.C. §§ 17501-17555, impacts both state and federal governments. The law's introductory language identifies six purposes: (1) to reduce criminal recidivism, to increase public safety, and to help "States, local units of government, and Indian Tribes [to] better address the growing problem of criminal offenders who return to their communities and commit new crimes"; (2) to rebuild offender family ties, with the objective of promoting stable families and communities; (3) to encourage and expand evidence-based programs that strengthen public safety and reduce recidivism; (4) to protect the public and promote law-abiding behavior by providing offenders with necessary services without conferring luxuries or privileges on those offenders; (5) to provide sufficient transitional services to assist offenders in establishing and maintaining a law-abiding life; and (6) to provide confined offenders with educational, literacy, vocational, and job placement services to help in their community reentry. The act provides for grants to be made to various entities, including states and units of local government.

From a specific legislative aspect, the act amends Title 18 U.S.C. Section 4042—Duties of Bureau of Prisons. The amended section specifically requires the Bureau of Prisons to establish both prerelease planning procedures—for example, helping offenders apply for federal and state benefits upon release, and securing such identification and benefits before release—and establishing reentry planning procedures to provide federal inmates with information in seven specific areas: health and nutrition; employment; literacy and education; personal finance and consumer skills; community resources; personal growth and development; and release requirements and procedures. While the act specifically states that none of its provisions are to be taken as creating any right or entitlement to assistance or services, the provisions do formally establish legally mandated requirements.[18]

SUMMARY

- Employment laws for a corrections agency are set by the statutes and policies of the jurisdiction (federal, state, or local) where that agency operates.

- The training of corrections staff is a vital part of maintaining a quality workforce. In addition, there are legal requirements for providing adequate training to staff members in the essentials of their work and especially in those aspects of their jobs that directly affect offenders and their family and friends who have dealings with them while they are in the corrections programs.

- Correctional agencies have standards of employee conduct that set out the expectations for its employees, including the identification of prohibited conduct. An employee may be held accountable, including job termination, for his off-duty actions that bring the mission of the employer and the professionalism of its staff into serious disrepute (*City of San Diego v. Roe*).

- Employees whose duties may require them to report to work before the start of their shift are entitled to compensation for walking time that occurs after the beginning of the employee's first principal activity and before the end of the employee's last principal activity (*IBP, Inc. v. Alvarez*).

- The Federal Civil Rights Act (Title VII) mandates that there be no discrimination in employment practices based on any individual's race, color, religion, sex, or national origin.

- The Supreme Court, in the case of *Dothard v. Rawlinson,* ruled that the minimum height and weight requirements set for hiring correctional counselors discriminated against female applicants under Title VII. Also, Alabama had not shown that those requirements were necessary for the performance of those jobs, based on strength requirements, which is what state officials had argued. However, the state prevailed because, under Title VII standards, the evidence did show a bona fide occupational qualification, requiring male staff to perform these jobs. This was because the jobs were in a maximum security penitentiary that was under-staffed, was beset by violent behavior on the part of inmates, many of whom were sex offenders, all of which justified the males-only hiring policy for the safety of all concerned.

- Appeals courts have held that correctional agencies may be held liable under Title VII for uncorrected inmate harassment of agency employees when such conduct creates a hostile work environment.

- Common law tort claims may be brought against governments if there is statutory permission to do so (if the legislature in that jurisdiction has waived its sovereign immunity to be sued). The most frequent tort claims made by inmates are for lost or damaged property, for injuries from assaults, and for medical malpractice. If the government is shown to be liable because of the negligent actions of its employees or agents, payment awards to the injured party are made by the government (not by the individuals who were negligent). This occurs provided the employee is acting within the scope of her employment.

- Congress may limit the remedy that persons may seek against particular individuals in certain circumstances. In *Hui v. Castaneda*, the Court held that Congress had made the Federal Tort Claims Act the exclusive remedy to be used for injury caused by the actions of a U.S. Public Health Services officer.

- The Americans with Disabilities Act of 1990 (ADA) prohibits discrimination against disabled individuals. In 2010, the ADA was revised, including the issuance of the 2010 ADA Standards for Accessible Design, parts of which specifically focus on corrections. The Act prohibits discrimination against disabled persons in employment and inmate programs and services. Regarding employment, reasonable steps must be taken to accommodate an applicant or employee who is a qualified individual with a disability. However, accommodations need not be made if to do so would create an undue hardship. For inmates, corrections officials must similarly take reasonable steps to include persons with disabilities in the programs and services that are provided to other inmates. The goal always is to "mainstream" inmates with disabilities, unless doing so would be significantly difficult or expensive; for example, an undue financial or administrative burden. The Supreme Court, in the case of *Pennsylvania Department of Corrections v. Yeskey*, ruled that the ADA applies to state prisons. In *United States v. Georgia*, the Supreme Court ruled that sovereign immunity does not prevent a state prison inmate from seeking money damages directly from the state for alleged violations of Title II of the ADA.

- In recent years, several other federal statutes have been enacted with provisions that have or are likely to have an effect on correctional administration (Prison Rape Elimination Act of 2003; Adam Walsh Child Protection and Safety Act of 2006; and Second Chance Act of 2007).

THINKING ABOUT IT

On June 4, 1995, Steve Hanson was arrested by the Springfield Police Department for possession of cannabis. Following his arrest, Hanson told the officers that he was deaf. He was taken to the county jail along with other arrestees. While at the jail, he was not advised of the amount of his bail, nor was he allowed, in a reasonable time, access to an interpreter, to a text telephone device (TDD), or to a TDD directory. It was not until several hours later that he was allowed to make telephone contact, at which time he was denied the private or confidential use of an accessible telephone. He was eventually released on bail, approximately 13 hours after his arrest and 9 hours after the release of the other persons transported and processed along with him. Hanson subsequently sued, in part, claiming a violation of his rights protected by the Americans with Disabilities Act (ADA). How do you think the court ruled? This case was reported as *Hanson v. Sangamon County Sheriff's Department*, 991 F.Supp. 1059 (C.D. Ill. 1998).

KEY TERMS

boot camp: A camp that emphasizes programs of intensive, militaristic regimens. It is used as an alternative to regular imprisonment. It has been used principally for younger offenders, and it requires a shorter term of confinement than ordinarily would be imposed.

prima facie: Literally, at first sight; on the face of it. A fact or matter presumed to be true, unless it is disproved by some evidence to the contrary.

ENDNOTES

1. Two actual examples are offered. In the first, a prison work supervisor spoke about his appreciation when treatment staff made informal visits to his shop, both to say hello and to learn more about the work done in his area. This had beneficial results in subsequent information exchanges regarding an inmate's work status. The second example involved an inmate whose caseworker told him no on a requested action. At a later point in their dealings, the inmate told his caseworker that while he disliked those decisions, he appreciated the caseworker providing reasons, saying he saw this as showing respect. Even a simple act of a staff member saying hello to an inmate as they pass one another can create a more positive prison environment, and can help lower the tension level within that prison.

2. In *Canton,* the Court hypothesized that a single incident, in a few circumstances, could be characterized as "deliberate indifference." As an example, the Court gave a situation where a city fails to train its officers in the constitutional use of deadly force, holding that the "obvious need" to provide such training, and the subsequent failure to do so, could be seen as deliberate indifference. The narrowness of this situation may be illustrated by *Connick v. Thompson,* 563 U.S. ___ (2011). In *Connick,* the Supreme Court considered whether "a district attorney's office may be held liable under § 1983 for failure to train based on a single *Brady* violation." [*Brady* requires the state to provide the defense with information in possession of the state that is favorable to the accused.] Both the district and appeals court found "a pattern of violations is not necessary to prove deliberate indifference when the need for training is 'so obvious.'" In reversing the lower courts, the Supreme Court in *Connick* held that a pattern of violations would need to be shown. In distinguishing a "single incident" from a "pattern," the Court concluded:

   > Failure to train prosecutors in their *Brady* obligations does not fall within the narrow range of *Canton's* hypothesized single-incident liability. The obvious need for specific legal training that was present in the *Canton* scenario is absent here. Armed police must sometimes make split second decisions with life-or-death consequences. There is no reason to assume that police academy applicants are familiar with the constitutional constraints on the use of deadly force. And, in the absence of training, there is no way for novice officers to obtain the legal knowledge they require. Under those circumstances there is an obvious need for some form of training. In stark contrast, "Attorneys are trained in the law and equipped with the tools to interpret and apply legal principles, understand constitutional limits, and exercise legal judgment."

3. Administrative Regulation 1450-01. *Code of Conduct.* Colorado Department of Corrections. Effective Date September 1, 2011. Accessed November 29, 2011 from http://www.doc.state .co.us/administrative-regulations.

4. Policy 103.220. *Personal Conduct of Employees.* Minnesota Department of Corrections. Effective Date April 5, 2011. Accessed November 29, 2011 from http://www.doc.state .mn.us/DOcpolicy2/html/DPW_toc.asp.

5. See endnote 3.

6. For example, in March 2011, a former correctional officer was sentenced on one count of bribery of a public official. While working as a correctional officer, this person accepted approximately $5,000 from the relatives of two inmates in exchange for providing those inmates with tobacco. Cellular phones were also given to an inmate, which, the judge noted, threatened institution security and the safety of staff. The former officer was sentenced to eight months in prison, four months of home confinement, and 120 hours of community service. At sentencing, the judge stated: "This case is not about the money. It's about the betrayal of the trust that was placed in [the officer]. When bad corrections officers abuse their trust, it causes others to distrust and disrespect all corrections officers and makes it much harder for them to do their jobs." News Release. *Former correctional officer sentenced for accepting bribes from inmates' relatives.* U.S. Attorney's Office, District of Minnesota, March 8, 2011. Accessed May 17, 2011 from http://www.justice.gov/usao/mn/ press/mar012.pdf.

7. In a prison context, there are occasional news stories about a correctional officer being terminated for posing nude in a magazine. The question that might be litigated in such cases is whether the employee's behavior brings, as stated in *Roe,* the "mission of the employer and the professionalism of its officers into serious disrepute."

8. Federal Labor Relations Authority. *United States Department of Justice, Federal Bureau of Prisons, United States Penitentiary, Marion, Illinois (Agency) and American Federation of Government Employees, Local 2343, Council of Prison Locals, Council 33, (Union).* September 13, 2006. It is worth noting that the arbitrator determined that staff in some departments, for example, food service and unit management, largely adhered to their work shifts and were not entitled to overtime pay.

9. Stephan, J. *Census of State and Federal Correctional Facilities, 2005.* Page 4. (Washington, DC: Bureau of Justice Statistics, U.S. Department of Justice, 2008). This report states that an estimated 445,000 employees worked in state and federal correctional institutions at the close of 2005.

10. 2010 Directory: Adult and Juvenile Correctional Departments, Institutions, Agencies, and Probation and Parole Authorities. (71st Ed.) *Adult Correctional Security Staff by Gender Supervision, Ratio to Inmates, Turnover Rate, and Vacant Positions on September 30, 2009.* Alexandria, VA: American Correctional Association, 2010.

11. Nondiscrimination on the Basis of Disability in State and Local Government Services, 75 Fed. Reg. 56164 (September 15, 2010) (to be codified at 28 CFR Part 35). The quoted material in this section is found on pages 56218-56219. This final rule document is a good resource for those interested in administrative law. Among the areas covered are the department's advance notice of proposed rulemaking, notice of proposed rulemaking, public comments, and the response to these, and the final rule.

12. The *Armstrong* decision also discussed several other areas. For example, the court rejected the state's contention that the state's arrangements were for the incarceration of persons, and not for the providing of aid, benefit, or service. The court held that the state's arrangements with counties were not only to confine, but to provide such persons with various positive opportunities, citing examples of treatment programs, the use of bathing facilities, and communication. The court also rejected the state's claim that the state was not being given the proper deference (*Turner v. Safley,* 482 U.S. 78 (1987)), that the ordered plan required parolees to be removed from the county jails and sent to California prisons when a jail showed a pattern of non-ADA compliance. The court disagreed, noting the order does not require placement in a state prison, only that the state either obtain an accommodation within that facility or move the inmate to an appropriate location, which could either be a California facility or a different county jail that can provide the appropriate accommodations.

13. The Architectural Barriers Act of 1968 is the federal law that requires accessibility to buildings designed, built, altered, or leased with federal funds.

14. *Americans with Disabilities Act—Questions and Answers.* Washington, DC: U.S. Equal Employment Opportunity Commission and United States Department of Justice, Civil Rights Division. May 2002, last updated November 14, 2008. Accesed January 18, 2011 from http://www.ada.gov/.

15. In *Edison,* the appeals court held that Title II (Public Services) of the ADA does not apply to private prison corporations. It is conceivable that, at some future time, an inmate may file similar litigation, but claim that the violation occurred under the ADA, Title III (Public Accommodations and Services Operated by Private Entities). Also to be noted is that the language of 28 CFR § 35.152(a), which is effective as of March 2011, specifically says section 35.152 applies to "public entities that are responsible for the operation or management of adult and juvenile justice jails, detention and correctional facilities, and community correctional facilities, either directly or through contractual, licensing, or other arrangements with public or private entities, in whole or in part, including private correctional facilities." Subpart (b) of this section is the one that covers *"Discrimination prohibited."*

16. National Standards to Prevent, Detect, and Respond to Prison Rape, 76 Fed. Reg. 6248 (February 3, 2011) (to be codified at 28 CFR Part 115).

17. The Federal Bureau of Prisons reports that sex offenders make up approximately 10.3% of its inmate population, with about 75% of these sex offenders meeting the Act's definition of sexually dangerous persons. With respect to the civil commitment process, the Bureau begins its review of sex offenders 18 months before their projected release dates. During fiscal year 2009, more than 6,400 case reviews were done, with 13 cases filed with the court. Two inmates were civilly committed as sexually dangerous persons. This information was taken from Federal Bureau of Prisons. *State Of The Bureau 2009—The Bureau's Core Values.* Pages 29–30. Washington, DC: Federal Bureau of Prisons, U.S. Department of Justice.

18. In an interesting twist to *Yeskey* (boot camp programs), discussed in the ADA section, the Second Chance Act authorizes a pilot program whereby an inmate who meets certain requirements, one of which is being at least age 65, may be released from a Bureau of Prisons facility and placed on home detention until expiration of the inmate's prison term. See 42 U.S.C. § 17541(g).

20 | Jails

Whether it be called a jail, a prison, or a custodial center, the purpose of the facility is to detain. Loss of freedom of choice and privacy are inherent incidents of confinement in such a facility.

U.S. Supreme Court, *Bell v. Wolfish*

Chapter Outline

- Constitutional Rights of Jail Inmates: *Bell v. Wolfish*
- Constitutional Issues in Jails
  - Visiting
  - Inmate Suicides
  - Searches
  - Legal Access
  - Personal Injury
- Using Excessive Force and Failure to Train
- Other Jail Issues and Cases
- Removing the Sheriff from Running the Jail

Jails are designed primarily to function as holding places for those who are held awaiting trial (those who are in custody, not having been released on bail or on recognizance). Because this is the primary function of jails, they are located as close as is feasible to the court(s) where detainees will be taken for trial. (In early days, jails were often built inside the county or city courthouse or just across the street. This is still the case in many jurisdictions, and even new jails are built as close to the courthouse as possible.) Jails also hold some persons who are serving sentences.

The security concerns for jails, because they may be required to hold any level and type of prisoner, are similar to those for prisons. The Supreme Court affirmed this in *Bell v. Wolfish*:

> There must be a "mutual accommodation between institutional needs and objectives and the provisions of the Constitution that are of general application." This principle applies equally to pretrial detainees and convicted prisoners. A detainee simply does not possess

> the full range of freedoms of an unincarcerated individual .... [M]aintaining institutional security and preserving internal order and discipline are essential goals that may require limitation or retraction of the retained constitutional rights of both convicted prisoners and pretrial detainees .... There is no basis for concluding that pretrial detainees pose any lesser security risk than convicted inmates. Indeed, it may be that in certain circumstances they present a greater risk to jail security and order.

Jail administrators must be aware of the court holdings and the constitutional and legal standards for both pretrial detainees and sentenced inmates, because both kinds of inmates are confined in jails. In this chapter, we will review holdings and standards that apply to jails, focusing on those that are peculiar to the main jail population: pretrial detainees.

■ Constitutional Rights of Jail Inmates: *Bell v. Wolfish*

In *Bell v. Wolfish*, 441 U.S. 520 (1979), the Supreme Court gave us the constitutional standards that govern the status of pretrial detainees, the major class of prisoners in jails. Let us review those standards that were set in the *Bell* case.

First of all, it is the due process clause that protects the pretrial detainee. Because he has not been convicted, he may not be punished. Under due process, he may not be deprived of his liberty without due process of law. Therefore, the legal inquiry is whether the detainee has been punished. If there are challenges to conditions in a jail, the question is whether those conditions amount to punishment. (There are some other protections retained by jail inmates, under other constitutional guarantees. We will look at those a little later.) How do we tell whether the inmate is being punished in the jail? Fortunately, the Supreme Court did not leave it to the lower courts to decide what amounted to punishment; it gave us some guidance on how to test the conditions in order to determine whether they are punishment. The test is this: Was the action taken, was the restriction imposed, or were the conditions created for the purpose of punishment, or, on the other side, was there a valid governmental purpose that supported the conditions?

> [I]f a particular condition or restriction of pretrial detention is reasonably related to a legitimate governmental objective, it does not, without more, amount to "punishment."

The government's objective in running a jail is usually to maintain security and order. If the conditions or restrictions that are complained about are necessary to maintain security and order, then there has not been unconstitutional punishment.

Based on these standards and measurements in assessing conditions at the federal jail in New York City, the Supreme Court in *Bell* concluded that crowding, including the double-bunking of inmates in single cells and even the bunking of inmates in recreation areas and corridors, did not amount to punishment.

In addition, as the Supreme Court indicated in *Bell,* factors other than just the number of inmates and the square footage in the cells are important. It also is important to look at such things as how long inmates are held at the jail, how much time they have to spend in their cells each day, whether there are activities for them outside of their cells, and whether the large number of inmates adversely affects the delivery of other important services, such as food, clothing, sanitation, and health care. It also is important to look at whether the crowded conditions are just temporary or long term and, if the latter is true, whether jail authorities (and local legislative and judicial authorities) are making plans to alleviate the crowded conditions.

From *Bell v. Wolfish*, we also know that jail inmates are protected when other rights, protected under specific constitutional provisions, are implicated. For example, inmates in *Bell v. Wolfish* complained of a rule at the jail that specified they could only order books and magazines from the publisher (books could not be sent in by family or friends). This raised a First Amendment question. The Supreme Court upheld the jail's publisher-only rule, saying that it was reasonably related to a security concern. Thus, the test used to support a restriction on First Amendment activities is virtually the same as that used to show no due process violation: whether the government had a legitimate, reasonable interest in protecting the security and order of the jail.

The same kind of justification for governmental restrictions was found in *Bell* with respect to two search issues: searching the living quarters of inmates (the exact question was whether the inmate had the right to be present during the search of his quarters) and conducting visual strip searches after contact visiting. The Fourth Amendment forbids unreasonable searches. The Supreme Court found that there were valid security reasons for both of these search procedures (not allowing the inmates to be present during the searches of their cells, and conducting the body cavity searches after visiting), so they were, in the jail context, reasonable. All issues in *Bell* were decided on the grounds that the government's actions were reasonable and necessary under the circumstances, because they were tied to the maintenance of security and order in the facility. It was the technical, legal analyses under different provisions of the Constitution that differed. The advice to jail administrators is clear: be certain that any regulations and practices used at the jail, particularly when they are in areas where constitutional rights might be claimed, are justifiable under concerns about keeping security and order at the facility.

Jails do not hold only pretrial detainees. (By the same token, it is not only the jails that hold pretrial detainees. For various reasons, correctional institutions sometimes hold offenders who are awaiting trial or sentencing.) The holdings we just reviewed of *Bell v. Wolfish* deal with detainees at that jail, those who were not yet convicted. But the jail in *Bell* held other inmates, as most jails do. There are usually persons at a jail who are serving short sentences. It just makes good sense, for economic and practical reasons, to keep short-term prisoners at a jail rather than transport them to a prison or other correctional institution. The length of time for holding those serving short terms differs: in some places it is all sentences of a year or less, six months or less, or some other time frame. But it is virtually a universal rule that jails will keep such short-term prisoners. Exceptions can be made for prisoners who are disruptive, those who pose an escape risk, or those who otherwise need to be moved to a different facility.

Exceptions have also been made in the opposite direction: because of crowding in prisons, prisoners who would otherwise be sent to a prison must be held in the local jails, often as required in court orders, until there is room for them at the prison. (On January 1, 2002, 17 corrections agencies reported that more than 9,900 inmates were being held in local jails, awaiting transfer.)[1] This, of course, has caused jail populations to swell, adding to the existing pressures. Jails also hold other sentenced prisoners—those who have been returned to the local court to be tried on additional charges or to testify in the cases of other persons; those who have challenged their convictions by appeal or by collateral attack and who are ordered back by the local court to consult with counsel or to be present for a hearing; and those who have been arrested as parole or probation violators and are being held locally, awaiting revocation hearings.

Finally, jail administrators may want to keep a core of sentenced inmates (sometimes called a "cadre") for maintenance and other work at the jail. These inmates may be serving a longer sentence than the ordinary jail term of a year or less; they may have volunteered to stay at the jail, rather than go to a state prison, in order to remain closer to home or, in some cases, even to have better living conditions.

In midyear 2010, there were 748,728 inmates confined in local jails. Reflecting the transient nature of jails, this population was a relatively small percentage of all admissions (an estimated 12.9 million) over the 12-month period ending June 30, 2010. About 39% of those confined were sentenced offenders or convicted offenders awaiting sentencing.[2]

The constitutional rights of those who are convicted and being held in the local jail are the same as those for prisoners held in prisons or correctional institutions. Therefore, the standards we have noted relating to inmate rights in all kinds of prison situations apply in jails, unless the jailer can show that local conditions (particularly related to security) require different considerations. In *Bell,* the Supreme Court found that the issues of mail (incoming publications and the receipt of packages) and searches (cell searches and strip searches) were all governed by the same concerns of security and order. For this reason, the government's policies and practices regarding convicted and sentenced prisoners were valid, just as they were for the pretrial detainees.

Within the past few years, there is a new policy that has been adopted in a few jails relating to incoming mail. This new policy restricts inmate correspondence (with a few exceptions, such as for legal mail) to postcards. One jail, which implemented its new policy in January 2010, said:

> Inmates are allowed to send and receive mail in order to maintain connection with their separated family, friends, acquaintances, etc. All mail will continue to be thoroughly checked for any violations. Incoming and outgoing mail must be in postcard format, no larger than 5.5" by 8.5". Other permitted forms of communication with inmates include phone calls and personal visits .... Prior to January 1, 2010 the Marion County [Oregon] Jail spent an average of nine (9) employee hours per day, Monday–Friday sorting and inspecting inmate mail. The process was costing the taxpayers between $55,000 and $60,000 per year in wages. By converting the vast majority of inmate mail from sealed envelopes to postcards we estimate the time spent handling inmate mail will be reduced by 50% for a savings to the taxpayer of nearly $30,000 per year. In addition, staff safety and security is enhanced by limiting the opportunities for introduction of contraband and/or biological and chemical agents into the jail in sealed envelopes. The benefits of converting from general enveloped mail to postcards: Saves tax dollars for reinvestment into our community. Enhances work place and public safety.[3]

As of 2010, this kind of postcard provision has been adopted by a number of jails. Some lower courts have considered this policy with varying results,[4] and further litigation is likely. The litigation will focus on the rights of inmates and their correspondents under the First and Fourteenth Amendments. In distinguishing jails from prisons, courts may consider such factors as the far larger number of jail admissions in any given year, the shorter inmate stays within a jail, and the security concerns that may occur over housing a population for which there is less background information, such as in presentence or law enforcement reports, or other reliable sources.

■ Constitutional Issues in Jails

In this section, we will consider some other court rulings related to constitutional issues in a jail context.

Visiting

Block v. Rutherford, 468 U.S. 576 (1984), raised the question of whether the sheriff of the Los Angeles County Jail could restrict pretrial detainees to noncontact visiting. The Supreme Court (reversing the lower courts) held that he could. The Court said that, because there was a legitimate government objective that was being pursued (the prevention of the introduction of contraband), the prohibition of contact visits was permissible. The Court specifically held that contact visits were not constitutionally required.

Houchins v. KQED, Inc., 483 U.S. 1 (1978), involved a request by a television station to visit and film an area of the county jail where an inmate had recently committed suicide. The Supreme Court restated its holding in the prison cases in which media representatives had requested individual interviews (*Pell v. Procunier*, 417 U.S. 817 (1974), and *Saxbe v. Washington Post*, 417 U.S. 843 (1974)). The Court held that the media did not have any right of access to the jail under the First Amendment. The sheriff was not required to give the media access to the jail because it was an area that was not open to the public generally, and the media has no more right of access to such areas (to prisons or to jails) than does the general public.

Grabowski v. Jackson County Public Defenders Office, 47 F.3d 1386 (5th Cir. 1995), dealt with Grabowski's challenges to his conviction and sentence. A portion of his challenges related to jail conditions. Grabowski claimed Section 1983 violations occurred when his visiting privileges with his girlfriend were revoked and when he was denied telephone and recreation privileges while he was a pretrial detainee. At the request of the public defender, Grabowski had been granted in-house visits with his girlfriend, who was also an inmate at the jail. His privileges were revoked when Grabowski had a shouting match with a paralegal, to whom he directed a racial slur in the presence of other (mostly black) inmates. Jail officials said his conduct was disruptive and certainly not in accord with the special visitation privileges that had been granted to him. The court held that no constitutional rights were violated in the revocation of visiting privileges, because the action was reasonably related to the maintenance of security and order in the jail. Regarding the withdrawal of Grabowski's telephone, recreation, and canteen privileges, the court held that the evidence showed that those actions were taken for his own safety and not for punishment (which would be the impermissible reason for any action taken against a detainee). Following the incident already referred to (with the paralegal), Grabowski was involved in altercations with other inmates (mostly black), a fire was set in his cell, and he was threatened. Officials moved him into protective custody, where the privileges in question were not available. Here too the court found good justification for the officials' actions, based on concerns for institutional security and order, as well as the safety of Grabowski himself.[5]

A jail inmate's loss of telephone privileges was also upheld in *Valdez v. Rosenbaum*, 302 F.3d 1039 (9th Cir. 2002). Valdez had been identified as the leader of a drug smuggling conspiracy. In pretrial detention, he was first housed in the jail's general population, with access to four telephones. In October 1998, the federal prosecutor asked the U.S. marshal to suspend Valdez's telephone privileges. New indictments were about to be issued; in addition to naming Valdez, five new defendants would be named, who were not yet in custody. The prosecutor wanted to curtail Valdez's ability to communicate with those people. Based on the request, Valdez was placed in administrative segregation, and his telephone contacts were limited to one daily attorney telephone call. His visits were not curtailed. Because there was a delay in arresting the other defendants, Valdez remained under the segregated restrictions for about four and a half months. He was returned to the general population after one of the captured coconspirators was released. The prosecutor saw this release on bail as making Valdez's restricted status unnecessary.

Following his conviction (he received a 30-year sentence), Valdez filed a Section 1983 suit, alleging, in part, that the telephone restrictions violated his constitutional rights to due process and freedom of speech. The trial court held that Valdez's constitutional rights had been violated. The appeals court disagreed, holding there was no violation of his constitutional rights.

The appeals court held that preventing Valdez from tipping off his coconspirators was a legitimate governmental interest, showing that the restrictions imposed were not for the purpose of punishing him (which, under *Bell*, would be improper). Another sign of reasonableness was shown by the fact that the restrictions were ended once one coconspirator was released on bail. The court (applying *Turner v. Safley*, 482 U.S. 78 (1987), factors) also held that there was no First Amendment violation of Valdez's freedom of speech, as the restriction was rationally related to a legitimate governmental interest. Furthermore, Valdez retained the right of communication through such means as visiting and correspondence; to allow him telephone access would have required prison officials to allocate additional resources for monitoring purposes. Consequently, there was no easy alternative to the restrictions that were used.

Inmate Suicides

The problem of suicides is one that is at least as pressing in jails as it is in prisons. Many of the reported cases that have dealt with inmate suicides came out of jails. The standard used to assess liability for constitutional violation of rights is deliberate indifference to the needs of the inmates. Whether in custody of the police, in jail, or in prison, staff must be on the lookout for suicidal tendencies and take steps to prevent suicides when indications of suicidal risk are clear, based on the circumstances of the individual case.

One court, in *Gish v. Thomas*, 516 F.3d 952 (11th Cir. 2008), held that deliberate indifference requires a "strong likelihood" rather than a "mere possibility" that self-inflicted harm will occur. That was certainly the situation in *Heflin v. Stewart County*, 958 F.2d 709 (6th Cir. 1992), where a deputy sheriff failed to cut down an inmate who was hanging himself. His failure to take steps to try to save the inmate (his decision was to wait until emergency medical staff arrived) was found to amount to negligent care and deliberate indifference. However, officers were not held liable in *Freedman v. City of Allentown*, 853 F.2d 1111 (3rd Cir. 1988), (there was no deliberate indifference found) when they did not realize there was a suicidal risk because of scars that were observable on the inmate's wrists and neck.

There was a similar finding in *Brumfield v. Hollins*, 551 F.3d 332 (5th Cir. 2008). This case also involved an inmate (Smith) who hanged himself. Smith, who had been arrested the previous evening for drunk driving, was being housed in the jail's drunk tank. His belt, watch, jacket, and hat were removed from his person. Around 1:30 a.m. the following morning Smith was found lying on the floor in his cell, his shoelaces around his neck. Without removing the shoe-laces, three different people felt for a pulse, found none and assumed Smith was dead. It wasn't until the ambulance crew arrived 20 minutes later that the noose was removed and life-saving techniques began. In considering this information, the appeals court said, "[w]hile the deputies' conclusion that Smith was already dead and their resulting failure to make any attempt to save Smith's life are arguably negligent, negligent conduct alone does not amount to deliberate indif-ference." In distinguishing *Heflin*, the court said that the Sixth Circuit (in *Heflin*) applied an objective analysis of "deliberate indifference" (what the actor should have known), which was rejected by the Supreme Court in *Farmer v. Brennan*, 511 U.S. 825 (1994). The *Brumfield* court applied the current subjective "deliberate indifference" test (what the actor actually knew), which was established in *Farmer v. Brennan*.

A Supreme Court case that deals with the suicide of a jail inmate is *Logue v. United States*, 412 U.S. 521 (1973). The decision in that case primarily dealt with whether the federal govern-ment could be held liable for the negligence (a common law tort) of local jail officials who were holding a federal prisoner who committed suicide. The Court said the government could not be held liable because the county jail staff were not agents or employees of the federal government. However, the Court said that there could be tort liability attributable to the United States if the federal agent (a deputy U.S. marshal) who placed the inmate in the jail knew that there were suicidal problems and did not alert the jail officials to those problems so that they could take appropriate precautionary, surveillance steps.

Searches

Bell v. Wolfish, as we have already noted, dealt with other issues besides the central issue of whether the crowded conditions at the jail were unconstitutional. Two of the issues dealt with searches. The standard for examining searches under the Constitution is determining whether the searches were reasonable. (The Constitution forbids "unreasonable searches and seizures.") The Supreme Court held that the room searches conducted at that jail were an "appropriate security measure" and were therefore reasonable. Inmates claimed that they should be present when their cells were searched, but the Court said that was unnecessary and, indeed, could be contrary to the security needs for conducting effective room searches. (That same issue, the right of an inmate to be present during the search of his cell, was raised again in *Block v. Rutherford*, and the Supreme Court affirmed and repeated its holding in *Bell*: that the inmate does not have a right to be present during the search of his cell.)

Another part of the *Bell* decision dealt with body cavity searches of inmates, which were conducted by jail staff after all contact visits. The Court upheld the necessity of conducting such searches in order to detect contraband. The searches were found to be reasonable under the

Constitution. The Court warned, however, that such searches might easily be abused and, therefore, cautioned that they should be conducted professionally and reasonably.

One court, the U.S. Court of Appeals for the Second Circuit, has ruled in two cases on the strip-search issue for jail inmates. In *Shain v. Ellison*, 273 F.3d 56 (2d Cir. 2001), a detention facility, the Nassau County (New York) Correctional Center (NCCC), strip-searched Shain when he arrived at the facility and again the next morning prior to his appearance in court. Shain had been arrested for a domestic disturbance and charged with a misdemeanor. This court of appeals agreed with the lower (federal district) court that the search was a violation of the Fourth Amendment. The sheriff could be held liable and was not entitled to qualified immunity, because the law (in this circuit) had been clearly established: persons charged with misdemeanors could not be strip-searched, unless there was a reasonable suspicion that they were concealing weapons or other contraband.

In *Hartline v. Gallo*, 546 F.3d 95 (2nd Cir. 2008), this court re-affirmed its position on strip searches. The "Fourth Amendment requires an individualized '*reasonable suspicion* [emphasis added] that [a misdemeanor] arrestee is concealing weapons or other contraband based on the crime charged, the particular characteristics of the arrestee, and/or the circumstances of the arrest' before she may be lawfully subjected to a strip search." Hartline had been stopped by the police because the truck she was driving was missing a license plate. The officer then noticed a stem of a marijuana plant on the floor of the truck, and Hartline was taken to the police station. There, she was strip-searched, with a video camera operating in the cell while she was searched. The appeals court agreed with Hartline that this search was contrary to the established law in this circuit. There was not a reasonable basis, because of her appearance or other circumstances surrounding her arrest, to conclude that she was concealing any type of contraband. (Hartline's misdemeanor marijuana charges were ultimately dismissed.)

More recently, however, the U.S. Supreme Court, in *Florence v. Board of Chosen Freeholders*, 566 U.S. __ (2012), upheld strip searches of detainees admitted to a jail's general population, absent reasonable suspicion, citing the government's substantial interest in preventing any new inmate from putting those who live or work at these institutions at even greater risk.

Lanza v. New York, 370 U.S. 139 (1962), dealt with the visit between a jail inmate and his brother. Their conversation during visiting was monitored and recorded. The Supreme Court upheld authorities' use of that taped conversation at hearings. The Court notably pointed out that a jail is not the equivalent of a man's house. Privacy is lost in a jail (or prison) setting, and surveillance throughout a jail (including in visiting areas) must be conducted. A similar case is *United States v. Hearst*, 563 F.2d 1331 (9th Cir. 1977), cert. denied, 435 U.S. 1000 (1978), in which a federal court of appeals upheld Hearst's conviction and the use at trial of an intercepted conversation during visiting that Hearst had had at a county jail. The court found that there was a valid governmental purpose (for security reasons) to monitor and record visiting room conversations and that the tapes from such monitoring could be turned over to law enforcement officials for their use.

Legal Access

A state prisoner was being held in a local jail, awaiting transfer to state prison to serve his term of imprisonment. He complained that the jail library holdings were inadequate (not nearly as large as those in the prison libraries) and that one hour per week of access time to the library was also inadequate. The federal court of appeals held, in *Strickler v. Waters*, 989 F.2d 1375 (4th Cir. 1993), that the library had a reasonable collection of law books, including state and federal codes, some reporters of cases, and legal encyclopedia sets, which were sufficient for the time the inmate was held in the jail. Perhaps anticipating *Lewis v. Casey*, 518 U.S. 343 (1996), the court also said that the inmate had not shown that he had suffered any actual prejudice in any pending or contemplated legal action.

A civil rights violation was claimed by a pretrial detainee who said that his incoming legal mail was opened and read in *Walker v. Navarro County Jail*, 4 F.3d 410 (5th Cir. 1993). The court held that opening and checking the incoming mail without censoring it did not amount to a constitutional violation. In *Kane v. Garcia Espitia*, 546 U.S. 9 (2005), a Supreme Court per curiam opinion, Garcia Espitia said he had received no law library access while in jail before trial and only around four hours during the trial (he had chosen not to be represented by an attorney). Garcia Espitia claimed his restricted library access violated his Sixth Amendment rights. Following conviction, he filed for a writ of habeas corpus, with the district court denying relief. The Court of Appeals for the Ninth Circuit reversed, saying that "the lack of any pretrial access to lawbooks violated Garcia Espitia's constitutional right to represent himself." The Supreme Court disagreed, holding there was no clearly established right of law library access to a defendant who was representing himself.

Personal Injury

There are two leading cases that limit the use of the due process clause to pursue injuries (to person or to property) as violations of the Constitution: *Daniels v. Williams*, 474 U.S. 327 (1986) and *Davidson v. Cannon*, 474 U.S. 344 (1986). Of those two cases, *Daniels v. Williams* was a jail case. The inmate, Daniels, sued officials when he was injured in a fall on a stairway at a city jail. He claimed that staff had been negligent in leaving a pillow on the stairs, which caused his fall. The Supreme Court said that such a claim does not amount to a constitutional violation. The Fourteenth Amendment (due process) is intended to apply against much more serious matters—the abuse of power by government officials, not their negligence. Claims like this one, asserting negligence on the part of the jail officials, did not state a claim for violation of due process of law.

Although negligent acts causing personal injury or loss of property did not state constitutional violations (under 42 U.S.C. § 1983), they could (and perhaps even should) be considered under traditional tort law. Most jurisdictions have waived their sovereign immunity and have made their tort claims acts (or the equivalent) available to prisoners, meaning that jail inmates may be able to recover damages in a tort claim or lawsuit for negligent acts of officials. (Remember that these claims would be brought against the state or government entity, not against the individual officials, as in a Section 1983 action.)

■ Using Excessive Force and Failure to Train

A county or city can be held liable under 42 U.S.C. § 1983 for constitutional violations committed by its employees when they are carrying out policy set by the county or city. In *Davis v. Mason County*, 927 F.2d 1473 (9th Cir. 1991), the county and the sheriff were held liable for failure to set up a program of adequate training for deputy sheriffs. Whether it occurred on the streets or inside the jail, the deputies themselves would be held liable for the beatings that were administered to persons they had arrested. But because they had had inadequate (virtually no) training regarding the proper use of force, the sheriff himself (who was responsible for setting training policy) and the county (which was ultimately responsible for training policy) were also found liable. The Supreme Court, in *City of Canton v. Harris*, 489 U.S. 378 (1989), has set the training requirement standard: a city or county may be held liable if it is shown that its failure to train "amounts to deliberate indifference to the rights of persons" with whom officers come into contact.

Gibson v. County of Washoe, Nevada, 290 F.3d 1175 (9th Cir. 2002), is a case involving several topics discussed in this chapter—health care, use of force, and training of staff. Two officers pulled over Stephen Gibson after observing his strange behavior, suspecting he was driving under the influence of alcohol or drugs. A search of Gibson's car found several prescription medications. What the officers did not know at the time was that the police had an "attempt to locate" (ATL) alert out on Gibson, that he suffered from manic depressive disorder, that he did not like police, and that, according to his treating physician, once located, he should have been taken to the hospital for emergency commitment.

At the jail, the arresting officers gave the medication they found to the jail nurse, who told one of the officers that the drugs were used to stabilize a person suffering from mental illness. The record does not indicate that this information was shared with anyone else at the jail. Twice during the evening, Gibson slipped out of his waist chain. The second time, jail staff ordered Gibson to be moved to a special watch cell, containing a bench with attached soft restraints and a helmet. Gibson resisted, and force was used. During this encounter, Gibson suffered a heart attack and died.

Gibson's wife filed a Section 1983 suit against the county and several officials, in their official and individual capacities. She did not sue the arresting officers or the nurse. She set forth three causes of action: (1) that the individual deputies used excessive force; (2) that they showed deliberate indifference to Gibson's serious mental health needs; and (3) that the deputies' actions resulted from policies, practices, or customs of the sheriff's department, which caused or contributed to his death. It was alleged that the county's "omission"—its lack of a system for staff to communicate relevant information—revealed deliberate indifference to the constitutional rights of the mentally ill and that the county failed to adequately train its staff on identifying and handling the mentally ill.

The appeals court affirmed the district court's finding that the individual deputies were not deliberately indifferent to Gibson's medical needs and that no excessive force was used. It was on the third issue of county liability that the appeals court reversed and remanded. Citing the standards of *City of Canton*, the court said that a plaintiff must show three things in order to impose liability. First, it must be shown that Gibson's constitutional rights were violated by a county employee. The court felt this could be shown—for example, a jury could find that the nurse on duty was deliberately indifferent to his special medical conditions and needs. Second, it must be shown that the county had customs or policies that amounted to deliberate indifference. The court said a jury could find deliberate indifference in the county's policies, which provided for the arresting officers to give the nurse any prescription medications found with an incoming detainee, but did not require the nurse to take action based on what the particular medication might reveal. Third, according to the *City of Canton* analysis, it must be shown that the county could have prevented the violation if it had had an appropriate policy.

> Had the County had a policy instructing the medical staff to use information obtained from a prisoner's medication to screen incoming detainees, the nurse, after observing Gibson's behavior in light of his medication, likely would have concluded that Gibson was in the midst of a manic phase and recommended transporting him to a mental hospital....Alternatively, the nurse could have considered administering the medication on an emergency basis.

In its opinion, the court in *Gibson* said that county liability also could be shown through a second method—by looking at a municipality's policies. In that context, the court held that drawing "all reasonable inferences from the record in favor of Ms. Gibson, [it could be concluded] that the County's policies and procedures regarding medical evaluations of incoming detainees violated Gibson's constitutionally protected right to receive medical care while in the custody of the County."

Failure to give proper training was also an issue in *Warner v. Grand County*, 57 F.3d 962 (10th Cir. 1995). This Section 1983 action was brought by two female plaintiffs, alleging constitutional violations when they were strip-searched following their arrest for possessing marijuana. The suit was brought against the police officer, a private citizen who assisted the police, the sheriff, and the county. After the arrest, the police officer called for assistance, which was given by the female director of a crisis center; she had assisted in the transfer and searches of female detainees on many occasions. One question was whether Parker (the female private citizen) was entitled to the qualified immunity defense that was available to state employees. The district court gave her such immunity, and the court of appeals agreed, saying that she had served as an officer's agent, carrying out an investigative function of the local government. The courts said that she should be shielded from liability in the same manner as the government employees. The arresting officer in this case was also granted qualified immunity, protecting him from the suit, because he had acted in accordance with the law that was established at the time. The legal standard was that strip searches could be performed (upon transfer of the arrestee to a detention facility soon after arrest) if there was reasonable suspicion that the suspect possessed drugs or other contraband or if the suspect was to be placed in the general jail population. The officer in *Warner* had reasonable suspicion, the courts said, that the two suspects possessed additional drugs (in addition to the marijuana found at the arrest scene); therefore, the strip search that he directed to be performed was in accordance with existing standards (in the 10th Circuit) for such searches.

The sheriff and the county were sued, because it was alleged that they had a policy and custom of not adequately training officers on constitutional arrest and search standards. (The sheriff and the county could not be held liable for the actual conducting of the searches.) The courts said that the plaintiffs might show that the defendants had failed to train officers as a deliberate or conscious choice. If that was the case, it could implicate the sheriff and county on the basis of setting policy (failure to train) that violated constitutional standards (citing *City of Canton*). The court of appeals, however, said that was not the case here. Grand County had a clear policy that there would be no warrantless strip searches of temporary detainees. That policy, conveyed to all officers, barred the conducting of strip searches of female detainees, because all female arrestees who required incarceration were taken to San Juan County Jail and were not kept in Grand

County. The evidence showed that no female arrestees had been kept in Grand County Jail since 1989 (more than five years earlier). There was nothing to show that either the sheriff or the county had reason to think there would be any female strip searches, because the policy prohibited female strip searches for temporary detainees and that policy had been consistently followed. Summary judgment for the sheriff and the county was affirmed on the grounds that they had not been shown to be deliberately indifferent to these plaintiffs' rights or to the need for more training for officers.

■ Other Jail Issues and Cases

In a case that combines elements of our discussion of inmate suicides and the health care that is owed to all inmates, a Louisiana appeals court overturned an award of $100,000 to the family of a detainee who died in jail from an overdose of the "ecstasy" drug in *Brown v. Lee*, 639 So.2d 897 (La. App. 1996). The detainee had been arrested for drunken driving and, when interrogated, had denied any drug use. He was presenting only the symptoms of intoxication. The appeals court refused to hold the sheriff liable, saying that it would be unreasonable to require him to provide medical treatment to every intoxicated person who was in his custody. Finding no such duty, there was no liability for negligent action or failure to act.

The case of *Anderson v. County of Kern*, 45 F.3d 1310 (9th Cir. 1995), presented three major issues about jail conditions and the treatment of detainees. The first issue involved the use of a "safety cell" at the Kern County Jail. There was one such cell, which was 10 feet by 10 feet, was covered with rubberized foam padding, and contained a pit toilet with a grate covering in the floor. There was evidence that violent inmates were sometimes chained to the floor grate. The cell was used mostly for the temporary holding of suicidal and mentally disturbed inmates when they became very disruptive or threatening. When an inmate was placed in the cell, staff were required to check on the inmate's condition and safety every 15 to 30 minutes. In addition, the supervisor in charge reviewed the inmate's placement in the cell (whether it needed to be continued) every four hours.

Inmates challenged the use of this cell, claiming that to use it was a violation of the Eighth and Fourteenth Amendments. The court noted that, because the jail held both pretrial detainees and sentenced prisoners, the questions to be addressed were whether placement in the cell constituted an intentional infliction of pain or a denial of basic human needs (which would show an Eighth Amendment, cruel and unusual punishment violation) and whether officials acted with deliberate indifference to the inmates' needs when they were placed in the cell, showing an intent to punish them (a Fourteenth Amendment violation, for pretrial detainees). The court of appeals affirmed the district court's holding that conditions in the safety cell were not unconstitutional. Even though the evidence showed that the conditions in the cell could be unsanitary and even though the court conceded that it was a very severe environment, the court said that it was needed to deal with very serious safety concerns. It was also noted that placement into the cell was temporary and short in duration.

A second issue in the *Anderson* case involved the conditions in the administrative segregation unit of the jail. Inmates were placed in administrative segregation for different reasons: because they were subject to attacks, they were high security risks, they were former law enforcement officers, or they were notorious criminals. The court noted that it was established in *Hewitt v. Helms*, 459 U.S. 460 (1983), that placement in more restrictive quarters was within the terms of confinement ordinarily contemplated for a prison sentence (and, one may assume from this court's approach, for a jailed inmate). The district court had ordered jail officials to determine whether some of these segregated prisoners could be allowed to exercise together or to use the day room together. (The jail practiced total separation of all segregation inmates. Officials testified that these inmates could never be allowed together, for fear of someone being harmed.) The court of appeals ruled that the district court order went too far. There was no constitutional violation in the use of the segregation unit and no need for any corrective action. Although conditions in isolated segregation confinement were not pleasant, they did not show deliberate indifference to the needs of the inmates, and they were required for safety and security reasons. Finding no constitutional level of violation, the court of appeals asserted that it was improper for the district court to order any corrective action. *Wright v. Rushen*, 642 F.2d 1129 (9th Cir. 1981), was cited to support that proposition.

A third issue in *Anderson* concerned health care. The district court had ordered a translator (an employee, and not an inmate, preferably from the medical staff) to translate, when requested by inmates, during medical and mental health interviews. The court noted that the U.S. Seventh Circuit Court of Appeals, in *Wellman v. Faulkner*, 715 F.2d 269 (7th Cir. 1983), had said that a failure to provide translators could constitute deliberate indifference to the medical needs of non-English speaking inmates. This circuit court agreed with that approach and with the district court, saying that it was necessary during medical interviews to have a translator (who is not an inmate, because inmate translators would be potentially inaccurate or unreliable in their translations).

In *Bryant v. Maffucci*, 923 F.2d 979 (2nd Cir. 1991), a New York detainee claimed a Section 1983 violation because she had not been promptly scheduled for an abortion and also because the physician had made an error in estimating her gestational age. The court of appeals held that these facts only showed negligence, which occurred when jail officials delayed her letter to the physician requesting the abortion appointment. Also, there was no evidence to show that the physician could not rely on the sonogram reading that had been made; at the most, any error in setting the inmate's gestational age was also negligence and not a violation of the inmate's right to privacy or a deliberate indifference to her medical needs (which are the constitutional standards). Thus, there was no showing of constitutional violations of the inmate's rights.

In *Cooper v. Dyke,* 814 F.2d 941 (4th Cir. 1987), a 16-year-old boy was shot during an altercation at a skating rink. The boy and his friends left the rink in a van and were stopped by police. While some in the van fled, Cooper and his friend Hill went towards the police, saying they had both been shot. The friend's injury was visible, Cooper's was not. An ambulance was called and the arriving paramedics began to examine the two boys. Meanwhile, the police had set up a roadblock and were detaining several busloads of people leaving the skating rink. The conditions became chaotic with disruptions and threats being made both to the boys and to the officers. Cooper's gunshot wound was not discovered at the scene (paramedics were afraid for their safety and were unable to conduct a thorough exam, at one point stopping their exam and going back towards the ambulance while the police regained control). Cooper and two others were taken to the police station where they were handcuffed to a detention rail. Although the three testified that they constantly complained that Cooper had been shot, he was not attended to until one of his friends vomited on Cooper and Cooper failed to respond. Taken by ambulance to the hospital, Cooper was found to be in "profound shock and in need of immediate surgery."

Police officers were found liable under Section 1983 for deliberate indifference to Cooper's repeated pleas for medical attention to his wound. The court of appeals affirmed the jury's verdict. The defense of the police officers had been that they relied on the paramedics' examination, and the fact there was an examination showed there was no deliberate indifference to the condition of the detainee. The court held, however, that it was permissible for the jury to make its conclusions, in effect finding that the police officers were not justified in relying on the paramedics since the examination had been performed under such chaotic conditions. The repeated complaints of Cooper under these circumstances should not have been ignored.

And, if we thought we had heard of every kind of medical complaint, in *Frohmader v. Wayne,* 958 F.2d 1024 (10th Cir. 1992), a Colorado inmate alleged constitutional violations because jail officials were deliberately indifferent to his complaints of claustrophobia and agoraphobia (apparently, his fears of being confined in close spaces and with lots of other persons). The court held that, even if it was shown that there was indifference to these complaints, the detainee had not proved that those fears constituted a "serious medical need," which is another aspect of the standard that the inmate must show in order to sustain a claim for Eighth (or Fourteenth) Amendment violations with respect to medical care.

◼ Removing the Sheriff from Running the Jail

A most unusual action with respect to a sheriff and a county jail was the subject of *Beck v. County of Santa Clara,* 204 Cal. App. 3d 789 (6th Dist. CA 1988). In this case, because of dissatisfaction with the repeated problems (including legal problems) at the county jail, the county board of supervisors transferred all duties relating to the jail from the elected sheriff and placed the jail under a nonelected, appointed department head. This matter had been submitted to popular vote and was approved. The court noted that ordinarily it would not be permissible to remove certain duties that were historically performed by an elected public official and place them under a person who was not elected to perform them. However, because the sheriff had no personal right to perform the jail duties (and there was nothing in state law that mandated that those duties be performed by the sheriff only), the court approved the action of the board of supervisors, which had been affirmed by popular vote in the county.

SUMMARY

- The leading case on constitutional requirements for jail conditions is *Bell v. Wolfish.* The Supreme Court ruled in that case that, because of due process clause protections, a pretrial inmate may not be punished. How do we tell if the inmate is being punished? If the condition complained about is reasonably related to a legitimate governmental objective (usually the objective is security or good order), then there has been no punishment.

- Other rights, protected by other constitutional provisions, are guaranteed to pretrial detainees, but they may all be limited by security concerns at the jail. In *Bell*, it was permissible for jail officials to limit incoming publications to publisher-only mailings. The Supreme Court also upheld jail practices of conducting cell searches without the inmates being present and conducting visual (body cavity) searches after contact visiting. In *Florence v. Board of Chosen Freeholders*, the Supreme Court upheld strip searches of detainees admitted to a jail's general population, absent reasonable suspicion, citing the government's substantial interest in preventing any new inmate from putting those who live or work at these institutions at even greater risk.

- Other Supreme Court cases have dealt with other constitutional claims by jail inmates. In *Block v. Rutherford*, the Court held that it was permissible for a jail to limit visiting to non-contact visiting. The Court also said that a television station did not have to be permitted to come into a jail to film a story on a jail suicide (*Houchins v. KQED, Inc*).

- Federal appeals courts ruled that, on claims arising out of suicides of jail inmates, deliberate indifference to the needs of the inmate is the constitutional standard for liability.

- Courts have held that no privacy is to be expected in jail visits, so it is permissible for authorities to monitor and tape conversations between inmates and their visitors (*Lanza v. New York; United States v. Hearst*).

- The Supreme Court held that, in a suit based on allegations of government negligence causing an inmate to fall on a stairway, mere negligence did not state a constitutional claim against the jail officials. For a constitutional (Fourteenth Amendment) violation, a more serious action must be shown, amounting to abuse by officials of their governmental powers, to sustain a liability judgment against the officials (*Daniels v. Williams*). Negligence by government officials would support a common law tort claim, if that procedure was available in the jurisdiction where the accident occurred.

- A county, a city, a sheriff, or other supervisory personnel may be held liable for failing to train employees on the basic rights of citizens and on the constitutional requirements of their jobs. Liability has been proved and affirmed in cases in which arrestees were beaten (where excessive force was used); in cases in which strip searches were performed in inappropriate and unnecessary circumstances; and in cases in which arrests were improperly made.

- A major federal appellate decision (*Anderson v. County of Kern*) held that severely austere conditions in a small padded cell with a pit toilet in the floor did not amount to Fourteenth Amendment violations (or Eighth Amendment violations, for sentenced inmates) when it was used for short-term confinement of severely disturbed inmates. That case also approved the jail's use of administrative segregation cells, where the inmates were not allowed to exercise together, because of the jail's concerns for the inmates' safety. The court did require the jail to employ a staff translator to assist non-English speaking inmates during medical and mental health interviews.

- Other jail cases dealing with claims of improper health care turned on the courts' conclusions of whether staff had shown deliberate indifference to the serious medical complaints of inmates.

- In *Beck v. County of Santa Clara*, a California court upheld the removal of a sheriff from running the county jail because of repeated difficulties at the jail, which included adverse court decisions and other legal problems. The removal was made by action of the county board of supervisors and was approved by county voters in a referendum.

THINKING ABOUT IT

On August 17, 1996, Prince George's County (PGC), Maryland police officers arrested Nelson Robles on an outstanding traffic warrant issued by neighboring Montgomery County. When the officers requested an informal prisoner exchange with the Montgomery County Police Department (MCPD), they were told that the MCPD officers were too busy and that formal procedures (taking him to a commissioner in the county where he was arrested and then transferring him to the sheriff's department in the county issuing the warrant) should be followed. Rather than doing this, the PGC officers drove Robles to a deserted shopping center parking lot in Montgomery County, tied him to a metal pole using three pairs of flex-cuffs, and left a note at his feet saying Robles had outstanding Montgomery County warrants. They then placed an anonymous call to the MCPD reporting the situation, but not reporting that they had tied Robles to the pole. Ten to fifteen minutes later, MCPD officers arrived, untied Robles, and took him into custody. Assuming, as the court did, that Robles' status was that of a pretrial detainee at the time of the incident, did the actions of the PGC officers violate Robles' federal constitutional rights? Did the officers' actions amount to punishment of Robles in violation of the due process clause of the Fourteenth Amendment? If so, are the officers entitled to qualified immunity for the violation of those rights? This case was reported as *Robles v. Prince George's County, Maryland*, 308 F.3d 437 (4th Cir. 2002).

ENDNOTES

1. Camp, C. G. *The 2002 Corrections Yearbook—Adult Corrections.* Pages 12–13. (Middletown, CT: Criminal Justice Institute, 2003.) The *Yearbook* also notes that 19 agencies reported that over 29,500 inmates were being held under contractual agreements.
2. Minton, T. *Jail Inmates at Midyear 2010—Statistical Tables.* Page 2, and Tables 1 and 7. (Washington, DC: Bureau of Justice Statistics, U.S. Department of Justice, 2011.)
3. Marion County, Oregon. *Inmate Mail Rules.* Accessed January 27, 2011 from http://www.co.marion.or.us/SO/Institutions/inmatemail.htm.
4. In *Covell v. Arpaio*, 662 F.Supp.2d 1146 (D. AZ 2009), the inmate, representing himself, claimed his First Amendment rights were violated by the Maricopa County Lower Buckeye Jail (Phoenix, Arizona) policy of restricting an inmate's incoming nonprivileged mail to metered postcards. The district court, applying the *Turner v. Safley* test, held there was no violation and granted the defendant's motion for summary judgment. Applying *Turner,* the court held that the jail's policy had a rational connection to a legitimate penological objective—preventing the smuggling of contraband into the jail; that there were alternative means for communication (metered postcards, visiting and telephone calls); that prison staff had shown that by allowing regular stamped mail there is an increased possibility of

contraband (e.g., various drugs were found contained on the back of postage stamps) being smuggled into the prison, with this possibly resulting in conflicts and potential violence between inmates; and that the inmate failed to meet his burden of showing obvious, easy alternatives to the postcard regulation. For an opposite finding, see *Martinez v. Maketa*, where inmates at the El Paso County Jail challenged the jail's policy of requiring that inmates use jail-supplied four-by-six inch postcards for their outgoing correspondence, with some exceptions. On December 20, 2010, the United States District Court for the District of Colorado issued a stipulated order granting a preliminary injunction to stop the postcard-only policy. That same day the jail dropped its policy of restricting inmate outgoing mail to postcards. *Stipulated Order Granting Preliminary Injunction* (Civil Action No. 10-cv-02242-WYD-KLM). Also see *Jail Drops Postcard-Only Policy Following ACLU Lawsuit*. American Civil Liberties Union. Accessed April 17, 2011 from http://www.aclu .org/print/prisoners-rights/jail-drops-postcard-only-policy-following-aclu-lawsuit.

5. In *Grabowski v. Jackson County Public Defenders Office*, 79 F.3d 478 (5th Cir. 1996), the full court looked at this case en banc, vacating the previous panel opinion. The only defendant in this new consideration was Jackson County, Mississippi, which was being sued for alleged constitutional violations. In ruling against Grabowski, the court stated that on the record before the court, there was no showing of the existence of a policy or custom of the county under which any employee violated the inmate's constitutional rights.

21 | Juveniles and Young Offenders

Under our Constitution, the condition of being a boy does not justify a kangaroo court.

U.S. Supreme Court, *In re Gault*

Chapter Outline

In this chapter, we examine the special considerations that are given in our criminal justice system to younger persons. Most of these (from a perspective of different, specialized treatment) are juveniles. In some jurisdictions, young offenders—those in age between juveniles and adults—are given some degree of special attention, both legally and correctionally. We will look at the practical and legal aspects of treating those more youthful offenders.

Juveniles: History and Background

Like so much of the legal system in the United States, including many aspects of the criminal justice area, the juvenile justice system can be traced to laws and practices in the law of England. The basic approach of old English law to the offenses committed by children was based on assumptions about criminal responsibility (whether the individual had the mental capacity to commit crimes). The English, by the 1700s, established the following principles for dealing with children in the criminal law: (1) Children under the age of seven were irrebuttably presumed to be incapable of having criminal intent. Those children, therefore, were never brought to court on criminal charges. (2) Children between the ages of 7 and 14 were rebuttably presumed to be incapable of having criminal intent. That meant that those children were not prosecuted for criminal acts unless the state could prove that they were mentally capable of forming criminal intent. (3) Persons over the age of 14 were presumed to be able to form criminal intent (that presumption, of course, as for adults, could be rebutted by the defendant, showing that he was not mentally able to understand right from wrong or to conform his behavior to requirements of the law) and were prosecuted as adults. These divisions between adults and children carried over to American law.

Along with the definitions of criminal responsibility according to age, legal concepts of guardianship were also developed. Early in English history, there was the concept of ***parens patriae***, which recognized the king as being the "father of the country." Within this concept, the king (later, more broadly, the government) was responsible for the welfare of children and of others (such as mental incompetents) who were not able to be properly cared for by their families. The persons needing such special care or protection were called **wards** of the state and were placed under the protection of the king (*parens patriae*). This concept developed into the guardianship of wards by the state. To determine the need for such protection, and to declare the legal status of the wards, the children were taken before chancery courts, not criminal courts. Chancery courts were established to keep the "king's conscience" and to decide matters based on ideas of fairness and doing the right thing, without strict adherence to established principles of statutory or common law. The rules for conducting proceedings were much more relaxed in these courts. The chancery courts took responsibility for looking out for the welfare of children (and others who needed protection), which, over centuries, developed into the law of juveniles.

■ Juvenile Court Concepts

Over time, the age of criminal responsibility was raised from 14 to 16 and then, in many places, to 18. In most states in the United States today, 18 is the age when children (juveniles) are presumed to become adults and are held responsible for their criminal behavior.[1] Some of the other legal concepts that have historically applied to juvenile court proceedings follow. Later in this chapter, we will discuss modifications that are being made to some of these concepts.

Juveniles are not found "guilty" of "committing crimes." Flowing from this concept (which really flows from the old English concept of children not being responsible for their acts) is an avoidance of using terms that connote criminality: A juvenile is not prosecuted, he is "proceeded against." There is not a crime involved; there is an act of delinquency. There is no verdict of guilty; there is a "finding of delinquency." A juvenile is not sentenced; there instead is a "disposition." The juveniles are not defendants in court, they are juveniles charged with being delinquents, at the worst, "criminal offenders."

The **juvenile court** (which may be a separate court, a separate division of a municipal or county court, or a court of general jurisdiction sitting in special session as a juvenile court) sits in protection of the welfare of the juvenile. These courts may be known by various names, such as district, superior, circuit, county, family, or probate. The court proceedings are much less formal than those for adults. They are often closed to public attendance to protect the privacy of the juvenile. The juvenile court sits in the position of judicial protector (guardian) of the rights, and the best interests, of the juvenile.

Disposition of the juvenile case is based on the concern for the welfare of the juvenile. She is not sentenced to punishment. The court will order what is needed, in the court's judgment, for the welfare of the child, and this is done in the name of treatment. Cases are disposed of quickly (the average juvenile case takes much less time in court than an adult case). **Table 21-1** identifies distinctions between the juvenile and criminal justice systems. For example, one distinction is the intake–prosecution stage. In the juvenile justice system, "[t]he decision to file a petition for court action is based on both social and legal factors;" in the adult criminal justice system, "[t]he prosecution decision is based largely on legal facts." In the juvenile justice system, "[d]isposition decisions are based on individual and social factors, offense severity, and youth's offense history." In the adult criminal justice system, "[s]entencing decisions are bound primarily by the severity of the current offense and by the offender's criminal history." With regard to the concept of guilt, in the juvenile justice system, "[i]f guilt is established, the youth is adjudicated delinquent regardless of offense." In the adult criminal justice system, "[g]uilt must be established on individual offenses charged for conviction."

Records of the court proceedings for juveniles are usually sealed. This means the public (including the media) may not peruse the court records. It also means that, under the historical protection of the juvenile's status, they may not be used in later court proceedings, for example, if the juvenile is prosecuted when he becomes an adult.

Juveniles are not sent to prison. They are placed, if they need institutional care, in facilities that have been called by many titles, including training schools, residential facilities, juvenile homes, shelters, cottages, and boys' (and girls') ranches, farms, and camps. There is some movement toward handling more juveniles in regular adult proceedings, as shown in **Table 21-2**. This table shows that the number of referrals of juveniles to adult or criminal courts increased over 500% from 1972 to 2000, and another 25% from 2000 to 2009.

The length of jurisdiction over a case is indeterminate. The juvenile court may retain jurisdiction in order to modify its orders or to do whatever else is in the best interest of the juvenile, ordinarily until the individual's 21st birthday. (In a few states, once juveniles are brought into juvenile court, they may be kept under the court's jurisdiction for some time past their 21st birthdays.) Commitments to facilities are for shorter periods than for most adults: a juvenile may be committed for a period of months or years (not to exceed his 21st birthday). In addition, a juvenile may be committed for an indeterminate amount of time, with his release to be determined (based on reports of his adjustment and betterment) by the court, juvenile parole or institutional authorities, or, at the maximum, until his 21st birthday.[2] If it is possible, he will be returned at the earliest feasible time to the community, with continued supervision and assistance from juvenile staff (government or private).

There are three ways in which juveniles are brought before juvenile courts. First, there are those who are charged with acts of delinquency, which would be crimes if they were committed by adults. (These are the ones we have mainly considered in the previous discussion—the persons who, but for their young age, would be treated as accused persons and criminals in the criminal justice system.) But flowing from the concept that the state should look after the welfare of all children who have special needs, there are two other categories of juveniles who may be

Table 21-1 Distinctions Between the Juvenile Justice System and the Criminal Justice System

Although the juvenile and criminal justice systems are more alike in some jurisdictions than in others, generalizations can be made about the distinctions between the two systems and about their common ground

Juvenile justice system	Common ground	Criminal justice system
Operating Assumptions		
• Youth behavior is malleable. • Rehabilitation is usually a viable goal. • Youth are in families and not independent.	• Community protection is a primary goal. • Law violators must be held accountable. • Constitutional rights apply.	• Sanctions should be proportional to the offense. • General deterrence works. • Rehabilitation is not a primary goal.
Prevention		
• Many specific delinquency prevention activities (e.g., school, church, recreation) are used. • Prevention is intended to change individual behavior and is often focused on reducing risk factors and increasing protective factors in the individual, family, and community.	• Educational approaches are taken to specific behaviors (drunk driving, drug use).	• Prevention activities are generalized and are aimed at deterrence (e.g., Crime Watch).
Law Enforcement		
• Specialized "juvenile" units are used. • Some additional behaviors are prohibited (truancy, running away, curfew violations). • Some limitations are placed on public access to information. • A significant number of youth are diverted away from the juvenile justice system, often into alternative programs.	• Jurisdiction involves the full range of criminal behavior. • Constitutional and procedural safeguards exist. • Both reactive and proactive approaches (targeted at offense types, neighborhoods, etc.) are used. • Community policing strategies are employed.	• Open public access to all information is required. • Law enforcement exercises discretion to divert offenders out of the criminal justice system.
Intake—Prosecution		
• In many instances, juvenile court intake, not the prosecutor, decides what cases to file. • The decision to file a petition for court action is based on both social and legal factors. • A significant portion of cases are diverted from formal case processing. • Intake or the prosecutor diverts cases from formal processing to services operated by the juvenile court, prosecutor's office, or outside agencies.	• Probable cause must be established. • The prosecutor acts on behalf of the State.	• Plea bargaining is common. • The prosecution decision is based largely on legal facts. • Prosecution is valuable in building history for subsequent offenses. • Prosecution exercises discretion to withhold charges or divert offenders out of the criminal justice system.

Table 21-1 (*Continued*)

Juvenile justice system	Common ground	Criminal justice system
Detention—Jail/lockup		
• Juveniles may be detained for their own protection or the community's protection. • Juveniles may not be confined with adults unless there is "sight and sound separation."	• Accused offenders may be held in custody to ensure their appearance in court. • Detention alternatives of home or electronic detention are used.	• Accused individuals have the right to apply for bond/bail release.
Adjudication—Conviction		
• Juvenile court proceedings are "quasi-civil" (not criminal) and may be confidential. • If guilt is established, the youth is adjudicated delinquent regardless of offense. • Right to jury trial is not afforded in all States.	• Standard of "proof beyond a reasonable doubt" is required. • Rights to be represented by an attorney, to confront witnesses, and to remain silent are afforded. • Appeals to a higher court are allowed. • Experimentation with specialized courts (i.e., drug courts, gun courts) is underway.	• Defendants have a constitutional right to a jury trial. • Guilt must be established on individual offenses charged for conviction. • All proceedings are open.
Disposition—Sentencing		
• Disposition decisions are based on individual and social factors, offense severity, and youth's offense history. • Dispositional philosophy includes a significant rehabilitation component. • Many dispositional alternatives are operated by the juvenile court. • Dispositions cover a wide range of community-based and residential services. • Disposition orders may be directed to people other than the offender (e.g., parents). • Disposition may be indeterminate, based on progress demonstrated by the youth.	• Decisions are influenced by current offense, offending history, and social factors. • Decisions hold offenders accountable. • Decisions may give consideration to victims (e.g., restitution and "no contact" orders). • Decisions may not be cruel or unusual.	• Sentencing decisions are bound primarily by the severity of the current offense and by the offender's criminal history. • Sentencing philosophy is based largely on proportionality and punishment. • Sentence is often determinate, based on offense.
Aftercare—Parole		
• Function combines surveillance and reintegration activities (e.g., family, school, work).	• The behavior of individuals released from correctional settings is monitored. • Violation of conditions can result in reincarceration.	• Function is primarily surveillance and reporting to monitor illicit behavior.

Source: Snyder, Howard N., and Sickmund, Melissa. (1999). *Juvenile Offenders and Victims: 1999 National Report.* Pages 94–96. Washington, DC: Office of Juvenile Justice and Delinquency Prevention, U.S. Department of Justice.

Table 21-2 Distribution of Juveniles Taken into Police Custody in 1972, 2000, and 2009

	1972	2000	2009
Distribution			
Referred to juvenile court jurisdiction	50.8%	70.8%	67.4%
Handled within department and released	45.0%	20.3%	22.3%
Referred to criminal or adult court	1.3%	7.0%	8.8%
Referred to other police agency	1.6%	1.1%	1.1%
Referred to welfare agency	1.3%	0.8%	0.5%

Source: Maguire, K., ed. *Sourcebook of Criminal Justice Statistics,* Table 4.26.2009. Available from http://www.albany.edu/sourcebook/pdf/t4262009.pdf. January 3, 2011

brought before the courts. The first group includes those juveniles who have violated societal rules that are not criminal for adults. These are called **status offenders**. A status offense (such as failing to attend school or violating a curfew for young people) may be grounds for bringing the juvenile before the court on a petition requesting that steps be taken to correct the situation or change the behavior of the child. There is also a group of juveniles who are **dependent children**. In most jurisdictions, these children may also be brought before juvenile courts to verify their dependency status in order for the courts to determine the best steps that can be taken for their welfare. Foster parents or group foster homes may be used for such children. They may be removed from the legal responsibility of their parents (or other relatives) and placed under the guardianship of designated alternative parents.

In 2007, approximately 1.7 million delinquency cases were handled in juvenile courts. Of these, approximately 36% were property offenses (e.g., burglary, larceny-theft); 25% were offenses against persons (e.g., criminal homicide, forcible rape, simple and aggravated assault); 28% were public order crimes (e.g., obstruction of justice, disorderly conduct); and 11% were drug law violations. Cases involving females have more than doubled since 1985, to the point that they now comprise 27% of all cases. (In 1985, females were 19% of the cases.) The significant increase in the number of females compares to a 30% increase in the number of cases involving males as compared to 1985 figures. In 2007, juveniles were adjudicated delinquent in 63% (more than 586,000) of the petitioned cases, a 74% increase over those adjudicated delinquent in 1985. (In juvenile cases, a **petition** is a document filed in juvenile court alleging that a juvenile is a delinquent, a status offender, or a dependent and asking the court to assume jurisdiction over the juvenile or asking that the juvenile be transferred to a criminal court for prosecution as an adult.) Of those juveniles adjudicated to be delinquent in 2007, 56% received probation. The use of residential placement has dropped since 1985, from 31% to 25% of the dispositions in 2007. The proportion of persons receiving other sanctions has increased, from 11% in 1985 to 19% in 2007.[3]

In these different kinds of dispositions, the terminology used in courts (and the mechanics of sanctioning, as well as the percentages spread among such dispositions) are very similar to those used for adult offenders. For juvenile delinquents, probation offices screen cases and submit reports to juvenile courts on recommended dispositions; they provide supervision to those placed on probation; and they deliver aftercare services to many juveniles when they are released from residential programs. How these duties are performed, and whether they are even performed by probation officers, varies from one jurisdiction to another. Not all probation officers, for example, provide aftercare services. In some jurisdictions, the prosecutor screens cases and makes recommendations to the court for dispositions. In all jurisdictions, probation officers are responsible for the supervision of probationers when probation is ordered by the juvenile courts.[4] Probation is, by far, the most commonly used sanction for juvenile delinquents, and especially so for first offenders.

More Sophisticated Juveniles

You will recall that, under English law, there was a rebuttable presumption that children over the age of 7 and up to the age of 14 were not criminally responsible and should not be tried or punished as adult criminals. That concept has been transformed, under the U.S. juvenile law system, into the presumption that juveniles should be processed in juvenile courts. What is the age ceiling for juvenile court jurisdiction? Ordinarily, the term "juvenile" refers to persons under the age of 18, although a few states have set a lower ceiling (3 states have set under the age of 16; 10 states under the age of 17).[5] Exceptions are possible, and it is permissible for a court to find that a juvenile is of sufficient maturity that she should be tried as an adult.

Every state has a means for juveniles to be tried in adult criminal courts under certain circumstances. There are three types of transfer laws. The first is legislative (automatic transfer), which is in effect in 29 states. These cases require the juvenile's transfer if statutory requirements are met. An example is a juvenile, who is 14 or older, and alleged to have committed a violent felony. In this instance, the case either begins in criminal court or, if it starts in juvenile court, it is transferred to criminal court.

The second type of transfer law is judicial transfer, operating in 45 states and the District of Columbia. A judicial transfer leaves to the juvenile court judge the discretion to decide whether a juvenile should be transferred after the prosecution files a motion to transfer. The third type is prosecutorial direct-file laws, in 14 states and the District of Columbia. In this instance, the discretion rests with the prosecutor, allowing her to decide whether to file charges in the juvenile or criminal court. (Twenty-five states also have reverse waiver laws, giving to the criminal court judge the discretion to transfer the case back to juvenile court, or, for sentencing purposes, to treat the defendant as a juvenile.[6])

For the traditional juvenile transfer to adult criminal court to occur, usually by motion of the prosecutor (but sometimes on motion of the court itself, or by the probation office, or even by the parents, or by the juvenile herself), the court hears evidence, reviews reports and recommendations, and considers arguments on the issue of whether the juvenile is of such a degree of maturity or sophistication that her case should be heard in adult court. If the court decides that adult proceedings are appropriate for the individual, the judge enters an order that waives jurisdiction over the juvenile by the juvenile court and transfers the case to the local court of adult criminal prosecution. In 2007, there were 8,500 juvenile cases judicially waived to criminal courts; this represents a 35% decrease since 1994.[7]

In the 1980s, there was a public perception that serious juvenile crime was increasing and that the system needed to "get tough." Many states began to pass more punitive laws. In the 1990s, as a result of this effort to crack down on juvenile crime, there were five areas of change:

1. Transfer provisions: Forty-five states passed laws to make it easier to transfer juvenile offenders from the juvenile justice system to the adult criminal justice system.

2. Sentencing authority: Thirty-one states gave criminal and juvenile courts expanded (tougher) sentencing options for juveniles.

3. Confidentiality: Forty-seven states modified their laws to make juvenile records and proceedings more open.

4. Victim rights: Twenty-two states expanded the role of victims of juvenile crime in the juvenile justice process.

5. Correctional programming: Due to new transfer and sentencing laws, adult and juvenile correctional administrators developed new programs for juvenile offenders.

In addition, some states have modified their juvenile code "purpose" clauses not only with respect to the underlying philosophies and assumptions, but also in how they approach their task. Most states fall within one of the following five purpose clauses. Components of Balanced and Restorative Justice (BARJ) are the most common in state purpose clauses. Supporters of this concept believe the balanced attention of juvenile courts should focus on three primary interests: public safety, individual accountability to victims and to the community, and the development of skills to help offenders live productive and law-abiding lives.

A second type of purpose clause is modeled on language from the Standard Juvenile Court Act and has more of the *parens patriae* concept: "each child coming within the jurisdiction of the court shall receive ... care, guidance, and control that will conduce to his welfare and the best interest of the state, and that when he is removed from the control of his parents the court shall secure for him care as nearly as possible equivalent to that which they should have given him."

A third group of states uses language found in the purpose clause of a 1960s document (Legislative Guide for Drafting Family and Juvenile Court Acts). This document lists four purposes: providing for the care, protection and the wholesome development of children involved with the juvenile court; removing from children committing delinquent acts the consequences of criminal behavior and substituting supervision, care, and rehabilitation; removing a child from his home only when necessary for his welfare or for public safety; and assuring that the involved parties have their constitutional and other legal rights.

Purpose clauses in some states focus on being "tough." These stress community protection, offender accountability, deterrence, or outright punishment. A final small group of states has purpose clauses that focus on the welfare and best interests of the child, with this being the primary purpose of the juvenile court system. An example is Massachusetts, which says accused juveniles shall be "treated, not as criminals, but as children in need of aid, encouragement and guidance. Proceedings against children ... shall not be deemed criminal proceedings."[8]

■ *Kent v. United States*

In comparison to adult criminal defendants and prisoners, there has been little attention paid to the rights of juveniles under the Constitution. Most of the decisions that exist are interpretations of requirements of the juvenile statutes in particular states, and many deal with the procedures that must be followed in cases of delinquency, status offenses, or dependency. Some have dealt with the programs that are offered to juveniles and the conditions under which juveniles are held when they are detained or committed.

In *Kent* (and *Gault*), the Supreme Court reviewed the rights of juveniles and the constitutional protections to which they are entitled. *Kent v. United States*, 383 U.S. 541 (1966), dealt with a youth of 16 whose case was waived by a juvenile court judge to adult court. Kent broke into an apartment, stole a wallet, and raped the woman who was there. He was interrogated by police (without presence of counsel) and admitted these offenses, as well as others that he had committed earlier. His mother thereafter retained counsel. The juvenile court held no hearing. The judge did not talk to Kent, his mother, or his counsel. The judge considered reports submitted by court staff, the social service department, and the probation section (Kent was on probation for an offense he committed when he was 14). Kent's counsel requested that he be allowed to review the file that the judge was considering, but that was denied. The Juvenile Court Act, under which the District of Columbia juvenile judge was acting, stated that the case of a juvenile who was 16 years of age or older and charged with an offense that would be a felony if committed by an adult could be waived to adult court, based on "full investigation" by the juvenile judge. No hearing was mandated by the statute or by court rules, and none was ordinarily conducted. Kent appealed the order waiving his case to adult court. The District of Columbia courts denied his appeals, holding that the juvenile court had complied with the juvenile statute and its purposes.

Kent was indicted in U.S. district court (the adult trial court for felonies in the District of Columbia) on eight counts, covering housebreaking, robbery, and rape. At trial, he was found to be not guilty by reason of insanity on the rape counts. He was convicted on the other counts and received a sentence of 30 to 90 years. (Under District of Columbia law, he was mandatorily committed to St. Elizabeth's Hospital for treatment on the basis of the insanity acquittal.) Kent again appealed his prosecution in adult court and his convictions there. The court of appeals upheld the procedures that had been followed. But the Supreme Court held that the transfer proceedings that had been used to send Kent from juvenile court to adult court were invalid.

> **While there can be no doubt of the original laudable purpose of juvenile courts, studies and critiques in recent years raise serious questions as to whether actual performance measures well enough against theoretical purpose to make tolerable the immunity of the process from the reach of constitutional guaranties applicable to adults....It is clear beyond dispute that the waiver of jurisdiction is a "critically important" action determining vitally important statutory rights of the juvenile....[A]s a condition to a valid waiver order, [Kent] was entitled to a hearing, including access by his counsel to the social records and probation or similar reports which presumably are considered by the court, and to a statement of reasons for the Juvenile Court's decision.**

This conclusion was reached based on "constitutional principles relating to due process and the assistance of counsel."

The Supreme Court noted in its review of Kent's case that the theory of the juvenile court statute was rooted in social welfare philosophy rather than in traditional criminal concepts.

> **The Juvenile Court is theoretically engaged in determining the needs of the child and of society rather than adjudicating criminal conduct. The objectives are to provide measures of guidance and rehabilitation for the child and protection for society, not to fix criminal responsibility, guilt, and punishment. The State is *parens patriae* rather than prosecuting attorney and judge. But the admonition to function in a "parental" relationship is not an invitation to procedural arbitrariness.**

For the first time, the Supreme Court set minimum constitutional (due process) requirements for juvenile waiver proceedings. It said, "Meaningful review [by the juvenile judge] requires that the reviewing court should review. It should not be remitted to assumptions." Further, there had to be a hearing, which could be informal. There was also a right to counsel, which could not be a mere formality; the counsel had to be given access to the records that were considered by the court. (In a strange twist for the disposition of the case, the Supreme Court noted that it ordinarily would have reversed the lower courts' rulings and sent the case back to the juvenile court for a proper determination, with a hearing, on the waiver decision. But Kent had by this time passed the age of 21, so the juvenile court no longer had jurisdiction over him. The Supreme Court resisted the suggestion by Kent that his conviction and sentence be totally vacated as improper and remanded the case to the [adult] district court for a hearing *de novo* (that is, as if there had been no earlier decision) on the waiver, in accord with the new constitutional requirements laid down by the Supreme Court.)

■ *In re Gault*

Gault, a 15-year-old, was taken into custody by a county sheriff in Arizona, without notice to his parents. When he was placed in a detention home, Gault's mother was advised that he was being held there for making an obscene phone call. His hearing in juvenile court was held the next day. The petition that was filed against him did not refer to any facts but only stated that he was a delinquent minor. At the hearing, an officer said that when he was questioned, Gault admitted making lewd remarks on the phone. Neither Gault nor his parents were advised of any right to have counsel. He was committed to the Arizona State Industrial School for the remainder of his minority (until he reached age 21). Gault's parents filed a petition for habeas corpus, which was denied in the Arizona courts (including the Supreme Court of Arizona).

The U.S. Supreme Court reversed in *In re Gault*, 387 U.S. 1 (1967). The Court held that Gault had been denied due process under the Constitution because his juvenile delinquency proceedings did not comply with minimum requirements for fair treatment.

> **Due process of law is the primary and indispensable foundation of individual freedom. It is the basic and essential term in the social compact which defines the rights of the individual and delimits the powers which the state may exercise.**

The Court noted that it was claimed by those arguing in favor of the informal juvenile proceedings that those proceedings were designed to benefit juveniles, not to punish criminal behavior, which is the purpose of criminal proceedings. The Court refused to accept the state's defense of the closed, informal juvenile proceeding. After all, the Court pointed out, this juvenile process resulted in a boy being committed to an institution, where he could be deprived of his liberty for years. Whatever the institution might euphemistically be called, the Court said (in this case, it was called an "Industrial School"), the boy's world became "a building with white-washed walls, regimented routine, and institutional hours."

> Under our Constitution, the condition of being a boy does not justify a kangaroo court....As [other commentators] have put it, "The rhetoric of the juvenile court movement has developed without any necessarily close correspondence to the realities of court and institutional routines."

The Court also observed that, in *Kent*, it was said (there, with respect to waiver of a juvenile to adult court):

> [T]here is no place in our system of law for reaching a result of such tremendous consequences ... without hearing, without effective assistance of counsel, without a statement of reasons [for the action taken].

The Court in *Gault* adopted this same view, with respect to the delinquency hearing for a juvenile.

> We do not mean...to indicate that the hearing to be held must conform with all of the requirements of a criminal trial or even of the usual administrative hearing; but we do hold that the hearing must measure up to the essentials of due process and fair treatment.

Well, if a juvenile hearing does not have to match the process of a criminal trial or even an administrative hearing, then what due process is required at a juvenile hearing? Fortunately, the Supreme Court gave us the minimum constitutional requirements:

1. There must be advance written notice to the child and to his parents of the specific charges and the factual allegations that support the delinquency petition or charges. These must be provided sufficiently in advance of the hearing to permit preparation for the hearing.
2. There must be notification to the child and to his parents of the child's right to be represented by counsel, either retained by them or, if they cannot afford counsel, appointed by the court.
3. The child must be entitled to the application of the constitutional privilege against self-incrimination.
4. Absent a valid confession, a determination of delinquency and an order of commitment must be based only on sworn testimony, subjected to the opportunity for cross-examination.

(As to another question that had been raised in *Gault*, the Supreme Court avoided the issue of whether there was a constitutional right to appellate review of the delinquency and commitment determination. This avoidance was based on procedural grounds, because the case had not developed in a way that permitted the Court to review that question.)

■ *In re Winship*

What should be the standard of proof in juvenile proceedings? This was the issue before the Supreme Court in the case of *In re Winship*, 397 U.S. 358 (1970). In this case, a 12-year-old boy was found to have stolen $112 from a woman's purse. The petition charging the boy with delinquency alleged that if the act had been committed by an adult, the crime would have been larceny. The governing New York law stated that "[a]ny determination at the conclusion of [an adjudicatory] hearing that a [juvenile] did an act or acts must be based on a preponderance of the evidence." The youth was subsequently ordered to be placed in a training school for 18 months, subject to possible annual extensions until his 18th birthday, which for Winship would have been six years down the road. The appeals courts affirmed.

In reversing, the Supreme Court noted that, for criminal cases, a guilty finding requires proof to be established beyond a reasonable doubt. The Court observed that the standard is important because the accused is facing a possible loss of liberty, and he also will be stigmatized if convicted.

> **Accordingly, a society that values the good name and freedom of every individual should not condemn a man for commission of a crime when there is reasonable doubt about his guilt.**

Thus, the question before the Court was whether juveniles also are constitutionally entitled to this same standard when charged with the equivalent of a criminal law violation. In answering yes, the Court rejected the contrary conclusions of the New York Court of Appeals. The appeals court had argued against stricter standards on the grounds that the delinquency adjudication was not a conviction; that the juvenile proceedings were designed not to punish, but to "save" the child; that to impose the higher standard (of proof beyond a reasonable doubt) would risk the "destruction" of the beneficial aspects of the juvenile process; that to allow a child to prevail was probably not in his best interest; and that there was only a "tenuous" difference between the two standards.[9]

> **In sum, the constitutional safeguard of proof beyond a reasonable doubt is as much required during the adjudicatory stage of a delinquency proceeding as are those constitutional safeguards applied in *Gault*—notice of charges, right to counsel, the rights of confrontation and examination, and the privilege against self incrimination. We therefore hold, in agreement with Chief Judge Fuld in dissent in the Court of Appeals, "that, where a 12-year old child is charged with an act of stealing which renders him liable to confinement for as long as six years, then, as a matter of due process... the case against him must be proved beyond a reasonable doubt."**

■ *McKeiver v. Pennsylvania; Breed v. Jones; Schall v. Martin*

Other Supreme Court decisions in the 1970s and 1980s addressed whether juveniles appearing before the juvenile court were constitutionally entitled to jury trials; whether an adjudicated delinquent could subsequently be referred to adult criminal court; and whether preventive detention may be used for juveniles.

McKeiver v. Pennsylvania, 403 U.S. 528 (1971), involved two separate lower court cases, later consolidated. McKeiver, age 16, was charged with robbery, larceny, and receiving stolen goods. At the adjudication hearing, his counsel's request for a jury trial was denied. McKeiver was adjudged a delinquent.

In a separate case, Terry, age 15, was charged with assault and battery on a police officer and conspiracy. His attorney's request for a jury trial was denied, and Terry was adjudged a delinquent. The state supreme court consolidated the two cases. The question considered by the court was "whether there is a constitutional right to a jury trial in juvenile court." The court held there was no such right. The United State Supreme Court affirmed, finding that the due process clause of the Fourteenth Amendment did not require jury trials in the juvenile court.

> **All the litigants here agree that the applicable due process standard in juvenile proceedings, as developed by *Gault* and *Winship*, is fundamental fairness. As that standard was applied in those two cases, we have an emphasis on factfinding procedures....But one cannot say that in our legal system the jury is a necessary component of accurate factfinding....**
>
> **The imposition of the jury trial on the juvenile court system would not strengthen greatly, if at all, the factfinding function, and would, contrarily, provide an attrition of the juvenile court's assumed ability to function in a unique manner.**

While the Supreme Court held no constitutional right exists to a jury trial in juvenile court, states do have the option to provide for such trials.

In *Breed v. Jones,* 421 U.S. 519 (1975), Jones, age 17, following a juvenile court adjudicatory hearing, was found to have violated a criminal statute (robbery). Two weeks later, he had a dispositional hearing and was found unfit for treatment as a juvenile. Prosecution as an adult was ordered. He was convicted in adult court of robbery in the first degree and committed to the state youth authority.

Through his mother as **guardian ad litem**, Jones filed a petition for a writ of habeas corpus, alleging his transfer to adult court and subsequent trial constituted double jeopardy. The district court denied the petition, holding that juvenile adjudication is not a trial. The appeals court reversed. In support of its finding that jeopardy attached at the adjudicatory hearing, the appeals court said the juvenile court had the power to "impose severe restrictions upon the juvenile's liberty" and that to hold jeopardy did not attach allows "the prosecution to review in advance the accused's defense and...hear him testify about the crime charged." The court found such a procedure "offensive to [its] concepts of basic, even-handed fairness."

In agreeing to hear the case, the Supreme Court stated a conflict existed on this issue between courts of appeals and the highest courts of a number of states and also mentioned "the importance of final resolution ... to the administration of the juvenile-court system."

The Court found a violation of the double jeopardy clause of the Fifth Amendment, as applied to the states through the Fourteenth Amendment. The Court opinion, which resulted in the vacating of Jones's adult conviction, pointed out that Jones went through two trials for the same offense and twice had to marshal his resources against those of the state. The Court held that juvenile court adjudication with a finding that the juvenile had violated a criminal statute is equivalent to trial in criminal court. The Court said to require transfer hearings prior to adjudicatory hearings does not affect the nature of such hearings or the quality of decision making at the transfer hearings, but did express concern when a transfer hearing occurs after the adjudicatory hearing.

> **Knowledge of the risk of transfer after an adjudicatory hearing can only undermine the potential for informality and cooperation which was intended to be the hallmark of the juvenile-court system. Rather than concerning themselves with the matter at hand, establishing innocence or seeking a disposition best suited to individual correctional needs...the juvenile and his attorney are pressed into a posture of adversary wariness that is conducive to neither.**

In *Schall v. Martin*, 467 U.S. 253 (1984), the Supreme Court examined whether preventive detention of juveniles under New York's Family Court Act (FCA) is compatible with the "fundamental fairness" required by due process. Section 320.5(3)(b) of that Act allowed pretrial detention of an accused juvenile delinquent upon a finding of serious risk that the juvenile "may before the return date commit an act which if committed by an adult would constitute a crime."

Martin, age 14, was arrested and charged with robbery, assault, and possession of a weapon. Finding a serious risk that Martin would commit another crime if released, the Family Court judge ordered Martin detained pending adjudication. While still in preventive detention, Martin filed a habeas corpus action in which he challenged the fundamental fairness of preventive detention. (The filing was done as a class action and the class was later certified by the district court.)

The district court held that pretrial detention under § 320.5(3)(b) violated due process. The court of appeals affirmed, commenting that most juveniles detained under the statute either have their petitions dismissed prior to adjudication or are released after adjudication, concluding that the statute is principally used "not for preventive purposes, but to impose punishment for unadjudicated criminal acts."

The Supreme Court reversed. The Court looked at whether preventive detention of juveniles under the FCA statute is compatible with the "fundamental fairness" required by due process. The Court held it was:

> **Every state [and the District of Columbia] permits preventive detention of juveniles accused of crime ....In light of the uniform legislative judgment that pretrial detention of juveniles properly promotes the interests of both society and the juvenile, we conclude...the practice serves a legitimate regulatory purpose compatible with the "fundamental fairness" demanded by the Due Process Clause in juvenile proceedings.**

As to the issue of punishment, the Court observed that the statute itself gave no indication that preventive detention is used or intended as punishment. Disagreeing with the lower court, the Supreme Court said pretrial detention did not have to be seen as punitive just because a juvenile was put on probation or subsequently released subject to conditions. The Court saw such actions as reinforcing the original determination of the need for close supervision and as protecting both the juvenile and society from the risks of pretrial crime. The Court found there were sufficient procedures (notice, hearing, and a statement of the facts and reasons) prior to any detention under the statute, with provisions for a formal probable cause hearing shortly thereafter, if the factfinding hearing is not scheduled within three days. The Court opinion also referenced the *parens patriae* state interest in promoting the welfare of children.

> **Children, by definition, are not assumed to have the capacity to take care of themselves. They are assumed to be subject to the control of their parents, and if parental control falters, the State must play its part as *parens patriae*.**

▓ Death Penalty for Juvenile Offenders

At the outset of this chapter, we noted we would be examining the special considerations our criminal justice system affords younger persons. A significant part of this chapter has examined Supreme Court decisions that have set the constitutional framework for the functioning of the juvenile court. In this section, and the next, we continue to look at these special considerations, but from a different perspective—that of sentencing.

From 1988 through 2005, the Supreme Court decided three cases dealing with the constitutionality of imposing the death penalty for a capital offense committed by a juvenile. In *Thompson v. Oklahoma*, 487 U.S. 815 (1988), the Court ruled that the death penalty could not be constitutionally imposed on persons for capital offenses committed at age 15 or younger. One year later, in *Stanford v. Kentucky*, 492 U.S. 361 (1989), the Court ruled that the death penalty could be constitutionally imposed on juveniles who committed capital offenses at age 16 or 17. In 2005, in *Roper v. Simmons*, 543 U.S. 551 (2005), the Court reversed *Stanford* and ruled that the Eighth and Fourteenth Amendments are violated when the sentence of death is imposed on a person for a capital offense committed while the person was younger than 18. We will discuss each case in the order in which it was decided.

In *Thompson v. Oklahoma*, the Court ruled that imposing the death penalty on a juvenile for a capital offense committed when the juvenile was 15 violated the Eighth Amendment. Thompson was one of four persons who had brutally murdered Thompson's former brother-in-law. Each of the four was convicted of murder and sentenced to death. In determining whether the death penalty could be constitutionally imposed on a person for a crime committed at age 15, the Court held that the prohibition against cruel and unusual punishments had to be interpreted "according to its text, by considering history, tradition, and precedent, and with due regard for its purpose and function in the constitutional design." This process involves a consideration of the "evolving standards of decency that mark the progress of a maturing society" to determine those punishments that are so disproportionate as to be cruel and unusual.

The Court next identified a number of areas—for example, death penalty states that set a minimum age (none had set the age lower than 16); the views of respected professional organizations; and jury actions (the last execution of a person who committed their crime while under the age of 16 had been done over 40 years earlier, in 1948)—to determine that current standards of decency did not allow executing a person under age 16 at the time of the crime. The Court further said in *Thompson:*

> **The reasons why juveniles are not trusted with the privileges and responsibilities of an adult also explain why their irresponsible conduct is not as morally reprehensible as that of an adult.**

The Court also concluded that two principal social purposes for imposing the death penalty are retribution and deterrence of capital crimes. It is not inconsistent with society's "respect for the dignity of man" to extract retribution by capital punishment for the moral outrage caused by "particularly offensive conduct." However, the Court ruled:

> **Given the lesser culpability of the juvenile offender, the teenager's capacity for growth, and society's fiduciary obligations to its children, this conclusion is simply inapplicable to the execution of a fifteen year-old offender.**

The Court also ruled that prohibiting the execution of persons who committed capital crimes at an age younger than 16 would not diminish the deterrent value of capital punishment. Because imposing the death penalty on juveniles who committed capital crimes at an age younger than 16 promoted neither of the societal purposes of retribution or deterrence, the offender's execution would be "nothing more than the purposeless and needless imposition of pain and suffering".

The next year, in *Stanford*, the Court held that the Eighth and Fourteenth Amendments did not bar the execution of a person over age 15 and under age 18. Stanford was seventeen when he participated in the rape and murder of a gas station attendant which occurred as part of a robbery. Stanford was waived into adult court pursuant to state law based on the seriousness of the offenses and his past delinquencies. Following a trial he was convicted and sentenced to death. The state supreme court affirmed the waiver into adult court, the conviction, and sentence. In upholding the constitutionality of the death penalty imposed for offenses committed while the person was 16 or 17, the Court pointed out that 22 of the 37 states that provided for the death penalty allowed the execution of 16 year-olds, and 25 states allowed for the execution of 17 year-olds. The Court said this indicated the absence of a national consensus that such executions would be cruel and unusual. The Court also declined the invitation that it bring its own judgment to this issue as to whether the death penalty for juveniles is acceptable or cruel and unusual.

Sixteen years after ruling that the Constitution did not prohibit the execution of persons for crimes committed when they were 16 or 17, the Court reversed its *Stanford* decision in *Roper v. Simmons*, 543 U.S. 551 (2005). In 1993, when Simmons was 17, he and a 15-year-old accomplice kidnapped and murdered a female victim. Prior to the crime, Simmons told his friends that he wanted to kill someone and that because he was a minor he could get away with it. He and the accomplice broke into the victim's home, bound her, took her to the Mississippi River, and threw her off a railroad trestle into the river. After the crime was committed, Simmons bragged to his friends about killing the woman, leading to his arrest and eventual confession.

At age 17, Simmons was outside the criminal jurisdiction of the juvenile court system in Missouri. Tried as an adult, the jury found him guilty of murder, and he was sentenced to death. His conviction and sentence were affirmed by the state supreme court. After the Supreme Court issued its opinion in *Atkins v. Virginia*, 536 U.S. 304 (2002), barring the execution of a mentally retarded (this is the term used by the courts) person, Simmons filed a new petition for postconviction relief, claiming that the reasoning of *Atkins* bars executing a juvenile who was under the age 18 at the time of the criminal act. The state supreme court agreed, holding that a "national consensus has developed against the execution of juvenile offenders." Simmons' death sentence was set aside and he was resentenced to "life imprisonment without eligibility for probation, parole, or release except by act of the Governor."

In affirming the lower court, the Supreme Court first re-stated the principles announced in *Thompson v. Oklahoma* (discussed above)—that the prohibition against cruel and unusual punishments had to be interpreted by considering the history, tradition, and precedent of the Eighth Amendment, and also whether the punishment was so disproportionate to the crime that the "evolving standards of decency" are offended. The Court would do this by looking at the objective indications of consensus and then, in the exercise of its own independent judgment, determine whether the death penalty is a disproportionate punishment for juveniles.

To assess national consensus, the Court used the same process it had used in *Atkins,* looking at where the states stood in regards to the execution of juveniles. The Court concluded that 30 states prohibited the death penalty for juveniles, including 12 states that prohibited the death penalty for all offenses. Even in those states with capital punishment, 18 states prohibited imposing the death sentence for crimes committed by juveniles. Of the 20 states that permitted the use of the death penalty for crimes committed by juveniles, it had been imposed only infrequently. Only six states since the *Stanford* decision had executed prisoners for crimes committed as a juvenile, and only three states had done so in the 10 years before the *Roper* decision.

The Court also looked at what was occurring in society from a broader perspective:

> Since *Stanford*, no State that previously prohibited capital punishment for juveniles has reinstated it. This fact, coupled with the trend toward abolition of the juvenile death penalty, carries special force in light of the general popularity of anticrime legislation…and in light of the particular trend in recent years toward cracking down on juvenile crime in other respects….

> As in *Atkins*, the objective indicia of consensus in this case—the rejection of the juvenile death penalty in the majority of States; the infrequency of its use even where it remains on the books; and the consistency in the trend toward abolition of the practice—provide sufficient evidence that today our society views juveniles, in the words *Atkins* used respecting the mentally retarded, as "categorically less culpable than the average criminal."

The Court held that imposing the death penalty on an offender for an offense committed as a juvenile is prohibited by the Eighth Amendment. Because the death penalty is the most severe punishment society can impose, the Court said that its application must be limited to persons committing the most serious crimes and whose "extreme culpability" makes that person the most deserving to be executed. The Court considered three general differences between juveniles and adults, using these differences to support its holding that juveniles cannot with reliability be classified among the worst offenders. First, as put forth by scientific and sociological studies, "[a] lack of maturity and an underdeveloped sense of responsibility are found in youth more often than adults and are more understandable among the young." Second, the Court pointed to juveniles being more vulnerable or susceptible to negative pressures, with this discussed in the context that juveniles have less control, or less experience with control, over their own environment. Third, the juvenile's character is less well formed compared to that of an adult; the personality traits are more transitory and less firmed up.

> **These differences render suspect any conclusion that a juvenile falls among the worst offenders. The susceptibility of juveniles to immature and irresponsible behavior means "their irresponsible conduct is not as morally reprehensible as that of an adult."... Their own vulnerability and comparative lack of control over their immediate surroundings mean juveniles have a greater claim than adults to be forgiven for failing to escape negative influences in their whole environment....The reality that juveniles still struggle to define their identity means it is less supportable to conclude that even a heinous crime committed by a juvenile is evidence of irretrievably depraved character. From a moral standpoint it would be misguided to equate the failings of a minor with those of an adult, for a greater possibility exists that a minor's character deficiencies will be reformed.**

As it had in *Thompson*, the Court concluded that the two social purposes served by the death penalty—retribution and deterrence of capital crimes by future offenders—were not as strong in cases involving juveniles.

The Court also rejected the argument that the death penalty determination should be made on a case-by-case basis, holding that the differences between juvenile and adult offenders are too significant and too well understood to risk allowing the "brutality or cold-blooded nature" of a particular crime to overpower mitigating arguments.

A final issue in *Roper* concerned the United States being the only country to still give official sanction to the juvenile death penalty. Acknowledging that this information was not controlling, the Court nonetheless saw the practices of other countries as instructive in the Court's interpretation of the Eighth Amendment's prohibition against cruel and unusual punishment.

> **The opinion of the world community, while not controlling our outcome, does provide respected and significant confirmation for our own conclusions.**

■ *Graham v. Florida*

Graham v. Florida, 560 U.S. (2010), continues our examination of the "evolving standards of decency." In *Roper*, the Supreme Court held it was unconstitutional to impose the death penalty on offenders who were under the age of 18 at the time of their crime. But does the Constitution allow a juvenile to be sentenced to life in prison without parole for a nonhomicide crime? This was the issue before the Court in *Graham*.

Terrence Graham, at age 16, was one of four youths who attempted to rob a barbecue restaurant. As allowed by state statute, he was charged as an adult. The specific charges were armed burglary with assault or battery, a first-degree felony carrying a maximum penalty of life in prison with no possibility of parole, and attempted armed robbery, a second-degree felony with a maximum penalty of 15 years.

Under a plea agreement, Graham pleaded guilty to both charges. The plea agreement was accepted by the trial court, and an adjudication of guilt was withheld, with Graham sentenced to concurrent three-year terms of probation. The first 12 months of his probation were served in the county jail.

Less than six months after release, at age 17, Graham was arrested for a home invasion robbery. It also was alleged he took part in a second robbery later that evening, during which one of his two accomplices (who also were involved in the first robbery) was shot.

The trial court found Graham had violated his probation by committing a home invasion robbery, possessing a firearm, and by associating with persons involved in criminal activities. The court sentenced Graham to the maximum sentence for his crimes, which was life imprisonment in the case of the armed burglary. Because Florida had abolished parole, this meant Graham had no possibility of release, other than executive clemency.

Graham filed a motion in the trial court, saying his sentence violated the Eighth Amendment's bar against cruel and unusual punishment. Not getting a response, the motion was considered denied, and Graham filed with the appeals court. That court affirmed, holding that Graham's sentence "was not grossly disproportionate to his crimes." The court found Graham incapable of rehabilitation. The state supreme court denied review. The U.S. Supreme Court granted certiorari, to review the case.

As in *Roper*, the Court said determining whether a punishment was cruel and unusual necessitated looking at the "evolving standards of decency that mark the progress of a maturing society." While the standard remains the same, its applicability changes as the basic mores of society change.

In making its analysis, the Court said, "[t]he present case involves an issue the Court has not considered previously: a categorical challenge to a term-of-years sentence....This case implicates a particular type of sentence as it applies to an entire class of offenders who have committed a range of crimes."

In looking at objective indicia, the Court found the majority of states (37 plus the District of Columbia) had legislation authorizing life sentences without parole for juvenile nonhomicide offenders in some circumstances. Federal law also allowed the possibility of life without parole for offenders as young as age 13. The state argued this showed the absence of a national consensus that such sentences are cruel and unusual. The Court disagreed, saying an examination of actual sentencing practice in the authorizing states shows a consensus against its use, that only 109 (later amended to 123) juvenile offenders were serving such sentences. Of these, 77 were in one state, with the remaining offenders (46) confined in just 10 states. Twenty-six states, the District of Columbia, and the federal government had not imposed such sentences, although they had the statutory authorization to do so. Further, the fact that states allow for this sentence, but don't impose it, should not be seen as viewing the sentence as appropriate. The Court said these findings show how rarely such sentences are imposed.[10] The Court concluded that it was fair to say that a national consensus had developed against authorizing life sentences without parole for juvenile nonhomicide offenders.

The Court next considered its responsibility to interpret the Eighth Amendment, looking at how culpable the offenders were with respect to their crimes and characteristics, along with the severity of the punishment. Also involved was a consideration of how the challenged sentencing practice serves legitimate penological goals.

Pointing out juveniles' "lack of maturity and...underdeveloped sense of responsibility," their being "more vulnerable or susceptible to negative influences..." and their characters being "not as well formed," the Court, citing *Roper*, said that "juvenile offenders cannot with reliability be classified among the worst offenders."

Having looked at the status of the offenders, the Court next considered the nature of the offense. While serious nonhomicide crimes can be devastating, such crimes were not seen as comparable to murder in their "severity and irrevocability."

[W]hen compared to an adult murderer, a juvenile offender who did not kill or intend to kill has a twice diminished moral culpability. The age of the offender and the nature of the crime each bear on the analysis.

The sentence of life without parole, the Court said, is "the second most severe penalty permitted by law"—there is an alteration of life that is irrevocable and a deprivation of basic liberties without significant hope of restoration. For a juvenile, because of her age, a sentence of life without parole was seen as especially harsh punishment, since, on average, she would serve more years and a higher percentage of her life in prison than an adult offender.

In looking at the penological justifications, the Court said:

A sentence lacking any legitimate penological justification is...disproportionate to the offense. With respect to life without parole for juvenile nonhomicide offenders, none of the goals of penal sanctions that have been recognized as legitimate—retribution, deterrence, incapacitation, and rehabilitation...—provides an adequate justification.

The Court said retribution is appropriate where the criminal sentence is directly related to the personal culpability of the criminal offender. Because a juvenile is less culpable than an adult, the case for retribution is not as strong with a juvenile. Further weakening the argument for retribution is the fact that the juvenile did not commit a homicide. The Court held that to impose the second most severe penalty (life in prison without parole) on the less culpable juvenile nonhomicide offender is not proportional to the crime.

Deterrence was not seen as viable as the juvenile's lack of maturity and underdeveloped sense of responsibility makes it less likely for them to consider the possible punishments when making decisions. Any limited deterrent effect provided by life without parole was held insufficient to justify that sentence.

Incapacitation of the juvenile nonhomicide offender for life without parole was not viable as it implies a judgment that the juvenile is incorrigible, incapable of change. This is contrary to earlier determinations, with the Court holding, "[a] life without parole sentence improperly denies the juvenile offender a chance to demonstrate growth and maturity."

As to the final rationale, the Court said a life sentence without parole cannot be justified by the goal of rehabilitation. "The penalty forswears altogether the rehabilitative idea" and was inappropriate when considering the "juvenile nonhomicide offender's capacity for change and limited moral culpability."

Based on its finding that penological theory does not justify life without parole for juvenile nonhomicide offenders, the limited culpability of juvenile nonhomicide offenders, and the severity of life without parole sentences, the Court held that life imprisonment without parole for a juvenile nonhomicide offender is unconstitutional under the Eighth Amendment.

> **This clear line is necessary to prevent the possibility that life without parole sentences will be imposed on juvenile nonhomicide offenders who are not sufficiently culpable to merit that punishment. Because "[t]he age of 18 is the point where society draws the line for many purposes between childhood and adulthood," those who were below that age when the offense was committed may not be sentenced to life without parole for a nonhomicide crime.**

> **[W]hile the Eighth Amendment forbids a State from imposing a life without parole sentence on a juvenile nonhomicide offender, it does not require the State to release that offender....Those who commit truly horrifying crimes as juveniles may turn out to be irredeemable, and thus deserving of incarceration....The Eighth Amendment does not foreclose the possibility that persons convicted of nonhomicide crimes committed before adulthood will remain behind bars for life. It does forbid States from making the judgment at the outset that those offenders never will be fit to reenter society.**

> **Terrance Graham's sentence guarantees he will die in prison without any meaningful opportunity to obtain release, no matter what he might do [to show otherwise]....The State has denied him any chance to later demonstrate that he is fit to rejoin society based solely on a nonhomicide crime...committed while...a child in the eyes of the law. This the Eighth Amendment does not permit.[11]**

As it did in *Roper*, the Court opinion also looked to global practices, finding that only the United States imposes life without parole sentences on juvenile nonhomicide offenders. Saying such findings are not dispositive as to what the Eighth Amendment means, the Court nonetheless found them to be relevant.

> **The Court has treated the laws and practices of other nations and international agreements as relevant to the Eighth Amendment not because those norms are binding or controlling but because the judgment of the world's nations that a particular sentencing practice is inconsistent with basic principles of decency demonstrates that the Court's rationale has respected reasoning to support it.**

Boot Camps

Boot camp programs are geared primarily to young offenders. This type of intensive institutional treatment is sometimes called "shock incarceration." It may be included in a special type of sentencing, called "intermediate sanctions" or "alternative sentencing." These terms are imprecise, and they are not clearly defined, but they are mentioned here because they are encountered in discussions about criminal justice, sentencing, and the role of corrections.

Boot camps are facilities that emphasize military drill, physical training, and hard labor. Their name comes from military boot camp training, and many aspects of such programs are patterned on military regimens. They have been geared to young male offenders who are sentenced for nonviolent offenses. The length of stay in a boot camp is intended to be short. Daily life is planned to be long and hard, with heavily structured activity.

Most agencies began operating their camps in the 1980s and 1990s. By 1995, there were 75 boot camps for adults operated by state correctional agencies. Thirty juvenile boot camps were operated by state and local agencies, and 18 boot camps in local jails were operated by larger counties. While the early camps stressed military discipline, physical training, and hard work, later camps added such components as alcohol and drug treatment and problem solving strategies. Some also added intensive post-release services such as electronic monitoring and home confinement.[12]

In a sense, boot camps replaced the specialized treatment of youth offenders that was favored by many penologists and corrections professionals after World War II. Patterned in the United States on the Borstal system in England, specialized youth facilities and programs were developed for youthful offenders—those in their late teens (older than juvenile offenders) and early twenties. California had a Youth Authority that was a model of this type of sentencing. Many states and the federal government also had special youth offender laws. Offenders in this category were committed, typically for indeterminate terms, for specialized treatment that emphasized education, vocational training, counseling, and work. They were to be released when corrections authorities concluded that they had successfully completed their needed treatment programs. They were released to parole-type supervision in the community. The length of time spent in an institution and under supervision was, in theory, geared to the needs of the offender and not to the seriousness of the offense. The offenders were usually convicted, like adults (and unlike juveniles), but were sometimes given sentences that could be set aside or sealed if the youths were successful in their programming.

As an alternative, boot camps have been supported with the following arguments: they are cheaper to run and thus reduce costs; they help to reduce the crowding in regular prison facilities; they are seen (by judges, legislators, the media, and the public) as being tougher on offenders and thus more fitting as punishment; they help to rehabilitate the offender; and they deter future crime and reduce recidivism. Like the specialized youthful offender programs described previously, the underlying concept is that concentrating on persons of this younger age, who are not criminally sophisticated and not entrenched in criminal careers, will produce good results, because they are still amenable to treatment programs and change. The boot camp programs teach respect for authority, self-discipline skills, accountability, pride in achievements, self-esteem, and good work habits.

For reasons discussed later in this section, the use of boot camps began to drop in the mid-1990s, and by the year 2000, nearly one-third of state prison boot camps had closed, with the average daily population in state boot camps dropping more than 30%.[13]

In the 1990s, correctional boot camps also became increasingly popular for juvenile delinquents, but, as with adult boot camps, the use of juvenile boot camps also has dropped. In 1996, 27 states were operating 48 residential boot camps for adjudicated juveniles. Offenders often wore military-style uniforms, marched to and from activities, and responded quickly to the orders of the "drill instructors." The daily schedule ordinarily included drills and ceremony practice, physical fitness activities, and challenge programs, as well as academic education. Misbehavior could be handled by summary punishment.[14] In 2007, juvenile boot camps operated in 11 states, with a total population of fewer than 1,400 juveniles.[15]

Evaluation of the arguments for boot camps brings mixed results but seems to suggest that boot camps are not a viable approach, especially for juveniles. Because of the shorter terms served, there are overall cost savings and the demand for regular prison beds is reduced. Obviously, if the program is large, the savings will be greater. (This assumes that those going into boot camps would otherwise be incarcerated. If these are inmates who would otherwise be on probation, then the cost savings are negligible.) As to the rehabilitation of inmates and the reduction of recidivism rates due to "shock incarceration" or deterrence, the studies do not show that boot camps are significantly different from traditional prison programs in terms of results. This was found to be true despite the fact that inmates who successfully completed boot camp programs reported that they had developed better attitudes toward authority, better self-esteem, and improved social attitudes.[16] (One aspect must be carefully assessed: because boot camp inmates are a selected group of offenders, they must be compared with offenders of similar backgrounds for valid assessments.)

Juvenile boot camps are also seen as unsuccessful in reducing recidivism. One study found "a preponderance of evidence showing that the boot camp and shock type of deterrence programs either did not affect subsequent offending or actually increased recidivism."[17]

There have been few legal challenges to the conditions of boot camp facilities and programs.[18] Where such programs exist, most offenders probably have been told (by their sentencing judges and probably by their lawyers) that they are fortunate to be given the opportunities afforded by boot camp, so they do not bring lawsuits (after all, their days are so long, and the purpose is to render them so exhausted, that few of them probably have the time or energy to draw up legal papers!). The main legal problems are sentencing ones, involving matters of equal protection or equal opportunity under the criminal law. Because the boot camp sentence is perceived as providing some advantages (including shorter terms, special programming, and early return to homes and family), the main legal questions are ones of parity. Specifically, does the sentencing or the opportunity for the program benefits discriminate against women offenders, against disabled persons, and against older offenders or others who are excluded by the definitions of eligibility for the boot camp program? It seems clear that, on the surface, it does. Government officials considering or operating such programs would probably be well-advised to examine their resources in advance of any legal challenge (because they certainly will be required to provide such evaluations and reports in defense against such a challenge). This examination of boot camp programs should include the following: the numbers of persons who would be included if the programs were expanded to include more offenders; whether the programs could include more offenders; and whether females, disabled offenders, or wider categories of offenders (in age or other criteria) might be included in the programs by special accommodations or other steps.

SUMMARY

- Juveniles in the U.S. criminal justice system are treated under special rules that are designed for their protection. These rules derive from concepts in the English legal system, in which children who committed offenses were taken before chancery court judges and were processed under the concept of *parens patriae*, which stipulates that the monarch (the government) is the protector of their rights and welfare.

- Special juvenile courts are the rule in the United States. Proceedings in these courts are usually not public. Juvenile records are sealed or specially protected. Specialized terms used in juvenile court proceedings reflect the ideas of treating juveniles differently from adults: juveniles are "proceeded against," not prosecuted; they are "found to be delinquent," not convicted; they are issued a disposition by the court, not a sentence; they are sent to training schools (or other similarly named facilities), not to prisons.

- Juveniles, especially those in the upper age ranges (although the ages vary from state to state, we refer here mostly to 16- and 17-year-olds), may be transferred to adult court for prosecution for violent or serious offenses. In recent years, when it has been widely perceived that juveniles are involved in more sophisticated criminal activity at younger ages, there has been a get-tough movement, which has resulted in procedures for the referral of larger numbers of juveniles to adult courts in many states.

- The Supreme Court, in 1966, after decades of deference in all levels of courts to the concepts of juvenile processing in which protective and informal procedures were the rule, said that transfers of juveniles to adult courts (waiver of juvenile court jurisdiction) must be accompanied with some due process protections. These protections include the right to a hearing, access by counsel to the reports used by the juvenile court in making its decision, and a statement of the reasons for the court's decision (*Kent v. United States*).

- In regular juvenile court cases (and not just the transfer cases, which *Kent* dealt with), the Supreme Court said that delinquency proceedings must also include minimal due process protections. Although not as extensive as adult criminal proceedings, these hearings require (at a minimum) the following: advance written notice to the juvenile and his parents; the opportunity to be represented by counsel; the availability of the privilege against self-incrimination; and a determination by the court of delinquency based on sworn testimony, subject to cross-examination (*In re Gault*).

- Juveniles, like adults, are constitutionally entitled to a standard of proof beyond a reasonable doubt during the adjudicatory stage of the juvenile court process (*In re Winship*).

- During the 1970s and 1980s, the Court held that jury trials were not constitutionally required for juveniles appearing before the juvenile court and that to require such trials could lessen the court's assumed ability to function in a unique manner (*McKeiver v. Pennsylvania*). The Court also held that an adjudicated delinquent could not subsequently be referred to adult criminal court, as this would constitute double jeopardy (*Breed v. Jones*); and that the use of preventive detention for juveniles properly promotes the interests of both society and the juvenile and that the practice serves a legitimate regulatory purpose compatible with the "fundamental fairness" demanded by the Due Process Clause in juvenile proceedings (*Schall v. Martin*).

- From 1988 through 2005, the Supreme Court decided three cases dealing with juvenile offenders and the death penalty. In *Thompson v. Oklahoma*, the Court held that the death penalty could not be imposed on persons for capital offenses committed at age 15 or younger. A year later, in *Stanford v. Kentucky*, the Court upheld use of the death penalty for persons committing capital offenses at age 16 or 17. In 2005, in *Roper v. Simmons*, this ruling was reversed, with the Court holding that the Eighth and Fourteenth Amendments are violated when the sentence of death is imposed on a person for a capital offense that was committed by a person under age 18. A guiding principle in each of these cases was the "evolving standards of decency that mark the progress of a maturing society to determine which punishments are so disproportionate as to be cruel and unusual."

- The "evolving standard of decency" also was used in determining that it is unconstitutional to impose a sentence of life imprisonment without parole on a nonhomicide juvenile offender (*Graham v. Florida*).

- Youthful offenders are those who are technically adults (above the age of juveniles in a particular jurisdiction) but who are at the lower range of adulthood (typically, those in their late teens and early twenties). Many states have had specialized programs mandated in corrections facilities for such younger adult offenders, based on the concept that they are usually less sophisticated and more amenable to treatment and rehabilitation programs.

- A special kind of corrections program is the boot camp. Boot camps feature military drills and hard labor. The per-day costs of boot camps may be slightly higher than those for regular corrections institutions, but because stays in boot camps are significantly shorter, the costs per inmate commitment are lower. Claims of higher rehabilitation (and lower recidivism) rates for those sent to boot camps have not been sustained by studies, which so far have shown about the same recidivism rates for both those who were placed in boot camps and those who were sent to traditional prisons. In recent years, the use of such camps has decreased.

THINKING ABOUT IT

In *Roper,* the Supreme Court referred "to 'the evolving standards of decency that mark the progress of a maturing society' to determine which punishments are so disproportionate as to be cruel and unusual." *Graham* also applied the "evolving standards" assessment. With your knowledge of the varieties of sentences imposed in different circumstances, identify some current punishments that you believe the Court may determine, in the next 10 years, to be so disproportionate as to be cruel and unusual. As one example, *Graham* held it was unconstitutional under the Eighth Amendment to sentence a juvenile nonhomicide offender to life in prison without the possibility of parole. Should this same determination apply to juveniles serving life-without-parole sentences who did commit homicides?

KEY TERMS

dependent children: Juveniles without family or support, or who have deficient family or support. These children may appear before juvenile courts to verify their dependency status so the courts may determine the best steps that can be taken for their welfare.

guardian ad litem: An individual appointed by the court to function on behalf of an incompetent or an infant and to represent the interests of that incompetent or infant in a suit to which that person is a party.

juvenile court: The term for courts that have original jurisdiction over persons statutorily defined as juveniles and alleged to be delinquents, status offenders, or dependents. It may be a separate court, established by constitution or by statute, it may be a division of a court, or it may be a court of broader or general jurisdiction sitting in special session on juvenile matters.

parens patriae: Literally, father (or parent) of the country. The concept that the king (the government) has protective responsibility for those who are not able to care for themselves, particularly children and mentally incompetent individuals.

petition (juvenile): A document filed in juvenile court alleging that a juvenile is a delinquent, a status offender, or a dependent and asking that the court assume jurisdiction over the juvenile or asking that the juvenile be transferred to a criminal court for prosecution as an adult.

status offender: A juvenile who has been adjudicated by a judicial officer of a juvenile court as having committed a status offense, which is an act or conduct that is an offense only when committed or engaged in by a juvenile (that is, it would not be a crime if committed by an adult).

ward: A person placed under the care of a guardian as a consequence of being legally unable to manage his own affairs. Used especially in juvenile law, meaning a child who is under special protection of the state or a juvenile court.

ENDNOTES

1. While most states set 17 as the oldest age for original juvenile court jurisdiction, a few states have set ages 15 or 16. Some states also set a minimum age (from ages 6 to 10) for original juvenile court jurisdiction in delinquency matters. Finally, states have set an upper age over which the juvenile court can retain jurisdiction for purpose of disposition in delinquency matters. This ranges from ages 18 to 24 or the full term of the disposition order. Office of Justice Programs. *Juvenile Offenders and Victims: 2006 National Report.* Page 103. (Washington, DC: Office of Juvenile Justice and Delinquency Prevention, U.S. Department of Justice, 2006. Accessed February 1, 2011 from http://www.ojjdp.gov/ojstatbb/nr2006/index.html.)

2. In some states, the juvenile court, under "blended sentencing" laws, may impose criminal sanctions on certain juvenile offenders. These laws broaden the sanctioning powers of the juvenile court so that certain juvenile offenders can be handled in the same manner as adult offenders, thus exposing these juvenile offenders to harsher penalties. Further information on blended sentencing may be found in Chapter 4: Juvenile justice system structure and process, *Juvenile Offenders and Victims: 2006 National Report* (endnote 1). [Endnote 1 also provides information concerning juvenile courts retaining jurisdiction past the juvenile's 21st birthday.]

3. Knoll, C. and Sickmund, M. *Delinquency Cases in Juvenile Court, 2007.* Pages 1–3. (Washington, DC: Office of Juvenile Justice and Delinquency Prevention, U.S. Department of Justice. 2010.)

4. Throughout the United States, probation officers (for adults as well as juveniles) have higher educational requirements than many other corrections officers. In most jurisdictions, there are degree requirements for entry-level probation officers. Correctional officers usually do not

have to meet such degree requirements, although caseworkers (whose work is closely tied to that of probation and parole officers) usually are required to have college degrees. In post-hiring training, corrections staff always receive on-the-job training, as do probation officers. Many corrections agencies now have training academies for entry-level correctional training for new staff. These are not yet as extensive or intensive, nationwide, as police training academies.

5. See endnote 1: *Juvenile Offenders and Victims: 2006 National Report.*

6. Redding, R. *Juvenile Transfer Laws: An Effective Deterrent to Delinquency?* Page 2. (Washington, DC: Office of Juvenile Justice and Delinquency Prevention, U.S. Department of Justice, 2010.)

7. Adams, B. and Addie, S. *Delinquency Cases Waived to Criminal Court, 2007.* Page 1. (Washington, DC: Office of Juvenile Justice and Delinquency Prevention, U.S. Department of Justice, 2010.)

8. See endnote 1: *Juvenile Offenders and Victims: 2006 National Report.* Pages 96–99. The quoted material on the Massachusetts law is taken from Mass. Gen. L. ch. 119, § 53.

9. But the Supreme Court commented that the trial judge had acknowledged that the proof might not show the boy's guilt beyond a reasonable doubt.

10. The Court observed that many states allow juveniles to be transferred to, or charged directly in adult court. Once there, the juvenile could receive the same sentence as an adult, including life without parole. While recognizing this could occur, the Court said such an action did not justify the judgment that many states intended for that result to take place.

11. The Court briefly considered, and rejected as inadequate, two alternative approaches. The first was the state's argument that state laws consider the juvenile offender's age. This argument was rejected based on the view that subjective judgments could still occur, for example that the crime showed an "irretrievably depraved character." The second approach was for a case-by-case assessment. Citing *Roper,* the Court held that "it does not follow that courts taking a case-by-case proportionality approach could with sufficient accuracy distinguish the few incorrigible juvenile offenders from the many that have the capacity for change." Another concern with the case-by-case approach dealt with juveniles having a greater distrust of adults and being less likely than adults to work effectively with their lawyers, thus impairing the quality of representation. The categorical rule avoids the risk that, as a result of such difficulties, a court or jury would erroneously conclude there was sufficient culpability to deserve life without parole for a nonhomicide offense. The Court also saw the categorical rule as giving "all juvenile nonhomicide offenders a chance to demonstrate maturity and reform."

12. *Correctional Boot Camps: Lessons from a Decade of Research.* Page 2. (Washington, DC: Office of Justice Programs, U.S. Department of Justice, 2003.)

13. See endnote 12.

14. MacKenzie, D., Gover, A., Armstrong, G., and Mitchell, O. *A National Study Comparing the Environments of Boot Camps with Traditional Facilities for Juvenile Offenders.* Page 1. (Washington, DC: National Institute of Justice, U.S. Department of Justice, 2001.)

15. Sickmund, M. 2010. *Juvenile boot camps, 1997-2007.* Pittsburgh, PA: National Center for Juvenile Justice.

16. A 2003 study found that participants in boot camp programs reported positive short-term changes in attitudes and behaviors and also better problem-solving and coping skills.

However, with few exceptions, these changes did not result in reduced recidivism. *Correctional Boot Camps: Lessons from a Decade of Research.* See endnote 12. With respect to the positive change reported by participants, let us share an anecdote that was told by an administrator of a boot camp. This camp had a graduation ceremony, to which family members were invited. An inmate's mother came to his graduation and was so impressed with the program and with her son's improvement that she asked the administrator, "How do I get my other son in?"

17. Austin, A., Johnson, K., and Weitzer, R. *Alternatives to the Secure Detention and Confinement of Juvenile Offenders.* Page 22. (Washington, DC: Office of Justice Programs, Department of Justice, 2005.)

18. A recent example, while not resulting in convictions, shows the concerns posed by boot camps and supports the need to make sure staff is sufficiently trained. According to court filings, a 14-year-old boy was committed to the state's department of juvenile justice and placed in a boot camp. Upon arrival, he was given a physical assessment consisting of two minutes of push-ups, two minutes of sit-ups, and a run of about 1.5 miles. Prior to completing the run, the youth fell to the ground. He was said to have been restrained by the guards at the camp and subjected to multiple uses of force. Drill instructors at the boot camp forced the youth to inhale ammonia on several occasions, each time with staff covering his mouth. The youth became unresponsive during the last forced application of ammonia. (The incident was recorded on videotape.) Taken to a medical center, then a hospital, the youth was unable to be revived and died the next day. An autopsy performed first reported a natural death due to complications of a sickle cell trait. A second autopsy, however, found that the victim's death was due to oxygen deprivation.

Eight staff were charged with manslaughter. In 2007, they were acquitted. A federal investigation was opened. In an April 16, 2010 press release, the U.S. Department of Justice announced that it would not pursue federal criminal civil rights charges against the eight staff. The press release said that prosecutors, under the applicable federal criminal civil rights laws, "must establish, beyond a reasonable doubt, that an official 'willfully' deprived an individual of a constitutional right, meaning that the official acted with the deliberate and specific intent to do something the law forbids....Neither accident, mistake, fear, negligence nor bad judgment is sufficient to establish a federal criminal civil rights violation." The evidence was found insufficient to pursue federal charges.

For more general information in this area, see the U.S. Government Accountability Office (GAO) 2007 report, *Residential Treatment Programs: Concerns Regarding Abuse and Death in Certain Programs for Troubled Youth.* Available from http://www.gao.gov/new.items/d08146t.pdf. The report refers to finding thousands of abuse allegations, covering the years between 1990 and 2007. GAO also looked at 10 closed civil or criminal cases involving the death of a teenager in a private residential treatment program between the years 1990 and 2004. For most of the 10 cases, GAO found there was ineffective management, with the needs of program participants and staff being ignored. The report also refers to the hiring of untrained staff, a lack of adequate nourishment, and reckless or negligent operating practices.

22 Privatization Issues in Corrections

Government has the ultimate authority and responsibility for corrections. For its most effective operation, corrections should use all appropriate resources, both public and private.

American Correctional Association, *Public Policy for Corrections*

Chapter Outline

- History of Privatization
- Contracting for Services
- Pros and Cons of Privatization
- Legal Issues in Privatization
- *Richardson v. McKnight; Correctional Services Corporation v. Malesko; Holly v. Scott; Pollard v. GEO Group*

In recent years, **privatization** has become a pressing issue in corrections. In the United States, and in several other nations, there have been moves toward using private prisons and jails. In this chapter, we will examine the background of the privatization movement, the pros and cons in the debate over its use, and the legal implications an administrator may encounter in privatizing.

History of Privatization

Using private facilities for confining offenders is by no means a new concept. In England, jails were run under what we would have to call private enterprise as far back as the Middle Ages, and probably before. There were some efforts (in the 14th to 17th centuries) to set some standards for the jails, but conditions were generally pretty miserable. By the 18th century, jails were run in England and jailers made their money by charging fees. Fees (set by the individual jailers) were demanded for all sorts of items and services, from food and clothing to certain aspects of special punishments (such as taking irons off) and even release from custody. Those with more money could purchase liquor, tobacco, and special family visits. Very little money was available from public funds. Prisoners without funds got money for jail services by working, by begging, or from charities.[1] This system led to many abuses.

There were reformers who proposed changing the conditions, the most notable of whom was probably John Howard. In the late 18th century, Howard proposed ideas for the betterment of English prisons and jails. Some of his ideas were gleaned from his visits to institutions on the European continent. He recommended the classification of prisoners (separating them by age, sex, and seriousness of offenses), work programs for the reformation of prisoners, and religious penitence as an underlying philosophy for running jails. He specifically recommended paying jailers a government salary, rather than running jails based on fees paid by inmates and their families.

In the colonies, criminal justice procedures, including the running of jails, were copied from the English practice without much change. Prisoners were rarely separated by type—women and children were often confined with hardened adult male criminals. Many jails were very crowded; most were unsanitary. Payments were extracted for special services, such as better meals or other privileges. The government gave some money to the jailer (often the sheriff) for basic services, but it was widely accepted that jailers could charge additional money for virtually any type of special benefit. In many places, inmates worked for jailers at their farms or other businesses. In some places, inmates were "rented out" for working for others in the community, with payments going to the jailers, not to the inmates.

In this climate of private exploitation in the jails, reforms came in the United States. They largely flowed from the ideas of John Howard and other reformers in Europe, and they were supported by strong voices for reform within the United States, particularly from religious groups. The Walnut Street Jail in Philadelphia and the Newgate and Auburn Prisons in New York were established as prototypes of the reformed (government-run) prison system. Solitary confinement (for personal reflection) and hard labor (not for wages but for its inherent therapeutic effect) were cornerstones of these new approaches. Thus, we arrived at the **penitentiary,** a place where prisoners with a strict code of silence (at Auburn) lived in separate cells, worked hard, were disciplined with corporal punishment, and had plenty of time to reflect on their mistaken ways and to repent.

Auburn became the model for prisons throughout the United States. The "silent system," along with a heavy work ethic, became a perfect environment for factories in the prisons, which produced all kinds of products. At some prisons, private companies on the outside provided raw materials, which were worked on at shops in the prisons and then sold by the private companies in the community. At other prisons, inmates were delivered to outside factories for work under contract at the private site. Alternatively, a shop area in the prison was rented to the private manufacturer, complete with prison labor, which was furnished at a very cheap rate. Other prisons performed the entire manufacturing process, from raw products through to finished goods and sales, from inside the prisons. Thus, prison industries were born. The industrial revolution meshed wonderfully with the cheap supply of labor in the prisons. Many private manufacturers made handsome profits from the prison labor pool. Not all prison labor occurred in factories, however. In many states, inmates worked in local stone quarries, in gravel pits, on logging operations, on road-building projects, or—in virtually all of the states—on farms, where goods were produced for prison consumption (to make the institutions self-sufficient to the extent possible) and, sometimes, even for the sale of prison farm products to the outside community.

Besides renting out shop areas inside prisons or renting out prisoners to work in outside factories, there were instances where the operation of an entire prison (primarily to save money) was leased to a private contractor. The first known instance of a completely private, leased institution in the United States was the Frankfort, Kentucky State Prison. In 1825, a local businessman leased the prison for five years and paid the state $1,000 a year to take over completely the management of the Auburn-style facility (and with it the labor of the 200 inmates who were his to use under rules he set and for production he devised).

In the 1800s, several other states did the same, leasing the prisons to private operators, usually to avoid the financial pressures of the government having to run them. After the Civil War, states in the South used such leases to private firms or individuals for economic savings. Besides leasing the facilities, private companies also rented prison laborers out of regular prisons run by the government. By the late 1800s and early 1900s, the leasing of convicts was generally phased out. But some practices—inmates being used on private projects for the personal benefit of wardens and sheriffs, work on the prison farm being performed for little or no pay, and prison labor being provided for the benefit of private citizens—continued into the 1900s.

What we see in this pattern of prisons and jails in Anglo-American history is a shift from largely private control (certainly very little governmental responsibility) in early English jails, through a reform period in the late 1700s and the 1800s when conditions for prisoners were improved in the penitentiary movement, mandated and financed at government expense. There were some elements of private enterprise pervading prisons in the later 1800s in America and then a shift to almost total government control and very little private involvement in the 1900s. With this historical perspective, we can see that our assumptions that prisons and jails are necessarily governmental in nature are not accurate, and that, indeed, private involvement in corrections facilities was, in past centuries, a common practice. The history of that fluctuating degree of private involvement is not a particularly positive one. It is rife with abusive treatment of prisoners and corruption, and it is indicative (in many instances) of facilities that were operated for personal gain rather than for any commitment to what we would consider today to be sound penological goals.

■ Contracting for Services

In recent years, there is one area of privatization that is widely used by corrections agencies. That is the practice of correctional facilities contracting for specific services within the walls of jails and prisons that are built by and otherwise operated by government appropriations and staff. Examples of such services are food, health care, mental health, commissary, substance abuse treatment, and education. This list is not all-inclusive, as other services, such as college, vocational, and work training, may also be provided.

As corrections facilities have become presumptively governmental agencies, authorized by statute, staffed by government employees, and funded solely with government monies, the assumption has been that all types of programs and services are provided by the agencies' staff. In the traditional prison or jail—let us say since the 1920s—government officials, under public laws and regulations and at government expense, have managed all functions of the institution. This has come to cover an immense range of activities. The largest function, in numbers of staff and in dollars spent, is the security function—providing custodial staff or guards to keep order and control in the facility. Beyond that, basic services for inmates are required: providing maintenance of the physical plant and the grounds, providing food and clothes, safety and sanitation, and health services of all kinds. In addition, there are programs, usually introduced under the umbrella of rehabilitative opportunities, which are so widespread as to be seen as essential in modern corrections. These include recreation and hobbies, religious services, education at many levels, vocational training classes, individual and group counseling, group support services (such as Alcoholics Anonymous and substance abuse programs), and other organization activities (such as Jaycees and Girl Scouts). Also, there are all kinds of work assignments, including those in factory settings (usually called prison industries), in maintenance and upkeep jobs, and on farms and other off-site locations.

The prevailing practice in all American correctional agencies has been to provide all of these corrections services as governmental activities in institutions that are constructed and maintained at government expense. In some program areas, the services provided are augmented by volunteer services. This is especially prevalent in religious and educational programs in many agencies. The traditional practice of funding, staffing, and providing services in all areas exclusively with government resources is currently challenged by the offer of private companies and individuals to perform many or all of these functions by means of contracts. As we saw in the preceding section in this chapter, such involvement of the private sector should not be surprising to us. But it is surprising, largely because we have come to accept the recent pattern in which the government performs virtually all corrections functions.

Corrections agencies have come to accept private performance of specific, isolated services as a matter of necessity. With regard to health services, for example, smaller jails and prisons cannot economically hope to provide the full range of medical care that is expected, both by individual inmates and by legal requirements, while competing for staff with the health care marketplace. At a minimum, contracts with medical specialists are entered to provide specialized care (for eye exams, orthopedics, dentistry, surgery, or whatever is needed). Contracts with local hospitals are usually necessary, unless there is a local, publicly funded hospital that is obliged to take inmate–patients. Even large corrections systems that have tried to maintain a health care staff of doctors, nurses, paraprofessionals, and some specialists have encountered staffing difficulties, usually in certain medical specialties. This has led many to contract with companies that provide a full range of health services.

Similarly, prisons and jails traditionally provided their own food services. They built their own kitchens and dining rooms and staffed them with trained food service personnel. Inmates performed much of the menial work in food preparation, such as serving food on cafeteria lines and cleaning duties. Because of difficulties (usually financial) in providing good food service, especially in certain areas of the country, agencies have turned to food service companies to provide all kinds of food service. ("All kinds" includes not only regular food service on the "main line," the main cafeteria line in the prison, but also special food preparation and service, such as for religious and medical diets and for persons who are restricted or segregated and cannot come to the regular dining area.)

Preparing and serving food and staffing medical examination and treatment rooms in a prison or jail setting involve special concerns, mainly regarding security and the supervision of inmates, that a typical private company is not trained or equipped to handle. For this reason, the contracts for these services (or for any other contracted services, such as education or counseling) must involve special elements. These include requirements for security precautions, training of the staff who are in contact with or who may even supervise inmates, and close coordination with other departments in the facility, especially the security department, to ensure proper oversight of the inmates. Such special requirements should be built into the contracts (specifically in the clauses that outline the specifications for the work, when bids are solicited, and the required standards of performance of the contracts). After the contracts are awarded and performance begins, the contracts must be closely monitored to be especially sure that any aspects of performance that may threaten security concerns or the orderly running of the institution are promptly corrected.

A firm that is not able to make such corrections in its performance must be terminated, which is always a special problem in the handling of private contracts for services. If a company is severely deficient in its performance—for example, regarding the quality of personnel who are provided or in the laxity of its approach to security concerns—what happens to the contract? How quickly can it be terminated? What happens to the parties involved during the termination period? Who will provide the services after the departure of the deficient contractor? These are all questions that, unfortunately, corrections facilities have had to face. If it was difficult to find health coverage in the first place, finding a quick replacement may be even more difficult or impossible. If a food service company is badly deficient, it is not that easy to step back in with agency staff and supplies or to find a good replacement from the private sector. These may be infrequent occurrences, but they are still events that must be anticipated by the agency contractor when entering any service contract. Counsel for the agency must make sure that contracts contain adequate details for ensuring that minimal performance standards are met by the contractor and that a cancellation of the contract is provided for, in the most expedient way possible within the law of the jurisdiction, when performance is seriously deficient.

Pros and Cons of Privatization

The provision of specific services (such as medical or food services) by private contractors has been widely accepted in the corrections field. In some jurisdictions, agencies lack legal authority to contract with private companies for work that is to be done directly with inmates inside prisons or jails. (Virtually all jurisdictions allow for private contracting for construction work for building, renovating, or repairing buildings.) In many places, administrators have become so dependent on private services that they do not see how they could survive without them.

But the real debate, and the area that still is a concern to many, is whether the operation of entire correctional facilities should be managed by private companies. When we talk about the controversy of privatization in corrections, we are focusing on the building and operation of private prisons and jails. This move (back) to private facilities dates only from the 1980s. In 1986, U.S. Corrections Corporation opened a private prison in Marion, Kentucky for minimum security inmates. Corrections Corporation of America, in the 1980s, operated a jail in Bay County, Florida (holding all levels of security), two detention facilities for the Immigration and Naturalization Service, and a halfway house for the Federal Bureau of Prisons. (Halfway houses and community corrections facilities had, for some time, been an exception to government operation of corrections agencies, because many of them were operated by private organizations. Some of these were for-profit companies, and many were nonprofit organizations, including religious groups. The Dismas Houses, Salvation Army, and Volunteers of America were leaders in the community corrections field. Persons working in corrections do not consider those types of operations as part of the central debate, which concerns the operation of traditional, secure corrections facilities.)

As of December 31, 2009, in the United States, there were more than 129,000 state or federal prisoners in private facilities. This represents 8% of all prisoners. This compares to 87,369 state or federal prisoners in private facilities as of December 31, 2000 (6.3% of all prisoners).[2]

Several factors led to the sudden growth of this industry. There was rapid growth in prison and jail populations and the aging of old prison buildings and jails. In the 1960s, there had been a strong push against traditional institutions and for alternatives to corrections or for non-incarcerative punishments. Prisons in many jurisdictions were scaled down, and legislatures were glad not to have to spend money on keeping up old buildings or building new ones. This trend continued into the 1970s. Then, with constant pressures resulting from increases in the crime rate, and especially increases in drug use and all kinds of drug offenses, tougher and tougher laws were passed to try to cope with the high crime rates. The construction of new prisons and jails became essential. Court decisions that criticized outmoded programs, often because those programs were housed in decrepit buildings, increased the pressure to build. In the 1980s and into the 1990s, new jail and prison construction was going on everywhere. However, simply building new prisons and jails was not sufficient: the new buildings had to be staffed and run from year to year, and those operating expenses were high. The U.S. General Accounting Office (GAO) reported that prison operating costs (state and federal) increased from about $3.1 billion in fiscal year 1980 to over $17 billion in fiscal year 1994, an increase of almost 550%.[3] In an October 2010 report, the VERA Institute of Justice said that the U.S. prison population grew from 424,000 in 1983 to over 1.5 million people in 2008, with this accompanied by a 674% increase in state corrections spending. Today, state corrections is the fourth-largest category of states' collective spending (behind education, Medicaid, and transportation).[4]

In most places in the mid-1990s, a "get-tough-on-crime" sentiment was prevailing in the legislatures. Such legislatures reversed earlier efforts to release more offenders to the streets and demanded that more offenders be locked up, and for longer periods of time. At the same time, inharmoniously, there was a push for greater fiscal economies and a downsizing of government functions. These various political pressures made privatization look appealing in many jurisdictions. The biggest selling point of private companies had been that they could provide a total facility cheaper than the government could. They also claimed that they could build and get a facility open and running more quickly than the government could. The latter claim seems to be supported by experience: because private firms are not bound by governmental rules that tend to slow down prison construction, such as political pressures from unhappy neighbors, environmental restraints, and requirements of competed bidding and construction contracting, private firms have shown an ability to open new facilities more quickly. They claim they can also raise the money to build new institutions more quickly from private investors or from lenders, while the government has to work more slowly, getting appropriations from the legislature or going through a bond-issuing process. In addition, working with existing designs ("cookie-cutter" plans), private firms can begin site preparation and construction more quickly.[5]

As with all of these claims and counterclaims, it is hard to establish exact comparisons, because we must use comparable facilities to make valid comparisons. Nonetheless, it is generally accepted that it takes the government at least two to three years to build a correctional facility, while some private companies claim they can do it in 12 to 18 months (and they, in fact, have done so). Minimum security facilities are built in even less time by private firms (as quickly as six months, in some cases). In order to conserve funds, private facilities are often designed to require the smallest possible staff, and this may make valid comparisons more difficult. Critics wonder if this low staffing level comes at the expense of security. Another concern that has been raised is whether private companies, in a rush to make quick deadlines, cut corners and do not use the same quality materials and construction methods that are present in government construction. This is a valid concern, and it should be met by stringent requirements in the contract with the private firm that will build the facility, just as it is when the government contracts with a private company to build a facility that it plans to operate itself. Writing a contract with strict, thorough specifications and then carefully monitoring it are the essential elements for all private work done for the government through contracting.

Another claimed advantage of privately operated prisons is that, by using private facilities, the government may more effectively and quickly respond to variations in prison population. We have already discussed the faster startup time in building private prisons. On the other hand, if the prison population decreases, the government may choose not to extend the contract. In some jurisdictions, public contracts may only be entered for one, two, or three years. It may be of some assurance to the government to know that it can get out of a situation if it proves to be undesirable.[6] Such contracts also avoid the need for the government to lay off its own staff if downsizing is required.

While private prisons appear beneficial in allowing the government to more efficiently expand and contract the number of prison beds, other privatization claims are more suspect. Privatization supporters have frequently claimed appreciable cost savings in building and operating private prisons. These claims are extremely hard to evaluate and prove.[7] One reason, which was already referred to, is the "apples and oranges" problem—the difficulty in making sure that comparisons are between facilities of truly comparable features. Another, even bigger problem is the hidden nature of many costs of corrections. These cover such things as capital costs (depreciation and amortization methods may be very different), employee benefits packages (particularly retirement plans, bonuses, insurance, and health plans), legal services, insurance, liability costs, staff training, transportation costs, interagency personnel costs (governments can often borrow some personnel, full- or part-time, from other agencies), and the true costs of programs and services, including agency monitoring for contract compliance. An agency would be ill-advised to conclude that it can contract out a jail or prison operation and then walk away and assume that the contracted cost is the end of the matter. Essential to a good contractual operation—and this cannot be overemphasized—is close, careful monitoring of all aspects of the private performance. That monitoring must be conducted by experienced persons; this is not a cheap aspect of privatization.

The experienced monitor is critical; one of her primary and obvious tasks is to ensure the contract guidelines are followed. The monitor, however, should not do the work or, unless specified in the contract, dictate the approach to be used. For the monitor to do either of these takes away from the purpose and integrity of privatization and skews any assessment of the process.

Another concern that is present in conducting a cost analysis is the lack of rigorous controls to prevent staff manipulation and to ensure that inmate behavior is measured in a standard manner.

In discussing the debate over the cost-efficiency of prisons, a Bureau of Justice Assistance's monograph on privatized prisons stated that many studies had "serious methodological flaws."[8]

How are the claimed savings achieved by private firms? The biggest savings, no doubt, are in personnel costs. The private firms typically employ nonunionized labor and offer the lowest benefits packages and wages that can be negotiated and maintained. Supervision and training are provided by experienced staff members, many of whom are hired from the ranks of state or federal agencies, or from the retirees' ranks of those government agencies. Savings also result from centralized management, which, especially in the large companies, can provide broader programs and services at cost savings, compared to what can be provided by a small jurisdiction, such as a county or a small state. Private companies claim that they are able to save because, unlike the government agencies, they do not have to be involved in political hassling, bureaucratic red tape (personnel requirements and financial accounting procedures, for example), and complex dealings with the legislature. Perhaps the most significant factor is that privatization promotes competition between companies, so minimizing costs is essential to obtaining contracts in the first place and to retaining them in the future.

These facts about the nature of private operations also serve to point out some of the arguments against privatization. For example, private firms are in business to make a profit, and they must do so in order to satisfy investors and to stay in business.[9] So they will look to cut costs and to cut corners, including the quality of services, at every conceivable point. One of the biggest concerns is the quality of staff. If staff are poorly paid, poorly motivated, poorly educated, and poorly trained, the consequences in job performance are predictable. Critics of privatization point to the private sector in police protection; how do you compare, in your experience, the quality of staff in "rent-a-cop" operations with those in government police forces? After all, a majority of security personnel [police] in this country are privately employed—at factories, shopping malls, universities, hospitals, and so on. No doubt, city, county, and state police officers are more professional in their appearance and probably in their performance. Overall, they have higher pay and benefits, along with higher morale and greater respect from the public. Is it worth the extra cost? Apologists for the private sector may say it is unfair to make these comparisons with private security forces, but we must look for whatever relevant information we can find and ask whatever tough questions we come across in this difficult debate over the privatization of facilities.

So far, we have not had enough experience to evaluate with certainty the quality of performance that can be expected from the private sector. We do know that there are problems unique to contracting for corrections work, which are not present in other kinds of government contracting, and there are probably problems that we have not yet even encountered. We also know there have been isolated failures, such as when the staff at a detention facility walked off the job when there was an inmate disturbance.

What of the right to strike? If the staff at a privately run facility want to organize and stage some kind of work action to achieve union goals, what should the position of the government be? Can such a situation be adequately covered by contract terms? If there is a nonstrike clause (as there is for most government workers, especially those in law enforcement), how can it be enforced against private workers? The experience we have with privatization is still too short to make a final, balanced assessment. Again, strict contract requirements and close monitoring are the keys to avoid sad consequences. When it comes to the quality of staff, one must wonder whether it is possible to ensure, by contract, that high standards are met and kept, when it is so hard to do when a government manager has direct control of hiring, training, promoting, and firing in a traditional government agency.

The following views are presented in the Bureau of Justice Assistance's monograph on privatized prisons:[10]

> What seems to have evolved in the United States is a privatization model that essentially mimics the public model but achieves modest cost savings, at least initially, by making modest reductions in staffing patterns, fringe benefits, and other labor-related costs. There is no evidence showing that private prisons will have a dramatic impact on how prisons operate....

> Despite these criticisms, privatization still provides a vital function within the correctional system.... [P]rivatization has forced the public sector to reexamine how it conducts business.... In this sense, privatization has served as a catalyst for change...

There are three reports which address the need for further research in this area. In September 2010, Arizona's Office of the Auditor General conducted a performance audit of the state's department of corrections. With respect to private prisons, the audit "[a]fter adjusting state and private rates to make them more comparable...found that rates paid to private facilities were higher [than for state-operated facilities] for both minimum and medium custody beds, the two categories of beds for which the Department contracts." The report also noted that the costs were not directly comparable, stating that private prisons "do not have all the same responsibilities and costs as state-operated facilities." One example was that private prisons do not accept inmates with serious medical needs.[11]

This report referred to a 2009 University of Utah article on prison privatization and the cost and quality of confinement indicators. That article reported on 12 studies. Eight of the studies that "met inclusion criteria provided information on cost of confinement." Four of these studies identified private prison cost savings, two studies found no difference in cost savings, and two found that publicly managed prisons cost less.[12]

Perhaps the clearest need for further and improved research on public-private prisons was shown by a 2008 Department of Justice publication reporting on two cost and performance analyses of the same four prisons (one privately operated and three publicly operated). The two analyses showed different cost findings. The two primary reasons for this were the different approaches used for handling the size of the inmate population and what was included in overhead costs. The article points out the need to develop a uniform performance measure.[13]

The VERA Institute for Justice reports that some states in fiscal year 2011 are cutting back on their use of private prisons. This report said it is a "subject of debate" on whether cost savings may be realized from using privately contracted facilities.[14] From a different perspective, one state has proposed selling several of its state prisons to private prison operators and then contracting with those companies to house inmates.[15]

■ Legal Issues in Privatization

The underlying issue of privatizing prisons, in a sense, is a quasi-legal one, or it may be labeled a philosophical question that is related to the function of government: Is it proper for private entities to exercise the function of confining, of punishing, fellow citizens? Privatization opponents believe it is not:

> In many instances, private prison operators are paid according to the number of inmates housed. Arguably, it is in the operator's financial interests to encourage lengthier sentences for inmates to keep bed spaces filled....Critics of prison privatization argue that firms will cut corners, from construction materials to hiring inexperienced personnel, forsaking security and quality of service in the process of making a profit.[16]

Providing particular services, such as food service or individual medical care, is one thing, but it is quite a different matter to take over an entire facility, both from the viewpoint of the individual inmates and in consideration of the protection of the public. The most difficult aspects of this issue are the ones involving custody and security. Can, or should, private staff members punish inmates for violations of rules—rules that may differ from those in government-run prisons? Can this be done to the extent that it is done by government staff, such as by placing offending inmates in solitary confinement, taking away all sorts of privileges (including some, such as correspondence and visiting, that affect the families as well as the inmates), and even affecting the length of time served (as in good-time allowances and parole recommendations)? Can, or should, private guards use force to control inmates, including deadly force, in cases of attempted escapes or riots? If they cannot do these things, how is the public to be protected? These are the most sensitive questions. The questions become more intense the higher the level of security of the institution and the higher the degree of sophistication or violent behavior that is present in the inmate population. In fact, private companies have so far operated in this country primarily at lower-security-level institutions. A 2005 census of correctional facilities under state or federal authority, by facility security level, identified only 8 (from a total of 415 private facilities) that operated at a maximum level of security and 43 that operated at a medium level of security.[17] It is at the maximum type of facility where the security concerns just mentioned would be the most pressing. But those same concerns are present in the lower level institutions—just to a lesser degree.

Some states have tackled the security issue by placing limits on the actions of private-sector staff: they are (in some places) only allowed to take summary and minor disciplinary actions against inmates; higher levels of disciplinary punishments are considered and imposed by regular government staff. (Some places use government staff for all disciplinary punishments against inmates.) As to the use of force, the private staff on the scene must be allowed to take immediate action in some situations. However, it is generally anticipated and provided for in the arrangements with the private company that, in the case of major disturbances, government staff (police or corrections officers) will be called on to handle the situation. Requirements on the use of deadly force (such as instructions for firing at fleeing prisoners) cannot be avoided, just because the officer with the weapon is a private rather than a government employee. Constitutional limits apply (see especially the discussion on the use of force and the cases of *Tennessee v. Garner*, 471 U.S. 1 (1985), and *Whitley v. Albers*, 475 U.S. 312 (1986)). To the extent that private corrections officers (or private security police in shopping malls, for that matter) are issued weapons and have authority to use them, they must be carefully trained in the standards for using force, especially the limitations on the use of potentially deadly force.

As we have repeatedly emphasized, the drafting of a good contract and the careful monitoring of that contract are essential to producing good results in private operations of prisons. They are, to a large degree, legal concerns. It is, of course, necessary to have a lawyer work closely with the appropriate government staff, such as the contract monitors and those working in the program areas, in order to prepare tight legal contracts, under the rules and standards of contracting in the jurisdiction. Ideally, the lawyer should be not only proficient in writing contracts, but also knowledgeable in criminal justice concerns and the demands of corrections operations. The legal staff should continue to be involved with the team that monitors the performance of a contract. Contract monitors do not have to be attorneys, but they should be trained by attorneys about the details of their jobs, and attorneys should be available to answer questions that arise from the actual monitoring.

In many situations, the corrections agency will assign at least one staff member to the private facility on a full-time basis. This monitor must have access to the inmates and the staff, to all areas of the institution, and to all records and reports at any time. Periodic (intermittent) inspections of facilities are less costly and cause less friction with private management, but they are less effective in ensuring good contract performance. "Constant monitoring of all aspects of internal performance is essential to a good contractual relationship."[18] A troubling aspect of contract drafting and implementation is providing for the handling of violations of the contract. Isolated, minor problems can, of course, be handled by warnings and negotiations, but there must be provisions in the contract for sanctions for serious abuses. These may be in the form of dollar penalties or withholding of some payment under the contract, which is deemed to be the most effective curative tool for a private corporation. If the violations continue, there must be provisions for additional sanctions, including termination of the contract.

As a practical exercise, if you were responsible for monitoring the performance of a contract and you found that the private company was cutting costs (obviously, trying to save money and increase profits) by buying low-quality food supplies, serving leftover foods, and repeating low-cost menu items, leading to little variety in meals for the inmates, what would you do to correct the situation? This, with endless varieties in details, is the sort of situation that underscores the complexity in drafting good contracts and in properly monitoring them. This exercise also points out a dilemma in contracting with private companies for services or to run whole facilities: on the one hand, it is desirable to allow a private vendor to be creative and to try new approaches, perhaps saving money in the process; on the other hand, there are certain attempts at cost savings that cannot be risked for fear of repercussions in security, safety, health, or protection of the public. This dilemma, along with the tension it creates, is another complicating factor in the debate over the use of private sector organizations and in the practical aspects of drawing up contracts and enforcing them.

Another significant legal issue is liability. Private companies will usually cover their exposure to liability by taking out liability insurance for all types of claims. As to ordinary, common law tort actions, such as medical malpractice or injuries from faulty equipment, the insurance should cover any losses due to inmate claims (or claims that may be made by visitors or by staff for injuries caused by negligent conditions or staff actions). The government, in the contract, will usually require the private company to be insured and to hold harmless the government for any such legal claims. In this portion of the contract, the language must be broad enough, and specific enough, to cover all types of claims that might be brought in relation to the operations of the private facility. The private company will typically have its own counsel, but property and injury claims will usually be handled by the insurance carrier.

The tougher legal question is the liability of the government or the contractor for constitutional violations. The language of 42 U.S.C. § 1983 allows such suits for claimed violations by any person who was acting under color of state law. It appears that liability cannot be escaped for constitutional violations by contracting the government service to a private entity. The leading case on this is *West v. Atkins*, 487 U.S. 42 (1988), where the Supreme Court said that the claimed violations of constitutional rights (a claim of deliberate indifference to the inmate's medical needs) were valid under Section 1983 because the private physician who was being sued in that case was performing a function for the state. The fact that he was under contract to perform medical services did not remove him (or the state) from obligations and liability under the civil rights law.

◼ *Richardson v. McKnight; Correctional Services Corporation v. Malesko; Holly v. Scott; Pollard v. GEO Group*

In *Richardson v. McKnight*, 521 U.S. 399 (1997), two prison guards who worked for a private firm claimed they were entitled to qualified immunity from inmate lawsuits charging a Section 1983 violation. McKnight, an inmate in a private prison in Tennessee, filed the constitutional tort action, alleging the officers placed him in "extremely tight physical restraints," causing a deprivation of his constitutional rights. The district court held the officers were not entitled to immunity because they worked for a private company, not the government. The appeals court, primarily for reasons of "public policy," agreed that immunity was inappropriate.

In affirming, the Supreme Court looked at several issues. One was whether there was a "firmly rooted" tradition of immunity for privately employed prison guards. As we discussed earlier, correctional functions have never been the exclusive domain of the government. The Court found "no evidence that the law gave purely private companies or their employees any special immunity from such suits."

The Court also considered whether the purposes of qualified immunity warranted a reversal. The officers correctly noted that state prison guards were entitled to qualified immunity; the officers therefore argued that, since they do the same work as state prison guards, they too should have this entitlement. In addressing the "functional approach" (people who do the same work), the Court acknowledged using the approach in some prior circumstances, but held that its prior applicability was more directed to the type of immunity—qualified or absolute—that the public official should receive. The Court recognized important differences between private and state workers with respect to immunity. The Court reviewed some of these differences and concluded:

> **Our examination of history and purpose thus reveals nothing special enough about the job or about its organizational structure that would warrant providing these private prison guards with a governmental immunity. The job is one that private industry might, or might**

not, perform; and which history shows private firms did sometimes perform without relevant immunities. The organizational structure is one subject to the ordinary competitive pressures that normally help private firms adjust their behavior in response to the incentives that tort suits provide—pressures not necessarily present in government departments.

In closing, the Court gave three caveats. First, the Court was not finding there was Section 1983 liability, but only that there was no entitlement to qualified immunity for a private prison guard. Second, the holding was narrowly drawn to apply to a private firm, "systematically organized" to perform a major administrative task, such as managing an institution, that receives limited direct government supervision and that undertakes the task for profit and potentially is in competition with other companies. Excluded from this case's coverage are those activities undertaken by a private person as an adjunct to government or acting under close government supervision (as in *West v. Atkins*). Third, the Court left open the issue of whether the defendants could successfully claim a "good faith" defense in this kind of lawsuit.

Richardson holds that private prison guards are not entitled to qualified immunity under 42 U.S.C. § 1983. The federal equivalent to a Section 1983 action is a *Bivens* lawsuit. *Correctional Services Corporation v. Malesko*, 534 U.S. 61 (2001), looks at the question of whether a private firm acting under color of federal law may be held liable under *Bivens*.

Correctional Services Corporation (CSC) contracted with the Federal Bureau of Prisons to house released federal inmates at its New York City halfway house. Malesko was sent to the halfway house to serve out the balance of his sentence. His verified heart condition limited his ability to climb stairs. While at the house, he lived on the fifth floor, taking the elevator to and from his room. In 1994, the facility changed its policy and authorized use of the elevator only for those residents living on the sixth floor or above. Malesko was exempted because of his heart condition. However, on March 28, 1994, CSC employee Urena told Malesko he could not use the elevator, requiring him to climb the stairs. He had a heart attack and fell, injuring his ear.

In 1999, Malesko filed a lawsuit against CSC and CSC employees. The district court considered the complaint under *Bivens* and dismissed it, saying "a *Bivens* action may only be maintained against an individual" and that it did not apply to CSC. The statute of limitations barred suit against the other, individual defendants. The appeals court affirmed with respect to dismissal of the complaint against the individual defendants, but it held that private corporations should be held liable under *Bivens*, thus providing a remedy for constitutional violations. The Supreme Court reversed, holding that the purpose of a *Bivens* action is to deter the officer, not the agency.[19] Whether such liability charges against private prison facilities should exist, as independent legal recovery actions, was seen by the Court as a question for Congress to address. The Court further noted that Malesko had not been without remedies, citing both the Bureau of Prisons' grievance procedure and a possible remedy in tort, allowing Malesko to allege negligence on the part of the CSC staff.

In both *Richardson* and, indirectly, in *Correctional Services Corporation*, we see the Supreme Court recognizing that private prison staff are not immune from litigation alleging constitutional violations. What the Court has not addressed is whether employees of a private prison operating under contract with a state or federal entity are acting under color of state law (allowing for a Section 1983 action) or federal law (allowing for a *Bivens* action). As to *Bivens*, the circuits are split.

The split we will discuss is in the Fourth and Ninth Circuits. Both cases involve federal inmates confined in private prisons (one in North Carolina, one in California). Both prisons are operated by the GEO Group under contract with the Federal Bureau of Prisons. Both cases involve medical issues and Eighth Amendment claims. In *Holly v. Scott,* 434 F.3d 287 (4th Cir. 2006), Holly argued that he received inadequate medical care for his diabetic condition. In *Pollard v. GEO Group, Inc.,* 607 F.3d 583 (9th Cir. 2010), Pollard was injured when he fell. He alleged that prison officials failed to provide timely and adequate medical and personal care (claiming that he was unable to feed or bathe himself), and that he was forced to return to his prison work assignment prior to an adequate period of recovery.

Lawsuits were filed by both Holly and Pollard, with each making Eighth Amendment claims against private prison employees at the inmate's institution. In each instance, the district court considered whether the inmate's suit should be dismissed for failure to state a claim. This is where the cases become more distinctive.

In *Holly,* the district court did not dismiss, finding that the inmate's claim met the three preconditions for a *Bivens* remedy as set out in the Fourth Circuit. The court held that Congress had not created an exclusive statutory remedy nor expressly barred money damages. As to the third precondition, the court found no special factors "counseling hesitation in the absence of affirmative action by Congress."

The appeals court reversed, saying there were two special factors warranting hesitation: first, that the defendants are private individuals, not government actors, and that their actions are not "'fairly attributable' to the federal government," and second, that the inmate had adequate remedies under state law for his alleged injuries. The court cited *Malesko*: "[t]he purpose of *Bivens* is to deter individual *federal* [court added emphasis] officers from committing constitutional violations." The court observed that *Bivens* is a judicially created remedy, not a legislative enactment like Section 1983. The court held that any extension of *Bivens* remedies into new contexts is better left to legislative determination.

In *Pollard,* the Magistrate Judge concluded a *Bivens* cause of action was not available to Pollard, finding that state law provided him with alternative remedies (tort action) and that GEO employees did not act under color of federal law. The district court adopted the Magistrate's recommendation that Pollard's suit be dismissed for failure to state a claim. The appeals court reversed, holding that *Bivens* "allows a federal prisoner to recover for violations of his constitutional rights by employees of private corporations operating federal prisons."[20]

Let's look at two examples of how, under very similar facts, the Fourth and Ninth Circuits came to opposite holdings. The first example involves whether the GEO Group is engaging in state action. The court in *Pollard* said yes, relying on the "public function" test—"a private entity may engage in state action where it exercises 'powers traditionally exclusively reserved to the State.'" The court held there was "no principled basis to distinguish the activities of the GEO employees... from the governmental action identified in *West*" (discussed earlier).

This statement directly conflicts with the holding in *Holly,* which said the relationship is very different "where the correctional facility is privately run, than in *West*... where the state itself was directly responsible for managing the prison." The court in *Holly* said, "The Supreme Court's analysis in *Richardson*... precludes argument that the operation of a prison is a traditionally exclusive state function."

A second distinction is whether the availability of a state law remedy alone precluded a *Bivens* cause of action. *Pollard* held that such action was not precluded, saying the issue has not been decided by the Supreme Court. The court in *Pollard* held it was necessary to consider "whether any alternative, existing process for protecting the interests amounts to a convincing reason for the Judicial Branch to refrain from providing a new and freestanding remedy in damages." The court further said that even in the absence of an alternative remedy, "federal courts must make the kind of remedial determination that is appropriate for a common-law tribunal, paying particular heed ... to any special factors counseling hesitation before authorizing a new kind of federal litigation."

The court of appeals in *Holly* had a different position. Pointing out that *Bivens* is a judicially created remedy, the court said that any extension of *Bivens* remedies into new contexts should be left to legislative determination, that "Congress has a greater ability to evaluate the broader ramifications of a remedial scheme by holding hearings and soliciting the views of all interested parties."[21]

With respect to private prisons, there also is one overriding question—does the government have the authority to contract away a government function? The ultimate answer, by U.S. Supreme Court decision, has not yet been given.[22]

Perhaps the most severe critic of privatization on a broad and legal front, Professor Ira Robbins, has concluded that contracting away functions probably can be legally supported on some levels but not on others.[23] The courts (including the Supreme Court) have usually upheld the delegation of authority by executive agencies at the federal and state levels. What is not allowed is the delegation of legislative or judicial functions. The management of individual correctional functions, such as food and health services, has been upheld legally. Some other functions that more directly affect the lives of inmates have also been upheld. States have commonly permitted private parties to perform law enforcement functions, such as in the case of private security police, and those functions have included the right to detain a person suspected of breaking the law (a shoplifter, for example). But then, a private citizen in the United States also has the right to perform a citizen's arrest. Confining persons in a jail or in a prison is a different matter, because it has been considered (in recent times, at least) to be a function for the government alone. This is an issue that will have to be litigated in each jurisdiction, but it can best be handled (legally) for now by having the legislature authorize the delegation of the function to private parties.

The delegation of rulemaking and decisions on inmate discipline are seen by Professor Robbins as very different matters, ones where the courts may say private contractors may not take over the government function (because they approach the nature of legislative and adjudicative functions). Private companies must be able to conduct routine activities concerning the management of inmates when they take over the running of an entire facility, such as record keeping, assigning inmates to housing and jobs, and scheduling activities (including visiting, recreation, work, and programs). Such routine functions, which must be done if any management of the inmate population is to be accomplished by the private company, would have to be accompanied also by the issuance of rules to cover them. These kinds of "routine" rules, Robbins predicts, will be upheld as a delegated function. When those rules cross over into the area of outlining the consequences for breaking the rules and exercising disciplinary authority, Robbins sees those as a more essential government function, because they entail adjudication of misconduct, they affect the terms to be served, and they embody strict constitutional standards of process.[24]

This whole area of the legality and constitutionality of private prisons and jails at the federal and the state levels is one that has only begun to be litigated. We agree that the provision of specialized services by contract, such as a food service department, does not present significant legal problems, as long as the jurisdiction has the legal authority (specifically found in statutes) to contract for such matters. Further, the contracting for lower security facilities and detention facilities is also defensible, again, as long as there is statutory authority to contract, the contracts are carefully drawn and monitored, and there is provision for disciplinary action to be taken (or at least supervised) by government corrections staff. Finally, we have serious reservations about the wisdom (although not necessarily the legality) of contracting with a private company to run a maximum security facility. We should work our way toward that step carefully, evaluating the performance of private companies in the lower security institutions. We should assess the ability of private corrections to perform at that lower level and move cautiously toward allowing private management of the highest level of institutions. This is necessary for the most important part of the mission of corrections: the protection of the public. Certain functions, such as inmate discipline and the use of deadly force, most often encountered at the higher level of security, should be kept under government regulation (government issuance of the rules) and probably government implementation to the extent possible. With time, private facility staff will gain more experience in dealing with inmates, and that experience will equip them better to deal with the more sophisticated inmates who are in the high-security prisons. Whether the Supreme Court will ultimately uphold the private operation of higher-security prisons remains an open question.

SUMMARY

- Privatization in corrections follows two paths: contracting for special services and programs (such as food services and health services), which is widely practiced and accepted and contracting for the building and operation of an entire correctional facility, which is of more recent vintage (since the 1980s) and is the focus of heated debate among corrections officials and commentators.
- Historically, the running of prisons and jails by private parties is a very old concept. In England, it goes back at least to the Middle Ages. Prison reformers argued for better conditions in jails and prisons in the 18th and 19th centuries, and improvements were achieved largely through legislation and the transition of all types of corrections facilities to management by state and local governments. It was only in the 1900s that we came to assume that corrections is, at all levels, a government function.
- There have always been exceptions to the government-only rule for corrections operations. Prisons and jails have been constructed, renovated, and expanded by private construction contracts. Some inmate services, especially in specialized health care, have been contracted to private organizations in many jurisdictions. Community facilities, especially halfway houses, have also been operated by private organizations.

- The main debate is over the operation by private companies of entire corrections facilities, jails, and prisons that confine sophisticated inmates in high-security surroundings. In recent years, a number of corporations have entered the corrections business, seeking to build (or remodel) and run jails and prisons.

- The private firms argued that, in a climate of heavy demand for prison and jail beds, they could get a facility running more quickly and at less expense than the government could. It is sometimes hard to get exact comparative figures, but studies do seem to support the claims that private companies can act faster than the government in getting new facilities into operation. What is open to more debate, and what needs more study and hard evidence, is whether the quality of operation provided by private companies is comparable to government operations. The quality of the staff is an extremely important factor and one that must be emphasized during the privatization process. The quality of all services and programs in a facility must be ensured, to the extent possible, by the terms of the private contract and by careful monitoring of the performance of the contract.

- As private firms move up the ladder into the operation of high-security institutions and the inmates under their supervision are more sophisticated, concerns about the abilities of private employees (and the underlying philosophical questions of what responsibilities in corrections should be turned over to them) increase. Of special concern are the questions of whether private-sector employees should be authorized to use deadly force, to take disciplinary actions that affect the freedom of inmates, and to issue rules for the management of inmates.

- Persons who provide services to inmates under contract are not immune from suits for constitutional violations (*West v. Atkins*). Officials and staff who run private prisons and jails may be sued for constitutional torts under 42 U.S.C. Section 1983, because they are operating under color of state law. They may also be sued for common law torts for injuries or losses caused by their wrongful actions.

- The Supreme Court has ruled that prison guards hired by a private firm are not entitled to qualified immunity from inmate suits charging a Section 1983 violation (*Richardson v. McKnight*). The Court has held that private firms operating under color of federal law are not subject to liability under *Bivens* suits (*Correctional Services Corporation v. Malesko*). What the Supreme Court has not yet addressed is whether employees of a private prison operating under contract with a state or federal entity are acting under color of state law (allowing for a Section 1983 action) or federal law (allowing for a *Bivens* action). Also, what has not been settled in the courts is the propriety of private firms running entire corrections facilities as a broad legal or constitutional question.

THINKING ABOUT IT

Should a private prison have direct responsibility for those actions that affect a person's loss of life, liberty, or property? For example, an inmate's loss of good time has the impact of extending his prison stay, and an inmate's disciplinary infraction may lead to placement in segregation.

KEY TERMS

penitentiary: In the United States, a place of imprisonment (historically, for those sentenced to terms of imprisonment with hard labor; more recently, for adults sentenced for felonies or for long terms). A penitentiary is a type of prison that historically dates back to a time when "penitence" (religious reflection) was the prime element of confinement of adult offenders, which was based on the Auburn, New York model. The name persists, usually in the titles of large facilities for high-security, long-term adult offenders.

privatization: The performance of governmental function by private enterprise (a nongovernmental person or corporation). The performance is arranged for by the government through contract or other agreement.

ENDNOTES

1. For a full review of the history of private jails and prisons, see *Punishment for Profit*, especially Chapter 2 (pages 19–44), "A Historical Review of Private Prisons." Shichor, D. *Punishment for Profit*. Thousand Oaks, CA: Sage Publications. 1995.
2. West, H., Sabol, W., and Greenman, S. *Prisoners in 2009*. Appendix Table 19. (Washington, DC: Bureau of Justice Statistics, U.S. Department of Justice, 2010.)
3. Austin, J. and Coventry, G. *Emerging Issues on Privatized Prisons*. Page 1. (Washington, DC: Bureau of Justice Assistance, U.S. Department of Justice, 2001
4. *The Continuing Fiscal Crisis in Corrections: Setting a New Course*. The Vera Institute of Justice. October 2010. Accessed February 25, 2011 from http://www.vera.org/content/continuing-fiscal-crisis-in-corrections. This report suggests that the fiscal crisis beginning in 2007 has motivated lawmakers to look at who is punished and how this is accomplished. Contributing to this reevaluation are the high recidivism rate, lower crime rates, and research reports examining how corrections may function more effectively at a lower financial cost. As stated in the VERA report (page 5): "State policy makers appear less inclined to be reflexively 'tough on crime.' Indeed, it is becoming more typical—if not expected—that policies are driven by the growing body of evidence about effective responses: a 'smart on crime' approach." In one instance, the report refers (on page 14) to "research and evidence suggesting that mandatory supervision and other prison alternatives are more effective and cost efficient for many lower-risk, nonviolent offenders."
5. One objection is that privatization allows prisons to be built without public agreement. Whereas the state has to seek voter approval for a construction bond for a publicly operated facility, the needed construction costs for a privately operated prison can be included in the state's prison operating budget. See endnote 3, page 15.
6. This is a serious threat to the financial profitability of the private corrections companies, because building and staffing a facility are expensive and must be amortized over a period of years. This short life of contracts, by the same token, is a spur to good contract performance for the benefit of the government.

7. This difficulty is compounded by ethical conflicts. In one instance, the State of Florida Commission on Ethics found that a college professor had violated Florida statutes by having "contractual relationships with private corrections companies, or companies related to the private corrections industry, which conflicted with his duty to objectively evaluate the corrections industry through his research with the University of Florida." As a result of its findings, the commission recommended a civil penalty of $20,000. In December 1999, the state governor issued Executive Order Number 99-318, imposing the $20,000 civil penalty. The order stipulated that the penalty could not be paid, or reimbursed, with public funds.

8. See endnote 3, page 37.

9. Two of the bigger companies involved in private corrections, Corrections Corporation of America (Accessed April 19, 2011 from http://www.cca.com) and the GEO Group, Inc. (Accessed April 19, 2011 from http://thegeogroupinc.com) each have an "investor" heading on their home page. The GEO Group home page also contains information on the current stock price. Each company's website provides information on its mission. The GEO group discusses this under the heading "Culture." It states, in part:

> All levels of government (federal, state and local) are being pressured to relieve prison over-crowding and by public opinion to impose longer sentences and resist early release programs based on insufficient bed space. Limited financial resources and resistance to tax increases compound this dilemma. The GEO Group, Inc. (GEO) and GEO Care offers privatized detention/correctional facilities as well as mental health and healthcare facilities as a viable solution.
>
> As a contractor in a competitive arena, GEO's cadre of corrections professionals is motivated to find cost effective and innovative approaches and also provide the highest quality service possible..."

The CCA website describes its mission as follows: "In partnership with government, we will provide a meaningful public service by operating the highest quality adult corrections company in the United States."

The reader may wish to compare these statements with those of government agencies (Departments of Corrections).

10. See endnote 3, pages 59–60.

11. *Department of Corrections—Prison Population Growth.* Phoenix, Arizona: Office of the Auditor General, State of Arizona. September 2010. Pages 19–21. This report notes that Arizona law requires the Department to consider contracting for private prisons. Title 41-1609.02, provides, in part:

> A. Before expanding an existing minimum or medium security level prison or before establishing a new minimum or medium security level prison, the director shall give consideration to contracting for private prisons for the incarceration of: [lists five categories, including female inmates and inmates over the age of 55].
>
> B. Before entering into a contract with a private prison facility contractor for the incarceration of prisoners listed in subsection A of this section, the director shall determine that the contractor will provide at least the same quality of services as this state at a lower cost or that the contractor will provide services superior in quality to those provided by this state at

essentially the same cost. In making this determination, the director shall consider the following: [lists 9 factors, among these being security, food service, inmate health services, and inmate discipline].

The complete language of § 41-1609.02 is available from <http://www.azleg.state.az.us/FormatDocument.asp?inDoc=/ars/41/01609-02.htm&Title=41&DocType=ARS. Accessed June 24, 2011.

12. Lundahl, B., Kunz, C., Brownell, C., Harris, N., and Van Vleet, R. "Prison Privatization: A Meta-analysis of Cost and Quantity of Confinement Indicators." *Research on Social Work Practice.* 19 (2009): 383–394. The study reported, on page 393, that the data reviewed "do not support a move toward privatization at this time. Similarly, the data do not clearly discourage privatization despite a slight advantage for publicly managed prisons in skills training." With respect to cost savings that may occur from privatizing prisons, the study found such savings were not guaranteed and "appear minimal."

13. Gaes, G. *Cost, Performance Studies Look at Prison Privatization.* (Washington, DC: National Institute of Justice, U.S. Department of Justice, 2008.)

14. See endnote 4. The report notes (on page 12) that as prison populations drop, the factors that make private prisons attractive as a means to solve prison overcrowding become less relevant. With respect to the decline in prison population, a December 2010 Bureau of Justice Statistics report, *Prisoners in 2009*, stated, on page 2, that 24 state departments of corrections reported a drop in prison population during 2009.

15. *Prisons for Profit—A look at prison privatization.* American Civil Liberties Union of Ohio. April 2011. Accessed April 21, 2011 from http://www.acluohio.org/issues/CriminalJustice/PrisonsForProfit2011_04.pdf. The ACLU, which does not support the proposed action to privatize state prisons, says its report "seeks to explore the many problems that plague prisons for profit, in the areas of fiscal efficiency, safety, contributions to the community, accountability and effect on recidivism."

16. See endnote 3, pages 16–17. A leading critic of privatized prisons, Professor Ira Robbins of the Washington College of Law, American University, asserts that "[b]y their very nature, private-incarceration companies are more interested in doing well than doing good." Robbins, I. "The Case Against the Prison-Industrial Complex." *Public Interest Law Reporter* (winter 1997): 44.

17. Stephan, J. *Census of State and Federal Correctional Facilities, 2005.* Appendix table 5. (Washington, DC: Bureau of Justice Statistics, U.S. Department of Justice, 2008.) Among its other findings is the following: about 90% of public correctional facilities and 60% of private correctional facilities offered academic and vocational training programs in 2005, and counseling programs were offered in nearly all public facilities and in about 75% of the private facilities. The inmate per correctional officer ratio was 5 to 1 in public correctional facilities and 6.9 to 1 in the private facilities. Excluded from this report were city, county, and regional jails, and private facilities that did not primarily hold state or federal inmates. Also not included were facilities for the military, U.S. Immigration and Customs Enforcement, Bureau of Indian Affairs, U.S. Marshals Service, and correctional hospital wards not operated by correctional authorities.

18. See endnote 3, page 16.

19. The Court cited *FDIC v. Meyer*, 510 U.S. 471 (1994), where it declined to extend a *Bivens* action to permit suit against a federal agency. The Court said that, if given a choice, a plaintiff would always sue a federal agency instead of a person, who could raise the affirmative defense of qualified immunity. Such a development was seen as resulting in the "evisceration of the *Bivens* remedy, rather than its extension."

20. In its decision, the Ninth Circuit in *Pollard* recognized that its holding directly conflicts not only with *Holly*, but also with *Alba v. Montford*, 517 F.3d 1249 (11th Cir. 2008). In *Alba*, the district court dismissed the inmate's complaint for failure to state a claim for relief under *Bivens* because he had adequate state remedies. The appeals court affirmed the decision of the district court.

21. Based on this split in the circuits, it was reasonable to expect that the Supreme Court would be asked to decide this issue, and that has occurred. In May 2011, the United States Supreme Court granted the petition for a writ of certiorari in *Pollard*, and the case (*Minneci v. Pollard*, 565 U.S. __ (2012)) was heard during the Supreme Court term beginning October 2011. The question presented was "[w]hether the Court should imply a cause of action under *Bivens* ... against individual employees of private companies that contract with the Federal government to provide prison services, where the plaintiff has adequate alternative remedies for the harm alleged and the defendants have no employment or contractual relationship with the government." In January 2012, the Court held that Pollard could not assert a *Bivens* claim, that his "Eighth Amendment claim focuses upon a kind of conduct that typically falls within the scope of traditional state tort law. And in the case of a privately employed defendant, state tort law provides an 'alternative, existing process' capable of protecting the constitutional interests at stake." The Court said, "the prisoner must seek a remedy under state tort law."

22. While the U.S. Supreme Court has yet to rule on this issue, in 2009, Israel's High Court of Justice ruled that privately run prisons are unconstitutional (*Academic Center of Law and Business v. Minister of Finance*). In its opinion, Israel's Supreme Court said (page 78), in part:

> When the state transfers the power to imprison someone, with the invasive powers that go with it, to a private corporation that operates on a profit-making basis, this action—both in practice and on an ethical and symbolic level—expresses a divestment of a significant part of the state's responsibility for the fate of the inmates, by exposing them to a violation of their rights by a private profit-making enterprise. This conduct of the state violates the human dignity of the inmates of a privately managed prison, since the public purposes that underlie their imprisonment and give it legitimacy are undermined, and, as described above, their imprisonment becomes a means for a private corporation to make a profit. This symbolic significance derives ... from the very existence of a private corporation that has been given powers to keep human beings behind bars while making a financial profit from their imprisonment ..."

23. Robbins, I. *The Legal Dimensions of Private Incarceration, Prisoners and the Law.* New York: Clark Boardman, 1989. I. Robbins, correspondence with author, June 9, 2003.

24. See endnote 23.

23 | Loss of Rights of Convicted Persons

No person convicted of a felony, or adjudicated in this or any other state to be mentally incompetent, shall be qualified to vote or hold office until restoration of civil rights or removal of disability.

Florida Constitution, Article VI, Section 4

No person is permitted to vote, serve as a juror, or hold any civil office who has, at any place, been convicted of a felony, and who has not been restored to the rights of citizenship, or who, at the time of such election, is confined in prison on conviction of a criminal offense.

Idaho Constitution, Article VI, Section 3

No person convicted of a felony, in any court within the United States, no person convicted in federal court of a crime designated, at the time of commission, under federal law as a misdemeanor involving a violation of public trust and no person convicted, in a court of a state, of a crime designated, at the time of commission, under the law of the state as a misdemeanor involving a violation of public trust shall be eligible to any office of trust, profit or honor in this state unless pardoned of the conviction.

Wisconsin Constitution, Article XIII, Section 3

Chapter Outline

- Background
- Bars to Employment and Other Impediments: *DeVeau v. Braisted*
- Voting Rights: *Richardson v. Ramirez; Hunter v. Underwood*
- Restoration of Rights

In this chapter, we will look at some of the restrictions that are placed on the rights of released offenders and the efforts that have been made in some places to remove many of those restrictions. Historically, there were times when persons convicted of serious (or "infamous") crimes were assumed to have forfeited all of their civil rights. After all, at one time in English history (particularly in the 17th and 18th centuries), most serious crimes carried the death penalty, and persons under sentence of death were presumed to have forfeited all of their rights—even to civilized treatment—while they were awaiting execution. The introduction of prisons was considered a highly enlightened advance over the widespread use of capital punishment.

By the 20th century, prison reforms advanced to the point where the principal purpose of incarceration was to rehabilitate the offender, to improve him to the point where he could function as a law-abiding citizen upon release. That penological philosophy, of course, assumed that virtually all offenders would be released from prison and that they would then be expected (from the positive and wonderful programs they had experienced in prison) to be productive citizens, avoiding all temptations to criminal conduct.

One of the things that stood in the way of those rehabilitative goals (idealistic as they always were) was the fact that, embedded in the laws of the country (and probably in the attitudes of most of its citizens), there were impediments to reentering society as an equal participant. Employment opportunities were especially a problem, and many other restrictions were also in place.

■ Background

More than 729,000 sentenced prisoners were released from state and federal jurisdiction during 2009. This is more than 20% higher than the approximately 605,000 sentenced prisoners released during the year ending December 31, 2000. More than 69% of the inmates released in 2009 were released under some form of supervision; the remainder, were released without supervision.[1] For these offenders, adjusting into mainstream American life without committing new crimes is a major challenge. Reducing recidivism is also a major goal of the judiciary, particularly during sentencing, when judges select the appropriate sentence for a convicted offender. It is also a major goal of the corrections professionals, whether they are probation or parole officers, community corrections staff, jail workers, or prison officials.

Many obstacles stand in the way of these offenders while they are adjusting to law-abiding life in the community. Some offenders have little education. Many of them have trouble finding decent jobs. Although, in some jurisdictions, there are resources to help released offenders find jobs (help may be available from probation and parole officers, other community corrections staff, private agencies, or individuals), many receive no help at all. Not only do they lack references of a good work history, their criminal records are held against them by many employers (even though this may be done very tacitly). Only a minority of offenders have an established home to return to (whether with a spouse, parents, or otherwise), so most must find housing on their own. Again, social service (welfare) agencies or other community organizations, governmental or private, may be of some help. But most offenders have been on their own.

Against these obstacles, which are well known and documented in the criminal justice field, it is not surprising that many offenders (more than 51%, according to a 2002 Bureau of Justice Statistics report[2]) are back in prison either serving time for a new prison sentence or for a technical release violation (e.g., failing a drug test; an arrest for a new crime) within three years of their release. A more recent study (the previous study looked at inmates released in 1994) examined the "three-year return-to-prison rates" for inmates released in 1999 and 2004 and included more than twice as many states (33 and 41 respectively) than the 1994 report (15 states). This study indicates that 45.4% of 1999 prison releasees and 43.3% of 2004 prison releasees were re-confined within three years of their release, either for a new crime or for violating their release conditions. The report states, "[i]f more than 4 out of 10 adult American offenders still return to prison within three years of their release, the system designed to deter them from continued criminal behavior clearly is falling short. That is an unhappy reality, not just for offenders, but for the safety of American communities."[3]

Efforts are being made to address these concerns. One significant example is the Second Chance Act of 2007. A stated purpose of this Act is to reduce criminal recidivism. Among the Act's other purposes are providing sufficient transitional services to offenders and providing offenders, while confined, with educational, literacy, vocational, and job placement services to help them upon reentry into the community.

Added to the impediments faced by released offenders are legal ones. In this chapter we will look at some of those legal restrictions on the rights of offenders following their convictions. As a general introduction, in the year 2000, the Office of the Pardon Attorney, United States Department of Justice, identified a number of the collateral consequences that federal law imposes on persons following a felony conviction.[4] These include the following:

- Ineligibility to vote in federal elections (determined by state law; for examples, see the opening quotations for this chapter). States may vary in their approach on this issue. The two ends of the spectrum—Vermont allows its prisoners to vote (see Title 17, Chapter 43, sections 2121 and 2122 of the Vermont Statutes), while in Kentucky, a person convicted of a felony is permanently ineligible to vote, unless they receive a pardon (see section 145 of the Kentucky Constitution).

- Ineligibility to serve on a federal jury; 28 U.S.C. § 1865(b) says "[the chief judge of the district court or other designated person specified in (b)] shall deem any person qualified to serve on...juries in the district court unless he....(5) has a charge pending against him for the commission of, or has been convicted in a State or Federal court of record of, a crime punishable by imprisonment for more than one year and his civil rights have not been restored."

- Possible loss of or ineligibility to hold federal office or employment (can depend on the type of position and the nature of the offender's crime); for example, the sentencing court may order disqualification from federal office when the person is convicted of bribing a public official or accepting a bribe (see 18 U.S.C. § 201(b)).

- Absent an exception being made, ineligibility to enlist in the military (10 U.S.C. § 504, discussed in the next section); loss of veterans benefits for mutiny, treason, sabotage, or rendering assistance to an enemy of the United States or of its allies (see 38 U.S.C. § 6104).

- Loss of federal firearms privileges; (18 U.S. C. § 922(g)(1) prohibits a person convicted in any court of a crime that has a punishment exceeding one year in prison "to ship or transport in interstate or foreign commerce, or possess in or affecting commerce, any firearm or ammunition; or to receive any firearm or ammunition which has been shipped or transported in interstate or foreign commerce."[5]

- Restrictions on occupation as a condition of probation (requires a "reasonably direct relationship" between a person's occupation, business, or profession, and the offense conduct; see 18 U.S.C. § 3563(b)(5)).

- Possible loss of or ineligibility to acquire a federal license (of different types) for particular convictions; for an example relating to a commercial motor vehicle operator's license, see 49 U.S.C. § 31310(b)(1)(C)—"using a commercial motor vehicle in committing a felony."

- For particular convictions (involving dishonesty, breach of trust, or money laundering), restrictions on being an "institution-affiliated party" (for example, a director, officer, employee, agent, or controlling stockholder) with respect to an insured depository institution (a bank or other financial institution); for an example, with respect to a person convicted of "any criminal offense involving dishonesty or a breach of trust or money laundering...", see 12 U.S.C. § 1829(a).

- Ineligibility to serve in various capacities relating to a labor organization or an employee benefits plan (for particular convictions); see 29 U.S.C. § 504, "Prohibition against certain persons holding office." Paragraph (a) says "[n]o person... who has been convicted of, or served any part of a prison term resulting from his conviction of, robbery, bribery, extortion, embezzlement,...[or] any felony involving abuse or misuse of such person's position or employment in a labor organization or employee benefit plan to seek or obtain an illegal gain at the expense of the members of the labor organization or the beneficiaries of the employee benefit plan,...shall serve or be permitted to serve—(1) as a consultant or adviser to any labor organization, (2) as an officer, director, trustee,... or representative in any capacity of any labor organization..."

- Restrictions on participating in certain federal contracts or programs; see 10 U.S.C. § 2408(a), which states, in part, "(a) PROHIBITION.—(1) An individual who is convicted of fraud or any other felony arising out of a contract with the Department of Defense shall be prohibited from...: (A) Working in a management or supervisory capacity on any defense contract or any first tier subcontract of a defense contract."

- Sexual offender registration and notification; every state has legislation that requires convicted sex offenders to provide their place(s) of residence to designated authorities.

- Restrictions on certain federal benefits; for example, a person is not eligible for federally assisted housing if subject to a lifetime registration under a state sexual offender registration program (see 42 U.S.C. § 13663). Other examples of federal benefits that may be affected relate to passports (see 22 U.S.C. § 2714) and to eligibility to receive food stamps or temporary assistance to needy families (see 21 U.S.C. § 862a).

- Possible ineligibility to enter the United States (for aliens convicted of crimes involving moral turpitude, see 8 U.S.C. § 1182(a)(2)(A)).

It is worth noting that some of the limitations or ineligibilities may be for a limited time. For example, the prohibitions in 29 U.S.C. § 504, relating to involvement in labor organizations and employee benefit plans, last for up to 13 years after conviction or after the end of such imprisonment. The statute discusses the means by which this period may be further reduced.

Of course, many states have similar types of restrictions on offenders' rights or even some additional ones. In the following sections, we will look at both federal and state law with respect to several types of disabilities.

■ Bars to Employment and Other Impediments: *DeVeau v. Braisted*

As noted above, there are statutes, federal and state, that bar offenders (usually felons) from holding certain kinds of jobs. Persons with felony records are generally barred from serving in the armed forces of the United States. Title 10, U.S. Code, Section 504, provides:

> **No person who is insane,... or who has been convicted of a felony, may be enlisted in any armed force.**

Exceptions can be made by the secretary (of any of the armed services) in "meritorious cases."

In *DeVeau v. Braisted,* 363 U.S. 144 (1960), the Supreme Court upheld a state law that prohibited a felon from serving as an officer of a waterfront labor union. New York had a statute that barred the collection of union dues from waterfront workers for any union that had an officer or agent who had been convicted of a felony (and had not been pardoned). This law was challenged, mainly on the ground that it conflicted with a federal law, the Labor–Management Reporting and Disclosure Act of 1959, which provided that no person who had been convicted of certain serious felonies could serve as a union official. The Supreme Court allowed the state law to stand and in its opinion noted:

> **Barring convicted felons from certain employments is a familiar legislative device to insure against corruption in specified, vital areas. Federal law has frequently and of old utilized this type of disqualification....[The Court noted the ban on enlistment into the armed forces.] A citizen is not competent to serve on federal grand or petit juries if he has been "convicted in a State or Federal court of record of a crime punishable by imprisonment for more than one year and his civil rights have not been restored by pardon or amnesty." 28 U.S.C. Sec. 1861. In addition, a large group of federal statutes disqualify persons "from holding any office of honor, trust, or profit under the United States" because of their conviction of certain crimes, generally involving official misconduct. [Citing numerous federal statutes.]**

Some states also have statutory or constitutional provisions that bar felons or persons convicted of certain offenses from holding public offices or from obtaining government jobs.

■ Voting Rights: *Richardson v. Ramirez; Hunter v. Underwood*

Three persons completed service of their prison sentences and paroles in California. They claimed that when the state denied them the right to vote because of their status as ex-felons, the state was denying them the equal protection of the laws that they were entitled to under the

Fourteenth Amendment. The Supreme Court of California agreed with them and found the ban on voting unconstitutional. The U.S. Supreme Court reversed that ruling in *Richardson v. Ramirez*, 418 U.S. 24 (1974).

The state constitution in California provided that, "[l]aws shall be made to exclude from voting persons convicted of bribery, perjury, forgery, malfeasance in office, or other high crimes." The California Elections Code required that an affidavit made at the time of registering to vote must show whether the prospective voter had been convicted of "a felony which disqualifies [him] from voting." The county clerk was authorized to cancel the registration of any voter who had been convicted of "any infamous crime or of the embezzlement or misappropriation of any public money." Other sections of the law allowed a voter to be challenged on the grounds that he was convicted of a felony or of the embezzlement or misappropriation of public money. State law did allow for the restoration of the right to vote to convicted persons by executive pardon or by judicial review.

The decision by the California Supreme Court, striking down the voting bans in the state laws, was based on other U.S. Supreme Court decisions that had held that there must be a compelling state interest in order to justify exclusion of a particular class from voting. The state supreme court had found no such state interest with regard to ex-felons. The U.S. Supreme Court disagreed. It relied primarily on little-used Section 2 of the Fourteenth Amendment. Section 2 provides that the right to vote for president and vice president, representatives in Congress, and all state officials shall not be abridged (or if it is abridged, there are penalties for doing so), "except for participation in rebellion, or other crime." Of course, the language in that amendment was adopted in the aftermath of the Civil War. Even considering that history, the Supreme Court said, in *Richardson*, that the language means just what it says: that participation in crime is a justifiable grounds for denying the franchise (the right to vote). Further, the Court noted that "29 states had provisions in their constitutions which prohibited, or authorized the legislature to prohibit, exercise of the franchise by persons convicted of felonies or infamous crime."

The justices of the U.S. Supreme Court recognized that they had been urged to endorse the more modern view, "that it is essential to the process of rehabilitating the ex-felon that he be returned to his role in society as a fully participating citizen when he has completed the serving of his term." They did not reject that notion. Rather, they pointed out that setting voting requirements, including the standards for registering voters, is the responsibility of the individual states. It is up to California, or any individual state, to decide whether it wants to adopt the "more enlightened" view that ex-felons should be allowed to vote, the Supreme Court said. Until that happened, it was not unconstitutional for a state, by its constitution or its statutes, to bar ex-felons from voting, the Supreme Court ruled.

A different result was reached by the U.S. Supreme Court in the case of *Hunter v. Underwood*, 471 U.S. 222 (1985). That case dealt with an Alabama constitutional provision that barred persons who had been convicted of a crime "involving moral turpitude" from voting. The history of that provision showed that it was adopted in 1901 in order to keep blacks from voting; it was believed (by the Alabama legislators) that more blacks than whites were convicted of such crimes. The Supreme Court struck down that provision in the Alabama constitution, because it was found to be a violation of the Equal Protection Clause of the Fourteenth Amendment. It was the discriminatory intent that was shown in adopting the voting clause, as well as its continuing discriminatory effect of excluding more blacks than whites, that led the Court to find it uncon-stitutional.[6]

Besides revoking voting rights, some states, by statute, bar convicted felons from serving on juries. For example, Chapter 9, Article I, Section 9.3 of the North Carolina General Statutes details such restrictions:

> All persons are qualified to serve as jurors and to be included on the jury list who are citizens of the State and residents of the county... who have not been convicted of a felony or pleaded guilty or nolo contendere to an indictment charging a felony (or if convicted of a felony or having pleaded guilty or nolo contendere to an indictment charging a felony have had their citizenship restored pursuant to law)....Persons not qualified under this section are subject to challenge for cause.

■ Restoration of Rights

Under the U.S. Constitution (Article II, Section 2), the president has power to grant pardons. The power to pardon is a very sweeping power. In the federal government, there is a pardon attorney, located in the Department of Justice, who receives applications for pardons from all over the country. After review, the pardon attorney makes recommendations to the president as to whether a pardon should be granted. A pardon discharges the offender from all aspects of the conviction (unless the pardoning authority places conditions or restrictions on the nature and extent of the pardon; legally, the pardoning authority can place restrictions of any kind on the grant of pardon). A pardon, therefore, usually acts to restore to the offender the right to vote, to serve on juries, and to hold public office.

Applications to the president are made with some frequency, but pardons are granted infrequently. For example, for the fiscal years covering the presidency of George W. Bush (2001–2009), 2,498 petitions for pardon were received, with 189 granted and 1,729 denied. For the first 28.5 months covering the presidency of Barack Obama (2009–2011), 708 petitions were received, with 17 petitions granted and 872 denied. (These numbers include pardon petitions carried over from the previous administration.) In addition to pardons, the pardoning authority (the president, for the federal government) also can grant commutations of sentences. Commutations are reductions in the terms of the sentence, without wiping out the conviction and sentence (wiping out or vacating the conviction and sentence usually happens with a pardon). During the presidency of George W. Bush, there were 8,576 petitions for commutation received in the Office of the Pardon Attorney, with 11 granted and 7,498 denied. During the first 28.5 months of the presidency of Barack Obama, 4,180 petitions for commutation were received, with none granted and 3,104 denied.[7]

In the states, the pardoning authority may be the governor of the state, or it may be a board of pardons or paroles. In the year 2001, 718 former and current inmates were pardoned in 20 jurisdictions. ("Former inmates" refers to those who were granted pardons after they were released from prison or after they had completed their paroles or their probation terms.) Executive clemency (this refers to releasing an inmate from incarceration) was granted to 1,000 inmates in 17 jurisdictions during the year 2001.[8] More recent examples include Minnesota, which granted 10 pardons in 2009 (compared to 7 in 2001) and Delaware, which granted 175 pardons in 2009.[9] Even though a person has been pardoned and his conviction and sentence have been legally vacated, the criminal behavior may still be taken into account in decisions about licensing for some occupations or professions. For example, embezzlement or other financial wrongdoing may be taken into account in deciding on public accountant licensing; likewise, violations of trust or "morally reprehensible" crimes may still be considered in licensing attorneys.

Some states have adopted statutes that operate to automatically restore the rights of convicted persons after they have satisfactorily completed their sentences or after a certain period of time elapses after they are released from their sentences. For example, Indiana Code § 3-7-13-4, *Disfranchisement of prisoners,* says that a person who is convicted of a crime and imprisoned following conviction is "deprived of the right of suffrage [vote]." Section 3-7-13-5, *Restoration of right to vote,* says that a person who is otherwise qualified to register [interestingly, this section doesn't say to vote] is eligible to register once the person is no longer imprisoned or subject to lawful detention. (In addition, section 3-7-13-6, *Disfranchisement of prisoners; exceptions,* provides the right to register and to vote to a person who is on probation, parole, subject to home detention, or in a community corrections program.)

These restoration-of-rights statutes serve to provide much of the same relief that pardons provide. Like pardons, the restoration of rights does not mean that all vestiges of the conviction are removed: licensing authorities for some fields may still consider the criminal record of the offender. It is always a tough, practical question as to how the offender who has been pardoned should answer when he is asked, on employment applications for example, whether he has ever been convicted. The best advice is for the offender to report the situation exactly as it is: he was convicted (on a certain date, for a certain offense) but he was pardoned for that offense, and his conviction and sentence were vacated (if that is the legal status in his case) on a certain date.

Other statutes provide that released offenders should not be discriminated against, either in their civil rights (such as voting) or in employment. An employment example is shown by Hawaii Revised Statute § 378-2.5(a), which provides that "an employer may inquire about and consider an individual's criminal conviction record concerning hiring, termination, or the terms, conditions, or privileges of employment; provided that the conviction record bears a rational relationship to the duties and responsibilities of the position." Paragraph (b) of § 378-2.5 says the inquiry into and consideration of the conviction records may occur *only* [emphasis added] after a conditional offer of employment has been made. Also, the Supreme Court, in *Schware v. Board of Bar Examiners,* 353 U.S. 232 (1957), has said that government employment for an ex-offender should not be denied unless there is a reasonable connection between the requirements of the job and the concerns over his particular criminal record.

There is a difficult question regarding whether ex-offenders should be employed in corrections agencies. Corrections officials do not agree on the answer. In fact, some agencies have employed ex-offenders in many different kinds of jobs. Probably the strongest concerns about their ability to work successfully would be in high-security facilities, and certainly in those facilities where the ex-offender had been recently confined. The nature of the offense and other information about the individual offender would enter into the hiring decision, and this would agree with the thinking of the Supreme Court in the *Schware* case. The same would be true with respect to different kinds of licensing: removal of license (or refusal to grant a new license) would be justified based on the nature of the work covered by the licensure and the criminal history of the offender. The constitutional protection in such circumstances is the due process clause; the equal protection clause may also be implicated.

As we have seen, juvenile records are generally sealed, and, indeed, in many places they are expunged after release from any juvenile commitment. (If the records are **expunged**, it means they may be sealed or destroyed, and they legally may not be referred to in any situation. If the records are **sealed**, it means that they will remain in existence, but they may not be accessed or referred to for any purpose absent specific authority, such as a court giving permission.) There has been some movement to provide for the sealing or expunging of adult criminal records. Some states have such provisions. There is a wide variation, however, as to how these provisions are applied. Some states apply sealing to probation records. An example is in Arkansas, where Ark. Code Ann. Sec. 16-93-303, paragraph (d) states "After successful completion of probation placed on the defendant under this section, a defendant is considered as not having a felony conviction except for...", listing five areas of exception, including a determination of habitual offender status, and for sentencing. (Ark. Code Ann. Sec. 16-90-902 states that following expungement of the person's record, she "shall have all privileges and rights restored.") Some apply sealing only to first-time, nonviolent offenders (for example, RI [Rhode Island] Gen. Laws Sec. 12-1.3-2(a)). Others authorize expunging for a misdemeanor with no other convictions or charges pending (for example, Okla. [Oklahoma] Stat. Ann., Title 22, Sec. 18, when at least 10 years have passed since the judgment was entered).

Appendix 7 contains a table showing the collateral consequences of a felony conviction in several areas: restoration of voting rights, for public employment, jury service, firearm ownership, and parental rights. The table also shows whether there is a registration requirement for convicted sex offenders.

The area of collateral consequences is receiving increased attention, which we believe is likely to continue. In 2009, the Uniform Law Commission[10] published the "Uniform Collateral Consequences of Conviction Act [UCCCA]." In summarizing the Act, the Commission states, in part:

> Concern about the impact of collateral consequences has grown in recent years as the numbers and complexity of these consequences have mushroomed and the U.S. prison population has grown. Collateral consequences are the legal disabilities that attach as an operation of law when an individual is convicted of a crime but are not part of the sentence for the crime. Examples of collateral consequences include the denial of government issued licenses or permits, ineligibility for public services and public programs, and the elimination or impairment of civil rights. There is a real concern on a societal level that collateral consequences may impose such harsh burdens on convicted persons that they will be unable to reintegrate into society.

> Indeed, the judge and lawyers in the case are frequently unaware of collateral consequences that will predictably have a substantial impact upon a defendant. Few jurisdictions provide a reliable way of avoiding or mitigating categorical restrictions based solely on conviction even years after the fact. Fewer still give decision-makers useful guidance in applying discretionary disqualifications on a case-by-case basis, or a measure of protection against liability. Jurisdictions are frequently at a loss about the effect to give relief granted by other jurisdictions.

The Uniform Collateral Consequences of Conviction Act, promulgated by the Uniform Law Commission in 2009, is an effort to improve public and individual understanding of the nature of this problem and to provide modest means by which people who suffer from these disabilities may, in appropriate circumstances, gain partial relief from those disabilities.[11]

The UCCCA, among other provisions, calls for the collection of a state's collateral consequences (both automatic bars and discretionary penalties) into a single document. The American Bar Association, by means of a National Institute of Justice grant, is in the process of categorizing the collateral consequences laws of each state for dissemination via publicly accessible website. This compilation will mark the first time this information is readily available. A second provision is that the Act, if implemented by the state, helps ensure that the defendant in a criminal case is aware of the collateral consequences, so she is better able to make an informed decision about how to proceed.

The UCCCA also provides a benefit to defense counsel, and, by implication, to a more efficient judicial process. In *Padilla v. Kentucky*, 559 U.S. ___ (2010), Padilla was a legal permanent resident of the United States and had been for more than 40 years. Following his arrest for drug distribution charges, Padilla pleaded guilty, a plea which made his deportation "virtually mandatory." Padilla claimed that his attorney did not advise him that by pleading guilty he faced the possibility of deportation. In fact, Padilla claimed that he was told that based on the period of time he had been in the United States, he did not need to worry about his immigration status. The Supreme Court of Kentucky denied Padilla postconviction relief, and held that "the Sixth Amendment's guarantee of effective assistance of counsel does not protect a criminal defendant from erroneous advice about deportation because it is merely a 'collateral' consequence of his conviction." The U.S. Supreme Court said it agreed with Padilla that constitutionally competent counsel would have advised him of the risk of deportation. The Court, however, said that whether Padilla was entitled to relief depended on whether he has been prejudiced. The Court remanded the case for further proceedings.

The UCCCA addresses two issues raised by *Padilla*. First, the Act helps ensure that counsel have a resource for identifying collateral consequences that may be faced by their clients. Second, although *Padilla* applies only to deportation, it is conceivable that courts in the future may extend the *Padilla* holding to other collateral consequences. This possibility was addressed in the concurring *Padilla* opinion: "criminal convictions can carry a wide variety of consequences other than conviction and sentencing, including … the loss of the right to vote, disqualification from public benefits, … and loss of business or professional licenses. … All of those consequences are 'seriou[s] …'"

SUMMARY

- The millions of offenders who are released into the community each year face many obstacles in reintegrating into mainstream community life. Finding housing and jobs upon release are immediate and universal problems. Discrimination against ex-offenders is prevalent in many areas.

- There are a number of collateral consequences that federal law imposes following a felony conviction. For example, there are laws that bar ex-felons from certain employment, such as in the armed forces or from serving as an officer of a waterfront labor union (*DeVeau v. Braisted*).
- Voting qualifications are, for the most part, left to the states. The Supreme Court upheld voting bans against ex-felons in California (*Richardson v. Ramirez*). An Alabama voting ban was disapproved, because the history of its enactment showed that it was used for racial disqualification, an impermissible purpose under the Constitution (*Hunter v. Underwood*).
- There are provisions in the U.S. Constitution and in the states for the restoration of rights to released offenders. The president (under the Constitution) and the governors (in most states) have the authority to grant pardons or commutations of sentences. Pardons usually act to wipe out all effects of convictions. Many states have also enacted laws that restore rights to many convicted persons, for certain offenses, upon release or after certain periods of time have elapsed without a new offense being committed.

THINKING ABOUT IT

From a legal perspective, consider the discretionary powers of the president in using his pardon authority. Do you think that there are any grounds under which Congress or the judiciary should or could place limitations on this presidential authority?

KEY TERMS

expunge: To seal or purge arrest, criminal, or juvenile record information.

seal (records): The removal, for the benefit of the individual, of arrest, criminal, or juvenile record information from routinely available status to a status requiring special procedures (usually approval by a judicial authority) for access.

ENDNOTES

1. West, H., Sabol, W., and Greenman, S. *Prisoners in 2009.* Appendix Tables 10 and 11. (Washington, DC: Bureau of Justice Statistics, U.S. Department of Justice, 2010.)
2. Langan, P. and Levin, D. *Recidivism of Prisoners Released in 1994.* Page 1. (Washington, DC: Bureau of Justice Statistics, U.S. Department of Justice, 2002.)

3. Pew Center on the States. *State of Recidivism: The Revolving Door of America's Prisons.* Pages 1–16. (Washington, DC: The Pew Charitable Trusts, 2011.) In its Executive Summary, the report speaks to economic forces and the other entities that have a role in recidivism:

> [A]s the nation's slumping economy continues to force states to do more with less, policy makers are asking tougher questions about corrections outcomes. One key element of that analysis is measuring recidivism, or the rate at which offenders return to prison. Prisons, of course, are not solely responsible for recidivism results. Parole and probation agencies, along with social service providers and community organizations, play a critical role.... This report seeks to elevate the public discussion about recidivism, prompting policy makers and the public to dig more deeply into the factors that impact rates of return to prison, and into effective strategies for reducing them.

4. *Federal Statutes Imposing Collateral Consequences Upon Conviction.* (Washington, DC: Office of the Pardon Attorney. United States Department of Justice, 2000.) This list is provided to give the reader a general idea of the type of civil disabilities that exist. For currency, your authors also reviewed relevant U.S. Code sections.

5. Title 18 U.S.C. § 922(g)(9) prohibits gun possession if a person has been convicted in any court of a misdemeanor crime of domestic violence. Law enforcement officers are not excluded from this provision, and such a conviction could impact the officer's future employment.

6. In *Farrakhan v. Gregoire*, 623 F.3d 990 (9th Cir. 2010) en banc, six minority citizens, including Farrakhan, claimed their loss of voting rights under Washington state's felon disenfranchisement law was a violation of section 2 of the Voting Rights Act (VRA), codified in 42 U.S.C. § 1973(a), resulting in a denial or abridgement of the right to vote based on race. No claim was made that the law was passed specifically to deny minorities the right to vote, nor that their convictions and subsequent disenfranchisement were based on intentional racial discrimination by the state's criminal justice system. Although the district court did find discrimination in the state's criminal justice system based on race, it held that this was only one factor in a section 2 (VRA) "totality of circumstances" analysis, and that other factors counterbalanced this evidence of racial disparities. Affirming the district court grant of summary judgment to the state defendants, the appeals court in its en banc per curiam opinion held that a "section 2 VRA challenge to a felon disenfranchisement law based on the operation of a state's criminal justice system must at least show that the criminal justice system is infected by *intentional* discrimination or that the felon disenfranchisement law was enacted with such intent."

7. *Clemency Statistics.* Washington, DC: Office of the Pardon Attorney, U.S. Department of Justice. Accessed June 25, 2011 from http://www.justice.gov/pardon/statistics.htm. Clemency petitions may carry over from one administration to the next administration.

8. Camp, C. G. *The 2002 Corrections Yearbook—Adult Corrections.* Page 68. (Middletown, CT: Criminal Justice Institute, 2003.)

9. *Minnesota Board of Pardons—Annual Report to the Legislature—2009 Activity.* (Saint Paul, MN: Minnesota Board of Pardons.) Also see *Delaware Statistical Information on Pardons/ Commutations 2000–2009.* (Dover, DE: Board of Pardons.)

10. The Uniform Law Commission (ULC), formerly known as the National Conference of Commissioners on Uniform State Law, has worked to advance uniformity of state law for more than a century. Originally created in 1892, the ULC assesses what areas of the law should be uniform from state to state, and drafts statutory text to propose for enactment by state legislatures. Commissioners are appointed from every state, the District of Columbia, the U.S. Virgin Islands, and Puerto Rico. The roster of commissioners includes state legislators, practitioners, judges, and law professors. Commissioners receive no salary or fees for their work with the ULC.

11. *Uniform Collateral Consequences of Conviction Act*. Uniform Law Commission. Accessed June 25, 2011 from http://www.law.upenn.edu/bll/archives/ulc/ucsada/2010final_amends. pdf. In August 2010, the American Bar Association approved the UCCCA as "an appropriate Act for those states desiring to adopt the specific substantive law suggested therein." As of early 2011, the UCCCA had been introduced in six states. The quoted material in the chapter is available from http://nccusl.org/ActSummary.aspx?title=Collateral Consequences of Conviction Act (accessed June 2, 2011).

24 | In Conclusion: A Postscript

Chapter Outline

- A History: Two Cases
- *Jones v. Wittenberg*
- *Morales v. Schmidt*
- Closing Comments

It is axiomatic that the law is an evolving, constantly changing, set of rules and principles. If the law is obtained from statutes, we know for certain that those laws can be amended, and they do change from one political generation to another. If the law is obtained from the courts—and that is the principal source of the law considered in this book—it too can shift from time to time or from place to place. The Supreme Court gives us most of what we have as a national set of legal rules and principles, but even that court can change its mind, overrule an earlier decision, or give us more "enlightenment" on what the law really is.

As we have seen, it is a basic premise from the Supreme Court that the Eighth Amendment concept of "cruel and unusual punishment" is a shifting standard, evolving along with changing (and presumptively improving) attitudes of the American public. This idea of evolving standards can be applied to other constitutional standards as well, though perhaps not as openly and not with Supreme Court assertion, as in the case of discussions of the Eighth Amendment. But it must be allowed that even the Constitution, our most solid base of legal authority and constancy, is open to different interpretations at different times by the Supreme Court, as the makeup of the Court changes by only a few justices, who bring very different views on some basic concepts and rulings. Or if the Supreme Court has not yet ruled on a question, or if its rulings are not crystal clear and broadly inclusive, the lower courts will give us differing interpretations of clauses in the Constitution. This has to be frustrating and sometimes confusing to many observers; but it does give a lot of work to lawyers!

All of this is done within the context of a legal system that relies heavily on the concept of **stare decisis.** It is the foundation of our common law that we rely on the value of precedent: If a court of controlling jurisdiction has spoken on a legal question and has given us the legal principles that control that question, then other courts will use that judicial ruling and will apply it in future cases that raise the same or a similar question. The rest of us, lawyers and nonlawyers alike, should be able to rely on the principle of "stare decisis": the decision has been made, so let it stand! This principle, as you can see, is in constant tension with the idea that the law is evolving and should be allowed to change. This state of tension means that we must turn to lawyers, who are trained to juggle these two concepts and to give us advice about what principles we can rely on, what questions have not been answered, which rulings are open to interpretation, and which law is likely to be changed.

A History: Two Cases

To further explore the idea of these shifting concepts of the law, let us present two court opinions that deal with leading corrections issues. Because they are about 40 years old, they give us some historical perspective of what courts were saying in those "olden times." They were considered, for many years and by many professors, judges, and corrections attorneys, as enlightened, persuasive rulings on difficult questions of prison and jail management. Not until the Supreme Court spoke on these questions, which these lower courts had addressed, did we find out how wrong they were![1]

Jones v. Wittenberg

The case of *Jones v. Wittenberg*, 323 F.Supp. 93 (N.D. Ohio 1971), dealt with numerous complaints about the conditions in the Lucas County, Ohio jail. The lawsuit was brought under Section 1983, alleging constitutional violations, and also under Title 28, U.S. Code, Section 2201, seeking declaratory judgment (a ruling as to the rights and duties of the parties); it was a class action suit, on behalf of all inmates at the jail. The U.S. district judge, in his published opinion, described many poor conditions and deficiencies at the jail. These included poor sanitary conditions, poor ventilation and lighting, inadequate food and clothing, crowded conditions in cells and in visiting areas, inadequate staff supervision, minimal medical coverage, and inmate discipline without notice or hearings. Expert witnesses presented by the plaintiffs testified that the jail was "outstandingly bad from every standpoint." The court reviewed what case law guidance there was at the time, including references to cases that cautioned that courts should be reluctant to interfere with the administration of detention facilities. (This was a passing reference to the old "hands-off" doctrine, which was virtually abandoned by this time, in 1971.)

The court in *Jones* noted that it would not refrain from dealing with allegations of constitutional violations (that is, it would not keep its hands off "vital issues of civil rights"). The court then observed that there were two classes of inmates at the Lucas County Jail: prisoners serving sentences and pretrial detainees. For the sentenced prisoners, the question was whether their treatment violated the Eighth Amendment—whether it amounted to cruel and unusual punishment. How the court was going to come out on that question was predicted by the (what shall we say?) vigor with which it described the conditions at the jail and by the following paragraph of "legal" discussion: "The official policy of the State of Ohio is that the standards of punishment which prevailed in medieval times are to be followed in dealing with those convicted of crimes. Insofar as possible, they are to be removed to remote places and confined in harsh and forbidding prisons. In constructing its newest prison facility, the State selected one of its more sparsely populated areas as a site, and a medieval French prison as the basic model for the building." (This discussion, in a case involving the Lucas County Jail, located in downtown Toledo!) With this as a preface, it was no surprise that the court concluded that the sentenced prisoners were being cruelly and unusually punished: "The cruelty is a refined sort, much more comparable to the Chinese water torture than to such crudities as breaking on the wheel."

The case, being a conditions-of-jail case, is better known for its ruling on the second category of inmates, the pretrial detainees. With respect to them, the court said, "they are not to be subjected to any hardship except those absolutely requisite for the purpose of confinement only, and they retain all the rights of an ordinary citizen except the right to go and come as they please." Using that standard, their treatment at the jail denied them the equal protection of the laws. (The court also said they were being punished "without any semblance of due process or fair treatment." That statement correctly anticipated the standard of *Bell v. Wolfish*, 441 U.S. 520 (1979), but this court in *Jones* seemed to rely more on the equal protection clause than the due process clause.) And what was the class of persons to whom the jail detainees were similarly situated for the purposes of "equal protection"? It was "ordinary citizens," the people of the free world, those in the outside community. (It is hard to think of any two classes of persons who are much more dissimilarly situated, for legal and practical analysis.) The court arrived at that conclusion because the jail inmates "are only in jail awaiting trial, and are, according to our law, presumed to be innocent of any wrongdoing."

These conclusions did not just affect the inmates, the staff, and the administrators of the Lucas County Jail. The words of the court in *Jones* were often quoted in articles analyzing the legal rights of jail inmates. In addition, the legal standards of *Jones* were adopted by judges in other parts of the country, who wanted to remedy the bad conditions they found in their local jails.

■ *Morales v. Schmidt*

The second case is *Morales v. Schmidt*, 340 F.Supp. 544 (W.D. Wis. 1972). The question in *Morales* was a fairly narrow one, although it was one of the first federal rulings on the important First Amendment issue of prisoner mail. Morales was an inmate in the Wisconsin State Prison. His wife's sister was on his mailing list, and he wrote a letter to her. A prison social worker read the outgoing letter and never mailed it. Some time later, the name of the sister-in-law was removed from Morales's list of approved correspondents.

Morales sued, claiming violation of his constitutional right to free speech. (This case was decided, of course, before the Supreme Court's first guidance on inmate correspondence in *Procunier v. Martinez*, 416 U.S. 396 (1974), and long before the further guidance of *Turner v. Safley*, 482 U.S. 78 (1987), and *Thornburgh v. Abbott*, 490 U.S. 401 (1989).) Prison officials justified interference with this correspondence on the grounds that they had discovered, after the disputed letter was read, that Morales was the father of an illegitimate child born to his sister-in-law, that he was then, and he remained, married to his wife Sandra (who was unaware that her husband was the father of her sister's child), and that Morales wanted to continue his illicit relationship with Sandra's sister. The prison authorities removed the sister-in-law from Morales's correspondence list because they believed he should not be permitted to correspond with the woman with whom he had the illicit sexual relationship (which he apparently wished to continue).

The federal district judge in *Morales* noted that there was (by 1972) "a flood of constitutional lawsuits by prisoners." This flood of suits had heavily burdened correctional authorities, as well as the federal courts. The court observed also the language from the Supreme Court decision in *Price v. Johnston*, 334 U.S. 266 (1948), which had been for many years the absolute foundation of many court actions dismissing prisoner suits: "Lawful incarceration brings about the necessary withdrawal or limitation of many privileges and rights, a retraction justified by the considerations underlying our penal system." The court in *Morales* also noted an even more rigid warning from the Supreme Court: "[I]t is not the function of the courts to superintend the treatment and discipline of prisoners in penitentiaries, but only to deliver from imprisonment those who are illegally confined." This statement was made in *Stroud v. Swope*, 187 F.2d 850 (9th Cir. 1951). But why did the court even refer to those cases advising deference to prison administrators and a "hands-off" attitude? This judge was not about to hold back from his review of claims by inmates of constitutional violations. And this was true, even though the court observed that there was virtually no guidance from other courts about what the rights of a prisoner were in this context.

The opinion in *Morales* may be most noteworthy for this language: "With respect to the intrinsic importance of the challenges, I am persuaded that the institution of prison probably must end. In many respects it is as intolerable within the United States as was the institution of slavery, equally brutalizing to all involved, equally toxic to the social system, equally subversive of the brotherhood of man, even more costly by some standards, and probably less rational." (Oh my. Well, with that sermon delivered, it may not be hard to guess how this judge decided this case—and, indeed, on which side he came down on most prison cases.)

The district judge's legal analysis of the correspondence rights of Morales was as follows: "[T]hose convicted of crime should continue to share with the general population the full latent protection of the Fourteenth Amendment." That protection would be equal protection of the laws and due process. But are prisoners to have unfettered access to the mails, under the First Amendment? And what of prison officials' concerns about security or other governmental interests? This court said, "I conclude that freedom to use the mails is a First Amendment freedom.... [A] member of the general population would be free to correspond by mail with his wife's sister [without regard to the 'illicit' circumstances present in this case].... [E]ach individual's interest in corresponding by mail with another is fairly to be characterized as a 'fundamental' interest. [If the government wants to deny this freedom to an inmate], the burden is upon the defendant [prison official] to show a compelling governmental interest in this differential in treatment."

Applying these standards to this case, the court concluded that the government's interest in banning this correspondence (and thereby "diminishing the likelihood of such future unlawful sexual activity by one convicted of a past crime") was not a compelling one. Denying Morales the opportunity to correspond with his sister-in-law was a deprivation of his rights under the First and the Fourteenth Amendments. Prison officials were enjoined from continuing the ban on that correspondence.[2]

Closing Comments

From these cases, the following points may be made: (1) The cases were well-written and were frequently quoted by others. Their influence was more than that of an ordinary district court ruling, which would be legally conclusive only in that court's home district. (2) The cases are strong examples of the principle, cynical as it may be, that judges decide cases according to their gut reactions to the facts they hear. Sometimes, they do not even hear the facts of the case before them. Sometimes, they have heard of conditions (in the local jail or in a nearby prison) from various sources—the media, attorneys, law clerks, or others around the courthouse, classes or seminars they have attended, or even comments from friends and acquaintances at social gatherings.

The point is, much as we insist on the principle that judges come to cases unbiased and without preconceptions about the outcome, the fact is that that principle is often not true. It especially is not true in many (if not most) prison and jail cases. These two highly influential cases, *Jones* and *Morales,* are very instructive on this point, because the judges said more than they needed to. They showed us quite clearly in their language their bias on the nature of jails and prisons. Of course, judges can be slanted as much to the other (government) side as these two judges seemed to be slanted to the inmates' side.

(3) The district judges in these two cases were not evil men or bad judges. Neither were they saints (as one of the authors heard some prisoner advocates refer to them) or great judges. Judges are human beings. Federal judges are sometimes considered, on overall assessment, to be the best of the lot. One of your authors knew the judge on the *Morales* case, Judge Doyle, personally; he was a fine man, a respected jurist, and an extremely careful and sensitive judge (perhaps too sensitive, as seen in the *Morales* case language, to deal realistically with criminal justice matters). Much as we would like to have our cases heard by judges who are absolutely impartial, who come to the case without any preconceptions, such ideal situations are, unfortunately, the exception more often than the rule.

After this discussion of these two corrections decisions, we come back to the point underlying this summary: do not think of "corrections law" as being a set of fixed rules. The Supreme Court gave us, in *Bell v. Wolfish* (for *Jones v. Wittenberg*) and in *Procunier v. Martinez, Turner v. Safley*, and *Thornburgh v. Abbott* (for *Morales v. Schmidt),* principles of constitutional interpretation that totally rejected the legal analyses and conclusions of those two federal district court judges. From *Bell,* we know for certain that jail inmates do not have all the rights of free citizens, except the right to come and go as they please (the concept underlying the *Jones* ruling). In addition, the Supreme Court flatly rejected the idea that the presumption of innocence for detainees had anything at all to do with evaluating the conditions of the jail where they were held. From *Turner* and *Thornburgh* we know that to restrict inmate correspondence there need be only a reasonable relationship to a legitimate government purpose (not a compelling government interest). (Judge Doyle's comparison of "the institution of prison" to slavery and prediction of its necessary end is interesting commentary but hardly sound legal or political principle, at least for the foreseeable future.)

The Supreme Court, in *Rhodes v. Chapman*, 452 U.S. 337 (1981), made the optimistic observation that the standards for interpreting the Constitution (in that case, specifically the Eighth Amendment) reflect the progress that is made in a maturing society. If viewed from a broad historical perspective, we can see that conditions in prisons have drastically changed over the decades. To some extent, improvements in prisons and jails can be attributed to the involvement of the courts in constantly assessing the conditions and programs in those facilities, pursuant to constitutional (and American society's) expectations. We have to continue with that optimism— that our society, as it matures, will produce prisons that are more civilized and decent.

Like it or not, the law is in constant flux. What you have in this book are three aspects of the law in its current state: (1) an identification of the issues that, from a legal standpoint, are the most challenging to the field of corrections; (2) a presentation of those legal principles that are the firmest, best guidance we have right now—the decisions of the Supreme Court and some controlling statutes (and even some treaties); and (3) some discussion of the lower court decisions, where the Supreme Court has not yet ruled. With those in mind, you will be equipped, it is hoped, to understand the current status of "corrections law." Just stay tuned for those changes and new rulings, which are sure to come!

KEY TERMS

stare decisis: Literally, to stand by decisions. This is the legal doctrine that courts will adhere to principles settled by court decisions in other cases in which the facts are substantially the same. It is a strong judicial policy that a point of law that is determined in a court will be followed by that court, or a court of lower rank, in a later case that presents the same legal question.

ENDNOTES

1. One of your authors has been involved in the development of correctional litigation since the early 1960s. Here is his "confession": It is true that I present these cases with a particular bias—that of a corrections attorney who was dismayed at the time by the mistaken assumptions and the legal approaches of these cases. Every author on corrections matters writes with some bias, based on her experience and the ideas she has about the purposes of corrections, the role of corrections staff, and the inherent status of prisoners. Every corrections lawyer (whether prisoner advocate, law professor, or government attorney) also approaches his work and his writing with bias, although precious few have ever admitted, or tried to describe, that bias in their writing. Here is my bias: I came into the corrections field in 1962, because of my interest in criminal justice matters broadly, and in prisoners' rights (more exactly, just how prisoners were treated) specifically. Over time, I became more and more informed about the demands of good prison management and the very difficult problems of working with prisoners. Of course, I also had some personal ideas about the role of the law: I thought the courts were right to tackle serious questions of constitutional rights, but I was appalled by the readiness of some judges to jump in and manage matters where they had no expert background (and, in my view, no legal business) to be intruding. For a fuller presentation of my view on activist judges, see C. Cripe, "Court, Corrections, and the Constitution: A Practitioner's View," in *Courts, Corrections, and the Constitution*, ed. J. J. DiIulio, Jr. (New York: Oxford University Press, 1990).
2. On appeal, *Morales* was reversed and remanded. The appeals court said the state was not required to show a compelling interest to justify its restriction on correspondence, but only had to show a reasonable and necessary relationship towards achieving a justified purpose of confinement. *Morales v. Schmidt*, 494 F.2d 85 (7th Cir. 1974).

Appendix 1

Sample Presentence Investigation Report

THADDEUS SMITH

Source: Administrative Office of the U.S. Courts. *The Presentence Investigation Report.* Available from http://www.fd.org/pdf_lib/publication%20107.pdf.

IN UNITED STATES DISTRICT COURT
FOR THE WESTERN DISTRICT OF ATLANTIS

UNITED STATES OF AMERICA	)	
	)	
VS.	)	PRESENTENCE INVESTIGATION REPORT
Thaddeus Smith	)	**Docket No.** CR 05-001-01-KGG

Prepared for: The Honorable Kelly G. Green
U.S. District Judge

Prepared by: Craig T. Doe
U.S. Probation Officer
Breaker Bay, Atlantis
(123) 111-1111

Assistant U.S. Attorney
Mr. Robert Prosecutor
United States Courthouse
Breaker Bay, Atlantis
(123) 111-1212

Defense Counsel
Mr. Arthur Goodfellow
737 North 7th Street
Breaker Bay, Atlantis
(123) 111-1313

Sentence Date: February 22, 2006

Offense: Count One: Bank Robbery (18 U.S.C. § 2113(a)) - 20 years/$308,270 fine

Count Two: Simple Possession of Cocaine (21 U.S.C. § 844(a)) - 15 days to 2 years/$250,000

Release Status: Detained without bail since 11/21/05

Detainers: Atlantis Parole Authority - Parole violation
Breaker Bay Municipal Court - Drunk Driving

Codefendants: Simon Brown - CR 005 - 0001-02-KGG
Veronica Pond - CR 005 - 0001-03-KGG

Related Cases: None

Date Report Prepared: 1/31/2006   **Date Report Revised:** 02/15/2006

Identifying Data:

Date of Birth:	3/15/1975
Age:	30
Race:	White
Sex:	Male
S.S. #:	111-11-1111
FBI #:	444-44-44B
USM #:	11111-111
Other ID #:	Not applicable
Education:	Vocational Degree
Dependents:	None
Citizenship:	U.S.
Legal Address:	111 Fifth St. #2B
	Breaker Bay, AT 99993

Optional Photograph

Aliases: None

Restrictions on Use and Redisclosure of Presentence Investigation Report. Disclosure of this presentence investigation report to the Federal Bureau of Prisons and rediscosure by the Bureau of Prisons is authorized by the United States District Court solely to assist administering the offender's prison sentence (*i.e.*, classification, designation, programming, sentence calculation, pre-release planning, escape apprehension, prison disturbance response, sentence commutation, or pardon) and other limited purposes, including deportation proceedings and federal investigations directly related to terrorist activities. If this presentence investigation report is rediscosed by the Federal Bureau of Prisons upon completion of its sentence administration function, the report must be returned to the Federal Bureau of Prisons or destroyed. It is the policy of the federal judiciary and the Department of Justice that further rediscosure of the presentence investigation report is prohibited without the consent of the sentencing judge.

PART A. THE OFFENSE

Charge(s) and Conviction(s)

1. Thaddeus Smith and codefendants Simon Brown and Veronica Pond were named in a five-count indictment filed by a Western District of Atlantis grand jury on November 30, 2005. Count One charges that from November 10, 2005 until November 18, 2005, the above-named defendants conspired to commit bank robbery, in violation of 18 U.S.C. § 2113(a) and 18 U.S.C. § 371. Count Two charges that on November 18, 2005, Smith, while armed with a revolver, robbed the Atlantis Credit Union, in violation of 18 U.S.C. § 2113(a). Count Three charges that on November 18, 2005, Smith used a firearm in a crime of violence, in violation of 18 U.S.C. § 924(c). Count Four charges that on November 21, 2005, he possessed with intent to distribute a controlled substance (cocaine), in violation of 21 U.S.C. § 841 (a)(1), and Count Five charges that on November 18, 2005, the defendant robbed the Williams Bank, in violation of 18 U.S.C. § 2113(a).

2. On December 7, 2005, in accordance with the terms of a written plea agreement, Thaddeus Smith pled guilty to a two-count Superceding Information, charging him with armed bank robbery, in violation of 18 U.S.C. § 2113 (a), and simple possession of cocaine, in violation of 21 U.S.C. § 844(a). The U.S. Attorney has filed an information charging Smith with a prior drug conviction, enhancing the penalty for this offense, in accordance with 21 U.S.C. § 851. The terms of the plea agreement call for the dismissal of the original Indictment. Codefendant Brown pled guilty to a one-count Superceding Information charging bank robbery, in violation of 18 U.S.C. § 2113(a). Codefendant Pond pled guilty to a one-count Superceding Information, charging simple possession of cocaine, in violation of 21 U.S.C. § 844(a). All of the defendants are scheduled to be sentenced on February 22, 2006.

The Offense Conduct

3. On November 10, 2005, Thaddeus Smith met with Simon Brown and Brown's girlfriend, Veronica Pond, at a bar in Breaker Bay. While at the bar, Smith discussed his plans of robbing the Atlantis Credit Union, located at 1948 Edgewater Street, Breaker Bay, Atlantis. Smith explained he had learned that on the following Friday, November 18, 2005, the credit union would have extra money in the safe to cash payroll checks and he planned to rob it on that date. To establish an alibi, Smith told Brown and Pond that he planned to leave the area for several days to visit relatives in a neighboring state, but would return to Breaker Bay early Friday morning, rob the credit union, and fly back to his relatives' residence before he was missed. He planned to travel using an alias to further avoid apprehension. Brown and Pond agreed to steal two getaway vehicles for Smith and to assist him in the robbery. Smith gave the couple a .357 magnum revolver, which he told them he had stolen from a friend's cabin, and asked them to leave it in the trunk of the getaway car. Smith promised to pay Brown and Pond $500 each for their help.

4. On November 14, 2001, Brown and Pond stole a 2001 sedan from a Chevrolet dealership in Surf City and, the following day, the couple stole a 1999 Ford truck from an apartment

complex in Surf City. On November 18, 2005, Brown picked Smith up at the airport in the Chevrolet and drove to a nearby shopping mall where Pond was waiting in the Ford. Brown told Pond to wait while he and Smith drove to the credit union.

5. Before the credit union opened, Smith, disguised with a wig and mustache, and Brown approached Patty Martinez, a teller, as she was exiting her vehicle. Armed with a revolver, Smith grabbed the teller's arm and escorted her to the rear door of the credit union. Ordering the teller to pretend that she was alone, Brown told her to knock on the door to the credit union. The teller complied and the manager opened the door. The defendants then forced them back inside, and, while pointing the revolver at two other employees, herded them into a corner near the vault.

6. Smith ordered the manager to open the vault and place five bags of cash into a duffle bag carried by Brown. Smith then directed the employees to the back of the credit union, ordered them to lie on the floor, placed his revolver inside his coat, and the two fled the credit union. Smith and Brown proceeded to the Chevrolet and immediately drove toward the shopping mall where Pond was waiting. En route, Smith threw the revolver into a vacant lot, later stating that he hoped some kid would find it, get caught, and be blamed for the robbery.

7. Smith and Brown abandoned the Chevrolet in the parking lot and left with Pond in the stolen Ford. While traveling to the airport, Smith changed his shirt and shoes, and threw them, along with his disguise, into a dumpster. As Smith began to count the money, Pond was shocked that over $100,000 had been stolen and demanded $5,000 for herself and Brown. Smith became angry and threatened to keep all of the money if they continued to complain. At the airport, Smith gave Brown and Pond a total of $1,000, and a small packet of cocaine as a bonus. Smith then left the couple and flew back to his relatives' residence that afternoon.

8. As Brown and Pond were driving home in the stolen Ford, they were stopped by the police for a routine traffic violation. When the police officer discovered the truck was stolen, Brown and Pond were placed under arrest. Brown and Pond each admitted their involvement in the offense and, during questioning, implicated Smith.

9. On November 21, 2001, Smith was arrested by federal agents at his relatives' home. The agents seized $78,690, along with 56 grams of cocaine, from Smith's suitcase. A subsequent laboratory analysis found the seized cocaine to be 64 percent pure. The revolver used by Smith in the robbery has not been recovered but was believed to be a .357 Smith & Wesson. Local police have no record of a theft of such a weapon on file. According to Smith, he purchased the weapon from an unknown individual at a gun show held at the Breaker Bay High School in October 2001.

10. Smith is the most culpable defendant in this case. Smith recruited his codefendants, Brown and Pond, and directed their activities in this offense. In addition, Smith compensated his codefendants for their participation in the offense with a small share of the bank robbery proceeds.

Victim Impact

11. The Atlantis Credit Union is the primary victim in this offense and sustained direct financial losses totaling $128,135. The credit union has recovered $78,690 seized from Smith at the time of his arrest, leaving a net loss of $49,445. According to credit union officials, Apex Insurance Company has reimbursed the credit union, except for a $5,000 deductible. In addition, the credit union paid a total of $900 for Ms. Martinez to receive 12 hours of psychological counseling.

12. Three tellers and the credit union manager are also victims in this offense. The tellers and the manager were interviewed by the probation officer and provided the following information.

13. Patty Martinez was the teller approached by Smith as she left her car in the credit union parking lot. While she was not physically injured, she was reportedly emotionally traumatized by the defendant's conduct. With her consent, the credit union arranged for Martinez to receive private psychological counseling. After 12 sessions, Martinez states that she began improving, and was able to sleep at night without nightmares and felt more comfortable at work. Nevertheless, Martinez decided to resign from the credit union, due in part to the offense, and has now returned to college to pursue her education.

14. The branch manager and the other two tellers inside the credit union stated that they were not physically injured by the defendant, but each expressed anger toward Smith for assaulting them. Each employee expressed experiences of being startled by strangers who entered the credit union, but the employees do not believe they are in need of professional counseling or treatment.

15. The two stolen vehicles in this case have been recovered without damages. A representative from the Chevrolet dealership was contacted and interviewed by the probation officer and advised that he has subsequently sold the sedan for $14,000. Similarly, the owner of the Ford truck reported no losses or expenses related to the theft of the truck.

Adjustment for Obstruction of Justice

16. The probation officer has no information to suggest that the defendant impeded or obstructed justice.

Adjustment for Acceptance of Responsibility

17. Shortly after his arrest, Smith made voluntary and candid admissions to the authorities concerning his involvement in this offense, including his recruitment of Brown and Pond to help him execute the robbery scheme. Smith also acknowledged using a weapon during the robbery, which he purchased from an unknown individual at a gun show. In addition, Smith admitted his possession of cocaine at the time of his arrest, explaining that he had purchased the narcotics with money stolen from the robbery. The defendant freely admitted his guilt in court at the time of his plea and appears to fully accept responsibility for his

conduct. During his interview with the probation officer, Smith explained that he committed this offense at the prospect of quick and easy financial gains, and expressed remorse for assaulting the credit union employees.

Offense Level Computation

18. The 2005 edition of the Guidelines Manual has been used in this case. Pursuant to the provisions found in USSG §3D1.1(a)(3), Counts One and Two are unrelated offenses and are treated separately.

Count One—Armed Bank Robbery

19. **Base Offense Level:** The guideline for an 18 U.S.C. § 2113(a) offense is found in USSG §2B3.1, which states that robbery has a base offense level of 20.   20

20. **Specific Offense Characteristic:** Pursuant to USSG §2B3.1(b)(1), because the property of a financial institution was taken, the offense level is increased by two levels.   +2

21. **Specific Offense Characteristic:** Pursuant to USSG §2B3.1(b)(2)(C), because a gun was possessed and brandished during the commission of this offense, the offense level is increased five levels.   +5

22. **Specific Offense Characteristic:** In preparation for this offense, Smith directed Brown and Pond to steal two vehicles, valued at a total of $26,000. Smith stole $128,135 from the credit union; thus the total loss attributable to this offense is $154,135. According to the provisions in USSG §2B3.1(b)(7)(C), the offense level is increased by two levels in accordance with the overall loss in this offense.   +2

23. **Victim-Related Adjustments:** None.   0

24. **Adjustment for Role in the Offense:** Smith was the organizer and leader in this offense. He provided instructions and directives to his codefendants and compensated them for their participation in this offense. In accordance with the provisions found in USSG §3B1.1(c), a two-level increase is recommended.   +2

25. **Adjustment for Obstruction of Justice:** None.   0

26. **Adjusted Offense Level (Subtotal):**   31

Count Two—Possession of Cocaine

27. **Base Offense Level:** The guideline for a 21 U.S.C. § 844(a) offense is found in USSG § 2D2.1(a)(2), which provides that the base offense level for the unlawful possession of cocaine is six.   6

28. **Specific Offense Characteristic:** None   0

29. **Victim-Related Adjustments:** None.   0

30. **Adjustment for Role in the Offense:** None.   0

31. **Adjustment for Obstruction of Justice:** None.   0

32. **Adjusted Offense Level (Subtotal):**   6

    Multiple-Count Adjustment (See USSG § 3D1.4)

		Units	
33. Adjusted Offense Level for Count One	31	1	
34. Adjusted Offense Level for Count Two	6	0	
35. Total Number of Units		1	
36. Highest Adjusted Offense Level			31
37. Increase in Offense Level:			0
38. **Combined Adjusted Offense Level:**			31

39. **Adjustment for Acceptance of Responsibility:** The defendant has shown recognition of responsibility for his criminal conduct and a reduction of two levels for Acceptance of Responsibility is applicable under USSG §3E1.1(a). Further, based upon the defendant's timely notification of his intent to plead guilty, and the Government's motion for an additional one-level reduction under USSG §3E1.1(b), a total reduction of three levels is recommended.   -3

40. **Total Offense Level:**   28

41. **Chapter Four Enhancements:** None.   0

42. **Total Offense Level:**   28

    Offense Behavior Not Part of Relevant Conduct

43. Smith was also charged in an unrelated robbery on November 18, 2005, of Williams Bank in Sun City, Atlantis, as summarized in Count Five of the original indictment. Bank surveillance cameras show a suspect, generally resembling the defendant, as he was approaching a teller, handing her a bag, accompanied by a demand note. The suspect then left the bank with $1,375 in the bag. While the defendant has declined to discuss this robbery, at the time of his arrest, federal agents recovered a shirt, pants, and shoes from the defendant's duffle bag matching those of the suspect in the surveillance photographs.

PART B. THE DEFENDANT'S CRIMINAL HISTORY

Juvenile Adjudication(s)

Date of Referral	Charge/ Court	Date Sentence Imposed/Disposition	Guideline/ Points
44. 04/15/1992 (Age 17)	Auto Theft, Breaker Bay Juvenile Ct., Atlantis Action #4732	05/15/1992 Youth Correction Center	4A1.2(e)(3) 0

According to court records, Smith was arrested after he stole and dismantled a vehicle and sold the part. Smith was represented by counsel.

Adult Criminal Conviction(s)

Date of Arrest	Conviction/ Court	Date Sentence Imposed/Disposition	Guideline/ Points
45. 04/20/1993 (Age 18)	Receiving Stolen Property, Breaker Bay Superior Court Atlantis, Dkt. # 57349	10/08/1994 2 years imprisonment; paroled 11/11/1995	4A1.1(a) 4A1.2(e)(1) 3

According to court records, Smith was arrested after he was found to be in possession of stolen automobile parts. The defendant was represented by counsel. Although Smith was arrested several times while under parole supervision, according to his supervision record, he made satisfactory adjustment to parole supervision and was discharged from parole on April 7, 1996.

Date of Arrest	Conviction/ Court	Date Sentence Imposed/Disposition	Guideline/ Points
46. 05/30/1993 (Age 18)	Petty Theft Breaker Bay Municipal Ct., Atlantis, Dkt. # 758924A	06/15/1993 1 year probation	4A1.2(e)(3) 0

Smith was arrested after he fueled his vehicle at a service station and left without paying. The defendant waived counsel, and successfully completed probation shortly before he was convicted on the unrelated charges of his previous arrest noted above.

Date of Arrest	Conviction/ Court	Date Sentence Imposed/Disposition	Guideline/ Points
47. 03/16/1994 (Age 19)	Petty Theft, Breaker Bay Municipal Ct., Dkt. #857234A	04/10/1994 1 year probation; 10/10/994 probation revoked; 90 days jail	4A1.1(b) 4A1.2(k)(1) 2

According to court records, Smith stole two packages of frozen vegetables valued at $3.00 from a local grocery store. He waived counsel, and his probation was later revoked after he absconded from supervision.

Date of Arrest	Conviction/ Court	Date Sentence Imposed/Disposition	Guideline/ Points
48. 08/20/1995 (Age 20)	Theft Breaker Bay Municipal Ct., Dkt. Dkt. #857234A	09/10/1995 Consolidated with Dkt. # 867330B; 20 days jail, consecutive	4A1.1(c) 1

According to court records, Smith was arrested after he offered to sell an undercover Breaker Bay police officer stolen automobile parts as detailed in his next conviction. At the time of the defendant's arrest, police officers also recovered a vehicle stolen from a local automobile dealership. Smith admitted that on July 5, 1995, he used a false driver's license and took the vehicle for a test drive, but never returned it. Smith was represented by counsel. The points assigned for this offense take into account the below-listed case which was consolidated for sentencing, in accordance with the provisions found in U.S.S.G. § 4A1.2, comment. (n.3.)

49. 08/20/1995	Theft,	09/10/1995	4A1.1 (c)	
(Age 20)	Breaker Bay	Consolidated with	4A1.2(a)(2)	
	Municipal Ct.,	Dkt. # 867329A;		0
	Dkt. #867330B	30 days jail, consecutive		

According to the arrest report and court documents, Smith and a codefendant were arrested after they convinced an intoxicated acquaintance to surrender his keys to a 1990 Buick Skylark. Smith and his codefendant dismantled the vehicle and offered to sell the parts to an undercover Breaker Bay police officer. Police also recovered a stolen vehicle which had been taken from a local dealership as detailed in the above arrest. Smith was represented by counsel. No points were assigned for this conviction because the case was consolidated with the case above and assigned one point.

50. 05/17/1997	Reckless Driving,	06/09/1997	4A1.1(c)	
(Age 22)	Breaker Bay	1 year probation	4A1.2(c)(1)	
	Municipal Ct.,			1
	Dkt. #875662			

According to court records, Smith was detained after he was observed by a Breaker Bay traffic officer driving a vehicle at 90 miles per hour in a 15-mile-per-hour school zone. Smith waived his right to counsel.

51. 05/15/1998	Possession of	07/10/1998	4A1.1(c)	
(Age 23)	Marijuana,	3 years probation		1
	Breaker Bay			
	Municipal Ct.,			
	Dkt. #879322A			

A Breaker Bay police officer arrested Smith after he was observed smoking marijuana at a concert. At the time of his arrest, Smith was found in possession of five grams of marijuana. According to local probation-department records, Smith successfully completed probation and, as a condition of his supervision, participated in a substance abuse treatment program. The defendant was represented by counsel. The probation term was terminated unsatisfactorily on April3, 2001, due to Smith's new arrest for criminal conduct.

52. 06/10/1998   Insufficient Funds/   06/30/1998   4A1.2(c)(1)
    (Age 23)   Bad Checks,   10 days jail   0
                        Breaker Bay
                        Municipal Ct.,
                        Dkt. # 875883A

According to the court and bank records, Smith established a checking account in his own name and deposited $500. He then wrote personal checks payable in amounts totaling $1,000. The funds were not recovered. He was represented by counsel.

53. 03/14/2001   Grand Theft,   07/15/2001   4A1.1(c)
    (Age 25)   Breaker Bay   3 years probation   1
                        Superior Court,   with 59 days jail;
                        Dkt. # 97456   probation terminated
                                                and deemed unsuccessful
                                                08/30/2002

According to court records, on March 14, 2001, Smith stole the keys to an automobile showroom. Later that night, he returned to the showroom and stole three vehicles, valued at $56,000. Smith was apprehended as he attempted to drive the third vehicle away from the lot, and assisted in the recovery of the other two stolen vehicles. Smith was originally charged with burglary, but he was later convicted of theft. The defendant was represented by counsel. His probation was later terminated and deemed unsuccessful after he was committed to prison on an unrelated offense.

54. 12/15/2002   Petty Theft,   12/20/2002   4A1.1(c)
    (Age 27)   Breaker Bay   20 days jail   1
                        Municipal Ct.,
                        Dkt. # 932741A

According to court records, a private store security officer arrested Smith after he stole a hat, valued at $14.00, from a local department store. Smith was represented by counsel.

55. 01/15/2003   Robbery,   08/27/2003   4A1.1(a)
    (Age 27)   Breaker Bay   5 years imprisonment;   3
                        Superior Court,   paroled 08/26/2005

According to available police reports and court records, Smith robbed a convenience store owner of $765.00 at gunpoint. As he attempted to leave the store, Smith was apprehended by a Breaker Bay patrolman. Smith was represented by counsel. He was later committed to the Allmont Correctional Facility and, according to institutional records, Smith was enrolled in a high school equivalency program but did not complete the course. During his incarceration, Smith received several incident reports, including the possession and use of a weapon, fighting, and possession of marijuana. Smith also worked in the facility kitchen, where he received above-average performance evaluations.

Smith was released to parole supervision on August 26, 2005, and committed the instant offense shortly thereafter. According to his parole officer, Smith reported as directed, but was unemployed and was not actively looking for work, although he had been repeatedly instructed to do so by his parole officer. The defendant has been charged with violation of his parole, based on this offense, and a warrant has been lodged as a detainer.

56. In addition, Smith was convicted five times, between 1993 and 1999, for public intoxication and ten times for traffic infractions. He was fined up to $150 for each traffic infraction and for two of the intoxication convictions. Smith was jailed for up to five days for the other three intoxication convictions, and he was represented by counsel for all of the convictions which resulted in imprisonment.

Criminal History Computation

57. The criminal convictions above result in a subtotal criminal history score of 12. In accordance with the provisions found in USSG. §4A1.1(c), only a total of 4 points have been added for the defendant's 5 prior convictions that resulted in a term of imprisonment of less than 60 days.

58. At the time that the instant offense was committed, Smith was on parole supervision for his August 27, 2003, sentence. In accordance with USSG. §4A1.1(d), two points are added.

59. The instant offense was committed less than two years following Smith's release from custody on August 26, 2005. Pursuant to USSG §4A1.1(e), one point is added.

60. The total of the criminal history points is 15. According to the sentencing table (Chapter 5, Part A), 13 or more criminal history points establish a criminal history category of VI.

Other Criminal Conduct

61. During the presentence interview, Smith admitted to the probation officer that he was granted pretrial diversion in 1994 for possession of marijuana. Probation department records indicated that Smith successfully completed the diversion program.

Pending Charges

62. On August 28, 2005, the defendant was arrested for driving under the influence of alcohol. Smith has been charged with a violation in the Breaker Bay Municipal Court under docket number 945789A. An arrest warrant was issued after Smith was taken into federal custody and failed to appear in municipal court. The warrant has been lodged as a detainer with the U.S. Marshals Service.

63. On December 1, 2005, a warrant was issued by the Atlantis Parole Authority, charging Smith with parole violations. This warrant has also been lodged as a detainer with the U.S. Marshals Service.

Other Arrests

Date of Arrest	Charge	Agency	Disposition
64. 11/14/2002 (Age 27)	Shoplifting	Breaker Bay Police Dept.	No charges filed

PART C. OFFENDER CHARACTERISTICS

Personal and Family Data

65. Thaddeus Smith was born on March 15, 1975, in Breaker Bay, Atlantis, to the union of Samuel and Edith Smith (nee Barker). The defendant's parents separated on numerous occasions, and Smith was often left in the care of his maternal grandmother, who has a history of severe depression. As a consequence, his childhood was chaotic. According to his juvenile record, Smith ran away from home several times and was eventually placed in his grandmother's custody. In 1989, the grandmother committed suicide and Smith discovered her body. He was returned to his mother's residence, located in a small housing project on the lower east side of Breaker Bay.

66. According to the defendant's mother, Smith was very respectful in the family home, although he did exhibit recurring signs of violence and temper tantrums, which she attributed to her son's inability to overcome the emotionally traumatic experiences associated with the loss of his grandmother. Smith and his grandmother had been extremely close. After an episode of delinquency, Smith was committed to the Breaker Bay Youth Correctional Center.

67. Since his release from the youth center, Smith has been residing with distant relatives, with friends, or alone in a series of small apartments in Breaker Bay. His last contact with his parents was in 1995 at his brother Frederick's funeral. Since 1998, Smith has lived at 111 Fifth Street, Apartment B, Breaker Bay, Atlantis 99993, with his cousin, Martin Johnson. A recent home investigation found this small, sparsely furnished apartment to be located in a high-crime section in northwest Breaker Bay. According to the defendant's cousin Martin Johnson, Smith rarely stayed in the apartment and did not contribute to their monthly living expenses; however, Johnson would welcome the defendant back into his apartment upon his release because of limited housing alternatives available to the defendant at the present time.

Physical Condition

68. Thaddeus Smith is a white non-Hispanic male who is 6'2" tall and weighs 210 pounds. He has brown eyes and brown shoulder-length hair. Smith has a surgical scar on his abdomen, and a tattoo of a skull with the motto "Born to Lose" on his right hand.

69. The defendant describes his overall general physical health as good. He was hospitalized briefly in 1996 for the repair of a hernia he suffered while working in the Breaker Bay jail laundry.

Mental and Emotional Health

70. Smith indicated that he has never been seen by a psychiatrist and described his overall mental and emotional health as good. There is no documented evidence to suggest otherwise.

Substance Abuse

71. The defendant describes a history of alcohol and drug abuse which began when he was approximately 10 years old. According to Smith, he stole alcohol from his parents' supply, adding, "…they were drunk so often, they never noticed." He stated that he often attended school under the influence of alcohol, and that he has been intoxicated "too many times to count."

72. Smith stated that he began smoking marijuana when he was 12 years old. When he discovered that it was easier to attend school under the influence of marijuana without detection than under the influence of alcohol, he became a daily marijuana smoker. The defendant reports the abuse of numerous substances, including hallucinogens, stimulants and depressants, methamphetamine, and cocaine. Smith said he never used opiates.

73. Smith reported he has often been under the influence of some substance while committing his crimes. Before the instant offense, he drank a pint of whisky and inhaled approximately one quarter gram of methamphetamine. Smith admitted that he used some of the proceeds from the robbery to purchase cocaine, and said that since his most recent release from prison, he has used as much as he could acquire. Smith estimates that he has spent at least $200 each week for methamphetamine (his drug of choice), alcohol, or cocaine. The results of a urine test administered by a pretrial services officer at the time of the defendant's arrest were positive for methamphetamine and cocaine.

74. Smith stated that he has been referred to several alcohol and substance abuse programs as a result of his criminal conduct. In 1994, he participated in a marijuana use and education program as a condition of diversion and in 1993, he underwent drug treatment as a condition of probation. Prison records reflect that during his most recent confinement, Smith attended Alcoholics and Narcotics Anonymous sessions regularly, but his correctional counselors noted that Smith seemed unmotivated and never selected sponsors. The defendant currently indicates that he would be willing to participate in a drug treatment program and adds that he is now motivated to address his narcotics dependency.

Educational and Vocational Skills

75. The defendant attended Kennedy High School for Boys in Breaker Bay in 1993, where he received poor grades and had a poor attendance record. After his commitment to the Breaker Bay Youth Center in 1992, Smith completed the 11th grade, but center records indicate that he reads at an 8th grade level. He has no other formal education or identifiable skills and is in need of remedial educational or vocational training.

Employment Record

76. Since his release from State custody on August 26, 2005, Smith has been unemployed. He acknowledges he has made no attempt to actively seek employment and has relied on others for financial assistance.

77. From September 15, 1996, until December 15, 1996, Smith was employed by Sam's SuperSave Gasoline, 333 Third Avenue, Breaker Bay, as a service station attendant and cashier, earning minimum wages. In addition, from January 10, 1997, until June 9, 1997 Smith was employed as a mechanic by Al's Auto Aid, 129 5th Street, Breaker Bay, earning $10.45 per hour, until his arrest on new criminal charges and subsequent commitment to state prison.

78. From June 15, 1993 until July 14, 1996, Smith was employed by Uriah's Cheap Heaps, 435 Ohio Street, Breaker Bay. He was first hired as a mechanic, but was later promoted to service manager at this dealership, where he earned $2,500 per month before he was terminated when the dealership learned of his arrest for stealing cars from a nearby dealership showroom. Smith's former employer, Uriah Dickens, advised that he was extremely disappointed in Smith, whom he hired despite his criminal record. Dickens described Smith as a likable employee who got along well with others. According to Dickens, hoping that a second chance would encourage Smith to reform, Dickens allowed Smith to continue in his employ, even after his 1993 conviction for petty theft.

79. From January 10, 1992, until June 9, 1992, Smith was employed by Prestigious Motors, Breaker Bay, where he worked detailing cars, earning $6.75 per hour. According to his immediate supervisor, Smith was knowledgeable but was terminated after he repeatedly failed to show up for work.

80. Overall, Smith has a sporadic work history, marked by substantial periods of employment. After his release from the Breaker Bay Youth Corrections Center, he worked sporadically as a mechanic. When unemployed, he supplemented his income by working on friends' and acquaintances' vehicles.

Financial Condition: Ability to Pay

81. According to the Personal Financial Statement and a credit bureau check, Smith has no known identifiable assets or liabilities. While he has no sources of income, Smith claims to have spent approximately $800 per month for drugs and alcohol. Prior to his arrest in this offense, Smith was living with his cousin and the defendant provided no financial assistance to the monthly living expenses. The defendant is unemployed and upon his release, he will be dependent upon others for financial assistance. Smith's attorney has been appointed by the court, and at the present time, Smith does not have the ability to pay a fine. Based upon his vocational training and skills, Smith does appear to have the ability to pay a minimal fine on a payment schedule. However, his ability to pay a fine may be limited by any restitution which the court may impose.

PART D. SENTENCING OPTIONS

Custody

82. **Statutory Provisions:** The maximum term of imprisonment for Count One is 20 years, pursuant to 18 U.S.C. § 2113(a). The minimum term of imprisonment on Count Two is 15 days, and the maximum term of imprisonment is 2 years, pursuant to 21 U.S.C. § 844(a) since the defendant has a prior drug conviction.

83. **Guideline Provisions:** Based on an offense level of 28 and a criminal history category of VI, the guideline range of imprisonment is 140 to 175 months.

Impact of the Plea Agreement

84. Had the defendant been convicted of all the charges in the original indictment, the guideline imprisonment range would be 140 to 175 months, plus a mandatory 60-month minimum term of imprisonment required for violations of 18 U.S.C. § 924(c)(1), which would be served consecutively to any other sentence imposed.

Supervised Release

85. **Statutory Provisions:** If a term of imprisonment is imposed on Counts One and Two, the court may impose a term of supervised release of not more than three years on Count One and not more than one year on Count Two, pursuant to 18 U.S.C. §§ 3583(b)(2) and (3), since they are Class C and Class E felonies, respectively. According to 18 U.S.C. § 3624(e), the terms of supervised release shall run concurrently.

86. **Guideline Provisions:** If the defendant is sentenced to a term of imprisonment of more than one year, the court must impose a term of supervised release, pursuant to USSG. § 5D1.1. The authorized term of supervised release for Count One is not less than two years nor more than three years, and the authorized term of supervised release for Count Two is one year, pursuant to USSG §§ 5D1.2(b)(2) and (3). Pursuant to 18 U.S.C. § 3624(e), the terms would be served concurrently.

Probation

87. **Statutory Provisions:** The defendant is ineligible for a term of probation in this offense, pursuant to 18 U.S.C. § 3561(a)(3) since he must be sentenced to at least a 15-day term of imprisonment on Count Two.

88. **Guideline Provisions:** The defendant is ineligible for a term of probation since Count Two requires a mandatory term of imprisonment of 15 days and the minimum guideline imprisonment range exceeds eight months, pursuant to USSG §§ 5B1.1(b)(3) and 5B1.1, comment. (n.2).

Fines

89. **Statutory Provisions:** The maximum fine for Count One is twice the gross loss, or $308,270, pursuant to 18 U.S.C. § 3571(d). The minimum fine for Count Two is $2,500, plus the cost of the investigation and prosecution (unless the defendant does not have the ability to pay), pursuant to 21 U.S.C. § 844(a), and the maximum fine is $250,000, pursuant to 18 U.S.C. § 3571(b).

90. A special assessment of $50 on each count for a total of $100 is mandatory, pursuant to 18 U.S.C. § 3013.

91. **Guideline Provisions:** Pursuant to U.S.S.G. § 5E1.2(c)(3), the fine range for this offense is from $12,500 to $ 125,000.

Restitution

92. **Statutory Provisions:** Pursuant to 18 U.S.C. § 3663A, restitution shall be ordered. In this case, restitution in the amount of $5,900 is outstanding to the Atlantis Credit Union and can be forwarded to the following address:

> Atlantis Credit Union
> Attention: Mr. Sam Claim
> 1948 Edgewater Street
> Breaker Bay, Atlantis 99996

93. In addition, restitution in the amount of $44,445 is outstanding to the Apex Insurance Company and can be forwarded to the following address:

> Apex Insurance Company
> Attention: Mrs. Cindy Claim
> 1950 Backstreet
> Breaker Bay, Atlantis 99995

94. **Guideline Provisions:** In accordance with the provisions of USSG § 5E1.1, restitution shall be ordered.

Denial of Federal Benefits

95. **Statutory Provisions:** Pursuant to 21 U.S.C. § 862, upon a second conviction for possession of a controlled substance, a defendant may be declared ineligible for any or all Federal benefits for up to five years as determined by the Court. In addition, the Court may require the defendant to participate and complete an approved drug treatment program that includes periodic drug testing, or to perform appropriate community service.

96. **Guideline Provisions:** Pursuant to 21 USSG § 5F1.6, the Court may deny eligibility for certain federal benefits of any individual convicted of distribution or possession of a controlled substance.

PART E. CIRCUMSTANCES THAT MAY WARRANT DEPARTURE

97. The probation officer has no information concerning the offense or the offender which would warrant a departure from the prescribed sentencing guidelines.

PART F. VARIANCES THAT MAY BE CONSIDERED IN IMPOSING SENTENCE

98. The probation officer has not identified any factors under 18 U.S.C. § 3553(a) that may warrant a variance and imposition of a non-guideline sentence.

Respectfully submitted,

CHIEF U.S. PROBATION OFFICER

By _____

Craig T. Doe
U.S. Probation Officer

Reviewed and Approved:

_____
Joan B. Fair
Supervising U.S. Probation Officer

ADDENDUM TO THE PRESENTENCE REPORT
UNITED STATES DISTRICT COURT FOR WESTERN DISTRICT OF ATLANTIS
UNITED STATES V. THADDEUS SMITH; DKT. NO. CR 01-001-01-KGG

OBJECTIONS

By the Government

On February 6, 2006, Assistant U.S. Attorney Robert Prosecutor advised the probation officer that he had no objections to the presentence report.

By the Defendant

On February 7, 2006, defense counsel Arthur Goodfellow provided the probation officer with a written objection to the initial presentence report. In summary, defense counsel objects to the adjustment for role in the offense and will argue that defendant Smith was not the organizer or leader within the meaning of USSG §3B1.1(c) and that all of the defendants in this offense are equally culpable.

The probation officer believes that Smith was an organizer and leader in this offense and there is not evidence to support defense counsel's contention that the defendants are equally culpable. The uncontested facts presented in this offense reveal that Smith recruited the codefendants in this offense and exercised clear decision making authority over the other participants when he planned the robbery. Moreover, he gave implicit instructions to Brown and Pond, defining their role in the offense, and claimed the right to a far greater share of the proceeds from the robbery. The probation officer relies on a review of the commentary found in USSG §3B1.1 that supports a two-level enhancement for Smith's role in this offense.

Respectfully submitted,

CHIEF U.S. PROBATION OFFICER

By _____
                    Craig T. Doe
                    U.S. Probation Officer

Reviewed and Approved:

_____
Joan B. Fair
Supervising U.S. Probation Officer

SENTENCING RECOMMENDATION
UNITED STATES DISTRICT COURT FOR WESTERN DISTRICT OF ATLANTIS
UNITED STATES V. THADDEUS SMITH; DKT. NO. 01-001-01-KGG

TOTAL OFFENSE LEVEL: 28
CRIMINAL HISTORY CATEGORY: VI

	Statutory Provisions	Guideline Provisions	Plea Agreement Provisions	Recommended Sentence
CUSTODY:	Ct.1: 20 yrs Ct.2: 15 days– 2 years	140–175 months	None	160 months
PROBATION:	Ineligible	Ineligible	None	Not applicable
SUPERVISED RELEASE:	Ct.1: 3 yrs Ct.2: 1 yr	Ct. 1: 2 to 3 yrs Ct.2: 1 yr	None	Ct.1: 3 years Ct.2: 1 year, cc
FINE:	Ct.1: $308,270 Ct.2: $2,500– $250,000	$12,500 to $384,405	None	$0
RESTITUTION:	Ct.1: $50,345 Ct.2: N/A	Ct.1: $50,345 Ct.2: N/A	None	Ct.1: $50,345 Ct.2: N/A
SPECIAL ASSESSMENT:	$200	$200	None	$200

Justification

The robbery of the credit union involved extensive planning in the design of the crime, as well as the recruitment of others to participate in the offense. These factors, as well as Thaddeus Smith's role in the offense, use of a gun, and the amount of loss, have been taken into account in determining the guideline range. The defendant has an extensive criminal record which is reflected in the fact that he is in the highest criminal history category. He accepts responsibility for his actions and expresses remorse for his actions in the instant case. Because the significant sentencing considerations, both aggravating and mitigating, have been factored into the application of the guidelines, a sentence near the middle of the guideline range is merited. Accordingly, a prison sentence of 160 months is recommended, which would reflect the seriousness of the offense and meet the sentencing objective of just punishment.

In the past, when Smith has been subject to community supervision, his overall adjustment has been poor, as evidenced by continued conflicts with the law. He has a history of drug and alcohol abuse and could benefit from intervention and treatment. A three-year period of supervised release is recommended for the protection of the public, as well as for the correctional treatment of the defendant when he is released to the community. Accordingly, a special condition for testing and substance abuse treatment is recommended.

In view of the defendant's inability to pay financial sanctions and his lack of employment stability, it is recommended that the fine be waived. However, in light of his expected lengthy jail sentence, it is recommended that the defendant be ordered to make restitution immediately to the Atlantis Credit Union in the amount of $5,900 and to the Apex Insurance Company in the amount of $44,445. The Federal Bureau of Prisons has a voluntary Inmate Financial Responsibility Program, and while incarcerated, if employed, Smith can begin immediate payment toward his restitution obligation.

Although the court may deny any or all Federal benefits for up to five years because Count Two is the defendant's second conviction for possession of a controlled substance, denial of Federal benefits is not recommended. If the court imposes a custodial sentence within the guideline range, the period of ineligibility for benefits would expire before the defendant's release from custody.

Voluntary Surrender:

Smith is subject to a substantial period of incarceration in this offense and he has been detained without bail since his arrest. Although he has family members in the community, his regular contact with them has been sporadic. As a result, the defendant does not appear to be a good candidate for voluntary surrender.

Recommendation:

It is respectfully recommended that sentence in this case be imposed as follows:

Pursuant to the Sentencing Reform Act of 1984, it is the judgment of the court that the defendant, Thaddeus Smith, is hereby committed to the custody of the United States Bureau of Prisons, to be imprisoned for a term of 160 months. The term consists of 160 months on Count One and a term of 24 months on Count Two, all to be served concurrently.

Upon release from imprisonment, the defendant shall be placed on supervised release for a term of three years. This term consists of three years on each of Counts One and Two and all such terms to run concurrently. Within 72 hours of release from custody of the Bureau of Prisons, the defendant shall report in person to the probation office in the district to which the defendant is released.

While on supervised release, the defendant shall not commit any Federal, state, or local crimes, and he shall be prohibited from possessing a firearm or other dangerous device, and he shall not possess a controlled substance. In addition, he shall comply with the standard conditions of supervised release as recommended by the Unite[d] States Sentencing Commission. The defendant shall also comply with the following special condition: The defendant shall participate in a program of testing and treatment for drug and alcohol abuse, as directed by the probation officer, until such time as the defendant is released from the program by the probation officer.

THE COURT FINDS that the defendant does not have the ability to pay a fine, but he will begin to make immediate restitution in accordance with the provisions of 18 U.S.C. § 3663 to the Atlantis Credit Union in the amount of $5,900 and to the Apex Insurance Company in the amount of $44,445. Any payment that is not paid in full shall be divided proportionately among the entities named. Upon release from custody, payment of any unpaid restitution balance will become a special condition of supervised release.

IT IS ORDERED that the defendant pay a special assessment in the amount of $200 for Counts One and Two, which shall be due immediately.

Respectfully submitted,

Chief U.S. Probation Officer

By _____

Craig T. Doe
U.S. Probation Officer

Approved:

_____

Joan B. Fair
Supervising U.S. Probation Officer

Appendix 2

Conditions of Supervised Release

§5D1.3. Conditions of Supervised Release

(a) Mandatory Conditions–

    (1) the defendant shall not commit another federal, state, or local offense (see 18 U.S.C. § 3583(d));

    (2) the defendant shall not unlawfully possess a controlled substance (see 18 U.S.C. § 3583(d));

    (3) the defendant who is convicted for a domestic violence crime as defined in 18 U.S.C. § 3561(b) for the first time shall attend a public, private, or private non-profit offender rehabilitation program that has been approved by the court, in consultation with a State Coalition Against Domestic Violence or other appropriate experts, if an approved program is available within a 50-mile radius of the legal residence of the defendant (see 18 U.S.C. § 3583(d));

    (4) the defendant shall refrain from any unlawful use of a controlled substance and submit to one drug test within 15 days of release on probation and at least two periodic drug tests thereafter (as determined by the court) for use of a controlled substance, but the condition stated in this paragraph may be ameliorated or suspended by the court for any individual defendant if the defendant's presentence or other reliable information indicates a low risk of future substance abuse by the defendant (see 18 U.S.C. § 3583(d));

    (5) if a fine is imposed and has not been paid upon release to supervised release, the defendant shall adhere to an installment schedule to pay that fine (see 18 U.S.C. § 3624(e));

    (6) the defendant shall (A) make restitution in accordance with 18 U.S.C. §§ 2248, 2259, 2264, 2327, 3663, 3663A, and 3664; and (B) pay the assessment imposed in accordance with 18 U.S.C. § 3013;

    (7) (A) in a state in which the requirements of the Sex Offender Registration and Notification Act (see 42 U.S.C. §§ 16911 and 16913) do not apply, a defendant convicted of a sexual offense as described in 18 U.S.C. § 4042(c)(4) (Pub. L. 105–119, § 115(a)(8), Nov. 26, 1997) shall report the address where the defendant will reside and any subsequent change of residence to the probation officer responsible for supervision and shall register as a sex offender in any State where the person resides, is employed, carries on a vocation, or is a student; or

(B) in a state in which the requirements of Sex Offender Registration and Notification Act apply, a sex offender shall (i) register, and keep such registration current, where the offender resides, where the offender is an employee, and where the offender is a student, and for the initial registration, a sex offender also shall register in the jurisdiction in which convicted if such jurisdiction is different from the jurisdiction of residence; (ii) provide information required by 42 U.S.C. § 16914; and (iii) keep such registration current for the full registration period as set forth in 42 U.S.C. § 16915;

(8) the defendant shall submit to the collection of a DNA sample from the defendant at the direction of the United States Probation Office if the collection of such a sample is authorized pursuant to section 3 of the DNA Analysis Backlog Elimination Act of 2000 (42 U.S.C. § 14135a).

(b) The court may impose other conditions of supervised release to the extent that such conditions (1) are reasonably related to (A) the nature and circumstances of the offense and the history and characteristics of the defendant; (B) the need for the sentence imposed to afford adequate deterrence to criminal conduct; (C) the need to protect the public from further crimes of the defendant; and (D) the need to provide the defendant with needed educational or vocational training, medical care, or other correctional treatment in the most effective manner; and (2) involve no greater deprivation of liberty than is reasonably necessary for the purposes set forth above and are consistent with any pertinent policy statements issued by the Sentencing Commission.

(c) (Policy Statement) The following "standard" conditions are recommended for supervised release. Several of the conditions are expansions of the conditions required by statute:

(1) the defendant shall not leave the judicial district or other specified geographic area without the permission of the court or probation officer;

(2) the defendant shall report to the probation officer as directed by the court or probation officer and shall submit a truthful and complete written report within the first five days of each month;

(3) the defendant shall answer truthfully all inquiries by the probation officer and follow the instructions of the probation officer;

(4) the defendant shall support the defendant's dependents and meet other family responsibilities (including, but not limited to, complying with the terms of any court order or administrative process pursuant to the law of a state, the District of Columbia, or any other possession or territory of the United States requiring payments by the defendant for the support and maintenance of any child or of a child and the parent with whom the child is living);

(5) the defendant shall work regularly at a lawful occupation unless excused by the probation officer for schooling, training, or other acceptable reasons;

(6) the defendant shall notify the probation officer at least ten days prior to any change of residence or employment;

(7) the defendant shall refrain from excessive use of alcohol and shall not purchase, possess, use, distribute, or administer any controlled substance, or any paraphernalia related to any controlled substance, except as prescribed by a physician;

(8) the defendant shall not frequent places where controlled substances are illegally sold, used, distributed, or administered, or other places specified by the court;

(9) the defendant shall not associate with any persons engaged in criminal activity, and shall not associate with any person convicted of a felony unless granted permission to do so by the probation officer;

(10) the defendant shall permit a probation officer to visit the defendant at any time at home or elsewhere and shall permit confiscation of any contraband observed in plain view by the probation officer;

(11) the defendant shall notify the probation officer within seventy-two hours of being arrested or questioned by a law enforcement officer;

(12) the defendant shall not enter into any agreement to act as an informer or a special agent of a law enforcement agency without the permission of the court;

(13) as directed by the probation officer, the defendant shall notify third parties of risks that may be occasioned by the defendant's criminal record or personal history or characteristics, and shall permit the probation officer to make such notifications and to confirm the defendant's compliance with such notification requirement;

(14) the defendant shall pay the special assessment imposed or adhere to a court-ordered installment schedule for the payment of the special assessment;

(15) the defendant shall notify the probation officer of any material change in the defendant's economic circumstances that might affect the defendant's ability to pay any unpaid amount of restitution, fines, or special assessments.

(d) (Policy Statement) The following "special" conditions of supervised release are recommended in the circumstances described and, in addition, may otherwise be appropriate in particular cases:

(1) Possession of Weapons

If the instant conviction is for a felony, or if the defendant was previously convicted of a felony or used a firearm or other dangerous weapon in the course of the instant offense—a condition prohibiting the defendant from possessing a firearm or other dangerous weapon.

(2) Debt Obligations

If an installment schedule of payment of restitution or a fine is imposed—a condition prohibiting the defendant from incurring new credit charges or opening additional lines of credit without approval of the probation officer unless the defendant is in compliance with the payment schedule.

(3) Access to Financial Information

If the court imposes an order of restitution, forfeiture, or notice to victims, or orders the defendant to pay a fine—a condition requiring the defendant to provide the probation officer access to any requested financial information.

(4) Substance Abuse Program Participation

If the court has reason to believe that the defendant is an abuser of narcotics, other controlled substances, or alcohol—a condition requiring the defendant to participate in a program approved by the United States Probation Office for substance abuse, which program may include testing to determine whether the defendant has reverted to the use of drugs or alcohol.

(5) Mental Health Program Participation

If the court has reason to believe that the defendant is in need of psychological or psychiatric treatment—a condition requiring that the defendant participate in a mental health program approved by the United States Probation Office.

(6) Deportation

If (A) the defendant and the United States entered into a stipulation of deportation pursuant to section 238(c)(5)*) or (B) in the absence of a stipulation of deportation, if, after notice and hearing pursuant to such section, the Attorney General demonstrates by clear and convincing evidence that the alien is deportable—a condition ordering deportation by a United States district court or a United States magistrate judge.

So in original. Probably should be 8 U.S.C. § 1228(d)(5)

(7) Sex Offenses

If the instant offense of conviction is a sex offense, as defined in Application Note 1 of the Commentary to §5D1.2 (Term of Supervised Release)–

(A) A condition requiring the defendant to participate in a program approved by the United States Probation Office for the treatment and monitoring of sex offenders.

(B) A condition limiting the use of a computer or an interactive computer service in cases in which the defendant used such items.

(C) A condition requiring the defendant to submit to a search, at any time, with or without a warrant, and by any law enforcement or probation officer, of the defendant's person and any property, house, residence, vehicle, papers, computer, other electronic communication or data storage devices or media, and effects upon reasonable suspicion concerning a violation of a condition of supervised release or unlawful conduct by the defendant or by any probation officer in the lawful discharge of the officer's supervision functions.

(e) Additional Conditions (Policy Statement)

The following "special conditions" may be appropriate on a case-by-case basis:

(1) Community Confinement

Residence in a community treatment center, halfway house or similar facility may be imposed as a condition of supervised release. See § 5F1.1 (Community Confinement).

(2) Home Detention

Home detention may be imposed as a condition of supervised release but only as a substitute for imprisonment. See §5F1.2 (Home Detention).

(3) Community Service

Community service may be imposed as a condition of supervised release. See §5F1.3 (Community Service).

(4) Occupational Restrictions

Occupational restrictions may be imposed as a condition of supervised release. See §5F1.5 (Occupational Restrictions).

(5) Curfew

A condition imposing a curfew may be imposed if the court concludes that restricting the defendant to his place of residence during evening and nighttime hours is necessary to protect the public from crimes that the defendant might commit during those hours, or to assist in the rehabilitation of the defendant. Electronic monitoring may be used as a means of surveillance to ensure compliance with a curfew order.

(6) Intermittent Confinement

Intermittent confinement (custody for intervals of time) may be ordered as a condition of supervised release during the first year of supervised release, but only for a violation of a condition of supervised release in accordance with 18 U.S.C. § 3583(e)(2) and only when facilities are available. See §5F1.8 (Intermittent Confinement).

Commentary

Application Note:

1. *Application of Subsection (a)(7)(A) and (B).—Some jurisdictions continue to register sex offenders pursuant to the sex offender registry in place prior to July 27, 2006, the date of enactment of the Adam Walsh Act, which contained the Sex Offender Registration and Notification Act. In such a jurisdiction, subsection (a)(7)(A) will apply. In a jurisdiction that has implemented the requirements of the Sex Offender Registration and Notification Act, subsection (a)(7)(B) will apply. (See 42 U.S.C. §§ 16911 and 16913.)*

Historical Note: Effective November 1, 1987. Amended effective November 1, 1989 (see Appendix C, amendments 276, 277, and 302); November 1, 1997 (See Appendix C, amendment 569); November 1, 1998 (See Appendix C, amendment 584); November 1, 2000 (See Appendix C, amendment 605); November 1, 2001 (See Appendix C, amendment 615); November 1, 2002 (See Appendix C, amendments 644 and 646); November 1, 2004 (See Appendix C, amendment 664); November 1, 2007 (See Appendix C, amendments 701 and 711); November 1, 2009 (See Appendix C, amendment 733).

Source: United States Sentencing Commission, Guidelines Manual, §5D1.3 (Nov. 2010)

Appendix 3

Example of an Inmate Complaint for Injunctive and Declaratory Relief

[Plaintiff],

v.

DEPARTMENT OF JUSTICE
     and
BUREAU OF PRISONS,
Defendants.

COMPLAINT FOR INJUNCTIVE AND DECLARATORY RELIEF

[Plaintiff] complains against the Department of Justice and Bureau of Prisons for violations of his First and Fifth Amendment rights to expression and due process. Jurisdiction is conferred under 28 U.S.C. sections 1331 and 2201. Venue is proper in this Court because the Defendants are located in Washington D.C.

1. [Plaintiff] is a federal prisoner serving a contested parole violation at the Federal Institution in Cumberland, Maryland.

2. [Plaintiff] is a professional musician who sings, writes, copyrights, publishes, and performs his own music. He has a record-deal offer from a well-known record label, and he has a First Amendment right to express himself through music.

3. For decades, the Bureau of Prisons (BOP) has had a music program, which either (1) allowed an inmate to purchase and maintain his own musical instrument or (2) use an instrument purchased and maintained by the BOP. An instrument could be either acoustic or electric, and inmates were allowed to keep their instruments in their rooms. This was codified in 28 C.F.R. section 544.30 and Bureau of Prison Policy Statement 5370.08. See attached Institutional Supplement as Exhibit A. Moreover, 28 C.F.R. section 551.80 allows an inmate to prepare lyric and music manuscripts. Thousands of inmates have participated in the music program and many have purchased electric guitars, keyboards, and amplifiers.

4. Many of the inmates in the music program participated in band activity and played live for the inmate population during the holidays. Bands played, rock, jazz, rap, reggae, country, blue-grass, gospel, folk, and Spanish music.

5. The music program was actively promoted by the BOP staff, because it enhanced the rehabilitative goals of the inmates by engaging them in constructive and positive behavior.

Many inmates used their time in prison to learn to play an instrument or write music and this enhanced their self-esteem.

6. During [Plaintiff]'s time in the custody of the BOP, he has never heard of or witnessed any problems caused by the music program.

7. As part of the 1996 fiscal year's appropriation bill for the BOP, Congress attached an amendment called the "Zimmer Bill," named after Republican Representative Dick Zimmer. That bill prohibited the BOP from using any of the general appropriations funds to provide the following amenities or personal comforts in the Federal prison system—

   (1) in-cell television viewing except for prisoners who are segregated from the general population for their own safety;

   (2) the viewing of R, X, and NC-17 rated movies, through whatever medium presented;

   (3) any instruction (live or through broadcasts) or training equipment for boxing, wrestling, judo, karate, or other martial art, or any bodybuilding or weightlifting equipment of any sort;

   (4) possession of in-cell coffee pots, hot plates, or heating elements; or

   (5) the use or possession of any electric or electronic instrument.

8. This amendment was part of a mean-spirited campaign against prisoners by lawmakers emboldened by the Republican sweep of Congress in 1994. Representative Zimmer was later soundly defeated in 1996.

9. The BOP opposed the Zimmer Bill, but it passed without hearings, findings or discussions as to how it advanced legitimate penological and rehabilitative goals.

10. The BOP began implementing the Zimmer Bill by telling its staff nationwide not to purchase, replace, or repair any electric musical equipment. It also informed the inmate population that no inmate could purchase an electric instrument, and all inmates had to send their instruments home by November 1, 1997. When a BOP instrument now breaks, no matter how minor, the BOP discards the entire instrument, amplifier, microphone, or keyboard. Over the past year, the BOP has discarded thousands of dollars worth of perfectly good or maintainable instruments and components. For example, the BOP will not even order a new tube for an amplifier or replace a key on a piano, or buy a new string for a guitar.[1]

11. At FCI Cumberland, where [Plaintiff] is temporarily detained on a contested parole violation, the Director of Recreation, _ _ _ _ _ _ _ _ _ , has let the music program deteriorate through attrition. For example, on October 7, 1997, when two electric guitars each needed a single string replaced, she chose to discard both electric guitars instead of replacing the strings from the stock of 80 in storage. She stated that she will discard the 80 strings and all electric instruments in the program. She has already discarded amplifiers, a keyboard, cords and generally let "Rome burn" in order to comply with the Zimmer Bill.

---

[1]Because of the Zimmer Bill's similar prohibition of using funds to purchase of exercise equipment, the BOP has also discarded hundreds of thousands of dollars, if not millions of dollars, worth of weightlifting equipment. If a $2.00 cable gets frayed on a $5000.00 Universal Machine, the entire machine is discarded.

12. When [Plaintiff] complained about the dismal state of the music program, he was fired twice from working in the band room and told that he was no longer needed.

13. When [Plaintiff] asked for the policy which allowed for the internal implosion of the music program, he was told by the Director of Education, _ _ _ _ _ _ _ _ , that no policy existed. She further told [Plaintiff] that the Zimmer Bill was responsible for the dismantling of the music program but that bill was "restricted" from inmate viewing. [Plaintiff] replied that if there were no policy countermanding the BOP's previous policies regarding the music program, then the BOP's action was arbitrary, capricious, and unconstitutional.

14. The BOP policy regarding the music program also includes other recreational programs such as hobbycraft, art, and athletics. In all of these programs, the BOP allows inmates to purchase with their own money the materials and equipment they use. When [Plaintiff] requested that he be allowed to purchase a guitar and strings with his own funds, he was falsely told that the Zimmer Bill prohibited such purchases. Prior to the Zimmer Bill, BOP policy allowed inmates to purchase their own instruments. Exhibit A, page 4.

15. The BOP has an Inmate Commissary Trust Fund that is funded by profits from the inmate Commissary. 31 U.S.C. section 1321. That fund is supposed to be used for the benefit of the inmates such as for their amusement, education, or general welfare. When [Plaintiff] requested that the money in that fund be used to fund the music program, he was falsely told that the Zimmer Bill prohibited the use of such funds.

16. When [Plaintiff] suggested other ways to fund the music program such as with funds from the inmate telephone profits or from funds from an Inmate Music Club, he was told that such funding would subvert the Zimmer Bill.

17. The BOP told [Plaintiff] that it would retain acoustic instruments but not electric instruments. There is no rational or penological reason for treating the two types of instruments different from one another. However, the Zimmer Bill singles out only electric instruments. Without electric instruments, the music program will be gutted because very few inmates play acoustic instruments and no bands are acoustic.

18. The BOP has not published its music policy change in the Federal Register nor allowed [Plaintiff] or the public to comment on that policy change. Furthermore, it has not reduced its policy to writing as required by the Administrative Procedures Act, 5 U.S.C. sections 552 and 553.

CLAIM 1

The Defendants have interfered with and intend to continue to interfere with [Plaintiff]'s exercise of his First Amendment right to expression through music and music writing by cutting off funding for the BOP music program and thereby effectively dismantling the program.

CLAIM 2

The Defendants, by refusing to fund the BOP music program through alternative means such as through the Inmate Commissary Trust Fund, have deprived [Plaintiff] of due process and equal protection under the Fifth Amendment.

CLAIM 3

The Defendants, by relying on the Zimmer Bill to deny [Plaintiff] his First and Fifth Amendment rights as stated in Claims 1 and 2, and by not officially changing BOP policy as required by the Administrative Procedures Act, have deprived [Plaintiff] of due process under the Fifth Amendment.

RELIEF

[Plaintiff] requests declaratory and injunctive relief as follows: (1) an order declaring that the Zimmer Bill is unconstitutional and invalid on its face and as applied; (2) an order enjoining the Defendants from relying on the Zimmer Bill to refuse to fund the BOP music program; (3) an order enjoining the Defendants from refusing to use the Inmate Trust Fund to fund the BOP music program; (4) an order declaring that the BOP has failed to comply with the Administrative Procedures Act by making policy without notice or an opportunity to be heard; and (5) an order declaring that the Defendants have violated [Plaintiff]'s First and Fifth Amendment rights and an injunction prohibiting them from doing so in the future.

Respectfully submitted,

_____

VERIFICATION

I, [Plaintiff], verify that the foregoing facts are true and correct to the best of my belief under the provisions of 28 U.S.C. 1746.

_____

Appendix 4

Example of an Inmate Complaint Under 42 U.S.C. § 1983

In The United States District Court For the Middle District of Atlantis*

FORM TO BE USED BY PRISONERS IN FILING A COMPLAINT

UNDER THE CIVIL RIGHTS ACT, 42 U.S.C. § 1983

In the United States District Court for the Middle District of Atlantis

Inmate [XXXXXX]

(Enter above full name of plaintiff—only one plaintiff

permitted per complaint)   Jury Trial Demanded

               V.

Officer [YYYYYY] in his official and individual capacities

(Enter above full names of defendant or defendants)

I.   Previous law suits

    A. Have you begun other lawsuits in state or federal court dealing with the same facts involved in this action or otherwise relating to your imprisonment?   Yes ( )   No (X)

    B. If your answer to A is yes, describe each lawsuit in the space below. (If there is more than one lawsuit describe the additional lawsuits on another piece of paper, using the same outline.)

       1. Parties to previous lawsuit:

         Plaintiffs: _____

         _____

         Defendants: _____

         _____

       2. Court (if federal court, name the district; if state court, name the county):

         _____

       3. Docket numbers: _____

       4. Name of judge assigned to case: _____

5. Disposition (for example, was the case dismissed? appealed? is it still pending?)

_____

_____

6. Approximate date of filing lawsuit: _____

II. Previous *in forma pauperis* lawsuits

    A. While incarcerated or detained in any facility, have you filed a lawsuit in any federal court in which you were allowed to proceed *in forma pauperis* (without prepayment of fees)?

        ( ) Yes   (X) No

        1. Name the court and docket number for each:_____

    B. Were any of these cases dismissed under 28 U.S.C. § 1915(d) on the grounds that they were frivolous, malicious, or failed to state a claim upon which relief may be granted? Yes ( ) No ( )

        1. If yes, how many? _____

        2. Name the court and docket number for each: _____

        _____

III. Exhaustion of Inmate Administrative Remedies

    A. Did you present the facts of each claim relating to your complaint to the Inmate Grievance Commission or any other available administrative remedy procedure?

        Yes (X)   No ( )

    B. If your answer is Yes:

        1. When did you file your grievance?   [--/--/----]

        2. What was your grievance? That I was unnecessarily assaulted by officer [YYYYYY].

        3. Did you appeal any adverse decision to the highest level possible in the administrative procedure? Yes (X)   No ( )

        If yes, when was the decision and what was the result? On [--/--/----] the final result was that it got dismissed for lack of supporting evidence

    C. If your answer to A is no, identify the claim(s), and explain why not: _____

    _____

(Please Attach Copies of All Filed Grievances)

IV. Parties

    A. Plaintiff(s)

    Name of plaintiff: [XXXXXX]

    Current address (place of confinement) [Atlantis State Correctional Facility, Atlantis] (You may lose important legal rights unless you immediately notify the court of any address change.)

B. Defendant(s) (NOTICE: A person must be identified in this subsection B in order to be considered and served as a defendant.)

Name of defendant 1:   Officer [YYYYY] who is sued in official and individual capacities

Position: Correctional Officer

Place of Employment: [Atlantis State Correctional Facility]

Current Address: Upon belief and info he is still employed at [Atlantis State Correctional Facility]

Additional defendant(s) (provide name, position, place of employment, and current address for each)

Defendant 2: _____

Defendant 3: _____

Defendant 4: _____

(Continue on a separate sheet if necessary)

V. Statement of Claim:

State here as briefly as possible the FACTS in your case. Do this by describing how each defendant named in section III.B. above is personally involved in depriving you of your rights. Include relevant times, dates, and places. YOU MAY, BUT NEED NOT, GIVE LEGAL ARGUMENTS OR CITE ANY CASES OR STATUTES. You may only combine claims involving events that relate to all defendants. Number and set forth each separate claim in a separate paragraph. Unrelated claims involving separate events must be set out in a separate complaint. (Attach extra sheets if necessary.)

On ZZ-ZZ-ZZZZ plaintiff was on maximum control at [Atlantis] confined in his cell. At approx 1:30 p.m., defendant escorted an inmate to his cell and began verbally disrespecting the block. Plaintiff asked for a grievance. At this time defendant became irate and said, "Shut the f___ up before I shut you up!" Plaintiff repeated his request for a grievance. Defendant returned to plaintiff's cell after securing the other inmate and began threatening to physically harm plaintiff if he kept talking.

Then defendant opened plaintiff's trap door for the sole purpose of misleading the control booth officer into thinking plaintiff was restrained and started waving to get his attention so that he would open the cell door.

Without any provocation defendant did maliciously and sadistically use unwarranted excessive force by attacking the unrestrained plaintiff once the cell was opened. Defendant snatched plaintiff off the ground and slammed him onto the concrete floor then proceeded to punch, kick, knee, and choke plaintiff until another officer had to physically restrain him from plaintiff.

As a result of the excessive force used by defendant, plaintiff sustained multiple physical injuries including a bruised heel, lower back pain, increased blood pressure, as well as migraine headaches and dizziness.

Plaintiff also suffered severe psychological trauma and mental anguish including depression, panic attacks, and nightmares of the assault.

VI. Relief:

STATE BRIEFLY EXACTLY WHAT YOU WANT THE COURT TO DO FOR YOU. YOU NEED NOT MAKE ANY LEGAL ARGUMENTS, OR CITE ANY CASES OR STATUTES.

Plaintiff respectfully prays that this court declare that the acts and omissions described herein violated plaintiff's rights under the constitution and laws of the United States

Also to enter judgment in favor of plaintiff for nominal, compensatory, and punitive damages as allowed by law against the defendant

Order such additional relief as the court may deem necessary

Signed this [--] day of [------], [----].

Prisoner No.   [1234567]   Signature _____ XXXXXX

*The complaint used here is similar to the complaint in an actual case that was decided by the Supreme Court. After the district court and court of appeals had dismissed the complaint because it alleged only a de minimis injury, the Supreme Court reversed and remanded the matter back to the lower court.

Instructions for Filing a Complaint by a Prisoner Under 42 U.S.C. § 1983

**UNITED STATES DISTRICT COURT
FOR THE DISTRICT OF COLUMBIA**

_____)
_____)
_____)
_____)

(Enter your full name, prison number,
and address)

v.

_____)
_____)
_____)
_____)

(Enter the full name and address(es),
if known, of the defendant(s) in this
action)

COMPLAINT FOR VIOLATION OF CIVIL RIGHTS

Instructions for filing a Complaint by a Prisoner

Under the Civil Rights Act, 42 U.S.C. § 1983

This packet contains one copy of a complaint form and one copy of an application to proceed *in forma pauperis.* To start an action, you must file an original and one copy of this complaint form.

Your complaint must be clearly handwritten or typewritten and you must sign and declare under penalty of perjury that the facts are correct. If you need additional space to answer a question, you may use another blank page.

Your complaint can be brought in this Court only if one or more of the named defendants is located within the District of Columbia. Further, you must file a separate [complaint] for each claim that you have unless they are related to the same incident or problem. The law requires that you state only facts in your complaint.

You must supply a certified copy of your prison trust account, pursuant to the provisions of 28 U.S.C. § 1915, effective April 26, 1996. The filing fee is $350.00. If insufficient funds exist in your prison account at the time of filing your complaint, the court <u>must</u> access, and when funds exist, collect an initial filing fee equal to 20 percent of the greater of:

(1) the average monthly deposits to your prison account, or

(2) the average monthly balance of your prison account for the prior six-month period.

Thereafter, you are required to make monthly payments of 20% of the preceding month's income. The agency having custody over you must forward payments from your account to the clerk of the court each time the amount in the account exceeds $10.00 until the filing fees are paid.

Therefore, before an assessment can be made regarding your ability to pay, you <u>must</u> submit a certified copy of your prison account for the prior six-month period.

When this form is completed, mail it and the copy to the Clerk of the United States District Court for the District of Columbia, 333 Constitution Ave., N.W., Washington, D.C. 20001.

I. SUCCESSIVE CLAIMS

Pursuant to the Prison Litigation Reform Act of 1995, unless a prisoner claims to be in "imminent danger of serious physical injury," he or she may not file a civil action or pursue a civil appeal *in forma pauperis* "if the prisoner has, on three or more occasions, while incarcerated or detained in any facility, brought an action or appeal in a court of the United States that was dismissed on the grounds that it is frivolous, malicious, or they failed to state a claim upon which relief could be granted."

II. PREVIOUS LAWSUITS

A. Have you begun other lawsuits in state or federal court dealing with the same or similar facts involved in this action?   Yes ( )   No ( )

B. Have you begun other lawsuits in state or federal court relating to your imprisonment?   Yes ( )   No ( )

C. If your answers to A or B is Yes, describe each lawsuit in the space below. (If there is more than one lawsuit, describe the additional lawsuits on another piece of paper, using the same outline.)

   1. Parties to this previous lawsuit.

   Plaintiffs: _____

   _____

   Defendants: _____

   _____

2. Court (If federal court, please name the district; if state court name the county.)

_____

3. Docket number: _____

4. Name of judge to whom case was assigned: _____

5. Disposition (for example: Was the case dismissed? Was it appealed? Is it still pending?)

_____

6. Approximate date of filing lawsuit: _____

_____

7. Approximate date of disposition: _____

_____

III. PLACE OF CONFINEMENT

_____

_____

A. Is there a prisoner grievance procedure in this institution?   Yes ( )   No ( )
   If your answer is Yes, go to Question III B. If your answer is No, skip Questions III, B, C, and D and go to Question III E.

B. Did you present the facts relating to your complaint in the prisoner grievance procedure?   Yes ( )   No ( )

C. If your answer is Yes to Question III B:
   1. To whom and when did you complain? _____

   _____

   2. Did you complain in writing? (Furnish copy of the complaint you made, if you have one.)   Yes ( )   No ( )

   3. What, if any, response did you receive? (Furnish copy of response, if in writing.)

   _____

   _____

   4. What happened as a result of your complaint? _____

   _____

   _____

D. If your answer is No to Question III B, explain why not.

   _____

   _____

E. If there is no prison grievance procedure in the institution, did you complain to prison authorities?   Yes ( )   No ( )

F. If your answer is Yes to Question III E:
   1. To whom and when did you complain? _____

   _____

2. Did you complain in writing? (Furnish copy of the complaint you made, if you have one.)   Yes ( )   No ( )

3. What, if any response did you receive? (Furnish copy of response, if in writing.)

_____

4. What happened as a result of your complaint? _____

_____

_____

IV. PARTIES

In item A below, place your name and prison number in the first blank and your present address in the second blank. Do the same for additional plaintiffs, if any.

A. Name of Plaintiff: _____

    Address: _____

In item B below, place the full name of the defendant(s) in the first blank, their official position in the second blank, their place of employment in the third blank, and their address in the fourth blank. Do the same for additional defendants, if any.

B. Defendant: _____

_____

    Address: _____

_____

    Defendant: _____

_____

    Address: _____

_____

    Defendant: _____

_____

    Address: _____

_____

    Defendant: _____

_____

    Address: _____

_____

V.   STATEMENT OF CLAIM

State here briefly as possible the facts of your case. Describe how each defendant is involved. Include the names of other persons involved, dates, and places. If you intend to allege a number of related claims, number and set forth each claim in a separate paragraph. Attach extra sheets, if necessary.

_____

_____

_____

_____

_____

_____

_____

_____

_____

_____

_____

_____

VI. RELIEF

State briefly exactly what you want the Court to do for you.

_____

_____

_____

_____

_____

_____

_____

_____

_____

_____

_____

_____

_____

Signed this _____ day of _____, _____.

_____   _____

                                      (Signature of Plaintiff)

I declare under penalty of perjury that the foregoing is true and correct.

_____   _____

      (Date)   (Signature of Plaintiff)

Appendix 6

Prohibited Acts and Disciplinary Severity Scale

Table 3—Prohibited Acts and Disciplinary Severity Scale

Code	Prohibited acts	Sanctions
	Greatest Category	
	The UDC (Unit Discipline Committee) shall refer all Greatest Severity Prohibited Acts to the DHO (Discipline Hearing Officer) with recommendations as to an appropriate disposition.	
100	Killing	A. Recommend parole date rescission or retardation.
101	Assaulting any person (includes sexual assault) or an armed assault on the institution's secure perimeter (a charge for assaulting any person at this level is to be used only when serious physical Injury has been attempted or carried out by an inmate)	B. Forfeit earned statutory good time or non-vested good conduct time (up to 100%) and/or terminate or disallow extra good time (an extra good time or good conduct time sanction may not be suspended).
102	Escape from escort; escape from a secure institution (low-, medium-, and high-security level and administrative institutions); or escape from a minimum institution *with* *violence*	
103	Setting a fire (charged with this act in this category only when found to pose a threat to life or a threat of serious bodily harm or in furtherance of a prohibited act of Greatest Severity, e.g., in furtherance of a riot or escape; otherwise the charge is properly classified Code 218, or 329)	B.1 Disallow ordinarily between 50–75% (27–41 days) of good conduct time credit available for year (a good conduct time sanction may not be suspended).
104	Possession, manufacture, or introduction of a gun, firearm, weapon, sharpened instrument, knife, dangerous chemical, explosive, or any ammunition	C. Disciplinary Transfer (recommend). D. Disciplinary segregation (up to 60 days). E. Make monetary restitution.
105	Rioting	F. Withhold statutory good time (Note—can be in addition to A through E—cannot be the only sanction executed).
106	Encouraging others to riot	
107	Taking hostage(s)	
108	Possession, manufacture, or introduction of a hazardous tool (Tools most likely to be used in an escape or escape attempt or to serve as weapons capable of doing serious bodily harm to others; or those hazardous to institutional security or personal safety; e.g., hack-saw blade)	G. Loss of privileges (Note—can be in addition to A through E—cannot be the only sanction executed).

109	(Not to be used)	
110	Refusing to provide a urine sample or to take part in other drug-abuse testing	
111	Introduction of any narcotics, marijuana, drugs, or related paraphernalia not prescribed for the individual by the medical staff	
112	Use of any narcotics, marijuana, drugs, or related paraphernalia not prescribed for the individual by the medical staff	
113	Possession of any narcotics, marijuana, drugs, or related paraphernalia not prescribed for the individual by the medical staff	
197	Use of the telephone to further criminal activity	
198	Interfering with a staff member in the performance of duties. (*Conduct must be of the Greatest Severity nature.*) This charge is to be used only when another charge of greatest severity is not applicable	
199	Conduct which disrupts or interferes with the security or orderly running of the institution or the Bureau of Prisons. (*Conduct must be of the Greatest Severity nature.*) This charge is to be used only when another charge of greatest severity is not applicable	

Table 3—Prohibited Acts and Disciplinary Severity Scale (*Continued*)

Code	Prohibited acts	Sanctions
	High Category	
200	Escape from unescorted Community Programs and activities and Open Institutions (minimum) and from outside secure institutions—*without* violence	A. Recommend parole date rescission or retardation.
201	Fighting with another person	B. Forfeit earned statutory good time or non-vested good conduct time up to 50% or up to 60 days, whichever is less, and/or terminate or disallow extra good time (an extra good time or good conduct time sanction may not be suspended).
202	(Not to be used)	
203	Threatening another with bodily harm or any other offense	
204	Extortion, blackmail, protection: Demanding or receiving money or anything of value in return for protection against others, to avoid bodily harm, or under threat of informing	
205	Engaging in sexual acts	
206	Making sexual proposals or threats to another	B.1 Disallow ordinarily between 25 and 50% (14–27 days) of good conduct time credit available for year (a good conduct time sanction may not be suspended).
207	Wearing a disguise or a mask	
208	Possession of any unauthorized locking device, or lock pick, or tampering with or blocking any lock device (includes keys), or destroying, altering, interfering with, improperly using, or damaging any security device, mechanism, or procedure	C. Disciplinary transfer (recommend).
209	Adulteration of any food or drink	D. Disciplinary segregation (up to 30 days).
210	(Not to be used)	
211	Possessing any officer's or staff clothing	E. Make monetary restitution.
212	Engaging in or encouraging a group demonstration	F. Withhold statutory good time.
213	Encouraging others to refuse to work, or to participate in a work stoppage	G. Loss of privileges: commissary, movies, recreation, etc.
214	(Not to be used)	H. Change housing (quarters).
215	Introduction of alcohol into BOP facility	I. Remove from program and/or group activity.
216	Giving or offering an official or staff member a bribe, or anything of value	J. Loss of job.
217	Giving money to, or receiving money from, any person for purposes of introducing contraband or for any other illegal or prohibited purposes	K. Impound inmate's personal property. L. Confiscate contraband. M. Restrict to quarters.
218	Destroying, altering, or damaging government property, or the property of another person, having a value in excess of $100.00 or destroying, altering, or damaging life-safety devices (e.g., fire alarm) regardless of financial value	

219	Stealing (theft; this includes data obtained through the unauthorized use of a communications facility, or through the unauthorized access to disks, tapes, or computer printouts or other automated equipment on which data is stored.)	
220	Demonstrating, practicing, or using martial arts, boxing (except for use of a punching bag), wrestling, or other forms of physical encounter, or military exercises or drill (except for drill authorized and conducted by staff)	
221	Being in an unauthorized area with a person of the opposite sex without staff permission	
222	Making, possessing, or using intoxicants	
223	Refusing to breathe into a breathalyzer or take part in other testing for use of alcohol	
224	Assaulting any person (charged with this act only when a less serious physical injury or contact has been attempted or carried out by an inmate)	
297	Use of the telephone for abuses other than criminal activity (e.g., circumventing telephone monitoring procedures, possession and/or use of another inmate's PIN number; third-party calling; third-party billing; using credit card numbers to place telephone calls, conference calling; talking in code)	
298	Interfering with a staff member in the performance of duties. (*Conduct must be of the High Severity nature.*) This charge is to be used only when another charge of high severity is not applicable	
299	Conduct which disrupts or interferes with the security or orderly running of the institution or the Bureau of Prisons. (*Conduct must be of the High Severity nature.*) This charge is to be used only when another charge of high severity is not applicable	

Table 3—Prohibited Acts and Disciplinary Severity Scale (*Continued*)

Code	Prohibited acts	Sanctions
	Moderate Category	
300	Indecent exposure	A. Recommend parole date rescission or retardation.
301	(Not to be used)	
302	Misuse of authorized medication	B. Forfeit earned statutory good time or non-vested good conduct time up to 25% or up to 30 days, whichever is less, and/or terminate or disallow extra good time (an extra good time or good conduct time sanction may not be suspended).
303	Possession of money or currency, unless specifically authorized, or in excess of the amount authorized	
304	Loaning of property or anything of value for profit or increased return	
305	Possession of anything not authorized for retention or receipt by the inmate and not issued to him through regular channels	
306	Refusing to work, or to accept a program assignment	B.1 Disallow ordinarily up to 25% (1–14 days) of good conduct time credit available for year (a good conduct time sanction may not be suspended).
307	Refusing to obey an order of any staff member (May be categorized and charged in terms of greater severity, according to the nature of the order being disobeyed; e.g., failure to obey an order which furthers a riot would be charged as 105, Rioting; refusing to obey an order which furthers a fight would be charged as 201, Fighting; refusing to provide a urine sample when ordered would be charged as Code 110	C. Disciplinary transfer (recommend). D. Disciplinary segregation (up to 15 days).
308	Violating a condition of a furlough	E. Make monetary restitution.
309	Violating a condition of a community program	F. Withhold statutory good time.
310	Unexcused absence from work or any assignment	G. Loss of privileges: commissary, movies, recreation, etc.
311	Failing to perform work as instructed by the supervisor	
312	Insolence towards a staff member	
313	Lying or providing a false statement to a staff member	H. Change housing (quarters).
314	Counterfeiting, forging or unauthorized reproduction of any document, article of identification, money, security, or official paper. (May be categorized in terms of greater severity according to the nature of the item being reproduced; e.g., counterfeiting release papers to effect escape, Code 102 or Code 200)	I. Remove from program and/or group activity. J. Loss of job. K. Impound inmate's personal property. L. Confiscate contraband. M. Restrict to quarters. N. Extra duty.
315	Participating in an unauthorized meeting or gathering	
316	Being in an unauthorized area	

317	Failure to follow safety or sanitation regulations	
318	Using any equipment or machinery which is not specifically authorized	
319	Using any equipment or machinery contrary to instructions or posted safety standards	
320	Failing to stand count	
321	Interfering with the taking of count	
322	(Not to be used)	
323	(Not to be used)	
324	Gambling	
325	Preparing or conducting a gambling pool	
326	Possession of gambling paraphernalia	
327	Unauthorized contacts with the public	
328	Giving money or anything of value to, or accepting money or anything of value from: another inmate, or any other person without staff authorization	
329	Destroying, altering, or damaging government property, or the property of another person, having a value of $100.00 or less	
330	Being unsanitary or untidy; failing to keep one's person and one's quarters in accordance with posted standards	
331	Possession, manufacture, or introduction of a non-hazardous tool or other non-hazardous contraband (Tool not likely to be used in an escape or escape attempt, or to serve as a weapon capable of doing serious bodily harm to others, or not hazardous to institutional security or personal safety; Other non-hazardous contraband includes such items as food or cosmetics).	
332	Smoking where prohibited	
397	Use of the telephone for abuses other than criminal activity (e.g., conference calling, possession and/or use of another inmate's PIN number, three-way calling, providing false information for preparation of a telephone list).	
398	Interfering with a staff member in the performance of duties. (*Conduct must be of the Moderate Severity nature.*) This charge is to be used only when another charge of moderate severity is not applicable.	
399	Conduct which disrupts or interferes with the security or orderly running of the institution or the Bureau of Prisons. (*Conduct must be of the Moderate Severity nature.*) This charge is to be used only when another charge of moderate severity is not applicable.	

Low Moderate Category		
400	Possession of property belonging to another person	B.1 Disallow ordinarily up to 12.5% (1–7 days) of good conduct time credit available for year (to be used only where inmate found to have committed a second violation of the same prohibited act within 6 months); Disallow ordinarily up to 25% (1–14 days) of good conduct time credit available for year (to be used only where inmate found to have committed a third violation of the same prohibited act within 6 months) (a good conduct time sanction may not be suspended).
401	Possessing unauthorized amount of otherwise authorized clothing	
402	Malingering, feigning illness	
403	(Not to be used)	
404	Using abusive or obscene language	
405	Tattooing or self-mutilation	
406	(Not to be used)	
407	Conduct with a visitor in violation of bureau regulations (Restriction, or loss for a specific period of time, of these privileges may often be an appropriate sanction G)	
408	Conducting a business	
409	Unauthorized physical contact (e.g., kissing, embracing)	
410	Unauthorized use of mail (Restriction, or loss for a specific period of time, of these privileges may often be an appropriate sanction G) (May be categorized and charged in terms of greater severity, according to the nature of the unauthorized use; e.g., the mail is used for planning, facilitating, committing an armed assault on the institution's secure perimeter, would be charged as a Code 101 Assault)	E. Make monetary restitution. F. Withhold statutory good time. G. Loss of privileges: commissary, movies, recreation, etc.
497	Use of the telephone for abuses other than criminal activity (e.g., exceeding the 15-minute time limit for telephone calls; using the telephone in an unauthorized area; placing of an unauthorized individual on the telephone list)	H. Change housing (quarters). I. Remove from program and/or group activity. J. Loss of job.
498	Interfering with a staff member in the performance of duties. (*Conduct must be of the Low Moderate severity nature.*) This charge is to be used only when another charge of Low Moderate severity is not applicable	K. Impound inmate's personal property. L. Confiscate contraband. M. Restrict to quarters.
499	Conduct which disrupts or interferes with the security or orderly running of the institution or the Bureau of Prisons (*Conduct must be of the Low Moderate severity nature.*) This charge is to be used only when another charge of low moderate severity is not applicable	N. Extra duty. O. Reprimand. P. Warning.

NOTE: *Aiding* another person to commit any of these offenses, *attempting* to commit any of these offenses, and *making plans* to commit any of these offenses, in all categories of severity, shall be considered the same as a commission of the offense itself.

Author's comment: We have learned that the Bureau of Prisons recently revised its listing of prohibited acts and available sanctions. The updated information may be found in Title 28 § CFR 541.3 (revised as of July 1, 2011).

SOURCE: Reprinted from the Federal Bureau of Prisons, published in Title 28 CFR §541.13 (revised as of July 1, 2010).

Collateral Consequences of a Felony Conviction

Collateral Consequences of a Felony Conviction

Legend: ■ = Yes

	Voting rights restorable	Public employment		Jury service duty		Firearm ownership		Sex offender registration	Offenses for which parental rights are terminated
		Barred	Restorable	Forfeited	Restorable	Forfeited	Restorable		
Alabama	■	■		■ For crime of moral turpitude		■ Concealed weapons		■ Also habitual offenders (3 or more felonies)	
Alaska	■		■	■ For crime of moral turpitude			■ Concealed weapons	■	Sexual or child abuse
Arizona	■	■ If public office, other public employment permitted			■		■	■[1]	
Arkansas		■			■		■	■	Abandonment, neglect, unfitness
California	■	■ For specified crimes			■	■ Concealed weapons		■	
Colorado	■		■		■		After 10 yrs	■	
Connecticut[2]	■	■ If public office, until rights regained		■ For 7 yrs		■ Concealed weapons		■	Abandonment or neglect
Delaware	■	■ If for conviction of infamous crime			■		■	■	Crime involved or harmed child
District of Columbia	■		■	■		■ Concealed weapons		■	
Florida	■	■ If directly related to position of employment			■	■		■	
Georgia	■	■ If felony involved moral turpitude		■			■	■	
Hawaii	■	■ If public office	■ With exceptions for specified crimes	■ If not pardoned		■		■ Certain sex crimes only	

Collateral Consequences of a Felony Conviction

Legend: ■=Yes

	Voting rights restorable	Public employment		Jury service duty		Firearm ownership		Sex offender registration	Offenses for which parental rights are terminated
		Barred	Restorable	Forfeited	Restorable	Forfeited	Restorable		
Idaho[3]	■		■		■		Can petition after 5 yrs	Certain sex crimes only	
Illinois	■		■		■ Must be free of legal exception		■	Sex offenders and specified murderers	
Indiana	■	■			■	■		■	
Iowa	■	■			■	■		■	
Kansas	■		■	■		■ Forfeit for 5 yrs, 10 yrs, or life		■	
Kentucky			■ Except if bribery		■	■		■	Abandonment, neglect, or abuse
Louisiana	■	■ If convicted while in state employment		■		■		■	
Maine	■		■		■		■ Can petition after 5 yrs for concealable	■	
Maryland	■		■	■ If fined over $500 or sentenced to 6+ months; restored via pardon		■		■	
Massachusetts	■		■ Except for judicial branch employment	For 7 yrs		■		■	
Michigan	■	■ From Dept. of Corrections		■ While serving sentence			After 3-5 yrs	■	
Minnesota	■	■ Where crime relates to position			■		After 10 yrs	■	Abandonment, murder, manslaughter, or assault of another child of the parent
Mississippi			■	If infamous crime		■ Unless pardoned		■	
Missouri	■		■ Except felony connected w/ right of suffrage	Unless restored to civil rights		■		■ Also crimes against minors	
Montana	■		■	■			■ Lifetime supervision	■	If unfit and convicted of violent crime
Nebraska	■		■		■	■		■	Abandonment, neglect, or abuse

Collateral Consequences of a Felony Conviction

Legend: ■=Yes

	Voting rights restorable	Public employment		Jury service duty		Firearm ownership		Sex offender registration	Offenses for which parental rights are terminated
		Barred	Restorable	Forfeited	Restorable	Forfeited	Restorable		
Nevada	■	■			■	■		■	
New Hampshire	■[4]		■		■	■		■	
New Jersey	■		■	■		■		■	Abandonment, neglect, or abuse
New Mexico	■	■ From elected or appointed office			■	■		■	Abandonment, neglect, or abuse
New York[5]	■		■ Except public officials	■		■ Rifles/ shotguns	■ After 5 yrs	■	Permanent neglect
North Carolina	■		■ Except police or sheriffs		■ Not "qualified" and subject to challenge for cause	■[6]		■ Also certain crimes against children	Abandonment, abuse, or neglect
North Dakota	■		■	■			■ After 10 yrs	■ Also crimes against children	Abandonment or neglect
Ohio	■	■			■	■		■	Abandonment
Oklahoma	■		■ Except public officials		■	■		■	Child abuse or death of a child
Oregon	■		■		■		■ Unless conviction expunged	■	Abuse, neglect, unfitness, extreme conduct, abandonment
Pennsylvania	■		■ Unless subversive person	■		■		■ Also child kidnapping	Abandonment or neglect
Puerto Rico			■	■			■	■	Misconduct
Rhode Island	■	■ For 3 yrs				■	After 2 yrs if non violent crime	■ Also crimes against children	Unfitness, abusive, or abandonment
South Carolina	■ Elected or appointed office	■			■	■		■	Abandonment, neglect, or abuse
South Dakota	■		■		■	■		■	Murder, sex offense, crimes against children
Tennessee			■		■	■		■	Abandonment, neglect, or abuse; incarcerated 10+ yrs & child under 8

Collateral Consequences of a Felony Conviction

Legend: ■ = Yes

	Voting rights restorable	Public employment		Jury service duty		Firearm ownership		Sex offender registration	Offenses for which parental rights are terminated
		Barred	Restorable	Forfeited	Restorable	Forfeited	Restorable		
Texas	■			■			■ After 5 yrs	■	Murder, assault, sexual offenses causing death or serious injury to a child
Utah	■ Not for treason, bribery, election fraud		■ May be removed from public office as part of sentence	■ Unless conviction expunged		■		■	
Vermont	■		■	■		■		■	Unfitness
Virginia	■		■	■ Unless pardoned		■ Unless pardoned		■ Also crimes against minors	Abandonment or neglect
Washington			■ Except for public officials			■	■	■	
West Virginia	■		■	■ If perjury or infamous crime		■		■	
Wisconsin	■		■			■	■	■	[7]
Wyoming	■		■			■	■	■	Unfitness

FOOTNOTES:

Arizona:
[1] Judges may require registration at time of sentencing.

Connecticut:
[2] Exception, civil rights are not impaired for failure to pay support (a felony).

Idaho:
[3] Still has "civil death" statutes for felons sentenced to life imprisonment. However, these laws have been partially abrogated by holdings of appellate courts that denial of access to courts is a violation of equal protection.

New Hampshire:
[4] Except bribery, treason, or willful violation of election laws, which require restoration by Supreme Court.

New York:
[5] Still has "civil death" statutes for felons sentenced to life imprisonment. However, these laws have been partially abrogated by holdings of appellate courts that denial of access to courts is a violation of equal protection.

North Carolina:
[6] Five years from the last of these events: conviction of that felony; unconditional discharge from prison; or termination of suspended sentence, or parole. No possession of firearms less than 26 inches in length or weapons of mass destruction for 10 years after final discharge if convicted of a violent felony except that any firearm is okay to keep in the home or lawful place of business.

Wisconsin:
[7] May terminate if parent has caused death/injury to a child/children resulting in a felony conviction or if parent intentionally/recklessly killed other parent.

Source: State Court Organization 2004. Table 47. Washington, DC: Bureau of Justice Statistics, United States Department of Justice. August 2006.

Glossary

Listed here are words and terms that are used in this text and that are often encountered in corrections, criminal justice, and the law. Many of the definitions were taken from the Dictionary of Criminal Justice Data Terminology, published by the U.S. Department of Justice, Law Enforcement Assistance Administration (1976, 1981). Other definitions are the authors'—you can spot them; they are the ones that are obscure and hard to understand!

abscond (corrections): To depart from a geographical area or jurisdiction prescribed by the conditions of one's probation or parole, without authorization. (*Caution:* this term is not to be used as a synonym for escape.)

abscond (court): To intentionally absent or conceal oneself unlawfully in order to avoid a legal proceeding.

accreditation: Recognition by an authority that an organization, program, or facility has achieved high professional standards. (In corrections, there is an accreditation program administered by a commission associated with the American Correctional Association.)

acquittal: A judgment of a court, based either on the verdict of a jury or a judicial officer, that the defendant is not guilty of the offense(s) for which he has been tried.

adjudication (criminal): The judicial decision that terminates a criminal proceeding with a judgment of conviction or acquittal or a dismissal of the case.

adjudication (juvenile): The juvenile court decision that terminates an adjudicatory hearing with a judgment that the juvenile is a delinquent, a status offender, or a dependent, or that the allegations in the petition are not sustained.

administrative law: The body of law created by administrative agencies (such as regulatory agencies). These laws are seen in the form of rules, regulations, orders, and interpretive decisions.

adult: A person who is within the original jurisdiction of a criminal court rather than a juvenile court because his age at the time of an alleged criminal act was above a statutorily specified limit.

affidavit: A written statement of facts, confirmed by oath or affirmation of the person making it (the affiant).

allocution: Inquiry made by a judge directly to a defendant who has been convicted as to whether there is any legal reason why judgment should not be rendered. More frequently today, asking the defendant at the sentencing phase of the criminal proceeding for any statement in mitigation of the sentence.

alternative facility: An alternative place of confinement (to traditional confinement institutions, such as prisons or jails), with lesser security controls, which may be used as an option in sentencing or in an inmate's placement by corrections authorities.

amicus curiae: Friend of the court. A person who is not a party but who has a strong interest in a legal matter and who asks permission to lodge his views with the court (usually in an appellate court) in an amicus brief.

answer (civil procedure): The pleading filed by the defendant, responding to the plaintiff's allegations in the complaint. It is a written statement that sets out the defendant's factual and legal grounds for his defense.

appeal: A request by either party that a case be removed from a lower court to a higher court in order for a trial proceeding to be reviewed by the higher court. It also refers to the review by an appeals court of a lower court's proceedings or outcome.

appellant: A person who initiates an appeal (ordinarily, the person who has lost in the lower court).

appellee: The opposing party to an appellant (usually, the person who has prevailed in the lower court and who defends in the higher court the results or rulings in that lower court).

arraignment: The appearance of a person (soon after arrest or after charges have been lodged) before a court in order that the court may inform him of the accusation(s) against him and in order that he may enter his plea to the charges.

arrest: Taking a person into custody by authority of the law for the purpose of charging him with a criminal offense or for the purpose of initiating juvenile proceedings, terminating with the recording of a specific offense.

assault: The unlawful intentional infliction, or attempted or threatened infliction, of injury upon another. (Also defined as an unlawful physical attack by one person upon another.)

attorney: A person trained in the law, admitted to practice before the bar of a given jurisdiction, and authorized to advise, represent, and act for other persons in legal proceedings. (Used interchangeably with lawyer or counsel.)

battery: The unlawful use of force against the person of another. Technically, offensive touching or bodily injury to another person.

Bill of Rights: A common term for the first 10 Amendments to the U.S. Constitution.

Bivens action: An action in federal court, alleging a civil rights violation by federal officials. Named for a Supreme Court opinion (*Bivens v. Six Unknown Narcotics Agents*) that allows a lawsuit for such federal agents' violations equivalent to the lawsuits authorized by 42 U.S.C. § 1983 for violations of civil rights by persons operating under color of state law.

bona fide: In good faith. Honestly, openly, without deceit.

bond (appearance bond): A written promise by a financially responsible person to pay the bail sum if the offender does not follow the terms of release. See also release on bail.

booking: An action by police that officially records an arrest and identifies the person, the place, the time, the arresting authority, and the reason for the arrest.

boot camp: A camp that emphasizes programs of intensive, militaristic regimens. It is used as an alternative to regular imprisonment. It has been used principally for younger offenders, and it requires a shorter term of confinement than ordinarily would be imposed.

brief: A written document prepared by counsel that presents facts, discussion of contested issues, legal references, and arguments pertaining to the case before a trial court or an appellate court.

burden of proof: The necessity of proving a fact or facts in dispute in a case. The obligation a party has to introduce sufficient evidence to convince the trier of fact that an essential fact or conclusion is true.

camp: A correctional facility, usually located in a rural setting and usually of a low-security level, for the confinement of adults or juveniles who have been committed after their adjudication.

canon law (church law): The body of law established by religious organizations, administered by religious officials, for the determination of rights and liabilities under matters subject to religious jurisdiction.

capacity (corrections): The number of inmates or residents that a correctional facility can house.

capital punishment: The sanction of the death penalty. Now used only with great procedural protections, in cases where it is authorized by criminal statute.

case (criminal court): A single charging document under the jurisdiction of a criminal court. Also used to refer to a single defendant or any individual who is the object of criminal prosecution. (Used in the same sense for a juvenile who is being processed in juvenile court.)

case (legal proceedings): The court proceeding, whether civil or criminal, in all its aspects. Also used to refer to a report of a court decision in legal publications, such as court reporters.

case law: The cumulated law, as given in the decisions of courts. The aggregate of reported cases on a particular subject, or from a particular source, or in toto.

caseload (corrections): The total number of clients registered with a corrections agency, or with an individual officer within an agency, during a specified time period. (Usually refers to persons under probation or parole supervision, or those assigned to caseworkers inside a corrections facility.)

caseload (court): The total number of cases filed in a given court, or before a certain judicial officer, during a given period of time.

caveat: A warning or notice to beware or to exercise caution or special care.

certiorari: A writ issued by a superior court to an inferior court of record, ordering the certification of the records and proceedings in the case, so that the record (the case) may be reviewed for any error and corrected, as needed. A form of appellate review. (Now, used principally to apply to reviews by the U.S. Supreme Court of actions by lower courts. To obtain a Supreme Court review, an applicant files a petition for a writ of certiorari.)

chancery (court of chancery): A court to hear cases in equity (in England and some places in the United States).

charge: A formal allegation that a specific person has committed a specific offense. (Inside a corrections facility, used to refer to allegations of misconduct against persons, under the facility's administrative disciplinary code.)

charging document: A formal written accusation, filed in a court, alleging that a specified person has committed a specific offense. (Inside a corrections facility, the written accusation alleging that inmates have committed certain acts of misconduct.) In court, there are three kinds of charging documents: complaint, information, and indictment. When the charging document is filed in a court, that initiates criminal proceedings against the accused.

checks and balances: Procedures established by constitutional requirements, whereby each of the three branches of government has some constraints on the other two.

citation (criminal court): A written order issued by a law enforcement officer directing an alleged offender to appear in a specific court at a specified time in order to answer a criminal charge.

citation (legal research): The reference to the exact place in legal reference books where a court decision can be found. Usually, a citation (also called a cite) refers to a certain collection of legal books and includes the volume and page numbers where a decision is located.

civil law: The body of law that determines private rights and liabilities, as distinguished from criminal law.

civil liberties (civil rights): Personal rights guaranteed by the Constitution. The liberties of any member of society, particularly against government encroachment, but restrained as need be for the protection of the rights of others.

class action: An action brought by one (or a few) plaintiff(s) on behalf of a large group of persons, all of whom have similar interests in pursuing the action.

classification (corrections): The systematic arrangement, usually prescribed by written policy, of persons or things into similar groups, based on specified criteria. There are two principal subjects of classification in corrections: (1) correctional facilities, or portions of facilities, usually grouped by security level (such as minimum, medium, maximum, high, or low) or special purpose (such as pretrial status, protective custody, or medical or mental health facilities); (2) inmates, whereby offenders are grouped according to their backgrounds, their special needs, their legal status, and their custody requirements (reflecting any requirements for special security precautions).

clemency: An act (usually by the executive) of forgiveness or leniency. The granting of a pardon or a commutation of sentence.

commitment: The action of a judicial officer ordering that a convicted adult, or an adjudicated juvenile, be admitted into a correctional facility. (May be used to refer to an order for the admission of a person before final adjudication for a temporary, special purpose, such as a commitment of a criminal defendant to a mental health facility to determine competency to stand trial. May also be used to refer to an order for admission of a patient for mental health observation and treatment, termed a civil commitment.)

common law: Those principles and rules, applicable to government and individuals, that do not rest for their original authority on statutes but on statements (rulings) found in decisions of courts. In a broader sense, it is sometimes used to refer to the Anglo-American system of justice and legal concepts.

community corrections: All of those organizations, facilities, and programs that operate in a locality outside of traditional confinement facilities.

community facility: A correctional facility from which residents are regularly permitted to depart, without escort, for the purpose of using community resources, such as schools or treatment programs, or seeking or holding employment. (May be used during preadjudication or for the commitment of adults or juveniles.)

community service: A sentence (or alternative to sentencing) in which the offender performs work benefiting a charity, a government operation, or another organization; the work is approved by the sentencing court as being in the public's (or community's) interest.

commutation: The act of clemency, reducing a sentence. Changing a sentence to one that is less severe.

compact: An agreement between persons, nations, or states. Often used to describe agreements between states concerning matters of mutual interest and concern (interstate compacts). Compacts between states must receive the approval of Congress, as required by Article I, Section 10 of the U.S. Constitution.

competent: With respect to the law, having sufficient ability to act or participate in a legal matter. With respect to court proceedings or administrative hearings, possessing sufficient understanding, especially the mental capacity, to be involved in the proceeding, whether as a party or a witness.

complaint (civil procedure): The initial pleading filed in court, by which a legal action is commenced. This is the pleading that sets out a claim for relief, including the factual and legal grounds for such relief.

complaint (criminal procedure): A formal, written accusation made by any person, often a prosecutor, and filed in a court, alleging that a specified person has committed a specific offense. (Usually used in misdemeanor cases or to initiate probable cause hearings in felony cases.)

concurrent sentences: Two or more terms of imprisonment that are served simultaneously, "running together," in whole or in part. (The opposite: consecutive sentences.)

confinement: The status of being in secured custody, where the person is not free to come and go, unless escorted.

confinement facility: A correctional facility from which the inmates are not permitted to depart unaccompanied. (This is a broad term for detention facilities [jails] and corrections institutions [prisons]. Some community facilities have such restrictions on their inmates, to the degree that they may be considered confinement facilities. Similarly, some jails and prisons allow some inmates to reenter the community unescorted to participate in work-release or other programs. Such jails and prisons are still considered to be confinement facilities if the majority of the inmates are not regularly released for such unescorted activities in the community.)

conjugal visits: Visits with a spouse. In corrections, the term has come to refer to programs that allow an inmate and spouse to be together in separate facilities, away from the common visiting room, where they have more privacy and the opportunity for sexual intimacy.

consecutive sentences: One term of imprisonment being served following another. (In some places, called "from and after" sentences.)

consent: Voluntary agreement to the proposal or request of another person.

consent decree: A decree (judgment or order of a court) that is agreed to by both parties in a lawsuit and, when approved by the court, is binding on them both.

constitution: A statement of the fundamental laws or principles that are agreed on to govern a nation, a state, an organization, or a society.

contraband (corrections): Material which is prohibited, either by law or regulation. It includes material which can reasonably be expected to cause physical injury or to adversely affect the security, safety, or good order of a prison or jail.

contract: An agreement, between competent persons, with consideration (that is, a price paid [not always money] for a promise) to do, or refrain from doing, a particular thing.

convict: An adult who has been found guilty and sentenced in criminal court and who is confined in a confinement facility. (Virtually a slang term today; inmate and prisoner are the preferred terms.)

conviction: A judgment of a court, based either on the verdict of a jury or a judicial officer or on the guilty plea of the defendant, that the defendant is guilty of the offense for which he has been tried.

coram nobis: Technically, a writ of error coram nobis. An order at common law to correct a judgment in the same court in which it was entered.

correctional agency: A federal, state, or local criminal justice agency, under a single administrative authority, of which the principal functions are the investigation, intake screening, supervision, custody, confinement, or treatment of alleged or adjudicated adult offenders, or juvenile delinquents or status offenders. (This includes probation agencies, parole agencies, juvenile agencies, and agencies that administer correctional facilities.)

correctional facility: A building, a set of buildings, or an area enclosing a set of buildings operated by an agency (public or private) for the custody or treatment of adjudicated and committed persons, or persons subject to criminal or juvenile justice proceedings.

correctional institution: A generic name for long-term adult confinement facilities (often called prisons, federal or state correctional institutions, or penitentiaries) and juvenile and youth confinement facilities (sometimes called training schools, reformatories, boys' ranches, and the like).

correctional officer: An employee of a correctional agency whose duties include one or more of the functions of the agency. Used most often to refer to those employees who are responsible for the security functions of correctional facilities and for the direct supervision of inmates. (A colloquial synonym is guard.)

corrections: A generic term that includes all government agencies, facilities, programs, procedures, personnel, and techniques concerned with the investigation, intake, custody, confinement, supervision, or treatment of alleged or adjudicated adult offenders, juvenile delinquents, or status offenders.

counsel: See attorney.

count (corrections): The procedure for "taking the roll" of all persons who are present in a correctional facility. Records of the facility show the exact number of persons who should be present at a given time; during regularly scheduled (and sometimes irregular or random) counting times, staff members verify that all persons assigned to the facility are accounted for. When a count is taken, all inmates are required to be and remain at their assigned location for that particular time until the count is "cleared"—that is, the correct count is verified.

count (court): Each separate offense, as listed in a complaint, information, or indictment.

court: An agency or individual officer of the judicial branch of government, authorized or established by statute or constitution, which has the authority to decide controversies in law and disputed matters of fact brought before it.

court of appeals: A court that does not try cases, but rather hears appeals.

court of general jurisdiction: A court that has the legal authority to try all civil cases and criminal offenses, including all felonies.

court of limited jurisdiction: A court with authority to try cases, but only cases of certain kinds. Such courts often have no authority to try felony cases, or they have authority that is limited to only certain kinds of felonies.

crime (criminal offense): An act committed or omitted in violation of a law forbidding or commanding it, for which an adult can be punished, upon conviction, by incarceration or other penalties, or for which a juvenile can be brought under the jurisdiction of a juvenile court and adjudicated as a delinquent or transferred to adult court.

criminal justice agency: Any court with criminal jurisdiction and any other government agency or subunit that defends indigents or of which the principal functions or activities consist of the prevention, detection, and investigation of crime; the apprehension, detention, and prosecution of alleged offenders; the confinement or official correctional supervision of accused or convicted persons; or the administrative or technical support of these functions.

criminal laws (penal laws): The body of state and federal statutes that impose penalties for offenses against the state. (Criminal law is the entire body of law—statutes, court opinions, rules—that defines offenses against the state, sets rules for their prosecution, and authorizes sanctions for committing offenses.)

criminal proceedings: Proceedings in a court of law, undertaken to determine the guilt or innocence of an adult accused of a crime.

cruel and unusual punishment: Excessive, inhumane penalties or correctional treatment, prohibited by the Eighth Amendment to the U.S. Constitution.

damages: Monetary awards in civil cases, given by court order (judgment) to a person who has been harmed by another.

deadly force: Force intended or likely to cause death or serious bodily harm.

decision: A determination or conclusion reached by a court. Usually used to refer to the written report of a court that states its conclusion or determination of the case. The decision reached by a court is reflected in its opinion. (See that definition.)

declaratory relief (declaratory judgment): A court judgment that sets out conclusively the rights and duties of parties but involves no coercive or monetary relief.

defamation: A tort, involving the unprivileged publication of false statements, which result in injury to another. The injury suffered may be contempt, ridicule, hatred, or damage to reputation.

defendant: A person against whom a criminal proceeding is undertaken or a person against whom a civil legal action is brought.

defense attorney: An attorney who represents the defendant in a legal proceeding.

delinquency: Juvenile actions or conduct in violation of criminal law (and sometimes also in committing status offenses).

delinquent: A juvenile who has been adjudicated by a judicial officer of a juvenile court as having committed a delinquent act, which is an act for which an adult could be prosecuted in a criminal court.

de novo: Anew, afresh, as if there had been no earlier decision.

dependent children: Juveniles without family or support, or who have deficient family or support. These children may appear before juvenile courts to verify their dependency status so the courts may determine the best steps that can be taken for their welfare.

deposition: The testimony of a witness taken under oath, not in open court, in response to oral questions, pursuant to a rule or order that authorizes such questioning. The testimony is transcribed and is usually intended for use at a later trial.

detainer: A notice that informs prison authorities that charges (or sometimes an unserved sentence, as for an escapee) are pending elsewhere against an inmate, and asks that the custodian notify the requesting jurisdiction before the inmate is released.

detention: The legally authorized holding in confinement of a person subject to criminal or juvenile court proceedings, until the point of commitment to a correctional facility, release to an alternative facility, or release to the community.

detention center: A facility that provides temporary care in a physically restricting environment for juveniles in custody pending court disposition.

detention facility: A generic term for all types of facilities that hold adults or juveniles in confinement pending adjudication; such facilities also often hold adults who are sentenced for a year or less of confinement, and, in some instances, postadjudicated juveniles. These facilities may variously be called jails, county farms, work camps, road camps, detention centers, shelters, or juvenile halls.

determinate sentence: A sentence, usually to a term of imprisonment, for a period of time that is fixed by statute. (Similar to a mandatory sentence, but not identical.)

deterrence: The act, or theory, of stopping action by frightening the potential actor. In penology (sentencing philosophy), deterrence refers to the discouragement of crime because of fear of its consequences (the sanctions that may be imposed). There are two aspects of deterrence: specific (or individual) deterrence—discouragement of the individual offender; and general deterrence—discouragement of a large number of persons who might consider the criminal conduct but who might be convinced not to engage in that conduct because of its adverse consequences, as shown by the punishment of others.

diagnosis (or classification) center: A unit within a correctional institution, or a separate facility, that holds persons in custody for the purpose of determining to which correctional facility or program they should be committed.

dictum (plural, dicta): A statement in a court opinion that is not essential to support the decision. A legal principle or conclusion (in an opinion) that is not necessary to the decision of the case.

disciplinary confinement: The act (and the place) of confining inmates separately because of their institutional misconduct. Segregation for disciplinary reasons. (Variously called disciplinary detention, disciplinary segregation, punitive segregation, and isolation.)

discipline (corrections): The program in a corrections agency or facility of punishing inmates who violate the internal code of conduct adopted for that agency or facility.

discovery (court procedure): A procedural tool or remedy used to compel an adverse party or a witness to answer allegations and interrogatories, to disclose facts within his knowledge, or to produce documents or records, all of which are designed to help the requesting party to better prepare and present his case.

dismissal: A decision by a judicial officer to terminate a case without a trial or without any further proceedings.

dissent: A disagreement with an opinion. Used most often to refer to the refusal of a judge (or judges) to agree with the majority of the court on the case being decided in an appellate court. If an opinion is written by the dissenter(s), it is called a dissenting opinion.

distinguish: In the law, used to point out essential differences. To distinguish a case means to show why a particular prior case (decision) is inapplicable to the case now before the court, usually when it would be damaging if the prior case were applicable or controlling.

diversion: The official halting or suspension of formal criminal or juvenile justice proceedings against an alleged offender and referral of that person to a treatment or care program administered by a nonjustice or private agency, or to a proceeding with noncriminal consequences.

double jeopardy: A prohibition against a person being prosecuted after there was a first trial for the same offense. The Fifth Amendment of the U.S. Constitution provides that no person shall "be subject for the same offence to be twice put in jeopardy of life or limb."

due process (due process of law): Exercise of the powers and authority of government in those ways that are prescribed by settled principles of law. There is a wide range of principles and procedures that may be prescribed (that is, process that may be due) according to the nature of the proceedings. The minimum process (principles and procedures) requires adequate advance notice of the proceeding, an opportunity to be heard and to assert one's rights, and consideration before a person or tribunal that is authorized by law to hear and determine the matter, according to established rules of good order.

due process clause: The constitutional statement that protects persons from certain governmental actions unless prescribed rules and procedures are followed. There are two such clauses in the U.S. Constitution; these appear in the Fifth Amendment (for federal government actions) and in the Fourteenth Amendment (for state actions). Almost all state constitutions also have such clauses.

electronic law library: A method of providing legal materials, such as statutes and court opinions, in an electronic format, rather than in paper volumes.

en banc (courts): A proceeding in which all members of a particular court will participate in hearing and deciding a case.

equal protection of the laws: A guarantee in a clause of the Fourteenth Amendment to the U.S. Constitution that persons in like circumstances should be given equal protection in their personal rights.

equity (courts): An alternative, established in English law, to the ordinary forms of civil law and justice. The emphasis in equity is to provide fair and just results in cases in which the common law or ordinary laws do not appear adequate. Equity concentrates on the persons who are present in court without trying to establish rights to govern other cases. (In the United States, in most jurisdictions, equity and law have been combined in courts of general jurisdiction.)

escape: The unlawful departure of a lawfully confined person from a confinement facility or from custody while being transported or officially escorted.

evidence: Any type of proof that is presented at trial, consisting of witnesses' testimony, records, documents, and other physical objects. Used to prove (or disprove) a fact relevant to the case being tried.

execution: The act of carrying out an order or judgment of a court. (Sometimes used in common parlance to refer to carrying out a sentence of death.)

exhaustion: A requirement that relief must be pursued in another procedure or place before it can be pursued in a particular court. Used especially for *exhaustion of administrative remedies* (requiring that such remedies be used, where they are available, before a lawsuit is filed) and *exhaustion of state remedies* (requiring that state remedies be pursued before federal actions are undertaken).

ex-offender: An offender who is no longer under the jurisdiction of any criminal justice agency.

ex parte: Used in the title of a case, or in an application to a court, to indicate that the action is brought on behalf of only one party, without notice to any adverse party.

ex post facto: Literally, after the act is committed. Used to signify something done after the fact, which is intended to affect something that was done before. An ex post facto law refers to a law that is enacted to impose a penalty for doing something that was lawful when it was done or to increase the punishment for a crime, making the sanction greater than when the crime was committed.

expunge: To seal or purge arrest, criminal, or juvenile record information.

extradition: The surrender by the authorities of one state (or country) of an accused or convicted offender to another state (or country), upon demand by authorities of that other state (or country). The surrender is usually made by the governor of the state where the offender is located, and it is initiated after an official request has been made to that governor and following a review of the legitimacy of the request. (Also known as rendition.)

facial challenge: A claim that a statute is unconstitutional on its face. A facial challenge does not get into the consideration of any specific facts, but is limited to the issue of whether the statute itself, as written, is unconstitutional.

false imprisonment: A tort, involving the unlawful restraint by one person of the physical liberty of another. (May also be a crime.)

federal: Pertaining to the national government of the United States of America. The government of a community of independent states, joined in a union having central and predominate authority.

felony: A criminal offense punishable by death or by incarceration in a confinement facility for a period of which the lower limit is prescribed by statute in a given jurisdiction, typically more than one year.

filing: In criminal proceedings, the commencement of legal action by entering a charging document into the official record of a court.

finding: The official determination of a judicial officer or administrative body regarding a disputed matter of fact or law. (Also called a ruling or a decision.)

fine: A penalty imposed on a convicted person by a court that requires payment of a specified sum of money.

forfeiture: The loss of something by way of penalty. (An example in corrections is good-time forfeiture. See good time.)

fugitive: A person who has concealed himself or fled a given jurisdiction in order to avoid confinement or prosecution. (Not exactly the same as an escapee—some but not necessarily all escapees may be fugitives.)

furlough: A temporary leave of absence, authorizing an inmate to depart from a correctional facility for a specified purpose, to a specific place, and with strict time limitations. These actions must be authorized by statute or, in rare cases, by judicial order.

good time: An award, authorized by statute, that reduces the length of time an inmate must spend in prison. It is given for satisfactory conduct in prison. There may also be authorization for *extra good time,* an additional award for particularly meritorious or outstanding actions or behavior. Good time does not usually reduce the total length of the sentence. Initially conceived as an incentive for good behavior, it has become virtually an automatic award in most places, lost only when the inmate misbehaves (withholding good time for current awards, forfeiture of good time for accumulated awards). In a few jurisdictions, the good-time allowance may reduce the maximum term of the sentence or even the parole eligibility date (the earliest date the inmate can be considered for parole release).

grand jury: A body of persons who have been selected and sworn to investigate criminal activity and the conduct of public officials and who hear evidence and legal advice from a prosecutor against an accused person to determine whether there is sufficient evidence to bring that person to trial. The decision of a grand jury that there is sufficient evidence for trial results in an indictment or "true bill," which is "handed up" by the grand jury. (See jury for a trial jury and petit jury definition.)

grievance (corrections): A complaint filed by an inmate in an informal procedure, which is reviewed in a mechanism established by a corrections agency. Relief may be given for conditions or actions that are found in the review process to have been wrongful.

guardian: A person who is given the legal authority to take care of another person.

guardian ad litem: An individual appointed by the court to function on behalf of an incompetent or an infant and to represent the interests of that incompetent or infant in a suit to which that person is a party.

guilt: Responsibility for wrongdoing. Guilty is used in criminal practice to denote a conclusion (by a defendant's plea or by a finding by a judge or jury) that an accused person is responsible for the crimes or offenses for which he has been charged.

habeas corpus: A writ (a court process or order) of ancient origin, used to obtain immediate relief by release from illegal confinement or custody. (Technically, this is the writ of *habeas corpus ad subjiciendum.* Other writs of habeas corpus are used to obtain a person in custody before a court, for prosecution [*habeas corpus ad prosequendum*] or for testifying [*habeas corpus ad testificandum*].)

halfway house: A residential facility for adjudicated adults or juveniles or those subject to criminal or juvenile proceedings that is intended to provide an alternative to confinement (in less secure surroundings) for persons not suitable for probation or other supervised release, or for those needing a period of readjustment to the community after confinement. A facility designed to assist a person to readjust to community life. (The same term may also be used for group homes for hospital releasees.) Most often used for those being released from correctional institutions ("halfway-out houses") but may also be used in lieu of placement into secure facilities ("halfway-in houses").

hearing: A proceeding in which arguments, witnesses, or evidence is heard by a judicial officer or by an administrative body.

hearing officer: The official who is given authority to conduct a hearing.

hold harmless: An agreement in which one party assumes the liability in a situation, relieving the other party of legal responsibility.

holding: The legal principle decided by a court's opinion or ruling.

immunity: Exemption by law. Freedom from a duty, or from liability, because actions are protected by law. Immunity from criminal prosecution may be either transactional immunity or use immunity. Transactional immunity provides immunity from prosecution for an offense to which a witness's compelled testimony relates. Use immunity bars a person's compelled testimony and its fruits from being used in any manner in connection with the criminal prosecution of the person.

incapacitation: The inability to act. In penology (sentencing philosophy), the justification for a term of imprisonment on the grounds that it renders the offender unable to commit offenses during the time of his imprisonment.

incarceration: Imprisonment. Confinement in a jail or prison.

indemnification: Compensation given to reimburse a person for a loss already sustained by him.

indeterminate sentence: A sentence imposed, not for a precise period of time, but often with a minimum and a maximum period of confinement, with the release of the offender usually controlled by correctional authorities, based on the behavior and successful achievement of the offender.

indictment: A formal, written accusation made by a grand jury and filed in a court, alleging that a specified person has committed a specific offense.

in forma pauperis: Literally, in the nature of a pauper. Indigent; lacking funds to pay certain fees or costs in court.

informant: A person, usually undisclosed to the accused, who provides information or accusations against another person. (Also called an informer.)

information: A formal, written accusation made by a prosecutor and filed in a court, alleging that a specified person has committed a specific offense.

infraction: An offense punishable by fine or other penalty, but not by incarceration. (In some places, this is called a violation.)

injunction (court action): A lawsuit brought, historically in a court of equity, to protect the rights of a plaintiff against the actions (or inactions) of a defendant, to avoid or right a wrong.

injunction (court order): A writ (order) to restrain a person from doing that which he should not do, or requiring him to do that which he should do. (The latter is sometimes called a mandatory injunction or mandamus.) This relief is entered to avoid irreparable injury (under the "rules of conscience" of an equity court) to any individual's person, or property, or other rights.

injury: Any wrong or damage done to another's person, rights, reputation, or property.

inmate: A person in custody in a confinement facility. (Prisoner is virtually a synonym, but see that definition for the difference.)

in re: In the matter of. In the titles of court cases, indicates those unusual actions that are brought without the traditional two opposing parties.

insanity: In the law, denotes a degree of mental disease or illness that renders a person not responsible for his conduct. It indicates a state of mental incapacity, which serves as a legal defense to criminal charges.

institutional capacity: The officially stated number of inmates or residents that a correctional facility is designed to house, exclusive of extraordinary arrangement to accommodate crowded conditions. (Also called design capacity.)

instructions: Rules and directions the trial judge gives to a jury to use in their deliberations on the facts of the case.

interrogatories (court procedure): A method of discovery. Written questions about facts of a case that an attorney submits in advance of trial to persons who are believed to have knowledge about those facts.

jail: A confinement facility, usually administered by a local law enforcement agency, such as a sheriff's department, that is intended for adults, but may sometimes contain juveniles, which persons are being detained pending adjudication or are committed, after adjudication, for a short period of time (usually a year or less).

jail sentence: The penalty of commitment to the jurisdiction of a confinement facility system for adults, where the custodial authority is limited to holding persons sentenced to a year or less of confinement.

judge: A judicial officer, either elected or appointed to the office, who presides over a court of law. The position is created by statute or by constitution. The decisions of a judge are final at that level of adjudication and may only be reviewed by a judge (or judges) of a higher court. (Some lower level judges are called magistrates, justices of the peace, or commissioners. If the decisions of these judicial officers (see that definition) are not subject to de novo review, but are reviewable only on appeal to a higher level court, and if their positions are created by statute or by constitution, then they are properly called judges under this definition. If any of those attributes of the office are missing, then they may be considered subjudicial or subordinate judicial officers, not judges.)

judgment: The statement of the decision of a court, amounting to final disposition of the case at that level. It is sometimes made orally in a courtroom, but it is finalized by entry into the records of the court. In a criminal case, it is an official, recorded statement that the defendant is convicted or acquitted of the offense charged.

judicial notice: The acknowledgment by a court that certain facts are accepted as true, without the taking of evidence, because of a wide acceptance of their reliability. Examples are the content of statutes and geographic and calendar facts.

judicial officer: Any person exercising judicial powers in a court of law.

jurisdiction: The precise geographic territory, subject matter, or person(s) over which lawful authority may be exercised, as defined by constitutional provisions or by statute.

jury, trial jury, petit jury: A body of persons, the number of which is defined by constitution, by statute, or by court rules, that is selected according to law, sworn to determine certain matters of fact in a criminal action, and sworn to render a verdict of guilty or not guilty (in a criminal case). (In civil cases, a jury, as defined by statute or by court rules, decides certain matters of fact and renders a verdict for either the plaintiff or the defendant, including, in most cases, the amount of damages that are awarded to the prevailing party.)

juvenile: A person subject to juvenile court proceedings or to certain other special status or treatment because his age is below the statutorily specified limit of adulthood.

juvenile court: The term for courts that have original jurisdiction over persons statutorily defined as juveniles and alleged to be delinquents, status offenders, or dependents. It may be a separate court, established by constitution or by statute, it may be a division of a court, or it may be a court of broader or general jurisdiction sitting in special session on juvenile matters.

juvenile justice agency: A government agency, or a subunit of an agency, of which the functions are the investigation, supervision, adjudication, care, or confinement of juveniles whose conduct or condition has brought or could bring them within the jurisdiction of a juvenile court.

law enforcement agency: A federal, state, or local criminal justice agency of which the principal functions are the prevention, detection, and investigation of crime and the apprehension of offenders.

law enforcement officer: An employee of a law enforcement agency who is an officer sworn to carry out law enforcement duties, or a sworn employee of a prosecutorial agency who primarily performs investigative duties. (Also called peace officer or police officer.)

lawyer: See attorney.

liability: The condition of being legally responsible for damages, or other relief, to the prevailing party in a tort or other civil action. (Also refers to the obligation to perform a contract or to pay indebtedness.)

libel: Defamation (see that definition) by means of print, writing, pictures, or signs. A publication that is injurious to the reputation of another.

liberty: Freedom from restraints. As provided in the Fifth and Fourteenth Amendments, no person shall be deprived of "life, liberty, or property, without due process of law."

license: Permission granted by a government (or other authorized) official to perform some act or to engage in some business activity. The written statement of such official permission.

magistrate: An official with limited judicial authority. In U.S. practice, an inferior judicial officer.

majority opinion: The opinion of an appellate court in which the majority of its participating members join. It therefore is the controlling opinion for the case. (See also plurality opinion.)

mandamus: A writ (order) requiring a person to do what he should do. Sometimes called a mandatory injunction. See also injunction (court order).

mandatory sentence: A sentence requiring, by statute, a defendant to be imprisoned for a period of time, allowing no (or little) discretion to the sentencing court. Often, these statutes provide that sentences may not be suspended and that probation and parole are not available to the offender.

master (court procedure): A person appointed by a court to assist in specified duties in a particular case. The duties to be performed are spelled out in an order and often include the gathering of facts and the taking of testimony. A master will then prepare a report of his actions for the court.

misdemeanor: An offense usually punishable by incarceration in a local confinement facility (jail), for a period of which the upper limit is prescribed by statute in a given jurisdiction; the period is less than that of a felony and is typically limited to a year or less.

monitor: A person who watches. In court proceedings, it is a type of master (see that definition) who is ordered to observe specified things, and then to report those observations to the court.

moot: A question that is unsettled, open to argument. In the law, a question not yet settled by judicial decisions. In common legal usage, it means an action or dispute has become uncontroversial, because the controlling issues or facts or questions have disappeared or become academic.

motion: An oral or written request made by a party to any action, before, during, or after a trial, that a court issue a ruling or an order on any matter of procedure or substance related to the case.

motion to produce documents (court procedure): A method of discovery. A motion to obtain from the opposing side any documents that may be relevant to the case.

municipality: A legally incorporated (or otherwise authorized) body of citizens, defined in a limited geographic area, organized for the purpose of local government. (May be in a particular state, a city, town, borough, township, or village.)

negligence: The failure to use such care as a reasonably prudent person would use under the same or similar circumstances. In the law, it is the doing of something that a prudent person would not have done, or the failure to do something that a prudent person would have done. It is the failure to live up to that standard of conduct that the law expects in order to protect other persons against unreasonable risk of harm.

nolo contendere: Literally, no contest. A defendant's formal answer (plea) in court to the charges in a complaint, information, or indictment, in which he states that he does not contest the charges. Although it is not a legal admission of guilt, it subjects the defendant to the same legal consequences as a plea of guilty.

offender: An adult who has been charged with (strictly, that person is an alleged offender) or convicted of a criminal offense.

officer (corrections): A corrections officer is a staff member in a corrections facility who is responsible for order and security in the facility and for the direct supervision of inmates. All of the corrections officers in the facility constitute the security force or the custody department. (Sometimes referred to as guard, but corrections officer is the preferred name, just as police officer is preferred to cop in law enforcement.)

opinion (court): The statement by a judge or a court of the decision reached in a case. It is usually given in writing and typically sets out the issue(s) presented in the case, the facts of the case, the law that applies, and the reasoning used to reach a conclusion or judgment. (See also dissent.)

order (court): A direction or command by a judge or court. The conclusion of a court on any motion or proceeding.

ordinance: Broadly, the same as a law or a statute. Most often used to refer to a municipal statute, the enactment of the legislative body of a municipality.

pardon: An executive act of grace that exempts an individual from the punishment the law inflicts for a crime he has committed. It may be issued as a full or a partial pardon, because it absolves all or a portion of the legal consequences of the crime. It may be absolute, or conditional, if it imposes a condition on the operation of the exemption.

parens patriae: Literally, father (or parent) of the country. The concept that the king (the government) has protective responsibility for those who are not able to care for themselves, particularly children and mentally incompetent individuals.

parole: The status of an offender who has been conditionally released from a confinement facility prior to the expiration of his sentence and placed under the supervision of a parole agency. The various aspects of parole—such as which inmates are eligible for parole and when, who is the paroling authority, the setting of parole standards (conditions), and the authority to revoke parole and to terminate parole—are defined by statute.

parole authority: A correctional agency or a person who has the authority to release on parole adults or juveniles committed to confinement facilities, to revoke parole, and to discharge from parole. (Usually, the parole authority is a parole board or a parole commission.)

parole violation: An act or a failure to act by a parolee that does not conform to the conditions of his parole and that may serve as grounds for the revocation of his parole.

parolee: A person who has been conditionally released from a correctional institution prior to the expiration of his sentence and placed under the supervision of a parole agency.

penalty: The punishment that is affixed by law or by judicial decision to the commission of a particular offense. It may be death, imprisonment (which may be a prison sentence or a jail sentence), an alternative facility sanction, a fine, restitution, or a loss of civil privileges. (Also called a sanction or punishment.)

penitentiary: In the United States, a place of imprisonment (historically, for those sentenced to terms of imprisonment with hard labor; more recently, for adults sentenced for felonies or for long terms). A penitentiary is a type of prison that historically dates back to a time when "penitence" (religious reflection) was the prime element of confinement of adult offenders, which was based on the Auburn, New York model. The name persists, usually in the titles of large facilities for high-security, long-term adult offenders.

per curiam: Literally, by the court. Used to denote an opinion of the whole court, rather than one written (as is usual) by a particular judge. Often used for a brief announcement of the disposition of a case, without a full opinion.

person: A human being or a group of human beings considered a legal unit, which has the lawful capacity to defend rights, to incur obligations, to prosecute and defend claims, or which can be prosecuted or adjudicated.

petition (juvenile): A document filed in juvenile court alleging that a juvenile is a delinquent, a status offender, or a dependent and asking that the court assume jurisdiction over the juvenile or asking that the juvenile be transferred to a criminal court for prosecution as an adult.

petition (legal proceeding): A document filed in a court having civil or general jurisdiction, asking that special relief within the jurisdiction of that court be granted. Used in habeas corpus proceedings as the document filed by a person who is in custody, asking for release from custody. Used in the Supreme Court as the document filed by a person requesting that the court issue a writ of certiorari, indicating that the case will be reviewed by that court.

petitioner: The party who files a petition.

petty offense: A minor criminal offense that is triable by a magistrate or subjudicial officer, without a jury. (The definition of the offenses so triable will be made by statute. In some places, it may include misdemeanors.)

plaintiff: The party who initiates a civil action. The person who files a complaint in court. (Technically, also the prosecutor, the state, or the United States in a criminal action, but it is seldom used in that context.)

plea: A defendant's formal answer in court to the criminal charges brought against him in a complaint, an information, or an indictment.

plurality opinion: An opinion of an appellate court, in which less than a majority of the justices (or judges) join, but in which more join than in any other opinion of the court.

police officer: See law enforcement officer.

population: The collective group of persons in a given status. A sentenced population is the body of adjudicated persons moving from courts into correctional facilities. The population of a jail or prison is the total number of persons confined at that facility at a given time.

precedent: A court decision that provides authoritative guidance or principle for a later case that has a similar question of law. A determination of a point of law made by a court, which is to be followed by a court of the same rank or of lower rank in a subsequent case that presents the same legal problem. (See stare decisis.)

preponderance of evidence: Evidence that is of greater weight than that offered on the other side. It is more convincing, or more probable than not, when weighed by the trier of fact.

presentence report: The document resulting from an investigation undertaken by a probation agency or other designated authority, at the request of a criminal court, into the past behavior, family circumstances, and personality of an adult who has been convicted of a crime, in order to assist the court in determining the most appropriate sentence. (For a juvenile, the same kind of report is called a predisposition report.)

presumption: At law, a rule that certain facts give rise to a conclusion that is assumed to be true unless it is rebutted.

prima facie: Literally, at first sight; on the face of it. A fact or matter presumed to be true, unless it is disproved by some evidence to the contrary.

prison: A confinement facility having custodial authority over adults sentenced to confinement for more than a year. An adult correctional institution is another name for the same type of facility. See also penitentiary.

prisoner: A person (either sentenced or unsentenced) in custody in a confinement facility, or in the personal custody of a criminal justice official while being transported from, to, or between confinement facilities.

prisoners' rights: Those privileges and rights that are legally, and especially constitutionally, retained by and guaranteed to inmates of correctional facilities.

privacy (records): The principles and procedures developed to ensure the security and confidentiality of record information relating to individuals, in order to protect the privacy of the persons identified in those records.

privatization: The performance of governmental function by private enterprise (a nongovernmental person or corporation). The performance is arranged for by the government through contract or other agreement.

probable cause: A set of facts and circumstances that would induce a reasonably intelligent and prudent person to believe that an accused person had committed a specific offense.

probation: The conditional freedom granted by a judicial officer to an alleged offender or an adjudicated adult or juvenile, as long as the person meets certain conditions of behavior, for a given period of time. The conditions and period of time are set by the judicial officer. The offender is released into the community, under the supervision of a probation officer.

probation (sentence): Probation given by a sentencing judge, requiring that a defendant fulfill certain conditions of behavior and accept the supervision of a probation agency. It is usually given in lieu of a sentence of confinement (along with a suspension of the execution of a sentence of confinement or with a suspension of the imposition of a sentence of confinement), although sometimes it is used along with (in addition to) a jail sentence. (As a rule, probation is tied to the suspension of a sentence; whenever a sentence is suspended, the defendant should be placed on probation.)

probation agency: A correctional agency of which the principal functions are the supervision of adults or juveniles who are placed on probation status and the investigation of adults or juveniles for the purpose of preparing presentence or predisposition reports to assist the court in determining the proper sentence (for adults) or the proper disposition (for juveniles).

probation officer: An employee of a probation agency whose primary duties include one or more of the probation agency functions.

probation violation: An act or a failure to act by a probationer that does not conform to the conditions of his probation. (It may be a grounds for revocation of probation—see that definition.)

probationer: A person required by a court or probation agency to meet certain conditions of behavior as required by a sentence or disposition of probation.

procedural law: Methods of proceeding, typically in a court, by which a legal right or duty is enforced. Distinguished from substantive law, which defines the rights, responsibilities, and duties of persons.

process: A broad term for any action by a court, usually in writing.

pro se: Acting as one's own attorney in legal or administrative proceedings.

prosecutor: An attorney employed by a government agency or subunit, whose official duty is to initiate and pursue criminal proceedings on behalf of the government against persons accused of committing criminal offenses.

public defender: An attorney employed by a government agency or subunit, whose official duty is to represent criminal defendants who are unable to hire private counsel.

punishment: See penalty.

purge: The complete removal of arrest, criminal, or juvenile record information from a given records system.

reasonable suspicion: A set of facts (used as the standard, for example, to stop a suspected offender in a public place) that would lead a prudent person under the circumstances to believe criminal activity is present.

rebut: To defeat, refute, or take away the effect of something. To contradict or deny, by facts or argument.

recidivist (recidivism): A repeat offender. One who habitually commits crimes.

reformatory: A correctional institution that is intended as a place of confinement for persons convicted of crimes of a less serious nature (and sometimes only for persons of a youthful age), who appear to be amenable to reformation by a course of treatment, education, work, and discipline during their confinement.

regulation: An order by competent authority, most often an agency of the executive branch, setting rules for actions that are under the agency's control.

rehabilitation: Restoring an offender to a law-abiding lifestyle. In penology (sentencing philosophy), rehabilitation refers to the theory that a purpose of sentencing is to help the offender live a crime-free life in the community. To that end, a corrections agency is expected to have rehabilitation programs, which improve the offender's prospects of being a productive and law-abiding citizen.

release (corrections): The authorized, lawful exit from detention or confinement facilities of persons subject to criminal or juvenile proceedings (detention) or those serving sentences (confinement facilities).

release on bail: The release, by a judicial officer, of an accused person who has been taken into custody, upon his promise to pay a certain sum of money if he fails to appear in court as required, the promise of which may or may not be secured by the deposit of an actual sum of money or property.

release on own recognizance: The release, by a judicial officer, of an accused person who has been taken into custody, upon his promise to appear in court as required for criminal proceedings.

relief (court procedure): A broad term used to describe the assistance, redress, or benefit that a complainant wishes to receive from a court. Examples are orders of injunction, declaratory relief, and money damages.

remand: To send back. To return the person or matter to the place from which it came.

requests for admissions (court procedure): A method of discovery. Written statements of facts about a case; these statements are formally sent to the opposing party, who is asked to admit or deny that certain facts are true. Those which are admitted usually will be accepted by the court as having been established and as not requiring proof at trial.

rescission: The abrogation, annulment, or cancellation of a contract. Nullifying a contract or an action, to put an end to it, as if it never took place.

residential treatment center: An alternative means of disposition or sentencing in a government facility that provides less strict controls than a training school (for juveniles) or a confinement facility (for adults), usually allowing the offenders greater contact with the community.

respondent: The party who files a response.

response: The pleading filed by the respondent in an equity action. An answer to a petition (such as a petition for a writ of habeas corpus) or other proceeding in equity or to a petition (for writ of certiorari) in the Supreme Court.

restitution: Compensation or reparation by one person for loss or injury caused to another. In criminal law, a court sanction requiring restoration by the offender to a person of that of which he has been wrongfully deprived, or payment by the offender of some monetary amount to the wronged person (victim) to compensate for injury or loss caused by criminal conduct.

retained counsel: An attorney who is not employed by a government agency for indigents or assigned by the court, but who is privately hired to represent a person in a legal proceeding.

retribution: In sentencing philosophy, the theory that every crime deserves a concomitant punishment.

reverse: To overturn by contrary judgment or decision. To set aside, repeal, or revoke.

revocation: Generally, the recall of some power or the voiding of something that has been granted. An administrative act by a parole authority removing a person from parole, or a judicial order by a court removing a person from probation in response to a violation on the part of the parolee or the probationer.

revocation hearing: An administrative (parole) or judicial (probation) hearing on the question of whether a person's probation or parole status should be revoked.

rights of defendants: Those powers and privileges that are legally, and especially constitutionally, guaranteed to every criminal defendant.

runaway: A juvenile who has committed the status offense of leaving the custody and home of his parents, guardians, or custodians without permission and failing to return within a reasonable length of time.

sanction: See penalty.

sanity: Soundness of mind. In criminal law, the opposite of insanity (see that definition).

scope of employment: The boundaries that define the actions that an employee (or agent) is expected to perform and the manner in which those actions are to be performed.

seal (records): The removal, for the benefit of the individual, of arrest, criminal, or juvenile record information from routinely available status to a status requiring special procedures (usually approval by a judicial authority) for access.

search: The close examination of a person, his house, or other property for the purpose of discovering any contraband, illicit property, or evidence of criminal activity. The act of looking for any thing that offends against the law (by law enforcement officials) or against misconduct codes (by corrections officers).

search warrant: A written order, issued by a judicial officer, authorizing the search and seizure of property, for evidence of criminal activity, including illicit goods and the fruits of crime.

security (corrections): The degree of restriction of inmate movement and the degree of custodial controls over inmates within a correctional facility, usually divided into maximum, medium, and minimum levels (of security).

segregation (corrections): The separation of inmates in correctional facilities from the regular population. It is usually done for disciplinary reasons, but it may be done for a variety of other reasons, such as awaiting transfer, for protection, or pending investigation. Also used to denote the place (the separate unit) in a facility where inmates are housed separately and under tighter control. This place is known in different facilities as disciplinary detention, administrative detention, punitive detention, segregation, isolation, and (colloquially) the hole.

seizure: The act of taking possession of property, usually from the possession of another person.

sentence (criminal law): The penalty (sanction) imposed by a court on a convicted person. This includes a court decision to suspend (defer) the imposition or the execution of a penalty and place the defendant on probation.

sentence, mandatory: A statutory requirement that a certain penalty, a certain minimum penalty, or a penalty with severe restrictions (such as no parole eligibility) shall be imposed and executed upon certain convicted offenders.

sentence, suspended: The court decision of either postponing the pronouncing of sentence upon a convicted person or postponing the execution of a sentence that has been pronounced by the court.

shakedown (corrections): Vernacular in correctional facilities for the search of a person or place.

show cause order: An order to appear and to give reasons to the court why a particular order contemplated by or requested from the court should not be entered or executed. An order to explain to the court why a proposed action should not be taken.

slander: Defamation (see that definition) by spoken words.

sovereign: The person (ruler) or body (government) in which supreme authority is vested. Sovereign immunity is the immunity (see that definition) of the sovereign from liability.

stare decisis: Literally, to stand by decisions. This is the legal doctrine that courts will adhere to principles settled by court decisions in other cases in which the facts are substantially the same. It is a strong judicial policy that a point of law that is determined in a court will be followed by that court, or a court of lower rank, in a later case that presents the same legal question.

status offender: A juvenile who has been adjudicated by a judicial officer of a juvenile court as having committed a status offense, which is an act or conduct that is an offense only when committed or engaged in by a juvenile (that is, it would not be a crime if committed by an adult).

statute: An act of a legislature declaring, commanding, or prohibiting something.

statutory law: The body of law created by the acts of the legislatures.

subjudicial officer: A judicial officer who is invested with certain limited judicial powers and functions but whose decisions in criminal or other cases are usually subject to de novo review by a judge.

subpoena: A written order issued by a judicial officer requiring a specified person to appear in a designated court at a specified time in order to serve as a witness in a case under the jurisdiction of that court or to bring material (documents, etc.) to that court.

substantial evidence: Evidence that a reasoning mind would accept as sufficient to support a particular conclusion. (It is more than a *scintilla* of evidence, but it may be less than a *preponderance* of the evidence.)

substantive law: The whole area of the law that creates and defines legal rights and obligations. Distinguished from procedural law, which is the methods of proceeding by which a legal right or duty is enforced.

summary judgment: The court's disposition of a case summarily—that is, without the need for a trial. Based on the facts shown in the pleadings and by affidavits, a court's determination that judgment can be entered before trial because the facts necessary to decide the case are already clearly presented and are not controverted, so that trial (which is intended to resolve disputed facts) is unnecessary.

summons: A written order issued by a judicial officer requiring a person accused of a criminal offense to appear in a designated court at a specified time to answer a charge. Also, an order in a civil case to respond or answer in court.

superintendent: In corrections, the person in charge of a correctional facility. In most places, it is used as the title for the manager of a lower security correctional facility. (Similar to warden—see that definition.)

supreme court: An appellate court at the highest level in most states and in the federal court system. The court of last resort in the particular jurisdiction. The U.S. Supreme Court is the highest court in the federal court system and the highest court in the nation.

suspect: A person considered by a criminal justice agency to be one who may have committed a specific criminal offense but who has not been arrested or charged.

suspend: To postpone, delay, or discontinue. A suspended sentence is one that is imposed but not executed.

suspicion: The belief that a person has committed a criminal offense, based on facts and circumstances that are insufficient to constitute probable cause.

time served: The time spent in confinement by a convicted person until a given date or until the date of release. (Sometimes used to refer only to the time spent in a confinement facility after a sentence is imposed.)

toll: To suspend or stop the requirements of any law.

tort: A wrong. An injury to the person or property of another, outside of any contractual agreement. A breach of duty that the law (by statute or by common law) has said is owed to another person. (Some acts may be either crimes or torts or both—crimes are offenses against the public, whereas torts are injuries to private persons, which may be pursued in civil courts.)

training school: A correctional institution for juveniles adjudicated to be delinquents or status offenders and committed to confinement by a judicial officer.

transfer (corrections): The movement of an inmate from one facility to another.

transfer to adult court: The decision by a juvenile court, resulting from a transfer hearing, that jurisdiction over an alleged delinquent will be waived by the juvenile court and that the individual should be prosecuted as an adult in a criminal court.

trial: The examination of issues of fact and law in a case or controversy, beginning when the jury has been selected in a jury trial, when the first witness is sworn, or when the first evidence is introduced in a court trial, and concluding when a verdict is reached or the case is dismissed.

trial by judge (court trial): A trial in which there is no jury and in which a judicial officer determines the issues of fact as well as the law in the case.

trial by jury (jury trial): A trial in which a jury determines the issues of fact in a case and renders a verdict.

trial court: A judicial officer who is authorized to conduct trials. (Usually used to distinguish from appeals courts.)

vacate: To cancel, set aside, annul (declare of no validity).

venue: The geographic area from which the jury is drawn and in which the trial is held in a criminal case. More broadly, the place (county, city, district) where a case is to be tried. Today, the proper venue for an action is set by statute, with the possibility for it to be changed by agreement of the parties or by court order upon application of a party. (Not to be confused with jurisdiction, which may not be changed by consent or waiver.)

verdict: In criminal proceedings, the decision made by a jury (in a jury trial) or by a judicial officer (in a court trial) that a defendant is either guilty or not guilty of the offense for which he has been tried. In civil proceedings, the decision made by a jury or by a judicial officer in favor of the claim of the plaintiff or the counterclaim or defense of the defendant.

victim: A person who has suffered death, physical or mental suffering, or loss of property as the result of an actual or attempted criminal offense committed by another person.

waiver: The relinquishing of a known right. The abandonment of a claim, right, or privilege.

waiver of summons: A process authorized in federal courts and some state courts allowing a plaintiff to request the defendant to waive service of the summons, eliminating some costs of the litigation. A defendant who waives service of summons is still required to respond or answer to the complaint.

ward: A person placed under the care of a guardian as a consequence of being legally unable to manage his own affairs. Used especially in juvenile law, meaning a child who is under special protection of the state or a juvenile court.

warden: Historically, a guardian; a keeper of wards. Today, used principally as the title of the person in charge (the chief executive officer) of a correctional facility. (In many jurisdictions, used for the title of such a person in a maximum or medium security facility, whereas superintendent is used for lower security facilities.)

warrant, arrest: A document issued by a judicial officer that directs a law enforcement officer to arrest a person who has been accused of an offense.

warrant, bench: A document issued by a judicial officer directing that a person (who has failed to obey a notice or a court order to appear in court) be brought before the court.

warrant, search: A document issued by a judicial officer that directs a law enforcement officer to conduct a search for specified property or persons at a specific location, to seize the property or persons, if found, and to account for the results of the search to the issuing judicial officer.

withholding (good-time withholding): See good time.

witness: A person who directly perceives an event or thing or who has expert knowledge relevant to a case. Also, such a person who is called to testify in a hearing or trial.

work release: A correctional program that allows an inmate to leave a facility for the purpose of working in the community during the day, but requires him to return to the facility for nights and weekends (for all nonworking hours). Similarly, study release allows the same kind of leave for attendance at educational activities in the community.

writ: An order requiring a specified act to be performed.

youthful offender: A person, adjudicated in criminal court, who is above the statutory age limit for juveniles but is below a specified upper age limit set by statute, for whom special correctional commitments (often indeterminate in nature), release supervision, and record-sealing procedures are made available by statute.

Table of Cases

These are the cases that are discussed and cited in this book. Decisions of the U.S. Supreme Court are in **bold** print. Decisions of all other courts are in regular print. References are to pages in this book. If a case appears at more than one place in the book, the number in **bold** print indicates where a principal discussion of that case is located.

Index

E